Private Wealth Management

The Complete Reference for the Personal Financial Planner

G. Victor Hallman, Ph.D., J.D.

Member of the Pennsylvania Bar
and Lecturer, Wharton School,
University of Pennsylvania

Jerry S. Rosenbloom, Ph.D.

Frederick H. Ecker Emeritus Professor of Insurance
and Risk Management, Wharton School,
and Academic Director of the Certified
Employee Benefit Specialist Program,
Wharton School, University of Pennsylvania

Eighth Edition

New York Chicago San Francisco Lisbon London
Madrid Mexico City Milan New Delhi San Juan
Seoul Singapore Sydney Toronto

The McGraw·Hill Companies

Previous editions of this book were published under the title *Personal Financial Planning.*

4 5 6 7 8 9 0 IBT/IBT 1 9 8 7 6 5 4 3 2 1

ISBN 978-0-07-154421-4
MHID 0-07-154421-6

This publication is designed to provide accurate and authoritative information in regard to the subject matter covered. It is sold with the understanding that neither the author nor the publisher is engaged in rendering legal, accounting, futures/securities trading, or other professional service. If legal advice or other expert assistance is required, the services of a competent professional person should be sought.

—From a Declaration of Principles jointly adopted by a Committee of the American Bar Association and a Committee of Publishers

McGraw-Hill books are available at special quantity discounts to use as premiums and sales promotions, or for use in corporate training programs. To contact a representative, please visit the Contact Us page at www.mhprofessional.com.

Contents

Preface

The publication of this new and completely revised eighth edition comes at a time of great economic uncertainty and new developments. Change is in the air. As the ballad goes, "the times they are a'changin."

As of this writing, we are in the midst (whether it is the beginning or the ending, we now do not know) of the most severe worldwide economic downturn (recession or depression) since the Great Depression of the 1930s. Central banks throughout the world have used the tools of monetary policy to provide liquidity to financial institutions, have expanded those eligible for loans and aid, and have driven short-term interest rates to historic lows (even virtually to zero). Governments have employed fiscal policy in the form of massive stimulus packages and have "bailed out" banks, insurance companies, and large industrial corporations in the forms of loans and by taking equity positions in them. In the process, governments have incurred very large budget deficits as a percentage of their countries' gross domestic product (GDP).

The impact of these developments on the current recession is unclear. Many economists and analysts believe they will succeed and the economy will begin recovery late this year (2009) and return to prosperity. We all certainly hope so, but others fear that the economy will slip back into recession and that the road to prosperity will take many years, as was true during the Great Depression. Thus, the overall theme of this book is to be ready for all kinds of economic environments through diversification in asset allocation and other financial strategies, and through careful planning in general.

All these issues have great impact on private wealth management. Therefore, the new edition begins in Chapter 2 with a discussion of the economic, institutional, and regulatory environments in which wealth management is practiced. These regulatory environments may well change in the future because of some of the economic failures we have experienced in recent years.

The "baby boom generation," born in the years after World War II, is now approaching retirement. This will cause great strains on Social Security and retirement systems in general. Therefore, this edition places greater emphasis on providing adequate retirement income, planning for distributions from retirement plans, and retirement planning in general.

In the preface to the first edition of this book, written in 1975, we noted that consumerism has been a rising tide and that personal financial planning really is consumerism applied to an individual's or a family's personal financial affairs. We also noted that since the end of World War II, our economy has developed an almost unheard-of level of affluence that has made wealth management important for larger and larger numbers of people. We further observed that the increasing role of women in the workforce, particularly at the executive and professional levels, and the rapid growth of multi-income-earner families in the United States are placing more and more persons in a position in which they need to apply sophisticated financial planning techniques to their personal and family affairs. It is surprising how well those statements apply today, even more than they did then. The impact of all these forces simply has become stronger in the intervening years.

In this edition of the book, as in the previous editions, we consider private wealth management as the process of determining an individual's or a family's total financial objectives, considering alternative plans or methods for meeting those objectives, selecting the plans and methods that are best suited for the person's circumstances, implementing those plans, and then periodically reviewing the decisions made and making necessary adjustments. In this process, a person's or family's overall financial affairs—investments, saving programs, financing arrangements, insurance and annuities, retirement plans, other employee benefits, income tax planning, estate planning, and so forth—should be considered on a coordinated whole, rather than on a piecemeal basis. This means that individual financial instruments, such as stocks, bonds, life insurance, annuities, mutual funds, real estate, trusts, and various kinds of employee benefits and compensation arrangements, should be considered in terms of a person's overall financial objectives and plans rather than in isolation. It also means that the professional in this field should be knowledgeable in a variety of disciplines. It is an objective of this book to help achieve these results.

In this spirit, the title of the eighth edition has been changed to *Private Wealth Management.* This reflects the term increasingly being used for this field today. It also reflects the level and breadth of the material covered in this edition.

A number of planning areas have been added or expanded in this edition. They include:

- Discussion of the planning ramifications of the "sunset" provisions of the Economic Growth and Tax Relief Reconciliation Act of 2001
- Discussion of possible estate tax changes before this "sunset"
- New material on the economic environment for wealth management
- New material on the regulatory environment for wealth management
- A new chapter on valuation concepts in wealth management
- New material on modern portfolio theory and asset allocation decision making
- New material on financial management, including a discussion of reverse mortgages
- Increased coverage of financing education expenses
- Increased coverage of retirement planning, including planning for retirement plan distributions
- Coverage of the Pension Protection Act of 2006
- Increased coverage of nonqualified individual annuities, including guaranteed minimum income benefits (GMIBs) and guaranteed minimum death benefits (GMDBs)
- Changes made in Medicaid planning by the Deficit Reduction Act of 2005
- Increased coverage of Roth IRAs
- Increased coverage of Social Security and planning for taking Social Security retirement benefits
- Increased coverage of individual life insurance, including no-lapse guarantee benefits, financed life insurance, and life settlement transactions
- Possible changes in marital deduction planning in the event of adoption in the future of "portable" unified credits between spouses

Thus, the reorganized and retitled eighth edition has not only been updated, but it has also been expanded in these and other areas.

G. Victor Hallman
Jerry S. Rosenbloom

PART I

Introduction

1

Nature and Objectives of Private Wealth Management

Competence Objectives for This Chapter After reading this chapter, planners should understand how to:

- Recognize the phases of a family's economic lifecycle
- Identify, evaluate, and use planning strategies for a person's or family's overall financial objectives, including:
  - Capital accumulation
  - Investment and property management (money management)
  - Income tax planning
  - Financing education expenses
  - Retirement planning (provision of retirement income)
  - Protection against personal risks (personal risk management)
  - Health-care decision making and property management in case of physical or mental incapacity
  - Estate planning
  - Charitable giving
  - Business planning
  - Managing special circumstances
- Employ the steps in the financial planning process
- Construct and use personal financial statements
- Recognize the ethical obligations of persons involved in private wealth management and to know well the ethical standards for his or her own area of expertise

Need for Wealth Management Services

Most people are in need of wealth management. They have various financial and personal goals they want to attain for themselves, their families, and perhaps for charitable entities and others. Of course, some persons and families have situations and objectives that are more complex than others. But virtually everyone has a need for planning to some degree.

To help meet their goals, the public is offered a sometimes-bewildering array of investment products, financing plans, insurance coverages, tax-saving ideas, retirement plans, trusts, charitable giving arrangements, and other products and ideas. However, these financial arrangements and ideas often are presented in a piecemeal fashion without overall coordination and planning. In contrast, the concept of private wealth management is the development and implementation of comprehensive plans for achieving a person's overall financial and personal objectives, as noted in this chapter and throughout this book.

Wealth Management over a Family's Economic Lifecycle

People deal with their objectives over their entire *economic lifecycle*. This cycle encompasses their *early years as an income earner* when they often are purchasing a home, concerned with debt management, protecting a young family with adequate insurance, and hopefully beginning their wealth accumulation program. When they enter their higher-earning years, they should have significant capital accumulation, but at this *midlife period*, they also often are faced with financing their children's higher education, planning in earnest for their own retirements, and perhaps needing to provide financial support (including possible custodial care) for aged parents or other relatives. Then there are their *immediate preretirement and retirement years*, when they must organize their affairs so that they will have adequate retirement income during the lifetimes of both spouses. They also may want to arrange their retirement plan distributions so that they can meet both their retirement income needs and their wealth-transfer objectives in a tax-efficient manner. Depending on how old people are when they have their children and the ages of their parents, they also may be faced with higher education expenses and the cost of caring for aged parents at the very time they need to be primarily concerned with income for their own retirements. Finally, people normally plan for the *transmission of their wealth* during their lifetimes and/or after their deaths to their children, grandchildren, or other heirs, again in a tax-efficient manner (estate planning).

This book covers planning strategies and techniques to meet the objectives just noted. While some of these techniques may apply primarily to higher-net-worth individuals and families,[1] most of them apply to virtually everyone.

Focus on Objectives and Planning Strategies

Private wealth management focuses on meeting a person's or family's overall financial objectives and the planning strategies for doing so. In this regard, the following classification of objectives provides a systematic way for determining, analyzing, and planning for these goals and expectations.

Capital Accumulation

People may want to accumulate capital for a variety of reasons. Some of these are listed below.

Emergency Fund An emergency fund may be needed to meet unexpected expenses, to pay for deliberately retained exposures to loss, and to provide a financial cushion against the risks of life (including economic recession or depression).

The size of an emergency fund varies and depends on such factors as family income, number of income earners, stability of employment, assets, debts, insurance deductibles, uncovered health and property exposures, and the family's general attitudes toward risk. It often is expressed as so many months of family income—such as 3 to 12 months—but may be a fixed amount.

Education Needs The cost of higher education has increased dramatically, particularly at private colleges and universities. The size of an education fund depends on the number of children or other recipients, their ages, their educational plans, any available financial aid, and the size of the family's available assets and income. It also depends on the attitudes of the family toward education. The issue of financing education costs is covered in Part IV of this book.

Retirement Needs Because of the importance and unique characteristics of this objective, it is dealt with as a separate objective in Part V of this book.

[1] Who constitutes a high-net-worth person or family varies among commentators. But just as an example, in its annual *World Wealth Report* Merrill Lynch and Capgemini Consulting consider high-net-worth individuals (HNWIs) to be people holding more than $1,000,000 in financial assets. Other wealth management professionals may use higher or lower amounts in their definitions.

General Investment Fund People often accumulate capital for general investment purposes. They may want a better standard of living in the future, a second income in addition to their earnings, greater financial security, the ability to retire early, or a capital fund to pass on to their children or grandchildren, or they may simply enjoy the investment process.

Investment and Property Management (Money Management)

Need for Management The desire to obtain professional investment and property management varies considerably among individuals and families. However, the increasing complexity of investments, volatility of financial markets, economic uncertainties, tax problems, and the like generally have increased the desire for professional management in this area.

Sources of Aid for Investment and Property Management

Use of Financial Intermediaries: Broadly speaking, a financial intermediary is a financial institution that invests people's money and pays them a return on that money. Such institutions serve as conduits for savings into appropriate investments. They may include the following:

- Investment companies (mutual funds, exchange-traded funds, closed-end investment companies, and unit investment trusts)
- Commercial banks (offering certificates of deposit, money market accounts, and various types of savings accounts)
- Life insurance companies
- Savings institutions
- In real estate, real estate investment trusts (REITs) and tenant in common (TIC) plans

Trusts: One of the basic reasons for establishing trusts is to provide experienced and knowledgeable investment and property management for the beneficiaries of the trust (who may include the creator of the trust).

Investment Advisers and Advisory Firms: There are many investment advisers and advisory firms, ranging in size and types of services provided, who offer their clients professional investment advice on a fee basis. Many commercial banks and securities firms also offer investment advisory services.

In terms of investment decision-making authority, investment advisers may operate (1) on a strictly discretionary basis, under which the adviser actually makes investment decisions and buys and sells securities for the client without prior consultation with the client, (2) under an arrangement whereby the adviser basically makes investment decisions but consults with the client before taking action, and (3) under an arrangement by which the adviser and client consult extensively before investment decisions are made, but clients reserve the actual decision making for themselves.

Investment advisers are regulated under the *Investment Advisers Act of 1940* and similar state laws. The 1940 Act defines investment advisers as persons who, for compensation, engage in the business of advising others, either directly or through publications or writing, as to the value of securities or as to the advisability of investing in, purchasing, or selling securities; or who, for compensation and as a part of a regular business, issue or promulgate analyses or reports concerning securities. Such advisers with $25 million or more under management must register with the Securities and Exchange Commission (SEC). Advisers managing lesser amounts must meet state registration requirements in states where they operate. The 1940 Act also regulates certain investment adviser activities, such as advisory contract terms, fees, advertising, client solicitation, disclosures to clients, and record keeping.

Some persons and entities are specifically exempted from the Act. They include bankers; attorneys; accountants, engineers, and teachers who provide investment advice that is incidental to the practice of their profession; brokers or dealers who provide investment advice incidental to the conduct of their business and who do not charge special compensation for such advice; publishers of bona fide newspapers, news magazines, or financial publications; and certain other exemptions.

Investment advisers have a fiduciary relationship with their clients. Thus, they must deal with clients in good faith and operate in the clients' best interests.

Independent Financial Planners: These are persons and organizations that provide coordinated planning services for their clients on a fee-for-service basis or as part of their services in connection with the sale of financial products. They often provide planning with respect to investments and property management, as well as in a number of other areas. Depending on the nature and size of their practice, financial planners may fall under the definition of investment adviser and would need to register with the SEC under the 1940 Act or under an applicable state law.

Securities Firms: Investors can obtain valuable investment and research advice from account executives and others with stock brokerage firms. It must be pointed out, however, that the relationship between stockbrokers and their clients is not the same as that of investment advisers or trust departments and their clients. Brokers often are paid commissions based on the transactions in their customers' accounts, while advisers and trustees usually are paid an annual fee that is a percentage of the assets under their management. However, professionally minded brokers recognize that their long-term success ultimately depends on the investment success of their customers, and they act accordingly. Also, other compensation arrangements for brokers now are being used.

Other Advisers: There are several other important sources from whom individuals can secure aid. Attorneys provide legal and other advice. Accountants provide advice concerning financial affairs, particularly in the tax area. Mutual fund representatives and persons offering tax-sheltered and other investments can provide advice on how these vehicles can be used in financial planning. Life insurance agents and brokers can offer advice concerning life insurance, health insurance, annuities, and other retirement plans, as well as other financial products and services. Similarly, property and liability insurance agents and brokers provide advice on personal risk management, property and liability insurance, and other financial products and services. Furthermore, real estate brokers and other professionals in that area can provide aid concerning real estate investments and management.

Costs and Investment Management It must be recognized that there are always charges, in one fashion or another, when people hire someone else (a professional) to manage their money. The charges may be in the form of an annual *asset-based percentage fee* (such as 1 percent of assets under management), like those charged by professional trustees and investment advisers, often with a minimum annual fee of, for example, $1,500 to $3,000. Investment companies (e.g., mutual funds) charge *annual expense ratios* as a percentage of fund assets for investment management and other expenses. Variable annuities and variable life insurance have asset-based fees at both the policy level (called mortality and expense risk charges) and the fund level (an expense ratio) for investment management services and other costs. Independent financial planners have various compensation arrangements.

Investment management costs also may be embedded in the structure of investment products and services. For example, investment expenses of banks, thrift institutions, and insurance companies are recovered based on the difference between the returns they earn on their own investments and the interest rates they pay to their customers on products like certificates of deposit (CDs), saving accounts, money market accounts, fixed-dollar life insurance policies and annuities, and the like. Stockbrokers usually are compensated for investment advice through the commissions they earn. Likewise, other professionals are compensated through fees or commissions for the services they provide. As different financial products are discussed throughout this book, their cost structures will be part of the analysis. The real question is not whether there are charges for investment services and advice—of course there are—but rather whether those charges are reasonable in relation to the returns and benefits achieved.

Income Tax Planning (Reducing the Tax Burden)

Most people have the legitimate objective of reducing their tax burden as much as legally possible. People may be subject to many different taxes. These include the federal income tax (including the alternative minimum tax), state and local income taxes, federal estate tax, state death taxes, federal gift tax, the federal tax on generation-skipping transfers (GSTs), and Social Security and other employment-related taxes. This objective is concerned with income tax planning. Estate, gift, and GST tax savings are dealt with under estate planning.

Financing Education Expenses

This has become an important objective for many individuals and families as the need for higher education has become increasingly recognized and its cost has risen dramatically. In response to this need, there also have arisen some attractive, tax-efficient plans for financing education costs, such as qualified tuition (Section 529) plans. Planning strategies for financing education expenses are covered in Part IV.

Retirement Planning (Provision of Retirement Income)

This objective also has become increasingly prominent. This is because today most people can anticipate living to enjoy a long period of retirement (possibly lasting into their 80s, 90s, or even beyond); retirement planning itself has become so complex; there is debate as to whether people are saving enough to finance their retirements adequately; and currently, economic recession or depression is depleting the value of many retirement accounts. Also, some people are thinking about retiring early (i.e., well before age 65). Consequently, much planning today has to do with the provision of adequate retirement income and planning for how to take distributions from various retirement plans. Retirement planning is covered in Part V.

Protection against Personal Risks

This objective involves planning for the many risks that may cause personal losses, such as medical expenses, disability of income earners, custodial care (long-term care) expenses, death, and property and liability losses. Dealing with these exposures often is called *personal risk management.*

Medical Care Expenses There is little need to convince most people of the importance of protecting themselves and their families against medical care costs. For planning purposes, we can divide medical costs into the following categories:

Normal or Budgetable Expenses: These are expenses the family can pay out of its regular monthly budget. Traditional thinking holds that, as a general principle, the more of these expenses a family can assume, the lower its overall costs will be. This is the concept of *retention* in personal risk management.

Larger-than-Normal and Catastrophic Expenses: These are expenses that exceed normal ones and may be so large as to cause severe financial strain (catastrophic expenses), even for high-net-worth families. They obviously are important to plan for, and normally cannot be deliberately retained. Planning strategies for these expenses are covered in Chapter 22.

Disability Income Losses Loss of earned income due to the disability of an income earner can be referred to as the *disability income exposure.*

Significance of the Disability Income Exposure: Such an exposure, particularly total and permanent disability, is a serious risk.[2] Many experts agree that consumers should give greatest attention to protecting against long-term disability rather than being unduly concerned with disabilities that last only a few weeks. Using the figures in Footnote 2, it may be suggested that not many families can afford the loss of one or both of the breadwinners' earnings for four or more years.

Planning Strategies: Disability income insurance is the main source of protection against the disability exposure, particularly long-term disabilities. Depending on the circumstances, part of this exposure (such as losses from short-term disabilities) can be retained through the emergency fund. Sometimes, investment income can replace part or even all of a disabled person's earned income in the case of high-net-worth persons. Most people with earned income are covered by Social Security disability benefits. Also, some employers provide their employees with disability benefits of various types.

[2] Interestingly, the probability that someone will suffer a serious long-term disability (of 90 days or more) prior to age 65 is considerably greater than the probability of death at all ages prior to age 65. As examples of the importance of the disability exposure, according to Society of Actuaries data, a person age 30 has a 24 percent probability of having a disability lasting 90 days or more before reaching age 65 and a person age 50 has a corresponding probability of 18 percent. These figures illustrate the *average frequency* of such a serious disability. Data on *average severity* are equally startling. For persons under age 40, the average duration (severity) of a disability lasting 90 days or more is four years, while the corresponding average duration for persons ages 50 to 54 is four years, six months.

However, many people with earned income find they must supplement these sources of disability protection by purchasing individual disability income policies.

In planning for this exposure, the adviser and the client may pursue the strategy of assuming the worst—that the client (or another income earner in the family) may become totally and permanently disabled (unable to have an earned income) from now until his or her normal retirement. In addition, consideration must be given to the impact that disability during a person's working years will have on his or her available retirement income. Given such a worst-case scenario, what the person will receive from existing disability income insurance, other benefits, and income from other sources can be determined. Recommendations then can be made to deal with any shortfalls in needed after-tax disability income. Chapter 22 covers planning for this exposure.

Custodial Care (Long-Term Care) Expenses These are expenses incurred to maintain persons when they are unable to perform at least several of the normal activities of daily living.

How It Differs from Medical Care: This category of expenses is for *custodial care,* when persons are no longer able to care for themselves, rather than for the treatment and potentially the cure of *acute medical conditions.* Custodial care can take a variety of forms, such as skilled nursing home care, intermediate institutional (assisted living facility) care, adult day care, and home health care.

Medical expense coverages, such as Medicare and private health insurance, provide little to no coverage for custodial care expenses. With increasing longevity and the high cost of custodial care, planning for these expenses has become an increasingly important objective.

Planning Strategies: *Long-term care (LTC) insurance* is the private insurance approach to meeting this exposure. Starting around age 50, or even younger, LTC insurance should be part of most peoples' insurance portfolio. Of course, very high-net-worth persons may be able to finance this exposure from their investment income or assets. At what level of wealth such self-funding may become an appropriate strategy is debatable.

Unfortunately, many older people do not have adequate LTC insurance or other income and resources to meet the custodial care exposure. A planning strategy in this situation may be to enable the person needing care to qualify for Medicaid (the federal-state medical assistance program for the needy), which does cover nursing home and other custodial care, while still planning to pass as much of the person's assets as possible to his or her family. This is referred to as *Medicaid planning.* For people who do not have other options, Medicaid planning may be an appropriate strategy. However, reliance on Medicaid to meet the custodial care exposure is highly problematic for most people. The *Deficit Reduction Act of 2005* has made Medicaid planning considerably more difficult. Public policy in this area clearly seems to be to encourage people to plan in advance by purchasing long-term care insurance.

Planning for custodial care expenses is covered in Chapter 23.

Death A major objective of most people is to protect their families or others from the financial consequences of their deaths. People also may be concerned with the impact of their deaths on their business affairs or their estate's liquidity and conservation picture.

Potential Losses and Needs at Death: These include the following:

- *Loss of the Deceased's Future Earning Power.* Most families live on the earned income from one or both spouses. The death of an income earner results in the loss of that person's future earnings. This has sometimes been referred to as a person's *human life value.* In addition, the death of a family member working in the home may result in increased expenses because of the need to replace his or her services.
- *Loss of Funds to Meet Future Needs or Objectives.* These may include funds for children's education and amounts needed to satisfy mortgages and other large debts.
- *Liquidity Needs of a Decedent's Estate.* Any federal estate tax due generally is payable no later than nine months after the decedent's death. It is payable by the executor or administrator of the estate. Depending on the jurisdictions involved, there also may be substantial state death taxes due. Thus, for high-net-worth persons, these taxes often will create substantial *liquidity needs* for their estates (i.e., the need for ready cash to pay taxes and other obligations). There also will be estate settlement costs and debts that must be paid from the estate.
- *Estate Shrinkage.* Even assuming an estate has adequate liquid assets or other resources with which to pay its taxes and other obligations, larger estates often suffer considerable reduction in value due to federal and state death taxes. This *estate shrinkage* will substantially reduce the wealth passing to the estate owner's heirs if steps are not taken to reduce the shrinkage or to make up for it. Strategies to deal with such shrinkage may be referred to as *estate conservation* measures.
- *Loss of Business Values.* When an owner of a closely held business dies, the business also may die financially or suffer considerable loss in value. Also, many businesses have key employees, whether owners or not, whose death can cause considerable financial loss to the business.

Planning Strategies: Life insurance is the primary vehicle for providing cash to meet the losses arising out of a person's death. Various strategies can be applied to determine the types and amounts of life insurance needed in a particular case. These strategies are discussed in Chapters 21 and 29.

Property Damage and Legal Liability Exposures There are a variety of such exposures, which can cause substantial financial loss. Most people carry insurance against basic exposures, like auto and homeowners' policies, but careful planning is necessary to consider all the exposures a person or family may have and to make sure their insurance coverages have adequate limits. This is particularly true for high-net-worth persons, who usually have diverse interests, highly valued properties and collections, and property held in trust. They also frequently serve on boards of directors.

Property Losses: Ownership of property brings with it the risk of loss to the property itself (*direct losses*) and loss of use of the property (*indirect or consequential losses*). A planning decision in this area is how much exposure should be assumed (usually through policy deductibles) and how much should be insured.

Liability Losses: By virtue of almost everything a person may do, he or she is exposed to possible liability claims by others. Such liability can arise out of the person's own negligent acts, the negligent acts of others for whom the person may be legally responsible, liability he or she may have assumed under a contract (such as a lease), liability imposed by statute (such as workers' compensation laws), liability from board memberships, and liability for certain intentional acts (intentional torts) done by the person. Since a large liability claim potentially can be financially devastating, identifying and evaluating liability exposures and planning for adequate liability insurance to cover these exposures are critical.

Planning Strategies: A risk management (insurance) survey, with a checklist of potential exposures, is an approach to identifying and evaluating these risks. Property appraisals for insurance valuation purposes may be called for. A strategic issue is determining which exposures should not be insured (retained) and what, if any, deductibles (cost sharing) should be used for the exposures that are insured. Risk management principles for property and liability exposures are covered in Chapter 24.

Health-Care Decision Making and Property Management in Case of Physical and Mental Incapacity These issues arise when people become physically and mentally incapacitated and unable to make important decisions for themselves. There generally is more concern about these issues as people age, but as some recent high-profile cases illustrate, adults of any age may find themselves in this unfortunate situation.

Health-Care Decision Making: This area of planning involves preparing directives and making arrangements for a person's health care and other matters if he or she becomes no longer capable of making decisions on such matters. The planning strategies used are also covered in Chapter 30.

Property Management: The incapacity of someone who owns property and has other financial affairs gives rise to special problems because the incapacitated person will be unable to handle his or her own affairs effectively. The planning strategies in this situation are covered in Chapter 30.

Estate Planning (Planning for One's Heirs)

Nature and Scope of Planning: An estate plan has been defined as "an arrangement for the devolution of one's wealth." For some people, such an arrangement can be relatively simple. But for high-net-worth persons who are or will be subject to the federal transfer tax system (and perhaps state transfer taxes as well), and for those whose estate situation can present special problems, estate planning can become complex.

Estate planning often involves planning during an estate owner's lifetime, at his or her death, and for the management and devolution of his or her property long after the owner's death. It thus is broad in scope and touches on planning for many of the other objectives noted here.

Planning Strategies: As noted, estate planning may be broad in scope and can involve planning over a person's or family's entire economic lifecycle and after death. The estate planning process and strategies are described in Part VIII.

Charitable Giving Most people have charitable objectives to some degree. Others, who may have larger resources, may establish sophisticated systems for their charitable giving. In many cases, charitable planning is integrated with other objectives, such as income tax planning, retirement planning, and estate planning. Strategies for charitable giving are discussed in Part VI and in other parts of the book.

Business Planning In situations where closely held business interests are the main or an important part of a person's or family's wealth, planning for those interests is an important objective. This planning can involve choice of business entity; business operations, compensation arrangements, and employee benefits to maximize wealth for the family; and business succession plans, among other issues. Part IX deals with this area of planning.

Special Circumstances A final objective is the possibility, even the probability, that clients will have one or more special circumstances that should be considered in their planning. These may include the following:

- Existing disabilities, incapacities, illness, and even terminal illness of the person or family members.
- Dependents with special needs. This relates to dependents who qualify or who may need to qualify for government-provided assistance based on need. Special-needs trusts (covered in Chapter 25) may be called for in such situations.
- Marital issues in the family. This may involve marital problems, such as separations or divorces of the person, his or her children and grandchildren, and possibly other family members.
- Related to the previous point is whether the person or his or her spouse has been married before and whether there are children from the previous marriage or marriages.
- In the case of nontraditional families, partnerships, unions, and companionships, special planning issues often arise.
- The nature of the person's employment and job security obviously has an effect on planning. It also is significant if the person is planning to change jobs or retire soon, and if both the person and his or her spouse are employed outside the home.
- The possibility of future gifts and inheritances also will affect planning.

These special circumstances will be discussed throughout the book as appropriate.

Financial Planning Process

The financial planning process involves the translation of personal objectives into specific plans and finally into financial arrangements to implement those plans. To this end, following is an overview of the steps in this process.

Establishing Client-Planner Relationships

A review of the preceding objectives and planning strategies reveals the broad scope and complexity of private wealth management. Naturally, not all of these objectives apply to all persons, but most of them do. It is virtually certain, therefore, that individuals and families who need comprehensive private wealth management will need to retain the services of one and very likely several professional advisers in the various planning areas just noted. No one person can be an expert in them all.

These professional advisers include lawyers, investment advisers and asset managers, financial planners, accountants, life insurance agents and brokers, trust officers, property and liability insurance agents and brokers, valuation experts, and others. In some cases, one professional or firm will initiate planning and then bring in other professionals as needed. In many cases, however, the client deals independently with a number of professional advisers in the areas of their expertise. Either way, it is important for the client and planner to establish the scope and nature of the services to be provided, the client's objectives, limits on the planner's responsibilities and when the planning will end, any potential conflicts of interest, and the compensation arrangements involved, if necessary.

Gathering Data and Determining Goals and Expectations

The kinds of information needed vary with the situation, but they may include information about the person's or family's investments; homes and other properties; retirement plans, employer stock plans, and other employee benefits; tax situation (income, estate, and gift taxes); life, health, long-term care, and property and liability insurance policies; wills, trusts, and other estate planning documents; powers of attorney and related instruments; and similar documents and information.

In summarizing a person's present financial position, it is helpful to prepare some personal financial statements. These are much like those businesses use, except that business statements normally are prepared on the basis of generally accepted accounting principles (GAAP), while personal or family statements normally reflect cash transactions (rather than on an accrual basis) and value assets at their fair market value (rather than at the lower of original cost less depreciation or fair market value).

Personal financial statements can include a *statement of financial position* (also called a personal balance sheet), which provides a picture of a person's or family's assets, liabilities, and net worth as of a given point in time, and a *statement of cash flow*, which shows the person's or family's cash income, cash expenditures, and resultant savings (or cash flow). This cash flow statement is similar in concept to a business's income statement, except it shows only cash transactions rather than income and expenses on an accrual basis, and has other differences. A sample statement of financial position (Table 1.1) and statement of cash flow (Table 1.2) for a hypothetical family are given in the next section of this chapter.

However, as noted, depending on the purpose and scope of the planning being done, a variety of other data may need to be gathered. Furthermore, information about the person, his or her family, and other persons or institutions the person may want to benefit will be needed for estate planning and other purposes. Gathering adequate data, particularly about personal matters, often is a challenge for private wealth management professionals. In this process, they may use checklists, questionnaires, work forms, and personal interviews or some combination of these techniques for this purpose.

Next, the person must determine his or her financial goals and expectations. This, in essence, is articulating his or her objectives as outlined in the previous sections of this chapter.

Determining the Person's Financial Status

This involves analyzing the person's general financial status in relation to his or her goals and expectations (objectives) as determined in the previous steps.

Developing and Presenting the Financial Plan

Given the facts of the case, the person's objectives, an analysis of his or her present financial position, and consideration of alternatives, recommendations can be made for a financial plan to meet the indicated objectives.

Implementing the Financial Plan

A financial plan, no matter how soundly conceived, is only as good as its actual implementation. Many excellent plans are only partly implemented or not implemented at all. For example, an estate plan may be developed and agreed to by the client, and wills, trusts, and other documents may be drafted and executed, but then asset titles and beneficiary designations may not actually be changed to correspond to the well-conceived plan. Clearly, wealth management professionals should do their best to make sure their agreed-upon recommendations are actually implemented for their clients.

Monitoring the Financial Plan

No plan should be considered "cast in bronze." Circumstances change. There are births, marriages, divorces, deaths, job changes, different economic conditions, and a host of other factors that may make revisions in financial plans desirable or necessary. Hence, monitoring the plan and making necessary revisions are important activities in the financial planning process.

Case Example – Personal Financial Statements

John and Mary Henderson, ages 52 and 48, respectively, are engaging in private wealth management and have the following personal financial statements: a *statement of financial position* and a *statement of cash flow*. John is a marketing manager for a large publicly traded corporation, while Mary has recently returned to high school teaching after taking time off to raise (with John) their two children and be a homemaker. Their two children are ages 14 and 19. The 19-year-old is now in college. John and Mary also are helping support John's 82-year-old mother.

The sample statements are for the combined assets, liabilities, income, and expenses of John and Mary. Statements for each of them separately could be prepared, if desired.

The categories of assets, liabilities, income, and expenses in these statements have been selected to facilitate the planning process. They normally are good starting points, but are not meant to be exhaustive. They, of course, can be modified to fit the planner's needs and purposes. In addition, financial concerns and wealth management professionals will have their own checklists, questionnaires, forms, and reports as appropriate for their areas of expertise.

Statement of Financial Position (Balance Sheet)

Table 1.1 is the statement of financial position for the Hendersons. Dollar amounts are stated in even thousands for the sake of convenience. Assets are valued at their current fair market values, account values, and cash values, except for John's vested and "in the money" stock options, which are valued at their intrinsic value (the stock's fair market value less the option exercise price times the number of vested unexercised options). See Chapter 18 for a discussion of valuing stock options.

Table 1.1. Statement of Financial Position (as of Present Date)

Assets		
Liquid assets (in own names and jointly owned):		
Cash and checking account(s)	$5,000	
Savings account(s)	—0—	
Money market funds (mutual funds and bank funds)	40,000	
U.S. savings bonds	—0—	
Brokerage account cash balances	—0—	
Other	—0—	
Total liquid assets		$45,000
Directly owned marketable investments (in own names and jointly owned):		
Common stocks	300,000	
Corporate bonds	—0—	

Table 1.1. Statement of Financial Position (as of Present Date)

Municipal bonds	—0—	
U.S. Treasury bonds	—0—	
Certificates of deposit	—0—	
Other	—0—	
Directly owned investment companies and similar funds (in own names and jointly owned):		
Common stock funds	100,000	
Corporate bond funds	—0—	
Municipal bond funds	40,000	
U.S. Treasury bond funds	—0—	
Balanced funds	20,000	
Real estate investment trusts (REITs)	—0—	
Other funds	—0—	
Total directly owned marketable investments and investment funds		460,000
Life insurance and annuity cash values:		
Life insurance cash values	25,000	
Annuity accumulations	—0—	
Total life insurance and annuity cash values		25,000
Directly owned "nonmarketable" investments and business interests (in own names and jointly owned):		
Active business interests (proprietorships, partnership interests, limited liability company memberships, and stock in closely held corporations)	—0—	
Investment real estate (other then REITs)	—0—	
Interests in limited partnerships	—0—	
Other alternative investments	—0—	
Total directly owned "nonmarketable" investments and business interests		—0—
Assets held in trust:		
Revocable living trusts	—0—	
Other trusts and similar arrangements in which the client has an interest	—0—	
Total assets held in trust		—0—
Retirement plan accounts:		
Pension accounts	—0—	

Table 1.1. (*Continued*) Statement of Financial Position (as of Present Date)

Savings plan accounts [Section 401(k) plans]	400,000	
Profit-sharing accounts	—0—	
IRA accounts (traditional and Roth)	100,000	
Other retirement plans [Section 403(b) plans]	20,000	
Total retirement plan accounts		520,000
Employee stock plans:		
Stock options (incentive stock options [ISOs] and nonqualified options valued at intrinsic value for vested options)	100,000	
Balance in employee stock purchase plan	15,000	
Restricted stock	50,000	
Other plans	—0—	
Total employee stock plans		165,000
Education plans:		
Qualified tuition programs (Section 529 plans) as owner	20,000	
Coverdell IRAs	—0—	
Other plans	—0—	
Total education plans		20,000
Personal real estate:		
Residence	600,000	
Vacation home	300,000	
Total personal real estate		900,000
Other personal assets:		
Auto(s)	20,000	
Boat(s)	5,000	
Furs and jewelry	16,000	
Art, collections, hobbies, etc.	10,000	
Furniture and household accessories	70,000	
Other personal property	2,000	
Total other personal assets		123,000
Total assets		$2,258,000
Liabilities		
Current liabilities:		
Charge accounts, credit card balances, and other bills payable	20,000	

Table 1.1. Statement of Financial Position (as of Present Date)

Installment credit and other short-term loans	—0—	
Unusual tax liabilities	—0—	
Total current liabilities		20,000
Long-term liabilities:		
Mortgage notes on personal real estate	300,000	
Mortgage notes on investment real estate	—0—	
Home equity loans and lines	100,000	
Bank loans	—0—	
Margin loans and other investment loans	80,000	
Life insurance policy loans	—0—	
Other liabilities	—0—	
Total long-term liabilities		480,000
Total liabilities		$500,000
Family net worth (assets minus liabilities)		$1,758,000
Total liabilities and family net worth		$2,258,000

Statement of Cash Flow

Table 1.2 shows the statement of cash flow for the Hendersons as of the most recent 12-month period. All transactions are recorded on a cash basis. The items of income and expenses are selected to show the family's economic activities over the time period and to facilitate planning. Other breakdowns of income and expenses can, of course, be used as desired.

Table 1.2. Statement of Cash Flow (for the Most Recent Year)

Income		
Salary(ies) and fees:		
John	$150,000	
Mary	50,000	
Others	—0—	
Total salaries		$200,000
Investment income:		
Interest (taxable)	2,000	
Interest (nontaxable)	2,000	
Dividends (common stock and mutual funds)	9,000	
Real estate	—0—	

Table 1.2. (*Continued*) Statement of Cash Flow (for the Most Recent Year)

Realized capital gains (on sales of assets and from mutual fund distributions)	8,000	
Other investment income	—0—	
Total investment income		21,000
Bonuses, profit-sharing payments, etc.		—0—
Other income:		—0—
Total income		$221,000
Expenses and fixed obligations:		
Ordinary living expenses (food, clothing, household maintenance, transportation, recreation, hobbies, vacation, and other personal expenses)		$46,000
Interest expense:		
Consumer loans	$1,000	
Bank loans	—0—	
Margin and other investment interest	6,000	
Mortgage notes	16,000	
Home equity loans and lines	5,000	
Insurance policy loans	—0—	
Other interest	—0—	
Total interest expense		28,000
Debt amortization (mortgage notes, home equity loans and lines, consumer debt, etc.)		12,000
Insurance premiums:		
Life insurance	4,000	
Health insurance (including contributions to employer-provided plans and HSAs)	3,000	
Long-term care insurance	—0—	
Property and liability insurance	5,000	
Total insurance premiums		12,000
Charitable contributions		5,000
Tuition and educational expenses		20,000
Payments for support of aged parents or others		6,000
Other gifts		—0—
Alimony and child support payments		—0—
Health-care expenses (unreimbursed)		4,000

Table 1.2. Statement of Cash Flow (for the Most Recent Year)

Retirement plan contributions:		
Employer-provided plans	12,000	
IRAs (traditional)	—0—	
IRAs (Roth)	—0—	
Personal annuities	—0—	
Other plans	—0—	
Total retirement plan contributions		12,000
Taxes:		
Federal income tax	40,000	
State and local income tax(es)	6,000	
Social security tax(es)	12,000	
Local property taxes	9,000	
Other taxes	—0—	
Total taxes		67,000
Total expenses and fixed obligations		$212,000
Cash flow from regular activities		$9,000
Larger capital expenditures	—0—	
Net additional debt		—0—
Net cash flow		$9,000

Other Planning Statements and Projections

The previously cited statements of financial position and cash flow give a picture of the person's or family's overall economic position as of a given point or period of time. However, a number of other forms, statements, or projections also may be prepared for in-depth planning in a variety of areas.

These might include the following items, among others:

- A listing of investments held by asset class (e.g., common stocks, bonds, investment companies, real estate, other alternative investments, and so forth), including current values, when acquired, tax bases, yields, and other investment data for asset allocation and investment planning purposes.
- Pro forma income tax returns for tax planning.
- Projections of future education costs and resources for education financing.
- Projections of retirement income needs and sources of retirement income (including distribution planning).
- A listing of employee stock options (and other stock compensation plans) for asset allocation purposes and for planning how and when to exercise options.

- An analysis of lump-sum and income needs in case of the client's and his or her spouse's deaths for life insurance planning.
- An analysis of income needs in case of the client's and his or her spouse's long-term disability for disability income planning.
- An analysis of potential transfer-tax (e.g., estate tax) liabilities and other estate settlement costs and probate and nonprobate asset distribution patterns, first on the assumption that the client dies first followed by the death of his or her spouse, then on the assumption that the order of deaths is reversed for estate planning purposes. Personal family data will also be gathered for estate planning and other planning purposes.

Ethics and Wealth Management

The various professionals who offer advice and services in this field are subject to codes of professional conduct and regulations. These codes and regulations vary among the professional groups, but often deal with:

- Competence required of a professional in the field
- Confidentiality regarding client information and other matters
- Conflicts of interest in dealing with clients and required disclosure of such conflicts
- Compensation for services rendered and any requirements for disclosure of such compensation
- Principles involved in proper professional conduct
- Compliance with and enforcement of rules and procedures

A discussion of the codes and rules of all relevant professions is beyond the scope of this book. However, as examples, following is a listing of some professions and groups, with accompanying Web sites where the reader can find the complete rules and practice standards for each (in alphabetical order).

Organization	Ethics Code	Web site
American Bankers Association	Institute of Certified Bankers Professional Code of Ethics	www.aba.com/aba/documents/ICB/Exam_Application/ExamApplication.pdf
American Bar Association	Model Rules of Professional Conduct (Specific rules vary by state)	www.abanet.org/cpr/mrpc/model_rules.html
American Institute of Certified Public Accountants	Code of Professional Conduct	www.aicpa.org/about/code/index.htm

Organization	Ethics Code	Web site
Certified Financial Planner (CFP) Board of Standards, Inc.	Code of Ethics and Professional Responsibility and CFP Board's Financial Planning Practice Standards	www.cfp.net/certificants/conduct.asp
Financial Planning Association (FPA) (now includes International Association for Financial Planning)	Code of Ethics	www.fpaforfinancialplanning.org/AboutFPA/CodeofEthics
National Association of Insurance & Financial Advisers (NAIFA)	Code of Ethics	www.naifa.org/about/ethics.cfm
National Association of Personal Financial Advisers (NAPFA)	Code of Ethics	http://www.napfa.org/about/codeofethics.asp
Society of Financial Service Professionals	Code of Professional Responsibility	www.financialpro.org/about/CodeOfProfResp.cfm

Trusts & Estates magazine publishes an "ethics matrix" for many such organizations. The latest matrix can be found on the public part of its Web site at www.trustsandestates.com.

2

Environment for Wealth Management

Competence Objectives for This Chapter After reading this chapter, planners should understand:

- The functions, products, services, and regulatory structure of commercial banks
- The role of the Federal Deposit Insurance Corporation (FDIC) in protecting bank deposits against insolvency of banks and how such insurance limits can apply to multiple deposits
- The functions, products, services, and regulatory structure of brokerage and securities firms
- The role of the Securities Investor Protection Corporation (SIPC) in protecting brokerage customers' securities and cash accounts against insolvency of brokerage firms
- The functions, products, services, and regulatory and tax structures of investment companies
- The types, functions, products, services, and regulation of insurance companies
- The role of state guaranty association laws in protecting policyholders, beneficiaries, and claimants in the event of insolvency of insurance companies
- The nature and functions of trust companies
- The distinction between microeconomics and macroeconomics
- The law of supply and demand and its role in price determination
- Some of the concepts of behavioral economics (or behavioral finance)
- The definitions of inflation, the inflation rate, and some of the price indexes used to measure general price changes
- The distinction between real and nominal interest rates and values

- The definitions of deflation and stagflation
- How to recognize the phases of the business cycle and possible wealth management strategies for dealing with the business cycle
- The nature of monetary policies and the role of the Federal Reserve in attempting to maintain economic growth and price stability
- The nature of fiscal policies in attempting to maintain economic growth
- Certain commonly used economic indicators
- The tax environment for wealth management
- Economic Growth and Tax Relief Reconciliation Act of 2001 (EGTRRA) and Jobs and Growth Tax Relief Reconciliation Act of 2003 (JGTRRA)

This chapter provides an overview of the institutional, economic, and tax environments in which wealth management is carried on.

Institutional Environment

A number of financial institutions provide the products and financial services embraced by private wealth management. These institutions operate in the economy's *capital markets,* in which the available supply of funds is allocated to those who wish to borrow or invest. They act as *financial intermediaries* in that they receive funds from savers and investors and then allocate them to those who want to consume, buy property, or invest in productive enterprises. These institutions include commercial banks; securities and brokerage firms; investment company (mutual fund) organizations; insurance companies; trust companies; credit unions and other thrift institutions; and newer entities, such as hedge funds and private equity firms.

Commercial Banks

Functions, Purpose, and Federal Deposit Insurance Commercial banks traditionally have accepted customer deposits and made loans to businesses and consumers. Their deposits include checking accounts (demand deposits), saving accounts, certificates of deposit (time accounts), and money market accounts. Current interest rates on these accounts for a number of banks are reported on the Internet at www.bankrate.com.

These accounts are insured against loss due to the insolvency of the financial institution by the FDIC. For many years, accounts were insured up to $100,000 for each depositor in each insured bank. However, on October 3, 2008, the *Emergency Economic Stabilization Act of 2008* temporarily increased this basic limit to $250,000 per depositor per bank, until December 31, 2009. It then is scheduled to return to the former limit. In addition, self-directed retirement accounts, such as individual retirement accounts, are insured by the FDIC up to $250,000 (which was not changed by the Emergency Economic Stabilization Act). The FDIC is an independent agency of the U.S. government, and FDIC insurance is backed by the full faith and credit of the United States.

A depositor can obtain up to $250,000 of insurance per bank for single accounts held in any number of insured banks. Furthermore, a depositor might have an account in an insured bank in his or her own name (a single account) and then another account in the same bank in the joint names of the depositor and someone else (a joint account), and each account would be covered by the FDIC up to $250,000 per depositor. There are other rules for covering accounts held in other ownership categories, such as revocable trust accounts, irrevocable trust accounts, employee benefit plan accounts, and others. Online sites for further information include www2.fdic.gov/edie (for calculating insurance coverage using the FDIC's electronic deposit insurance calculator) and www.fdic.gov/deposit (for information on FDIC insurance).

CASE EXAMPLE

Marie Napoli's asset allocation planning calls for her to hold $400,000 in 12-to-36-month traditional certificates of deposit (CDs). Upon investigation of their respective yields, Marie decides to buy a $150,000 12-month insured CD in Bank "A," a $100,000 24-month insured CD in Bank "B," another $100,000 24-month insured CD in Bank "C," and a $50,000 36-month insured CD in Bank "D." In addition, Marie and her husband, Paul, have a joint insured checking account in Bank "A" with a $10,000 balance. Finally, Marie has a $200,000 IRA account invested in 36-month CDs in Bank "E." As of this writing, all of these accounts would be fully covered by FDIC insurance. However, depending on what happens to the Stabilization Act temporary limit increase, $50,000 of the 12-month CD in Bank "A" would not be covered under the former $100,000 basic limit.

Commercial banks also have a unique role in the execution of monetary policy by the Federal Reserve. They maintain *reserves* in the form of deposits with the 12 regional Federal Reserve Banks. The Federal Reserve then conducts monetary policy by affecting the levels of commercial bank reserves.

Products and Services As just noted, the traditional services of commercial banks are accepting deposits and making loans. However, in recent years, commercial banks, through their affiliates, now offer a wide variety of other products and services, including brokerage services, investment banking and other securities activities, mutual funds, insurance and annuities, private banking (wealth management services), and others. Commercial banks traditionally have also had trust departments and provided trustee and other fiduciary services.

Regulation Commercial banks may be chartered by the federal government and called *national banks,* or chartered by a state, in which case they are called *state banks.* Three federal agencies may regulate commercial banks. The Comptroller of the Currency charters and regulates national banks. Also, all national banks must be members of the Federal Reserve System and hence subject to the regulations of the board of governors of that system. Finally, all member banks of the Federal Reserve System are insured by and subject to the regulations of the board of directors of the FDIC.

State banks are regulated under the banking laws of their respective states. In addition, state banks may elect to join the Federal Reserve System and thus be insured by the FDIC. In this case, they also would be regulated by these two federal agencies.

Securities and Brokerage Firms

Functions, Purpose, and Securities Investor Protection Corporation (SIPC) These firms provide brokerage services in buying and selling securities, commodities, and the like for their customers, for which they usually charge commissions. In this role, they are also referred to as *broker–dealers.* Securities firms also engage in investment banking in which they originate (underwrite) securities issued by corporations, government bodies, and other entities and then distribute those securities to the investing public. They provide other investment and financial services as well.

Following several sizable brokerage-house failures, in 1970 the *Securities Investor Protection Act* was passed, which created the *Securities Investor Protection Corporation (SIPC).* The SIPC is intended to protect customers of SIPC member firms if a firm becomes insolvent and is liquidated under the provisions of the Act. If a member firm is to be liquidated, a trustee is appointed to supervise the liquidation. The trustee attempts to return to customers the securities that can be "specifically identified" as theirs. (Generally, these are fully paid securities in cash accounts and excess margin securities in margin accounts that have been set aside as the property of customers.) SIPC pays any remaining claims of each customer, up to $500,000, except that claims for cash are limited to $100,000. In general, customers' securities and cash are covered by the Act. Other kinds of property, such as commodities accounts, are not covered. The SIPC, of course, does not provide any protection to investors against losses from fluctuations in securities prices. The SIPC is funded by the member brokerage firms. In addition, many brokerage firms voluntarily provide private insolvency insurance protection for their customers above the SIPC coverage, up to much higher limits.

Products and Services Like commercial banks, securities firms have broadened their offerings to include a wide range of financial products and services, such as mutual funds, insurance and annuities, wealth management services, mortgages and other loans, credit cards, check writing, and others. Some of these firms also operate trust companies. With respect to their brokerage operations, securities firms may be full-service brokers, discount brokers, or exclusively online electronic brokers.

Regulation Following the onset of the Great Depression of the 1930s, the federal government enacted several important statutes, which remain the basis of federal securities law today.

Securities Act of 1933: The first was the *Securities Act of 1933,* which requires that securities offered for public sale by an issuing company or any person in a control relationship with the company, with some exceptions, must be registered with the Securities and Exchange Commission (SEC). This is done by filing a *registration statement* with the SEC that discloses required material information about the new issue. It also requires that a *prospectus* (a selling document) containing essential information from the registration statement be supplied to purchasers of the new issue. The Act further prohibits misrepresentations, deceit, and other fraudulent acts in the sale of securities (a general antifraud provision).

Private Placements and Other Exemptions from Registration: From the viewpoint of private wealth management, an important exception to the registration requirements of the 1933 Act is for private offerings to certain persons or entities who presumably have adequate information or investment sophistication so that they can protect themselves and who do not plan to redistribute the securities—commonly called *private placements.* There is a commonly used safe-harbor rule contained in Rule 506 of Regulation D issued by the SEC that defines the private placement exemption. Under this rule, an issuer can sell securities (in any amount) to an unlimited number of "accredited" investors (for whom no disclosures or sophistication requirements are imposed) and to no more than 35 "nonaccredited" investors (who the issuer reasonably believes have sufficient knowledge and experience to evaluate adequately the investment and who receive specified written disclosures about the securities). *Accredited investors* include individuals who (with their spouse, if applicable) have a net worth of more than $1 million or who have had and expect to have an annual income of $200,000 or more, or $300,000 or more including their spouse. Accredited investors also include institutional investors, key inside persons (such as directors and executive officers of the issuer), certain trusts, and others. The securities issued in a private placement are *restricted securities* and cannot be resold in the public market without SEC registration or complying with another rule exempting them from registration.

Other exemptions from registration include offerings restricted to residents of the state in which the issuing company is located (intrastate offerings); small offerings; offerings by small business investment companies; certain exempt categories of assets, such as U.S. government notes and bonds, state and local government securities, securities issued by banks and regulated savings and loan associations, insurance and annuity policies, and qualified retirement plans; and others. Even if an offering is exempted from registration, the Act's antifraud provisions still apply.

Securities Exchange Act of 1934: This was the second basic pillar of federal securities regulation. The 1934 Act, with its many amendments, is wide-ranging and regulates national securities exchanges and trading markets, securities firms and registered representatives, periodic disclosure by public companies, fraudulent and abusive practices, and many other matters. The Act also created the *Securities and Exchange Commission (SEC)*, which is an independent federal agency charged with administering the federal securities laws.

The Securities Exchange Act requires the registration of national securities exchanges, broker–dealers, and their sales associates with the SEC. However, actual day-to-day regulation of these exchanges, of the over-the-counter market, of broker–dealers, and of registered representatives is mainly done through self-regulation by the firms themselves and private *self-regulatory organizations (SROs)* under the administrative supervision of the SEC.

Because of this rather unique regulatory system, broker–dealers and their registered representatives are subject to a wide range of regulation through the SEC, SROs, court decisions, and federal antifraud rules.[1] For example, these securities professionals are subject to several *rules of conduct*, which include the need to know their customers' financial situation, ability, and desire to assume

[1]The 1934 Act defines a *broker* as any person engaged in the regular business of affecting securities transactions for the account of others. A *dealer* is defined as any person engaged in buying or selling securities for his or her own account as part of his or her regular business. Neither definition includes a bank. As noted earlier in Chapter 1, *investment advisers* are regulated by the SEC under the Investment Advisers Act of 1940.

risk ("know your customer"); to have reasonable grounds for investment recommendations based on their customers' situation; to know the securities they recommend; to not "churn" (frequent buying and selling of securities for little or no investment reason and mainly to earn commissions) in discretionary customer accounts; to not charge "unreasonable" commissions or markups; and to execute customer orders properly, among others.

Rule 10b-5 Fraud Actions: A wide-ranging SEC rule concerning the antifraud provisions of securities law is *Rule 10b-5.* This important rule prohibits any person from engaging in fraudulent activities or making untrue statements of material facts with intent to deceive in connection with securities transactions. Much securities litigation is based on Rule 10b-5.

Arbitration Agreements: Securities disputes may be settled through *arbitration,* rather than in the courts, if the parties so agree. As a result, the account agreements between securities firms and their customers routinely contain a provision requiring arbitration of disputes. These arbitration clauses have been enforced by the courts.

Regulation of Publicly Traded Companies: The 1934 Act also extends disclosure requirements and substantive securities regulation on an ongoing basis to publicly traded companies. Thus, companies whose securities are listed on an exchange or are traded over the counter and meet certain size requirements must *register their securities* and *file periodic disclosure statements* with the SEC. These are called *reporting companies.* The periodic statements include an annual report (on *Form 10-K*), quarterly reports, and special reports on certain material events affecting the company. The Sarbanes-Oxley Act requires certain certifying officers of the company (the CEO and CFO) to certify that they have reviewed the annual and quarterly reports and, based on their knowledge, that they are not false or misleading and "fairly represent" the condition of the company. Reporting companies also are subject to other reporting and conduct requirements.

Insider Trading: Another important area of regulation in the 1934 Act and other securities law involves *insider trading.* This occurs when a corporate insider who has a duty of confidentiality buys or sells his or her company's securities (or the securities of another company—called "outsider trading") using material, nonpublic information secured from his or her insider status. Insider trading may give rise to Rule 10b-5 liability. Such liability may attach not only to insiders themselves, but also to others who obtain material, nonpublic information due to their relationship with the company (such as lawyers, bankers, and accountants) or who obtain such information from persons who have a duty of confidentiality (such as someone receiving an improper tip). Of course, once information becomes public, there is no insider trading issue.

Other aspects of insider trading are the requirements in Section 16(b) of the Exchange Act for specified insiders to report to the SEC and on the company's Web site their trading in their company's securities, and to pay to the corporation any "short-swing" profits from company securities. Such short-swing profits arise from the purchase and sale of company securities within any six-month period.

Market Practices: The 1934 Act also regulates certain *market practices.* For example, the Act prohibits *market manipulation,* which can involve certain activities that intentionally create misleading appearances of market movements in listed securities. Similarly, the Act regulates *issuer repurchases* of a company's own securities. Furthermore, the Exchange Act authorizes the Federal Reserve Board to set *margin requirements* for the extension of credit to purchase securities. The Federal Reserve Board has done so in Regulation T for securities market intermediaries (such as broker–dealers). As of this writing, the initial margin requirement is set at 50 percent. Buying securities on margin is discussed in Chapter 5.

Other Federal Laws Affecting Investments: A number of other federal laws deal with securities, investments, and wealth management. Soon after passage of the Securities Act of 1933, the *Glass-Steagall Act* was passed in 1934. Glass-Steagall required the separation of commercial banking and investment banking, and created the FDIC. However, in 1999, this separation was reversed by passage of the *Financial Services Modernization Act (Gramm-Leach-Bliley Act),* which repealed this part of Glass-Steagall.

Two important laws were passed in 1940. The *Investment Advisers Act of 1940* has already been described in Chapter 1. The other was the *Investment Company Act of 1940,* which created the regulatory framework for the mutual fund industry. This law is described in more detail later in the chapter in the discussion of investment companies.

Another federal law of note is the *National Securities Markets Improvement Act of 1996.* This law preempts state securities law in important areas involving "covered securities." This, in large measure, ends dual federal-state regulation for most categories of securities. This law also divides regulation of investment advisers into federal regulation of advisers managing $25 million or more of client assets and advising registered investment companies, and state regulation of all other advisers.

State Securities Regulation ("Blue Sky Laws"): Every state has securities laws that cover subjects such as the offering of securities intrastate, registration of broker–dealers, regulation of investment advisers, and securities antifraud laws.[2] State agencies administer these laws. Thus, except for the areas preempted for federal regulation by the National Securities Markets Improvement Act just noted, there is dual federal-state securities regulation.

Investment Companies

Functions and Purpose Investment companies are organizations that gather assets from investors and invest those assets in specified categories of investment media, such as common stocks, preferred stocks, various types of bonds, money market instruments, and other kinds of assets. The investors are shareholders in the investment company. The investment company provides its shareholders with professional investment management or an indexed fund that mirrors a particular market index, diversification over a number of individual securities, convenience and ready marketability of their shares, and the ability to invest reasonable amounts in the fund.

There are four basic types of investment companies. By far, the most important is *mutual funds,* which legally are called "open-end investment companies." These are structured either as corporations or business trusts. Mutual funds do not have their own staff, but instead are operated by separate management companies that serve as a fund's investment adviser, act as the fund's principal underwriter to distribute the fund's shares to the public (as a broker–dealer), and perform other administrative functions for the fund. These management companies have contracts with the funds and may be compensated based on fees expressed as a percentage of a fund's net assets. Mutual funds also have boards of directors who are elected by the shareholders and have responsibility for overseeing the fund's affairs, including approving the contracts between the fund and its management company and other service providers.

Mutual funds are required to redeem their shares at the request of shareholders on a daily basis. This is done at a price equal to the net asset value (NAV) of the shares (in a few cases, less a redemption charge), the value of which is determined at the close of New York Stock Exchange trading—normally at 4 p.m. eastern standard time. The funds also normally stand ready to sell shares to investors at the same NAV per share (plus a sales charge in the case of load funds) on a daily basis as of the same time.

Mutual funds can be sponsored by fund management companies, brokerage firms, banks, and insurance companies. These organizations normally sponsor a number of individual funds, called "families of funds." In terms of

[2] The term "blue sky laws" reputedly comes from an old saying that unethical securities dealers sold no more than a piece of the blue sky.

distribution, many funds are sold through third-party sales operations, such as brokers, fund management company sales representatives, banks, insurance agents, and financial planners. Load funds (containing sales charges) are sold in this way because it is necessary to compensate the marketing representative. Some no-load funds (generally containing no sales charges) are also sold in this manner. Other funds are sold directly from the fund itself without a third-party marketing representative. These would include most no-load funds.

The second type of investment company is *exchange-traded funds (ETFs).* ETFs are like mutual funds except that they are bought and sold by investors on organized exchanges rather than through the funds themselves. Thus, ETFs do not redeem or sell their shares based on their NAVs. The prices of ETFs are determined by supply and demand for their shares in the market, and may differ from the funds' NAVs.[3] Also, ETFs are continuously traded during market hours and their prices are determined for each trade, just like other stocks and bonds that are on organized exchanges. Furthermore, ETFs can be bought on margin and sold short. ETFs are bought and sold through brokers, so a commission normally is charged on each trade.

The third type of investment company is the *closed-end fund.* Closed-end funds are corporations with a fixed number of shares that are actively and continuously traded on organized exchanges. Their share prices are determined for each trade based on the supply and demand for their shares in the market. Thus, the prices for closed-end fund shares may be greater (trade at a premium), about the same, or less (trade at a discount) than the funds' NAVs, depending on the market's perceptions concerning a fund's management and prospects. Since they are market traded, closed-end funds can be bought on margin and sold short. Furthermore, many closed-end fund companies use borrowed money to attempt to enhance their investment returns (i.e., are leveraged). This may increase or decrease their returns, depending on market conditions.

The final category is *unit investment trusts (UITs).* This type of investment company holds a fixed portfolio of securities or investments. Units in the trust are then sold to investors. UITs often have a fixed termination date, at which time the unit holders receive a distribution of their proportionate share of the trust's net assets.

Products and Services As just noted, the main products of investment companies are pooled, diversified investment funds sold to investors in

[3] As a practical matter, since most ETFs are index funds and not actively managed, their market prices generally should not deviate much from their NAVs.

convenient units. The investment characteristics of mutual funds and other investment companies are discussed in detail in Chapter 8.

Like banks and brokerage firms, some mutual fund management companies have broadened the financial services they offer through subsidiaries or contractual arrangements. These might include sale of insurance and annuity policies, brokerage services, and providing trust services.

Regulation The principal federal law regulating investment companies is the *Investment Company Act of 1940.* This law requires investment companies to register with and report to the SEC, maintain proper records, have a majority of independent directors on mutual funds' boards of directors (in most cases), and other matters.

Investment organizations whose investors meet certain requirements are exempt from registering as an investment company under the Investment Company Act of 1940 and other laws. Such an exemption applies if all the investors are "qualified purchasers." In general, a *qualified purchaser* is any natural person who owns $5 million or more in investments; certain family-owned entities that own $5 million or more in investments; certain trusts whose trustees and persons contributing assets to the trust meet any of the previous requirements; and any person who is acting for his or her own account or for other qualified purchasers and who owns, in the aggregate, $25 million or more in investments.[4]

Thus, we have now dealt with the concepts of accredited investors (to whom an issuer can sell securities without registration under the 1933 Act and other laws as a private placement) and qualified purchasers (to whom an issuer can sell investments without being classified as an investment company under the 1940 Act and other laws). A significant aspect of these definitions is that hedge fund and private equity fund managers usually restrict sales of their investment interests only to persons and entities that are both "accredited investors" and "qualified purchasers." By so doing, they avoid having to register their offerings under the 1933 Act and other laws, and do not have to register as an investment company under the 1940 Act and other laws. The same restrictions on eligible purchasers also normally apply to sales of private placement life insurance for the same reasons.[5]

Investment companies also are subject to other federal and state securities laws. They must register public offerings of their securities, such as mutual fund

[4] There is another exemption from registration without limiting sales to "qualified purchasers" that requires a fund not to admit more than 100 investors, but such investors still must meet the definition of an "accredited investor."

[5] Hedge funds, private equity, and other alternative investments are covered in Chapter 8; private placement life insurance is covered in Chapter 21.

shares, under the 1933 Act and deliver a current prospectus to all prospective purchasers. Their principal underwriters and other sales agents are regulated as broker–dealers under the 1934 Act and other laws. Their investment advisers are regulated under the Investment Advisers Act of 1940.

Taxation The tax status of regulated investment companies is dealt with under Subchapter M of the Internal Revenue Code of 1986 (IRC of 1986). To qualify as a regulated investment company (RIC) for tax purposes, a fund must be registered under the Investment Company Act of 1940 as a management company, unit investment trust, or certain other entities; at least 90 percent of its gross income must come from investment sources; it must distribute at least 90 percent of its annual investment company taxable income and all of its net tax-exempt interest income to its shareholders; and it must meet certain investment diversification requirements. Regulated investment companies are allowed to deduct from their ordinary taxable income and net realized capital gains (entity-level income) the dividends they pay to their shareholders. As a result, RICs generally distribute all of their earnings each year as dividends to their shareholders and thus avoid corporate-level taxation. The funds' shareholders are then taxed on the dividend distributions they receive as ordinary income dividends, qualified dividends, capital gains, or exempt interest dividends, whichever the case may be. (The taxation of RIC shareholders is described further in Chapter 8.) Thus, RICs serve as a conduit for their shareholders for tax purposes.

Insurance Companies

Functions, Purpose, and State Guaranty Associations Insurance companies sell contracts (policies) that financially protect individuals and businesses against many of the perils of life (insurable risks). As a general principle, insurers can effectively insure against these perils because they cover large numbers of insureds (exposure units) and so by employing the principles of probability (including the law of large numbers), they can reasonably and accurately predict their losses on whole groups by insureds. This is the concept of *pooling.*

In the United States, insurance companies generally are divided into life insurance companies (which write life insurance, annuities, and health insurance), property and liability companies (which write personal lines and commercial lines of insurance covering property losses, legal liability claims, and other exposures), health insurers (writing medical expense and other health coverages), and monoline or specialty insurers (such as title insurers and bond insurers).

In terms of organizational and ownership structures, insurers are unique among financial institutions in that there are stock insurance companies, mutual insurance companies, and reciprocal insurance exchanges. Like other for-profit corporations, *stock insurance companies* have stockholders who own the company, elect the board of directors, and are entitled to their proportionate share of any dividends declared by the board on their stock. The stock generally is traded on organized exchanges or markets. *Mutual insurance companies* also are structured as corporations, but they are organized to provide insurance for their policyholders and not for profit. They are like cooperatives. Mutual insurers do not have common stock outstanding or stockholders, but rather are technically owned by their policyholders, who elect the board of directors, may receive policyholder dividends on insurance purchased from the company, and are entitled to their proportionate share of the company's surplus if the mutual insurance company should be converted into a stock insurance company under state law (referred to as *demutualizing*), or in the unlikely event the insurer should be liquidated. *Reciprocal insurance exchanges* are entities of policyholders who technically exchange insurance contracts with each other and share in any cost savings from the insurance operation. Reciprocals resemble mutual insurance companies, but are not structured as corporations. Rather, reciprocals are managed by outside management companies that are referred to as attorneys-in-fact. In life insurance, there are also fraternal companies and benefit societies that sell insurance within religions or other groups to their members.

In terms of distribution systems, most insurance is sold through insurance agents and insurance brokers, who typically are independent businesspersons or corporations. *Insurance agents* legally are agents of one or more insurance companies and have agency contracts with the companies they represent. Independent agents have contracts with a number of insurers, while exclusive agents generally represent only one insurer. *Insurance brokers* legally are agents of their insureds and can secure insurance contracts for them from any one of a number of insurance companies that will accept brokerage business. Both agents and brokers typically are compensated by commissions paid by the insurers with whom they place the policies they have sold. As a practical matter, many insurance marketing persons (often referred to as "producers") act as both agents and brokers, and have agency contracts with some insurers but also place brokerage business with others.

A few large insurance companies sell policies directly to consumers without an agent or broker. This may be done through the Internet or by mail. In addition, insurance may be distributed through securities firms, banks, and investment companies.

Insurers generally have had a good record for financial strength and solvency. However, in recent years, several high-profile insurance companies have become insolvent, so when purchasing insurance or recommending coverage for clients, due diligence must be paid to the financial strength of the insurers being considered. Such due diligence is covered in Chapter 20.

If an insurer should experience financial difficulty, the state insurance regulator normally becomes involved and may take various actions to rehabilitate the insurer. If this is successful, the policyowners are not seriously harmed. However, if rehabilitation is not practical or successful, the regulator will liquidate an insolvent insurer.

In order to protect policyholders, beneficiaries, and claimants of insolvent insurers, every state has enacted some type of guaranty association law. The National Association of Insurance Commissioners (NAIC) has created two model statutes: one for life and health insurance and the other for property and liability insurance. The state guaranty association laws are largely based on these model acts, but individual state laws may differ in important respects. These laws generally apply to policyholders of insolvent or impaired insurers who are residents of the state where the insurer is deemed insolvent. However, they apply to life and accident insurance beneficiaries, regardless of their state of residence. The laws have limits on the amounts of insolvency losses they will cover. For example, many state laws cover up to $300,000 of life insurace death benefits, $100,000 of life insurance cash values, and $100,000 of annuity cash values per insured person; various limits on health insurance; and various limits on other insurance coverages.

Benefits paid from state guaranty associations are financed by post-insolvency assessments against the insurers writing the business involved in the state. Thus, there is no advance funding of the associations. In addition, the laws put limits on insurer assessments in a calendar year, such as no more than 2 percent of an insurer's annual premiums on covered business. Assessments can also be limited if they would harm an insurer's ability to carry out its obligations. It can be seen that these state guaranty association plans differ in important respects from the insolvency protection provided by the FDIC and SIPC discussed earlier.[6]

Products and Services Of course, the main products of insurance companies are various insurance policies. In the United States, insurers normally are organized and licensed either as life and health insurers (or only health insurers) or as property and liability insurers, or monoline insurers. However, groups of insurers containing life and health companies and property and liability companies are frequently organized under common ownership.

Like other financial institutions, insurers have broadened the products and services they offer to the public. For example, insurers or groups of insurers might own securities firms, management companies for families of

[6] They also differ materially from the insolvency protection for defined benefit pension plan participants provided by the Pension Benefit Guaranty Corporation (PBGC) discussed in Chapter 13.

mutual funds, investment advisory firms, banks or thrift institutions, trust companies, and other financial services firms.

Regulation Insurance companies and their representatives are primarily regulated at the state level through state government departments headed by an official typically called the insurance commissioner, director of insurance, superintendent of insurance, or some similar title. The nature and quality of state insurance regulation varies markedly among the states. Some regulatory coordination among the states is achieved through the *National Association of Insurance Commissioners (NAIC).* However, the actions of the NAIC are advisory only and its model laws and regulations only become operative when, and if, they are actually enacted by the individual states.

Trust Companies

Acting as trustees, estate administration and other fiduciary activities may be carried out by individuals (i.e., individual trustees) or corporate trust companies (often referred to as "professional trustees"). An important issue in planning for trusts is whether individual trustees, corporate trustees, or a combination of both should be named as trustee(s). This issue is discussed in Chapter 25.

Most corporate trustees operate as trust departments of commercial banks. However, some corporate trustees operate solely as trust companies. Also, as noted previously, other trust companies may be subsidiaries of securities firms, investment companies, and life insurance companies.

Trust companies generally operate under state law. The trust departments of state banks are regulated under state banking law. The Comptroller of the Currency may authorize national banks to operate trust departments, but they must do so within the confines of state trust law where they are located.

Trust companies perform a number of *fiduciary functions.* Primarily, they act as trustees under various kinds of trusts, in which capacity they invest trust assets, prepare trust tax returns, make discretionary and mandatory distributions to trust beneficiaries, and generally administer the trust according to its terms and state trust law. They also may act as executor or administrator of estates, serve as guardian of property for those not able to act for themselves, act as investment and property managers, serve as registrar of stocks and bonds, and other similar functions.

Savings Institutions and Credit Unions

Savings (thrift) institutions include savings banks and savings and loan (S&L) associations. The primary functions of these institutions are to accept deposits from the public (such as savings accounts and certificates of deposit) and make loans from those deposits. Their lending traditionally has been primarily for home mortgage loans, but over the years, their lending authority has been expanded to include other types of loans. However, like other financial services organizations, many thrift institutions have broadened their products and services to include insurance sales, mutual funds, trust services, and other financial services.

These institutions may be organized as stock companies (owned by stockholders) or as mutual fund associations (technically owned by their depositors). However, there has been a distinct trend for mutual fund associations to demutualize and become stock companies. Thrift institutions may be chartered by states or by the federal government, in which case they are regulated by the federal Office of Thrift Supervision. Accounts in thrift institutions generally are insured by the FDIC, in which case the institutions themselves also are regulated by the FDIC.

Credit unions are nonprofit organizations that both accept deposits from and make loans to members. The members have some common association with each other, such as working for the same employer, belonging to the same union, belonging to the same fraternal group, and so forth. It is argued that such member associations make loan defaults less likely. The loans may be personal loans, mortgage loans, installment loans, and others.

Credit unions may be state-chartered and regulated by the state or chartered by the federal government and regulated by the National Credit Union Administration. Member accounts usually are insured against insolvency of the credit union, on the same terms that the FDIC insures commercial bank and thrift institution accounts, now up to $250,000 per account by the National Credit Union Share Insurance Fund, which is a federal agency backed by the full faith and credit of the U.S. government.

Deregulation of Financial Institutions and the Financial Services Movement

Prior to 1999 in the United States, there were various regulatory boundaries between commercial banks and other financial institutions. Perhaps best known was the Banking Act of 1933, commonly called the *Glass-Steagall Act,* which prohibited commercial banks from associating with any business organization that engaged principally in the issue, floatation, underwriting, public sale, or distributions of securities. Furthermore, the Bank Holding Company Act of 1956 and its 1970 Amendments generally limited bank holding companies to activities "closely related" to commercial banking.

This changed in 1999 with passage of the *Financial Services Modernization Act* or *Gramm-Leach-Bliley Act of 1999.* This law allowed banks and bank holding companies to engage in various financial activities that previously had been denied to them, with some limitations. First, it repealed the securities activities prohibitions on commercial banks in Glass-Steagall. In addition, it created a new type of bank holding company called a *financial holding company,* which has the authority to engage in various financial activities, such as underwriting or dealing in securities, and others. The Act further allowed national banks to have *financial subsidiaries* to engage in many of these financial activities. It also allowed other financial institutions, such as insurance companies, securities firms, and investment companies, to own commercial banks and thrift institutions.

As of this writing, the economy is suffering through a "credit crunch" (and recession), characterized by loan defaults, restricted bank lending, liquidity problems, and potential insolvencies of banks and other financial institutions resulting in massive federal "bailouts." How these developments will affect the regulation of financial institutions remains to be seen.

Economic Environment and Wealth Management

Implicit in any wealth management or financial planning are at least some assumptions as to what the economy may look like in the near and distant future. These assumptions may or may not be explicitly stated, but they are imbedded in the recommendations made and actions taken.

Of course, no one can know what the future may bring. This gives rise to two foundational principles of planning: (1) the need for *caution* in making financial decisions and (2) the desirability of *diversification* in asset allocation and other planning. It also means that a basic understanding of economics is an important backdrop for wealth management.

Microeconomics and Macroeconomics

The field of economics is broadly divided into two areas: microeconomics and macroeconomics. *Microeconomics* deals with the actions of individuals and firms in purchasing and selling specific products and services. It involves supply, demand, costs, and price considerations for individual products and industries. Price theory (supply and demand) is part of microeconomics.

Macroeconomics, in contrast, involves the study of aggregate or "macro" (large) economic forces, such as overall production, economic growth (or decline), employment, money supply, government revenues and expenditures, general price levels (i.e., inflation, deflation, or stable prices), and so forth. Monetary policy and fiscal policy are part of macroeconomics.

Supply and Demand–Price Determination

The price paid and quantity sold for a product in any given market are equal to the point where the supply curve and demand curve for the product intersect. This is called the equilibrium price and quantity. In competitive markets, the actual price will tend to move to this price until supply and demand are at the equilibrium price. This is referred to as the *law of supply and demand.*

This is illustrated in Figure 2.1. The demand curve (D_1 D_2) slopes downward and to the right, indicating consumers will demand more of a product as its price decreases.

The supply curve (S_1 S_2) slopes upward and to the right, indicating that firms normally are willing to supply more of a product as its price increases. The equilibrium price and quantity sold in this market are determined at the point where the demand curve (D_1 D_2) and supply curve (S_1 S_2) intersect, or at point E. At this point, the equilibrium price is $3 per unit, 10 million units will be sold, and there will be no unsold units in the market.

The previous discussion assumes competitive markets and is referred to by economists as the *competitive model.* This is considered economically the

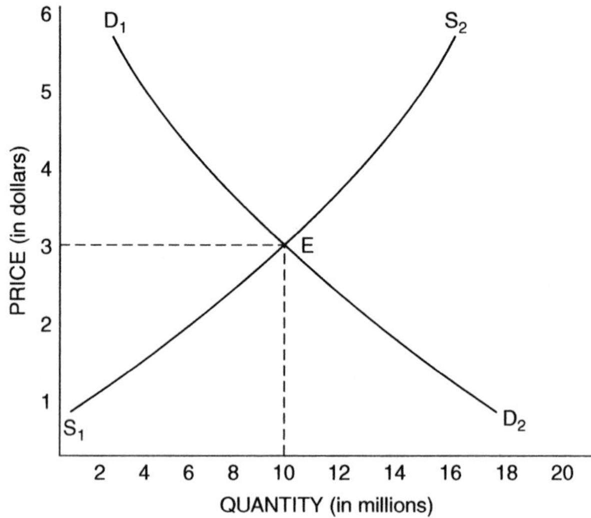

Figure 2.1. Demand and Supply Curves and Market Prices and Quantity Equilibrium

most efficient market structure. In this regard, economists define *perfect competition* as a market structure in which there are many individual buyers and sellers so that no one individual can affect the price paid and quantity sold as determined by the law of supply and demand. Some markets for agricultural products (e.g., wheat, corn, soybeans, etc.) may be examples of this. Properly functioning organized securities exchanges, such as the New York Stock Exchange and others, also probably come close to this definition.

However, in many other markets, the strict definition of perfect competition does not hold. For example, in a *monopoly,* only one firm supplies the whole market and can determine the quantity supplied and influence the price. A *natural monopoly* exists when it would be inefficient to have two or more firms competing in the same market. Some utilities may be examples of this. In the United States, government regulation is often the way such natural monopolies are controlled.

In many markets, however, there is competition, but it is imperfect. One form of imperfect competition is *oligopoly,* where there is a small number of firms supplying the market; when making moves in the market, they each must be concerned with the reactions of the others. The automobile industry may be an example of oligopoly. The other form of imperfect competition is *monopolistic competition.* Here there are a larger number of firms than in an oligopoly and each firm does not need to be concerned about the market reactions of the others, but each firm is sufficiently differentiated from the others (through product design, advertising, and so forth) so that competition is limited. Many markets probably fit this model.

Price and output determination in monopoly and imperfect competition are different in varying degrees from that just described for the competitive model. In general, under these market structures, the economic results will be less efficient (with a lower amount produced and at higher prices) than under the competitive model.

Behavioral Economics (Behavioral Finance)

This is a comparatively new field and combines psychology with economics and finance. It is concerned with how people actually make economic decisions and recognizes that their decision-making process may not be entirely "rational," as assumed in the preceding discussion.

Studies in this field have developed a number of concepts, such as the following:

- Anchoring (use of irrelevant information in decision making)
- Loss aversion (people are more concerned with avoiding losses than with making gains)

- Favoring the status quo (a tendency to accept things as they are rather than make changes)
- Regret theory (people make irrational choices because they fear making wrong ones)

Some of these concepts may help explain certain attitudes clients display in making wealth management decisions. For example, some investors want to continue holding a losing stock that should be sold, hoping that its market price will somehow return to the price they originally paid. This original price is irrelevant to the current investment quality of the stock (an example of anchoring). Also, some investors tend to sell stocks with gains too soon while tending to hold losing stocks too long (loss aversion). An example in the employee benefits field might be the situation where an employer's 401(k) savings plan (see Chapter 13) provides that eligible employees will be automatically enrolled to make elective contributions to the plan (automatic enrollment) unless they affirmatively elect not to do so. Then enrollment in the plan will be greater than if eligible employees initially had to affirmatively elect to participate (an example of the bias in favor of the status quo). (The Pension Protection Act of 2006 allows such automatic enrollment for this reason.)

Inflation, Deflation, and Stagflation

The section "Supply and Demand—Price Determination" dealt with the determination of the prices of individual goods and services. In this section, we will deal with changes in overall average prices of many or all goods and services in the economy. Here we will take a macroeconomic view of prices.

Inflation *Inflation* is the increase in the general level of prices in the economy. The *inflation rate* is the percentage rate at which the general price level increases from one period to another.

Price Indexes: In order to measure inflation (or deflation) in average prices over time, economists construct *price indexes,* which show average weighted price changes in a given "basket," or grouping, of goods and services as compared to their average prices in a selected base period, which is given an index value of 100. An important price index is the *consumer price index (CPI),* which measures the prices of baskets of goods and services assumed to be important to U.S. urban households (retail consumers). The CPI is widely cited as an inflation measure and is used to index a number of tax, benefit, and financial product values for inflation. These include, for example, federal income tax brackets and other tax values, Social Security benefits, some pension benefits (usually for state and local government plans), retirement plan contribution and benefit limits, the federal gift-tax annual exclusion and other transfer tax limits, the changes in values for Treasury Inflation Protected Securities (TIPS), and I series U.S. savings bonds, among others.

Other commonly used price indexes include the *producer price index (PPI)* and the *gross domestic product (GDP) deflator.* The PPI shows changes in average prices of goods sold by producers. The GDP deflator measures changes in the weighted average prices of all goods and services produced within the United States. It is said to be closely watched by the Federal Reserve authorities for inflationary trends. There also are commodity price indexes. Perhaps the best known is the Reuters Commodity Research Bureau (CRB) Futures Price Index, which tracks the prices of 19 commodities.

Rates of inflation, as measured by the CPI, are often cited as both *overall inflation* (sometimes called *headline inflation*) and *core inflation.* Overall inflation considers the prices of all goods and services included in the index. Core inflation excludes items of food and energy from the calculated rates. The theory behind this is that the prices for food and energy are thought to fluctuate considerably from one period to another (i.e., they are volatile) and hence might distort any inflationary trend in the economy. Some believe central banks (like the Federal Reserve) rely more on the core rate in making monetary decisions.

Economic Effects of Inflation: Persistent inflation tends to distort economic activity over time. One of the goals of the Federal Reserve is to control inflation (or to keep average inflation "low," depending on one's economic philosophy) through monetary policy.

A major adverse effect of persistent inflation is to reduce over time the real value (value in terms of purchasing power) of assets or benefits expressed in terms of a fixed number of dollars (fixed-dollar assets). These include saving accounts, CDs, currency and checking accounts, nonindexed bonds, and nonindexed pension payments, among others. Economists refer to this loss of purchasing power as an *inflation tax.*

Inflation also adversely affects taxpayers since the U.S. tax system is only partly indexed for inflation (see Chapters 10 and 26 for information on the structure of the tax system). This means inflation causes more income and estate and gift tax values to exceed nonindexed limits and deductions, resulting in greater taxation. A good example is the alternative minimum tax (AMT) exemption amount, which is not indexed for inflation.

Consumers are adversely affected when their cost of living increases and their incomes do not keep pace. This is particularly true for persons on a fixed income, such as retirees. Consumers also may be encouraged to increase current consumption beyond normal levels to "beat" future price increases. This, along with the loss of purchasing power of fixed-dollar assets, may discourage aggregate saving in the economy.

Finally, inflation usually results in higher nominal interest rates in the economy. First, bondholders and other lenders will demand higher interest rates to offset the loss of purchasing power in their bonds and other debt securities. In other words, they will seek to maintain an appropriate real interest return on their loans, as discussed in the next section. Second, the Federal Reserve, in fighting inflation (or "excessive" inflation), will act to increase the federal funds rate and the discount rate, which will increase short-term interest rates. Higher interest rates will put a "brake" on economic activity.

Everything considered, it seems that inflation (or perhaps "excessive" inflation) is bad for the economy. One of the objectives of wealth management is to consider the impact of inflation on clients' affairs and to plan for potential purchasing power risk.

Real versus Nominal Interest Rates and Values: *Nominal interest rates* (or yields) are the periodic percentage dollar returns on bonds (generally the current yield), savings accounts and CDs, and other fixed-dollar type securities without considering inflation. *Real interest rates* (or yields) are such returns minus the current rate of inflation or plus the current rate of deflation (discussed in the next section). For example, if the current yield on the 10-year U.S. Treasury note is 4.5 percent and the current rate of inflation (measured by the CPI) is 3 percent, the real rate of interest on such notes is 1.5 percent [nominal interest rate (4.5%) – rate of inflation (3%) = 1.5% real current yield]. On the other hand, if the current yield on the 10-year note is 2.5 percent and the current rate of deflation is 3 percent, the real rate of interest on the note is 5.5 percent [nominal rate of interest (2.5%) + rate of deflation (3%) = 5.5% real current yield]. It can be seen then that depending on nominal interest rates and inflation rates or deflation rates at any given time in the economy, it is possible to have positive or even negative real rates of return. However, bond investors and other savers normally will seek high enough nominal returns to more than offset the effects of inflation and produce a positive real rate of return.

Other economic values also may be stated in nominal terms or in real terms (adjusted for inflation). For example, comparisons of economic indicators over time, like gross domestic product, may be stated in inflation-adjusted terms in order to compare actual output from one period to another. The prices of commodities, like oil or gold, similarly may be inflation-adjusted for purposes of comparison.

CASE EXAMPLE

Assuming that inflation fears for the economy are rising, the dollar is falling in value relative to other currencies, and interest rates are low, Maria Rodriquez, age 45, is considering investing in gold and perhaps other precious metals for perhaps 5 to 10 percent of her overall asset allocation. (How she can do so is discussed in Chapter 6.) She notes that on March 13, 2008, the price of gold for April delivery on the Comex was $993.80 per ounce. This was well in excess of the previous peak in the nominal price for gold on January 21, 1980, of $850 per ounce. Maria wonders then if the current price of gold is at an all-time high. However, when inflation from 1980 to 2008 is considered, the inflation-adjusted price of gold on March 13, 2008, would be $2,239.67 per ounce in real terms, or more than double the current price.[7]

Adjusting for Inflation in Planning

Future Dollar Amounts: In several areas of wealth management, we are essentially planning to meet a need for funds many years in the future. Retirement income needs and education needs are examples. Therefore, considering past long-term inflationary trends in our economy, many planners view it as only realistic and prudent to adjust nominal future needs for anticipated future inflation in order to maintain the purchasing power of future funds.

CASE EXAMPLE

David Jones, age 50, and his wife Sara, age 48, are engaged in retirement planning. After considering their current expenditures and taxes (using the cash-flow analysis discussed in Chapter 1) and how their outlays might change during retirement, David estimates that he and his wife will need a retirement income of about $6,000 per month (in today's dollars) when he is 65, in 15 years, when they both plan to retire.

However, in view of past inflationary trends, David and Sara recognize that, to be realistic, their retirement income objective should be adjusted for inflation to maintain the planned-for-retirement income's purchasing power. David and Sara, with the help of their wealth management advisers, decide to assume a 3 percent average annual inflation rate for the next 15 years. Given this assumption, $1 today will be worth only 64.19 cents

[7] See *The Wall Street Journal*, March 14, 2008, p. C1.

in 15 years. This is the present value of $1 due at the end of 15 years at 3 percent compound average annual interest. (See Table 3.2 in Chapter 3.)

Therefore, to convert their objective of $6,000 per month in current dollars to a corresponding dollar amount of equal purchasing power 15 years hence, we should divide the $6,000 per month by the present value of $1 due at the end of 15 years at 3 percent compound interest (or 0.6419). The result is an inflation-adjusted retirement income objective of $9,347 ($6,000 ÷ 0.6419) per month. David and Sara also should consider possible inflation during their retirement years. They might want to plan for a reserve investment fund or account balance, which could be used to provide additional retirement income as needed depending on conditions then. Possible purchase of an immediate life annuity later in life also might be used to make up any future shortfall in needed retirement income. (See Chapter 17 for planning techniques with respect to immediate annuities.)

Hedges against Inflation: In their asset allocation planning, investors may attempt to include investments or property that they believe increase in value along with inflation (i.e., are "inflation hedges"). Gold is often thought of in this category. The same also might be said for other physical commodities and property investments whose prices may rise as costs rise in the economy. Some believe real estate is a good hedge against inflation.

It is often suggested that common stocks serve as a "hedge against inflation." However, it seems more logical to say that common stocks tend to perform well during periods of economic prosperity when business profits are rising. Such periods of prosperity may or may not be associated with rising inflation.

As noted earlier, most fixed-dollar investments suffer diminishing purchasing power during inflationary periods and might better be characterized as "deflation hedges." However, some fixed-dollar investments are structured as *inflation-protected securities* and are designed to increase in value during inflationary times. These include TIPS, Series I U.S. savings bonds, and a few CDs and corporate bonds. These are discussed in Chapter 7.

Deflation: Deflation is the opposite of inflation and is the decline in the general level of prices in the economy. Deflation has been much less common in the United States than inflation. In fact, as of this writing, there has not been a meaningful deflationary period in the United States since the Great

Depression of the 1930s.[8] Historically, deflation has been associated with economic depression and banking and credit crises. However, again as of this writing, there is concern by some that the current economic recession could develop into a period of deflation.

Stagflation: Some analysts believe there is at least a short-term tradeoff between unemployment and inflation. That is, when economic policymakers pursue policies intended to keep the economy growing and unemployment low (such as monetary policies to reduce interest rates), they must be ready to accept a "reasonable" rate of inflation because of the stimulative effects of their policies. The same is true of fiscal policies discussed later in this chapter.

However, during certain times, there has been both high inflation and high unemployment (no tradeoff). This situation has been dubbed *stagflation.* For example, during the 1970s, the inflation rate averaged more than 7 percent per year, while the unemployment rate averaged more than 6 percent per year.

United States Experience with Inflation, Deflation, and Stagflation Since the beginning of World War II, the United States has experienced persistent inflation. In fact, the CPI has increased each year from 1941 through 2007 (except for small declines in 1949 and 1955). During that time, the average annual percentage increase in the CPI was 3.1 percent.

At certain times during this post–World War II period, inflation has been severe. This was true, for example, during much of the 1970s and early 1980s. From 1979 through 1981, the average annual inflation rate was 11.7 percent and reached 13.6 percent in 1980. This period also was characterized by high interest rates as the Federal Reserve sought to rein in this rampant inflation. In 1981, for example, the federal funds rate reached 14 percent and the rate on the then-benchmark 30-year U.S. Treasury bond was 16 percent (the highest interest rates in the United States since the Civil War). As noted earlier, this period also included a period of stagflation. For those interested in knowing the impact of inflation over various periods, the Bureau of Labor Statistics provides an inflation calculator online that shows how much it would cost now to purchase goods that cost $100 at some earlier date. This inflation calculator is at www.bls.gov/cpi.

Also, as noted earlier, there has not been a significant period of deflation in the United States since the Great Depression (particularly 1929 through 1934). However, despite the lack of deflation and depression for many years and the view of some that they cannot recur in the United States, prudent financial

[8] Other countries, however, have experienced significant deflationary periods during this time. In Japan in the 1990s, for example, there was deflation and recession for a number of years following large real estate and other asset price increases (a "bubble") in the previous decade.

planning requires consideration of the possibility that they may, in fact, come again. In view of this uncertainty, it seems wise in asset allocation planning to hold at least some conservative asset classes that will maintain, or perhaps even increase, their values during a severe recession or depression. These might include U.S. Treasury and other high-quality bonds; insured savings accounts, CDs, and money market accounts; conservatively invested money market funds; fixed-dollar cash values in life insurance and annuity policies issued by highly rated insurers; and the like. These might be referred to as "deflation hedges." Again, diversification seems to be the key to prudent planning.

Business Cycles

An economy has fluctuations in overall economic activity. These fluctuations range from *expansions* (prosperity) to a peak in economic activity, from which output begins to decline during the *recession* (depression) phase, until a *trough* occurs, at which time the economy begins a new expansion phase. These periodic fluctuations are called the business cycle. Our economy has always had business cycles. The generally accepted dates for the phases of the business cycle in the United States are set by a private, nonprofit organization: the Business Cycle Dating Committee of the National Bureau of Economic Research (NBER). This organization has set these dates from 1854 to the present, and they are available on its Web site at www.nber.org/cycles.html.

Expansion (Prosperity) Expansions (sometimes also called "booms") are periods of growth in real GDP and are often characterized by low unemployment, rising wages, rising values and income from equity-type assets, low insolvencies and credit losses, a rising general price level, and higher interest rates.

Peaks and Then Recessions The *peak* is the turning point when the expansion reaches its highest level and the cycle turns toward recession. Unfortunately, no one really knows at the time when this peak has occurred, and there will be differing opinions as to whether a recession has begun.

A *recession* may be said to have occurred when there is a significant decline in economic activity. It is characterized by a reversal of the factors noted previously for an expansion. Recessions traditionally are defined as beginning when real GDP declines for two consecutive quarters, and this has often been true for recessions identified by the NBER. However, in recent years, the Business Cycle Dating Committee has used a broader definition and labeled a recession as "... a significant decline in economic activity spread across the economy, lasting more than a few months, normally visible in real GDP, real income, employment, industrial production, and wholesale-retail sales." A *depression* is generally thought of as a severe (deep) and prolonged recession.

Trough Leading to a New Expansion As with peaks, no one really knows at the time when a trough has occurred, the recession is over, and the economy is on the mend. According to the NBER, post–World War II recessions have had relatively short durations (ranging from 6 to 16 months) and have been relatively mild. Expansions, on the other hand, have been longer (ranging from 12 to 120 months), and the overall economy has shown great growth during this time.

The Business Cycle and Public Policy It is the public policy of most industrialized countries to use government policies to try to moderate (manage) the business cycle, promote economic stability and growth, and reduce unemployment as much as possible. In the United States, this was the implicit policy of the Roosevelt administration's "New Deal" during the Great Depression. This policy was formally adopted after World War II in the *Full Employment Act of 1946* and the *Full Employment and Balanced Growth Act of 1978* (the Humphrey-Hawkins Act). Government actions to do this are in the realm of macroeconomic policy—namely, fiscal policy and monetary policy, which will be discussed later in this chapter.

Planning Strategies Blessed indeed would be the hypothetical investor who, over a substantial period, can accurately predict the course of the business cycle. This person would sell their equities and buy high-grade bonds and accumulate cash at the peak and do the reverse at the trough. Such an investor almost certainly does not exist—at least your authors do not claim this kind of clairvoyance.

While there are a number of theories, economists really do not know what causes the business cycle and cannot predict in advance when its phases will occur. There almost always is disagreement and controversy at the time among economists, government officials, and investment professionals as to whether the economy is going into a recession or is recovering from one (i.e., when the peaks and troughs have occurred). As an extreme example, in the first few months of the Great Depression in 1929, some government officials and investment advisers were telling people who wanted to sell their stocks that the economy was "fundamentally sound" and "don't sell America short."

Given the virtual certainty that the business cycle will continue (as it always has in the past), but the uncertainty as to when downturns will occur and how severe they will be, it seems appropriate to repeat the strategy discussed previously. This involves a cautious, diversified asset allocation strategy that contains some secure, guaranteed asset classes that can be counted on during "hard times." Of course, the specific percentage allocations in given situations will depend on the factors discussed in Chapter 9. Also, investors normally will apply their own good judgment and common sense and become more conservative when they perceive the economic storm clouds gathering and perhaps more venturesome when they perceive the economic skies brightening. But that limited amount of market timing should be within the overall strategy of cautious, consistent diversification among asset classes.

Monetary and Fiscal Policies

These are the tools of macroeconomics to attempt to control the business cycle and maintain reasonable price stability.

Monetary Policy In the United States, this is the province of the Federal Reserve, which is an independent system created by the *Federal Reserve Act of 1913.*

Federal Reserve System: This consists of the 7-member Federal Reserve Board of Governors in Washington, D.C., and the 12 regional Federal Reserve banks. The members of the Federal Reserve Board are appointed by the president, subject to Senate confirmation; the president, with the consent of the Senate, also names one of these governors to serve as chairman. The chairman of the Federal Reserve Board is the chief official conducting monetary policy. The 12 regional Federal Reserve banks technically are owned by the commercial banks, who are members of the Federal Reserve System and who elect a majority of the directors of the regional banks. The directors appoint the president of each regional bank.

The Fed and Monetary Policy: The Federal Reserve conducts monetary policy by affecting the level of market interest rates (in the past, mainly short-term rates) in the economy and by controlling the money supply.[9] In recent years, the Fed's actions have been directed mainly at affecting interest rates rather than at controlling the money supply.

The Federal Reserve affects interest rates (and the money supply) by controlling the *reserves* that member banks have as non-interest-bearing deposits at the regional Federal Reserve banks. Member banks are required

[9]The definition of the money supply in this context includes currency in circulation and demand deposits (checking accounts), which is called M1. The Fed directly affects M1. A more expansive definition is M1 plus savings deposits up to $100,000 (or $250,000), money market accounts, money market mutual funds of individuals, CDs, and Eurodollars (U.S. dollars deposited in European banks). This is M2 and is substantially larger than M1. The most expansive measure is M3, which includes M2 plus institutional money market funds, large savings accounts, and some other items.

to maintain such reserves equal to specified percentages of deposits they hold from their customers (their liabilities to their depositors). These are *required reserves.* When a member bank's reserves exceed its required reserves, it has *excess reserves.*

Banks normally lend out these excess reserves on a short-term basis to other banks that need reserves to meet their reserve requirements. This lending and borrowing of excess reserves by commercial banks constitutes the *federal funds market,* and the prevailing interest rate for such funds is the *federal funds rate.* The federal funds rate thus is determined by the supply and demand for funds in the federal funds market, and traditionally has been the only market interest rate the Federal Reserve directly controls through its open market operations (described next). However, other interest rates, particularly short-term rates such as the prime rate, are much affected by the federal funds rate and tend to follow it, so the Fed, in fact, affects the overall level of market interest rates. The *prime rate* is the interest rate commercial banks charge their best business customers for short-term commercial loans. It is higher than the federal funds rate, but in practice moves in tandem with it. A similar rate is *London Interbank Offered Rate (LIBOR),* which is the rate at which English banks lend to each other on a short-term unsecured basis. The prime rate and LIBOR often are used as benchmark rates for indexing other interest rates in the economy. Hence, they are of considerable importance in world credit markets.

CASE EXAMPLE

Mary Henderson is planning to construct an addition to her residence. The construction cost will be $100,000. She is considering a fixed-rate mortgage on her home with an interest rate of 6½ percent or an adjustable rate mortgage (ARM) with an interest rate of prime plus ¾ of 1 percent. If the prime rate currently is 5 percent, the rate on the ARM will be 5¾ percent and lower than that of the fixed-rate mortgage. But if the prime rate rises to, say, 7 percent, the rate of the ARM will become 7¾ percent and Mary's financing costs will rise above the rate of the fixed-rate mortgage. (Read more on such loans in Chapter 9.)

If member commercial banks need reserves, they can also borrow them on a short-term basis directly from the Federal Reserve. The Fed charges an interest rate on such loans, called the *discount rate,* and requires acceptable collateral. The Fed sets the discount rate and periodically changes it in the face of monetary conditions, but as a practical matter, the Fed affects interest rates primarily through its actions to control the federal funds rate. The federal funds rate and the discount rate move together. Borrowing from the

Federal Reserve sometimes is referred to as the Fed's "discount window." Again as a practical matter, historically, commercial banks generally have preferred to borrow needed reserves through the federal funds market rather than from the Fed's "discount window." However, this depends on conditions in the financial (credit) markets.[10]

The Federal Reserve's Tools of Monetary Policy: The Fed may control the level of member bank reserves and hence their ability to expand deposits by making new loans through open market operations, discount rate changes, and changes in member-bank reserve requirements.

Open market operations. The most important of these is *open market operations.* Here the Fed buys and sells government securities it holds in the open market through government bond dealers. When the Fed buys securities, it pays for them with funds drawn on itself, which the bond dealers ultimately deposit in commercial banks. The banks, in turn, present these funds to the Fed for payment, and the Fed does so by crediting the commercial banks' reserve accounts with the Fed. This increases member bank reserves. The reverse occurs when the Federal Reserve sells securities. In this case, the bond dealers pay for the securities with funds drawn on commercial banks. The Fed then presents this obligation to the banks for payment and deducts the amount from their reserve accounts. Thus, member bank reserves are reduced when the Fed sells securities in the open market.

These open market operations are planned by the *Federal Open Market Committee (FOMC),* which consists of the Board of Governors and five Reserve bank presidents. The FOMC sets a *target rate* for the federal funds rate, and then open market operations are conducted to control the supply of member bank reserves to achieve the target rate. A summary of economic conditions in each Federal Reserve district is prepared for each FOMC meeting to assist in its deliberations. This is referred to as the *Beige Book.* The latest Beige Book can be found at www.federalreserve.gov/fomc/beigebook/2008 (with the year being the latest year available). Of course, when interest rates are raised, it will increase the cost of borrowing and reduce inflationary pressures. It will also tend to strengthen the dollar (raise its value relative to that of other currencies) because foreigners may have an incentive to deposit their interest-bearing funds in the United States to take advantage of the higher interest rates relative to those elsewhere. Lower interest rates, on the other

[10] For example, during the "credit crunch" existing as of this writing, commercial banks have increased their borrowing from the Fed. Also, in March 2008, the Fed began for the first time to lend directly to certain investment banks through its temporary, separate primary-dealer credit facility. The Fed also expanded the types of eligible collateral it would accept for its loans (such as mortgage-backed securities and commercial paper). All of this was to provide liquidity (ready cash) for the troubled credit markets.

hand, lower the cost of credit, tend to make loans more available, and provide stimulus to the economy, but may enhance inflationary pressures and weaken the dollar relative to other currencies.

Discount rate changes. As noted previously, member banks (and, temporarily, investment banks) may borrow directly from the Fed through its "discount window." The interest rate set by the Fed for these loans is the *discount rate.* When the Fed wants to tighten credit, it raises the discount rate; when it wishes to loosen credit conditions, it lowers the discount rate. Of course, banks may or may not want to borrow from the Federal Reserve.

Changes in reserve requirements. The Federal Reserve sets the reserve requirements for member banks. An increase in reserve requirements will reduce credit availability, while a reduction will have the opposite effect. The Fed rarely uses this tool of monetary policy.

The Federal Reserve as a Lender of Last Resort: The Fed also is charged with maintaining liquidity (available reserves) in the banking system by serving as a "lender of last resort" for commercial banks. Thus, member banks can meet short-term, emergency needs for cash (like a "run on the bank") by borrowing from the Fed through the discount window.

As noted in Footnote 10, the Fed temporarily extended this lender of last resort concept to investment banks in March 2008 by allowing direct loans to them through a separate credit facility ("lending window"). This was a dramatic and controversial departure from past practice. It may be noted that the Fed does not regulate investment banks as it does commercial banks.

The Federal Reserve also has brokered rescue arrangements for financial institutions (both informally and sometimes formally) when it felt their collapse would harm the overall financial system. This was true, for example, in encouraging banks to provide emergency loans to the hedge fund, Long-Term Capital Management, in 1998 and in engineering and providing backup funding for the emergency purchase of the investment banking and brokerage firm Bear Stearns by JPMorgan Chase in 2008.

Fiscal Policies These involve the use of *federal government expenditures, borrowing,* and *tax policy* to attempt to stabilize the economy and promote steady economic growth. Such policies are referred to as *discretionary policies* since they are deliberately undertaken by the federal government to control the economy.

When the economy is or appears to be heading toward a recession, it is suggested that increasing government expenditures will expand aggregate demand and stimulate economic activity. However, such increased expenditures (along with declining tax revenues and perhaps tax cuts) will result in greater federal budget deficits and borrowing.

Perhaps the clearest examples of substantially increased government spending to combat a depression were New Deal programs during the Great Depression. During this time, the federal government spent massive sums on roads, schools, parks, rural electrification, huge hydroelectric dams, and other infrastructure projects. Another aspect of such spending was to provide work for the large number of unemployed (as high as 25 percent of the labor force in 1933) through programs such as the Works Progress Administration (WPA) and Civilian Conservation Corps (CCC). However, these programs were controversial because some felt they were wasteful, harmful to individual initiative, and not well organized or effective.

In the area of tax policy, when recession exists or threatens, it is argued that cutting tax rates (particularly income tax rates) will expand aggregate demand and thus stimulate the economy.[11] Here again, however, the result is higher federal budget deficits and debt, which may cause inflation and higher real interest rates.

In recent years, there have been a number of examples of such tax cutting motivated at least in part by the desire to stimulate the economy. After World War II, the first was the *Kennedy tax cut.* President John F. Kennedy proposed and carried out an income tax rate cut in 1964 to combat what was then viewed as unacceptably high unemployment. Another was the *Economic Recovery Tax Act of 1981 (ERTA),* which was President Ronald Reagan's massive tax reduction measure. As its name implies, this law was intended to aid recovery from the severe recession then existing, as well as to further President Reagan's general philosophy of lowering taxes. A similar law was the EGTRRA, which was a tax-cutting and other tax-provisions measure of President George W. Bush intended at least partially to combat the economic weakness at the time.

A recent tax-oriented stimulus measure was the *Economic Stimulus Act of 2008.* This law provided for nontaxable rebate checks in 2008 to lower-income persons filing a 2007 income tax return. This included persons with

[11] Tax policy, of course, embraces many other issues than just its role as a part of fiscal policy. Some of these will be discussed in other parts of this book. Another theory related to tax cutting is what some have called "supply side economics." This theory proposes that tax cutting is desirable in and of itself, regardless of fiscal policy. Advocates argue that low tax rates will result in greater investment, expanding businesses and employment, higher income and wealth, and greater economic growth generally. They further argue that while tax rates will decline, total tax revenues will increase due to the economic growth caused by the tax cuts. For examples of this theory, see "Reaganomics 2.0," *The Wall Street Journal,* August 31, 2007, p. A8 and "Tax Cuts Helped Economy Stay Afloat," *Barron's,* July 16, 2007, p. 45. On the other hand, critics of the theory have called it "voodoo economics."

little or no tax liability, including those who otherwise did not have to file a tax return but who had at least $3,000 of qualifying income.

The most recent stimulus plan is the *American Recovery and Reinvestment Act of 2009.* This law contains a new *Making Work Pay Credit* for 2009 and 2010. This credit is equal to the smaller of 6.2 percent of a taxpayer's earned income or $800 for joint returns and $400 for other returns. It is phased out for higher income taxpayers.

On the other hand, during the expansion or prosperity phase of the business cycle, sound fiscal policy calls for reduced government expenditures and raising tax rates to serve as a brake on "excessive" economic expansion and so-called economic bubbles, which, when they "pop," may result in a recession. These actions also will result in reduced federal budget deficits, or even budget surpluses and reduced federal government borrowing. At this time, the Federal Reserve also should be following a monetary policy of raising interest rates for the same reason. This sometimes is referred to as "leaning against the economic wind." Unfortunately, as a practical matter, it seems that it is much easier for politicians to lower taxes and increase government spending than the reverse.[12]

However, in recent years, there have been examples of more conservative fiscal policies. One was the *Revenue Reconciliation Act of 1990* (RRA of 1990). This law was a compromise between a Republican president, George H. W. Bush, and a Democratic Congress, which raised income tax rates to a top rate on ordinary income of 31 percent and also reduced government spending. Another was the Clinton administration's *Revenue Reconciliation Act of 1993,* which again raised federal income tax rates on ordinary income to a top rate of 36 percent with a 10 percent surcharge, or a total top rate of 39.6 percent, and also reduced government spending. These deficit-cutting laws and the economic expansion of the late 1980s and 1990s resulted in federal budget surpluses in 1997 through 2000.

Automatic Stabilizers In contrast to discretionary policies, these are government expenditures that automatically increase, tax payments that automatically decrease, and benefit payments that remain fixed or increase when the economy turns down. During the expansion phase, the reverse is true.

For example, during recessions, progressive income tax payments decline proportionally more than income, unemployment benefits increase, welfare

[12] The early foundation for many of these macroeconomic ideas for dealing with the business cycle was first developed by the economist and businessman Sir John Maynard Keynes in his landmark 1936 book, *The General Theory of Employment, Interest, and Money.* These ideas have been called "Keynesian economics," and many credit the beginning of the separate study of macroeconomics to the publication of this book. While Keynesian economics was once quite controversial, its fundamental ideas are generally accepted by most economists today.

benefits increase, Social Security and similar benefits continue unreduced, and bank insurance protects most depositors if banks fail. The opposite occurs during the expansion phase.

Interventionists versus Noninterventionists There are differences of opinion among economists concerning the value and effectiveness of government macroeconomic policies in controlling the business cycle and stabilizing the economy.

Probably the most prevalent line of thought is that of the *interventionists* (sometimes called "Neo Keynesians"). They believe that discretionary government policies and automatic stabilizers are effective in the short run in moderating the business cycle.

On the other hand, the *noninterventionists* generally believe that discretionary macroeconomic government policies either are unnecessary (because markets adjust and correct themselves) or are actually harmful (due to uncertainty and delay in implementing the policies and possible disruption of free markets). This probably is the minority view today.

Economic Indicators

There are a number of measures of economic activity that are commonly cited by economists, financial commentators, and others. They are used to measure economic trends and perhaps help predict where the economy may be heading. The following are some examples:

- *Gross domestic product (GDP).* This is the overall measure of the value of the final goods and services produced within a country in a given period. When expressed in current dollars (i.e., unadjusted for price changes), it is known as *nominal GDP.* But when it is adjusted for changes in the general level of prices from a given base period, it is called *real GDP.*
- *Personal income and personal consumption data.*
- *Various price and cost indexes.* For example, these may include:
  - Consumer Price Index and Producer Price Index.
  - Employment Cost Index (ECI), which measures changes in employees' compensation (the cost of labor). Larger-than-normal increases in this index are considered a possible indicator of future inflation.
- *Money supply.* This includes M1, M2, and M3, as defined in Footnote 9. Large increases in the money supply may also indicate future inflationary trends.
- *Various stock market indexes and averages.* These measure overall movements in groups of stocks, depending on the particular index or average, including indexes such as Standard & Poor's 500, Russell 2000, Dow Jones

Wilshire 5000, NASDAQ Composite, MSCI, and MSCI EAFE and averages such as the Dow Jones Industrial Average, among others.

- *Commodity price indexes.* For example, the CRB, as discussed previously.
- *Institute for Supply Management (ISM) report that measures manufacturing activity.* A reading below 50 often is regarded as a recessionary signal.
- *Manufacturers' new orders (factory orders).*
- *Durable goods orders.*
- *Status of the labor market.* Weekly initial jobless claims, the moving average of such claims, average duration of unemployment, the total number of unemployed, and the average workweek are measures of the status of the labor market.
- *Status of the housing market.* Pending home sales (for existing homes and new homes), housing starts, inventory of unsold homes, and Standard & Poor's/Case-Shiller Home Price Index for 20 large cities are measures of the status of the housing market.
- *The University of Michigan Consumer Sentiment Index.* This is a monthly index of consumer confidence in terms of how consumers see their own finances and how they view the economy and its future direction. The Conference Board also publishes such a confidence index.
- *Index of Leading Economic Indicators.* This is a composite index consisting of 10 components, some of which are listed previously. It is widely regarded as an important forecasting tool for estimating the future course of the economy.

Tax Environment and Wealth Management

Tax laws obviously are an important force affecting wealth management, and they are constantly changing. Thus, possible future changes in tax policy may present uncertainties in planning. This has been particularly true in recent years because important tax-cutting and exclusion provisions of EGTRRA, JGTRRA, and other laws are scheduled to "sunset" (i.e., terminate with the former law returning) for years after 2010. However, most commentators believe there will be important tax legislation enacted before this "sunsetting" occurs.

Economic Growth and Tax Relief Reconciliation Act (EGTRRA)

EGTRRA of 2001 is an unusual and uncertain piece of tax legislation. This is because many of its original provisions were not effective until years in the future and it contained a "sunset provision" stating that all its terms and provisions will no longer apply after December 31, 2010. In summary, some changes (among others) made by EGTRRA are as follows:

- Provided for reductions in individual income tax rates. For example, the top rate on ordinary income was reduced from 39.6 percent to 35 percent and a new 10 percent lower bracket was added.
- Allowed *tax-free* qualified education distributions from qualified tuition programs (Section 529 plans) and education saving accounts (education IRAs). These favorable tax rules for education plans were made permanent (i.e., no sunset) by the Pension Protection Act (PPA) of 2006.
- Substantially increased contribution and deduction limits for qualified retirement plans, IRAs, and other retirement plans. These also were made permanent by PPA.
- Provided that all 401(k) plan participants could make all or part of their employee elective contributions as after-tax Roth contributions if the plan permits (i.e., created the Roth 401(k) plan). This also was made permanent by PPA.
- Increased federal estate tax and GST tax applicable exclusion amounts in stages from 2002 through 2009, provided repeal of the federal estate tax and GST tax entirely in 2010, and provided reinstatement of these taxes as they were in 2001 for 2011 and thereafter. Reduced the top federal estate tax rate (and GST tax rate) in stages from 50 percent to 45 percent.
- Repealed the step-up in income tax basis at death rule and adopted a modified carryover basis at death rule for 2010 only with reinstatement of the step-up in basis rule for 2011 and thereafter.
- Separated the gift tax and estate tax exclusion amounts and rates, with the gift tax applicable exclusion amount being kept at $1,000,000, the gift tax not being repealed in 2010, and the tax rate falling to 35 percent in 2010.

Jobs and Growth Tax Relief Reconciliation Act (JGTRRA) of 2003

This law, along with others, was a further tax-cutting measure. In summary, important changes (among others) made by JGTRRA and other laws are:

- Reduced long-term capital gains tax rates for individuals from 20 percent (top rate) and 10 percent to 15 percent (top rate) and 5 percent, with no capital-gains tax for taxpayers in the 10 and 15 percent income tax brackets for gains realized from 2008 through 2010.

- Reduced the income tax rates on "qualified" dividends received by individuals from a top rate of 35 percent to 15 percent (top rate) and 5 percent, with no tax on "qualified" dividends received by taxpayers in the 10 and 15 percent income tax brackets from 2008 through 2010.

Again, all terms and provisions of JGTRRA of 2003 will terminate (sunset) after December 31, 2010.

Sunset Provisions and Planning Strategies

In order to conform to the so-called Byrd Amendment,[13] Congress originally provided that all provisions of EGTRRA would expire on December 31, 2010. At that time, the tax law as it existed in 2001 would again become the law of the land. Congress modified this somewhat in the Pension Protection Act of 2006 by making the education and retirement plan provisions of EGTRRA permanent. Similarly, all provisions of JGTRRA and related laws are to "sunset" after December 31, 2010. Prior law is to return at that point.

These "sunset provisions" obviously create uncertainty in planning. Several possibilities may occur, depending on what the White House and Congress do prior to 2011. They could do nothing and allow the "sunset provisions" to take effect. Most commentators do not believe this will happen. Rather, it is generally believed that sometime before 2011, probably in 2009, new tax legislation will be enacted. It is expected by many that this new legislation will retain the federal estate tax and GST tax (with exclusion accounts retained at the 2009 level of $3,500,000), retain many provisions of EGTRRA and JGTRRA (but possibly increase the tax rate on capital gains and qualified dividends), retain step-up in basis at death, reduce income tax rates on lower and middle income taxpayers, and enact other provisions.

[13] The Congressional Budget Act of 1974, as amended.

3

Valuation Concepts in Wealth Management

Competence Objectives for This Chapter After reading this chapter, planners should understand:

- Simple and compound interest
- The future value of a sum
- Present value concepts
- Distinction between ordinary annuities and annuities due
- The future value of annuities
- Present and future values involving uneven cash flows
- Internal rates of return
- Actuarial factors for calculation of present values for annuities, income interests, unitrust interests, remainder interests, and reversionary interests under IRC Section 7520
- Applicable federal rates (AFRs) for the tax treatment of intrafamily loans and other purposes

A number of concepts concerning how amounts of money may be built up or distributed are important to many aspects of private wealth management. For example, they affect capital accumulation and investment planning, accumulating funds for educational expenses, and accumulating assets for retirement, among others. In addition, the tax law requires the use of certain valuation factors in determining present values for estate planning purposes and for the tax treatment of below-market loans. These concepts will be briefly discussed in this chapter.

Capital Accumulation Concepts

Simple Interest versus Compound Interest

Simple interest (return) is just the application of an interest rate (or rate of return) to a sum of money for a given period. For example, if an investor buys a $100,000 one-year certificate of deposit that pays 6 percent interest at the end of the year (i.e., no interest accrued before then), the investor will have $106,000 at the end of the year ($100,000 × 1.06 = $106,000).

On the other hand, *compound interest* (return) involves accumulating (compounding) the interest (or rate of return) on a sum of money at stated intervals (e.g., monthly, semiannually, or annually) over a given time when the interest earned is not paid out currently but instead is added to the fund at the end of each compounding period. In effect, interest is earned on the interest. Stated differently, with compound interest, the sum of money is not growing at a linear rate, as with simple interest, but at a geometric rate. This can produce powerful results when funds are invested at compound rates of return over a substantial period. Simple and compound returns can easily be determined on financial calculators.

Future Values

The *future value* of a sum is the amount to which an investment fund will grow over a certain period at a given rate of return, assuming compounding of returns. Table 3.1 shows the values to which a $1,000 investment fund will grow at various net rates of return for given periods, assuming annual compounding of returns.

Table 3.1. Values of a $1,000 investment fund invested for specified numbers of years at various rates of return (future value of a sum)

Percent Annual Net Rate of Return (Compounded)	Number of Years the $1,000 Is Invested							
	5	8	10	12	15	20	25	30
3%	1,159	1,267	1,344	1,462	1,558	1,806	2,094	2,427
4%	1,217	1,369	1,480	1,601	1,801	2,191	2,666	3,243
5%	1,276	1,478	1,629	1,796	2,079	2,653	3,386	4,322
6%	1,388	1,594	1,791	2,012	2,397	3,207	4,292	5,744
8%	1,469	1,851	2,159	2,518	3,172	4,661	6,848	10,064
10%	1,611	2,144	2,594	3,138	4,177	6,727	10,835	17,449
15%	2,011	3,059	4,046	5,350	8,137	16,367	32,919	66,212

For example, suppose a person age 35 has $10,000 to invest. If the *net rate of return* (after investment expenses and income taxes) is only 4 percent, the person can accumulate $14,800 by age 45, $21,910 by age 55, and $32,430 by age 65. But if this net rate of return can be increased to 6 percent (a 50 percent increase in rate of return), the person can accumulate $17,910 by age 45, $32,070 by age 55, and $57,440 by age 65 (or a 77 percent increase in the accumulation for age 65). With an increase of this net return to 10 percent (a 250 percent increase in return), the comparable figures would be $25,940 by age 45, $67,720 by age 55, and $174,490 by age 65 (or a 538 percent increase in the accumulation for age 65). This illustrates the importance of increasing net investment returns when feasible. Such future values can be determined on a financial calculator by solving, for example, for future value (FV) on an HP12C calculator.

We can approach this calculation somewhat differently. If, say, a mother, Mary Smith, with a $50,000 investment fund, feels she needs approximately $100,000 in 12 years for her children's education, she can see from Table 3.1 that she will have to earn a net rate of return of about 6 percent on the money to achieve her goal ($50,000 at 6 percent per year for 12 years = $100,120). This same result can be determined more accurately by using a financial calculator and solving for interest (i) on an HP12C calculator.

Present Values

Present values are really the reverse of future values. They are the value today of amounts to be received in the future, assuming the amounts will earn given rates of return. Table 3.2 shows the present value of $1 for different periods at various rates, assuming interest is compounded annually.

Table 3.2. Present values of $1 at the end of specified numbers of years at various interest (discount) rates (present value of a sum)

Percent Annual Net Discount Rate (Compounded)	Number of Years the $1 Is Discounted							
	5	8	10	12	15	20	25	30
3%	0.8626	0.7894	0.7441	0.7014	0.6419	0.5537	0.4776	0.4120
4%	0.8219	0.7307	0.6756	0.6246	0.5553	0.4564	0.3751	0.3083
5%	0.7835	0.6768	0.6139	0.5568	0.4810	0.3769	0.2953	0.2314
6%	0.7473	0.6274	0.5584	0.4970	0.4173	0.3118	0.2330	0.1741
8%	0.6806	0.5403	0.9632	0.3971	0.3152	0.2145	0.1460	0.0994
10%	0.6209	0.4665	0.3855	0.3186	0.2394	0.1486	0.0923	0.0573
15%	0.4972	0.3269	0.3269	0.1869	0.1229	0.0611	0.0304	0.0151

Again as an example, suppose John Henry, age 50, estimates he will need approximately $500,000 in 15 years to assure that he and his wife will have a comfortable retirement. In the current economic climate, John assumes conservatively that he can earn only about a 5 percent net return on investments for this period. He wants to know how much of an investment fund he needs now to meet his goal.

John can estimate this amount by determining the present value of $500,000 15 years from now, assuming 5 percent compound interest for this period. From Table 3.2, this would be $500,000 multiplied by 0.4810 (the present value of $1 at the end of 15 years at 5 percent interest), or $240,500. This amount may also be determined more easily by using a financial calculator and, for example, solving for present value (PV) on an HP12C calculator.

Future Value of Annuities

As a general definition, an annuity is a stream of periodic payments over a given period. With *annuities certain,* the payments are made, regardless of whether the recipient lives or dies during the period. With *life annuities,* the payments are made only during the lifetime(s) of the annuitant(s) and cease at his or her death or at the death of the last annuitant to die, in the case of joint and survivor annuities. Life annuities are discussed in Chapter 17.

Annuities certain may be ordinary annuities or annuities due. With an *ordinary annuity,* the periodic payments are made at the end of each payment period. With *annuities due,* the payments are made at the beginning of each period. Thus, for annuity payments for a certain period, say, 10 years or 10 payments, an annuity due will produce one more year of compounding interest for the payments at the end of 10 years.

The future value of an ordinary annuity or an annuity due is the amount to which the periodic payments will grow over a certain period at a given rate of return, assuming compounding of returns. Table 3.3 shows the future values of an ordinary annuity compounded annually.

For example, assume a person age 35 can save $2,400 per year (about $200 per month). If the person receives a *net* rate of return of 6 percent on the money, he or she can accumulate $31,632 (1,318 × 24) by age 45, $88,296 by age 55, and $189,744 by age 65.

Again, we can approach this calculation in a different way. A person may want to know how much he or she must invest (save) each year in order to reach a desired amount in a given number of years, assuming a certain net annual rate of return. Suppose, for example, a father wants to know how much he needs to invest by the end of each year to produce $200,000 for

Table 3.3. Values of a periodic investment of $100 per year at the end of specified numbers of years at various rates of return (future value of an annuity)

Percent Annual Net Rate of Return (Compounded)	Number of Years the $100 Is Invested							
	5	8	10	12	15	20	25	30
3%	531	889	1,146	1,419	1,860	2,687	3,646	4,758
4%	542	921	1,201	1,503	2,002	2,978	4,165	5,608
5%	553	955	1,258	1,592	2,158	3,307	4,773	6,644
6%	564	990	1,318	1,687	2,328	3,679	5,486	7,906
8%	587	1,064	1,449	1,898	2,715	4,576	7,311	11,328
10%	611	1,144	1,594	2,138	3,177	5,728	9,835	16,449
15%	674	1,373	2,030	2,900	4,758	10,244	21,279	43,474

his children's education in 12 years. If he assumes a net rate of return of 5 percent, he can see from Table 3.3 that he will need approximately $12,563 by the end of each year to produce the $200,000 in 12 years [($200,000 ÷ $1,592) × 100]. Again, this amount can be determined more easily and accurately by using a financial calculator and solving for payment (PMT) on an HP12C calculator.

A rather dramatic illustration of the power of compounding is presented in Table 3.4. Assume that Mary Jones wants to begin saving $5,000 per year. The second column shows the result at age 65 if she saves only from age 21 through age 30 and then stops. The third column shows the result at age 65 if she saves $5,000 per year starting at age 31 (10 years later) until age 65. In both cases, it is assumed she earns a net return of 7 percent on the investment funds. It may be noted that 7 percent is less than the average annual total return over a long period on common stocks, as described in Chapter 4.

Of course, Mary should try to save every year. This table only illustrates the advantage of saving early rather than putting it off. If Mary feels she cannot afford to save in these early years, perhaps her parents or grandparents could make gifts to her (within the gift tax annual exclusion) to enable her to do so. This is a good giving strategy. Perhaps Mary's contributions could be to an earnings-related traditional IRA or Roth IRA, if she is eligible to do so. Then her investment earnings can grow tax deferred or tax free.

Present Value of Annuities

This is the value today of even periodic annuity payments to be received in the future, assuming the payments will earn given compounded rates of

Table 3.4. Example of the advantage of early saving versus later saving—again, the power of compound return (assuming 7 percent net return)

Age	Early Contributions	Later Contributions
19	$0	$0
20	$0	$0
21	$5,000	$0
22	$5,000	$0
23	$5,000	$0
24	$5,000	$0
25	$5,000	$0
26	$5,000	$0
27	$5,000	$0
28	$5,000	$0
29	$5,000	$0
30	$5,000	$0
31	$0	$5,000
32	$0	$5,000
33	$0	$5,000
34	$0	$5,000
35	$0	$5,000
36	$0	$5,000
37	$0	$5,000
38	$0	$5,000
39	$0	$5,000
40	$0	$5,000
41	$0	$5,000
42	$0	$5,000
43	$0	$5,000
44	$0	$5,000
45	$0	$5,000
46	$0	$5,000
47	$0	$5,000
48	$0	$5,000
49	$0	$5,000
50	$0	$5,000
51	$0	$5,000
52	$0	$5,000
53	$0	$5,000
54	$0	$5,000

Table 3.4. Example of the advantage of early saving versus later saving—again, the power of compound return (assuming 7 percent net return)

Age	Early Contributions	Later Contributions
55	$0	$5,000
56	$0	$5,000
57	$0	$5,000
58	$0	$5,000
59	$0	$5,000
60	$0	$5,000
61	$0	$5,000
62	$0	$5,000
63	$0	$5,000
64	$0	$5,000
65	$0	$5,000
Total invested:	$50,000	$175,000
Value of investment fund at age 65	$737,560	$691,184

return. Table 3.5 shows this for different periods and compounded interest rates for ordinary annuities.

Present Values and Future Values for Uneven Cash Flows

For example, the prices of bonds equal the present value of the future cash flows from the bond. This would be the present value of its interest payments (essentially an ordinary annuity until the bond matures) plus the present value of the face of the bond when it matures. An example of future values would be when a person invests unequal amounts from year to year.

Internal Rates of Return

An internal rate of return (IRR) is simply the annual rate of return on sums of monies starting at the beginning of a period until the end of the period, assuming compounding interest. Stated differently, it is the average annual compound total rate of return on the cash flows from the beginning of the period to the end. This is also called the geometric average rate of return. The distinction between the geometric average and the arithmetic average is presented in Chapter 4.

Table 3.5. Present values of a periodic investment of $1 per year at the end of each year for specified numbers of years at various rates of return (present value of an annuity)

Percent Annual Net Discount Rate (Compounded)	Number of Years							
	5	8	10	12	15	20	25	30
3	4.5797	7.0197	8.5302	9.9540	11.9379	14.8775	17.4131	19.6004
4	4.4518	6.7327	8.1109	9.3851	11.1184	13.5903	15.6221	17.2920
5	4.3295	6.4632	7.7217	8.8633	10.3797	12.4622	14.0939	15.3724
6	4.2124	6.2098	7.3601	8.3838	9.7122	11.4699	12.7834	13.7648
8	3.9927	5.7466	6.7101	7.5361	8.5595	9.8181	10.6748	11.2578
10	3.7908	5.3349	6.1446	6.8137	7.6061	8.5136	9.0770	9.4269
15	3.3522	4.4873	5.0188	5.4206	5.8474	6.2593	6.4641	6.5660

Valuation Factors for Estate Planning and Wealth Transfer

We will now shift focus and consider various valuation factors used in estate planning, as required by tax law.

Actuarial Factors for Present Values of Certain Interests

A number of estate planning strategies (and other tax needs) require the calculation of the present value for one or more of an annuity interest or an income (or use) interest for a term of years or for life, a unitrust interest, a remainder interest, or a reversionary interest. These strategies are discussed in more detail in subsequent chapters of the book. Some examples, given just to illustrate the valuation issues, are as follows:

- The creator (grantor) of an irrevocable trust gives property that is expected to appreciate in value to the trust and retains an annuity interest (i.e., a fixed percentage of the original trust property) for a period of years. At the end of that time, any remaining trust property goes to other beneficiaries (remainderpersons). This is referred to as a grantor retained annuity trust (a GRAT) and is discussed in Chapter 27. To determine whether a taxable gift for gift tax purposes has been made when the GRAT was created, and if so, how much, it is necessary to calculate the present value of the retained annuity interest and then subtract this present value from the value of the property given to the GRAT. This determines the present value of any remainder interest given to the other beneficiaries (remainderpersons).

- The creator (grantor) of an irrevocable trust gives his or her principal residence to the trust, retains the right to live in the residence rent free for a term of years, and retains the right to have the house return (revert) to his or her estate if he or she should die within the period of years. At the end of the term of years, the residence would remain in the trust for the benefit of other beneficiaries (remainderpersons). This is referred to as a qualified personal residence trust (a QPRT) and is discussed in Chapter 27. In this case, to determine the amount of the taxable gift when the QPRT was created, it first is necessary to calculate the present value of the retained use (income) interest for the term of years and the present value of the retained reversionary interest (to the grantor's estate) in the event the grantor should die during the term of years. Then we must subtract the sum of these present values from the value of the residence when it was contributed to the QPRT to determine the present value of the remainder interest given to the other beneficiaries (e.g., the grantor's children as remainderpersons).

- As a final example, the creator (grantor) of an irrevocable charitable trust gives appreciated property to the trust, and retains the right to receive an annuity interest or a unitrust interest (i.e., a percentage of the current value of the trust property each year) for the creator's lifetime and his or her spouse's lifetime. After the last of their deaths, the remaining trust property passes to the designated charity. This is referred to as a charitable remainder trust (a CRT) and is discussed in Chapter 19. In this example, to determine the amount of the federal income tax and gift tax charitable deductions allowed to the creator when the CRT is created, it is necessary to calculate the present actuarial value of their annuity interest or unitrust interest for the remainder of their lifetimes (which, of course, does not go to the charity) and then subtract this present value from the value of the property originally placed in the CRT. This determines the present value of the remainder interest going to the charity (which is a charitable income tax deduction).

The actuarial factors involved in determining such present values are an interest rate at which future values can be discounted and a mortality table for determining life expectancies. Both of these actuarial factors are determined under the rules of Section 7520 of the Internal Revenue Code.

Section 7520 Discount Rate This is the interest rate the government prescribes for valuing the interests noted at the beginning of this section. It is determined by the IRS, is published monthly in a Revenue Ruling, and applies to gifts made during the month in which it is effective. For charitable deduction purposes, the taxpayer may elect to use the rate for the current month or one of the two preceding months.

The Section 7520 rate equals 120 percent of the federal midterm rate for the month to which it applies.[1] In effect, it is the rate the IRS assumes will be earned on the assets producing these interests. As of this writing, the Section 7520 rate was set at 3.4 percent. Of course, the assets in these trusts may actually earn less, but hopefully more, than this Section 7520 rate. The planning techniques described in Chapter 27 are based on the expectation that the actual rate earned will be higher than the applicable Section 7520 rate.

Section 7520 Mortality Assumption For the present values of interests affected by the life expectancies of one or more persons, it is necessary to make assumptions as to the probability of persons surviving to each age and correspondingly to the probability of death at each age. This is done through mortality tables,

[1] The federal midterm rate is the AFR, determined on the basis of the average market yield on outstanding marketable obligations of the United States, with remaining maturities of three to nine years for each calendar month. It is discussed later in this chapter.

which are constructed from statistical studies of survival and death rates for large numbers of people so the statistical law of large numbers can apply.[2]

Under Section 7520, the IRS also publishes a gender-neutral (unisex) mortality table every 10 years based on census data that is required to be used (along with the Section 7520 discount rate) in calculating the present values of interests when life expectancies are involved. As of this writing, the latest table is Life Table 90CM.

Tables of IRS Valuation Factors Section 7520 requires the IRS to publish Valuation Tables showing the actuarial factors to be used in calculating the present values for annuity interests, life interests or interests for a term of years, remainder interests, or reversionary interests.[3] The tables reflect the previously described mortality assumptions (for one or two lives) at a series of interest rates (Section 7520 discount rates), from 2.2 percent to 22 percent. The tables must be revised for recent mortality experience at least every 10 years. They also reflect values for terms certain.

The three books of tables are named "Aleph," "Beth," and "Gimel." "Aleph" provides actuarial present-value factors for remainder, income, and annuity interests for one life, two lives, and terms certain. "Beth" provides unitrust remainder factors for one life, two lives, and terms certain. ("Gimel" provides depreciation adjustment factors, which are not relevant here.) The following is just an example of the kinds of factors shown in "Aleph," assuming a person age 50 and 4 percent interest.

ACTUARIAL VALUES BOOK ALEPH IRS PUBLICATION 1457

Table S (4.0)

Single Life Factors Based on Life Table 90CM

Interest at 4.0 Percent

Age	**Annuity**	**Life Estate**	**Remainder**
50 (an example) from ages 0 to 88	16.0685 (present value of an annuity of $1 per year for a person age 50's lifetime	0.64274 (assuming $1 is deposited at age 50, this represents the portion of $1 equal to the life income from the $1, assuming 4% is earned on the fund)	0.35726 (again assuming $1 is deposited at age 50, this represents the portion of $1 that will be left (remain) after the death of life estate holder (or $1 – 0.64274 = 0.35726)

These factors, as well as others in the IRS tables, are used for valuing various interests, as noted previously.

[2] In insurance, the same concepts (but different tables) are used to determine the premiums for life insurance and life annuities.

[3] IRC Section 7520. Valuation Tables.

Estate and Financial Planning Software Programs Several organizations have proprietary software programs that can be used to perform calculations and illustrations for a large number of estate planning and financial planning strategies. These programs incorporate the latest IRS actuarial values just discussed. Many practitioners use such software programs to perform needed calculations and prepare illustrations for their professional activities. The programs are valuable for this purpose.

Applicable Federal Rates for Valuing Below-Market Loans

In the same Revenue Ruling in which the IRS announces the Section 7520 rate each month, it also sets the AFRs for the month. There is a federal short-term rate (based on the average market yield on outstanding marketable obligations of the United States with remaining maturities of three years or less), a federal mid-term rate (based on a similar calculation for U.S. marketable securities with remaining maturities of at least three years but not more than nine years), and a federal long-term rate (similarly based on average yields on U.S. marketable securities with remaining maturities of more than nine years). The appropriate AFR depends on the term (duration) of the debt instrument under consideration. For example, the interest rate on a demand note would be compared with the short-term AFR, the rate on an eight-year term note with the mid-term AFR, and so forth.

AFRs are used for several purposes, but one is to determine the tax consequences of so-called below-market loans. These are defined in Section 7892(e) of the IRC as *demand loans* when the interest rate (if any) is less than the AFR (short-term rate in this case) and as *term loans* when the amount of the loan is more than the present value of the payments due under the loan (discounted at the appropriate AFR for the term of the loan and compounded semiannually). The tax consequences depend on the nature of the below-market loan (e.g., gift loans, compensation-oriented loans, corporation-shareholder loans, etc.).

CASE EXAMPLE

Assume that Henry Johnson makes a $1,000,000 interest-free loan payable in eight years (a term loan) to his son, Peter. The idea is that Peter can invest the $1,000,000 and keep the investment earnings.

This is an example of a below-market gift loan (i.e., a below-market loan where the foregoing of interest is "in the nature of a gift"). In this case, Section 7872(a) provides that the foregone interest (i.e., the difference between the amount that would have been due using the appropriate AFR and the amount actually payable under the loan; here, this is the difference between the amount loaned and the present value of the payments under the loan) is treated (imputed) as a *gift* from the lender (Henry) to the borrower (Peter) and also as a payment of interest by the borrower (Peter) to the lender (Henry) and taxable as interest income to the lender.

To avoid the tax consequences of making below-market loans, the loan should contain an interest rate that is at least equal to the appropriate AFR. Thus, intrafamily loans for wealth transfer purposes normally charge the borrower an interest rate equal to the appropriate AFR. This then becomes the so-called hurdle rate that the yield on the borrower's investment of the borrowed funds must exceed for the strategy to work. This strategy is further discussed in Chapter 27.

PART II

Investment Planning and Financial Management

4

Basic Investment Planning and Strategies

Competence Objectives for This Chapter After reading this chapter, planners should understand:

- The basic investment objective
- Basic principles of modern portfolio theory, such as:
  - Expected returns
  - Some measures of investment risk
  - The degree of correlation among investments and asset classes
  - The concept of the efficient frontier
- The nature and limitations of the efficient market hypothesis (EMH)
- Factors in the choice of investments
- Types of investment risks, including:
  - Systematic (nondiversifiable, market) and unsystematic (diversifiable, nonmarket) risks
  - Interest rate risk
  - Reinvestment risk
  - Purchasing power risk
  - Exchange rate (currency) risk
  - Political risk
  - Tax risk
  - Financial (credit) risk
  - Business risk
  - Liquidity and marketability risks
  - Investment manager risk

- Measures of investment returns:
  - Annual rates of return, such as current yield, yield-to-maturity, yield-to-call, and real versus nominal returns
  - Total returns and holding period returns (HPRs)
  - Geometric average versus arithmetic average returns
  - After-tax yields
  - Tax-exempt income and taxable equivalent yields (TEYs)
  - Returns from capital gains
- Risk adjusted returns, including:
  - Capital asset pricing model (CAPM)
  - The Alpha (Jensen), Sharpe, and Treynor ratios
- Benchmarkers for measuring performance
- Other asset pricing models
- Forms and methods of investment diversification
- Other factors affecting investment decisions

Basic Investment Objective

The basic objective of most people is to earn the maximum possible total, after-tax rate of return on the funds available for investment, consistent with the investment limitations and constraints under which they must operate. In other words, most investors want to earn as much on their investments as they can relative to the level of risk they can assume. In general, the higher the expected returns on an asset class (e.g., common stocks, bonds, cash equivalents, real estate, and so forth), the greater the level of investment risk. This is referred to as the *risk-return tradeoff* (i.e., to get greater returns, the investor normally must assume greater risk). Obviously, the level of risk investors should assume varies greatly, depending on a host of factors, including their status within their economic lifecycle. For example, a young couple with both parties having successful careers outside the home normally can assume more investment risk than a couple with both parties age 65, who have just retired.

Investment Theories

Before discussing the specific factors involved in the choice of an investment portfolio and the characteristics, uses, and taxation of various investment vehicles (asset classes), it will be helpful to consider some investment theories that shape investment thinking today.

Modern Portfolio Theory

Investment thinking today is largely based on modern portfolio theory (MPT), which was pioneered by Professor Harry Markowitz in 1952.[1] MPT is also the basis for the *prudent investor rule,* which is the common legal standard today for the investment of trust funds, as explained in Chapter 25.

Prior to the development of MPT, investments for a portfolio were evaluated individually based on their individual characteristics of risk and return. Risk (and return) was considered on an asset by asset basis. Thus, some investments, or even asset classes, might have been regarded as "too risky" or "too speculative" to be included in a portfolio, regardless of what other assets were in the portfolio. This thinking also was important support for the "prudent man standard" (and particularly the "legal list rules") that formerly governed trust investment law, again as explained in Chapter 25.

On the other hand, MPT focuses on the expected returns, risk, and correlations (or covariance) among asset classes for the portfolio as a whole. It evaluates total portfolio risk rather than the risk presented by each component in the portfolio. Thus, the overall objective of MPT is to achieve the highest possible return on the whole portfolio for an acceptable level of risk (which depends on the investor's characteristics, objectives, and tolerance for risk). Or, stated somewhat differently, for a given level of risk, the rational investor will seek to organize his or her portfolio to secure the greatest expected return. This is accomplished through *efficient diversification* of the portfolio.

Expected Returns The *expected returns* considered in MPT are often based on long-term historical average (mean) annual total returns for different asset classes (such as, average annual returns on a common stock index, government bonds, and cash equivalents for a long period, such as 1926 through the present). Other estimates of expected returns may also be used. These expected returns often assume reinvestment of income and do not consider investment expenses or taxes. Naturally, it is impossible to know what future returns on any asset class will be. Thus, expected returns are difficult to determine. But many analysts believe that long-term experience over various economic cycles and events is the best guide. Of course, any analysis is only as good as the validity of the inputs going into it, and clearly, the length and representativeness of any historical period used will have a major impact on the validity of the expected returns produced.

[1] See, for example, Dr. Markowitz's seminal article, "Portfolio Selection," *Journal of Finance* 7, No. 1 (March 1952), pp. 77-91.

Risk In this context, *risk* is defined as the variation of actual returns for an individual investment, an asset class, or a portfolio around their expected returns. Thus, risk is the *variance*, or dispersion, of investment returns.[2] Note that variance includes both positive (gains) and negative (losses) percentage variations from the average (i.e., expected returns). Another concept is *semivariance*, which measures only negative percentage variations from the average.

Standard Deviation and Related Concepts: The main measurement of risk is the statistical concept of the *standard deviation.* The standard deviation is a measure of the dispersion (or distance from the average) of a series of returns (such as investment returns).[3] The greater the standard deviation, the greater the potential variation of actual returns from expected returns (average returns), and hence the greater the investment risk.

For example, assume that over the previous 40 years a portfolio consisting entirely of large-cap common stocks (as measured by, say, the S&P 500 index) had an average annual total return (expected return) of 10 percent and a standard deviation of 18 percent. On the other hand, assume that over the same period a portfolio consisting entirely of long-term U.S. government bonds had an average annual total return (expected return) of 6 percent and a standard deviation of 11 percent. Given these numbers, the next question might be within what range of the expected returns might we expect the actual returns in any given year (i.e., period) to fall? In other words, what is the likely maximum level of dispersion of the actual returns around the expected returns in a given year?

This is a question of probabilities. Statistical theory tells us that assuming a normal distribution of items (in this case, annual investment returns), the probabilities are that approximately two-thirds (say, 67 percent) of the items will fall within plus or minus one standard deviation of the arithmetic mean (average), approximately 95 percent will fall within plus or minus two standard deviations of the arithmetic mean, while approximately 99 percent will fall within three standard deviations. These are known as *confidence intervals.* Therefore, based on these probabilities, we can estimate that almost all (95 percent) of the actual annual total returns will fall within plus or minus two standard deviations of the expected (average) return. Thus, there is a 95 percent probability that the common stock portfolio's *actual annual total returns* will range from a gain of 46 percent (10 percent expected return +

[2] Technically, *variance* is the sum of the squared percentage deviations from the mean. The mathematical formula for the variance of returns is $\sigma^2 = E[r - E(r)]^2$.

[3] Technically, the *standard deviation* is the square root of the variance, or $\sigma = \sqrt{\sigma^2}$. Actual calculations of the variance and standard deviation are beyond the scope of this book.

36 percent for two standard deviations) to a loss of 26 percent (10 percent expected return – 36 percent for two standard deviations). The corresponding range for the government bond portfolio would be from an annual gain of 28 percent (6 percent expected return + 22 percent for two standard deviations) to an annual loss of 16 percent (6 percent expected return – 22 percent for two standard deviations). Thus, the hypothetical stock portfolio has a greater expected return but involves more risk than the bond portfolio.

It may be noted that these probabilities (confidence intervals) assume a normal distribution of variable items (annual investment returns) around the arithmetic mean of the items. A *normal distribution* is a bell-shaped frequency distribution of the items, with approximately an equal range of items above and below the mean (average) item. A distribution is *skewed* when there is a greater range of items either above or below the mean. In other words, the skewed distribution is not bell-shaped but has a "tail" of items extending either above or below the mean. The concept of *Kurtosis* refers to the shape of the distribution (i.e., how pointed or flat the frequency distribution is).

A distribution may also be a *lognormal distribution*, which is a probability distribution of items whose logarithms are normally distributed. If items are determined to be lognormally distributed, the geometric mean (e.g., average annual compound rates of return) and the geometric standard deviation can be used to estimate confidence intervals, as shown previously.

As just explained, the standard deviation is a commonly used measure of total investment risk. However, some cautions on such use might be noted.

First, the data used to calculate expected returns and standard deviations ideally should cover a relatively long period that encompasses a variety of economic conditions (prosperity, recession, depression, peace, and war). Periods that are not representative of differing economic conditions can produce misleading results that may not be duplicated in the future. Furthermore, the standard deviation normally measures anticipated *annual deviations* from the mean (expected returns). However, common stock "bear markets" often last longer than one year and produce steeper declines (from peak to trough) than one year's standard deviations. For example, the "bear market" at the start of the Great Depression of the 1930s lasted 35 months (from the peak in September 1929 to the trough in July 1932) and resulted in an 89 percent decline in the Dow Jones Industrial Average during that time. It took 25 years (until November 1954) for the market to recover to its previous peak of September 1929. In the post–World War II period, to take a more recent example, the severe "bear market" that started in January 1973 (peak) and lasted until December 1974 (trough) had a duration of 23 months and resulted in a decline in the Dow Jones Industrial Average of 45 percent. This time, it took the market 95 months to return to its previous high.[4] The suggestion here is that the use of the statistical concept of the standard deviation to measure risk should be tempered with consideration of what history has taught us about past severe bear markets.

A statistical measure related to the standard deviation is the *coefficient of variation (Cv)*. It is the ratio of the standard deviation to the mean of a distribution of data, and is often expressed as a percentage.[5] It may be referred to as the relative standard deviation or the percentage standard deviation. This measure will result in a single number (a percentage) that may be useful for comparison purposes in certain situations.

Beta: Another important statistical measure of investment risk is the *beta coefficient* or *beta*. This measures the volatility of the market prices of an individual common stock, a portfolio of stocks, or a mutual fund relative to those of a given market index (which may represent the whole market or a segment of the market).

The idea is that when market prices as a whole (which have a beta of 1) go up or down, the prices of individual stocks or mutual funds correspondingly may go up or down more than or less than those of the market as a whole, or they may move in sync with the market. This volatility relationship is measured by the stock's or fund's beta.[6] Thus, for example, if a stock or fund has a beta of 1.5 relative to the Wilshire 5000 Stock Index, it is more volatile (risky) than the index (representing most of the market), so if the Wilshire 5000 declines, say, by 10 percent, it is expected that the subject stock or fund will decline by 1.5 times that, or 15 percent. Correspondingly, if the Wilshire 5000 should go up, say, by 20 percent, the subject stock or fund should increase by 30 percent (20% × 1.5). Similarly, if a stock or fund has a beta of 0.75 relative to the Wilshire 5000, it is less volatile (risky) than the index and so is expected to move only 0.75 (75 percent) of any increase or decrease in the Wilshire 5000. If a stock or fund has a beta of 1, it is expected to move to the same degree as the market index. In a few cases, a stock or fund may move in the opposite direction to the market in general. Such stocks or funds might have a negative beta.

R-Squared (Coefficient of Determination): This is a statistical measure that indicates the fraction of the variance of a dependent variable (e.g., return

[4] Data on common stock bear market durations, percentage declines, and recovery periods are presented in Chapter 5.

[5] In this case, its mathematical formula would be $Cv = \frac{\sigma}{N}(100)$ where σ is the standard deviation and N is the mean.

[6] Technically, the beta (β) is the standard deviation of the individual stock or fund (σ_i) divided by the standard deviation of the market index (σ_m) and then multiplied by the correlation coefficient between the individual stock or fund and the market index [Corr (σ_i, σ_m)]. Thus, the formula for beta is $\beta = \sigma_i/\sigma_m$ [Corr (σ_i, σ_m)]. The concept of correlation is discussed next in this chapter. Again, the actual calculation of the beta is beyond the scope of this book.

on a stock or mutual fund) that is explained by the variance of an independent variable (such as the return on a stock market index). Thus, for example, it measures how much of a stock's or fund's past returns can be explained by the returns of the market generally (as measured by a stock market index). In the unlikely event that a stock's or fund's past total returns moved exactly with those of the index, its R-squared (R^2) would be 1.

It has been suggested that a fund's beta is related to its R^2. Since R^2 indicates the degree of correspondence (correlation) of returns of a fund and the index, it also indicates how reliable the beta is in measuring the fund's price volatility. The higher the R^2, the more reliable the beta; the lower the R^2, the less reliable the beta.

CASE EXAMPLE

The use of some of these statistical measures in wealth management can be shown by the following situation.

Mark Schwartz is age 55 and would like to retire in about five years. He and his wife Alice, age 53, own about $2,000,000 worth of various mutual funds and common stocks. These include seven mutual funds with several different investment objectives and eight individual common stocks. The overall portfolio is allocated more than 90 percent in common stock funds and common stocks. Mark and Alice are concerned about the current economic environment, particularly in light of their planned retirement in just five years. They would like to have some idea of how much investment risk they are assuming and what their expected investment returns might be. Their investment adviser has prepared a report for them covering their asset allocation, portfolio characteristics, and the characteristics of individual securities in the portfolio to evaluate their risk-return situation, among other things.

Just as examples, the report contains the following statistical information on two of their mutual funds (along with much more information).

Fund A	**3 years**	**5 years**	**10 years**
Mean (average annual total return)	15.03%	13.69%	9.78%
Standard Deviation	6.62%	11.44%	13.84%
	Fund Compared with a Broad Index		Fund Compared with a Similar Index
Beta	0.84		0.91
R-Squared	0.83		0.92

Fund B	3 years	5 years	10 years
Mean (average annual total return)	8.20%	13.80%	10.42%
Standard Deviation	12.38%	16.14%	19.96%
	Fund Compared with a Broad Index		Fund Compared with a Similar Index
Beta	1.48		1.35
R-Squared	0.78		0.88

In addition, the report gives the following statistical information on their overall portfolio (along with much more information).

	3 years	5 years	10 years
Mean (average annual total return)	14.20%	12.78%	10.38%
Standard Deviation	11.35%	15.54%	17.86%
Beta	1.21	1.28	1.32
R-Squared	0.74	0.76	0.85

Just using this information, it can be seen that Fund A has had almost the same average annual total return over the last 10 years as Fund B (9.78% compared with 10.42%) and better returns for the last three years, while experiencing lower risk. Fund A's standard deviation for the last 10 years was 13.84, while Fund B's was 19.96. Thus, Fund A experienced less variation from the mean (investment risk) than Fund B. Similarly, Fund A's beta (e.g., compared with a broad market index) was less than 1 (i.e., 0.84), while Fund B's beta was substantially greater than 1 (i.e., 1.48). Meaning that the prices of Fund B are more volatile relative to the index then those of Fund A. Furthermore, the R^2 of Fund A is somewhat higher than that of Fund B, so the returns of Fund A are somewhat better correlated with the index than Fund B. Thus, from these data it would appear that at least for the last 10 years, Fund A has had a better risk-notion relationship than Fund B.

Their investment adviser also points out to Mark and Alice that the standard deviation and beta for their overall portfolio are reasonably high, indicating significant variability of returns from the mean and from the market index.

Given this information and considerable further analysis, their investment adviser suggests that Mark and Alice consider revising their asset allocation to reduce their exposure to common stocks and stock funds. He suggests they move more of their asset allocation into less volatile (less risky) asset classes, such as investment-grade bonds and bond funds. By doing so, they could reduce their overall portfolio risk (as measured by the portfolio's standard deviation) while not greatly reducing their portfolio's expected return. That is, while overall expected return can be expected to decline (because long-term returns on investment-grade bonds normally are lower than on common stocks), portfolio risk will decline proportionally more. This is because the price movements of common stocks and bonds are poorly or even negatively correlated (i.e., they do not move together).

Cautions on Use of Statistical Measures Some cautions concerning the use of standard deviations have already been noted. It also should be borne in mind that these are theoretical measures based on past experience, which may or may not be repeated in the future. Also, betas may change over time. Investment research has indicated that, over time, betas tend to move toward the market beta of 1 (which is referred to as "regressing to the mean"). Also, as noted previously, betas should be analyzed in conjunction with the R^2 measure of correlation of returns to the market.

Furthermore, measures of expected returns and the standard deviations are more reliable when taken over reasonably long time periods (such as at least 10 years). It is interesting to observe that the returns for mutual funds with similar investment objectives tend to move much closer together when viewed over a 10-year time span.

The main point is that while these statistical measures can provide useful insights concerning risk and return, they are only part of the analytical picture. Their use should be tempered with sound judgment based on the facts of the particular case, the time horizons and other investment constraints involved, and the perceived general economic and investment climate.

Capital Market Line (CML) We have noted that there is always a tradeoff between risk and return in investing. Investment theorists illustrate this by considering a portfolio consisting of a risk-free asset (such as U.S. Treasury bills or insured bank accounts) and a hypothetical "risky" asset consisting of an optimal portfolio of all "risky" assets. The expected returns and risks (as measured by the standard deviation) of all combinations of these two assets are plotted on a straight line called the *capital allocation line (CAL).* This is part of the threshold decision of how much of a portfolio should be allocated to safe but low-yielding assets and how much to riskier assets, such as common stocks or real estate. This sometimes is referred to as the capital allocation decision.

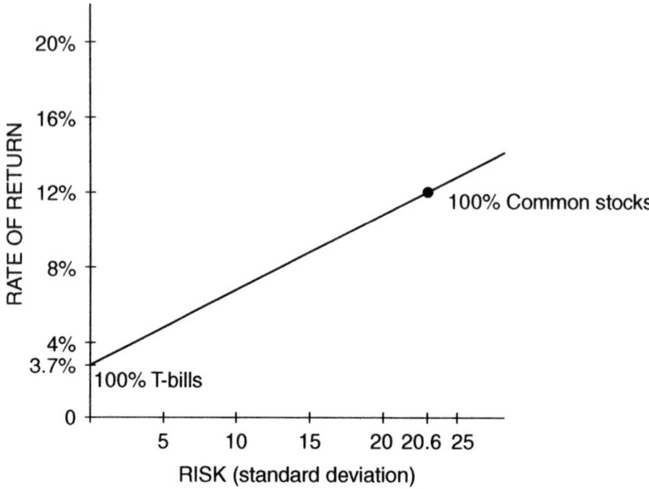

Figure 4.1. Capital Market Line (CML)

The capital market line (CML) is a capital allocation line that shows the expected returns and risk of all combinations of a risk-free asset (e.g., 30-day Treasury bills) and a broad market index of common stocks. The expected return and standard deviation for the common stocks are from long-term historical studies. The same is true for the expected return for the T-bills, but since they are the risk-free asset, their standard deviation is assumed to be zero.

Figure 4.1 shows such a capital market line. The vertical axis shows the expected returns and the horizontal axis the risk (as measured by the standard deviations). A portfolio of 100 percent T-bills would have an expected return of 3.7 percent and an assumed standard deviation of zero (i.e., is risk-free, although in reality 30-day bills would have some variability). A 100 percent common stock portfolio would have an expected return of 12 percent and a standard deviation of 20.6 percent. The various combinations of these two assets corresponding to the points on the line between these limits would have correspondingly weighted returns and risk.

The *risk premium* of an asset or asset class is the difference between its expected return and that of risk-free assets. It compensates the investor for the risk inherent in the "risky" asset. In this example, the risk premium is 8.3 percent (or 12 percent expected return on common stocks less 3.7 percent risk-free return on T-bills).[7]

[7] Another measure used in this context is the reward-to-variability ratio. This is the risk premium divided by the standard deviation, and it shows the increase in expected return for each point of standard deviation. In this example, it would be 8.3 ÷ 20.6 = 0.403. It also is the slope of the CAL or CML.

A variation of the CML is sometimes used by analysts to show the risk-return characteristics of other asset classes (such as alternative investments) in comparison to, say, combinations of the risk-free asset and common stocks. The idea is to show how such asset classes might fit into an investment portfolio in terms of risk and return.

Covariance and Correlation Coefficient (Correlation) It was noted previously that modern portfolio theory is concerned with expected return and risk for a portfolio as a whole (portfolio risk-return) rather than for individual securities considered separately. The goal is to achieve the best return possible on the entire portfolio for a given level of risk. This risk level depends on the individual investor's personal circumstances and risk aversion. In this context, the concepts of covariance and the correlation coefficient are important.

Covariance (or correlation) is a number (such as +80) indicating the degree to which the returns of two assets or asset classes move with each other. A positive covariance means the returns move together, while a negative covariance means they move in opposite directions. The size of the number indicates the intensity of the correlation.

The *correlation coefficient* is an easier number to use in analysis because it measures correlation between +1 (the returns move exactly in the same direction or are perfectly correlated) and −1 (the returns move exactly in opposite directions or are perfectly negatively correlated).[8] Thus, if there were two common stocks in the same industry with a correlation coefficient of +1 (an unlikely event), when one stock increases in price by, say, 20 percent, the other also will increase by 20 percent, and when one declines in price by 20 percent, the other also will fall by 20 percent. On the other hand, if one stock was an oil exploration company and the other a manufacturer of solar panels and they had a correlation coefficient of −1 (an equally unlikely event), when one stock increases in price by, say, 20 percent, the other will decline in price by the same 20 percent, and when the first stock declines, the other will rise by the same percentage.

Correlations normally fall somewhere between +1 and −1. If the correlation coefficient lies between +1 and 0, the assets are positively correlated, and the size of the correlation coefficient (how close it is to 1) indicates the degree of correlation. If the correlation coefficient lies between 0 and −1, the assets are negatively correlated (inversely correlated). Most assets and asset classes are positively correlated, but the degrees of correlation can vary considerably. For example, for a given period, the S&P 500 stock index may have a

[8] Technically, the correlation coefficient between two items is their covariance divided by the product of their standard deviations. However, such calculations are beyond the scope of this book.

0.81 correlation coefficient with the MSCI EAFE index,[9] indicating a relatively high positive correlation. On the other hand, for the same period, the S&P 500 may have a 0.50 correlation coefficient with an index of fund of hedge funds, indicating a positive but much lower degree of correlation. In fact, one of the arguments for including hedge funds in an asset allocation (if eligible to do so) is that they may have relatively low correlations with other asset classes (such as common stocks), yet may have relatively attractive expected returns. Hence, they may lower portfolio risk relative to their possible returns. (Hedge funds and private equity are discussed further in Chapter 8.) As a final example, the S&P 500 stock index may have a –0.21 correlation coefficient with intermediate-term U.S. Treasury notes, indicating a negative correlation. This may demonstrate a countercyclical movement in stock and bond prices (i.e., during the business cycle, when the market prices of stocks fall, such as during a recession, the market prices of investment-grade bonds may rise), as noted in Chapter 7.

Efficient Frontier We noted previously that the risk-return characteristics for an asset or asset class can be shown by its expected return (mean) and variance of returns around the mean or risk (as measured by the standard deviation). However, for a portfolio of assets or asset classes, the risk-return characteristics for the whole portfolio depend not only on the expected returns and variance of returns of the assets or asset classes individually, but also on the covariance (correlation) of the assets or asset classes to each other.

This covariance factor usually results in a reduction of portfolio risk through diversification. The expected return of a portfolio is equal to the weighted arithmetic average return of the assets or asset classes in the portfolio. However, the variance of returns of the portfolio (or portfolio standard deviation) will be less than the weighted arithmetic average standard deviation of the assets or asset classes in the portfolio, provided these assets or asset classes have a correlation coefficient of less than 1 (i.e., are not perfectly correlated with each other). As noted previously, assets or asset classes are almost never perfectly correlated. This general concept can be referred to as *efficient diversification.* Also, the lower the level of correlation among the assets or asset classes in the portfolio, the lower the overall portfolio variance (risk) will be. This is the theoretical basis for including otherwise risky assets or asset classes in a portfolio provided they have low correlations (or possibly are even uncorrelated, i.e., have a negative correlation coefficient) with the other assets in the portfolio.

[9] The MSCI EAFE is the Morgan Stanley Capital International index covering stock markets in Europe (E), Australasia (A), and the Far East (FE). It is often compared with the S&P 500 when comparing stock market performance in the United States and elsewhere.

The *efficient frontier* is a graph showing a given set of assets or asset classes with the lowest possible portfolio variance for the expected return for each possible combination of the assets or asset classes. This also may be referred to as the *minimum-variance frontier* or *mean-variance optimization.*

The inputs for this frontier are the expected returns, variances (standard deviations), and covariances (correlation coefficients) for the assets or asset classes involved. As stated previously, these inputs usually are taken from historical data. This means the historical period selected can have a major impact on the outcomes. Sometimes, the inputs are based on a scenario analysis where logical estimates are made of possible returns or are based on market forecasts made for the data by the preparer of the frontier or others. There also are many computer programs that can generate efficient frontiers from the inputs for specified assets or asset classes.

Figure 4.2 is an example of an efficient frontier (with inputs based on historical data) for a common-stock large-cap index and 20-year U.S. Treasury bonds. This frontier is the set of portfolios that for any given expected return (mean) on the vertical axis will produce the lowest standard deviation (risk) on the horizontal axis. As noted previously, this may be referred to as the variance minimization approach, or *mean-variance optimization.* Alternatively, the frontier shows the portfolio for any given risk level (standard deviation) that will produce the greatest expected return. The two approaches produce the same result. These concepts that developed a formalized diversification theory were first put forward by Professor Harry Markowitz in 1952. He earned the Nobel Prize for Economics in 1990 for this work.

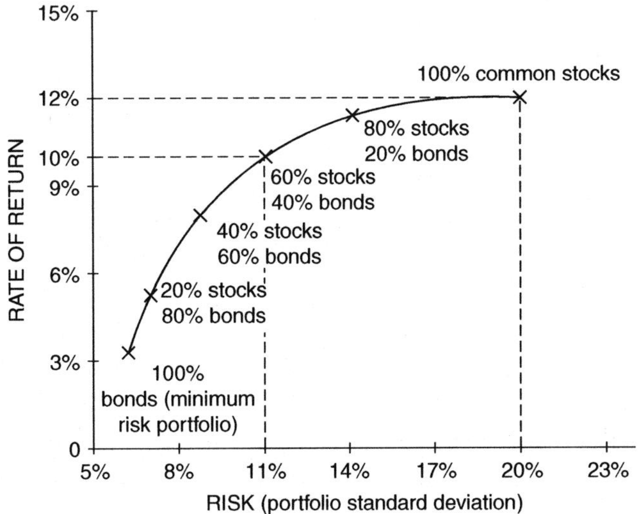

Figure 4.2. Efficient Frontier

Efficient Market Hypothesis (EMH)

This controversial theory attained prominence in the 1960s and has continued to be advanced since then, particularly in academic circles. It holds that common stock prices already reflect all information available to market participants and, therefore, it is not possible to consistently outperform the market using such information.

When new information emerges (such as mergers or dividend increases), stock prices will be affected, but they will adjust quickly to new values based on the new information. Thus, stock prices will be affected only by new, unpredictable information and the resulting effect in stock prices will be random and unpredictable (i.e., not discoverable through security analysis). Some have referred to this idea as stock prices following a *random walk.*

Depending on the form of EMH being advanced, it suggests that those efforts to pick undervalued securities (fundamental analysis and value investing) and to pick stocks based on their past price movements (technical analysis) generally are fruitless in an efficient market. It also would seem to favor passive investment approaches (such as index investing) and pursuing a buy-and-hold strategy in common stock investing generally. Thus, this theory argues against active stock management and security analysis.

Forms of Efficient Market Hypothesis Proponents of EMH are not uniform in how they apply the theory, particularly in terms of what information is presumed to be "available." There are three forms of EMH: weak, semistrong, and strong.

Weak Form: As its name implies, this is the least vigorous application of the theory. It assumes that stock prices already reflect publicly available information concerning past stock prices, trading volumes, and similar data. Therefore, technical analysis (attempting to predict future stock price movements from their past movements) cannot be effective in producing superior returns, but fundamental analysis (security analysis) can identify stocks that are temporarily undervalued or overvalued, allowing investors to profit from such analysis.

Semistrong Form: This form tightens the theory considerably and assumes that stock prices already reflect all publicly available information concerning the companies and their stocks. This would include information commonly used in security analysis, such as financial statements, product lines, market shares, management information, earnings forecasts, and so forth. Therefore, neither technical analysis nor fundamental analysis can be effective in producing superior results. This form does allow, however, that private information (e.g., held by corporate insiders) may allow holders of such information to earn superior returns because such information is not already reflected in stock prices. Of course, as noted in Chapter 1, trading on such insider information is often illegal, but as a practical matter, determining and proving insider trading may be difficult.

Strong Form: This is the most extreme (and controversial) form of EMH. It holds that stock prices already reflect all information (public and private) concerning companies and their stocks.

Anomalies of EMH: EMH theory is quite controversial, particularly in its strong form. Critics suggest there are reasons for market inefficiencies, such as slow diffusion of information and the power of some market participants. They also note that some sophisticated investors seem to consistently outperform the market over a significant period. Warren Buffett, for example, has been a critic of EMH.

Some who believe in security analysis (such as value investors) also argue that markets are not inherently efficient, but are often irrational so that prices of stocks can vary significantly from their true or intrinsic values. This group suggests that irrational behavior by market participants is, in fact, the norm. Thus, fundamental analysis can produce superior returns. This may be particularly true at the end of a bull market (when many investors are irrationally optimistic) or of a bear market (when they are irrationally pessimistic).

Finally, behavioral finance teaches that market participants may be driven by irrational psychological factors in addition to rational economic analysis. Behavioral economics and finance were discussed in Chapter 2.

Investment, Speculation, and Gambling

At one time, it was common to draw a rather sharp distinction between *investment* and *speculation.* For example, high-grade bonds were considered investments, while common stocks were viewed as speculative. Now, however, such distinctions are passé, and high-quality ("blue-chip") common stocks generally are looked upon as investment-grade securities. Also, as we have seen from the previous section, modern portfolio theory views risk in terms of the whole portfolio rather than in terms of individual assets or asset classes.

In general, however, the term *speculation* probably can be used to mean the purchase of securities or other assets involving the assumption of considerable risk in the hope that they will produce similarly large profits in a comparatively short time. In other words, the speculator takes considerable risk in the hope of immediate and sizeable gains.

Are prudent investors to avoid speculation, as we have just defined it? The answer seems to be "not necessarily"; it depends on such things as how much of the total investment portfolio the investor wants to risk in speculation, what other kinds of assets are available for the family, how good the investor or his or her advisers are at speculating, and whether the investor has the temperament to take speculative losses as well as speculative gains. Thus, a modest portion of a portfolio, say, 5 to 10 percent, might be allocated to speculative assets. However, it also seems reasonable to say that most people are not prepared to speculate successfully. They generally are better off investing more conservatively for the long term.

Gambling, on the other hand, involves creating the risk by the transaction itself. In playing roulette, for example, there is no risk until the player puts his or her money on, for example, the red seven. But when a speculator buys a hot new stock issue in hopes of a quick profit, the stock already presents a business risk and the speculator is simply assuming it in hopes of considerable gain.

Factors in the Choice of Investments

A number of factors may be considered when choosing among categories of investments or individual investments. Some of these are listed below.

- Security of principal and income
- Rate of return (yield)
- Marketability and liquidity
- Diversification
- Tax status
- Size of investment units or denominations
- Use as collateral for loans
- Protection against creditor's claims
- Callability
- Freedom from care

The following sections discuss these factors in detail.

Security of Principal and Income

For many investors, security of principal and income is of paramount importance. They want to be able to get their money back or not lose money on their investments. But when this factor is analyzed more closely, other questions arise, such as what kinds of "security" and over what time frame. Thus, investors and their advisers really need to keep in mind a number of different types of risks to investment values.

Types of Investment Risk

Systematic and Unsystematic Risks This category broadly defines and separates risks that remain after diversification (i.e., are *nondiversifiable*), which are called *systematic risks*, and those that can be reduced or even eliminated by diversification (i.e., are *diversifiable*) and are called *unsystematic risks*. Systematic risks are also referred to as *market risks*, while unsystematic risks are called non-market risks or *firm-specific risks*. Thus, market risk implies price fluctuations for a whole securities market, regardless of the financial soundness or investment merits of individual securities. Bull and bear markets (when most stocks go up or down at the same time) are examples of this phenomenon.

Some other types of systematic risk are discussed next.

Interest Rate Risk This risk involves price changes of existing investments because of changes in the general level of interest rates in the capital markets. In general, a rise in general market interest rates tends to cause a decline in market prices for existing securities; conversely, a decline in interest rates tends to cause a rise in market prices for existing securities. Thus, market prices for existing securities tend to move inversely with changes in the general level of interest rates.

CASE EXAMPLE

It is not difficult to see why this is true. Assume, for example, that 10 years ago Helen Johnson purchased a newly issued, high-grade corporate bond with a 7 percent interest rate for $1,000 (at par). The bond was to come due (mature) in 30 years. Therefore, Helen receives interest of $70 per year from the bond. At the time she bought the bond, the prevailing level of interest rates in the capital markets for bonds of this type, grade, and duration was around 7 percent. Otherwise, this bond issue could not have been sold successfully. But in the meantime, assume the general level of interest rates in the capital markets for bonds of this type, grade, and remaining duration has risen, and now the prevailing interest rate for comparable bonds with a 20-year duration is about 9 percent.

What effect does this have on Helen's existing bond? First, the 7 percent interest rate (coupon rate) does not change. So Helen will still get interest of $70 per year until the bond matures 20 years from now. Also, when the bond matures, Helen will get the full $1,000 maturity value from the issuing corporation. Therefore, if Helen simply holds the bond until maturity, she will continue to receive a 7 percent return and will have lost no principal (her $1,000). Unfortunately, however, the current market price of the bond in the bond market will have declined to somewhere near $816.[10] Why is this so? Because at about this price, the yield to maturity (in 20 years) of this bond would be 9 percent and this is the prevailing market interest rate. Therefore, since we assume investors can buy newly issued bonds at around 9 percent, the prices of existing bonds carrying lower interest rates must decline to the point where they will offer generally comparable yields to maturity for a buyer. When the market price of bonds declines in this manner below their maturity value, they are said to be selling *at a discount* and are called *market discount bonds*.[11] This decline in market price does, of course, have some impact on Helen, depending on the circumstances. In determining her current personal net worth (from her statement of financial position), the bond should be valued at $816. If she should need or want to sell the bond or use it as collateral for a loan, it is worth only $816 (not $1,000). However, if Helen sells this market discount bond, she will have a capital loss for tax purposes and can engage in a *tax swap bond strategy*.

Now, what will happen if interest rates in the capital markets should decline? Assume, for example, that five years pass and during that time the prevailing interest rate for comparable bonds moves from 9 to 6 percent. This would mean that the current market price of the existing 7 percent bond with 15 years left until maturity would rise to somewhere around $1,098 (or to a premium). Why? Because at about this price the yield to maturity (in 15 years) of this bond would be 6 percent, and this is now the prevailing market interest rate.

Applications: We have illustrated interest rate risk in terms of a 30-year corporate bond. Does it also apply to other types of securities? Yes! Changes in the general level of interest rates have some influence on the prices of all securities and other investments. For example, when interest rates generally rise, bonds may become more attractive than common stocks for some investors, thus exerting a downward pressure on the stock market. Higher interest rates also make it more expensive for corporations to borrow, thus lowering their profits. Correspondingly, investment real estate generally is financed by mortgage loans. Thus, higher mortgage interest rates lower the returns from real estate.

[10] A calculator or table shows that a 20-year bond with a 7 percent coupon rate will yield 9 percent to maturity if it is priced at $81.60 ($816).

[11] Bonds also may be originally issued at a discount from their ultimate maturity value so that some or all of their annual interest return comes from the gradually accruing increase in their value as the bond approaches maturity. These are called *original-issue discount (OID) bonds* and are of a different nature than the point being made in this section.

Of course, the reverse is true when market interest rates fall. For example, lower interest rates generally are considered good for the stock market.

In general, prices of securities that are of high quality because of their low financial risk tend to be most affected by changes in interest rates. This is because the financial risk factor has relatively little impact on their market prices. High-grade bonds fall into this category. However, prices of other securities, such as high-quality preferred stocks and certain types of common stocks (such as high-grade utility stocks), also may be significantly influenced by changes in interest rates.

Furthermore, the longer the maturity of bonds, the more influenced their prices will be by changes in market interest rates. This is because once a bond matures, it will be paid off by the issuer at par, regardless of the prevailing level of interest rates. Thus, for example, a 30-year U.S. Treasury bond will be much more affected by interest rate risk than will, say, a 5-year U.S. Treasury note. In addition, bonds issued with no current interest payments (zero coupon bonds) and bonds with low coupon rates will be more affected by interest rate risk than otherwise comparable bonds with higher coupon rates. These concepts are illustrated in Table 4.1. Finally, when bonds and preferred stocks are likely to be called, they will be less affected by interest rate risk.

Bond Duration and Interest Rate Risk: A bond's *duration* is the weighted average maturity of the bond's cash flows. It considers current interest payments as well as maturity value in determining these cash flows. Since interest payments are received earlier than the principal at maturity, a bond's or bond portfolio's duration will be less than its maturity (when the face or par value is payable) or a bond portfolio's weighted average maturity assuming the bond or bond portfolios pay current coupon interest. For example, as of a given date, an international bond mutual fund had a weighted average maturity of 8.3 years, a weighted average duration of 6 years, and an average quality of AA (bond quality ratings are discussed in Chapter 7). On the other hand, if a bond is a zero-coupon original issue discount bond (with no current interest payments), its duration will equal its maturity (the number of years until it matures).

Portfolio managers use a bond's or bond portfolio's duration to assess its price sensitivity to interest rate risk. This sensitivity can be approximately determined by multiplying the bond's or bond portfolio's duration by the percentage point change in market interest rates. For example, for the international bond fund noted previously with a duration of 6 years, if market interest rates fall by 2 percentage points (or 200 basis points), the fund's price per share will increase about 12 percent (6 years duration × 2 percentage points = 12 percent increase in price). Correspondingly, if market interest rates should rise by 1.5 percentage points (150 basis points), the fund's price will fall about 9 percent (6 × 1.5 = 9 percent decline in price).

Duration also can be used in bond *portfolio immunization strategy* to coordinate an investor's bond portfolio's duration with his or her needs for funds.

Analysis: Possible Interest Rate "Shocks" and Their Convexity: Table 4.1 shows the hypothetical volatility in market prices for 5-year Treasury notes (coupon), 10-year Treasury notes (coupon), 10-year Treasury notes (zero coupon), and 30-year Treasury bonds (coupon) in the event of 100, 200, and 300 basis point increases and decreases in market interest rates. (One percentage point of interest rate equals 100 basis points, two percentage points equal 200 basis points, and so on.)

It can be seen from Table 4.1 how bond maturity and coupon status affect interest rate risk. For example, in the face of a 200 basis point increase in market interest rates, the 5-year Treasury note's price will decline about 8.5 percent, the 10-year (coupon) Treasury note's price will decline about 14.34 percent, while the fall in price of the 30-year Treasury bond reaches 23.2 percent. This illustrates the impact of maturity on interest rate risk. Furthermore, showing the impact of coupon status, a 200 basis point increase in market interest rates will produce approximately a 14.34 percent decline in the price of the 4.75 percent 10-year (coupon) Treasury note, while it will cause, approximately, a 17.56 percent decline in price for the 10-year zero coupon note. Of course, declines in market interest rates will produce corresponding increases in bond and note prices, as shown in Table 4.1. As stated previously, the prices of fixed-income securities move inversely with market interest rates.

Another characteristic of bond valuation that can be seen from Table 4.1 is that of *bond convexity*. This means that when there is an increase in market interest rates, the decline in bond prices is less than the corresponding increase in bond prices for the same amount of decline in market interest rates. For example, if market interest rates increase by 200 basis points (2 percentage points), the 30-year Treasury bond price will decline approximately 23.2 percent, while if market rates decline by the same 200 basis points, the 30-year bond price will increase approximately 35.01 percent. This concept is called *convexity* because if the relationship between bond price and market rates were plotted in a graph, the bond price–market rate curve would be convex in shape.

Reinvestment Risk: From the viewpoint of maintaining the income in an investment portfolio, changes in interest rates may present a different kind of risk—the reinvestment risk. This risk can arise from bonds and preferred stocks that are *called* (redeemed) by their issuers prior to maturity when rates are lower than when they were issued or purchased, and from securities that

Table 4.1. Interest Rate Risk Volatility for Various U.S. Treasury Securities

Basis Point	5-year 3.875% Coupon Rate			10-year 4.75% Coupon Rate			10-year Strips (zero coupon T-note) 0.00% Coupon Rate			30-year (actual 27 year) 5.375% Coupon Rate		
Change	Yield	Price	% change	Yield	Price	% change	Yield	Price	% change	Yield	Price	% change
+300	6.81	87.84	−12.41%	7.68	79.86	−20.58%	8.06	45.55	−25.09%	8.38	68.13	−31.82%
+200	5.81	91.77	−8.50%	6.68	86.13	−14.34%	7.06	50.13	−17.56%	7.38	76.74	−23.20%
+100	4.81	95.92	−4.36%	5.68	93.01	−7.50%	6.06	55.20	−9.23%	6.38	87.18	−12.75%
Actual	3.81	100.29	—	4.68	100.55	—	5.06	60.81	—	5.38	99.92	—
−100	2.81	104.88	4.58%	3.68	108.85	8.25%	4.06	67.03	10.23%	4.38	115.56	15.65%
−200	1.81	109.74	9.42%	2.68	117.97	17.32%	3.06	73.91	21.54%	3.38	134.90	35.01%
−300	0.81	114.84	14.51%	1.68	128.02	27.32%	2.06	81.55	34.11%	2.28	158.93	59.06%

These figures are based on U.S. Treasury notes and bonds as of June 2004.

U.S. Treasury securities are considered free of default risk, so they would not be subject to financial or credit risk. For U.S. investors, they also would be free of exchange rate (currency) risk. These securities are free of other risks noted later as well. However, the price changes in Table 4.1 do not account for bid-offer spreads or other market factors, so they are hypothetical in nature.

SOURCE: Janney Montgomery Scott, LLC, *Volatility Report*

mature when interest rates are lower than they were when the maturing securities were originally issued. In both cases, the investor is presented with a principal sum, which he or she must reinvest at a lower rate than was enjoyed in the called or maturing securities.

Redemption or Call Risk: The issuers of callable bonds and preferred stocks normally will redeem them when comparable market interest rates fall significantly below the coupon rates being paid on the securities. As noted, this is disadvantageous for investors in callable securities because issuers will surely call them if interest rates fall, but, of course, will not do so if interest rates rise.

> **CASE EXAMPLE**
> Suppose Tina Rinaldi invested $100,000 in investment-grade, 30-year municipal bonds that paid 6 percent interest (coupon rate). Thus, her interest income from the bonds was $6,000 per year. Assume further that the bonds are callable at par (i.e., they can be redeemed by the municipality for the $1,000 face amount of each bond) any time after 10 years from time of issue. Suppose further that 10 years after these bonds were issued, interest rates for comparable bonds (i.e., 20-year, investment-grade, callable municipal bonds) have fallen to 4 percent. Under these conditions, the municipality will call these bonds. Now Tina has her $100,000 back, but if she wants to invest in similar bonds, she can secure only 4 percent interest, which means an income of $4,000 per year, rather than the $6,000 per year she enjoyed for 10 years.

It can be seen that call risk is important when investors would like to lock in current interest rates or yields for a reasonably long time, such as during their retirement years or in saving for a child's education. Strategies for dealing with call risk are discussed in Chapter 7.

Maturity Risk: When securities and other investments mature at a time when market interest rates are lower than those provided by the maturing investments, the investor must reinvest the proceeds at lower yields. This reinvestment risk really arises from investing in shorter-term securities and other investments.

> **CASE EXAMPLE**
> Suppose George and Martha Wilson place $75,000 of their retirement savings in a three-year insured CD that pays 6 percent interest. Thus, their annual income from this CD is $4,500. However, at the end of the three-year period, when the CD comes due and

> the Wilsons are ready to roll it over into a new CD, assume the economy is in recession, the Federal Reserve has pushed shorter-term interest rates down to try to stimulate a recovery, and the interest rates currently being paid on comparable CDs and other similarly secure investments are around 3 percent. Now if the Wilsons place their $75,000 into a comparable new CD, their annual interest income will drop from $4,500 to $2,250, or a 50 percent decline. Of course, if shorter-term interest rates should rise, the reverse would be true and the Wilsons would be better off with their shorter-term investments.

Strategies for dealing with interest rate risk and reinvestment risk, as well as other strategies for investing in fixed-income securities, are discussed in more detail in Chapter 7.

Purchasing Power Risk This is uncertainty over the future purchasing power of the income and principal from an investment. Purchasing power depends on changes in the general price level in the economy. When prices rise, purchasing power declines; when prices decline, purchasing power rises. As a practiced matter, however, since around 1940, the United States has experienced a rather steady inflationary trend (with an average annual increase in consumer prices of around 3 percent).

This has led many investors to seek investments whose principal and income they hope will increase during inflationary periods so that the purchasing power of their investment dollars at least will not decline. Such investments are often called *inflation hedges* and were discussed in Chapter 2.

Exchange Rate (Currency) Risk Investors may buy securities, have bank accounts, or have other investments that are denominated in currencies other than their own (foreign currencies). They also may own shares in investment companies (e.g., mutual funds) that invest in foreign securities or currencies (international funds) and that do not hedge against currency fluctuations. Such investors will be exposed to exchange rate risk in addition to other investment risks.

Exchange rate risk arises from market fluctuations in the value of one currency in terms of other currencies—in other words, fluctuations in how many units of one currency will be received for a unit of other currencies.

For example, as of this writing, the euro is worth $1.4233 and the dollar is worth 107.22 yen in the foreign exchange market. Now if six months later the euro is worth $1.50 in the foreign exchange market, the dollar would have weakened relative to the euro (because a euro will buy more dollars or, conversely, it takes more cents to buy a euro). Suppose now that a U.S. investor holds European bonds or stocks worth 100,000 euros (or owns shares in a mutual fund that owns such securities). In this case, the investor would have gained from the currency fluctuation because previously his or her European bonds or stocks would have been worth $142,330 (100,000 euros × $1.4233), while six months later (assuming all other factors remain the same), they would be worth $150,000 (100,000 euros × $1.50).

On the other hand, using the same example, if six months later the euro is worth $1.30, the dollar would have strengthened relative to the euro because a euro will buy fewer dollars. Now the U.S. investor would have lost due to the currency fluctuation because previously his or her European bonds or stocks would have been worth $142,330, while six months later (again assuming all other factors remain the same), they are worth only $130,000. This loss illustrates the exchange rate risk. Of course, no one objects to an exchange rate gain. It can be seen then that weakening of the U.S. dollar relative to foreign currencies is advantageous for U.S. investors in assets denominated in these foreign currencies, while strengthening of the U.S. dollar is disadvantageous to such U.S. investors.

Political Risk This risk arises out of uncertainty concerning possible unfavorable changes in the government, cultural, and business climates of a country. It can arise from hostile diplomatic or military actions, possibility of or actual expropriation of business assets, restrictive trade policies, unfavorable changes in tax policy, limits on foreign investment, limitations on currency exchanges, and manipulation of exchange rates, among other things.

Tax Risk This is the risk posed by possible unfavorable changes in the tax laws. Tax rates and the tax system obviously have an important bearing on investment decision making. The tax environment for wealth management and some upcoming future issues have been discussed in Chapter 2.

Unsystematic (or diversifiable) risk includes various types, as the following sections explain.

Financial (or Credit) Risk This unsystematic risk arises because the issuers of investments may run into financial difficulties and not be able to live up to their promises or expectations. For example, an investor who buys a corporate bond runs the financial risk that the issuing corporation will default on the interest payments and/or the principal amount at maturity. The buyer of common stock runs the financial risk that the corporation will reduce or eliminate its dividend payments or go bankrupt so that its stock becomes worthless.

Financial (credit) risk varies considerably among different classes of investments and over time. U.S. government securities generally are considered default-free and hence have no financial risk. Thus, their interest rates are lower than otherwise comparable securities. Investment-grade municipal securities are probably next lowest in financial risk because the states and municipalities issuing them have the taxing power. However, some municipalities have defaulted on their debt. Investment-grade corporate bonds generally have relatively low financial risk, but below-investment-grade corporate bonds ("junk bonds") have varying degrees of high financial risk. The financial risk of common stocks depends on the financial strength of the issuing corporation, but as an investment class, common stocks are the equity portion of a corporation's capital structure and, hence, are paid last in the event of a corporate default or bankruptcy (e.g., after bonds and preferred stock). For example, as of this writing, the common stockholders of Fannie Mae and Freddie Mac have been virtually wiped out because of the federal takeover of those institutions.

Financial risk also varies considerably with economic conditions. The likelihood of defaults, reduced or eliminated dividends, and bankruptcies is much greater during recessions and depressions than during prosperity.

Financial risk can be diversified by an asset allocation strategy that balances more risky assets (such as common stocks, real estate, and hedge funds) with more secure assets (such as U.S. Treasury securities, municipal securities, and high-grade corporate bonds). Diversification can also be secured by investing in a number of different issues so that a default in any one issue will cause only limited harm to the portfolio.

Business Risk This unsystematic risk involves the nature of the industry in which a firm operates and the management and operations of the firm itself. Some industries are more stable than others, and the firms in those industries tend to have more dependable sales and profits. Consumer products companies, food companies, and utilities may be examples of this. On the other hand, other industries, by their nature, are more volatile and the sales and profits of firms in those industries tend to fluctuate widely. Industrial equipment and farm equipment manufacturers and property and liability insurance companies may illustrate this group.

Stable industries normally suffer less volatility during the business cycle than less stable industries.

Within any industry, there are well-managed firms and firms that are not so well managed. A firm's quality of management, business model, products and services, financial strength, and competitive position within its industry are critical to its financial success and hence its quality as an investment. The extent to which firms are deficient in their characteristics presents a business risk for investors.

Like financial risk, business risk can be diversified by a balanced asset allocation strategy and by spreading the risk among a number of different issues so there is not undue concentration in one industry or in one or a few common stocks. Careful security analysis (with attention paid to quality of management) also can help reduce business risk.

Liquidity and Marketability Risks Sometimes, the terms *marketability* and *liquidity* are used to mean almost the same thing, but they do have different meanings. *Marketability* means the ability of an investor to find a ready market should he or she want to sell an investment in a short time. *Liquidity* means an investment is not only marketable, but also highly stable in price. In other words, an asset is liquid when an investor feels reasonably sure he or she can dispose of it quickly and also can receive approximately the amount put into it. Investors normally desire to keep some percentage of their overall portfolio in liquid assets (also called *cash equivalents*).

Marketability and liquidity risks represent the uncertainty that assets may not be marketable or may not be liquid when it is desired to convert them into cash. Securities listed on organized exchanges normally are marketable, but closely held corporate stock (such as in a family controlled corporation) generally has little marketability. That is why the Internal Revenue Service (IRS) will allow discounts for lack of marketability in valuing closely held stock for tax purposes. Real estate generally is not very marketable since sales must be individually negotiated and normally take time to consummate. Other alternative investments, such as interests in hedge funds and private equity funds, also generally restrict marketability since hedge funds often have a one-year lockup period for initial investments and may otherwise restrict redemptions, while private equity may be more restrictive on marketability by not allowing redemptions during the first few years of investment, not paying investment returns for some time, and having a commitment period during which the fund may call for more capital from investors. There also may not be secondary markets for such investments. The IRS also may permit lack of marketability discounts for gifts of such interests.

Liquid assets include asset classes such as insured bank savings accounts and money market accounts, high-quality mutual fund money market accounts, insured traditional CDs, Treasury bills, short-term Treasury notes and high-quality corporate bonds, nonvariable life insurance cash values (through policy loans), and other similar stable-value assets.

The marketability risk can be diversified by balancing marketable and nonmarketable asset classes in a portfolio. Thus, portfolios that are heavily concentrated in relatively nonmarketable assets, such as real estate or closely held business interests, may find it difficult to raise cash quickly from such assets if necessary. As noted, liquidity risk can be reduced (diversified) by maintaining a percentage of a portfolio in liquid assets (cash equivalents).

Investment Manager Risk This risk arises from possible variations in performance by persons or institutions retained directly or indirectly to manage an investor's assets. As explained in Chapter 1, investment management can come from many sources.

Investment management often produces good results and sometimes produces superior results, but in some cases, the results may be mediocre or even poor, particularly during difficult economic times. And in any event, investment manager performance must be judged in relation to its cost. Also, investment manager performance should be evaluated over a reasonably long time (such as 5 to 10 years), not just over 1 or 2 good years.

Investment manager risk would appear to apply mainly to an active management investment strategy. Such a strategy involves periodic buying and selling of securities in an attempt to secure above-average returns for a portfolio or fund. An active management strategy involves either *market timing* (forecasting bull and bear markets for stocks and bonds and buying when low and selling when high) and/or *security selection* (analyzing the fundamental aspects of individual securities in attempting to select undervalued securities in the market or securities with above-average growth potential). Active management necessarily depends on the skill of investment managers to produce better-than-average results (net of their costs), and hence, implies the existence of investment manager risk.

Passive investing, on the other hand, involves holding a well-diversified portfolio of securities without making many, if any, active trading decisions and generally without trying to "beat the market." Passive investing is perhaps best illustrated by *indexing* (buying a fund or funds whose investments mirror a broad market index). Thus, since passive investing involves modest, if any, security selection, it implies little investment manager risk.

Measures of Investment Returns (Rates of Return)

The primary purpose of investing is to earn a return on one's capital. Investors normally want to maximize their *total after-tax returns* (investment income and capital gains combined) consistent with the level of risk they wish to assume. As we have seen in this chapter, the goal of modern portfolio theory is to attain the highest return for a given level of risk considering the correlations of the assets in a portfolio.

Annual Rates of Return from Income (Yield) There are several ways of measuring annual rates of return represented by the periodic income from an investment. They include *nominal yield, current yield, yield to maturity,* and *yield to call.*

Nominal Yield: This is the annual amount of interest or dividends paid compared with a security's par, or face, value, shown as follows:

$$\text{Nominal yield} = \frac{\text{annual interest or dividends}}{\text{investment's par or face value}}$$

The nominal yield is called the *coupon rate* when applied to bonds and the *dividend rate* when applied to preferred stocks with a par value. For example, a bond with a maturity value (face amount) of $1,000 that pays interest of $70 per year has a nominal yield (coupon rate) of 7 percent. Nominal yield really has no meaning for common stocks and other forms of investment.

Current Yield: The current yield is the annual amount of income received from an investment compared with its current market price or value. It normally is used for common and preferred stocks and frequently for bonds as well. It can be calculated as:

$$\text{Current yield} = \frac{\text{annual investment income}}{\text{investment's current price or value}}$$

As examples of current yield, a common stock selling at $50 per share with an annual dividend rate of $1 has a current yield of 2 percent, and a 5 percent bond (coupon rate) that is selling for $800 has a current yield of about 6.25 percent.[12]

Yield to Maturity: Another measure of yield commonly applied to bonds is the yield to maturity. Bonds have a definite maturity date when their par or face amount is to be paid by the issuer. However, investors can purchase bonds in the market for less than their maturity value (at a discount) or for more than their maturity value (at a premium). Thus, the concept of yield to maturity for a bond can be illustrated by taking the bond's annual interest income and either adding the annual gain (discount) or deducting the annual loss (premium) that will be realized if the bond is held to maturity. The result is divided by the average investment in the bond. Just to illustrate the principle involved, the following formulas show the approximate yields to maturity for bonds selling at a discount and at a premium.

For a bond selling at a discount:

$$\text{Yield to maturity} = \frac{\text{annual coupon interest} + (\text{discount} \div \text{number of years to maturity})}{(\text{current market price of bond} + \text{par value}) \div 2}$$

[12] Annual bond interest of $50 ($1,000 maturity value × 5%) divided by $800 equals 0.0625, or 6.25%.

For a bond selling at a premium:

$$\text{Yield to maturity} = \frac{\textit{annual coupon interest} - (\textit{premium} \div \textit{number of years to maturity})}{(\textit{current market price of bond} + \textit{par value}) \div 2}$$

An accurate yield to maturity is really the internal rate of return (IRR), as described in Chapter 3, for the bond's cash flows until maturity. It is the compound rate of return until maturity, assuming bond interest payments are reinvested in the bond at an interest rate equal to the yield to maturity being calculated. This accurate yield-to-maturity calculation can be done on a financial calculator.

For bonds selling at a discount, the yield to maturity is greater than the current yield, which, in turn, is greater than the coupon rate. For bonds selling at a premium, the opposite is true. When a bond is selling at or near par, the coupon rate, current yield, and yield to maturity will be essentially the same. In most cases, when an investor plans to hold a bond until maturity, the yield to maturity is considered the most accurate measure of annual investment return.

Yield to Call: For callable bonds, this is the same concept as yield to maturity, except it is assumed that the bond will be called (redeemed) under the bond's call provisions prior to maturity. Therefore, the IRR calculation uses the earliest call date (sometimes called "yield to first") and the value at call (including any "call premium") in the calculation. Of course, bonds will mature, but if they are callable, they may or may not actually be called, based on prevailing market interest rates.

Real versus Nominal Returns: The distinction between real (inflation-adjusted) and nominal returns and values was discussed in Chapter 2. As explained, the real return on an investment is the stated periodic return (e.g., current yield) or nominal return minus the current or anticipated rate of inflation.

While we normally think of real returns during inflationary economic periods (when real returns are less than nominal returns), the same principle applies during deflationary periods, but in the opposite direction. That is, the real return would be the nominal return plus the current or anticipated rate of deflation.

Capital Gains and Total Rates of Return People often invest for capital gains as well as regular annual income. Capital gains generally result from the appreciation in the value of assets. Of course, there can be capital losses, too.

Advantages of Taking Returns as Capital Gains: Capital gains present a number of tax and nontax advantages for the investor, as follows:

- Capital gains are not taxed until actually realized and recognized for tax purposes, such as by a sale or exchange of a capital asset. Therefore, an investor generally can determine when, if ever, the gain is to be taxed.
- If an investor does not sell and realize a gain, but instead holds appreciated property until his or her death, the estate or heirs will get a stepped-up income tax basis in the property equal to its value for estate tax purposes (generally the value at the date of death), and the appreciation prior to death will forever escape taxation.[13]
- If an investor needs current income from investments (or cash for other purposes), he or she can periodically sell (at capital gains tax rates) a portion of his or her appreciated property to produce the same result as a stream of interest or dividend income. The investor in this situation can select the best investment assets to sell for both investment and tax considerations.
- The income tax rates are lower on long-term capital gains than on ordinary income. The top tax rate on long-term capital gains currently is 15 percent, while the top rate on ordinary income now is 35 percent.
- Numerous planning techniques are aimed at avoiding capital gains taxation entirely, deferring taxation, or stretching out any gain over a period of years. These techniques are discussed in Chapter 11.

Limitations on Taking Returns as Capital Gains: On the other hand, capital gains as a form of investment return can have disadvantages.

- Capital gains are inherently uncertain. There is no assurance an investment will appreciate. Thus, capital gains involve a higher degree of investment risk (in terms of variability of outcomes) than other forms of investment returns, such as interest and dividends.
- Once a person has achieved unrealized capital gains and holds highly appreciated assets in his or her portfolio, a dilemma may result. The person may hesitate to sell for fear of capital gains taxation. This may be referred to as the *capital gains lock-in problem,* which is further discussed in Chapter 11.
- It can be argued that investing for capital gains places greater emphasis on investment skill, since these returns are less certain.

Measuring Total Returns and Holding Period Returns (HPRs): Rates of return from capital gains are difficult to measure. First, no one can know

[13] The federal income tax system, including how capital gains are taxed, is described more fully in Chapter 10.

what, if any, future capital gain there may be on a given investment. An investor really can only reason from experience with the particular investment or similar investments, and possibly from estimates of expected returns based on historical studies. Second, there is no assurance that past results will be repeated in the future. Finally, most investors suffer some capital losses as well as realize capital gains, and this will be affected by current economic conditions (e.g., the stage of the business cycle). Despite these problems, however, it is important to measure capital gains returns because they constitute an important part of total returns from some important asset classes, such as common stocks and real estate.

An investment's *total return* for a given year is the change in its price or value (up or down) in that year plus any cash flow (dividends, interest, or rents) for the year. For example, if a common stock's price is $40 per share at the beginning of the year and $44 at the end of the year, and if the stock paid $1.20 in dividends during the year, its total return for the year is $5.20 per share, or 13 percent (10 percent capital gain plus 3 percent dividend income) on the initial share price. This same approach can be used for calculating total returns on other assets, such as bonds.

An investment's HPR is its rate of total return over a given period (called the holding period). There may be annual HPRs or HPRs for longer periods.

Geometric Average versus Arithmetic Average Returns: When measuring investment returns for an asset or asset class over time, it often is desirable to determine the *average annual total return* over the given period. This would be the average holding period return for that period. This average return can be calculated as a geometric average or as an arithmetic average.

The *geometric average* (or average annual compound rate of total return) is the annual rate at which an initial investment will accumulate to equal the final value of the investment at the end of the period considered, assuming reinvestment of the cash flows received during the period. To calculate this annual rate, one needs the initial value of the asset or assets, any annual cash flows (e.g., dividends, rents, etc.) during the period, and the final value of the asset or assets at the end of the period. The geometric average can be determined by solving for i (INT) in an internal rate of return calculation on a financial calculator.

The so-called rule of 72 is sometimes noted as a way of estimating this average annual rate of return. This is done by dividing 72 by the number of years it takes for an investment to double in value. Or, using the same concept, one can estimate how long it will take for an investment to double in value by dividing 72 by the investment's expected rate of return. Or, to triple in value, divide 116 by the expected return.

The *arithmetic average* is just the average value of a series of annual total returns (or the sum of the total returns divided by the number of years). This does not involve the compounding of returns, and unless the annual total returns are the same, the geometric average will be less than the arithmetic average.

CASE EXAMPLE

Suppose that 10 years ago Henry Potter started an investment portfolio with $100,000 (after taxes) that he received as a bonus from his employer. He invested it in a diversified portfolio of good quality ("blue-chip") common stocks. The following table shows the value of Henry's portfolio at the beginning of each year and the total return (dividends plus capital appreciation, or minus capital depreciation) on the portfolio for each year. All dividends and realized capital gains were reinvested in the portfolio, and any income taxes on this investment were paid from other sources (i.e., they did not reduce the value of the portfolio). Henry would like to know what the average annual total return was on his portfolio for these 10 years.

Year	Value of Portfolio at Beginning of the Year	Percentage Total Rate of Return for the Year
1	$100,000	10%
2	110,000	20
3	132,000	5
4	138,600	8
5	149,688	12
6	167,650	6
7	177,710	–4
8	170,602	–10
9	153,542	9
10	167,361	20
11	200,833	—
		76 (total rates of return)

The geometric average annual total return on Henry's portfolio for this period was 7.22 percent. This was determined from an IRR calculation on a financial calculator. According to the rule of 72, the rate of return would be approximately 7.2 percent (72 ÷ 10 years) since the portfolio approximately doubled in 10 years. To apply this rule, one must already know when the investment will double or the expected rate of return. The arithmetic average annual total return on the portfolio was 7.60 percent. This is the sum of the annual total returns of 76 percent divided by 10 years.

After-Tax Yields Up to this point, we have not considered the effect of income taxes on investment returns. As a practical matter, however, investors want to know what their investment returns are after taxes.

For purposes of estimating after-tax yields, we shall view the returns from investments as income that is taxable currently as ordinary income, income that is entirely tax-exempt, and returns that are taxable when realized (and recognized), if ever, as capital gains or as qualified dividend income. The taxation of returns in and distributions from various tax-deferred (advantaged) plans are discussed in Part V.

Taxable Ordinary Income: Investment income that is fully taxable as ordinary income, such as interest on CDs, taxable money market funds or accounts, corporate bonds, and U.S. Treasury bonds, is easy to express on an after-tax basis. The *after-tax yield* can be determined by multiplying the current yield by 1 minus the investor's highest marginal income tax rate. Thus, if a married taxpayer's highest tax bracket is 28 percent, a CD paying 4 percent interest would provide the following after-tax yield:

$$\begin{aligned}\text{After-tax yield} &= \text{current yield } (1 - \text{tax rate})\\ &= 0.04\ (1 - 0.28)\\ &= 0.04\ (0.72)\\ &= 0.0288 \text{ or } 2.88\%\end{aligned}$$

Tax-Exempt Income and Taxable Equivalent Yields: The after-tax yield for a fully tax-exempt investment equals the current yield. Thus, the after-tax yield for a 4.5 percent current yield municipal bond is 4.5 percent.

It is common practice also to express what a fully taxable security would have to earn to equal the yield from a tax-free security at different income tax rates. For example, a 4.5 percent tax-free yield received by an investor in a 35 percent tax bracket is worth 6.92 percent to him or her on a fully taxable basis.[14]

Capital Gains Returns and Total Returns: It becomes more complicated to determine after-tax yields when investment returns are in the form of

[14] Any similar tax-equivalent yields can be calculated by dividing the tax-free yield by 1 minus the investor's highest marginal income tax rate. In this case, 4.5% ÷ (1 – 0.35 or 0.65) = 6.92%. The highest marginal income tax rate used also can include state and local top marginal income tax rates if the income from the security also is exempt from those taxes as well as from the federal income tax.

capital gains or losses; or quite likely are part ordinary income, part tax-exempt income, part qualified corporate dividends, and part long-term capital gains or losses for an investment portfolio as a whole.

Tax Impact of Capital Gains Net short-term capital gains (net gains realized and recognized on capital assets held for 12 months or less) are taxed at the same rates as ordinary income. Therefore, they present no special tax advantage.

Net long-term capital gains (technically, these are *net capital gains*, as defined in Chapter 10) are net gains realized and recognized[15] on capital assets held for more than 12 months. As of this writing, they generally are taxed at a top rate of 15 percent through 2010, after which the top rate becomes 20 percent. However, the actual impact of income taxes on capital gains depends on whether a gain is ever realized and recognized for tax purposes, how long an asset has been held before the gain is realized and recognized, the applicable capital gains tax rate, and other factors. Thus, after-tax total returns depend on the circumstances.

A logical question at this point is how capital gains can completely escape income taxation. The answer lies in provisions of the tax code that allow taxpayers or their estates and heirs to avoid potential capital gains taxation entirely and other provisions that permit assets to be disposed of or arranged without current capital gains taxation and perhaps ultimately with no capital gains taxation at all. These planning techniques are described in Chapters 10 and 11.

Combination of Circumstances For most investors, the situation regarding taxation of their investment portfolio will be a mixed bag. In terms of capital gains and losses, some assets will be bought and sold in a fairly short time; others will be bought and held for the long term and then sold; while still others will be bought and held until death, or capital gains will be avoided in some other fashion. Furthermore, some assets will yield ordinary income; others will yield tax-exempt income; while still others will have special tax advantages, such as real estate and other alternative investments.

Planning Considerations Regarding Investment Returns From this discussion, some general planning issues emerge:

- It generally is better to take investment returns as long-term capital gains than as ordinary income.

[15] The terms *realized* and *recognized* are technical but important in tax terminology. A gain is realized when there is an actual sale or exchange of a capital asset at a gain. The gain also is recognized for tax purposes, unless there is a specific nonrecognition provision in the tax code that delays recognition of the gain. The taxation of capital gains and losses is treated more fully in Chapter 10.

- It generally is better taxwise to allow capital gains to accumulate over time before taking them. But this is always subject to the investment merits of holding the security.
- When consistent with other goals, it is desirable to avoid capital gains taxation entirely.
- An analysis should be made of the relative attractiveness of tax-free investment income (e.g., interest on most municipal bonds) as compared with taxable investment income for the particular investor. This depends on the investor's marginal income tax rates (federal, state, and local), the current yield (or yield to maturity) on tax-free bonds, and the total after-tax yield on comparable investments.

Of course, these general planning considerations should always be taken within the context of the investor's overall objectives, investment strategies, and general financial constraints.

Yields on Mutual Funds The principles just discussed also generally apply to assets held in mutual funds. However, there are some special tax rules applying to mutual funds, which are explained in Chapter 8.

Assets Held in Tax-Advantaged Plans Some of the principles just described also apply to assets held in income tax–deferred plans, such as qualified retirement plans, IRAs, Roth IRAs, and investment annuities. However, different tax rules apply to these plans, which will affect their after-tax returns. These plans and the tax rules applying to them are discussed in later chapters.

Risk-Adjusted Returns and Performance Measures The previous discussion of rates of return in investments did not take investment risk (volatility) into consideration. A number of theoretical models and formulas have been developed to help adjust and evaluate investment returns in relation to the risk involved.

Equity Risk Premium (Excess Return): This preliminary concept shows the return in an individual investment or portfolio that exceeds what could have been earned in risk-free assets. Thus, the equity risk premium (excess return) on an investment portfolio is the portfolio's total return minus the risk-free rate (typically the yield on short-term Treasury bills). It is the extra return an investor receives for taking an investment risk. For example, if the total return on a portfolio in a given year is 8 percent and the risk-free rate is 2 percent, the equity risk premium would be 6 percent.

Capital Asset Pricing Model (CAPM): This theoretical model is designed to measure the expected return on an individual security or investment portfolio considering the security's or portfolio's investment risk as measured by its beta. The formula for CAPM, which for this purpose is also known as the *security market line (SML),* is as follows:

$$ER = r + \beta\,(RM - r)$$

where

ER = the stock's or portfolio's expected return
r = the risk-free rate
β = the stock's or portfolio's beta
RM = the stock market return;

therefore,

RM − r = the equity risk premium for the market or the market premium

The SML is an upward-sloping graph of various combinations of the risk-free asset and the particular security or portfolio, with the expected return on the vertical axis and the beta on the horizontal axis. Thus, it shows that increasing expected returns correspond to increasing investment risk (security or portfolio beta).

As an example of the CAPM, if the risk-free rate is 2 percent, the rate of total return for the entire stock market is 7 percent, and a given portfolio of stocks has a weighted average beta of 1.25 relative to the market (i.e., it is more volatile than the market), the portfolio's expected return (ER) would be:

$$ER = 2 + 1.25\,(7 - 2) = 8.25 \text{ percent}$$

The actual returns from the portfolio then can be compared with the expected returns from the CAPM. In the preceding example, if the portfolio's actual return is greater than 8.25 percent, it has exceeded expectations and the investment management has been good, but if the actual return is less than 8.25 percent, the portfolio has not met expectations.

The concept of the CAPM is theoretical in nature and may or may not be correlated to actual investment experience. There is some controversy on this point.

Alpha (Jensen Ratio): This number shows how a security or portfolio (e.g., a mutual fund) performed, given its level of risk as shown by its beta, as compared with the stock market (or a benchmark index) as a whole. The formula for a stock's or portfolio's alpha is as follows:

$$A = R - [r + \beta\,(RM - r)]$$

where

A = the stock's or portfolio's alpha
R = the stock's or portfolio's actual return

r = the risk-free rate
β = the stock's or portfolio's beta
RM = the stock market return;

therefore,

$$RM - r = \text{the equity risk premium for the market or the market premium}$$

For example, assume a stock mutual fund had an actual return of 9 percent, has a beta of 0.70 (i.e., it is less volatile than the benchmark index), the risk-free rate is 3 percent, and the stock market return (based on the benchmark index) is 10 percent. In this example, the portfolio's alpha would be:

$$A = 9 - [3 + .7\ (10 - 3)] = 1.1\%$$

A positive alpha, as in this example, means the fund performed better than the market (the expected return) when its return is adjusted for the risk taken as measured by its beta. A negative alpha means the reverse. Therefore, alphas are often cited as risk-adjusted performance measures relative to the expected return in judging investment managers.

Sharpe Ratio: This measure divides a portfolio's excess return by its standard deviation as a measure of risk.

Treynor Ratio: This measure is similar to the Sharpe ratio, except that it divides excess return by the portfolio's beta. The Sharpe and Treynor ratios are useful when comparing one investment or portfolio with others. Taken by themselves, these ratios do not measure a portfolio's risk-adjusted return relative to the market's (or benchmark's) return.

Appropriate Benchmarks: Benchmarks are typically indexes of securities prices, assuming dividends and interest are reinvested. An index is a statistical measure showing the change over time of its component items relative to a base date, which has an index value of 100. We have already noted price indexes (like the consumer price index) in Chapter 2.

Securities indexes track values of groups of stocks or bonds over time. They may include large numbers of securities (like the Standard & Poor's 500 stock index) or be limited to a more narrow market segment (like the Wilshire Real Estate Securities or CS First Boston High Yield Bond indexes). Indexes are widely reported and are used by investors and the public to track day-to-day movements and long-term trends in securities prices. They also provide the basis for many indexed securities and insurance products, such as index mutual funds, most exchange-traded funds (ETFs), equity indexed annuities and life insurance policies, among others. These products are discussed in Chapters 17 and 21.

In the context of performance measures, benchmarkers serve as a point of comparison for the returns or risk-adjusted returns from securities or portfolios (like mutual funds). They can represent the "market" in the various performance concepts and measures just discussed. In this role as a standard of comparison, it is important that the index be similar or comparable to the portfolio that is being compared to it. In analyzing the performance and risk level of mutual funds, for example, the alpha, beta, and R^2 of the fund may be compared to a "standard index" (such as the S&P 500) and a "best fit index" (such as the Russell 1000), depending on the investment objective of the fund.

Some commonly used indexes (among others) include the following:

- Wilshire 5000
- Standard & Poor's 500
- Standard & Poor's Mid-Cap 400
- Standard & Poor's Small-Cap 600
- Russell 2000
- MSCI EAFE
- MSCI Emerging Markets Free Global
- CS First Boston High Yield Bond

An *index* is different from an average. As just noted, an index charts percentage change from a base line. An *average*, like the widely quoted Dow Jones Industrial Average (DJIA), is the arithmetic mean of the prices of the securities included in the average at a given time.

Time-Weighted versus Dollar-Weighted Returns: *Time-weighted returns* represent the average annual compound rate of return on a fixed dollar fund (such as $100,000) for a given period (such as 10 years). It does not consider any additional investments or withdrawals from the fund during that time. This is the geometric mean over that time. Mutual funds report such returns over various periods.

Dollar-weighted returns take into consideration that amounts may be added to or subtracted from an investment fund during the period involved. This probably is the more likely scenario for most investors. In situations like 401(k) plans or periodic investing under dollar-cost averaging, periodic contributions are routinely made to the investment fund. In this case, the return is the IRR on the cash flows going into and out of the investment fund.

Other Asset Pricing and Option Models: The CAPM, which is a cornerstone of much modern theoretical thinking in finance, was discussed earlier in this chapter. Another asset-pricing model is the *arbitrage pricing theory (APT)*. In addition, there is the well-known *Black-Scholes option valuation* *model*, which is discussed in Chapter 18 in connection with employee stock options. There also is a *binomial option pricing model*.

Diversification

The basic purpose of diversification is to reduce or minimize an investor's risk of loss (variability of overall returns and values). It is primarily a defensive policy and is discussed in detail in Chapter 9.

Tax Status

An investment's tax status can have an important bearing on its attractiveness. This is discussed more fully in subsequent chapters of this part.

Size of Investment Units (or Denominations)

In some cases, an investment can be made only in certain minimum amounts. For example, municipal bonds frequently are sold in lots of $5,000 or more. Direct investments in real estate require a down payment and payment of closing costs, as well as adequate mortgage financing. Also, hedge funds and private equity require large minimum investments.

Use as Collateral for Loans

Many forms of property can be used as collateral for loans. However, some kinds serve better than others. For example, good-quality securities (other than municipal bonds), life insurance policies, and improved real estate may operate well in this regard. In contrast, some types of property are unattractive. For example, tax-free municipal bonds involve tax pitfalls when used as collateral, or even when they are owned and other property is used as collateral for loans, as discussed in Chapter 7.

Callability

As discussed earlier in the section "Reinvestment Risk," callability (or redeemability) can be an important factor when investing in bonds and preferred stocks. Many issuers of corporate and municipal bonds have reserved the right to call or redeem the bonds before maturity, usually subject to certain conditions. Most issues of preferred stock also are callable. On the other hand, most U.S. government securities and some municipal and corporate bonds are not callable prior to maturity.

5

Common Stocks

Competence Objectives for This Chapter After reading this chapter, planners should understand:

- Some commonly used valuation measures for common stocks, such as:
  - Earnings per share
  - True cash flow per share
  - Sales per share
  - The price-earnings (P/E) ratio
  - The price-earnings to growth (P/EG) ratio
  - Other commonly used ratios
  - Book value per share
  - Liquidation value per share
- Some common stock valuation models
- The common stock investment process
- Some common stock diversification techniques, including dollar-cost averaging
- Various types of orders when buying or selling common stocks
- The nature of margin accounts
- The nature of selling stocks short
- Some categories of common stocks
- Some theories or approaches to common stock investment
- The case for long-term investment in common stocks
- Some caveats concerning common stock investment, including data on significant stock market declines (bear markets)

Characteristics of Common Stocks

Common stock may be defined as the residual ownership of a corporation that is entitled to all assets and earnings after other claims have been paid and that generally has voting control. In short, common stock is the fundamental ownership equity.

In modern asset allocation planning (see Chapter 9), it is recognized that common stocks as a group historically have provided superior total returns over reasonably long periods as compared with certain other investment media (e.g., bonds and Treasury bills). However, as noted in the preceding chapter, they also involve more risk in terms of volatility than these other asset classes. Therefore, common stocks are included in most investment portfolios for their superior returns, but other asset classes also may be included to reduce portfolio volatility and for diversification generally.

Stock Valuation Concepts

In selecting common stocks for an investment portfolio, it obviously is important to understand the techniques and models that may be used to estimate the value of individual stocks. Such techniques and models are discussed in this section.

Per-Share Data, Ratio Analysis, and Book Value

Several basic calculations may serve as indicators of the worth of a common stock, including earnings per share, free cash flow per share, price-earnings ratio, price to free cash flow ratio, sales per share, price to sales ratio, price-earnings ratio divided by the stock's growth rate (P/EG), book value per share, liquidating value per share, and earnings yield, among others.

Earnings Per Share The traditional way to compute earnings per share (EPS) is to divide the income available to common shareholders (net corporate profits after taxes minus any preferred dividends) by the average number of common shares actually outstanding. This may be illustrated as follows.

Over the most recent 12 months in which it reported earnings, XYZ Company had a net profit of $2,300,000 after deducting expenses, interest, taxes, and share-based compensation expenses. Preferred dividend requirements for the year were $200,000. The remaining $2,100,000 amounted to $3 per share on the average 700,000 shares actually outstanding for the year ($2,100,000 ÷ 700,000 = $3). These are the company's *basic earnings per share.* Earnings per share are computed in the same way for quarterly or semiannual periods.

Nonrecurring items (write-offs) contained in current income may or may not be excluded when computing earnings per share. When write-offs are excluded from the calculation, the earnings are called *operating earnings.* When they are included, the earnings are referred to as *reported earnings.*

The example just given is based on what are called *trailing earnings* because the earnings figure is for the most recent past actual earnings. However, sometimes analysts will estimate future earnings and base their calculations in whole or in part on these estimated (forward) earnings.

Corporations also report *diluted earnings per share.* Diluted earnings per share are computed by dividing net income by the average common shares actually outstanding plus the potential common shares that would be outstanding if the dilutive effect of employee stock options and other stock awards outstanding, convertible securities, and warrants were considered. Thus, the potential effect of these plans and securities (called *dilutive potential common shares*) on average outstanding common shares is taken into account by this adjustment. This can be significant, depending on the corporation. When discussing corporate earnings per share, analysts often use diluted earnings per share.

Starting in 2006, the Financial Accounting Standards Board requires corporations to recognize as an expense in their reported earnings the value of share-based compensation awards granted to their employees and directors. Such awards include employee stock options and employee stock purchases under an employee stock purchase plan (both discussed in Chapter 18). This is referred to as the "expensing of stock options." Such options usually are valued for this purpose by use of an option pricing model, such as Black-Scholes or some variation of it.

The impact of expensing stock options on reported earnings depends on the extent to which a firm uses stock-based compensation plans. It can have a significant impact in some cases. Analysts sometimes consider earnings without expensing stock options. This, of course, is a less conservative practice.

Investors and analysts generally place great emphasis on earnings per share and particularly on the trend of earnings per share in evaluating common stocks. It can be argued that a going business's value lies mainly in its potential earning power and that any present and future dividends depend on earnings. Thus, a stock's market price ultimately tends to keep pace with the growth or decline of its earnings per share.

Free Cash Flow Per Share Analysts also calculate a figure called *cash flow per share.* This is derived by adding back depreciation expense and possibly other noncash expenses to net profit minus preferred dividends and then dividing by the average number of common shares. The idea is to be able to better compare companies with varying depreciation policies. Other figures that some may use include *earnings before interest and taxes* (EBIT) (to adjust for differences in capital structures) and *earnings before interest, taxes, depreciation, and amortization* (EBITDA) (to adjust for differences in capital structures and depreciation and amortization policies).

Other Per-Share Data A number of other per-share figures may also be found in analyses of common stocks. They may include sales per share, dividends per share, capital spending per share, research and development (R&D) costs per share, working capital per share, and cash per share.

Price-Earnings (P/E) Ratio The price-earnings (P/E) ratio of a common stock is its market price divided by the current earnings per share of the corporation. Thus, if XYZ Company common stock is selling for $42 per share at a time when its reported earnings over the latest 12 months amounted to $3 per share, its P/E ratio (on a "trailing earnings" basis) would be 14 ($42 ÷ $3). The price-earnings ratio is a commonly used measure of stock value because it gives an indication of stock price measured against the earning power of the stock.

An investor may find a review of past price-earnings ratios of a stock helpful in estimating its current value relative to the past. Assume, for example, that over a 10-year period, XYZ Company common stock has shown generally consistent growth in earnings per share and market price and that its P/E ratios have ranged from around 12 on the low side to 30 on the high side. Therefore, since this stock currently is selling for a price-earnings ratio of 14, that ratio is historically relatively low (perhaps because of a temporary reversal in the company's fortunes or a general market decline–market risk), and thus the stock might be a good buy at this time. On the other hand, if XYZ common stock were selling for $84, its P/E ratio (28) would be on the high side historically (perhaps because of excessive market exuberance). Of course, investors must consider other factors about the stock when making a final decision. For example, the past trend of a corporation's earnings per share is significant. The factors involved in fundamental analysis (security analysis) of common stocks are covered later in this chapter. Also, economic and stock market conditions and what those conditions are expected to be in the future naturally are important.

P/EG Ratio A variation of the price-earnings ratio is the P/EG ratio, which is the P/E ratio divided by the company's historical average annual profit growth. For example, if ABC Company's P/E ratio is 14 and its average annual rate of growth in per-share earnings for the last 10 years is 7 percent, its P/EG ratio would be 2 (14 P/E ratio ÷ 7 = 2 P/EG). This number reflects the growth prospects of the company as well as the relationship between its stock price and current earnings. The P/EG ratio can be compared with other firms in its industry and analyzed over time.

Other Ratios Analysts use several other price ratios as well. For example, there is the stock's market price divided by its free cash flow. There also is sales per dollar of common stock market value, which is determined by dividing sales (revenue) by the average shares outstanding multiplied by the average stock price. Such sales ratios may be useful, for example, in evaluating companies in the developmental stage when they have no profits yet.

In terms of common stock yields, the *dividend yield* has already been described in Chapter 4. The *earnings yield* is the stock's earnings per share divided by the stock's market price.

Net Asset Value (Book Value) Per Share The net asset value per share, commonly referred to as the *book value* per share, attempts to measure the amount of net assets a corporation has for each share of common stock. It is calculated by taking the *net balance sheet values* of corporate assets, subtracting the face value of creditors' and preferred stockholders' claims, and dividing the remainder by the average number of outstanding common shares.

For example, XYZ Company at the end of its last fiscal year had total assets of $33 million and debts and preferred stock totaling $12 million. The remaining $21 million indicated a net asset value (book value) of $30 for each of its 700,000 common shares outstanding.

In most cases, book value per share is much less important than the ability of those assets to generate a stream of earnings. The market prices of common stocks of successful companies normally are several times the book value per share. On the other hand, for declining firms, market price may be less than book value. Overall, net asset value per share is not a very useful measure for evaluating the investment merits of a company's common stock. However, investors may measure the current market price level of a stock, an industry group, or the whole market in relation to past price levels by a measure often called *price to book* (market price per share divided by book value per share).

Liquidating Value Per Share This measure is determined by using the market or liquidating value of a corporation's assets rather than the balance sheet values (which generally are based on historical cost or market value, whichever is lower). Thus, this is the estimated amount that could be realized per share if the corporation's assets were sold off, its liabilities paid, and the balance distributed to the shareholders. It is not a going concern value, but rather a liquidation value after winding up the affairs of a business or venture. It also may be the starting point in arriving at discounts for gifts of closely held business interests.

Common Stock Valuation Models

In most cases, for corporations that are operating as profitable, going concerns are valued on the basis of their expected future earning power represented by future income (cash flow) or future dividends. This is an *income approach* to valuation. In the discussion that follows, the capitalized net earnings, discounted cash flow, and dividend discount models illustrate this approach to valuation.

In certain situations, however, other approaches to valuation may be useful. These include a *market approach* in which valuations are based on or analyzed in relation to the prices paid for, or price-earnings ratios, or P/EG ratios of comparable companies in the same industry. They also include a *cost or balance sheet approach* where valuations are based on or modified by the values of a company's assets and liabilities. In some cases, the break-up value or liquidated value of a company (as defined in the preceding section) may be significant. In a few industries, the price of a company's stock is greatly affected by the values of assets held by the company—such as gold mining companies, for example. Analysts may also note the amount of cash per share or other assets per share in evaluating a company.[1]

All these valuation approaches can be applied to publicly held corporations and private (closely held) corporations. Of course, the stock prices of publicly held corporations are determined daily by supply and demand for their shares on organized exchanges for all to see. Analysts value these stocks to determine their investment merits and to set price targets for them. The stocks of private corporations, on the other hand, are not publicly traded, so their prices are not determined regularly by market action. However, their values must be determined from time to time for various purposes, such as for the sale or merger of the company, to set prices in buy–sell agreements, for values in employee stock ownership plans (ESOPs) and phantom stock plans, for giving to family members, and at the death of an owner for estate tax and other purposes, among others. These values normally are estimated by business valuation experts. Planning for closely held corporations is considered in detail in Chapter 31.

Various theoretical models have been developed to value common stocks on the basis of their earnings or dividends (an income approach) and some will be discussed next.

Capitalized Earnings (Net Income) Model This approach discounts the expected future earnings (net income) of a corporation for the indefinite

[1] In general, these valuation techniques also can be used for other types of business entities, such as partnerships and limited liability companies (LLCs) as discussed in Chapter 31.

future at a discount rate which reflects the rate of return investors expect to receive from this kind of stock (required return). Assuming the corporation's earnings are expected to grow at a generally constant rate into the future, the formula for such a constant growth model can be expressed as:

$$V = \frac{E}{r - g}$$

where

V = the value of the stock (sometimes called the "intrinsic value" or "true value")

E = the current year's net income (or cash flow)

r = the discount rate, which is the rate of return investors require for the kind of stock being valued

g = the assumed growth rate in the stock's net income (or cash flow)

As an example, suppose Close Corporation is a private (closely held) company owned equally by three unrelated stockholders: Harry, Ann, and Walter. They are negotiating a buy–sell agreement among the three owners so that when one of them dies, the two survivors can purchase his or her stock from the deceased's estate for a fair value as determined in the agreement. Their advisers and a business valuation expert have recommended that they use a capitalized net earnings valuation formula in the agreement and assume a discount rate of 25 percent (for the risk involved in a small, closely held company) and an average annual growth rate of 5 percent.

Assume further that at the death of one of the owners, the Corporation's current year's net income (possibly with some adjustments) is \$1,200,000. Given these facts, the value of Close Corporation as a whole using the capitalized earnings approach would be:

$$V = \frac{\$1{,}200{,}000}{0.25 - 0.05}$$

$$= \frac{\$1{,}200{,}000}{0.20} = \$6{,}000{,}000 \text{ (or 2,000,000 for the decendants 1/3 share)}$$

It may be noted that the same result occurs in this case when the annual earnings are multiplied by 5 (or 1 ÷ 0.20 = 5).

Discounted Cash Flow (DCF) Model In this case, the analyst makes a year-by-year forecast of a corporation's net income or cash flow for a certain period in the future, say, five to seven years. The forecast income in each of these years can vary during this period. Each of these figures is then discounted back to its current present value. Then, at the end of the period a "terminal value" (capitalized earnings value) is calculated on the assumption that the corporation's income will grow at a constant rate from then on for the indefinite future. This terminal value is also discounted back to the present. The sum of these present values then is the estimated fair market value of the corporation under the DCF model. This may also be referred to as a multiple-growth model.

Dividend Discount Models (DDMs) This model discounts at an appropriate rate (the rate of return required by investors for the kind of stock involved) the expected future stream of dividends from a stock. The present value of this infinite stream of dividends is the estimated fair market value of the stock (intrinsic value). The rationale for using dividends in this model is that dividends represent the cash flow that stockholders receive from their investments in common stocks.

A stock could have a constant stream of dividends, such as from preferred stock; however, investors normally expect the dividends on common stocks to increase over time (a dividend growth model). The formula for a *constant growth dividend discount model is*:

$$V = \frac{D(1+g)}{r-g}$$

where

V = value of the stock (intrinsic value)

D = the current year's dividend

r = the discount rate required by investors

g = the assumed growth rate of the stock's dividends (normally based on past experience)

For example, assume an investor is considering buying Acme Corporation common stock with a current annual dividend of \$2 per share, and for the last 20 years, this dividend has been increased at an average annual rate of 6 percent and the investor expects it will continue to do so in the future. The investor also expects a 10 percent rate of return from Acme stock. Given these facts, the constant-growth DDM would produce the following estimated fair market value for Acme common stock:

$$V = \frac{2(1+0.06)}{0.10-0.06}$$

$$= \frac{2.12}{0.04} = \$53 \text{ per share}$$

If the actual market price for the stock is less than $53 per share, the model suggests it is undervalued by the market. On the other hand, if the market price is greater than $53, theoretically the stock is overvalued.

Developing the Discount Rate In utilizing the models just discussed, it is clear that many estimates and forecasts are necessary. Some of them are for many years in the future.

One important estimate is the discount rate (in the preceding formulas), which is the rate of return investors are assumed to require for the kind of stock being valued. As the divisor in the preceding formulas, it has a great impact on the values produced (as do estimates of future earnings or dividends). The discount rate used by analysts often is composed of several elements (a so-called build-up approach). These elements may include the risk-free rate (often the U.S. Treasury bill rate) to reflect the time value of money, the equity risk premium (defined in Chapter 4) to reflect the risk structure of common stocks, and additional adjustments to reflect the risk characteristics of the particular stock (like an additional rate for smaller closely held stocks).

Price-Earnings Ratio Models A number of analysts calculate an estimated value for a stock by multiplying its current year's earnings per share times an estimated, hypothetical or "normal" price-earnings (P/E) ratio. This estimated value then can be compared with the stock's actual market price per share to see if the stock is undervalued, appropriately valued, or overvalued in the market relative to the estimated value. Of course, much depends on the accuracy of the analyst's estimate of the "normal" P/E ratio for the stock.

Portfolio Development and Analysis (The Investment Process)

Successful investing in common stocks cannot be based on hunch, hope, or rumor (tips). It is founded on studying the economy and then studying industries and particular companies.

Fundamental Analysis

Fundamental analysis involves selecting stocks based on the many variables that will affect the fortunes of particular companies. It considers both external and company-specific factors that will influence the profitability and, hence, the investment value of companies. As noted earlier, however, the whole concept of fundamental analysis and security selection is called into question by the efficient market hypothesis, depending on which form of this hypothesis one is considering. However, the efficient market hypothesis itself is controversial, and many investors and their advisers believe in fundamental security analysis. Fundamental analysis, of course, involves active investment management as opposed to passive investing, such as through index funds.

Fundamental analysis begins with an evaluation of the general economy, then an analysis of the industries in which the companies being considered are operating, and finally a study of the particular company or companies being evaluated. This approach is referred to as *top-down analysis.*

Consider the Economy Chapter 2 dealt with the economic climate for wealth management. Naturally, the economy is a key element in investment planning in general and security selection in particular. The business cycle is especially significant in this regard. Stock prices decline during recessions and depressions (see Table 5.2 for some significant stock market declines during bear markets). They then recover and move higher during the prosperity phase. In general, however, stock prices tend to precede turns in the business cycle by about 11 months, on average, since the end of World War II. That is, they begin declining before the economy itself turns down and begin advancing before the economy starts to recover. Thus, they tend to be a leading economic indicator.

However, as noted in Chapter 2, forecasting the business cycle and bull and bear stock markets is very difficult, if not impossible. Many believe that most investors cannot successfully engage in such market timing. Therefore, investors may follow a buy-and-hold strategy for long-term investing over the various phases of the business cycle.

On the other hand, asset allocation and security selection normally will be different in the face of recession or depression than during prosperity. Asset allocations will shift more toward bonds and cash equivalents. Security selection will become more conservative and perhaps shift toward a defensive stock approach. More attention may be paid to the financial soundness (credit quality) and balance sheet values of companies during hard times. In fact, the basic premises of present-day value investing (discussed later in this chapter) were articulated in 1934 during the Great Depression by legendary investors Benjamin Graham and David Dodd in their seminal book *Security Analysis: Principles and Techniques* (McGraw-Hill, Inc.).

Such analysis of financial soundness will involve attention to various liquidity ratios. These may include the *current ratio* (current assets divided by current liabilities), the *quick ratio* (current assets minus inventory divided by current liabilities), and the *cash ratio* (cash items divided by current liabilities). Debt ratios are also significant. Some examples are the *coverage of senior charges* (pretax earned income divided by senior charges) and *debt service coverage* (after-tax cash flow from operations divided by interest, rent, current maturities, and sinking fund payments). The ratio of a corporation's debt to its capital (debt divided by assets minus liabilities) also is often cited.

Consider the Industry The next step is evaluating the industry or industries involved. The following are some questions to consider in doing so:

- Does the industry provide products or services for which demand is substantial and growing?
- Is the industry cyclical or relatively stable?
- Is the industry likely to be affected by new developments?
- Is the industry growing rapidly, growing at a more stable rate, or perhaps declining relative to other industries?
- Is the industry subject to rapid technological change or development?

Analyze the Company The characteristics to look for depend largely on the common stock investment strategy being followed. Some investors are looking for short-term speculations. Others want turnaround situations or are following the depressed-industry approach. Still others may be investing primarily for income. A large group of investors, however, are looking for good quality, financially strong, and profitable companies that they believe are temporarily undervalued by the market relative to the company's intrinsic (or fundamental) value. These are *value investors.* On the other hand, many other investors are looking for strong, high-quality companies with above-average growth prospects over a reasonably long period. They are generally following a buy-and-hold growth stock approach. Given which kind of philosophy is involved, the following are some characteristics that investors might consider in selecting common stocks:

- The company should have good, stable management.
- The company should provide good products or services that have strong competitive positions in their industry.
- The company should be reasonably diversified and not largely dependent on only one product or patent.
- The company should have had consistent earnings growth over a reasonable period, such as the last 10 years. This does not mean the company cannot have had declines in earnings for one or two years, but they should be exceptions and the trend should be decidedly upward (particularly for growth stocks).
- The previous characteristic can be quantified by saying there should be an average annual compound rate of growth in earnings per share over the period being considered of at least a certain figure, such as ranging from 15 to 20 percent (particularly for growth stocks).

- As far as can be determined, the company should have good prospects for growth of earnings in the future.
- The company should have a good return on equity over a period of years.
- The company should have a strong financial position.
- Depending on the industry, companies usually should be devoting reasonable resources to research and development (particularly for growth stocks).
- Investors who want current dividend income should consider the stock's current dividend yield and past record of dividend increases or decreases.
- Finally, the stock's purchase price should be reasonable. The "reasonableness" of a common stock's price is often measured in terms of its P/E ratio (or perhaps in terms of one of the valuation models described previously). This is especially pertinent for value investors who are looking for stocks they believe are temporarily undervalued by the market.

As a practical matter, it is difficult for most individual investors to research and analyze personally such factors as industry characteristics, competitive positions of companies, and the investment characteristics of a given company. However, various professional investment services, stockbrokers, and investment advisers are in a position to do such research, and this type of investigation frequently is available to individual investors. Investors should make it a practice not to buy a stock unless they have determined its fundamental position from such sources or perhaps from their own research.

Technical Analysis

As opposed to fundamental analysis, technical analysis attempts to predict changes in stock prices, up or down, based on movements or activity of the price or trading volume of a stock itself or of the stock market generally. It can focus on a particular stock or stocks or on the aggregate market. The concept is that the market itself is the best predictor of its future course because there are recurrent movements in stock prices. It is a market timing philosophy and attempts to predict stock price movements and then buy or sell accordingly.

A number of techniques are used in technical analysis. One is *charting*, in which records of past stock prices are analyzed. For example, high and low prices of a stock for each day may be studied to determine its "momentum." Other charting techniques employ so-called point-and-figure charts. In other cases, the structure of the market itself may be studied to determine future trends. The Dow theory is the genesis of most technical analysis. Its originator was Charles Dow, who established *The Wall Street Journal* and is the *Dow* of the Dow Jones Industrial Average. It seeks to predict long-term trends in stock prices by studying peaks and troughs in the market averages.

Other techniques involve *flow of funds indications.* One example would be studying volumes of stock trading and comparing the average volume of declining issues to the average volume of advancing issues. Another possibility would be sentiment indications, such as the analysis of insider trading activity.

Diversifying a Common Stock Portfolio

Assuming an investor wants to hold stocks directly, investment diversification does not mean that he or she should arbitrarily buy stock in a large number of companies. Investors normally should not own stock directly in more companies than they or their investment advisers can reasonably follow. It probably would be sensible to put the investor's directly owned common stock allocation into, say, 10 to 15 individually owned stocks. Of course, diversification can also be secured by investing through financial intermediaries.

Decisions Concerning Selling Common Stocks

Although much of the emphasis concerning common stock investment has been on buying, the question of when to sell also is important. There may be many reasons for selling stocks. One is the need for cash. Another is to take a profit (or reduce a loss) when an investor thinks a stock, or the market as a whole, has reached an upper limit. Or, investors may sell if they believe other stocks will perform better or their money can earn a higher rate of return if invested elsewhere. Furthermore, an important reason to sell may be that the investor's portfolio is too heavily concentrated in one or a few stocks.

It should be remembered, however, that there are transfer costs (i.e., brokerage commissions) and capital gains taxes on any profits when a stock is sold. This means the attractiveness of any alternative investment must, over time, outweigh the costs of selling.

Dollar-Cost Averaging

One diversification technique for long-term common stock investing is dollar-cost averaging. This is the investment of a certain sum of money at regular intervals in the same stock or stocks or the same investment intermediary. The method normally results in a lower average cost per share than the average market price per share during the period in question, because the investor buys more shares with the periodic fixed amount of money when the stock is low in price than when it is high. Then, when the stock rises again (if it does), the investor shows a profit on the greater number of shares

Table 5.1. Illustration of Dollar-Cost Averaging

Date	Amount Invested	Market Price Paid	Number of Shares Purchased
First period	$500	$20	25
Second period	$500	$12½	40
Third period	$500	$10	50
Fourth period	$500	$12½	40
Fifth period	$500	$25	20
	$2,500		175
Total amount invested over five periods			$2,500
Number of shares purchased			175
Average market price per share			$16.00
Average cost per share ($2,500 ÷ 175 shares)			$14.29

purchased at the lower prices. Table 5.1 shows how the principle of dollar-cost averaging could work.

Dollar-cost averaging frequently works, unless the stock goes into a persistent decline. However, it takes a certain strength of conviction. The investor must be convinced that, whatever happens from time to time, the stock or investment intermediary is a good long-term investment.

Types of Orders in Buying and Selling Common Stocks

Various kinds of buy and sell orders may be used in common stock transactions. The most common is the *market order,* which is an order to buy or sell securities at the best price obtainable in the market now. It is expressed to the broker as an order to buy or sell *at the market.* For many stock transactions, a market order is reasonable.

However, when market prices are uncertain or are fluctuating rapidly, it may be better for an investor to enter a *limit order* that specifies the maximum price the investor is willing to pay or, if selling, the minimum price the investor is willing to accept.

Most types of orders include a time reference. *Open orders* are good until canceled. Another type is the *day order,* which is good only for the day on which it is ordered.

Another common type of order is a *stop-loss order.* It is generally used to sell a stock once its price reaches a certain point, usually below the current market price. As an example, suppose a stock's current price is $100 and the investor feels the stock market is so uncertain that the price of the stock could fluctuate markedly in either direction. To minimize potential loss from the $100 level, the investor might enter a stop order at, say, $90. If the market price declines, the stock will be sold if the market price reaches $90. A stop-loss order becomes a market order once the specified price is reached, and the stock will be sold immediately at whatever price the broker can secure. Of course, if the market price goes up or never declines to the stop-loss price, the investor would have lost nothing by placing the order.

An investor who wishes to use a stop-loss order only at a specific price would enter a *stop limit order*. In the preceding illustration, this order would instruct the broker to sell only at $90. If the transaction cannot be executed at $90, it will not be executed at all.

Margin Accounts

Investors may open *cash accounts* with their brokerage firms. As the name implies, all transactions are for the full amount of the trade in cash. That is, a $10,000 trade requires a $10,000 cash settlement within three full business days after the trade is made.

A *margin account* allows investors to put up some of their own money and borrow the remainder. Margin accounts for listed securities can be opened through either a brokerage house or a commercial bank. The minimum down payment, or *margin requirement,* is set by the board of governors of the Federal Reserve system.

CASE EXAMPLE

Suppose the margin requirement is 50 percent and Mr. Baker buys 100 shares of ABC Corporation common stock at $70 per share. If this is a margin trade, he is required to come up with only $3,500 in cash (or its equivalent in other securities). He then borrows the rest ($3,500) from a bank or broker at the interest rate for this type of loan. Margin interest rates charged by different brokers can vary considerably and they often are less for larger loan balances. The entire $7,000 worth of securities is then put up as collateral for the $3,500 loan. Federal Reserve requirements specify only the *initial margin,* the minimum margin required at the time a loan is made.

But if the price of ABC common stock declines so that Mr. Baker's equity in the account decreases, he may get a maintenance margin call. *Maintenance margin* is the minimum equity position investors can have in their accounts before they are asked to put up additional funds. In this illustration, for example, assuming maintenance margin is 30 percent, ABC common could fall to a price as low as 50 without a margin call.[2] It can be seen that by borrowing to buy securities, investors stand a chance of magnifying their losses, just as they do of magnifying their gains. Thus, it is a more risky (aggressive) investment strategy.

Selling Short

Selling short means selling securities that the investor either does not possess, and therefore must borrow to settle the account, or does possess but does not wish to deliver.[3] The former is the typical short sale when an investor expects the stock to decline in price. The latter is called *selling short against the box*, and formerly was often used to lock in a profit on a stock and postpone paying taxes on the capital gain. However, the Taxpayer Relief Act of 1997 eliminated the selling-short-against-the-box technique for this purpose, except in limited circumstances. (The planning techniques for deferring or avoiding capital gains are covered in Chapter 11.)

The reason for selling short is that the investor anticipates a declining market price for the security. A typical example would be selling today at 100 with the hope of covering the sale, say, a year from now, at a lower price, for example, 70 or less. Covering involves buying securities to replace the borrowed ones. Of course, the reverse may occur and the price of the stock may not decline—it may rise, thereby making it necessary to buy the stock later at a higher price than that at which it was sold. Short sellers also must pay the equivalent of any dividends payable on the borrowed stock to the owner. Selling short is normally considered an aggressive investment policy.

Investment Categories of Common Stock

Securities firms and investment analysts use many different categories to classify the investment characteristics of common stocks. The basic categories used here are (1) growth, (2) value, (3) income, (4) growth (moderate) and income, (5) defensive, (6) cyclical, (7) blue chip, (8) speculative, (9) special situations,

[2] Since Mr. Baker must maintain an equity position of 30 percent in his margin account, he can borrow up to 70 percent of the value of the securities. His present loan is $3,500. Therefore, $3,500 divided by 0.70 (70 percent) equals the minimum value of securities Mr. Baker can have in his margin account without having to add more margin (cash or securities). In this case, the amount is $5,000 ($3,500 ÷ 0.70), or $50 per share.

[3] In the common parlance of transactions, when investors buy a security they hope eventually to sell at a higher price, they have assumed what is called a long position. When the order of these transactions is reversed—sell first and hope to cover the sale later by buying at a lower price—the investor has taken a short position.

(10) small and medium-sized companies, and (11) foreign. It should be recognized that these categories are not mutually exclusive.

Growth Stocks

The term *growth stock* is hard to define, but such a stock is usually considered from a company whose sales and earnings are expanding faster than the general economy and faster than those of most stocks. The company usually is well managed, is research- or innovation-oriented, and plows back most or all of its earnings into the company for future expansion. For this reason, growth companies often pay no or relatively small dividends. Over time, however, investors hope that substantial capital gains will accrue from the appreciation of the value of their stock. The market price of growth stocks can be volatile. They often go up faster than other stocks, but at the first hint that the rate of increase in their earnings is not being sustained or that they will not meet the expectations of investors or analysts, their prices can come down rapidly.

Value Stocks

As noted earlier, these typically are stocks of established, well-managed companies with strong balance sheets that are temporarily undervalued by the stock market. Thus, their market prices are temporarily below their so-called intrinsic value, based on their fundamental economic value. They usually pay reasonable dividends and have a good current yield.

Income Stocks

Sometimes people buy common stocks for current income. Stocks may be classified as *income stocks* when they pay a higher-than-average current yield. When general economic conditions become uncertain, investors often become more interested in current dividend income from stocks.

Growth (Moderate) and Income Stocks

These stocks pay reasonable dividends and offer reasonable growth potential.

Defensive Stocks

Some stocks are characterized as *defensive*. Such stocks are regarded as stable and comparatively safe, especially in periods of declining business activity. Their products tend to be staples and thus may suffer relatively little during recessions or depressions. The shares of utilities and food companies are examples of defensive issues.

Cyclical Stocks

Considerably different from defensive stocks are cyclical stocks. A *cyclical company* is one whose earnings and share price tend to fluctuate sharply with the business cycle or with a cycle peculiar to its own industry. Automobile manufacturers, machine tool companies, and property and liability insurers have been examples of cyclical companies.

Blue-Chip Stocks

Blue-chip stocks generally are considered high-grade, investment-quality issues of major, well-established companies that have long records of earnings stability or growth and dividend payments in good times as well as bad. *Blue chip* is a rather vague term that is not very helpful in investment analysis.

Speculative Stocks

Speculative stocks are those presenting far greater risks for the investor than common stocks generally. Some high-flying glamour stocks are speculative. Likewise, some hot new issues and penny mining stocks are speculative. Other types can be identified from time to time as they come and go. Some are easy to identify; others are more difficult.

Also, there usually comes a point in a bull market when small, hitherto unknown companies go public or new small companies are formed. The public offering of their shares may find a fierce speculative demand, and their prices often rise precipitously. Unfortunately, a day of reckoning usually follows.

Special Situations

There are stocks that may show rapid price appreciation due to some special and unique development that will affect the company positively. There might be a new process or invention, a natural resource discovery, a new product, a dramatic management change, a turnaround situation, and so forth. Companies normally in other categories can become a special situation in the face of such a development.

Small and Midsize Company Stocks

As the name indicates, small and midsize company stocks are stocks of smaller corporations—sometimes called *small-cap* or *mid-cap* (market capitalization) stocks. Some studies of stock returns over relatively long periods have shown that, on average, the performance of small company stocks has been better than that of their larger counterparts but with greater volatility.

Foreign Stocks

Americans can buy the stocks of foreign companies through American Depositary Receipts (ADRs). An ADR is a negotiable U.S. certificate representing ownership of shares in a foreign corporation. ADRs are quoted and traded in U.S. dollars on markets in the United States, and associated dividends are paid to investors in U.S. dollars. ADRs were created to make it easier for U.S. investors to buy, hold, and sell foreign stocks.

The shares of some foreign companies may be traded on U.S. stock exchanges and can be purchased directly by U.S. investors. Also, larger stockbrokers can purchase shares of foreign companies on foreign exchanges for their U.S. customers.

Some Theories of Common Stock Investment

There are many theories of how to invest in common stocks. They tend to rise and fall in popularity, depending on market and economic conditions. Clearly, there is no agreement on any one theory. Some examples of such theories follow. This listing of theories is not meant to be exhaustive; others could be given.

In structuring the common stock portion of an investor's asset allocation, he or she (or his or her adviser) may primarily want to follow one of these theories, such as value investing or growth investing. However, many investors may want to diversify their stock holdings among several categories of common stocks, such as some growth stocks or funds and some defensive stocks or funds.

Growth Theory

The growth theory has been popular. This theory advocates analysis of corporate and industry data to select those quality issues that show continuing growth from one business cycle to another and a growth rate that well exceeds that of the overall economy. Implicit in this theory is that the investor is seeking returns primarily in the form of capital growth rather than dividend income.

Another approach for the growth theory investor is to purchase mutual funds (or accounts through other financial intermediaries) that specialize in certain industries the investor considers growth industries or in funds with growth or aggressive growth as investment objectives. This way, the investor gets (and pays for) professional management in selecting growth stocks.

Value Investing

The value investing theory also is popular. It generally calls for investing in the stocks of good-quality companies that have strong balance sheets and whose stocks appear to be temporarily undervalued by the stock market. This undervaluation often results from some temporary setback for the company or its industry. This theory requires careful security analysis and considerable patience. Value investors also argue that their theory involves lower market risk because the stocks they consider are already selling at low prices relative to other stocks.

As noted earlier, the value investing approach was popularized by Benjamin Graham and David Dodd in their classic work, *Security Analysis: Principles and Techniques,* originally published in 1934. The Graham and Dodd book, with its subsequent editions, has influenced value theory investors to this day.

Moderately Growing Industries and Income Approach

Other investors prefer a policy of purchasing common stocks of good-quality companies that pay reasonable dividends and have prospects for at least some growth.

Depressed-Industry Approach

Almost the opposite of the growth stock theory is the depressed-industry approach, where the investor endeavors to select comeback industries and companies. As of this writing, shares of companies in the U.S. auto industry may be an example of this approach.

The Case for Long-Term Investments in Common Stocks

To many people, *investment* has almost come to mean buying common stocks. There are several historical reasons for this. First is the long-term general decrease in the purchasing power of the dollar (inflation). Second, generally rising stock markets during much of the 1950s and 1960s, and particularly during the later 1980s and the 1990s, provided substantial (and sometimes spectacular) capital gains for many people who were in the market.

Studies of Historical Returns

The case for long-term investment in a diversified portfolio of common stocks as the best way to accumulate wealth is often based on a number of studies comparing past total returns from common stocks with those from certain other asset classes. These studies have found that the average annual compound rates of total return for large groups of common stocks were considerably higher than the corresponding rates of total return for long-term U.S. Treasury bonds, U.S. Treasury bills, and gold over certain long periods. However, they also show that common stocks (and particularly U.S. small stocks) display much greater volatility (i.e., standard deviations) than these other asset classes. An excellent exposition of this thesis is contained in the book, *Stocks for the Long Run* by Jeremy J. Siegel.[4]

A number of other studies have reached the same general conclusions. They include the 1964 study by Lawrence Fisher and James H. Lorie that contained rates of return for all common stocks listed on the New York Stock Exchange for 22 periods between January 1926 and December 1960.[5]

Another important study along the same lines was that of Roger G. Ibbotson and Rex A. Sinquefield in 1976.[6] The average annual rates of return and standard deviations for common stocks and other investment media, along with other statistical data, are updated annually by Ibbotson and Associates.[7] These data are widely used in the securities and mutual fund industries and by financial commentators generally. They are sometimes referred to as Ibbotson yields. The Center for Research of Security Prices at the University of Chicago also makes available online similar data. There have been other studies as well.[8]

Some Conclusions Regarding the Studies

These studies have shown that average annual total rates of return and standard deviations have varied considerably among different asset classes (stocks, bonds, U.S. Treasury bills, gold, and so forth) and have varied over different periods. But what they also universally show is that over relatively long periods diversified portfolios of common stocks have performed

[4] Jeremy J. Siegel, *Stocks for the Long Run,* 4th Edition (New York: McGraw-Hill, 2008).

[5] Lawrence Fisher and James H. Lorie, "Rates of Return on Investment in Common Stocks," *Journal of Business,* University of Chicago, January 1964.

[6] Roger G. Ibbotson and Rex A. Sinquefield, "Stocks, Bonds, Bills, and Inflation: Year-by-Year Historical Returns (1926–74), " *Journal of Business,* University of Chicago, January 1976.

[7] The source is *Stocks, Bonds, Bills, and Inflation Yearbook,* Ibbotson and Associates, Chicago.

[8] For example, William Greenough did similar research, which provided the conceptual foundation for the College Retirement Equities Fund (CREF).

significantly better than the other investment media studied (mainly U.S. Treasury bonds and U.S. Treasury bills).

As an example, consider the period 1926 through 2005. This (or perhaps a period with a somewhat earlier starting year) is widely cited because it is of long duration, covers all kinds of economic conditions (prosperity, depression, and recession), and includes long periods of peace but also several times of war. During this period, the average annual arithmetic total return for U.S. large-cap common stocks was 12.15 percent, while the comparable return for long-term U.S. Treasury bonds was 5.68 percent. However, the risk factor (volatility) for common stocks for this period, as measured by the standard deviation of yearly returns, was also significantly higher for common stocks than for bonds. The standard deviation for these stocks for this period was 20.26, while for bonds it was 8.09.[9]

This means that although a diversified portfolio of common stocks can be expected to perform much better over a relatively long period than a portfolio of investment-grade bonds, the price of this better return is greater volatility of results from year to year and, therefore, higher risk.

These studies of historical returns have had a profound impact on investment thinking. They have helped make common stocks the preferred investment medium for many investors and their advisers. While the studies are based on historical data and there is no guarantee that the results shown will be repeated over long periods in the future, the consistency of the studies' results, the careful research that has gone into them, and the characteristics and variety of the long periods covered by the studies make them quite persuasive. It is hard to argue with the facts. After all, as the saying goes, "Those who do not learn from the lessons of history are doomed to repeat them."

These studies, which we shall refer to as the *historical yield approach,* relate particularly to asset allocation decisions. They may encourage investors to allocate as large a percentage of their investable assets as possible (given their time frames, tolerance for risk [volatility], and other considerations) to common stocks for the long term. This is discussed further in Chapter 9. Our tax system also tends to favor common stock investment over the long run.

Some Caveats

While the case just presented for a diversified portfolio (or index) of common stocks for superior long-term returns is persuasive, caveats always apply to any planning strategy. The first—that there is no guarantee history will repeat itself—has already been discussed.

[9] See Zvi Bodie, Alex Kane, and Alan J. Marcus, *Investments,* 7th Edition (New York: McGraw-Hill, 2008), p. 146.

Need for Diversified Long-Term Approach

The second is that the studies have been done using large numbers of stocks (e.g., all stocks listed on the New York Stock Exchange, the S&P 500, and so forth) and therefore would seem to be valid only if an investor has a reasonably diversified portfolio of common stocks. A portfolio heavily weighted in only one or a few stocks may not perform like the general averages.

Third, the studies' results are obtained only for relatively long holding periods. Thus, an investor should be prepared to hold a consistent stock position over a relatively long time, which may include bad times as well as good. However, this historical yield approach does not seem to imply that a reasonably diversified portfolio cannot be actively managed by selling some stocks and buying others.

Need to Be Aware of Bear Markets

Fourth, it must be recognized that over the periods being analyzed, there have been significant bear markets for common stocks. A bear market may be defined as a reasonably long period during which common stocks in general consistently decline by a significant amount. What amount is "significant" can be a matter of opinion, but many consider it a bear market when the decline is 20 percent or more over a period of six months or longer.[10]

We noted earlier the concept of degree of risk based on the standard deviation of yearly returns over a given period. However, since we are looking at history, a number of bear markets in stocks have lasted longer than a year. Investors must deal with actual, possibly sustained stock market declines, rather than just with statistical yearly deviations from the average.

Therefore, it will be fruitful in evaluating the possibility and extent of declines in a stock portfolio to look at some past bear markets in common stocks. Table 5.2 presents selected actual bear markets based on the Dow Jones Industrial Average, except where indicated. It starts with the famous (or infamous) Great Depression of the 1930s and then moves to post–World War II bear markets. Finally, it looks at the decline in the Japanese stock market (the Nikkei 225) for some international perspective.

These data may be useful in helping to estimate how large a potential stock market decline investors need to be prepared for in investment planning. It would be splendid, of course, if one could forecast when bear markets were coming and what the bottom was going to be and then sell high and buy low.

[10]Another term sometimes used in this respect is a market correction. In general, a market correction is not as severe as a bear market and is a sudden, sharp decline in stock prices of at least 10 percent that lasts a shorter time (such as a few days or weeks).

Table 5.2. Significant Stock Market Declines* (Bear Markets)

Date of Market Decline	Length of Market Decline (Bear Market Duration)	Percentage Decline	Recovery Period (to Previous High)**
Sept. 1929–July 1932	35 months	89	25 years (to Nov. 23, 1954)
Post–World War II U.S. Stock Market Declines*			
April 1956–Oct. 1957	19 months	19	11 months
Dec. 1961–June 1962	7 months	27	14 months
Feb. 1966–Oct. 1966	8 months	25	73 months
Dec. 1968–May 1970	18 months	36	29 months
Jan. 1973–Dec. 1974	23 months	45	95 months
Sept. 1976–Feb. 1978	17 months	27	37 months
April 1981–Aug. 1982	16 months	24	3 months
Aug. 1987–Oct. 1987	2 months	36	22 months
July 1990–Oct. 1990	3 months	21	6 months
Jan. 2000–Sept. 2002	33 months	38	82 months
Oct. 2007–Present	16 months (to date)	45 (to date)	Unknown
Nikkei Average			
1990-Present	18 years (to date)	80	Unknown

*These data are based on the Dow Jones Industrial Average, except where indicated.
**These recovery periods are based on stock prices only. They would be shorter if dividends paid on common stocks were considered. Dividends were not considered because interest or other income could have been earned on the funds had they not been placed in stocks.

Unfortunately, like the weather, everyone talks about bear markets but no one does anything about them. No one really knows when bear markets will occur and how severe they will be. However, it seems only prudent to assume that they will occur periodically, as they have in the past.

So the difficult question is how large a stock market decline should an investor plan for. As just admitted, no one really knows. However, history has helped us estimate long-term stock market returns, so it can give us some clues here as well. We previously noted that based on the lengthy period of 1926 through 2005, we have 95 percent confidence that common stocks will not decline more than about 20 percent from their expected return in any one year (the standard deviation). However, we also have seen from Table 5.2 that bear markets often have lasted longer than one year. Considering only post–World War II U.S. stock market declines, the most severe percentage declines so far have been about 45 percent during the 23 months between January 1973 and December 1974 and the current decline that began in October 2007. Therefore, to take a worst-case post–World War II kind of scenario for the U.S. market, we might assume just for planning purposes that common stocks could fall somewhere between 40 and 50 percent during a given bear market. However, given the lessons of the Great Depression of the 1930s (when common stocks declined about 89 percent and did not recover to their previous high for 25 years) and the current Japanese decline, it seems only prudent to be even more cautious in the current economic environment. How severe and how long the bear market existing as of this writing will be no one knows. However, for planning purposes (and in our asset allocation decision making) we might assume a potential decline of as much as 60–75 percent. This in no way means common stocks should be avoided in a portfolio. It just gives a benchmark to test for how much of a decline an investor can tolerate in his or her portfolio in asset allocation planning.

Before ending the discussion of bear markets, it should be noted that there also have been bear markets in asset classes other than common stocks. This has been true of bonds (particularly during the late 1970s and the 1980s) and real estate (particularly in the late 1980s, early 1990s, and at present).

6

Real Estate and Other Equity Investments

Competence Objectives for This Chapter After reading this chapter, planners should understand:

- The advantages and limitations of real estate as an investment
- How real estate investments can be held
- Kinds of real estate investments
- Various options for disposing of or exchanging real estate
- The nature of oil and gas and other tax shelter ventures
- The passive activity loss (PAL) rules and how they may affect certain investment returns
- The nature of put and call options and their investment and speculative characteristics
- The nature of initial public offerings (IPOs)
- The characteristics of commodity future trading
- The nature of investments in gold and other precious metals
- The nature of investments in collectibles

Real Estate

Historically, real estate has been a widely used investment medium for income and capital gains. Many people have an investment in real estate, in a sense, in that they own their house, or their condominiums, or cooperative apartments. Many people also own a second or vacation home. Others own income-producing properties or REITs as an investment. A few have larger real estate interests of various kinds.

Advantages of Real Estate as an Investment

Attractive Total Returns on Equity It is possible to earn a higher-than-average total after-tax return on well-selected real estate investments. This may result from the inherent advantages of owning well-selected real estate, the use of financial leverage, and tax advantages. One difficulty in comparing the yields on real estate with those of other investments is that there are specialized concepts for measuring real estate returns, and some of them are quite complex. They are beyond the scope of this book. However, to give a point of reference, here is a simple formula used in real estate as a rough rule of thumb for comparing the operating yields on different investment properties:

$$\text{Operating rate of return} = \frac{\text{net operating income from property before interest and depreciation}}{\text{purchase price for property}}$$

CASE EXAMPLE

To illustrate, suppose an investor purchased a small apartment house for $800,000. To finance the property, the investor paid $120,000 down in cash and took a $680,000 25-year, 7.5 percent mortgage on the property. Considering the local real estate market, the investor expects net operating income (NOI) and the market price for the real estate to increase at about 2 percent per year (perhaps an optimistic expectation considering the economic envirornment as of this writing). Thus, if current annual NOI—annual revenue (rents) minus property taxes, other expenses of operation, and minus an allowance for apartment vacancies, but before interest, depreciation, and income taxes are deducted—is $64,000, the operating rate of return is as follows:

$$\text{Operating rate of return} = \frac{\$64{,}000}{\$800{,}000} = 0.08 \text{ or } 8.0\%$$

The taxable income for federal income tax purposes for the first year of operation would be as follows:

NOI	$64,000
Minus:	
Depreciation	24,400
Interest paid	51,000
Taxable income (loss)	($11,400)

The depreciation in this example assumes that about $672,000 of the $800,000 purchase price (84 percent) is allocated to the building and its improvements (the depreciable portion of the property).

Land cannot be depreciated. Depreciation is taken on a straight-line basis over a 27.5-year useful life. Note that depreciation is a noncash expense that serves to reduce current taxable income. This is the main *tax-shelter* aspect of real estate as an investment.

It can be seen that this real estate investment will produce a loss for federal income tax purposes in its first year. An important issue is whether the investor will be able to deduct this loss against other taxable income (i.e., use it to shelter other income). This issue is explored later in this chapter with respect to the passive activity loss (PAL) rules. However, unless the investor is a real estate professional or the individual taxpayer exception applies, this loss would be a PAL and deductible currently only against passive activity income.

The taxable income (loss) from this property will change over time. The NOI may rise or fall, depending on real estate market conditions and operating expenses. The interest paid will decline as the amortizing mortgage is paid off, and depreciation will reduce the basis for the property.

Availability of Substantial Financial Leverage *Leverage* is simply the use of borrowed funds to try to increase the rate of return that can be earned on the investor's own funds invested in a project. In general, when the cost of borrowing is less than what can be earned on the investment, it is considered *favorable leverage* (or a *positive carry*), but when the reverse is true, it is called *unfavorable leverage* (or a *negative carry*).[1] The example just given has favorable leverage because the operating rate of return on the property is greater than the interest rate being paid on the mortgage.

Real estate investors typically employ substantial financial leverage—often from 60 to 90 percent of a property's value. They may also use leverage to pyramid their real estate holdings through refinancing of appreciated properties, reinvestment, and tax-free exchanges (covered later in this chapter). In the simple illustration used here, 85 percent of the initial purchase price was financed through a mortgage loan, while the investor's initial equity in the property was $120,000 ($800,000 value minus $680,000 mortgage).

Favorable Cash Flow Good-quality income property normally will produce a *favorable cash flow*. This is because it should produce a reasonable NOI and because depreciation is a noncash expense that will diminish taxable

[1] Leverage can also be viewed as the use of borrowed funds with the hope that the value of the real estate will increase at a faster rate than the cost of borrowing the funds. This is a more risky view of leverage.

income but not cash flow. *Cash flow* for the first year of our example can be calculated as follows:

NOI (first year)	$64,000
Minus:	
Annual debt service (principal and interest on mortgage loan)	53,900
Cash flow before tax	$10,100
Minus:	
Income tax payable	(3,990)[2]
Cash flow after tax	$14,090

If, however, the investor cannot take the $11,400 loss against other income because of the PAL rules and has no passive activity income to reduce, the first year's cash flow will be the same as the before-tax figure. Even in this case, however, the investor can reduce future taxable income through the accumulated, suspended PALs (if he or she later has passive activity income to offset), by selling the real estate in a fully taxable transaction, or to some extent at death.

Hedge against Inflation Real estate, like other equity investments, is considered a hedge against inflation. This is because property values and rents tend to rise during inflationary periods.

Tax Advantages First, as just noted, improved real estate allows the investor to take depreciation as a noncash income tax deduction. However, if the real estate is later sold in a taxable transaction, the depreciation previously deducted will reduce the property's income tax basis and result in a correspondingly higher capital gain (or lower capital loss). Thus, in the case of a subsequent sale, the depreciation deduction really defers the tax and converts gain from ordinary income to a capital gain.

Second, the costs to operate and maintain property, such as property taxes, management fees, insurance, and repairs, are deductible. Third, real estate can be traded or exchanged for like-kind property on a tax-free basis under Section 1031 of the IRC.

Fourth, on the sale of investment real estate, any gain normally is a capital gain.[3] In addition, an installment sale can be arranged so that any capital gain

[2] The income tax payable figure here is negative because it represents the reduction in the tax otherwise payable by the investor, due to the $11,400 loss for tax purposes. It assumes the investor is in the 35 percent marginal income tax bracket ($11,400 × 0.35 = $3,990).

[3] However, for certain depreciable real property (such as residential real property), net capital gain attributable to allowable depreciation on the property will be taxed at a maximum rate of 25 percent rather than the normal 15 percent maximum rate on net capital gains.

will be spread over the installment period. Finally, since borrowing against real estate is not considered a sale or exchange for tax purposes, refinancing real estate traditionally has been a way for taking value out of the real estate without incurring capital gains taxation.

Limitations of Real Estate as an Investment

Lack of Marketability There is usually relatively slow marketability in real estate. It can take substantial time to buy or sell real estate. Furthermore, the expenses of buying and selling are relatively high.

Need for Large Initial Investment A relatively large initial investment often is required. In the illustration used previously, for example, the investor would need $120,000 (equity) to purchase the apartment house.

Real Estate Cycles and Leverage It may be difficult to determine the proper value for real estate, particularly for the uninitiated. Real estate is not uniform and there are definite cycles in the real estate market. Also, during the down phase of the cycle, the very financial leverage that was so attractive when real estate prices (and rents) were rising works against the investor.

High Risk Level Real estate is considered by many to be an inherently risky form of investment. It is fixed in location and character. Also, real estate values will fall during a period of economic recession or depression as rapidly as, or perhaps even more rapidly than, other kinds of equity investments.

How Investments in Real Estate Can Be Held

Individual and Joint Ownership First, investors can simply buy property in their own names or as joint tenants or tenants in common with someone else. This is the traditional way of holding real estate, but it limits the size of the investment that can be made to the amount of capital the investor and perhaps a few others can raise.

Partnerships Many individuals invest in real estate by buying units in limited partnerships (LPs) that hold real estate. The LP has been a common vehicle for real estate investment, with investors as the limited partners and a promoter, builder, or developer as the general partner. In this way, the limited partners can invest their capital with only limited liability for partnership debts, and the earnings or losses from the real estate can be passed through the partnership organization to the individual limited partners without being taxed to the partnership. The earnings or losses are taxable to (or, to the extent permitted by tax law, deductible by) the individual partners.

The general partners manage the real estate investment. But note the importance of the character, ability, and experience of the general partners because they are in control. Also, real estate LP interests generally have limited marketability and liquidity. There are some secondary markets for these interests, but investors who dispose of their LP interests before the partnership itself terminates usually must accept large price discounts. Real estate could also be owned through limited liability companies (LLCs), which are also pass-through entities for tax purposes (see Chapter 31).

Tenant in Common Interest In this arrangement, real estate managers acquire properties and then sell or exchange interests in the properties to investors. The investors hold their interests as tenants in common, which is a partial ownership interest in the whole property (such as a 2 percent ownership interest, for example). (See Chapter 25 for a description of the legal nature of tenancy in common.) The real estate manager then manages the property for the tenant-in-common owners.

This arrangement is a way for investors to diversify their real estate investments among a number of properties. It also enables them to invest in larger properties that they might not be able to afford on their own or through partnerships or LLCs. The IRS has ruled that tenant-in-common interests are eligible for Section 1031 exchanges, which are described later in this chapter.

Real Estate Investment Trusts (REITs) A REIT is similar in concept to a closed-end investment company. (See Chapter 8 for a description of closed-end funds.) It is a corporation or business trust that meets the tax law requirements to be a REIT and invests primarily in real estate. A REIT can give investors the advantages of centralized management, limited liability, continuity of interests, and transferability of ownership (marketability). Furthermore, a REIT can avoid the corporate income tax by distributing most or all of its earnings to its shareholders. The distribution is then taxed to the shareholders as ordinary income or capital gains. However, unlike partnerships or LLCs, REITs are not allowed to pass losses through to their shareholders for tax purposes.

REITs vary considerably in size, origin, and types of real estate investments made. Therefore, investors should consider the investment objective of any REIT. Also, the management of a REIT is critical. Shares of many REITs are traded on organized stock exchanges.

There are three general types of REITs, in terms of their investment approach. *Equity REITs* derive their revenues primarily from rental income and capital gains from properties they own. *Mortgage REITs* receive their revenues mainly from interest income from mortgage loans they make. *Hybrid REITs* are combinations of the equity and mortgage approaches. REITs may also specialize in particular kinds of real estate or mortgage loans.

Subaccounts in Tax-Advantaged Plans Some qualified retirement plans, variable annuities, and possibly variable life insurance plans have subaccounts invested in real estate that participants or owners can select. However, since the investment income of these plans is not taxable currently and all distributions from them are taxed as ordinary income, the tax advantages of direct real estate investments or investments through partnerships or LLCs essentially are lost when real estate is held through these plans.

Kinds of Real Estate Investments

In terms of investment and tax considerations, real estate can be classified as follows:

- Unimproved land (bare land)
- Improved real estate (held for rental), including:
  - New and used residential property (apartment houses and the like)
  - Low-income housing
  - Old buildings and certified historic structures
  - Other income-producing real estate (such as office buildings, shopping centers, warehouses, hotels and motels, and various industrial and commercial properties)
- Mortgages
- Vacation and second homes

Disposition of Investment Real Estate

At some point, real estate investors may want to dispose of properties. Depending on the circumstances and the owner's objectives, there are several approaches to doing so.

Cash Sale In this case, the investor sells the property and gets the purchase price within one year. Using the previous case example, suppose our investor holds the apartment house for 10 years and then sells it for cash. Assuming the market price increases by 2 percent per year, the sale price would be approximately $975,000. The outstanding mortgage has declined to about $600,000 and the investor's income tax basis in the property now is $556,000 (which is the original basis of $800,000 reduced by annual depreciation of $24,400 for 10 years, or $244,000).[4]

[4] This assumes there have been no other changes in basis (such as improvements to the property that would increase basis).

Given these facts, the tax status of this sale would be as follows:

Sale price	$975,000
Minus:	
Transaction costs (at 7%)	68,250
Adjusted basis ($800,000 minus accumulated depreciation of $244,000)	556,000
Long-term capital gain	$350,750
Amount of gain attributable to depreciation taxed at 25% ($244,000 × 25% = $61,000)[5]	61,000
Remainder of net capital gain taxed at 15% ($106,750 × .15)	16,012
Total tax payable	$ 77,012

In addition, if the investor has suspended PALs,[6] he or she can use them against passive and nonpassive income in the year the entire interest in a passive activity (the apartment house, in this case) is disposed of. The suspended PALs are used first against the income or gain from the passive activity disposed of, then against passive income from any other passive activities, and finally against nonpassive income or gain (e.g., salary, interest, or dividends).

The after-tax equity position of the investor then would be as follows:

Sale price	$975,000
Minus:	
Transaction costs (at 7%)	68,250
Mortgage loan balance	600,000
Capital gains tax payable	77,012[7]
Net after-tax equity position	$229,738

As a result, the investor would have this cash for other investments or other purposes. However, the investor would realize and recognize capital gain in the year of the sale. The investor also would have received the annual cash flow from the property for the 10 years.

Installment Sale An *installment sale* occurs when payment for an asset is made over more than one taxable year.[8] Any taxes due are payable pro rata as each installment payment is made as described next.

[5] See Footnote 3. This portion of the gain is referred to as "unrecaptured IRC Section 1250 gain." There would be no ordinary income in this case because the residential real estate always has been depreciated on a straight-line basis.

[6] See the discussion of the PAL rules later in this chapter.

[7] This would be reduced by any tax savings from suspended PALs, as just explained.

[8] If a sale so qualifies, the installment method of taxation must be used unless the taxpayer (seller) affirmatively elects not to use it.

When the installment method of taxing gains (not losses) from sales is used, each payment is divided into parts for tax purposes consisting of untaxed return of basis, taxable capital gains (taxed at 15 percent or 25 percent depending on the circumstances), and interest on the installment payments (at least equal to the applicable federal rate as described in Chapter 3), which is taxable as ordinary income.[9] To determine the amount of capital gain that is taxable each year, a gross profit ratio (percentage) is calculated. This is the gross profit on the sale divided by the price paid for the property. The gross profit ratio is then multiplied by each installment payment to determine the portion of the payment that is a taxable gain. The remainder of the payment (after considering the interest) is the untaxed return of basis. As an illustration, in the previous Case Example, if an installment sale were being made, the profit ratio for the apartment house would be the gross profit ($350,750) divided by the sale price ($975,000) or 35.97 percent.

If a part of any taxable gain on depreciable property is taxable at 25 percent, this is taken into account before the 15 percent gain part. Interest on the installment payments is taxable as ordinary income.

The installment method can be used for most kinds of property, with some important exceptions. One exception is sales of stock or securities that are traded on an established securities market. Thus, publicly held (traded) stocks and other securities are not eligible for installment sale treatment. Also, to the extent provided by IRS regulations, sales of other kinds of property that are regularly traded on established markets are not eligible. Furthermore, dispositions of real or personal property by dealers in such property are excluded.

Real estate is often sold on an installment basis. Sales of closely held (private) corporation stock and other such business interests also can receive installment sale treatment, as can other kinds of property. To the seller, the main advantage of an installment sale is the deferral of the capital gains tax on the payments still to be made over the installment period. The buyer, on the other hand, does not have to have the entire purchase price available when the sale is made but can pay it over the installment period. However, when property is sold in this fashion, the seller still retains some credit risk that the buyer may not make the future payments.

Like-Kind Exchanges These are tax-deferred exchanges of similar (*like-kind*) property held for productive use in a trade or business or for investment under Section 1031 of the IRC. These transactions are often called *like-kind*

[9] In some cases, a portion of the gain will be taxable as ordinary income referred to as "recaptured ordinary income under IRC Section 1250." This usually comes from "excess depreciation" which results from taking depreciation deductions (when permitted) in excess of that which would be allowed under straight line depreciation.

exchanges or *Section 1031 exchanges.* They are important in real estate because they allow a property owner to exchange property for other real estate without recognizing capital gain on the property exchanged. Thus, an investor can change holdings with no or limited tax consequences by selling his or her property (called the relinquished property) and then buying other real estate (called the replacement property). These transactions are carried out through "qualified intermediaries" who handle the sale and purchase. The tax rules for like-kind exchanges are complex and must be carefully followed to secure nonrecognition treatment. The income tax basis of an owner in the property being exchanged carries over to the new property received.

These Section 1031 nonrecognition exchanges do not apply to stocks, bonds, notes, other securities, and similar property. They also do not apply to exchanges of property held for personal use (such as a family residence). However, if, say, a personal residence is converted to use as a business or investment property for a substantial period, it may become eligible for like-kind exchange treatment.

Like-kind exchanges may involve the receipt of *boot* in addition to the exchanged properties. Boot is cash or personal property (unlike property) received in addition to the like-kind exchanged real estate. Boot may be necessary to even out the values in an exchange. The receipt of boot will result in current taxation to the extent of the boot. The remainder of the gain will not be recognized.

Refinancing of Properties While not technically a disposition of real estate, refinancing allows owners of appreciated real estate to get cash out of their properties without taxation. However, it also means they will increase their leverage (debt), with the resulting risks or benefits.

If, for example, after 10 years the investor in our previous case example decided to refinance the apartment house with a mortgage at 85 percent of its current appraised value ($975,000) instead of selling or exchanging it, the following would be the result (ignoring the expenses of refinancing):

New mortgage loan (85% of $975,000)	$828,750
Minus:	
Current mortgage loan balance	600,000
Cash available from refinancing	$228,750

The investor could use this cash as equity for the purchase of additional real estate (and thus pyramid his or her real estate portfolio), invest it elsewhere, or use it for other purposes.

Gifting of Property Interests Real estate, like other property, can be given away to family members as part of an estate-planning gifting program. The advantages and disadvantages of lifetime giving are explored in Chapter 27.

Oil and Gas Ventures

These can be risky investments, but they can yield handsome returns if successful. They tend to be specialized investments, and their economic characteristics are beyond the scope of this book.

Some basic tax incentives exist for oil and gas investments.

- The deduction from income of intangible drilling costs (IDCs), which could be up to 80 or 90 percent of the initial cost of a productive well. The tax law permits persons with a *working interest* in oil and gas drilling operations (i.e., persons who generally have unlimited liability for their own share of the costs) to deduct their losses from these operations against other taxable income. This also may be true if the investor agrees to become a general partner (with unlimited liability) in the venture. However, a limited partnership interest (with limited liability) is not such a working interest, and losses of limited partners normally would be PALs.
- A percentage depletion allowance of 15 percent of gross revenue, which taxpayers can deduct from their gross incomes from oil and gas investments.
- However, the amounts an investor writes off for IDCs and depletion reduce his or her basis in the oil and gas interest. Under certain conditions, these amounts also may be tax-preference items for alternative minimum tax purposes.

People can, of course, invest directly in oil and gas operations. However, oil and gas partnerships are offered to the public as a way of investing in oil and gas.

Other Tax Shelters

Other kinds of tax-sheltered investments include cattle feeding and other farming enterprises; horse and cattle breeding; timber, mineral and mining operations; equipment leasing; movies; and research and development ventures, among others. Space does not permit a discussion of each of them in this book.

Impact of Passive Activity Loss Rules

The kinds of investments just described traditionally have been called *tax-sheltered investments* because losses (even though they may not have been real economic losses) were used to reduce an investor's other taxable income.[10]

[10] While the term *tax-sheltered investments* traditionally has been used as just described, it may also be loosely used to describe many other tax-favored arrangements.

Such tax losses might arise, for example, from depreciation in real estate investments and intangible drilling costs and percentage depletion in oil and gas ventures.

The Issue

The result was that many high-income persons invested in tax shelters with the aim of reducing their taxable income. They may have used nonrecourse loans to finance their investments. Naturally, it was hoped that the tax-sheltered investments would show a profit at some point; then the investor could sell them and take the gains at least partially as capital gains. Investors could also continually make new tax-sheltered investments and get new losses.

Because of alleged abuses in tax-sheltered investments, the Tax Reform Act of 1986 adopted the PAL rules. The main concept of the PAL rules is to prohibit taxpayers (with some exceptions) from using what are defined as *passive activity losses* to offset, or *shelter*, other kinds of taxable income.

What Constitutes a Passive Activity

For purposes of these rules, a passive activity is (1) a trade or business in which the taxpayer does not *materially participate* on a regular, continuous, and substantial basis[11] or (2) an activity primarily involving the rental of property, whether the taxpayer materially participates or not. Thus, rental activities (including rental real estate) generally are passive, regardless of material participation by the owners. There is an exception to this rule for real estate in the case of real estate professionals who materially participate in the rental activity. The law defines such persons quite strictly. There is also an individual real estate investor exception, as explained shortly.

Who Is Affected

Taxpayers affected by these rules include any individual acting as an individual, a partner in a partnership, a member of an LLC, or a stockholder in an S corporation; estates; trusts; and certain closely held C corporations. When there is passive activity, the tax law provides that expense deductions in excess

[11] There also are objective tests in the income tax regulations as to what the statutory term *materially participates* means. For example, a taxpayer is considered to materially participate in an activity if he or she participates more than 500 hours during the year, or if he or she participates more than 100 hours and no one else had greater participation, or if his or her participation during the year constituted substantially all the participation of anyone, among other tests.

of income (i.e., passive activity losses) generally may be used only to offset passive activity income from other passive activities. Thus, PALs may not be used to offset income from other sources, such as salary or personal earnings (called *personal service income*), taxable interest and dividends (referred to as *portfolio income*), and taxable income from *active business pursuits* (i.e., a trade or business in which the taxpayer materially participates).

However, unused PALs are not lost entirely. They are merely suspended until the taxpayer can use them against passive activity income in the future (if any) or until the taxpayer sells the passive activity in a fully taxable transaction (at which time they can be taken against other income as previously described) or to a certain extent at the death of the taxpayer.

Individual Real Estate Investor Exemption

There is a special exemption from these rules that allows an individual taxpayer who "actively participates" in a rental activity to deduct up to $25,000 of losses from rental real estate each year from his or her taxable income from other sources, provided the taxpayer's adjusted gross income (AGI) is less than $100,000. For taxpayers with AGIs over $100,000, this $25,000 exemption is phased out by reducing it by 50 percent of the amount the taxpayer's AGI exceeds $100,000.[12]

Put and Call Options

Trading in options to buy or sell common stocks (*calls* or *puts*) on organized exchanges is a technique used by some investors. A *call* is an option allowing the buyer to purchase from someone a certain stock or other asset at a set price (called the *exercise* or *strike price*) at any time within a specified period. A *put* is an option allowing the buyer to sell to someone a certain stock or other asset at a set price at any time within a specified period. Options normally are for round lots (100 shares) of common stock. The expiration date is the last day on which the holder of an option can exercise it. Listed options have standardized quarterly expiration dates.

Buying Options

People may buy options when they want to speculate on whether a stock is going up or down or is going to fluctuate beyond certain limits or for other reasons. The price paid for the option is called the premium.

[12] Thus, the phase-out occurs with AGIs between $100,000 and $150,000.

For example, suppose a person thinks XYZ common stock is too low and the price soon will go up. In this case, he or she might buy a call option for XYZ common. Furthermore, suppose that on June 1, XYZ common is selling at $62 a share and that a listed XYZ common October 60 call option is purchased for a premium of $7 per share, or $700 for the 100-share option. This means that for $700 (excluding commissions, for the sake of simplicity), the person has purchased a standardized contract allowing him or her to buy (call) 100 shares of XYZ common stock at $60 per share (the exercise price) at any time prior to the end of October (the expiration date). Now if XYZ common climbs to $72 a share by September 1, the October 60 call will become more valuable in the listed options market and, let us say, the premium for this option is $13 per share on September 1. If the person decides to close out the option position on September 1, he or she would sell the call option for $13 per share. In this case, the profit (excluding commissions) would be as follows:

June 1—Purchased call option for	$700
September 1—Sold call option for	1,300
Profit on the three-month transaction	$600

It can be seen that this profit is 85 percent of the $700 premium for the option, while the price of the underlying stock rose only 16 percent (from $62 to $72 per share). But if the price of XYZ common stays around $62 or declines during the five-month period, the option buyer will lose the $700 premium and suffer a 100 percent loss. However, the option buyer's risk of loss will be limited to the premium paid for the option.

While leveraged speculation is the main reason for buying calls, there are other possible reasons, such as to sell some existing investments to release cash while still maintaining a short-term market position, to protect against short-term market uncertainty, and to have a hedge against short sales.

On the other hand, if the person thinks XYZ common stock is overpriced and soon will fall substantially, he or she might buy a put option. It would work the same way as a call, except in the opposite direction.

Another reason for buying puts may be to protect an investment position from the risk of a declining market. As explained in Chapter 11, buying put options can be part of investment *collar transactions* designed to protect the value of highly appreciated stocks from market declines without actually selling the stocks and realizing capital gains.

More sophisticated traders can engage in a variety of option techniques. One is the *straddle,* in which a put and a call on the same stock are purchased with the same exercise price and expiration month. Here the speculator will profit if the underlying stock's price moves far enough in either direction to more than offset the premiums on both options.

Selling (Writing) Options

The motivation for selling call options normally is entirely different from the motivation for buying them. The option writer typically wants to secure an attractive yield on an existing investment. This increased yield comes from the premiums received by the option writer on the options granted to buyers. The option writer, however, gives up the opportunity for capital appreciation on stock he or she owns that is called away. But if the price of the stock declines, the option writer bears this risk (except that the writer still has the premium for the call).

But writing so-called *naked* call options is highly speculative. These are options where the writer does not own the underlying security. Generally, calls should be sold only on securities in the option writer's portfolio or on securities purchased for this purpose. Also, puts should be sold only against cash and only on stock the writer would otherwise want in his or her portfolio.

Selling call options is the other part of investment collar transactions noted previously and described in Chapter 11.

New Issues or Initial Public Offerings

Stocks and bonds offered by corporations for the first time are called *new issues* or *initial public offerings (IPOs).* Some have been offered by corporate giants, but most new issues are made by smaller, lesser known, or newly formed corporations. Many of them do not have an established track record of operations and earnings. Hence, they are often speculative. Some investors, however, like to buy such new issues as speculations. Those that prove successful offer phenomenal gains for their original buyers. There also may be rapid, initial run-ups in price immediately after an IPO. But many such issues do not prove successful in the long run.

Commodity Futures Trading

People usually engage in commodity futures trading in the hope of profiting from price changes in one or more basic commodities, including wheat, corn, oats, soybeans, potatoes, platinum, copper, silver, orange juice, cocoa, eggs, frozen pork bellies, lumber, and iced broilers. One can speculate on price changes in these commodities by buying and selling futures contracts.

A *futures contract* is an agreement to buy or sell a commodity at a price stated in the agreement on a specified future date. While futures contracts call for the delivery of the commodity (unless the contract is liquidated before it matures), this is rarely done. Speculators in commodity futures usually close out their positions before the contracts mature. This way, the commodity itself never actually changes hands among speculators. On the other hand, contracts to buy or sell the physical commodities are made in the cash (or *spot*) market.

As an illustration, suppose a person thinks the price of corn is going up. He or she might enter into a futures contract to buy 5,000 bushels of corn (a full contract in corn) for delivery in December at a price of $3 per bushel, which would be the market price for December corn at the time the buy order was executed (assuming it was a market order). This is referred to as being *long* in the commodity. Now suppose the person is correct and in a month the price of December corn futures rises 20 cents per bushel to $3.20. The speculator now might decide to close out the transaction by selling 5,000 bushels of December corn and taking a profit of 20 cents per bushel, or a total of $1,000 (5,000 × 0.20 = $1,000), excluding commissions and other costs. However, the speculator could have magnified this profit through the leverage of trading on margin. Margin requirements in commodities are relatively low—usually 5 to 10 percent of the value of the commodity traded. If the margin requirement in this example had been 10 percent, the speculator would have had to deposit with the broker only $1,500 as security for the futures contract that had a value of $15,000. Thus, such leverage can magnify a speculator's potential profits (and losses) in terms of the amount the speculator actually puts up. Of course, if the price of December corn futures had declined and the speculator had closed out the transaction, he or she would have suffered similar speculative, leveraged losses.

Suppose, instead, that the speculator thinks the price of corn is too high and is going down. In this case, he or she would sell short and might, for example, enter into a futures contract to sell 5,000 bushels of corn for delivery in December at a price of $3 per bushel. Of course, if the price of December corn futures rises and the speculator covers the short position, he or she will lose on the transaction. Many other techniques for dealing in commodity futures exist but are not discussed here.

A word of caution is in order. While the opportunities for speculative profits in commodity futures trading can be enormous and quick, the risks are equally so. Trading in commodity futures is inherently speculative and risky.

Gold and Other Precious Metals

In their asset allocations, some investors want to have a portion (such as 5 to 10 percent) of their portfolios in gold or other precious metals. In recent years, the price of gold has fluctuated widely. Gold is regarded by some as a hedge against inflation, with its price expected to rise when inflation threatens. On the other hand, gold also is viewed by some as a "safe haven" investment during uncertain and difficult economic times. There is no consensus regarding the desirability of gold or other precious metals as an investment class.

Individuals can invest in gold by buying coins or perhaps even the bullion itself. They can also buy the common stocks of gold and precious metals mining companies whose share prices presumably move with changes in the prices of the metals themselves. These stocks can be purchased directly or through intermediaries like mutual funds. In addition, there are some ETFs whose assets consist of actual gold and whose share prices move with the price of gold.

Art, Antiques, Coins, Stamps, and Other Collectibles

Some people are interested in investing in more unusual items. In recent years, properly selected items in some areas have shown substantial increases in price. Some of these items are unique and specialized, so buying them successfully requires a knowledge of what one is doing. Also, these items produce no investment income—only possible price appreciation. Of course, many people have a collector's interest in such property anyway, so it may be quite logical for them to acquire these items. When such property is sold at a gain, however, the long-term capital gains tax rate is 28 percent, rather than the 15 percent rate applying currently to most long-term capital gains.

7

Fixed-Income Investments

Competence Objectives for This Chapter After reading this chapter, planners should understand:

- How returns can be taken from bonds
- Nature and call provisions of corporate bonds
- Income tax status of corporate bonds
- Taxable equivalent yields for municipal bonds
- Kinds and call provisions of municipal bonds
- Income tax status of various categories of municipal bonds
- The types and call provisions of U.S. government obligations
- Income tax status of U.S. Treasury notes and bonds
- The nature and income tax status of inflation-indexed Treasury notes and bonds (TIPS)
- The nature and tax status of U.S. savings bonds
- The nature of pass-through securities
- The nature and income tax status of market discount bonds
- The nature and income tax status of zero coupon (OID, original issue discount) bonds
- The characteristics of preferred stocks
- The types and income tax status of certificates of deposit (CDs)
- The types of cash equivalents (liquid assets)
- Conversion privileges in fixed-income securities
- Investment quality, bond ratings, and high-yield bonds
- Strategies for fixed-income portfolios, including:
  - Laddering and barbell strategies
  - Taxable versus nontaxable securities

- Strategies for call protection
- Investment quality considerations (high-yield securities)
- Overall strategies

The previous two chapters have dealt with various equity-type investments. Yet, for most individuals, equity investments should form only part of their overall asset allocation strategy. One or more types of fixed-income securities generally should also be included. Simply stated, fixed-income investments generally promise the investor a stated amount of income periodically, and in most cases, also promise to pay the face amount at its maturity date.

Types of Fixed-Income Investments

Fixed-income securities and investments include the following:

- Corporate bonds
- Municipal bonds
- Marketable U.S. government obligations
- U.S. savings bonds
- U.S. government agency securities
- Mortgage- and asset-backed securities (pass-through securities)
- Zero-coupon bonds (corporate, municipal, and U.S. government)
- CDs
- Stable-value funds
- Liquid assets (cash equivalents)
- Preferred stocks

Ways of Taking Returns from Bonds

Before discussing the various types of bonds, it will be helpful to note the ways in which investors can purchase marketable bonds and take returns from them. This discussion will help explain the income tax status of various bonds. Furthermore, as with common stocks, the total return from a bond over a given period is the market price at the end of the period minus the market price at the beginning of the period (capital gain or loss) plus interest paid during the period.

Bonds Purchased at Par

When the purchase price of a bond is equal to its value at maturity (par value or face amount), it is purchased at par. The investor receives the interest payments (coupon rate) until maturity, at which time the investor receives the face amount. If the investor sells or redeems the bond prior to maturity, the investor will realize a capital gain (or loss) if the sale price is more (or less) than his or her tax basis (cost) in the bond.

Market Discount Bonds

These are bonds purchased in the open market after issuance at a price less than the face amount of the bond (assuming the bond was originally issued at par). For example, an investor might purchase a 4.5 percent $1,000 face-amount bond due to mature in 10 years for $937. In this case, the investor receives the interest payments (coupon rate of 4.5 percent times $1,000 or $45 per year) until maturity, at which time the investor will receive the $1,000 face amount, which includes $63 of market discount.

If the investor sells or redeems the bond prior to maturity, he or she will realize a gain (or loss) if the sale price is more (or less) than his or her adjusted tax basis in the bond. A gain may be partially a recovery of market discount and partially a capital gain. A loss will be a capital loss.

Original Issue Discount (OID) Bonds

Here the bonds are originally issued at a price less than the face amount of the bond. When these bonds pay no current interest (they have a coupon rate of zero), they are called *zero coupon bonds* or *zeros*. For example, an investor might purchase a $1,000 bond with a zero percent coupon rate due to mature in 20 years for a price of $255. In this case, he or she receives no current interest payments, but at maturity receives the $1,000 face amount, which includes $745 of original issue discount. If the investor sells the bond prior to maturity, he or she will realize a gain (or loss) if the sale price is more (or less) than his or her adjusted tax basis in the bond.

Bonds Purchased at a Premium

These are bonds purchased in the open market after issuance at a price greater than the face amount. For example, an investor might purchase a 6.25 percent $1,000 face-amount bond due to mature in 28 years for a price of $1,091. Here, the investor receives the interest payments (coupon rate of 6.25 percent times $1,000 or $62.50 per year) until maturity, when he or she receives the $1,000 face amount. If the investor sells and redeems the bond prior to maturity, he or she will realize a capital gain (or capital loss) if the sale price is more (or less) than the adjusted tax basis in the bond.

Bonds Held by Intermediaries

When bonds are held in mutual funds, in variable life insurance and variable annuity products, or in qualified retirement plans, their returns are generally treated like returns in these funds or accounts.

Corporate Bonds

These are bonds issued by private corporations and usually are based on the creditworthiness of the issuing corporation. They are viewed as less secure than U.S. Treasury issues (the most secure) and less secure than most municipal bonds.

Security for Corporate Bonds

Some bonds, such as equipment trust certificates and mortgage bonds, are secured by a lien on all or a portion of the property of the company. Many bonds, however, are *debentures,* bonds backed by the full credit of the issuing corporation but with no special lien on the corporation's property. Debentures generally have first claim on all assets not specifically pledged under other bond indentures. *Subordinated debentures* have a claim on assets after claims of senior debt. Bond issues may have sinking-fund provisions designed to retire a substantial portion of the bonds before maturity.

Call Provisions

Many corporate bonds can be redeemed, or *called,* before maturity. However, many corporations now issue securities that offer investors call protection for a specified period. Investors are willing to accept lower yields in exchange for some call protection or for bonds that are not callable at all. Call protection in bonds tends to vary with economic conditions. Unfortunately, no one really knows how interest rates will move in the future.

Tax Status of Corporate Bonds

As a general principle, the investment income from corporate bonds is fully taxable for federal income tax purposes. It also is generally fully taxable for state income tax purposes. (Some states do not have income taxes.) The *current interest paid* (coupon rate) is taxable as ordinary interest income. *Market discount* also is generally taxed as ordinary income. *Original issue discount* (OID) is taxed as ordinary income.

If a corporate bond is purchased at a premium, the investor may elect to amortize the premium over the remaining life of the bond (or sometimes until an earlier call date). Depending on when the bond was purchased, the investor may use the amount amortized each year to reduce the otherwise taxable interest on the bond or as an itemized deduction. Either way, the amount amortized serves to reduce otherwise taxable ordinary income. The amount amortized also reduces the investor's tax basis in the bond.

If the investor does not elect to amortize the premium, it is added to the basis and either reduces capital gain on disposition of the bond for more than the basis or produces a capital loss on disposition for less than the basis.

If a corporate bond is sold or redeemed prior to maturity, amounts received in excess of the basis generally are taxable as capital gains. However, in the case of market discount bonds or OID bonds, part or all of any gain may be taxed as ordinary interest income.

Municipal Bonds (Munis)

Tax-Free versus Taxable Returns

An important feature of municipal bonds is that interest is exempt from federal income tax and from state and local income taxes in the states in which the bonds are issued. Municipals are particularly attractive to persons whose income tax brackets enable them to realize greater after-tax return from tax-free interest than from interest that is fully taxable. Columns 2, 3, and 4 of Table 7.1 illustrate the relationship between the effective after-tax returns on municipal bonds and those of certain other fixed-income investments. Column 5 shows the equivalent taxable yields to a 5.5 percent tax-free yield at various marginal federal income tax rates applicable in 2009.

For example, a husband and wife who file a joint return and are in a 33 percent federal income tax bracket would keep, on an after-tax basis, all the income from a tax-free municipal bond (or 5.5 percent, as shown in Table 7.1). But this same couple could keep only 3.35 percent from a CD paying 5 percent (taxable) and only 4.69 percent from a 7 percent corporate bond (taxable). Based on these figures, this couple should consider municipals. Note that while yields will change over time, it is the investor's top marginal tax rate combined with the relationship between municipal bond yields and comparable taxable yields that are the basic points for the investor to consider.

If state and local taxes are considered, the after-tax yields on municipals that are free from federal, state, and local taxes are even more attractive.[1] To determine the combined effective federal and state top marginal income tax rate, assuming an investor itemizes federal income tax deductions, it is necessary to adjust the top marginal state tax rate to reflect the fact that state and local income taxes are deductible in arriving at federal taxable income. This adjustment involves multiplying the state rate by 1 minus the marginal federal rate to determine the effective state rate.

[1] These are sometimes called *triple-tax-free* municipal bonds. They are free of federal income tax, and states and municipalities generally do not tax the interest (and sometimes the capital gains) on municipal bonds issued in the state.

Table 7.1. After-Tax Returns on Fixed-Income Investments*

1	**2**	**3**	**4**	**5**†
Federal tax bracket	After-tax return from a municipal bond paying a tax-free yield of 5.5%	After-tax return from a bank paying 5% taxable	After-tax return from a corporate bond paying 7% taxable	For the investor to keep 5.5% (tax-free) from a taxable investment, it would have to pay an equivalent taxable yield of
15	5.5	4.25	5.96	6.47
25	5.5	7	5.25	7.33
33	5.5	3.35	4.69	8.21
35	5.5	3.25	4.55	8.46

*All values are in terms of percentages. These yields do not consider the possible effects of state or local government income taxation, which can vary considerably among the states.

†This equivalent taxable yield is calculated by dividing the tax-free yield (5.5%) by 1 minus the top marginal federal income tax rate.

If we assume the married couple in our example has a top marginal state and local tax rate of 6 percent and itemizes federal deductions, their effective state rate is 6 percent × (1 – 0.33) or 4.02 percent. Their combined effective federal and state rate then is 37.02 percent (33 percent federal rate + 4.02 percent effective state rate). In this event, the after-tax (federal, state, and local) return from the 7 percent corporate bond from Table 7.1 would be 4.41 percent and the equivalent taxable yield for a 5.5 percent municipal would be 8.73 percent.

If an investor does not itemize deductions for federal tax purposes and, hence, state and local income taxes are not deductible, the combined effective federal and state rate can simply be stated as the top federal rate plus the top state rate (or 33 + 6 = 39 percent in the previous illustration). Note that this analysis does not apply to U.S. Treasury securities or other direct U.S. government obligations because their interest is exempt from state and local income taxation.

Call Provisions

Like corporate bonds, municipals are often callable. However, they may be callable only after a certain date and/or have other call protection. Also, some municipals are not callable at all.

Kinds of Municipal Bonds

General-Obligation Bonds This is an important category of municipal bonds; they are secured by the full faith, credit, and taxing power of the issuing state or municipality. General-obligation bonds are normally considered to offer a high level of security for the investor, consistent, of course, with the credit rating of the issuer.

Special Tax Bonds These bonds are payable only from the proceeds of a single tax, a series of taxes, or some other specific source of revenue.

Revenue Bonds Revenue bonds are issued to finance various kinds of projects, such as water, sewage, gas, and electrical facilities; hospitals; dormitories; hydroelectric power projects; and bridges, tunnels, turnpikes, and expressways. The principal and interest on such bonds are payable solely from the revenues produced by the project.

Housing Authority Bonds These bonds are issued by local authorities to finance the construction of low-rent housing projects and are secured by the pledge of unconditional, annual contributions by the Housing Assistance

Administration, a federal agency. Housing authority bonds are considered top-quality investments.

Industrial Development Bonds (IDBs) These bonds are issued by a municipality or other authority but are secured by lease payments made by industrial corporations that occupy or use the facilities financed by the bond issue.

Insured Municipal Bonds Many municipal bonds carry insurance to protect investors against the risk of default on the bonds. Such insurance enhances the creditworthiness of the bonds and normally gives them the highest-quality rating. Three large insurers of municipal bonds are the Financial Guaranty Insurance Company (FGIC), Municipal Bond Investors Assurance (MBIA), and the American Municipal Bond Assurance Corporation (AMBAC). It is the financial strength of these private insurers that stands behind their insurance of municipal bond issues. In the uncertain economic conditions as of this writing, however, some questions have been raised concerning the financial strength of some bond insurers. It seems prudent, therefore, for municipal bond investors to consider the fundamental credit quality of the bond itself and not rely solely on the bond insurance.

Municipal Bond Ratings

Quality ratings on municipal bonds are provided by Moody's and Standard & Poor's, the financial services that also rate corporate bonds. (See the section in this chapter, "Bond Ratings and Investment Quality.") In general, high-grade municipals rank second in quality only to securities issued by the U.S. government and government agencies.

Tax Status of Municipal Bonds

Interest on all municipal bonds issued prior to August 8, 1986, generally is exempt from all federal income taxation. However, for municipal bonds issued after August 7, 1986 (or other applicable dates), there is a three-tiered system of federal income taxation, as follows: (1) interest on public-purpose municipals remains free from all federal income taxation; (2) interest on tax-exempt private-activity municipals (*qualified bonds* or *alternative minimum tax bonds*) is exempt from regular federal income taxation, but generally is a preference item for AMT purposes; and (3) interest on taxable private-activity municipals is fully taxable for federal income tax purposes. To date, relatively few fully taxable municipals have been issued.

Since the interest on AMT bonds (private activity bonds used to finance such projects as airports, stadiums, and student loan programs) is a preference item for AMT purposes, it will cause AMT at either a 26 or a 28 percent rate for those subject to the AMT system.[2] For those investors, AMT bonds are not attractive. However, since AMT bonds normally have higher yields than comparable public-purpose bonds, they may be attractive for investors who are not subject to the AMT.

For municipal bonds purchased after April 30, 1993, accrued market discount generally is taxed as ordinary income upon sale, redemption, or maturity of the bond. For bonds purchased before May 1, 1993, market discount is treated as capital gain.

OID in municipal bonds is not taxable, but for municipal bonds issued after September 3, 1982, and acquired after March 1, 1984, the owner's tax basis is increased by accrued tax-exempt OID.

If a fully tax-exempt, coupon-paying, municipal bond is purchased at a premium, the owner must amortize the premium over the remaining life of the bond (or sometimes until an earlier call date). However, the amount amortized each year is not deductible, nor does it reduce otherwise taxable interest. Instead, it simply reduces the tax-free interest received. Also, the owner must reduce his or her basis in the bond by the amount amortized each year.

If a municipal bond is sold or redeemed prior to maturity, amounts received in excess of basis generally are taxable as capital gains. However, for market discount bonds, part or all of any gain may be interest income.

U.S. Government Obligations

Treasury Bills

Treasury bills are issued on a discount basis and are redeemed at face value at maturity. They generally have maturity periods of 13 weeks, 26 weeks, and 52 weeks, and are considered highly liquid (cash equivalents).

Treasury Notes

Treasury notes have maturities from 1 to 10 years. They are issued at or near par, and their interest is paid semiannually.

Treasury Bonds

Treasury bonds mature in more than 10 years. They also are issued at or near par, and their interest is paid semiannually.

[2] The AMT system is described in Chapter 11. As part of the economic stimulus program in 2009, the American Recovery and Reinvestment Act provides that tax-exempt interest or private activity bonds issued in 2009 and 2010 will not be treated as AMT preference item.

Call Provisions

In general, Treasury notes and bonds are not callable. Some long-term bonds are callable at par five years before maturity; otherwise, they are not callable. This lack of call risk and their highest credit standing can be important factors in planning a bond portfolio. They may lead investors to use long-term Treasury notes and bonds for the longest-maturity rung in laddering a bond portfolio, as explained later in this chapter.

Tax Status of Treasury Notes and Bonds

The interest income from U.S. Treasury notes and bonds is taxable for federal income tax purposes. However, it is exempt from state and local income taxation. This somewhat increases the after-tax yields from Treasury notes and bonds, depending on the level of state and local taxation (if any) where the investor resides.

The current interest paid (coupon rate) is taxable as ordinary interest income. Market discount is generally taxed as ordinary income. In addition, OID is taxed as ordinary income. If Treasury notes or bonds are purchased at a premium, the investor may elect to amortize the premium over the remaining life of the bond. This operates in the same way as for corporate bonds. The sale of Treasury notes and bonds also produces the same general federal tax results as for corporate bonds.

Inflation-Indexed Treasury Notes and Bonds

The Treasury has issued Treasury inflation-protected securities (TIPS). These are Treasury notes or bonds with a fixed interest rate applied to a principal amount that is adjusted periodically for inflation or deflation based on an adjusted Consumer Price Index for urban consumers (CPI-U). They pay semiannual interest and then the principal amount (including any inflation or deflation adjustments) at maturity. However, there is a minimum guarantee payment at maturity if the principal at that time is less than the principal at issuance.

As an example, suppose the Treasury issued a $1,000 10-year inflation-indexed note with a fixed interest rate of 3.5 percent. Furthermore, assume that during the first year inflation was at 3 percent. At the end of the year, the note's principal amount would be adjusted to $1,030 and 3.5 percent interest would be paid on that amount ($36.05 per year). The principal amount would be adjusted regularly over its duration and paid to the bondholder at maturity. For tax purposes, the investor has gross income each year equal to the current interest paid plus any adjustment to principal for inflation (or less any deflation adjustment), even though the adjusted principal is not paid until maturity. Thus, an investor can have tax liability on an inflation adjustment without current cash from the note or bond with which to pay the tax. Thus, TIPS may be best suited for tax-advantaged vehicles, such as IRAs.

Savings Bonds

U.S. savings bonds are registered, noncallable, and nontransferable (i.e., nonmarketable) securities. Two kinds of savings bonds now being issued are Series EE (or E) and Series I, which are inflation-indexed. There are also Series HH bonds, but they are no longer being issued.

Series EE bonds are sold in face-volume denominations of $50 to $10,000, with the purchase price of paper bonds being 50 percent of the face amount, while electronic EE bonds are sold at face value. EE paper bonds pay no current interest; instead, they are issued at a discount and are redeemable at face value on the maturity date. The interest rate on EE bonds issued prior to May 1, 2005 is a *market-based rate* and is set by the Treasury every six months. Bonds issued after April 30, 2005 carry the *fixed interest rate* that was in effect when the bonds were purchased and that continues for the 30-year lifetime of the bond. Such EE bonds are guaranteed to double in value in 20 years. EE bonds are redeemable at any time starting six months after issue, but redemption within the first five years reduces the effective yield.

Series I bonds are sold at face amount and accrue earnings until they are redeemed or mature (in 30 years). They accrue annual earnings at a composite rate consisting of a fixed rate for the bond's duration and a semiannual inflation rate (or deflation rate). When investors redeem EE and I bonds, or when they mature, investors normally are taxed on the difference between the purchase price and the redemption value as ordinary interest income. However, investors can elect to be taxed annually as bond interest accrues, but few do so. In addition, interest on Series I bonds and some EE bonds used for tuition and fees at colleges, universities, and qualified technical schools can be excluded from the bond owner's income under certain conditions. Also, savings bond interest is exempt from state and local income taxes.

Series HH bonds are interest-paying savings bonds that pay interest every six months. Previously, they could be secured at par in exchange for EE and similar bonds. HH bonds can be redeemed six months after issue, but they may be held to earn interest for as long as 20 years.

Other U.S. Government and Agency Securities

U.S. Government Agency Securities These securities are not issued directly by the federal government, but some have government guarantees. They typically carry somewhat higher yields than comparable U.S. government securities. Some of the governmental agencies that issue these securities are the federal home loan banks, Ginnie Mae (formerly the Government National Mortgage Association), and the International Bank for Reconstruction and Development (World Bank).

Flower Bonds These were U.S. government bonds that the federal government formerly accepted at par in payment of federal estate taxes. However, they are no longer being issued, and the last issue outstanding matured in 1998. Therefore, they now are of historical interest only.

Mortgage- and Asset-Backed Securities (Pass-Through Securities)

This is a participation in a pool of assets (e.g., mortgages) in which the investor receives a certificate evidencing his or her interest in the underlying assets. Probably the most important are the Ginnie Mae pass-throughs (which are backed by the full faith and credit of the U.S. government and are considered as safe as U.S. government securities), Fannie Mae pass-throughs, and Freddie Mac pass-throughs. These certificates permit investors to earn higher mortgage yields.

A special feature of these securities is that part of the principal is returned with the interest each month as the underlying mortgages in the pool are amortized by the borrowers. Thus, these securities provide a higher level of secure income. On the other hand, there is inherent reinvestment risk in pass-throughs, in that if market interest rates decline significantly, mortgage borrowers will tend to pay off and refinance their loans at the lower rates. This will cause higher principal payments to the pass-through investors, who then must reinvest these payments at the current, lower interest rates. It also means the prices of pass-throughs will be less sensitive to declines in interest rates than for other bonds.

There are several categories of these securities. *Mortgage-backed securities* are participations in pools of mortgages, *asset-backed securities* are similar participations in pools of consumer or other loans, and *collateralized mortgage obligations* (CMOs) are a form of mortgage-backed security that may consist of portions with different investment characteristics. Another category is collateralized debt obligation (CDOs). These have caused considerable problems in recent years.

Market Discount Bonds

General Characteristics

As noted previously, market discount bonds sell in the market for less than their face amount (par value). Investors may like such bonds for several reasons. First, in effect, they provide automatic call protection because their coupon rates are relatively low, compared with current market interest rates. Also, their issuers normally must pay at least par value on redemption, which increases the cost of a call. In addition, they provide built-in income (or gain) upon maturity. Any kind of bond—corporate, municipal, or U.S. government—may sell at discount in the open market. The availability of such bonds and extent of the discounts depend on movements of interest rates. Rising interest rates—and hence, declining bond prices—tend to produce market discount bonds.

Tax Status of Market Discount Bonds

For taxable bonds issued after July 18, 1984, or for bonds issued on or before July 18, 1984, and purchased on the open market after April 30, 1993, any gain on sale, redemption, or maturity to the extent of accrued market discount will be taxed as ordinary interest income rather than capital gain.[3] Any gain in excess of this amount will be taxed as capital gain, and any loss will be treated as capital loss. (For other taxable bonds, accrued market discount on sale, redemption, or maturity will be taxed as capital gain.)

However, cash-basis bondholders may elect to include accrued market discount each year in their gross income and have it taxed then, rather than deferring taxation until sale, redemption, or maturity of the bond. Most bondholders will not make this election; however, it might be made if the bondholder has unused interest expense to carry investments that can only be deducted against investment income (e.g., taxable interest) or in certain other situations.

For tax-exempt obligations purchased after April 30, 1993, any gain on sale, redemption, or maturity to the extent of accrued market discount will be taxed as ordinary interest income rather than as capital gain.

Zero Coupon Bonds (Zeros)

General Characteristics

These are OID bonds sold without any stated coupon rate; hence, they pay no current interest income. They are sold originally at usually substantial discounts from par, and their return to the investor is measured by their yield to maturity. Zeros may be U.S. government bonds (taxable), corporate bonds

[3] There is a *de minimis* rule that ignores any market discount of less than one-quarter of 1 percent of the stated value at maturity times the number of years until maturity.

(taxable), or municipal bonds (tax exempt). The main advantage of zeros for investors is to lock in current interest rates for the duration of the bond.

Tax Status of Zero Coupon Bonds

For taxable bonds issued after July 1, 1982, an annual amount of accrued original issue discount (calculated by applying the bond's yield to maturity to an adjusted issue price) is currently taxable to the owner as ordinary interest income, even though the investor currently receives no cash income from the bonds.[4] This treatment of taxable zeros has caused them to be used almost entirely in tax-protected vehicles, such as IRAs, qualified retirement plans, variable annuities, and variable life insurance, because in these vehicles, otherwise taxable income is not taxed currently.

For tax-exempt zeros (municipal bonds), accrued OID is not included in gross income. It is tax exempt, just like interest on other tax-free munis. This treatment of tax-exempt zeros results in investors holding them directly, since the accrued OID is not taxable.

Preferred Stocks

Preferred stocks (or *preferreds*) represent equity capital of a corporation. The claim that preferred stockholders have against the assets of the corporation follows the claim of bondholders but precedes that of common stockholders. In almost all cases, a company must pay dividends on its preferred stock before paying anything on its common stock. However, a corporation can pass (omit) its preferred dividends without becoming insolvent. Thus, it is less risky for a corporation to issue preferred stock than bonds or some other debt instrument. On the other hand, the corporation cannot deduct preferred dividends for corporate income tax purposes, although it can deduct interest on bonds or other true indebtedness.

The dividend rate on preferred stock is usually fixed. When dividends are *cumulative,* any arrears of preferred dividends must be paid before dividends can be paid on the common stock. On the other hand, when dividends are noncumulative, common dividends can be paid even though preferred dividends have been omitted in the past and remain unpaid. Although preferreds typically do not have fixed maturities, they may be subject to call. Preferred

[4] There is a *de minimis* rule here, too, like that indicated in Footnote 3. Also, for OID bonds issued before July 2, 1982 (and after December 31, 1954), OID is included in gross income when the bond is sold, is redeemed, or matures.

stockholders normally do not have voting rights, but they may have them in some cases or under certain conditions. Some preferreds are convertible into common stock.

Guaranteed Principal Fixed-Income Investments

The types of fixed-income investments we have discussed so far provide guaranteed investment income and/or a promised value at maturity, but during the term of the investment (e.g., until a bond matures), the market price of the security can fluctuate, depending on market interest rates and other economic conditions.

The fixed-income investments we are now considering have both a guaranteed principal value throughout their term and certain guaranteed investment income. Such investments do not have any market risk or interest risk to their principal value. They may, however, have some financial risk in that their security (in the absence of government insurance) depends on the ability of the issuer to meet its financial commitments.

Certificates of Deposit (CDs)

Traditional Fixed-Dollar CDs These are interest-bearing, redeemable evidences of time deposits issued and sold through banks and savings institutions. They are sold in varying amounts and with maturities ranging from a few months to 10 years or more. The interest rate usually is fixed and guaranteed for the duration of the CD, with the rate normally being higher the longer the maturity. There is an interest penalty for early withdrawal if these CDs are redeemed prior to maturity, but any penalty is deductible by the investor from gross income to arrive at adjusted gross income. As of this writing, most CDs are insured up to $250,000 per eligible account through the FDIC. Also, an investor may purchase insured CDs up to $250,000 each from multiple banks and still be fully insured. Interest payable on CDs is fully taxable for federal and state purposes as ordinary interest income.

Negotiable CDs These are CDs that are not redeemable by the issuer before maturity but can be traded in a secondary market prior to maturity. If they are sold before maturity, the value received may be less (if market interest rates rise) or more (if market rates fall) than the face amount (purchase price). However, the full face amount is payable at maturity. In this sense, they are much like bonds. Negotiable CDs are issued by banks but usually sold through investment firms.

Market-Linked CDs Some banks issue CDs whose principal (original investment) is guaranteed by the issuer and often is insured up to $250,000 by the FDIC, but whose investment return is based on some equity index (like the S&P 500 stock index), provided the purchaser holds the CD until maturity. In other words, if the market goes up, the investor receives his or her original principal plus an investment return based on the appreciation of the applicable market index. If the market goes down, the investor is guaranteed to receive at least his or her original investment back. However, these CDs, which are often called *market-linked deposits* (MLDs), may not pay 100 percent of the original investment, or any investment income, if an investor withdraws from them prior to maturity.

A difficulty with MLDs is that the depositor does not receive any investment returns until maturity, but those gains are taxed currently as ordinary income. For this reason, MLDs are often considered for tax-protected accounts. Also, as of this writing, MLDs are not generally available.

Guaranteed-Dollar Life Insurance Cash Values

As noted in Chapters 9 and 21, the cash values of guaranteed-dollar life insurance contracts (traditional whole life, universal life, or interest-sensitive whole life) can be viewed as a guaranteed principal fixed-income investment.

Guaranteed-Dollar Annuity Cash Values

Guaranteed-dollar (or fixed-dollar) annuity cash values also can be considered guaranteed principal fixed-income investments. The characteristics of investment annuities are discussed in Chapter 17.

Stable Value Funds

These are investment options for employees under certain kinds of qualified retirement plans provided under a contract with a life insurance company or other financial institution. The issuer guarantees the principal and interest of the fund for the specified period. Employees should remember, however, that the security behind a stable value fund is the financial soundness of the company providing it.

Cash Equivalents (Liquid Assets)

Cash equivalents should be highly liquid (convertible into cash immediately with no loss of principal) and financially secure (low or no financial risk). On the other hand, these assets are short-term and tend to offer a lower yield than other fixed-income securities.[5] Investors may want liquid assets for possible emergencies, as security in times of severe economic uncertainty, to quickly take advantage of investment opportunities, as an investment strategy if interest rates are expected to rise significantly, or as a repository for cash while deciding on an investment or other large expenditure.

Some common types of cash-equivalent assets include:

- *Shorter-term CDs* (insured).
- *Bank savings accounts* (insured).
- *Money market funds.*
- *Treasury bills.*
- *Commercial paper.* These are short-term unsecured loans normally made to large creditworthy corporations. Commercial paper often is purchased by money market mutual funds.
- *Banker's acceptances.* These are time drafts usually used to finance international trade that are "accepted" (guaranteed) by a bank. They also are often purchased by money market mutual funds.
- *Eurodollars.* These are dollar-denominated accounts or CDs in Europe that are issued by foreign banks or foreign branches of U.S. banks.
- *Yankee CDs.* These are dollar-denominated accounts or CDs that are issued by branches of foreign banks in the United States.

Conversion Privileges in Fixed-Income Securities

Investors may consider whether to buy *convertible bonds* or *convertible preferred stocks,* which provide the security of a bond or a preferred, but also provide an opportunity for capital appreciation through anticipated appreciation of the underlying common stock. Convertible bonds and preferreds give the holder the right to convert the security into a certain number of shares of common stock at a predetermined price for the common.

But this opportunity is not free. The price effectively is the difference between the yield on a convertible bond or preferred and the yield on an

[5] This statement reflects the general principle that for a given quality of fixed-income investment, the yield will rise with duration. This may be referred to as a positive (or normal) yield curve. However, under certain economic conditions, this yield curve can be quite flat (with little or no difference in yields between shorter-term and longer-term securities of the same type) or even inverted (with shorter-term yields higher than longer-term yields). A flat or inverted yield curve may occur, for example, when investors generally believe that interest rates will fall significantly in the future and thus are seeking to lock in the present rates by buying (and hence bidding up the prices of) longer-term securities with adequate call protection (such as longer-term Treasury notes and bonds).

otherwise comparable nonconvertible security. Convertible securities generally are callable.

Bond Ratings and Investment Quality

Bonds issued or guaranteed by the U.S. government are considered the safest of investments. Other bonds have varying quality ratings in terms of financial risk.

Bond Rating Systems

To help investors assess the investment quality of many corporate and municipal bonds, bond ratings are published, periodically reviewed, and revised when needed by independent rating agencies. The two main rating agencies are Moody's and Standard & Poor's.[6] The corporate and municipal debt-rating systems of these two agencies are outlined in Table 7.2. These ratings consider the creditworthiness or financial ability to meet the specific obligations of the issuer of the particular bonds involved. Bonds with one of

Table 7.2. Bond Rating Systems

Quality	Standard & Poor's†	Moody's†
Investment grade:		
Highest quality*	AAA	Aaa
High quality	AA	Aa
Upper medium grade	A	A
Medium grade	BBB	Baa
Below investment grade:		
Moderately speculative*	BB	Ba
Speculative	B	B
Highly speculative	CCC	Caa
Lowest quality (including in default)	C, D	C

*These are abbreviated terms used to describe these rating systems and are not the complete descriptions used by the rating agencies themselves to describe their ratings.

†There may be subclasses within these letter ratings, designated as 2 or 3 by Moody's and + or – by Standard & Poor's.

[6] These agencies also rate many insurance companies for financial soundness or claims-paying ability. They also rate commercial paper.

the top four ratings from one or both agencies are often considered investment grade.[7] Bonds with lower ratings are considered by the rating agencies to have varying degrees of speculative elements.

High-Yield Bonds

High-yield, or *junk, bonds* generally are considered those with ratings below investment grade. As can be seen from Table 7.2, however, this can embrace a wide range of financial risk. Therefore, in evaluating high-yield bonds, the investor should consider the relative degrees of financial risk involved. In other words, some bonds are "junkier" than others. Of course, the spread between the yields on investment-grade bonds and high-risk bonds should be evaluated to see if the extra financial risk is worth it.

Bond Ratings and Yield

General Considerations A major question in high-yield investing is whether the higher yields on lower-quality bonds at least make up for the higher default rates on such bonds. Part of this question, of course, is what the real, long-term, average annual default rates are on bonds of lower quality. While a review of the research on this issue is beyond the scope of this book, it appears at this writing that no one really knows.

Diversification Issues Diversification seems to be the key idea in this area. First, to be a successful investor in high-risk bonds, it seems necessary to be reasonably diversified over a number of issues and perhaps maturities. The investor really has no way of knowing which particular bond or bonds may default. For investors with relatively small amounts of these bonds, mutual funds may be a logical answer to their diversification needs. It may also be desirable to invest only a small percentage of one's overall portfolio in high-risk bonds.

Strategies for Investing in Fixed-Income Securities

As the discussion in this chapter has unfolded, it can be seen that there are several areas where investors need to develop strategies with respect to the fixed-income portions of their overall asset allocations.

[7] Moody's judges bonds in its top two ratings to be of high quality.

Investment Duration Considerations

One approach to duration issues would be to adjust maturities, at least to some degree, with regard to expected changes in interest rates. As a rule, maturities should be lengthened when interest rates are expected to decline and should be shortened when interest rates are expected to rise. In this way, investors will have committed their funds at the present high rates, when future rates are expected to be lower, and will have funds available to commit later at the expected higher rates, when it is anticipated that interest rates will be higher. Of course, no one really knows which way interest rates will move in the future. On the other hand, investors can follow a *diversified approach* toward the maturity structure, such as laddering a bond portfolio.

Laddered Diversification to Deal with Interest Rate and Reinvestment Risks In view of the uncertainties concerning interest rates just noted, one possible approach for the risk-averse investor is to diversify the bond or bond-and-CD portion (the fixed-income portion) of the overall portfolio according to the maturity of the instruments in the portfolio. This is referred to as *laddering* a bond portfolio.

Thus, just as an example, the bond-and-CD portion of an investor's overall portfolio might be laddered, as shown in the table.

Maturity Range	Percentages of Bond-and-CD Portion of the Overall Fixed-Income Portfolio
1–5 years (short-term bonds or CDs)	33%
5–15 years (intermediate-term bonds)	33%
15–30 years (long-term bonds)	34%

With this kind of allocation, there would be some protection for the investor, no matter which way interest rates went. If market rates declined, the investor would benefit at the long end of the portfolio and be harmed only at the short end. The portion of the portfolio with longer maturities could provide a locked-in interest income stream and bond market prices would rise. However, for these benefits to remain, the securities at the long end should be noncallable or have reasonable call protection. (See the following section on "Strategies for Call Protection and Reinvestment Risk".) On the other hand, if interest rates rose, in terms of bond prices, the investor would not be greatly harmed at the short end of the portfolio and would be significantly harmed only at the long end, although there would be at least some bond price declines at all maturity levels. The values of any bank-distributed CDs would not change, except for possible interest penalties for early redemption. Furthermore, at the short end of the portfolio, there would be some bonds or CDs maturing each year whose maturity values then could be reinvested at the current higher rates.

The allocation of maturities in a portfolio could be periodically reviewed in light of the investor's expectations for future interest rates. If rates are expected to rise, relatively greater weight can be given to shorter maturities; the strategy can be reversed if rates are expected to decline. Or the investor can simply stick with a more balanced and longer-term allocation, as shown in the example, and not try to outguess the economy. This is an example of *immunizing a bond portfolio* against fluctuating interest rates.

Barbell Strategy A variation of this approach is the so-called *barbell strategy*. This essentially involves buying only short maturities and long maturities.

Taxable versus Nontaxable Considerations

Investors need to evaluate the relative after-tax attractiveness of taxable as compared to tax-exempt securities. This should be done considering federal, state, and local income taxes, particularly in states with high income taxes. The factors involved in this analysis were discussed earlier in this chapter.

Strategies for Call Protection and Reinvestment Risk

Investors also need to evaluate their exposure to interest rate and reinvestment risks. Some strategies for doing this have already been discussed (e.g., laddering). The following are some approaches investors can use to protect themselves from the call (or redeemability) risk:

- Investors can buy noncallable securities (such as U.S. Treasury notes and bonds). When municipal and corporate bonds are issued on a noncallable basis, they usually are for relatively shorter maturities. Zero coupon bonds may not be callable.
- They can buy securities with call protection.
- Investors can buy bonds or preferreds selling at a deep discount (market discount) from their maturity or par value. However, sometimes, such deep discount securities are scarce in the bond markets, and the investor normally must accept a lower yield on them than for comparable securities selling around par.
- Investors may be able to diversify their purchases over time so that only a small portion of the portfolio will be called at any one time.
- They may purchase high-quality, higher-yielding common stocks, which, of course, have no maturity date and are not callable. However, dividends on common stocks could be cut or eliminated by the corporation during "hard" economic times.

Investment-Quality Considerations

We have already discussed the relationship between yield and bond ratings, and have noted that there do not seem to be any pat answers. Much depends on an investor's personal circumstances, investment objectives, and tolerance for risk. On the other hand, modern portfolio theory tells us that if lower-quality bonds have low correlations with other asset categories in a portfolio, overall portfolio risk may not be increased (and may even be decreased) by the addition of high-return, high-financial-risk, but low-correlation bonds.

There can be a variety of strategies regarding investment quality. Highly risk-averse investors may decide to purchase only bonds rated in the top two or three grades according to Moody's or Standard & Poor's and U.S. Treasury notes and bonds or U.S. government-guaranteed or backed bonds, or to invest only in mutual funds or other financial intermediaries that have these investment objectives. In contrast, other investors may decide to allocate the bulk of their bond portfolio—say, 75 to 80 percent—only to such investment-grade securities, while allowing the balance to be in below-investment-grade bonds if market conditions and yield spreads seem propitious. At the other end of the scale, investors who are more aggressive may be willing to allocate a larger portion of the fixed-income part of their portfolio to higher-yield bonds when they think market conditions and yield spreads warrant it.

Overall Diversification Strategies

Investors should decide when and how they want to diversify their fixed-income investments. This might include diversification by maturities (laddering), by high-quality and high-yield issues, by investing in municipal securities, and by investing in a number of different issues.

8

Other Investment Companies and Alternative Investments

Competence Objectives for This Chapter After reading this chapter, planners should understand:

- The kinds of investment companies
- The advantages and limitations of mutual funds
- Distributions from and exchanges of mutual funds
- Mutual fund investment objectives
- The nature of index funds and exchange-traded funds (ETFs)
- The nature of tax-managed funds
- Measures of mutual fund performance
- The nature of mutual fund expenses
- Factors involved in selecting mutual funds
- Income tax aspects of mutual funds
- The nature of hedge funds and private equity funds as "alternative investments"

Kinds of Investment Companies

In popular usage, the term *mutual fund* often is used to refer to any kind of investment company. Actually, however, there are three basic kinds of investment companies: those that sell *face-amount certificates* (the issuer promises to pay the investor a stated amount at maturity or a surrender value if tendered early), those that sell *unit investment trusts* (the fund invests in a fixed portfolio of securities), and so-called *management companies*. The most important of these are the management companies, which, in turn, can be classified as *closed-end funds* and open-end, or *mutual funds.* The open-end or mutual fund is, by far, the most important variety.

Why Invest in Mutual Funds?

A number of advantages are given for investing in mutual funds. First, by pooling their investable capital, persons investing smaller amounts are able to enjoy a degree of diversification they could never achieve on their own. Second, mutual funds may offer experienced professional managers to select and manage the securities in which the funds' resources will be invested. And, third, mutual funds offer convenience and ready marketability through the funds' obligation to redeem their shares. Furthermore, funds provide investors with reasonable investment unit size so that many persons can invest through them. In addition, fund distributions normally can be reinvested systematically and investors' holdings can usually be liquidated systematically.

Limitations of Mutual Funds

As with any financial intermediary, there are costs associated with investing through mutual funds. Expenses vary among funds, as discussed later in this chapter. Second, investors still must find those funds whose investment objectives are consistent with their own and whose performance and costs are satisfactory. Thus, the investor still has a selection issue, even though the choice of individual investments is transferred to the fund's management. Also, investors who want to make their own investment selections for part or all of their portfolios would not use investment intermediaries for this. Finally, as noted in Chapter 2, investment companies are essentially pass-through entities for tax purposes. Hence, investors often have capital gains distributions from their funds that they cannot control.

Types of Funds and Planning Considerations

Open-End Funds

A mutual fund is, by definition, an open-end investment company. They are called *open-end* because the number of outstanding shares is not fixed. Instead, the number of shares is continually changing as investors purchase or redeem shares. When people buy shares in an open-end fund, they buy them from the fund itself. And when they want to redeem shares, the fund must stand ready to buy them back. The price for purchase or redemption is based on the most recent net asset value (NAV) of the shares. NAV per share is the total value of all securities and other assets held by the fund, minus any fund liabilities, divided by the number of outstanding shares. It is calculated daily.

Closed-End Funds

A closed-end investment company is similar in many respects to a typical corporation. It issues a fixed number of shares, which does not fluctuate except as new stock is issued. The company can issue bonds and preferred stock to leverage the position of the common shareholders. The closed-end fund uses its capital and other resources primarily to invest in the securities of other corporations.

The shares of closed-end funds are bought and sold in the market, just like the stock of other corporations. The price for closed-end shares is determined by supply and demand in the market and is not tied directly to a fund's NAV per share. When the market price of a fund's shares exceeds its NAV, the fund is said to sell *at a premium.* On the other hand, when the stock price is less than a fund's NAV, it is said to sell *at a discount.* At any given time, some closed-end funds may sell at a premium while others sell at a discount.

Open-End versus Closed-End Funds

It is debatable as to which fund is better; there are no pat answers. But here are some things to consider.

First, both types provide professional investment management, diversification, and periodic distributions of investment income and capital gains to investors. They both are readily marketable, but in different ways—an open-end fund through redemption of its shares by the fund itself and a closed-end fund by sale of its shares on the open market. There are many more open-end funds than closed-end funds from which to choose, and open-end funds often are sold by sales representatives or brokers who handle mutual funds.

When an investor buys or sells a closed-end fund, he or she pays stock market commissions and other costs. Sales charges paid for mutual fund shares depend in part on whether it is a *load* or *no-load fund,* as described next. What fund shares are worth at any given time is determined differently. In the case of a mutual fund, it is the NAV of the fund shares at that time; for a closed-end fund, it is the price on the stock market at that time. Investors cannot buy a mutual fund for less than its NAV per share, but they frequently can buy a closed-end fund at a discount or at a premium.

Load and No-Load Mutual Funds

Open-end funds are sold on either a load or a no-load basis. A *load* generally refers to the sales charge levied on an investor by a fund for executing a transaction.

A common arrangement is when the investor pays the charge when purchasing shares but then pays no charge when redeeming them. This is referred to as a *front-end load* (or class A shares). Front-end loads might range from 4 to 8.5 percent of the offering price, but generally are about 4 to 5 percent.[1] Thus, when a load fund is purchased, the investor pays the net asset value plus the load. No-load funds traditionally do not charge a sales commission (load) when the shares are purchased or redeemed. Thus, both transactions occur at the fund's NAV per share.

Some funds levy what are called *12b-1 fees* or level loads (referred to as class C shares). These are annual sales fees taken against fund assets to reimburse the fund for distribution and servicing costs.

Other funds charge a contingent-deferred sales fee (called a *back-end load*) if shares are redeemed within a few years of their purchase or at any time (called class B shares). These fees may or may not decline over time. Finally, some funds are known as *low-load* funds because they charge lower loads (3 percent or less) at purchase.

Open-end fund values and prices are given daily in the financial pages of many newspapers and online. Prices are quoted on the NAV basis and an offering price (offer) basis. Any spread between the NAV and the offering price is the load. For a no-load fund, the quoted NAV and the offering price would be the same.

For load funds, the percentage load is normally reduced as an investor makes larger dollar purchases. The purchase amounts at which the percentage sales charge declines are called *breakpoints.* Also, an investor may be entitled to an *accumulation discount* or *right of accumulation* based on previous fund purchases. Thus, all fund shares held at the time an additional purchase is made may be taken into account in determining the sales load.

In addition to the sales loads of load funds and any annual 12b-1 sales fees, both load and no-load funds charge investment management fees and other expenses annually as a percentage of the fund's net assets. These annual fees are referred to as a fund's *expense ratio.*

Assuming an investor has decided to invest in mutual funds, he or she should consider whether to buy a load fund or a no-load fund. This is a controversial question; again, there are no pat answers. The greater part of the load paid by investors is received as a commission by the sales representative

[1] Note that this results in a slightly higher percentage load based on the net amount actually invested (i.e., the offering price minus the sales load, or the NAV per share). The NASD limits the loads mutual funds can charge. The limit on front-end loads is 8.5 percent and the limit on 12b-1 fees for load funds is 1 percent.

or broker. No-load funds frequently are not sold through sales representatives. Their shares normally are purchased and redeemed directly through the fund itself.[2] Thus, no-load funds avoid the sales representative's commission. On the other hand, the mutual fund purchaser loses the advice and sales efforts of the representative.

Unit Investment Trusts

Unit investment trusts (UITs) are registered investment companies that generally buy and hold a relatively fixed portfolio of stocks, bonds, or other securities until termination of the UIT. Thus, a UIT does not actively manage the investment portfolio over its lifetime. UITs also have a stated date for termination, which is not usually the case for other investment companies. UITs can have a number of different types of investments, such as corporate bonds, equities, mortgage-backed securities, municipal bonds, U.S. government securities, and others. Investors may redeem their UIT units from the trust at any time for their NAV.

UITs may or may not charge a sales load. Their annual expenses (expense ratios) generally are low. Since they have a relatively fixed portfolio, there are few or no investment management fees. Also, their transaction costs are low, and since there is virtually no turnover of investments in their portfolios, investors' taxes are kept low. Thus, for investors who want diversification and initial portfolio selection but who do not want continuing active portfolio management, UITs may be attractive because of their lower costs. Most UITs have been municipal bond funds.

Regulation of Investment Companies

Investment companies are primarily regulated under federal securities laws. As noted in Chapter 2, sales of shares or units are regulated under the Securities Act of 1933 and the Securities Exchange Act of 1934. A prospectus must be delivered to investors who purchase shares or units. The companies' day-by-day operations and structures are regulated under the Investment Company Act of 1940. Furthermore, fund investment managers are governed by the Investment Advisers Act of 1940. The SEC administers these federal laws. There may also be state securities regulations.

[2] Brokerage houses through which load funds channel their business are generally willing to handle transactions for affiliated no-load funds.

How to Invest in Mutual Funds

There are a number of ways to invest in mutual funds, including outright purchase; various accumulation plans; reinvestment of dividends and realized capital gains payable from the fund; and through certain insurance products, such as variable annuities and variable life insurance. Mutual funds are also frequently held in tax-advantaged retirement accounts and education accounts.

It was noted previously that for load funds (i.e., class A shares), the front-end load may be reduced (i.e., discounts given) for large purchases of fund shares. These discounts (called breakpoint discounts) often begin at purchases of around $50,000, but this varies among load funds. For example, a fund may have a normal front-end load of 5 percent, but the load is reduced to 4½ percent for purchases of $50,000, to 4 percent for purchases of $100,000, and by further discounts for larger purchases. Thus, these breakpoint discounts can be significant for load fund investors.

Some planning approaches investors can take to help reach breakpoints, depending on the rules of the particular fund or funds, include:

- The right of accumulation (already discussed) which allows past fund purchases to count in reaching a breakpoint.
- Letters of intent. In this case, the investor signs a letter of intent that he or she will purchase a certain amount of shares over a specified period (such as 13 months) and receives the appropriate breakpoint discount for the investor's actual periodic purchases over this time.
- Counting purchases by other family members (e.g., spouse and children) of the investor in the same fund family.
- Counting purchases by the investor for different accounts, such as outright purchase, 401(k) plans, IRAs, and education savings accounts.

Withdrawals from and Redemptions and Exchanges of Mutual Funds

Mutual funds may offer *systematic withdrawal plans* to investors. An investor, for example, might establish a plan to pay a periodic amount to himself or herself, such as $4,000 per month, as long as there are fund shares to do so. Remember, however, that such a systematic withdrawal plan is not the same as a life annuity. The periodic payments are not guaranteed for the investor's or a spouse's lifetime. Also, if an investor cashes in fund shares (either for periodic payments under a withdrawal plan or otherwise), he or she may have a capital gain or loss for income tax purposes, depending on whether the fund shares have appreciated or depreciated in value.

Management companies that handle several mutual funds (a *family* of funds) often permit investors to exchange all or part of their shares in one fund for those in another fund or funds they manage at net asset value. Thus, an investor who may have purchased shares in a growth stock fund during his or her working years might exchange them for shares in an income fund at retirement. Such an exchange, however, will be considered a sale or exchange of a capital asset for income tax purposes and, hence, normally will result in the investor's realizing and recognizing a capital gain or loss at that time. Furthermore, load funds may require the investor to pay any difference in the sales loads between the fund the investor had and the one into which he or she is exchanging shares. Exchange fees also may be involved, but they often are waived. Finally, funds may place other restrictions on this exchange privilege to avoid excessive trading by investors.

Mutual Funds and Their Investment Objectives

There are mutual funds to meet just about any investment goal. A fund's investment objective and policies are described in its prospectus.

Equity Funds

Equity funds invest their assets in common stocks and corresponding assets. They may include the following categories.

Growth Funds The primary objective of these funds is capital appreciation rather than current dividend income. Growth funds hold the common stocks of more established, larger growth-type companies.

Aggressive Growth Funds Again, the primary investment objective is capital appreciation. However, the investment policies tend to be more aggressive and riskier than the growth funds. These funds may hold common stocks in startup companies, newer industries, and turnaround situations, as well as regular growth-type stocks. They also may use other investment techniques, such as option writing.

Growth and Income Funds These funds are in the category referred to as *total return funds.* They invest in common stocks of well-established companies that are expected to show reasonable growth of principal and income and that pay reasonable current dividends. Their risk level is moderate.

Income-Equity Funds These are another type of total return fund. They tend to invest in common stocks of companies with stable and good dividend returns. The emphasis is on secure and reasonable dividend yields and not on capital appreciation. Risk tends to be relatively low.

Option-Income Funds These funds also invest in dividend-paying common stocks, but they seek to maximize current return by writing call options on the stock they hold.

International Equity Funds These funds invest mainly in the stocks of foreign companies.

Global Equity Funds These funds invest in the common stocks of both foreign and U.S. companies.

Small-Stock (Small-Cap) Funds As the name implies, the objective of these funds is to invest in common stocks of smaller, lesser-known companies. Some argue that over the years small-cap stocks have generally performed better than their larger-cap brethren have but are more volatile. This has been shown in the historical yield studies described in Chapter 5. Mutual funds seem to be a particularly appropriate vehicle for investing in smaller stocks, because most investors probably do not have the time, knowledge, or resources to evaluate a large number of lesser-known companies.

Precious Metals Funds The investment objective here is to invest primarily in the common stocks of gold-mining companies and companies that produce other precious metals. These stocks can be viewed as surrogates for holding gold or other precious metals directly, since the prices of these stocks tend to move with the market prices of the precious metals they produce rather than with the stock market in general. Thus, investors can use these funds for any gold or precious metals component of their asset allocation, if they desire such a component.

Sector Funds These funds invest in common stocks of companies in particular fields or industries, such as financial services, health care, science and technology, natural resources, utilities, and so forth. They give investors an opportunity to concentrate their holdings in fields they view as attractive.

Hybrid Funds

These funds maintain a diversified portfolio in terms of kinds of investment media.

Asset Allocation Funds Funds of this type are required to maintain a fixed weighting (asset allocation) of stocks, bonds, and perhaps money market instruments. Thus, they may enable investors to implement an asset allocation strategy largely through the purchase of one mutual fund, rather than through several funds or other assets. One mutual fund group, for example, maintains four separate asset allocation funds, ranging from one with a growth orientation (80 percent stocks and 20 percent bonds) to one designed mainly for income (20 percent stocks, 60 percent bonds, and 20 percent cash reserves).

Balanced Funds The investment approach of these funds is to have a diversified portfolio of common stocks, preferred stocks, and bonds. The asset allocation of these investment media will be indicated in the fund's prospectus or elsewhere, and may change, depending on the investment policies of the fund's management. The objectives of these funds are to conserve principal, pay reasonable current income, and achieve long-term growth in principal and income consistent with the prior two objectives. They differ from asset allocation funds in that they do not maintain a fixed weighting of asset classes.

Flexible Portfolio Funds These funds differ from balanced funds mainly in that they may change their asset allocation more rapidly and may hold up to 100 percent of their assets in only one type of asset at any given time.

Income-Mixed Funds The investment objective of these funds is high current income. This is achieved by investing in good dividend-paying common stocks and corporate and government bonds.

Taxable Bond Funds

These funds invest primarily in taxable bonds of various kinds, depending on the investment objective of the particular fund. It may be noted that when an investor invests in bonds through a mutual fund or other pooled intermediaries, rather than owning the bonds directly, there is no fixed maturity date for the mutual fund shareholder. The NAV of the bond-fund shares fluctuates with the current market prices of the bonds in its portfolio.

U.S. Treasury Bond Funds These funds invest primarily in U.S. Treasury bonds. They are, therefore, viewed as completely safe in terms of financial risk, while their interest rate risk depends on their average duration. As noted earlier, U.S. Treasury bonds normally are not callable prior to maturity. In terms of duration, U.S. Treasury bond funds can have varying maturities, such as short-term, intermediate-term, and long-term. Such funds can be used to diversify a bond portfolio by duration and to provide call protection.

U.S. Government Income Funds These funds seek a somewhat higher yield by investing in a variety of U.S. Treasury bonds, federally guaranteed securities, and other government securities.

Ginnie Mae (Government National Mortgage Association) Funds As the name implies, these funds are invested mainly in government-backed, mortgage-backed securities.

Corporate Bond Funds The objective of some corporate bond funds is to invest in a diversified portfolio of high-quality bonds. In this case, the fund's financial risk is low and its interest rate risks depend on the bonds' maturities and call protection. Maturities can be short-term, intermediate-term, or long-term.

High-Yield (High-Risk or Junk) Bond Funds The objective of these funds is to secure a higher yield by accepting the greater financial risk of buying lower-quality bonds. However, not all high-yield bond funds are equally risky. They vary in the average quality of the bonds in their portfolios and the levels of their cash reserves.

Income Bond Funds These funds invest in a combination of corporate bonds and government bonds for greater yield.

International Bond Funds These funds invest in the bonds of foreign companies, foreign governments, or both. The market prices of the bonds are expressed in the currencies of the foreign countries whose bonds are held by the fund. Thus, as the value of these countries' currencies changes in relation to the dollar, so will the share value of these funds expressed in dollars. As a result, there can be three kinds of investment risk in these funds: financial risk, interest rate risk, and currency risk. Thus, purchase of these funds enables investors to take an indirect position in foreign currencies and diversify their portfolios in terms of currencies. (Of course, an investor could buy directly one or more foreign currencies or purchase some mutual funds that invest in foreign currencies.) This currency exposure is also present in international stock funds and, in varying degrees, in global equity funds and global bond funds. Some international bond funds seek to hedge against this currency risk in various ways. In this case, investors may not have full exposure to currency fluctuations.

Global Bond Funds These funds invest in bonds of foreign companies and countries as well as in those originating in the United States.

Municipal Bond Funds

National Municipal Bond Funds These funds invest in the bonds and other securities issued by states, cities, and other municipalities throughout the nation. In terms of duration, there are long-term, intermediate-term, and short-term funds. There are also funds that invest only in investment-grade municipal securities, while others may buy lower-quality (junk) municipals.

State Municipal Bond Funds These are municipal bond funds that invest only in the securities of a particular state. This enables the residents of that state to buy a fund for their state only and thus have tax-free interest income from the fund for federal, state, and local income tax purposes.

Money Market Mutual Funds

General Considerations These funds are highly secure, liquid investments that frequently are used by investors for the cash portion of their portfolios. They are generally viewed as cash equivalents because the mutual fund management companies selling their shares expect and intend to be able to redeem them at all times at a fixed value, normally $1 per share. Many money market funds also offer investors check-writing privileges. Thus, these funds are intended to be safe, liquid, and convenient. They also typically provide higher yields than bank money market accounts.

However, there is no guarantee that the shares of money market mutual funds will be redeemed at the fixed value or par. It is possible that a fund's expense ratio or poor investments could result in its not redeeming its shares at par. Thus, investors should pay attention to the expense ratios and the nature and quality of the underlying short-term assets of money market mutual funds. Bank money market accounts, on the other hand, technically are accounts in the bank that, as of this writing, are insured up to $250,000 per eligible account by the FDIC.

Taxable Money Market Funds The dividends paid by these funds are gross income to shareholders for federal income tax purposes and perhaps for state and local income taxes as well. Some taxable funds invest only in direct *U.S. Treasury obligations.* These would be the safest in terms of financial risk. Others invest in *U.S. Treasury obligations and other obligations guaranteed by the U.S. government or its agencies.* Still others invest in a *variety of money market investments,* such as CDs, commercial paper, and bankers' acceptances.

Tax-Exempt Money Market Funds The dividends paid by these funds generally are excluded from shareholders' gross income for federal income tax purposes and may be excluded for state and local income tax purposes. These funds may be national tax-exempt money market funds or state tax-exempt money market funds.

Index Funds

Active versus Passive Investment Management

The mutual funds we have considered thus far are *actively managed funds.* That is, fund managers attempt to select investments that will show superior results and outperform their particular benchmark indexes.

However, a newer concept in mutual funds is for a fund's portfolio to duplicate or track a specific group or index of securities. These are *index funds.* They are considered *passively managed* because the fund manager does not attempt to pick individual securities but only to track the outside index.

General Considerations

Index funds can invest in common stocks, bonds, and other securities, but they generally have been common stock funds. They can be based on a variety of indexes, such as Standard & Poor's (S&P) 500 (consisting of large-company stocks), the Wilshire 5000 (generally all stocks traded in the U.S. stock markets), the Wilshire 4500 (the Wilshire 5000 minus the S&P 500), the Russell 2000 (small-cap stocks traded in the U.S. stock markets), and various international indexes, such as the EAFE® (stocks from Europe, Australia, and the Far East).

Rationale for Index Funds

Several arguments have been advanced in favor of index funds.

Cost Index funds have significantly lower expense ratios than actively managed funds. Since they are passively managed, their investment management and research expenses are much lower. Furthermore, since they have a low turnover of securities, their transaction costs are low.

Alleged Difficulty in Beating the Market Commentators have suggested that, as a practical matter, it is difficult for a managed fund (or for other investors) consistently to outperform the overall market for any sustained period. Also, actively managed funds, in some cases, may not even perform as well as the overall market. Therefore, the argument goes, one might just as well invest with the overall market or a part of it and reap the advantage of lower costs of index funds. This argument, of course, fits well with the efficient market hypothesis discussed in Chapter 4.

Tax Considerations Since index funds have low turnover, there are relatively few sales of stocks by the fund and hence, relatively low capital gains being passed through to shareholders. This tax advantage essentially applies to any fund or security portfolio with low turnover.

Limitations of Index Funds

Naturally, arguments against index funds also exist.

Alleged Superior Investment Performance of Actively Managed Funds Proponents of actively managed funds argue that their particular fund will outperform the overall market, as some in fact have. Thus, the counterargument goes, their superior performance will more than justify any increased costs. This is the crux of the argument. An investor can evaluate this argument by analyzing past comparable performance over a substantial period for the particular actively managed fund or funds and the index fund or funds being considered. Of course, as with any analysis of past performance, investors must recognize that it may not be repeated in the future.

Loss of Investor Selection Some investors like to select among actively managed mutual funds to try to identify the better performers. Also, investors may want to buy some actively managed sector funds in areas or industries they view as particularly attractive.

Market Risks By their nature, stock index funds are fully invested in equities at all times because they simply mirror a stock index. During bull markets, this will result in good returns. However, during market declines or bear markets, the reverse may be true, since the index fund will remain in the market. Actively managed funds, on the other hand, may hold varying proportions of their assets in cash or other securities, depending on their view of market conditions and their investment objectives.

Exchange-Traded Funds (ETFs)

Unlike mutual funds, the newer ETFs are traded on an organized exchange, bought and sold through brokerage firms that charge commissions, and their market prices may be more or less than the NAV of the securities in the ETF. The market prices of ETF shares are determined by the values of the securities in the fund, as well as supply and demand conditions in the stock market for fund shares. Their market prices should be reasonably close to underlying fund values, but there is no assurance of that. ETFs are not redeemable from the funds, as are mutual funds. The arguments made for ETFs are that they have continual pricing, can be traded through limit orders, can be sold short, and can be bought on margin. They also may have lower operating costs. ETFs generally are index funds and so, in effect, can be used to "short the market" if that is desired.

The original ETFs were index funds and so share the advantages and limitations just cited for index funds in general. Most of the ETFs today are still index funds. Some track broad indexes (like the S&P 500), but others track narrower-sector indexes. A few actively managed ETFs have recently been created.

Tax-Managed Funds

Another newer concept is the tax-managed mutual fund. These funds operate with the objective of minimizing the impact of income taxes on the investment returns to their shareholders. Dividends and interest received and capital gains realized by mutual funds each year are passed through and taxable to the shareholders. The mutual fund itself pays no income taxes. Tax-managed funds follow investment policies intended to minimize this impact on shareholders. Such policies might include the following:

- *Minimizing the realization and distribution of capital gains.* This essentially involves a buy-and-hold approach that minimizes portfolio turnover.
- *Emphasizing lower current yielding securities.* Current dividends are taxable each year to shareholders. Hence, they are deemphasized. This tends to favor a long-term growth-type approach.
- *Adopting a tax-efficient selling selection policy.* When these funds sell appreciated securities for investment reasons, they seek to sell particular lots of securities that will produce long-term capital gains (as opposed to short-term gains) and that have the highest income tax bases (thereby reducing the long-term gains). They also seek to offset gains by realizing capital losses on other securities in the same year, when feasible.
- *Meeting shareholder redemptions by distributing appreciated securities in kind.* Some funds may follow this policy.

It is noteworthy that these policies can be employed just as effectively by individual investors managing their own investment portfolios tax efficiently.

Other Types of Funds

One specialized type of fund is the dual fund. A *dual fund* is organized as a closed-end investment company and is really two funds in one. Dual funds are based on the premise that some investors are interested exclusively in capital gains, while others are interested only in income. Thus, half of a dual fund's shares are sold as capital shares and the other half as income shares. The capital shares benefit from any capital appreciation of the entire fund, while the income shares receive all the income.

Mutual Fund Performance

Several areas of performance should be of interest to investors.

Administrative Performance

One area is the investment management fees and other administrative costs to the investor. This is generally evaluated by expressing total operating expenses as a percentage of a fund's net assets (the *expense ratio*) or as a percentage of fund income (the *income ratio*).

Investment Performance

A commonly used measure of investment performance is to analyze the *total return* (annual income dividends paid, realized capital gain distributions, and price fluctuations of the fund's shares) over a period. For example, assume a fund's purchase price at the beginning of a period—say, a year—is $40 and at the end of the year is $42. Also, assume the fund paid $1.00 in annual income dividends and had $1.80 in realized capital gain distributions for the year. In this case, the fund's total return for the year would be $4.80. Assuming the investor did not redeem the shares at the end of the year, $1.00 of this total return would be taxable to the shareholder as ordinary income or qualified dividends and $1.80 would be taxable as either short-term or long-term capital gains (depending on how long the fund held the securities sold).[3] Thus, in this example, the before-tax total return for the year, based on the original purchase price, would be 12 percent ($4.80 ÷ $40 = 0.12 or 12 percent).

Funds usually show total return performance data over several periods, such as 1 year, 3 years, 5 years, and 10 years. Longer periods probably are more

[3] The change in the fund's share price would not be subject to income taxation until the shareholder actually redeemed the shares. At that time, the total change would be a short-term or long-term capital gain or short-term or long-term capital loss, depending on how long the shareholder held the fund shares redeemed and whether there was a gain or loss at redemption. Of course, if the fund shares were held in a tax-protected vehicle, like an IRA or Section 401(k) plan, there would be no income taxation until distributions are taken from the tax-protected plan, and then they would be taxed as ordinary income (except for Roth IRAs).

meaningful for comparison purposes, since one- or even three-year periods may include unusual years, either up or down.

One way in which funds show total return performance is *cumulative total return* (as a percentage of initial share value) over a given period. This is the total change in the value of the fund's shares over the period, assuming reinvestment of income dividends and capital gain distributions.

Another common way to show total performance is *average annual compound rate of total return* (usually called *average annual total return*) over the period. This is the same rate of total return concept explained in Chapter 4. It is the compound level rate of return required each year to cause the initial share value to equal the share value at the end of the period, assuming reinvestment of income dividends and capital gain distributions. It is an internal rate of return (IRR) concept. These figures for cumulative total percentage return and average annual compound rate of total return for a particular fund often are compared with similar data for other indexes and averages. In the case of load funds, these performance measures can be *load-adjusted* to reflect the fund's sales charges. Such an adjustment can substantially reduce one-year returns, but it tends to diminish in importance over longer periods.

To illustrate these concepts, Table 8.1 shows performance data from the prospectus of a load-growth stock mutual fund for various periods.

It can be seen from this illustration that when a longer time horizon is used (such as 10 years), differences among the performances being compared narrow considerably. This also often is true for mutual funds in general.

Table 8.1. Performance Data from the Prospectus of a Load-Growth Stock Mutual Fund

Average Annual Total Returns (%)	**1 Year**	**Over the Past 5 Years**	**10 Years**
This fund	9.11%	14.92%	13.79%
This fund (load-adjusted)*	5.84	14.22	13.44
Lipper growth funds (average)	11.76	13.09	11.33
S&P 500 Stock Index	19.82	16.42	13.37
Cumulative Total Returns (%)			
This fund	9.11%	100.45%	263.91%
This fund (load-adjusted)*	5.84	94.44	252.99
Lipper growth funds (average)	11.76	87.43	203.06
S&P 500 Stock Index	19.82	113.93	251.11

*This fund has a 3 percent front-end load.

Tax-managed funds and other funds may show average annual total returns on a before-tax and an after-tax basis.[4] For example, one tax-managed growth stock mutual fund showed the following comparison for a 10-year period:

Average annual total returns (before shareholder taxes):
This tax-managed growth fund: 14.9%
Average of 190 growth funds: 13.5%

Average annual total returns (after assumed shareholder taxes):
This tax-managed growth fund: 14.2%
Average of 190 growth funds: 10.9%

It may be noted in the above that comparisons were made between the particular fund and other averages or indexes (Lipper growth funds average and S&P 500 Stock Index in Table 8.1) and the average of 190 growth funds for the tax-managed fund. These comparison averages and indexes are called *benchmarks* and are commonly used in mutual fund performance comparisons.

Volatility Various measures of volatility of mutual fund share prices are used. These include the beta, R-squared, alpha, and standard deviation. They are described in Chapter 4.

Considerations in Evaluating Investment Performance

Mutual fund investment performance data should be evaluated before investing in a fund. However, certain cautions are in order in making such evaluations. First, comparisons should be made based on several years' performance, such as 5, 10, or even 20 years. Be careful, too, about evaluating performance only during good times. Second, it is important to consider investment objectives of a fund. For example, a balanced fund should do better than a growth fund in a declining market, while the opposite should be true in a sharply advancing market. Also, consider the risks of market volatility involved.

Mutual Fund Expense Ratios

Fund expenses are required to be summarized and illustrated at the beginning of each fund's prospectus. The following summary of expenses for a load-growth stock fund is given only as an illustration.

[4] Such comparisons, of course, require assumptions concerning taxes and tax rates. In this example, the highest historical individual federal income tax rates were assumed. State and local income taxes and any taxes due on redemption of shares were ignored.

Summary of fund expenses:

A. Shareholder buying and selling expenses:
Sales charge on purchases (the front-end load for a low load mutual fund): 3.00%
Sales charge on reinvested distributions: None
Deferred sales charge on redemptions (the back-end load used by some funds): None
Exchange fee (imposed by some funds for exchanges into another fund within a family of mutual funds): None

B. Annual fund operating expenses (as percentage of average net assets):
Management fee (investment management fees generally charged by mutual funds): 0.45%
12b-1 fee (sales and marketing fees charged by some mutual funds instead of or in addition to any front-end sales load): None
Other expenses (such as administrative or servicing fees): 0.21%
Total fund operating expenses: 0.66%

The *expense ratio* of the fund illustrated is 0.66 percent. Expense ratios vary considerably among funds. They should be evaluated in conjunction with a fund's overall investment performance over a significant period.

Transaction Costs

These are the costs incurred by the fund in buying and selling securities for its portfolio, such as brokerage charges. Transaction costs are not included in a fund's published expense ratio. They are deducted from fund assets and so are an additional annual expense for the shareholders. They are not disclosed to shareholders in fund reports, but a fund's turnover rate is disclosed. They are directly related to fund turnover, as noted next.

Factors Involved in Selecting Mutual Funds

Here are some ideas that may be helpful in this important choice of selecting mutual funds:

- Determine whether the fund's objectives, investment style, and investment policies generally coincide with the investor's objectives and asset allocation strategy.
- Decide whether the investor wants an actively managed fund or a passively managed index fund.

- Consider the fund's past performance in light of its objectives.
- Ascertain the qualifications and experience of the people managing the fund's portfolio. The tenure of the portfolio manager (how long the manager has been managing the fund) also is significant.
- Briefly look over the securities in the fund's portfolio to see how well selected they seem to be.
- If it is a load fund, consider its sales charges to see how they compare with those of similar funds.
- Consider the fund's annual operating expenses (expense ratio) in comparison to those of similar funds and in light of fund performance.
- Consider the shareholder services the fund will make available to investors, including the right of accumulation, available investment plans, systematic withdrawal plans, and any exchange privilege.
- Remember that funds normally are considered long-term investments. Therefore, do not be too concerned with strictly short-term changes in fund values.
- Consider the fund's turnover rate for its portfolio. The turnover rate is calculated by dividing the smaller of the fund's total purchases or total sales of securities by its average monthly assets. A turnover rate of 100 percent, for example, means the fund has sold and replaced 100 percent in value of its assets during the year. A high turnover rate may mean the fund will have large capital gain distributions, and hence tax liabilities, for its shareholders. It also will increase transaction costs for the fund. And finally, it implies an active investment management style.
- Look out for style slippage in fund investment policies. Style slippage exists when a difference develops between the investment style or policies proclaimed by a fund and those actually followed. As a practical matter, this may be difficult for an investor to detect.
- Consider how long the fund has been in existence. Recent funds have not had much time to develop a track record for investors to consider.
- Consider any minimum investment amounts required by the fund.

Tax Aspects of Mutual Funds

Mutual funds are taxed as regulated investment companies, as noted in Chapter 2. Thus, funds pay out investment income to shareholders as various kinds of dividends, and the shareholders report those dividends on their tax returns as taxable or nontaxable, depending on the nature of the dividends. The fund itself pays no tax and operates essentially on a pass-through basis.

Types of Distributions for Tax Purposes

There are several kinds of such dividends: ordinary income dividends from the fund's net ordinary investment income and short-term capital gains, qualified dividend income, tax-exempt interest dividends (provided at least 50 percent of the fund's assets are in tax-exempt securities), and capital gains dividends (as long-term capital gains to the fund, regardless of how long the shareholder owned the fund's shares). Ordinary income dividends and qualified dividends are taxed to shareholders, tax-exempt interest dividends are not included in shareholders' gross income (except for AMT purposes in the case of certain private activity municipal bonds), and capital gains dividends are taxed as capital gains of shareholders in the year they are received.

Dividends that are automatically reinvested in additional fund shares are treated as constructively received by the shareholder and are taxed currently to the shareholder. However, if mutual fund shares are used as the investment medium for a plan that itself is tax sheltered (e.g., an IRA), the net investment income and capital gains dividends are not taxable until paid out from the tax-sheltered plan. The same, of course, would be true for any investments used in such plans.

Redemptions and Exchanges of Mutual Fund Shares

The preceding discussion dealt with taxation of distributions to shareholders of the investment income of funds. However, a mutual fund shareholder may have a taxable capital gain or a capital loss in the event he or she sells, exchanges, or redeems his or her mutual fund shares.

> **CASE EXAMPLE**
> Suppose Harry Wilson invested $10,000 in a growth stock mutual fund 15 years ago and all dividends were automatically reinvested. The shares are now worth $55,000; Harry's income tax basis in them (the initial $10,000 purchase price plus the dollar amount of the reinvested dividends) is $17,000. Harry is planning to retire and would now like to pursue a more conservative asset allocation approach. Therefore, he is planning to exchange his growth stock fund for shares in a growth and income fund maintained in the same family of funds. The fund permits such exchanges without another sales load and with no exchange fees. However, this exchange of one fund for another is a sale or *exchange* of a capital asset for capital gains tax purposes and results in a long-term capital gain in this case. Therefore, Harry has an amount realized of $55,000 and an adjusted income

tax basis of $17,000, which results in a long-term capital gain realized and recognized in the year of the exchange of $38,000 ($55,000 – $17,000 = $38,000). The result would be the same had Harry exchanged his growth fund for any other mutual fund or had redeemed his shares from the fund. But if the growth stock fund were inside a plan that is tax sheltered—say, an HR-10 plan or a rollover IRA—the exchange (or a redemption) would not result in any capital gains tax. Instead, the assets would be taxable as ordinary income when they are finally distributed from the tax-sheltered plan.

Income Tax Basis of Fund Shares

When a mutual fund shareholder sells, redeems, or exchanges all of the shares he or she owns, the total income tax basis of the shares is used to calculate any capital gain or loss, as just illustrated. If a shareholder acquires all of his or her shares at the same time and with the same basis, the sale, redemption, or exchange of only part of the shares owned will be at the shareholder's basis and holding period for that part of the shares.

However, if the mutual fund shares were acquired over time and for different prices, as in an automatic dividend reinvestment plan, the taxpayer has some flexibility in determining the income tax basis in the case of a sale, redemption, or exchange of only part of the shares owned. If the shareholder can adequately identify the group from which the shares sold, redeemed, or exchanged came, that basis and holding period can be used (as is true of securities in general, as noted in Chapter 10). If the shareholder cannot identify the group adequately or elects not to use this specific identification method, he or she has three other choices in determining the basis and holding period for the shares disposed of. The shareholder may assume that the earlier acquired shares were those sold. This is a *first-in, first-out (FIFO) concept.* Or, the shareholder may elect to use either one of two *average cost methods* for determining basis and holding period. The two alternative averaging methods are a *double-category method* and a *single-category method.* The shareholder qualifies to elect one of these averaging methods if the shares are held in a custodial account maintained for the acquisition or redemption of fund shares and the shareholder purchased or acquired the shares at different bases.

Once a shareholder elects to use one of these four methods for the shares of a particular fund, he or she is not permitted to switch to another method for that fund. However, an investor may employ different methods for different funds.

Closed-End Companies

If a closed-end company elects to be taxed as a regulated investment company, its shareholders will be taxed as described previously for mutual fund shareholders.

Look Out for Buying a Dividend

The situation referred to as *buying a dividend* occurs when a purchaser of fund shares buys them shortly before the *ex-dividend date* (or *record date*) of a distribution from the fund. This normally is not tax efficient, because the value of the shares usually will fall by about the amount of the dividend payable, but the dividend will be taxable to the purchasing shareholder. Thus, the purchaser's total position (shares plus after-tax dividend) will be reduced by the amount of the income tax on the dividend, as compared with the purchaser's total position (shares ex-dividend) if he or she had waited until after the ex-dividend date to buy the fund shares. Mutual funds often will provide the dates and estimated amounts of future distributions so investors can plan accordingly. This same general principle also applies to purchases of common stocks.

Hedge Funds and Private Equity Funds

The term "alternative investments" usually means investments in real estate (which was covered in Chapter 6), hedge funds, and private equity funds. However, it may also include other investment classes, such as oil and gas, timber, other natural resources, and so forth. Here we shall discuss hedge funds and private equity funds.

Hedge Funds

Hedge funds differ from mutual funds in several respects. First, while mutual funds are registered investment companies whose operations are regulated under the Investment Company Act of 1940, domestic hedge funds are normally organized as *investment limited partnerships* or *limited liability companies,* with the investors being limited partners or members and the investment manager being a general partner or managing member who runs the fund's affairs. Hedge funds are largely unregulated. Second, while hedge funds charge management fees that are a percentage of assets under management, they also commonly charge *incentive fees,* which are a percentage (such as 20 percent) of the realized and unrealized gains of the fund. In addition, for regulatory reasons, hedge funds and private equity funds accept only a limited number of investors and those investors generally must be accredited investors and qualified purchasers. These kinds of investors were defined and explained in Chapter 2.

Hedge funds have traditionally been characterized by their investment strategies. The classical concept is that hedge funds have an advantageous risk-return situation because they may take opposite investment positions at the same time and thus profit from their hoped-for superior investment selection models and techniques, whether an overall market goes up or down. They hope to have very low or no correlations in investment risks and returns among investment positions they take. As an example, hedge funds may purchase (be long in) common stocks they believe will outperform the market and at the same time sell short (be short in) other stocks they believe will underperform the market. If the overall stock market rises, investors hope that the good long positions will rise more than any losses in unfavorable short positions (which may even be profitable if well selected) and thus investors will make money. Correspondingly, if the overall market declines, it is hoped the good short positions (the favorable ones in this scenario) will fall more than the now-unfavorable long positions (which may even hold their value or rise if well selected) and thus again the fund investors will make money. Thus, hedge fund investors hope for superior and stable returns. This may be referred to as a long/short strategy.

In addition to short sales, hedge funds may make extensive use of financial leverage (debt) to magnify their positions. They also may use arbitrage, options, futures, and other derivatives to enhance returns and help control risk. There are many different kinds of hedge funds, and each uses a variety of financial techniques and invests globally.

Some hedge funds are structured to invest in other hedge funds. They are called *funds of funds.* This relieves the investor of the problem of selecting appropriate hedge funds (investment manager risk), but increases costs because both the funds of funds and the funds selected charge sizeable fees. In recent years, some securities firms have established funds of funds with smaller required initial investment amounts.

Hedge funds are not liquid or marketable investments. They generally are not publicly traded and may have, for example, a one-year lock-up period for initial investments.

Since they are organized as partnerships or LLCs, they operate as flow-through income tax entities. Thus, their profits and losses pass through to the investors. Profits often are short-term (one year or less) and so are taxed as ordinary income to taxable investors. Thus, hedge funds generally are not tax-efficient entities for taxable investors.

One of the arguments made by advocates of including hedge funds (or private equity) in an individual's or trust's investment portfolio is that the funds produce above-average returns but have low correlations with other asset classes such as stocks and bonds. Thus, using modern portfolio theory, they produce above-average returns with less overall portfolio risk. On the other hand, they are not readily liquid or marketable, have high costs, are not regulated or transparent, are highly leveraged, and have not really been tested during severe economic conditions. Of course, people have opinions on both sides of this issue.

Private Equity or Venture Capital

These funds are structured and operate much like hedge funds. They invest in other companies (sometimes called "portfolio companies") at various stages of the portfolio companies' development.

There are general categories of private equity. Probably the earliest was *venture capital* (VC), where the private equity firm helped finance and advised startup companies. In recent years, private equity funds have engaged in *leveraged buyouts* (LBOs) of established businesses. Typically, the acquired business would take on a large amount of debt because of the buyout. The private equity firm then would sell the business or conduct an IPO of its shares. The final category is *mezzanine financing,* where the private equity firm lends money with a fixed maturity date to the portfolio company.

9

Asset Allocation Strategies and Financial Management

Competence Objectives for This Chapter After reading this chapter, planners should understand:

- Use of investment policy statements
- The personal factors involved in asset allocation
- Possible asset classes and investment vehicles for asset allocation
- Asset allocations within investment classes
- How asset classes should be held (location analysis)
- Some illustrations of asset allocation strategies
- Cash flow management and budgeting
- Some strategies for promoting individual savings
- Types of debt and some debt management strategies
- Use of reverse mortgages to provide retirement income

Fundamentals of Asset Allocation

Asset allocation is a system for determining what percentages of an investment portfolio should be in different asset classes and subclasses. The system is based on the expected after-tax total returns on various asset classes and their correlations, the investor's financial situation, the time horizon involved, personal factors and investment constraints, the person's investment objectives and policies, and the person's ability to tolerate risk (volatility of returns).

Steps in the Asset Allocation Process

The following are possible steps in this process:

1. Develop an investment policy statement.
2. Consider the investor's personal situation, including investment constraints, time horizon, financial position, tax status, and liquidity and marketability needs.
3. Consider the person's investment objectives and strategies.
4. Review the investor's present asset allocation.
5. Consider and select the asset classes deemed suitable for the particular investor's allocation.
6. Estimate, to the extent possible, the long-term return-risk features of the asset classes selected. Logically, this step might be done concurrently with the preceding one since long-term return-risk characteristics are important in deciding which asset classes to include in a portfolio.
7. Consider the current and expected economic climate.
8. Decide on the percentage allocations of the selected asset classes in the portfolio. This, of course, is the critical step.
9. Decide on suballocations within each asset class selected.
10. Consider, to the extent possible, how the various asset classes should be held (i.e., directly owned, through financial intermediaries, or in tax-advantaged accounts or plans).
11. Implement the plan.
12. Periodically review and reevaluate the plan.

Investment Policy Statements

It is desirable for investors and their advisers to develop a formal *investment policy statement* to help guide the investor's asset allocation and other investment decisions. Such a statement might include:

- Asset classes deemed suitable for the portfolio
- Asset allocation targets for the approved asset classes
- Personal factors and attitudes affecting the investor's portfolio and his or her time horizons
- Risk-return considerations for the investor and desired overall after-tax rate of return desired; this may include an estimate of how much of a portfolio decline (e.g., during a "bear market") the investor feels he or she can tolerate
- Diversification standards to be followed

- Cash flow requirements from the portfolio
- Portfolio liquidity and marketability requirements

Personal Factors and Asset Allocation

Overall Financial Situation and Tax Status As for most forms of financial planning, one's personal or family financial situation—personal balance sheet and cash flow statement—is a valuable starting point. Tax status also is important since it is the after-tax returns from investments that are critical.

Time Horizon The longer the time horizon, the more discretion and flexibility there can be in asset allocation. There are several reasons for this. First, the long-term total return and variability data for common stocks, bonds, and cash equivalents (from such studies as those discussed in Chapter 5), which are so important in modern asset allocation thinking, are based on long-term historical studies for those asset classes. Hence, they need a long investment horizon in which to work. Second, since no one can be sure when short-term economic declines or personal problems may arise, it seems prudent to be ready for them today. Therefore, if one has only a short time (such as up to five years) to prepare for an economic need, such as college expenses, a more conservative asset allocation strategy may be in order, at least until the short-term need is met.

Investment Constraints, Investor Attitudes, and Other Factors Here are some investment constraints and other factors that might be considered:

- The investor's ability to risk loss of investment income and principal. This, in turn, is influenced by a number of factors, such as:
  - Personal earnings and the nature and stability of his or her employment, as well as the personal earnings, if any, of his or her spouse
  - Other sources of income
  - Age, health, family responsibilities, and other obligations
  - Ownership of closely held business interests
  - Any likely (or possible) inheritances
  - Plans to use investment principal for particular purposes, such as education expenses, retirement, or other large expenditures
  - The extent to which current investment income is needed for living expenses
- The degree of liquidity and marketability needed in the portfolio.
- How well the investor is able to weather the ups and particularly the downs in the securities markets.
- The quality of available investment management services.
- The investor's attitudes and emotional tolerance for risk.

Investment Objectives

Making investment decisions without defining the person's objectives is like trying to steer a ship without a rudder. Also, people's investment objectives normally change over their lifecycles and as circumstances change. Finally, a person may have a combination of objectives at the same time. The following can be listed as typical investment objectives.

Maximum Current Income This objective emphasizes current yield over other factors. It is typical of people who must rely on investment income for part or all of their livelihood.

Preservation of Capital This is a commonly heard objective. In its purest form, it means that the dollar value of the portfolio should not fall. This is a rather rigorous form of this objective. In a more flexible form, it means investing so that the potential for declines in the overall value of the portfolio is within tolerable limits. In this form, it is a common and quite logical objective.

Reasonable Current Income with Moderate Capital Growth This modifies the first objective, in that current investment income is not the only aim. While current income is important, capital gains also are sought.

Long-Term Capital Growth This objective aims primarily at capital gains over a relatively long time. It may be typical of investors who do not need current investment income to meet their living expenses. This objective implies a greater degree of risk in the portfolio.

Aggressive Capital Growth This objective seeks maximum capital growth and implies making riskier investments with considerable investment analysis and management.

Tax-Advantaged Investments A person's top marginal income tax bracket may make tax-free or tax-sheltered investments attractive.

Investment Policies and Strategies

Investors should establish policies and strategies to meet their objectives within the framework of their investment constraints. In setting such policies and strategies, the following kinds of issues might be considered.

Aggressive versus Defensive Policies *Aggressive policies* seek to maximize returns and, thus, accept above-average risks. On the other hand, *defensive policies* seek to minimize investment risks and, perhaps, accept correspondingly lower returns. In general, aggressive and defensive policies can be distinguished as follows. To maximize returns, an aggressive portfolio includes securities of greater financial risk than would be true of a defensive portfolio.

Again, to earn maximum returns, an aggressive investor tries to make profits by timing purchases and sales of securities according to his or her views on how the market will go. A defensive investor, on the other hand, tends to follow a buy-and-hold philosophy or use dollar-cost averaging or other such plans, pursues index investing, and usually does not try to outguess the market. An aggressive investor may use many techniques and investment media, such as stock warrants, puts and calls, IPOs, and short sales, that often are not used in portfolios that are more defensive. An aggressive policy may involve borrowing to increase profit potential, while a defensive policy generally does not use credit in this way. Finally, an aggressive policy may concentrate purchases in a relatively small number of securities to maximize the investor's skill at selection.

Probably few people consistently follow only aggressive policies or only defensive policies. However, many investors probably tend more toward defensive-type policies in general.

Liquidity and Marketability Setting the proper degree of liquidity in a portfolio is largely a matter of judgment. It can be done by deciding to hold a certain number of dollars, say, $20,000, in liquid assets; or to hold a certain percentage of assets, say, 10 percent, in liquid form; or some combination of the two. In asset allocation models, liquid assets (such as cash equivalents) often are stated as a percentage of the overall portfolio. The investment policy statement should also indicate what percentage of a portfolio may be in asset classes that generally lack marketability, such as real estate or other alternative investments.

Diversification versus Concentration As just stated, diversification is a defensive policy. The opposite of diversification is *concentration.* A portfolio may be concentrated in only one asset class (like common stocks or real estate) or even in just one or a few issues within an asset class. Sometimes events cause investment concentration—albeit unconsciously without its being a conscious policy. This may occur, for example, when a corporate executive's portfolio becomes overweighted in his or her company's stock. The problem then becomes how to diversify in an efficient manner.

Possible Asset Classes to Be Considered

Each investor needs to select those asset classes he or she feels might be suitable to include in his or her asset allocation decision making. The following are some possible asset classes:

- Domestic common stocks
- Foreign common stocks

- Domestic bonds (investment grade)
- Foreign bonds
- High-yield (junk) bonds
- Cash-type assets (cash equivalents)
- Longer-term fixed-dollar (guaranteed principal) assets
- Investment real estate
- Other alternative investments
- Convertible securities
- Gold and precious metals
- Other assets

Investment Vehicles to Be Considered

These asset classes can be found in a number of different investment vehicles. Each of them needs to be considered in asset allocation planning because a person is exposed to an asset class no matter how it is held.

Directly Owned Assets These are assets owned by a person in his or her own name or jointly with another. They may be titled to the person or held in brokerage or other accounts in the person's name.

Assets Held through Financial Intermediaries Here the person owns shares or interests in a financial intermediary that owns and manages the investment assets. Mutual funds and REITs are common examples.

Assets Held in Qualified Retirement Plans Many employer-provided retirement plans are *defined contribution* or *individual account plans* where specific accounts are allocated to individual employees. Participating employees often have control over how these account balances are invested.

IRAs IRA owners can invest their account balances in a broad array of investment vehicles and annuities. However, they cannot be invested in life insurance policies or collectibles.

Life Insurance Cash Values Traditional fixed-dollar policies and universal life (UL) policies have fixed-dollar (portfolio product) cash values. They are guaranteed principal assets. On the other hand, the asset classifications of variable life (VL) and variable universal life (VUL) policies depend on the subaccounts into which their cash values are placed.

Investment Annuity Cash Values Traditional fixed-dollar annuities have fixed-dollar (portfolio product) cash values and thus are guaranteed principal assets. Variable annuities (VAs) have cash values that the annuity owner can elect to place in one or more subaccounts. The subaccounts chosen determine the asset class.

Employee Stock Options and Stock Plans Some employees have been granted stock options or are eligible for other stock plans (e.g., restricted stock, employee stock purchase plans, stock appreciation rights, and so forth). Such options and plans clearly represent an investment interest in the employer's stock, but they may be difficult to value. (These plans and their valuation are discussed in Chapter 18.)

For our present purposes, we shall value unexercised stock options by subtracting the exercise price at grant (option price) from the current market price of the stock and multiplying by the number of shares for which the option can be exercised. This is referred to as the *intrinsic value* of the option.

For example, assume that two years ago John Herrera was granted nonqualified stock options (NQSOs) with a duration of 10 years to purchase 1,000 shares of his employer's stock at a price of $20 per share (grant price) and the market price of the stock is now $45 per share. The options' present intrinsic value is $25,000 ($45 – $20 = $25 × 1,000 shares). Of course, if an option already has been exercised or stock has been acquired under some other plan, the stock is simply counted as directly owned common stock.

Trust Assets Some people are beneficiaries of trusts. This can involve many different arrangements. Some people have set up funded revocable living trusts. The assets in these trusts (which can be terminated or amended by the creator at any time) should be counted in the creator-beneficiary's asset allocation because for all practical purposes they are still owned by the creator-beneficiary. Other times, a person may be a beneficiary of an irrevocable trust established by someone else. These trust assets may or may not be counted for asset allocation purposes, depending on what kinds of rights the beneficiary has in the trust's property. This is a judgment call.

How Investments (Asset Classes) Should Be Held (Location Analysis)

The issue here is whether investments should be held directly or in tax-advantaged vehicles. This is also referred to as *location analysis.* How much planning can be done in this area depends largely on the circumstances. Some people have almost all their investable assets in tax-advantaged plans, so their choices are limited. Others have few tax-advantaged plans available to them. In a few cases, participants in tax-advantaged plans may have limited or no choice as to how their plan assets are to be invested. The tax-advantaged vehicles we are considering include qualified retirement plans, IRAs, variable annuity contracts, and variable life insurance policies, among others.

Advantages of Directly Owned Assets

- Capital gains are not realized and recognized (taxable) until the asset is sold or exchanged in a taxable transaction.
- Long-term capital gains are taxed at favorable rates.
- Capital assets presently get a stepped-up income tax basis at death.
- Planning can be done to postpone or even totally avoid capital gains taxation.
- Capital losses can reduce or eliminate capital gains, and then any remaining losses can reduce ordinary income by up to $3,000 per year. Unused capital losses can be carried forward.
- Investors have control over the investment of their assets.

Limitations of Directly Owned Assets

- Dividends and taxable interest are taxable each year as received. But, as of this writing, qualified dividends are taxed at a lower rate.
- In order to change investments or an asset allocation, it will be necessary to realize and recognize capital gains (and pay capital gains taxes) if appreciated assets are sold or exchanged.
- Mutual funds and other investment companies may produce capital gains for shareholders through fund turnover.

Advantages of Holding Assets in Tax-Advantaged Plans

- All investment income (dividends, taxable interest, and capital gains) is not taxed currently to the participant. Taxation (as ordinary income) is deferred until distributions are actually made from the plan. Distributions from Roth IRAs and Roth 401(k) plans are tax free.
- Changes in investments or in asset allocation can be made tax free as long as they are made within the tax-favored plan. Thus, if assets have gains, these plans may be a good place to make changes in asset allocation. On the other hand, if assets have losses, directly owned assets may be the better ones to sell since the realized losses can offset other capital gains or up to $3,000 per year of ordinary income.
- Distributions usually can be deferred a long time, resulting in long periods of tax-deferred earnings. An example is the "stretch IRA" concept described in Chapter 16.

Limitations of Holding Assets in Tax-Advantaged Plans

- All investment income (dividends, taxable interest, and capital gains), as well as any taxable principal in these plans, will be taxed as ordinary income when distributed. [Roth IRAs, 401(k)s, and education IRAs are exceptions; their distributions are tax free.] Also, the balances in these plans must be distributed at some point (the minimum distribution rules are covered in Chapter 16).

- There is no step-up in basis at death for investments in these plans, and lower capital gains rates do not apply even though investment returns in the plan may have come in the form of capital gains.
- Participants must abide by the terms of the particular plan, and employers can change plan terms for the future.
- There may be penalty taxes for taking premature distributions (10 percent penalty tax) or for failure to take required minimum distributions (50 percent penalty tax).

Some Observations Concerning Location Analysis

While it can be seen from the preceding discussion that there are few hard and fast certainties in this area, the following are some general observations:

- Tax-free municipal bonds should always be held directly since their interest is tax free.
- Zero-coupon taxable bonds should be held in tax-advantaged accounts. Otherwise, their annual accrued interest will be taxed currently to the owners even though it has not yet been received in cash.
- An argument can be made that growth-type common stocks (with low or no current dividends) that are intended to be held for the long term probably should be held directly. The investor then would get tax-deferred or tax-free compounding of hoped-for capital gains, lower capital gains tax rates (if sold or exchanged before death), and at present, a step-up in basis if held until death. (Investors also may engage in other techniques to delay or avoid capital gains taxation, as described in Chapter 11.)
- An argument can be made that taxable bonds and guaranteed principal investments that pay current interest should be placed in tax-advantaged plans so that the tax on the current interest payments can be deferred.
- If changes are to be made in investments or in asset allocation, and appreciated assets are involved, it is better to try to make them in tax-advantaged plans so no capital gains taxes will be incurred. On the other hand, if assets with investment losses are involved, it is better to sell directly owned assets so capital losses can be realized to offset any capital gains or up to $3,000 per year of ordinary income.

Case Examples of Asset Allocation Strategies

There can be wide differences of opinion concerning asset allocation strategies, even with a given factual situation. The two case situations given here are meant simply to illustrate general asset allocation techniques.

A Young Professional Couple

Let us assume that Harry and Susan Modern are married; both have careers outside the home; and they have two children, ages six and four. Harry, age 40, is a lawyer with his own practice (a sole proprietor). Susan, age 38, has an undergraduate degree in chemical engineering and an MBA. She is an executive with a large pharmaceutical company. They each earn approximately $200,000 per year. Harry has recently established a retirement plan for the self-employed (an HR-10 plan), and Susan has a qualified pension plan and a qualified 401(k) plan (with five separate investment options including employer stock, among which she can select) from her employer.

Her employer's matching 401(k) contribution goes into the employer stock option. Half of her account balance is in her company's stock and half is in a diversified stock fund.

Harry carries $500,000 face amount of life insurance on his life, with $100,000 from a VUL policy (with an $8,000 cash value in its common stock account) and $400,000 as term insurance. Susan also carries $500,000 face amount of life insurance on her life, with $100,000 from a traditional fixed-premium whole life policy (with a $2,000 cash value) and the remainder as group and individual term insurance.

Four years ago, Susan's employer granted her NQSOs to purchase 1,000 shares of the company's stock at an option price of $50 per share. The market price of the stock is now $90 per share. The NQSOs are vested, but Susan has not yet exercised them.

From an employee stock purchase plan at Susan's employer, a lump-sum distribution from Harry's former employer's profit-sharing plan when he left the firm, their personal savings, and a small inheritance from Harry's mother, they have accumulated other investable assets of $300,000. They own their own home, valued at $700,000, on which there is now (after refinancing) a $500,000 fixed-rate mortgage with interest currently at 4.5 percent. As of now, they have decided not to use their investable assets to pay off the mortgage.

Susan and Harry file a joint income tax return and are in the 35 percent federal and 40 percent combined federal, state, and local top marginal income tax brackets. They also have indicated that they wish to plan their asset allocations on a combined basis, rather than individually.

With respect to their investment objectives and policies, the Moderns first plan to accumulate assets for their children's educations. For this purpose, they plan to set up Section 529 plans for each child. They then want to prepare for their own comfortable retirement at around age 60, and finally to establish a general investment fund. Since their oldest child is age six (with about 12 years before he begins college), all of these goals have a reasonably long time horizon. Both Harry and Susan believe in the long-term growth and superior returns of the stock market. Harry wants to put all their available assets in common stocks, but Susan is concerned about the volatility of the market. Both agree that current dividend income is not important to them. Harry eventually would like to invest in and manage sound income-producing real estate, which he says he comes across from time to time in his law practice. Susan agrees with this idea, but they both agree that investment real estate is for the future.

As of now, they both agree that they might consider the following asset classes for their portfolio:

- Growth common stocks (including the stock of Susan's employer, Growth Drugs)
- Value oriented common stocks (as a second choice to growth stocks)
- Investment-grade corporate bonds (if held in tax-advantaged plans or accounts)
- Investment-grade municipal bonds (held directly)
- Guaranteed principal assets (if held in tax-advantaged plans or accounts)
- Cash equivalents (liquid assets)
- Investment real estate (for the future)

Considering the long-term return-risk estimates suggested to them by their investment adviser, and their own situation and opinions, Harry and Susan have decided that for now they would like to plan for the following percentage allocations:

Growth and value common stocks (with mostly growth stocks)	70 percent
Corporate bonds (held in tax-advantaged accounts)	15 percent
Guaranteed principal assets (held in tax-advantaged accounts)	10 percent
Cash equivalents	5 percent

They also prefer not to have more than 10 percent of their portfolios in any one stock or security.

The Moderns presently have an overall investment portfolio of about $460,000. Almost all of this is in growth (or diversified) common stocks, as follows: $40,000 account balance under Harry's HR-10 plan; $70,000 account balance under Susan's Section 401(k) plan; $8,000 cash value of Harry's VUL policy; the $40,000 intrinsic value of Susan's stock options ($90 – $50 = $40 × 1,000 shares = $40,000); and almost all of their $300,000 of directly owned assets (which include $95,000 of Growth Drug stock purchased under Susan's employee stock purchase plan), growth-type stock mutual funds, and other growth-oriented common stocks. Only the $2,000 cash value of Susan's traditional whole life policy is otherwise invested.

However, according to their asset allocation goals, they should have approximately $322,000 in growth (or perhaps value) common stocks, $69,000 in bonds, $46,000 in guaranteed principal assets, and $23,000 in cash equivalents. Furthermore, they have a concentration problem with respect to Susan's Growth Drug stock. They now have $170,000 in Growth Drug stock—$35,000 under Susan's 401(k) plan, $95,000 held directly, and the $40,000 value of her stock options—which is almost 37 percent of their portfolio.

To implement their desired asset allocation strategy, Harry and Susan should add bonds, guaranteed principal assets, and cash equivalents to their portfolio. Correspondingly, they should reduce their stock holdings, particularly in Growth Drug. Naturally, they want to incur as little in the way of capital gains taxes as possible. With these thoughts in mind, the following actions might be suggested to the Moderns:

- Harry might change the investments in his HR-10 plan and VUL policy from stocks to investment-grade corporate bonds or bond funds. This would not result in current taxation.
- Susan might change the allocation of her contributions to her 401(k) plan from stocks (particularly Growth Drug stock) to the plan's stable value fund.
- She might also change her present account balance to the plan's stable value fund or corporate bond account. Note that under PPA of 2006 (as explained in Chapter 13), she can do this with respect to employer stock in the plan both from her contributions and from the employer match (since she has been with the company more than three years). Again, this would not result in current taxation.
- When Susan exercises her NQSOs, she might use presently owned Growth Drug stock as part of the purchase price (to the extent permitted by the plan). Or she might sell part or all of the stock received after exercise so no capital gains will be realized. These actions will reduce her exposure to Growth Drug stock with lessened taxation. (See Chapter 11.)
- When Susan and Harry have savings, proceeds from sales of securities, or other funds available for investment, they might first place the funds in a tax-free money market account (cash equivalent) until it reaches the desired level and then acquire directly held investment-grade municipal bonds until the overall bond portion reaches the desired level.

- If Harry and Susan are making charitable gifts, they might consider giving the most appreciated Growth Drug stock instead of cash. This will help reduce their investment exposure to Growth Drug stock. (See Chapter 11.)
- Finally, Susan and Harry may have to just bite the bullet and sell some appreciated stock and pay any capital gains taxes due. They probably do not have enough assets and possibly are too early in their lifecycle to consider more sophisticated techniques for deferring capital gains, as discussed in Chapter 11.

A More Mature Retired Couple

Now let us consider an entirely different case. Assume that John and Martha Senior are married, their three children are out of their home and self-supporting, and John and Martha are retired. John is age 67 and Martha is 64. John receives Social Security retirement benefits and a pension for his and Martha's lifetimes (with a 50 percent survivor's benefit for Martha if he should predecease her) from his former employer. Martha has not yet begun to receive Social Security retirement benefits, but she will begin to do so when she reaches full benefit retirement age. Martha receives a small pension of her own and is the income beneficiary for her lifetime of a modest trust established for her under her mother's will. John is covered by Medicare, and Martha presently has COBRA continuation coverage under John's former employer's medical plan. Martha will be eligible for Medicare when she reaches age 65. John carries $200,000 face amount of traditional whole life insurance that has a cash value of $40,000.

At John's retirement, he rolled over all of his account balance under his former employer's qualified savings plan into a regular rollover IRA. He now has $300,000 in this rollover IRA, with $200,000 invested in two-year insured CDs and $100,000 in investment-grade corporate bonds. From their personal savings, John and Martha have another $200,000 in directly owned assets, of which $100,000 is in three-year insured CDs and $100,000 is in a diversified common stock mutual fund.

Regarding investment objectives and policies, Martha and John would like to preserve their capital as much as possible, receive reasonable current income with moderate capital growth, protect their investment income against declines in interest rates as much as possible, maintain reasonable liquidity, and have reasonable diversification. They do need a reasonable income from their investment portfolio to maintain a comfortable standard of living. They do not wish to consider the corpus of Martha's trust in their asset allocation planning.

The Seniors file a joint income tax return and are in the 28 percent federal and 32 percent combined federal, state, and local top marginal income tax brackets. They want to consider their asset allocation decisions together.

For now, John and Martha agree that they would consider the following asset classes for their portfolio:

- Diversified income-producing common stocks or stock funds
- Investment-grade corporate bonds
- U.S. Treasury bonds
- Guaranteed principal assets
- Cash equivalents (liquid assets)

Considering the return-risk estimates provided by their investment adviser and their own situation and opinions, the Seniors have decided that they would like to plan for the following percentage allocation of their portfolios:

Investment grade corporate bonds (5- to 15-year maturities)	25 percent
U.S. Treasury bonds (20- to 30-year maturities)	25 percent
CDs (2- to 3-year maturities)	20 percent
Diversified income-producing common stocks	20 percent
Other guaranteed principal assets (e.g., life insurance cash values)	5 percent
Cash equivalents	5 percent

In this allocation, they are planning to ladder their bond and other fixed-income portfolio to protect themselves against call and reinvestment risks, as well as against interest rate risk to bond values. Hence, they plan to have about 25 percent of their assets in shorter-term securities (cash equivalents and 2- to 3-year CDs), 25 percent in intermediate-term bonds (5- to 15-year corporate bonds), and 25 percent in long-term bonds (20- to 30-year U.S. Treasury bonds). Their bonds could be held directly (outright or through mutual funds) or in the IRA.

To implement their desired asset allocation strategy, Martha and John need to move some of their assets now in CDs to U.S. Treasury bonds, corporate bonds, and a money market account in the appropriate amounts. These assets can be held directly or in the IRA. These shifts probably can occur as the CDs mature, so no early withdrawal penalties need to be paid. There also should be no tax consequences.

John has more cash value in his traditional whole life policy than he would like (5 percent of their $540,000 portfolio equals $27,000). He has indicated that he wants to keep the insurance in force to protect Martha against a reduction in retirement income if he should predecease her. Generally, one tries not to take taxable amounts from life insurance contracts. With these factors in mind, John has several options with respect to this policy. They are discussed more fully in Chapters 21 and 29.

Finally, John and Martha already have about the desired amount of common stocks. These could be held outright or through mutual funds.

Financial Management

In addition to asset allocation in investment planning, most people need to develop financial strategies for managing their cash flow and expenditures (budgeting), to facilitate saving, and to meet their financing needs (debt management). In addition, during their retirement years some people may need to consider reverse mortgages as a way to supplement their retirement income.

Cash Flow Management and Budgeting

A primary tool of cash flow management is the *personal or family budget*. This is a listing of expected cash flows to be received and expected expenditures in a given period of time, often monthly.

Such cash flows and expenditures were listed in the discussion of the personal cash flow (income) statement in Chapter 1. Some cash flow and expenditure items do not fit neatly into a monthly pattern (such as bonuses and semiannual or quarterly investment returns on the cash flow side and semiannual real estate taxes, quarterly federal and state estimated income tax payments, tuition bills, and perhaps some insurance premiums on the expenditure side). Such larger, irregular items can be prorated on a monthly basis for planning purposes or planned for separately.

Budgeting allows the person or family to keep their expenditures within their expected cash flow. The difference between cash flow and expenditures is net saving. It is desirable to have positive net savings. Obviously, allowing expenditures to exceed cash flow for a sustained period (i.e., living beyond one's means) is very bad financial management. Unfortunately, this simple truth is lost on some people who clearly need professional help in this regard. For some recent years, the savings rate in the United States has been very low or even negative.

Another aspect of cash flow management is *emergency fund planning*. This was discussed previously in Chapter 1.

Savings Strategies

As a general principle, saving is much better than debt as a financial policy. The economic situation as of this writing is a good illustration of this point.

Of course, for many people it is easier to spend than to save. However, there are a number of strategies that can aid in saving, such as:

- Follow a "pay yourself first" strategy. This means that each month or other period a person or couple makes at least a minimum payment to their savings before any other payments or expenditures.

  This really is part of the budgeting process. If necessary, this minimum saving can be reduced for a month or so, but there is always some saving. This creates the habit of thrift. Benjamin Franklin famously argues for this habit in his autobiography.
- Take full advantage of benefit plans requiring automatic employee contributions if they are otherwise favorable. Contributions to such plans are made through payroll deductions. The prime example would be IRC Section 401(k) plans discussed in Chapter 13. In many cases, employers also provide matching contributions to such plans. Employers now can require automatic employee enrollment in such plans unless employees affirmatively elect not to enroll. It has been reported that automatic enrollment substantially increases employee participation in such plans and hence automatic retirement savings through them. Of course, employees can, and probably should, contribute more than the automatic minimum contributions.
- Make allowable contributions to individual tax-advantaged plans, such as traditional and Roth IRAs.
- Repay debt in an organized fashion such as through amortizing first mortgages and home equity loans where an increasing portion of each payment goes to reduce the loan principal. Paying off debt is a form of saving.
- One of the arguments advanced in favor of fixed-premium whole life insurance is that the policyowner tends to view the fixed premium as a periodic financial obligation and thus pays it. This keeps the policy in force and causes the cash value to grow year by year. This has been described as a form of semicompulsory saving. Of course, any increase in life insurance or individual annuity cash values is a form of saving.
- As a lifetime giving strategy for estate planning purposes, parents, grandparents, or others may consider making gifts to their children, grandchildren, or others to enable them to start their own tax-advantaged plans, like IRAs, if they are eligible. This will enable the donees to start these plans early and help instill in them the habit of thrift. People also may give or lend children, grandchildren, or other family members part or all of the down payment on their first home. The donees then will have more equity in their homes and can pay off their amortizing mortgages.

Financing Strategies

People may want or need to borrow for a number of valid reasons. Most people need to borrow to finance the purchase of a primary residence or a secondary residence. Many people may borrow to finance other large purchases, such as automobiles or vacations. Many others must take loans to finance their children's educations, although now there are attractive ways to prefinance education costs. (Read more on education planning in Chapter 12.) Sometimes people unfortunately need to borrow to meet emergencies, such as for extraordinary medical costs or expenditures during temporary unemployment. However, meeting the costs of such emergencies is one reason to maintain an adequate *emergency fund* as explained in Chapter 1.

An entirely different reason for taking loans is to finance an investment position or start or maintain a closely held business. Borrowing to carry an investment position that is larger than investors otherwise could have with their own funds (financial leverage) will magnify investment gains, but also magnify investment losses. It is a risky investment strategy. In some areas, like real estate investing, it is common to use financial leverage as noted in Chapter 6. Many small businesses find they must borrow to provide capital for their businesses.

Long-Term versus Short-Term Debt As it's name implies, *short-term debt* is due within, say, three years. The borrower needs to prepare to be able to pay off debt within a relatively short period. In the case of credit card debt, for example, the carrying charges become very high if the card balance is not paid within about 25 days.

Another category is *intermediate-term debt* with a maturity between short-term and long-term debt.

Long-term debt might be thought of as debt that must be repaid in more than 10 years. In many cases, such debts (for example, mortgage loans) are amortizing. That is, they are paid off through level monthly payments which consist partly of principal repayment and partly of interest on the remaining loan balance. Thus, the interest portion of each level payment constitutes most of the payment in the beginning but diminishes as the loan is paid off. The reverse is true of the principal portion. Of course, long-term debt normally is used for long-term commitments, such as the purchase of a home.

Secured versus Unsecured Debt Assets of the debtor are pledged as collateral to protect the creditor in the case of secured debt.

Mortgages and margin loans are examples of secured debt. Sometimes the security behind secured loans is subsidiary or behind that of other secured loans, such as second mortgages, for example. Home equity loans and lines are second mortgages on residences.

A secured creditor can levy against or sell the pledged asset for payment if the debtor defaults on the loan. If the secured loan is *recourse indebtedness*, the creditor also can recover any unpaid amounts from the debtor's other assets (i.e., can go against the debtor personally) as well as from the pledged asset. On the other hand, nonrecourse indebtedness does not allow the creditor to go against the debtor personally, but only against the pledged property. Residential mortgages normally are recourse indebtedness.

For *unsecured debt*, the creditor only relies on the debtor's personal ability to repay the loan (the full faith and credit of the borrower). No property is pledged as security. Unsecured debt involves more credit risk than recourse secured debt, assuming the same credit circumstances of the borrowers.

Types of Debt There is a wide variety of kinds of debt persons can incur.

Mortgage Debt: Most people incur mortgage debt to finance the purchase of their primary residence and perhaps a secondary residence. Real estate investors typically finance their investments with a mortgage as discussed in Chapter 6.

There are several types of mortgage indebtedness on residences, including:

- *Fixed-rate mortgages.* These are amortizing longer-term loans whose interest rate remains fixed (level) for the duration of the loan. Thus, they protect the borrower against increases in interest rates. On the other hand, if interest rates decline, these mortgages can be refinanced at the prevailing lower rates. Thus, the interest rates on these fixed-rate mortgages normally are higher than for the comparable adjustable-rate mortgages described next.
- *Adjustable-rate mortgages (ARMs).* These are amortizing longer-term loans where the interest rates are indexed or tied to some market-based interest rate, such as LIBOR or the yield on certain U.S. Treasury securities. The rate then will be the benchmark rate plus, say, 1 or 2 percentage points. Thus the interest rate on these loans will "adjust" to the indexed market rates. If the indexed market rates decline, this will benefit the borrower. If they go up, the reverse will be true. However, if the indexed rates go up, the borrower *may* be able to refinance the loan with a fixed-rate mortgage. The danger in relying on this strategy is that if home prices decline (so the borrower does not have enough, or any, equity in the home) or credit conditions worsen, the borrower may not be able to refinance and will be stuck with a rising interest rate. This will be particularly true if the adjustable-rate loan had a below market (unusually low) "teaser" interest rate in the beginning which in a few years converted to a higher adjusted rate.

As of this writing, many homeowners with such adjustable-rate mortgages have been unable to refinance into fixed-rate loans when interest rates rose because the prices of their homes had declined to below the amounts of the mortgage (i.e., were "under water"), and so the homeowners had no equity in their residences.

It is also possible that if interest rates rise substantially, the monthly mortgage payments on the ARM will not be able to cover the increased interest, and so the principal balance of the loan will actually increase rather than decrease as is normally true for amortizing mortgages.

ARMs may also have limits on the increase in the loan's interest rate over a one-year period and for the life of the loan. These limits are called interest rate caps.

- *Hybrid ARMs.* This is a combination of the previous two types. There is a fixed rate for a period of time and then the loan becomes an ARM.
- *Home equity loans.* These are second mortgages because they are an additional lien on the residence (after the first mortgage) and are separate from the first mortgage. They are generally fixed-rate amortizing loans.
- *Home equity lines of credit.* In this case, the lender makes available an amount (a line of credit) that can be drawn down (borrowed) by the borrower. The monthly charge is the adjustable interest rate on the loan balance. The borrower can also pay off part or all of the loan balance as he or she wishes. These are also second mortgages on the residence.

Prepayment of Mortgage Loans: Borrowers may prepay the principal on mortgage loans before they are due. Frequently this can be done without any payment penalty. This may be done gradually to pay off the loan balance sooner than otherwise would be the case, like doubling up on monthly payments when there are funds to do so (i.e., making extra payments). This may be an effective saving strategy for some families.

For amortizing mortgages, prepayment results in a reduced number of payments with the monthly payment amount unchanged. For home equity lines, payment over and above the current monthly interest due reduces the outstanding loan balance.

Prepayment reduces further interest costs. Therefore, it should be evaluated in terms of the after-tax investment returns otherwise expected to be available from the funds that will be used for prepayments.

Refinancing of Mortgage Loans: As was noted previously, refinancing of mortgage loans may be a viable strategy when interest rates decline. One fixed-rate mortgage may be paid off and refinanced with another fixed-rate mortgage carrying a lower interest rate. Just as a rule of thumb, some commentators suggest that such refinancing may be worthwhile when current interest rates are 1 percent or more lower than the existing fixed rate. An analysis of this would involve comparing the yearly after-tax savings as compared with the time estimated for the after-tax savings to recover any closing costs for the refinancing.

Also, as discussed previously, an ARM may be refinanced with a fixed-rate loan and vice versa.

Margin Loans: These are loans from brokers and banks using eligible securities as collateral. The interest rate normally is indexed to a benchmark market rate (like the prime rate) plus several percentage points. The terms can vary considerably among brokers. Margin loans may be used for general credit purposes (because their interest rates may be relatively low), but they are generally used to finance additional purchases of securities (i.e., to leverage an investment position). This use of margin loans is more risky and is an aggressive investment strategy. Margin loans were discussed in Chapter 4.

Life Insurance Policy Loans: Cash-value life insurance policies offer policy-owners the right to borrow from the insurer an amount up to the cash value. Interest rates on policy loans normally are relatively low and the policy stipulates the amount of the rate or how it is determined. Life insurance policy loans are further described in Chapter 21.

Retirement Plan Loans: It is noted in Chapter 13 that qualified retirement plans, such as 401 (k) plans and profit-sharing plans, may permit participants to borrow a portion of their account balances. Such plan loans must carry a "reasonable" interest rate and be repayable under certain conditions as specified in ERISA. They represent an exception to the prohibited transaction rules or ERISA and are described in more detail in Chapter 13.

Participants may be tempted to borrow from their qualified plans because the money is available and the interest rate charged by the plan, while "reasonable," may be relatively low. Also the amount borrowed continues to earn an investment return inside the plan.

However, care must be taken with respect to such loans because if they are not repaid when due, they are considered distributions from the plan and are taxed as ordinary income to the participant with perhaps an additional 10 percent penalty tax if they are premature distributions. Also, if they are not repaid, they deplete the participant's funds in retirement.

Credit Card Debt: Many people have one or more credit cards. Some use these cards as a convenient way to budget their expenses for the month but are careful to pay off the card balance when due at the end of the month before any finance charges are due. This is a logical budgeting strategy.

On the other hand, if card payments are not paid immediately when due, normally very high finance charges will be charged often for several months. When this happens, credit card debt is very expensive, and many commentators, including your authors, suggest it should be avoided.

Other Debt: There are a variety of other sources for borrowing, such as unsecured bank loans, loans and mortgages from credit unions (often at relatively low rates), education loans (again perhaps at low rates, depending on the program involved as discussed in Chapter 12), auto loans, and other secured debt, among others.

Intra-Family Loans: These may simply result from family members and friends providing needed credit to someone who needs it. It may be an act of family loyalty or friendship.

On the other hand, such loans may be part of tax-effective intra-family wealth transfer techniques as described in Chapter 27. In this case, as described in Chapter 3, such loans should carry at least the applicable federal rate (AFR) to avoid gift and income tax consequences.

Reverse Mortgages for Retirement Income

Basic Characteristics A relatively new financing approach is to take a mortgage on the person's or couple's residence that makes a single lump-sum payment, a series of monthly cash advances for the borrower's lifetime, a credit line that lets the borrower draw on the account balance as he or she wishes, or some combination of the these payment methods to the borrower. The borrower does not make any monthly payments on the mortgage. The loan also does not need to be repaid until the last surviving borrower dies, the home is sold, all borrowers permanently move to a new principal residence, the last surviving borrower fails to live in the home for 12 months due to physical or mental illness, or in certain other circumstances. Basically, the loan is not due until the last borrower leaves the home. Thus, there is no fixed due date for the mortgage. Interest is charged in the outstanding balance of the reverse mortgage and is added to this balance. Therefore, the amount owed (principal balance) will increase over the life of the mortgage and the borrower's equity in the home will probably decline. It can be seen that in all these respects it operates in a reverse fashion to conventional amortizing mortgages.

Reverse mortgages are *nonrecourse loans* in that they are paid when due solely from the proceeds from the sale of the home. If these proceeds are less than the loan balance, the borrower or his or her estate is not responsible for paying the shortfall. The Federal Housing Administration (FHA) covers this loss for loans provided under the federal insured Home Equity Conversion Mortgage (HECM) program. Private lenders must absorb it for proprietary private sector plans. On the other hand, if the sale proceeds are more than the reverse mortgage balance, the difference belongs to the borrower or his or her estate (and thus heirs).

Sources of Reverse Mortgages Reverse mortgages are available from several sources. Most are originated through private lenders under the federal HECM program and are the only reverse mortgages insured by the FHA. This insurance covers the lenders for losses on sale of the homes and also covers the borrowers against loss because of default by lenders in making mortgage payments. For this insurance, borrowers are charged an upfront premium of 2 percent of the loan. The adjustable interest rate or HECMs loans is set monthly by the government and is the same for all HECMs lenders. These rates tend to be lower than for private home equity loans. However, origination fees and servicing fees vary among lenders, and so a potential borrower might want to check this with several lenders. A listing of HECM lenders for each state can be found on the HUD Web site: www.hud.gov/11/code/11plcrit.html.

Private lenders also provide *proprietary reverse mortgages* that are not insured by the government. These typically are for larger loans on more valuable properties than would be available under the HECM program. The terms and underwriting for these loans are determined by the private lenders. The Web site for the National Reverse Mortgage Lenders Association (NRMLA) is www.reversemortgages.org.

There also are *single-purpose reverse mortgages* offered by some state and local governments. The mortgages discussed previously can be used by the borrower for any purpose, but these are for special purposes like paying property taxes or making home repairs. Also, eligibility is limited for these loans where they are offered.

Eligibility Requirements, Amounts, and Costs The eligibility requirements for HECM mortgages include:

- The borrower and other current owners of the home must be age 62 or over and live in the home as a principal residence.
- The home must be a single family residence in a one- to four-unit dwelling, a condominium, or part of a planned unit development.
- The residence must meet minimum property standards.
- The borrower must discuss the program with a counselor from a HUD-approved agency.

The maximum amounts of HECM loans is set by the FHA and is based on:

- The value and location of the home (the borrower's income and personal credit rating are not considered because the home is the entire security for the mortgage).
- The maximum amount depends on median home values in the county involved.
- The age or ages of the borrower(s).

As noted previously, proprietary loans can be made for larger amounts than HECM loans.

The costs for HECM loans include initial charges, such as origination fees (which are limited by law to 2 percent of the loan up to $200,000 and 1 percent over that with a $6,000 overall limit); cost of property appraisals, title search, and so forth; and the 2 percent mortgage insurance premium. Except for the insurance premium, these costs vary among lenders, so comparisons may be in order. Again, except for the mortgage insurance premium, these are the initial costs normally associated with originating a mortgage loan. The interest rate charged on HECM loans has already been discussed.

Planning Issues Reverse mortgages are a relatively new concept and are somewhat controversial. They are basically a way for people at or close to retirement age to tap the equity in their homes (which by that time may be debt free or with relatively low mortgages) so as to provide a retirement income they cannot outlive, in the case of monthly cash advances, a lump sum to use for any purpose in the case of a single-sum payment, or a credit line to draw on as needed for that payment form, and still remain in their homes for as long as they live or until they wish or need to move. For federally insured reverse mortgages, there is no credit financial risk for either the lender or the borrower. If the lifetime monthly cash advance payment form is selected, the borrower has no mortality risk because the advances will continue as long as the borrower lives, but if he or she dies earlier than expected, the balance of the home's value will go to the borrower's estate and heirs. No depletion of the retiree's financial resources (stocks, bonds, etc.) is required to produce the life income. The payments from a reverse mortgage also are income tax–free because they are loans which are not considered gross income for federal income tax purposes.

The main argument against reverse mortgages is the relatively high initial cost of originating the mortgage which typically is added to the loan balance. Of course, heirs (and perhaps the retiree as well) may object because the heirs' inheritance will be gradually depleted.

Other strategies for dealing with a retiree's primary residence would be to sell the residence and perhaps buy a smaller home, possibly in another part of the country, or rent living quarters. In some cases, retirees may want or need to move into assisted-living facilities. In such cases, and possibly others, reverse mortgages would not be appropriate. Another possibility would be for the retiree simply to take a conventional home equity line of credit and borrow against it as needed. However, there is no assurance that such a line would last the borrower's lifetime.

Because of the guaranteed life income feature, reverse mortgages are analogous to other financial arrangements designed to produce such income. These include immediate life annuities sold by life insurance companies (covered in Chapter 17) and charitable gift annuities provided by many charitable organizations (discussed in Chapter 19). In these cases, the life annuities are guaranteed by the insurance company or the charity, respectively. However, both of these arrangements have mortality risk when the annuitant or annuitants die because the principal paid for the annuity is liquidated at death. Charitable remainder trusts (CRTs) also provide retirement income (as described in Chapter 19), but this income is not guaranteed except by the assets inside the CRT.

In all these situations, planning might include a strategy for replacing lost inheritances for heirs. This might be done, for example, through an irrevocable life insurance trust (ILIT) as covered in Chapter 29. Such an ILIT can be arranged so as not to be included in the retiree's gross estate for federal tax purposes, while the vehicle providing lifetime retirement income will actually deplete the gross estate for tax purposes.

It can be suggested that reverse mortgages, when appropriate, can be used in combination with other arrangements, like immediate life annuities or charitable gift annuities. Reverse mortgages can supplement them. On the other hand, reverse mortgages can be viewed as a reserve or contingent source of retirement income in case of economic downturn or other shortages of retirement income in the future.

PART

Income Tax Planning

10

Income Tax Fundamentals

Competence Objectives for This Chapter After reading this chapter, planners should understand:

- The federal income tax structure for individuals
- The alternative minimum tax (AMT) for individuals
- The corporate federal income tax structure
- Taxation of pass-through entities
- Federal income taxation of trusts and estates

The Federal Income Tax on Individuals

Basic Tax Structure

The federal income tax law is detailed and complex. However, the basic formula for determining an individual's tax can be shown briefly as follows.[1]

Gross income: This means all income from whatever sources derived, unless specifically excluded by a provision of the tax code. This approach can be described as gross income being an "all-inclusive concept." It is defined in this way in the IRC Section 61. The courts have further defined gross income as the accretion to a taxpayer's wealth over a given period, with some exceptions.

[1] The basic income tax structure presented here is not meant to be exhaustive. There are a number of excellent income tax publications and computer programs that taxpayers can consult to obtain detailed information on the deductions, exemptions, and so on due them. Also some of the items and limits discussed here may be phased out in the future.

Less: Deductions to arrive at adjusted gross income (referred to in tax parlance as "deductions above the line"), including (but not limited to):

- Trade or business expenses (not incurred as an employee)
- Expenses of producing rents and royalties
- Losses from sale or exchange of nonpersonal property
- Contributions to retirement plans for self-employed persons, including HR-10 or Keogh plans, Simplified Employee Pension (SEP) plans, and Savings Incentive Match Plan for Employees of Small Employers (SIMPLE) plans
- Contributions to individual retirement accounts or annuities (IRAs) for eligible persons (i.e., contributions that are tax deductible, but not the non-tax-deductible contributions that may be permitted)
- Alimony paid
- Interest penalty on early withdrawal from time savings accounts
- Contributions to health savings accounts (HSAs)
- Moving expenses
- Contributions to Archer medical savings accounts (MSAs)
- Interest paid on "qualified education loans" with an annual limit and income limits
- Qualified higher education expenses up to $3,000 per year with income limits

Equals: Adjusted gross income (AGI).

Less: Itemized deductions,[2] which are referred to as "deductions below the line" (or the standard deduction at the option of the taxpayer). The itemized deductions include:

- Medical and dental expenses (in excess of 7.5 percent of AGI)
- Nonbusiness taxes
- Charitable contributions (subject to certain limitations described in Chapter 19)
- Certain nonbusiness interest expense

Deductible interest for individuals includes *qualified residence interest*, which is mortgage interest on a taxpayer's principal residence and a second residence for acquisition or home equity indebtedness. *Acquisition indebtedness* is debt incurred to acquire, construct, or substantially improve a qualified residence. Refinanced debt is considered acquisition debt to the extent that it does not exceed the principal amount of acquisition debt immediately

[2] The overall amount of certain itemized deductions is phased out in the case of higher-income taxpayers.

before the refinancing. *Home equity indebtedness* is nonacqisition debt that does not exceed the fair market value of the qualified residence reduced by any acquisition indebtedness. There are dollar limits on the deductibility of such mortgage interest of $1,000,000 on the aggregate amount of acquisition indebtedness and $100,000 on the aggregate amount of home equity indebtedness. Interest on debt over these limits is not deductible. However, the dollar limit on acquisition indebtedness does not apply to debt incurred before October 14, 1987. But any such "grandfathered" acquisition indebtedness reduces the limit on new acquisition indebtedness.

However, *consumer interest or personal interest* (other than qualifying residence interest just described) is not deductible by individuals.

On the other hand, interest expense for loans on personal investments—*investment interest* or *portfolio interest*—is deductible, but only to the extent of investment income (if the taxpayer itemizes).

- Casualty losses (in excess of $100 for each loss and 10 percent of AGI for all losses)
- Miscellaneous deductions (in excess of 2 percent of AGI with certain exceptions)

Less: Personal exemptions.[3]

Equals: Taxable income.

Federal income tax (determined by applying income tax rates to taxable income).

Less: Credits (i.e., amounts deducted from the tax itself), including:

- Credit for the elderly or permanently and totally disabled
- Child care and care of disabled dependent or spouse credit
- Child tax credit and adoption credit
- Education credits (Hope credit and Lifetime Learning credit)
- Earned income credit
- Credit for qualified retirement savings contributions

Equals: Federal income tax payable.

Plus: Other taxes payable, including:

- AMT to the extent that it exceeds the regular income tax
- Self-employment tax (social security tax paid by the self-employed on their earnings subject to social security taxes)

Equals: Total federal taxes payable.

[3] As with certain itemized deductions, the overall amount of a taxpayer's personal and dependency exemptions are phased out for certain higher-income taxpayers.

Federal Income Tax Rates

Scheduled Tax Rates As of this writing, under the EGTRRA of 2001 and subsequent tax laws, the federal income tax rates for various filing statuses (see later discussion of filing status) are 10 percent, 15 percent, 25 percent, 28 percent, 33 percent, and 35 percent through 2010. For 2011 and thereafter, they are scheduled to "sunset" and return to the tax rates existing in 2001. Of course, new tax legislation may change this.

Thus, the *top nominal marginal* individual federal income tax rate now is 35 percent. The *average* income tax rate for a taxpayer is the total tax payable divided by the taxpayer's taxable income. For individuals, trusts, and estates, the average rate will always be less than the marginal rate. The top marginal rate normally is used for planning purposes. This assumes that the income or deductions being considered come at the top bracket, or are the last items received or paid. This assumption may tend to overstate the effect of taxes on ordinary income since the tax rates are quite progressive.

Indirect Rate Increases The situation becomes more complex, however, when we consider certain indirect rate factors. Certain itemized deductions (i.e., deductible taxes, deductible interest other than investment interest, charitable contributions, job expenses and most other miscellaneous deductions, and other miscellaneous deductions other than gambling losses) are phased out (not allowed) for higher-income taxpayers. For taxpayers in the phase-out range (AGI over $166,800 for most taxpayers for 2009 taxes), the rate of reduction in these itemized deductions is 3 percent but no more than 80 percent of allowable itemized deductions. Therefore, the effective tax rate is the nominal rate increased by about 3 percent. For example, for taxpayers subject to phase-out who are in the 35 percent bracket, the effective federal tax rate (considering only the itemized deduction phase-out) would be 36.05 percent [35% + (3% × 35% or 1.05%) = 36.05%].

In addition, the Medicare tax rate, which is currently 1.45 percent (2.90 percent on earnings from self-employment), is now applied to all earned income without limit. Therefore, higher-income taxpayers effectively must pay an additional 1.45 percent (2.90 percent for self-employed persons) on *personal earnings* over the earnings cap.

Finally, personal and dependency exemptions are also phased out for higher-income taxpayers. This increases the actual tax rate for persons in the phase-out range.

Trust Tax Rates Most irrevocable trusts are taxed as separate entities with their own tax rates.[4] Trust and estate tax brackets are steeply progressive. For example, in 2009, trust taxable income reaches the top tax bracket when it exceeds only $11,150. This rapid progression of trust tax rates has planning implications. It may not be desirable tax-wise to accumulate sizeable amounts of taxable income in trusts. It may be better to have such income distributed currently to trust beneficiaries so it will be taxable to them at possibly lower brackets. Also, when trust income is to be accumulated (such as for a minor), it may be desirable to invest trust corpus so as to produce as little taxable income as possible (such as in municipal bonds, growth common stocks, or tax-deferred vehicles).

Filing Status

There are separate federal income tax rate schedules for various categories of individual taxpayers. These include married individuals filing joint returns (and also a qualified surviving spouse during the first two years after the year in which the other spouse died), heads of households, single individuals, married individuals who elect to file separate returns, and estates and trusts. This is referred to as the taxpayer's *filing status*. Determining the appropriate filing status is one aspect of income tax planning.

Indexing for Inflation

The tax law adjusts annually, for the effects of inflation, the individual tax brackets, standard deduction amounts, the amount of personal and dependency exemptions, the thresholds for phasing out certain itemized deductions and the personal and dependency exemptions, and certain other limits or features in the tax law. This is referred to as *indexing* the tax schedules and other amounts.

Taxation of Children and the Unearned Income of Certain Children (Kiddie Tax)

When children receive income, it normally is taxable to the child at the child's tax rate. This has made planning to shift taxable income from higher-bracket taxpayers to lower-bracket children (or to others in lower brackets) reasonably attractive.

[4] Depending on their terms, certain irrevocable trusts can be *grantor trusts*. These trusts are defined in IRC Sections 671 through 679. Grantor trusts are trusts whose assets (corpus) are deemed to be owned by the grantor or creator of the trust for federal income tax purposes only. Therefore, the income and deductions of grantor trusts are treated as income and deductions of the grantor and are taxable to or taken by him or her. Revocable trusts are an example of grantor trusts.

However, there are tax limitations on income shifting to lower-bracket children.[5] First, the tax law provides that an individual who is eligible to be claimed as a dependent on another taxpayer's return may not take a personal exemption on his or her own return. Furthermore, such a dependent's standard deduction may not exceed the larger of (1) a specified amount, which is indexed for inflation, or (2) the dependent's earned income plus $300 in 2009 (indexed), subject to the regular standard deduction limits.

Finally, there is the so-called kiddie tax. This novel concept provides that the net unearned income of children age 18 or younger, or under age 24 if the child is a full-time students, (unless the child's earned income exceeds one-half of his or her support), is taxed to the child, but at the child's *parents'* top marginal federal income tax rate, assuming this rate is higher than the child's tax rate. However, this special rule can apply only when a child has unearned income in excess of a specified amount ($1,900 for 2009), which is indexed for inflation. Therefore, normally there would be no income tax advantage in shifting unearned income that will be subject to this kiddie tax.[6]

However, despite these limitations, planning is still possible. For example, earned income can still be received by a child and taxed at the child's rate. Also, shifting unearned income over the annual limit can be delayed until after a child reaches age 19 or 24. Furthermore, income can be accumulated in a trust for the child (and hence be taxable to the trust rather than the child) until the child reaches one of these ages. In this case, however, the highly progressive tax rates applying to trusts must be considered. Planning may involve distributing just enough trust income to a child (or to a custodial account for the child) to avoid the kiddie tax while allowing the remainder to be accumulated and taxed to the trust. Finally, the investment of property transferred to minors under these ages can be planned to produce as little currently taxable unearned income as possible. Such investments might include growth common stocks, municipal bonds (such as zero coupon municipals), series EE or I U.S. savings bonds, and tax-deferred vehicles (such as life insurance).

Income in Respect of a Decedent (IRD)

This is a commonly encountered but easily misunderstood concept. Income in respect of a decedent (IRD) will arise when a deceased person was entitled to items that would have been gross income for federal income tax purposes to the

[5] The subject of gifts to minors as part of estate planning is covered in Chapter 27.

[6] Parents in some cases may elect to include their children's unearned income over the greater of $1,900 for 2009 or $950 (the standard deduction) for 2009 in their own returns to avoid having to have the child file a return.

decedent, but which were not includable in the decedent's gross income for the year of his or her death. IRD items generally are treated as gross income to the recipients after the decedent's death. The recipients do *not* receive a step-up in basis following the decedent's death, as do capital assets at present.

There are numerous IRD items. Some common examples are:

- Distributions after an employee's or former employee's death from qualified retirement plans. This is an important source of IRD in many cases.
- Distributions from a decedent's IRA, other than a Roth IRA. This is another important source of IRD.
- Distributions after an employee's or former employee's death from tax-sheltered annuity [TSA or Section 403(b)] plans.
- Accrued, and as yet untaxed, interest on U.S. savings bonds as of the death of the owner.
- Death benefits under nonqualified deferred compensation plans.
- Distributions of as yet untaxed investment income from investment annuity contracts after the death of the annuitant.
- The taxable portion of payments made after death from sales made on the installment method.

An IRD item will not only produce gross income to the recipient of the item (e.g., a beneficiary or the decedent's estate or heirs), but it also will be included at full value in the decedent's gross estate for federal estate tax purposes (and counted for GST tax purposes as well). Thus, IRD items are heavily taxed at death. Some relief is provided, however, by allowing the recipient to take an itemized income tax deduction on his or her federal income tax return for any federal estate or GST tax attributable to the IRD item in the decedent's estate. The amount of this itemized deduction is determined by calculating the federal estate or GST tax payable with the IRD item included in the decedent's estate, and then calculating the estate or GST tax without the IRD item. The difference is the income tax deduction. Of course, if no federal estate or GST tax is payable, there will be no deduction.

CASE EXAMPLE

Suppose that Joan Martin, who is divorced, is a participant in a qualified savings plan with a Section 401(k) option. She has a current account balance in the plan of $200,000, and her adult daughter, Amy, is named as beneficiary in the event of Joan's death. Joan also has other property so that the total value will place her in a 45 percent top marginal federal estate tax bracket. Suppose now that Joan dies. Amy, as the plan's beneficiary, will receive the $200,000 account balance, which is IRD to her. Furthermore, the $200,000 is in Joan's gross estate for federal estate tax purposes. Thus, the $200,000 is gross income (ordinary income) to Amy in the year she receives it, but she will have an itemized deduction of $90,000 for the estate tax attributable to the account balance.[7] If Amy receives the account balance over more than one taxable year (such as over her life expectancy), she will receive gross income as it is paid out to her and also a proportional part of the itemized deduction each year.[8]

Actual and Constructive Receipt of Income

There are two generally accepted methods for recognizing income and expenses for income tax purposes. They are the cash basis and the accrual basis. Most individuals and many smaller businesses are cash-basis taxpayers.

For *cash-basis taxpayers,* items of income (or expenses) are considered received (or paid), and hence taxable for income tax purposes, in the year they are actually or constructively received. *Actual receipt* means a taxpayer is in actual possession of the income. *Constructive receipt* is when the income has been credited to the taxpayer or set apart for him or her so that the taxpayer can actually receive it at any time without any substantial limitation or restriction on the taxpayer's right to do so. For example, if Martha Jones is paid her salary this year and cashes her payroll check during the year, she is in actual receipt of the compensation this year and will be taxed on it this year. If, instead, Martha's employer this year places, say, 10 percent of her salary in an investment account in Martha's name from which she has the unrestricted right to withdraw the money at any time, Martha will be in constructive receipt of the 10 percent placed in this account even if she does not actually withdraw it this year.

This concept of constructive receipt can be important for planning purposes. Assume, for example, the same facts as just noted for Martha Jones, except that Martha will be entitled to the 10 percent of her salary placed in the investment account (and the earnings on the account) only in the event of her termination of employment, disability, death, the passage of time, or other substantial limitation or restriction. In this case, Martha would not be

[7] This assumes the full $200,000 account balance falls in the 45 percent estate tax bracket in Joan's estate. There is no GST tax in this case because Amy is not a "skip person" with respect to Joan. (See Chapter 26 for an explanation of the GST tax and the definition of a skip person.) We are also assuming Joan has no income tax basis in her Section 401(k) plan.

[8] In planning for distributions from qualified retirement plans, a common strategy is to defer the distributions and the income taxes thereon for as long as possible under the circumstances. In this case, this would normally be for Amy's life expectancy. (See Chapter 16 for a discussion of planning for taking distributions from retirement plans.)

in constructive receipt this year of the 10 percent of her salary because her right to receive it was subject to a substantial limitation or restriction.[9] She will be taxed only when the funds are actually paid to her or made available to her without restriction, which normally would be many years in the future. This is the principle underlying nonqualified deferred compensation plans offered by many employers to certain employees. The doctrine of constructive receipt applies only to cash-basis taxpayers.

For *accrual-basis taxpayers,* items of income are included in gross income for the year in which the right to receive the income becomes fixed and the amounts receivable become determinable with reasonable accuracy.

Assignment of Income

In general, income from property is taxable to the owner of the property. Thus, if one wishes to transfer the income from property to another, ownership of the property must be transferred (given or sold) to the intended recipient or to a trust for the recipient.

Merely assigning only the income from property while retaining ownership will not shift the tax liability on that income to the donee. The tax liability will remain with the property's owner. Similarly, income from personal services (personal earnings) is taxable to the person rendering the services. The tax liability on personal earnings cannot be transferred to another by assigning the right to receive the earnings to the other person. To use the famous analogy of Justice Oliver Wendell Holmes, if one wishes to transfer the fruit from a tree (for tax purposes), one must transfer the whole tree.[10]

Capital Gains Taxation

General Considerations Capital gains and losses are realized from the sale or exchange of capital assets. With some exceptions, capital assets include the property taxpayers own. Some examples are common stocks, bonds, preferred stocks, investment real estate, collectibles, partnership interests (generally), personal residences, and other personal assets. These gains and losses also are recognized in the year of the sale or exchange, unless there is some specific nonrecognition provision in the IRC that defers recognition. The common nonrecognition provisions are outlined in the next section. The difference between the amount realized from the sale or exchange and

[9] In general, an amount is not constructively received if it is only conditionally credited to the taxpayer, it is indefinite in amount, it is subject to substantial limitation or restriction, or the payer lacks funds.

[10] See *Lucas v. Earl,* 281 U.S. 111 (1930).

the adjusted basis of the asset in the hands of the taxpayer is the amount of the capital gain or loss.

Amount Realized and Adjusted Basis The *amount realized* generally is the value received from the sale or exchange of a capital asset.

It normally includes any cash received, the value of any property received, and any indebtedness assumed from the seller.

The *adjusted basis* depends on how the taxpayer acquired the property. In general, adjusted basis is determined in certain common situations as follows:

- If a taxpayer originally purchased the property, its adjusted basis is its cost plus any purchase commissions.
- If a taxpayer acquired appreciated property as a lifetime gift from another (i.e., the donor's basis is less than the property's fair market value), its adjusted basis for the donee is its basis in the hands of the donor (a carryover or substitute basis), plus any gift tax on unrealized appreciation of the gift property.

  On the other hand, if the donor's basis is greater than the fair market value of the gift property (i.e., it is loss property), the donee's basis is the smaller of the fair market value or the donor's basis assuming the donee sells the property at a loss (i.e., for less than its fair market value at the time of the gift).

  There is a carryover basis for gifts between married persons and for transfers of property incident to a divorce.
- If a taxpayer inherited the property from a decedent, its adjusted basis at present is the property's fair market value at the date of death (or the alternative valuation date for federal estate tax purposes). This is the important step-up or step-down in income tax basis at death rule.
- If a taxpayer receives new stock or securities in a tax-free reorganization or merger (as one of those tax-free reorganizations defined in the IRC), the new stock's or securities' basis will be the former basis of the stock or securities the taxpayer exchanged for the new stock or securities (a *carryover basis*).
- If a person acquires a partnership interest by a contribution of property (including money) to the partnership, the basis of the person's interest in the partnership generally is the money contributed plus the adjusted basis to the contributing partner of the property contributed (a carryover basis from the property contributed).
- If a partner receives a distribution of property in kind from his or her partnership, the partner takes the partnership's basis in the property (a carryover basis), but not greater than the partner's basis in his or her partnership interest.
- If a person or persons transfer property to a corporation solely in exchange for stock in such corporation, and immediately after the exchange, the

person or persons have control of the corporation (at least 80 percent ownership), the basis of the person's stock in such corporation generally is the same as the basis of the property transferred.

- If a person or entity owns an interest in a pass-through business entity (i.e., partnerships, S corporations, or LLCs), his or her basis in the interest will be adjusted to reflect the profits, losses, and other operations of the pass-through entity. (See Chapter 31 for a more complete description of these entities.)
- A taxpayer may increase his or her adjusted basis in property by the cost of any improvements and reduce it by any depreciation, depletion, or amortization.

These statements do not include all of the situations or rules for determining basis. They are intended to be representative of common situations. Other rules for determining basis are discussed elsewhere in this book. Finally, a taxpayer may increase his or her basis at sale or exchange by any expenses of sale (such as brokers' fees, commissions, transfer taxes, and the like), unless these expenses were taken from the amount realized.

Calculation of Capital Gains and Losses *Net capital gains* are net long-term capital gains (long-term capital gains minus long-term capital losses) minus any net short-term capital losses (short-term capital losses minus short-term capital gains). For this purpose, short-term capital gains and losses are those gains and losses on capital assets held for one year or less; the taxpayer first determines any net short-term capital gain or loss for the year. Long-term capital gains and losses are those gains and losses on capital assets held for more than one year; the taxpayer determines any net long-term capital gain or loss for the year. Thus, under this system, capital losses offset capital gains and, to the extent of $3,000 per year, other ordinary income of the taxpayer.

CASE EXAMPLE

Assume a taxpayer had the following gains and losses during a year:

Long-term capital gains	$12,000
Long-term capital losses	$3,000
Short-term capital gains	$1,000
Short-term capital losses	$2,500

Thus, this taxpayer has net long-term capital gains of $9,000 ($12,000 – $3,000), net short-term capital losses of $1,500 ($2,500 – $1,000), and net capital gains of $7,500 ($9,000 – $1,500). The importance of this calculation is that as of this writing the tax rate on capital gains for individuals is 15 percent (or 5 percent for individual taxpayers in the 10 and 15 percent brackets), while the rate on ordinary income and net short-term capital gains can be as high as 35 percent.

As just noted, capital losses are first used to offset capital gains of the same type and then any net capital loss (short-term or long-term) can be used to reduce the taxpayer's other ordinary income, dollar for dollar, up to a maximum of $3,000 in any one year. Any unused net capital losses may be carried forward by the taxpayer indefinitely and used in future years, first to offset any capital gains, and then to offset ordinary income, up to $3,000 per year.

CASE EXAMPLE

Suppose Harry Baker had the following capital gains and losses on his stock and bond transactions this year:

Long-term capital gains	$1,000
Short-term capital gains	$2,000
Short-term capital losses	$15,000

In addition, Harry and his wife had other ordinary taxable income of $250,000. Harry first can offset his capital gains against his capital losses so that he has a net capital loss for the year of $12,000. He then can use up to $3,000 of this net capital loss to reduce the other ordinary taxable income. Since Harry and his wife file a joint return and are in a 33 percent top marginal tax bracket, this would be worth $990 in income tax saving this year. Also, they can carry the remaining $9,000 of net capital loss forward to the next and subsequent tax years. Thus, a taxpayer with capital losses can use these losses to save on income taxes by realizing them at the proper time. This is sometimes called *tax loss selling.*

Tax Rates on Capital Gains At present, the tax rate for individuals on net capital gains generally is 15 percent, except for taxpayers in the 10 and 15 percent brackets for ordinary income, in which case the rate is 5 percent. However, for 2008 through 2010, the 5 percent rate becomes 0 (i.e., no tax on net capital gains). Under EGTRRA and subsequent laws, these rates will "sunset" in 2011 and become rates as of 2001 unless the law is changed before then.

There are some exceptions to these capital gains tax rates. One is that net capital gains on collectibles (art, coins, stamps, etc.) are taxed at a maximum rate of 28 percent. Also, for sales or taxable exchanges of certain depreciable real estate (such as residential rental property), the portion of the net capital gain attributable to allowable depreciation is taxed at a maximum rate of 25 percent, as illustrated in Chapter 6. Net short-term capital gains are taxed at the same rates as ordinary income.

Constructive Sales Normally, a capital gain or loss is not realized and recognized for tax purposes until there has been a sale, exchange, or other taxable disposition of a capital asset. At this point, the difference between the amount realized and the adjusted basis of the asset is the capital gain or loss.

However, the Taxpayer Relief Act of 1997 introduced a new concept of constructive sales of appreciated financial positions. The idea behind this provision is generally to prohibit the use of certain hedging techniques that essentially allowed holders of highly appreciated assets (mainly securities) to eliminate the risk of owning the securities without actually selling the securities and realizing a sizeable capital gain. Thus, realizing the gain could be deferred or perhaps even eliminated (through the step-up in basis at death rule or other techniques). Under the constructive sale rules, however, transactions that use these techniques are considered sales and are taxed at the time of sale.

For this purpose, an *appreciated financial position* is a position in any stock, debt instrument, or partnership interest (with certain exceptions) where there would be a gain if the position were sold or otherwise terminated at its fair market value. A *constructive sale* of an appreciated financial position is considered to occur if the holder (or a related person) (1) enters into a *short sale* of the same or substantially identical property (in effect, selling short against the box), (2) enters into an *offsetting notional principal contract* (a *swap*) with respect to the same or substantially identical property, (3) enters into a *futures or forward contract* to deliver the same or substantially identical property, (4) has entered into one of the previous transactions and acquires the same property as the underlying property in the position, or (5) to the extent prescribed in regulations, enters into other transactions with substantially the same effect as the transactions previously named.

This provision has essentially eliminated several formerly popular techniques (particularly selling short against the box) for deferring and perhaps eliminating significant capital gains.[11] However, some other techniques still may be available. They are discussed in Chapter 11.

[11] The law does provide that certain short-term hedges that close before the end of 30 days after the tax year in which the transaction was entered into and where the taxpayer is at risk on the appreciated financial position for an additional 60 days will not be considered constructive sales. However, this "safe harbor" is expected to be of limited usefulness to taxpayers.

Nonrecognition Provisions

It was noted at the beginning of this discussion that capital gains are realized as a result of the sale or exchange of a capital asset and also are recognized for tax purposes in the year of the sale or exchange, unless there is a specific provision in the tax code that defers recognition. Such provisions are called *nonrecognition provisions.* The effect of a nonrecognition provision is to defer income taxation on any gain to some future transaction or event when, depending on the property involved and the circumstances, there may or may not be a tax due.

When a nonrecognition provision applies, there normally is a *carryover of income tax basis* from the property sold or exchanged to the new property acquired, so, in effect, the new property takes the old property's basis. In this way, the nonrecognized gain is not forgiven; it is simply deferred until some future transaction or event. Nonrecognition provisions can be important in financial planning. Some of the more commonly used nonrecognition provisions are briefly listed here to illustrate the concept.

- *Section 1031: Exchange of property held for productive use or investment.* These exchanges are referred to as *like-kind exchanges* and are used for property held in a trade or business, or for investment, with certain exceptions. The exceptions include the important categories of stocks, bonds, notes, and other securities or evidences of indebtedness. These categories of assets are not eligible for like-kind exchange treatment. Like-kind exchanges are commonly used for investment real estate, as explained in Chapter 6.
- *Section 1035: Certain exchanges of insurance policies.* While it does not involve capital gains, this important provision states that no gain or loss shall be recognized on the exchange of certain life insurance policies or the exchange of certain annuity contracts.
- *Section 354: Exchanges of stock and securities in certain reorganizations.* This and other code provisions allow stockholders to exchange their stock for other stock, with no gain or loss being recognized, in the case of certain corporate reorganizations and mergers, as specified in the IRC. It permits tax-free reorganizations and mergers in these cases.
- *Section 351: Transfer to corporation controlled by transferor.* This provision permits a tax-free exchange of appreciated property for corporate stock if the combined transferors are in control of the corporation immediately thereafter. This nonrecognition provision is important in the formation of corporations.
- *Section 721: Nonrecognition of gain or loss on contribution to a partnership.* This provision permits a tax-free exchange of appreciated property for a partnership interest upon contribution of the property to the partnership.

This provision is important in the formation of, and in adding partners to, partnerships. It also can be significant in other areas, such as the creation of family limited partnerships and the use of exchange funds for deferring gains on securities.

- *Section 1041: Transfers of property between spouses or incident to divorce.* This provision specifies that no gain or loss shall be recognized on a transfer of property from an individual to his or her spouse or to his or her former spouse, provided in the case of a former spouse the transfer is incident to a divorce. This nonrecognition provision permits the tax-free sale of property between spouses and the tax-free transfer of property from one spouse to another as part of a divorce settlement.
- *Section 1036: Stock for stock of same corporation.* This provides that no gain or loss shall be recognized if common stock in a corporation is exchanged solely for common stock in the same corporation, or if preferred stock in a corporation is exchanged solely for preferred stock in the same corporation. This nonrecognition provision can be used, for example, to allow use of previously owned common stock in a corporation to exercise a stock option for common stock in the same corporation. Such an exchange will defer any gain in the previously owned stock.
- *Section 1042: Sales of stock to employee stock ownership plans or certain cooperatives.* This provision allows nonrecognition of gain on the sale of non-publicly–traded employer securities to an employee stock ownership plan (ESOP), under certain conditions. It allows stockowners of closely held C corporations to defer capital gains by selling their appreciated stock to their corporation's ESOP.

Alternative Minimum Tax (AMT) for Individuals

An AMT may be imposed on individual taxpayers, estates, and trusts with certain tax preference items and adjustments.[12] This minimum tax applies if it exceeds a taxpayer's regular income tax.

Calculation of the AMT The AMT is calculated by starting with a taxpayer's regular taxable income for the year. To this amount certain tax preference items are added back, and certain adjustments are added to or subtracted from it to arrive at the taxpayer's alternative minimum taxable income (AMTI) for the year. It may be noted that adjustments are different from tax preferences. Adjustments may involve only differences in timing for AMT and regular tax purposes, while preferences always increase AMTI.

[12] Taxable corporations may be subject to a corporate AMT, which is discussed later in this chapter.

Some common adjustments in arriving at AMTI include the following: (1) adding back personal and dependency exemptions, which are not allowed for AMT purposes; (2) adding back certain itemized deductions, which are not allowed or are cut back for AMT purposes (such as income and property taxes imposed by state and local governments, home equity loan interest on loans up to $100,000, employee business expenses deductible for regular tax purposes, and otherwise deductible medical expenses up to 10 percent of AGI); (3) adding back the standard deduction for those who do not itemize (the standard deduction is not allowed for AMT purposes); (4) adding the amount by which the value of stock purchased under incentive stock option (ISO) plans exceeds the option price; and (5) various other items.

The tax preferences that are added to regular taxable income to arrive at AMTI include: (1) otherwise tax-free interest on certain private-activity municipal bonds (AMT bonds) issued after August 7, 1986 (see Chapter 7, but this preference is suspended for 2009 and 2010); (2) accelerated depreciation on property placed in service before 1987; (3) 7 percent of the otherwise excluded gain from the sale of qualified newly issued small business stock held for at least five years; and (4) certain other items.

An AMT exemption amount, which is based on the taxpayer's filing status, then is deducted from AMTI. This amount was $69,950 for married taxpayers filing jointly and surviving spouses, and $46,200 for single taxpayers and heads of households for 2008.

However, this exemption is phased out when AMTI reaches certain levels. For example, for married taxpayers filing jointly, the exemption is reduced by 25 percent of the amount by which AMTI exceeds $150,000. The AMT rates are applied to the amount resulting from these calculations. These rates are 26 percent of the first $175,000 and 28 percent for amounts above $175,000. The taxpayer then subtracts his or her regular income tax liability for the year from this amount. If the result is positive, the excess over the regular tax is the AMT owed for the year.

Finally, there is a *minimum tax credit* (MTC) that taxpayers may be able to take against their regular income tax only for AMT paid on AMT items involving timing differences (such as on ISOs at exercise) when future regular tax exceeds future AMT.

CASE EXAMPLE

Assume that John and Mary Costa file a joint return and have regular taxable income for federal income tax purposes of $160,000 and that their regular federal income tax payable on this amount for the year is $37,926. In arriving at their taxable income, the Costas took personal and dependency exemptions, an itemized deduction for state and local income and property taxes, and an itemized deduction for interest on a home equity mortgage loan. The total for these exemptions and itemized deductions is $26,000. In addition, this year John exercised ISOs that his employer had granted to him nine years ago for 500 shares of employer stock at an exercise price of $20 per share. The fair market value of the stock at exercise was $80 per share. Finally, a municipal bond mutual fund that the Costas own reported that $2,000 of the dividends credited to them during the year were from AMT bonds.

Given these facts, the calculation of the Costas' AMT in 2008 would be as follows:

Regular taxable income	$160,000
AMT adjustments	+ 56,000[13]
AMT preferences	+ 2,000[14]
AMTI	$218,000
AMT exemption	– 52,950[15]
	$165,050
Tax ($165,050 × 0.26)	42,913
Regular tax liability	– 37,926
	$4,987

The Costas must pay a total tax for the year of $42,913 ($37,926 regular tax + $4,987 AMT).

AMT Planning Taxpayers may wish to time certain transactions (such as the exercise of ISOs) so that they will not produce AMT or produce as little AMT as possible. Of course, the AMT may be only one factor in such decisions. Persons who are likely to be subject to the AMT normally should not invest in AMT bonds or in mutual funds that have significant positions in such bonds. Also, taxpayers should make sure to take advantage of the MTC against the regular tax when it is available.

Additional planning ideas regarding stock options and the AMT are presented in Chapter 18.

[13] These would be the total of $26,000 of personal and dependency exemptions, state and local income and property taxes, and interest on the home equity mortgage loan, plus the $30,000 bargain element on the exercise of the ISOs. This bargain element is the difference between the fair market value of the stock at exercise and the exercise price paid ($80 per share – $20 per share × 500 shares = $30,000).

[14] This is the AMT bond interest. This amount would not be included for 2009 and 2010.

[15] This is the $69,950 exemption amount for married taxpayers filing a joint return for 2008 reduced by 25 percent of the amount by which AMTI exceeds $150,000 ($218,000 – $150,000 = $68,000 × 0.25 = $17,000; $69,950 – $17,000 = $52,950 AMT exemption in this example).

The Federal Income Tax on Corporations

Taxable corporations have their own federal income tax structure.[16] They also are subject to state (and perhaps local) income taxes in many states.

What Is a Taxable Corporation?

While this seems like a relatively simple question, it has not always been so in practice. However, with the "check-the-box" regulations issued by the IRS and effective January 1, 1997, this issue has been simplified for many entities.

A corporation that is incorporated under a state statute and that has not elected for S corporation status will be taxable as a corporation under the IRC. Correspondingly, a corporation that has elected for S corporation status will not be taxed as a corporation. It will have pass-through status, as described in the next section. Finally, most unincorporated businesses, such as partnerships and LLCs, can simply elect under the check-the-box regulations whether they wish to be taxed as corporations or as partnerships. If no election is made, it is presumed they have elected to be taxed as partnerships. These regulations have simplified this matter considerably for most unincorporated businesses.[17]

Basic Corporate Income Tax Structure

C corporations must pay tax on their taxable income at corporate income tax rates. The C corporation itself is a separate tax-paying entity apart from its shareholders. A C corporation's *taxable income* is its gross income subject to tax minus deductions allowable to corporations. For example, corporations normally may deduct their ordinary and necessary business expenses, with some exceptions. However, a corporation's taxable income may not be the

[16] The corporate tax rules are found in Subchapter C of the Internal Revenue Code. Therefore, corporations that are subject to federal income taxation are commonly called *C corporations*. On the other hand, the rules for electing small business corporations that have opted not to be taxed as corporations are found in Subchapter S of the IRC. Hence, they are commonly called *S corporations*.

[17] Formerly, if an unincorporated business (such as an LLC) had more corporate characteristics than noncorporate characteristics, the IRS would seek to tax it as an association taxable as a corporation (i.e., it would be subject to the corporate income tax, which generally is undesirable). There were four significant corporate characteristics in this regard: limited liability, centralized management, continuity of life, and free transferability of ownership interests. Thus, if an unincorporated business had any three of these four characteristics, it would be taxed as a corporation; if it had two or fewer, it would be taxed as a partnership. This resulted in a facts-and-circumstances test for most unincorporated businesses, which could cause uncertainty and complexity. Fortunately, these problems generally have been eliminated by the check-the-box regulations.

same as its income reported to shareholders (book income), because some items of corporate income may not be subject to tax and some deductions may not be allowable for tax purposes.

A C corporation may have an operating loss when its business deductions exceed its business gross income, with certain adjustments. This is referred to as a *net operating loss (NOL).* A corporation (as well as most taxpayers carrying on a trade or business) may carry back an NOL to each of the two preceding years and then any remaining loss may be carried forward to each of the following 20 years. Note, however, that these losses can be used to offset only corporate profits, not the income of the individual shareholders.

Corporations can also have capital gains and losses from sales or exchanges of capital assets. C corporations, however, can deduct capital losses only to the extent they have capital gains. Any unused net capital loss from a year can be carried back to each of the three preceding years and then any remaining loss can be carried forward to each of the five following years. The tax rate on net capital gains is the same as for other corporate taxable income.

The fact that the C corporations are separate tax-paying entities gives rise to the well-known *double taxation of C corporation income.* The taxable income of a C corporation is subject to corporate income tax. Then, to the extent a C corporation pays dividends to its shareholders from its after-tax income, those dividends are again taxed to the shareholders individually as dividend income. The corporation gets no tax deduction for dividends paid as it does for interest paid to its bondholders.

Corporate Income Tax Rates

Under the corporate tax system, unlike the tax rates for individuals, surtaxes are imposed at certain levels of corporate income to phase out the benefits of lower corporate tax brackets. Following are the federal tax rates for C corporations.

Taxable Income (Brackets)		Tax Rates
$0–$50,000	15%	
$50,000–$75,000	25%	
$75,000–$100,000	34%	
$100,000–$335,000	39%	(34% + 5% surtax to phase out benefits of 15% and 25% brackets)
$335,000–$10,000,000	34%	
$10,000,000–$15,000,000	35%	
$15,000,000–$18,333,333	38%	(35% + 3% surtax to phase out benefits of 34% bracket)
Over $18,333,333	35%	(Flat tax on all taxable income)

Other Corporate Taxes

In addition to the regular corporate income tax, several other federal taxes may apply to C corporations.

Accumulated Earnings Tax This tax is intended to apply to corporations that have accumulated earnings inside the corporation to avoid income taxation on dividends that might otherwise have been paid to shareholders. It applies only to earnings and profits that are accumulated beyond the reasonable needs of the business. There is an accumulated earnings credit, which is the greater of (1) earnings and profits accumulated during the year for the reasonable needs of the business or (2) $250,000. Thus, only accumulated income that exceeds a minimum of $250,000 per year is potentially subject to this tax. Furthermore, payment of dividends will reduce accumulated taxable income. The accumulated earnings tax rate, which is the top rate for individual taxpayers, is applied to accumulated taxable income. Any accumulated earnings tax is paid in addition to the regular corporate income tax.

AMT Taxable corporations are subject to their own AMT. It generally operates like the individual AMT, except that some adjustments and preferences are different and the minimum tax credit against the regular tax is allowed for the entire corporate AMT liability. The corporate AMT exemption is $40,000 and is phased out at various income levels. The tax rate is a flat 20 percent. A corporation pays AMT only when it exceeds its regular tax liability.

The corporate AMT does not apply to small business corporations for taxable years beginning after 1997. For this purpose, a "small business corporation" generally is one that has average gross receipts no greater than $5 million for three consecutive taxable years beginning after 1994. Once the $5 million test is met, the corporation will continue to be a small business corporation as long as its average gross receipts do not exceed $7.5 million.

Special Forms of Corporations for Tax Purposes There are a variety of such corporations. For example, in the case of *personal service corporations* (a corporation whose principal activity is the performance of personal services and such services are substantially performed by employee-owners of the corporation and whose principal purpose is avoiding taxes) the IRS may reallocate tax benefits of such corporations between the corporation and its employee-owners under certain conditions. Also, *personal holding companies* (PHCs) are corporations whose income is mainly (60 percent or more) from personal holding company income (dividends, interest, rents, royalties, annuities, payments under personal service contracts, taxable income from estates and trusts, etc.) and where more than 50 percent of its stock is owned by five or fewer individuals. A 15 percent surtax is imposed on the undistributed personal holding company income of a PHC in addition to the regular corporate income tax.

Furthermore, there are regulated investment companies (e.g., mutual funds), which were discussed in Chapter 8; REITs, which were covered in Chapter 6; and real estate mortgage investment conduits (REMICs). These are essentially pass-through corporations for their shareholders. S corporations are covered in the next section as a pass-through entity.

Pass-Through Business Entities

These are entities that are not themselves taxable, but rather report their profits, losses, and other tax items to their owners, who pay taxes on them or deduct them on the owners' individual tax returns. They are tax-reporting but not tax-paying entities.

Partnerships

For tax purposes, a partnership generally is a syndicate, group, pool, joint venture, or other unincorporated organization through which any business, financial operation, or venture is carried on and that is not a trust, estate, or corporation. It usually exists when two or more persons join together to carry on a trade or business and to share profits and losses as agreed, and with each contributing cash, property, or services to form the partnership. Aside from taxation, there are state law definitions of partnerships, often coming from the Uniform Revised Partnership Act and the Uniform Revised Limited Partnership Act.

A partnership itself does not pay taxes, but rather reports each partner's *distributive share* of the partnership's taxable income or loss, as well as certain separately stated items to the partner. The partner then includes this distributive share (whether or not any distributions are actually paid to the partner) in the partner's income and any other tax items on his or her own return. A partner also is taxed on any guaranteed payments (e.g., salary) paid to him or her by the partnership. Partnerships may be general partnerships, limited partnerships (LPs), or limited liability partnerships (LLPs). They are all taxed under the same tax rules.

A special kind of partnership for tax purposes is the *publicly traded partnership* (PTP) or *master limited partnership*. A partnership is a PTP if interests in the partnership are traded on an established securities market or on a substantially equivalent secondary market. The general rule is that PTPs are taxed like corporations. However, there are significant exceptions to this. For example, if 90 percent or more of a PTP's gross income comes from passive sources (e.g., rent, interest, dividends, or mining and natural resource income), it will be taxed as a partnership. Also, beginning in 1998, if a PTP existing in 1987 elects to pay a 3.5 percent tax on its gross income from the active conduct of a trade or business, it will not be taxed as a corporation. Some large corporations have spun off certain of their operations into PTPs, in which investors can purchase limited partnership interests on organized securities markets.

S Corporations

Eligible domestic corporations can elect (with the initial consent of all shareholders) to be taxed under Subchapter S of the IRC, rather than Subchapter C, and hence not pay any corporate income tax. The profits, losses, and other tax items of an S corporation are passed through to the shareholders in proportion to their stockholdings and are taxable to them on their own individual returns. This is true whether the shareholders receive any dividends or not. In all other respects, an S corporation is organized like any other corporation under state law.

Only some corporations are eligible to make an S election. These eligibility requirements are noted in Chapter 31; however, generally speaking, smaller, closely held corporations can elect S corporation status.

Limited Liability Companies (LLCs)

These are a relatively new kind of business entity. The owners are called *members,* and the LLC is managed by its members or by a manager. LLCs are organized by filing articles of organization with a state. All states now have statutes allowing LLCs. The unique characteristics of LLCs are that their members can manage the entity, have limited liability for the debts and obligations of the LLC, and generally can elect to be taxed like partnerships for federal income tax purposes under the check-the-box regulations.

Federal Income Taxation of Trusts and Estates

Estates and many trusts are taxed as separate entities with their own tax rate schedule. The rules regarding taxation of trusts and estates are complex and are only briefly reviewed here.

A *trust* is a fiduciary arrangement whereby a person (the grantor or creator) transfers property (the corpus) to a trustee (a fiduciary and "legal owner" of the trust property) to be administered under the terms of the trust for the benefit of trust beneficiaries (who are the "equitable owners" of the trust corpus). The corpus of a trust normally will produce income and perhaps capital gains, and the issue here is how such income and capital gains will be taxed for federal income tax purposes. Depending on the terms of a trust, trust income may be taxed to the trust, the trust beneficiaries, or the grantor of the trust.

Grantor Trusts

A *grantor trust* is one whose income is taxed to and whose deductions may be taken by the grantor, creator, or settlor of the trust, regardless of whether the grantor receives such income. The various kinds of powers over a trust possessed by the grantor (or in some cases by a "nonadverse party") that will cause the trust to be a grantor trust are spelled out in Sections 673 through 677 of the IRC and are called the *grantor trust rules.* In general, these powers include the power to revoke, alter, or amend the trust; the power to control beneficial enjoyment of the trust; use of trust income for the benefit of the grantor, a greater than 5 percent reversionary interest in the grantor; and certain administrative powers. The idea is that the grantor should be treated as the owner of a trust's corpus for income tax purposes (and hence be taxable on trust income and eligible for trust deductions) when the grantor can benefit from the trust or has too much power over the trust, as defined in the grantor trust rules.

It should be noted that the grantor trust rules just described for federal income tax purposes may be different from the rules regarding inclusion or noninclusion of a trust's corpus in the grantor's (or a beneficiary's) gross estate for federal estate tax purposes. Thus, sometimes a trust is deliberately structured to be a grantor trust for income tax purposes, but also structured so that the corpus will not be included in the grantor's gross estate for federal estate tax purposes. These are called *intentionally defective grantor trusts* and they may have several estate planning uses as described in Chapter 27.

Simple and Complex Trusts

General Tax Principles These are irrevocable trusts that are not grantor trusts. As a general principle, the income of such trusts is taxable to the beneficiaries to the extent it is distributed to them, and the trust gets a corresponding income tax deduction for such distributions. However, the gross income of trust beneficiaries and a trust's deduction for distributions to beneficiaries are limited by the trust's distributable net income (DNI) for the year (not counting items not included in the trust's gross income for tax purposes, such as tax-exempt interest on municipal bonds). Taxable income that is accumulated in a trust is taxed to the trust itself at the trust's rates.

A trust has an income tax basis in the property held by the trust, just as individuals do. Essentially, a trust's basis is determined in the same ways as for individuals. Trusts may realize and recognize capital gains on sales or exchanges of their property. Under the Revised Uniform Principal and Income Act (which has been adopted by most states), unless the trust document provides otherwise, capital gains are allocated to principal (corpus) and are not included in income for trust accounting purposes. They are then taxed to the trust. Of course, capital gains can be distributed to and be taxable to trust beneficiaries if the trust document so provides or if state law permits unitrust payments from a trust, as explained in Chapter 25.

When a trust distributes income with a special tax status, such as tax-exempt municipal bond interest, the income retains that status in the hands of a beneficiary. Thus, the trust beneficiary can exclude such items from his or her own gross income for tax purposes.

The overall idea underlying the income taxation of trusts is that trust income is taxed only once—to the beneficiaries if distributed, to the trust if accumulated, or possibly partly to each if distributed in part and accumulated in part.

Simple Trusts These are trusts that must distribute all income currently, whose trustee does not distribute corpus currently, and that have no charitable beneficiaries. In this case, the beneficiaries are taxed on the current income distributed and the trust gets a tax deduction for those distributions.

Complex Trusts and Estates Complex trusts are those that are not simple trusts or grantor trusts. They include trusts where income can be accumulated, where corpus is distributed, or that have charitable beneficiaries. Thus, trusts that give the trustee discretion to pay out or to accumulate current income and to distribute corpus to beneficiaries would be complex trusts for tax purposes. The income of complex trusts and estates may be taxed to the beneficiaries, who receive distributions, or to the trust or estate, depending on the circumstances.

State and Local Income Taxes

In addition to the federal income tax system just outlined, many states and some cities and other localities levy personal income taxes or wage taxes on individuals. They also may levy corporate income taxes.

State personal income taxes vary greatly. Most states have graduated rates like the federal system, but some have flat rates on all taxable income. The top effective tax rate varies among the states, from as low as 2 percent to as high as 10 percent (without counting local income or wage taxes). Some states do not have any income tax.

11

Income Tax Reduction and Management Techniques for Individuals

Competence Objectives for This Chapter After reading this chapter, planners should understand:

- The basic income tax planning techniques
- Planning sales of securities for tax losses
- Tax planning for sales of principal residences
- Techniques for shifting the income tax burden to others
- Methods for postponing income taxation
- Taking returns as capital gains and the capital gains lock-in problem
- Methods for deferring capital gains and dealing with concentrated equity positions

The income tax planning techniques considered in this chapter can be broken down into those that essentially involve (1) tax elimination or reduction; (2) shifting the tax burden to others; (3) allowing wealth to accumulate without current taxation (postponing taxation); (4) taking returns as capital gains; and (5) deferring, and perhaps even eliminating, potential capital gains on appreciated property. Some plans involve a combination of these ideas.

Tax Elimination or Reduction

Techniques aimed at producing income tax deductions, exemptions, and credits that reduce otherwise taxable income (or the tax itself) and techniques that result in nontaxable income or in economic benefits that are not taxable are perhaps the most desirable because they avoid tax altogether. Following are some such techniques.

Use of Checklists of Deductions, Exemptions, and Credits

Many specific income tax deductions, exemptions, and credits are available to taxpayers. Space does not permit discussion of all of them here, but some are mentioned in this and other chapters. Also, there are checklists available from the government and from commercial publishers for the following: items included in gross income; nontaxable income (and other items); deductions to arrive at adjusted gross income; itemized deductions; nondeductible items; other taxes (federal, state, and local); and various taxable or deductible items that apply particularly to certain occupations or businesses.

Use of Proper Filing Status

A related matter is the choice of the most advantageous filing status. For example, a taxpayer should be sure to claim head of household status or special surviving spouse status if he or she qualifies. Also, although married persons usually file joint returns, they can elect to file separate returns.

Receipt of Nontaxable Income

There are various forms of nontaxable income. Perhaps the most important for many taxpayers is interest paid on most state and local government bonds (as discussed in Chapter 7). However, in order to safeguard their tax break on municipal bonds, investors should watch their borrowing policies. If taxpayers borrow money "to purchase *or carry* tax-exempts," they cannot deduct the investment interest on the loan.

But when is a taxpayer borrowing to buy or carry municipals? In general, if a taxpayer has debt outstanding that is not (1) incurred for purposes of a personal nature (such as a mortgage on real estate held for personal use) or (2) incurred in connection with the active conduct of a trade or business, and if the taxpayer also owns tax-exempt bonds, the IRS may presume the purpose of the indebtedness is to carry the bonds and deny an income tax deduction for the interest on the indebtedness. Suppose, for example, a taxpayer owns debt-free municipal bonds but borrows money to buy common stock on margin. Under these circumstances, the IRS may deny part of the investment interest deduction on the loan, even though the common stock dividends are taxable income.

Nontaxable Employee Benefits

One of the great advantages of many kinds of employee benefits is that they provide real economic benefits for covered persons; but in many cases, there is no taxable income to the employee on the value of the benefits. In other cases, income taxation is deferred.

Among the employee benefits that provide protection for employees and their families, but that may involve no taxable income for employees, are:

- Group term life insurance (up to $50,000 of insurance)
- Medical expense coverage (except that benefits may reduce otherwise deductible medical and dental expenses if deductions are itemized)
- Disability income insurance (except that benefits provided through employer contributions are taxable)
- Noninsured sick-pay plans (again, benefits are taxable)
- Group accidental death and dismemberment and related plans
- Dependent care assistance plans (up to $5,000 per year), educational assistance plans (up to $5,250 per year), and adoption assistance programs (generally up to $12,150 per child in 2009).[1]

Planning Sales of Securities for Tax Losses

This involves using the capital gain and loss rules to the taxpayer's best advantage. We should state at the outset, however, that tax considerations should not outweigh sound investment decisions in buying or selling securities. The tax "tail" should not wag the investment "dog." But in many cases, investors can plan their securities transactions so as to realize tax savings and yet not significantly affect their basic investment decision making.

Unrealized Capital Losses Tax savings can take some of the sting out of unrealized investment losses that investors really have, even though they have not actually sold the security. Psychologically, this is hard for some investors to accept. For example, if an investor buys a stock at $90 per share and over time it falls to, say, $45 per share, the stock has declined 50 percent in value, and each share actually is worth only $45 in cash, not $90. It may never again rise to $90. Some investors somehow feel they have not really had a loss unless they sell the stock. But this is not true; they really do have the loss—the only question is whether they realize and recognize the loss by selling the stock. From an investment standpoint, investors must consider the investment merits of their securities *at the current prices,* not at what they paid for them.

Thus, investors who have an unrealized loss on a security and are lukewarm on the immediate future performance of the security, or who can make a satisfactory tax exchange (explained later), should seriously consider

[1] The tax advantages of adoption assistance programs are phased out for higher-income taxpayers.

selling the security, realizing the loss, and taking an income tax deduction for it now.

CASE EXAMPLE

Suppose that Mrs. Bailey, who is in the 33 percent income tax bracket, owns a stock she purchased for $10,000 and which now is worth $7,000 in the market. She has no capital gains for the year. If she sells this stock now, she will realize a $3,000 capital loss, which she can deduct from her other ordinary income and save $990 in taxes (minus selling expenses). Her actual after-tax loss then is $2,010.

Tax-Loss Selling The preceding example illustrates the general concept of *tax-loss selling* of securities (it works with bonds as well as stocks). The following are some ideas on how to maximize tax savings in this area:

- If investors already have taken capital gains on securities or other property, they can offset these gains by taking losses on other securities they own. Thus, investors can plan the purchase and sales of securities or other capital assets to minimize or even eliminate any taxable capital gains for a given year. Of course, it must be remembered that net capital gains generally are taxed at 15 percent, while other income (which might be offset by capital losses up to $3,000 per year) may be subject to as high as a 35 percent tax rate.
- If investors do not have any capital gains in a given year (or enough capital gains to absorb all their capital losses), they can still offset up to $3,000 per year of otherwise taxable ordinary income (dollar for dollar) with their capital losses. They can also carry any unused capital losses forward to be used in future tax years without any time limitation.
- Investors can use so-called tax exchanges to enable them to sell a security for a tax loss and yet still keep an investment position in the same field or industry.

In connection with the previous idea, suppose, for example, that Mr. Brown owns a stock in which he has a capital loss that he would like to take now for tax purposes, but he also feels the stock has investment merit for the future and would like to retain it or one like it. So he asks himself, "Why not sell the stock, take my tax loss, and then immediately buy it back again?" The reason is that this would be a *wash sale,* and the loss would be disallowed for tax purposes. The tax law does not recognize losses taken on the sale of securities if the taxpayer acquires, or has entered into an option or contract to acquire, substantially identical securities within 30 days before or after the sale. Therefore, Mr. Brown would have to wait at least 30 days after the sale or else run afoul of the wash sale rule.

However, when a loss has been disallowed because of the wash sale rule, the security's basis is increased by the disallowed loss. Therefore, if the investor sells the security in the future, the increased basis will result in a smaller gain or a larger loss than would otherwise be the case.

Undaunted, Mr. Brown then asks, "Why not sell the stock to my wife (or other family member), take my tax loss, but still keep the stock within the family?" Unhappily, this will not work either. The tax law disallows all losses on sales within the family (that is, those made directly or indirectly between husband and wife, brothers and sisters, and ancestors and lineal descendants).

Mr. Brown, however, can maintain approximately the same investment position in the field or industry, even for the 30-day period before or after the tax sale, by selling the stock in which he has the loss and then immediately purchasing a different stock of about the same (or perhaps even greater) investment attractiveness. This often is referred to as a tax exchange. Many investment firms maintain lists of suggested tax exchanges to aid investors.

Tax Benefits on Sales of Principal Residences

For tax purposes, a personal residence is considered a capital asset, but one held for personal use. Therefore, while a gain on the sale of a personal residence is taxable (unless excluded), a loss on the sale of such a residence is not deductible because the loss was not incurred in a trade or business or in connection with a transaction entered into for profit. The same is true for other assets held strictly for personal use, such as cars, boats, airplanes, or furniture.

Exclusion of Gain from Sale of Principal Residence However, the tax law does allow relief from the rigor of these rules in connection with gains on the sale or exchange of a residence (including a cooperative apartment, condominium, yacht, or houseboat) that is the taxpayer's principal place of abode. In this case, there is an optional exclusion of gain provision under certain conditions. This provision applies to sales and exchanges after May 6, 1997.[2]

An individual of any age may exclude from income up to $250,000 of gain realized on the sale or exchange of a principal residence. To be eligible for this exclusion, the individual must have owned the residence (ownership test) and occupied the residence as a principal residence (use test) for an aggregate of at least two of the five years preceding the sale or exchange. The exclusion applies to only one sale or exchange every two years (frequency test).

[2] This provision was enacted in the Taxpayer Relief Act of 1997 and replaces the former rollover-of-gain provision (a nonrecognition provision) of Section 1034 and the former one-time $125,000 exclusion of gain for taxpayers age 55 and older.

Married persons of any age filing joint returns may exclude up to $500,000 of gain from the sale or exchange of a principal residence if (1) either spouse meets the ownership test, (2) both spouses meet the use test, and (3) neither spouse has made a sale or exchange of a principal residence within the last two years (i.e., is ineligible due to the frequency test). However, the $250,000 exclusion is applied on an individual basis. Therefore, in the case of married persons filing joint returns, if either spouse meets the ownership and use requirements, he or she will be eligible for the $250,000 exclusion. Also, if an otherwise eligible individual marries a person who has used the exclusion within the last two years, the eligible spouse still can take the $250,000 exclusion. Of course, once two years have elapsed since the last exclusion was taken by either of them and they are otherwise eligible, the full $500,000 exclusion applies again. For divorced and separated couples, if one of the spouses or former spouses has met the two-out-of-five-year rule, each spouse or former spouse can exclude up to $250,000 of gain on sale or exchange of the residence.

To the extent that depreciation was allowable for the rental or business use of a principal residence, after May 6, 1997, the exclusion does not apply and gain will be recognized on the sale of the property. The exclusion may be prorated if a taxpayer does not meet the ownership or use requirements due to a change in place of employment, health, or unforeseen circumstances. Starting in 2010, EGTRRA extends this exclusion to sales by estates, heirs of deceased owners, and qualified revocable trusts.

Planning Issues There would appear to be a number of planning opportunities with regard to this provision.

- Taxpayers can sell appreciated principal residences and move to more expensive ones, less expensive ones, or perhaps to other living arrangements, with no or reduced capital gains.
- Land next to a principal residence will qualify for the exclusion as long as it is regularly used as part of the residence.
- If taxpayers have a second home (vacation or rental property), they could sell their principal residence (using the exclusion), move to the second home and convert it to their new principal residence, and then sell that home after two years, again using the exclusion.
- When an appreciated principal residence is placed in a qualified personal residence trust (QPRT) for estate planning purposes,[3] it would appear

[3] A qualified personal residence trust involves the gift of a personal residence by the owner to an irrevocable trust under which the owner (the grantor of the trust) can live in the property for a set period, at the end of which the property passes to the donee(s), often children of the grantor, or continues in trust for the benefit of the donees. This estate planning technique is covered in Chapter 27.

that after the grantor's use period ends, the trust can continue for the donees (often children of the grantor) as a defective grantor trust. Thus, any gain on the sale will be taxable to the grantor and the grantor could avail himself or herself of the exclusion.

- One of the purposes of the exclusion was to eliminate the need for homeowners to maintain records of home improvements (the cost of which would increase their basis for income tax purposes). However, it still may be desirable to maintain such records, because in some cases, the gain might exceed the exclusion, the person may not be eligible for the exclusion, and depreciation may result in gain.

Conversion to Income-Producing Property If property held for personal use is converted to property used for the production of income, as when a residence is rented to others, depreciation is allowed as a tax deduction from rental income, and at least part of any capital loss on a subsequent sale of the property is deductible. Thus, if owners of a residence actually rent it, they can treat a loss on its sale as at least a partially deductible capital loss.

The tax status of an inherited residence depends on the use made of it by the person inheriting it. If the new owner does not use it as a residence but immediately attempts to sell or rent it, the property is considered held for profit, and a loss on its sale is a potentially deductible capital loss. The same also is true when two persons own the residence jointly and use it as a personal asset and one of them dies. The tax status of the residence in the hands of the survivor depends on how the survivor then uses it.

Making Charitable Contributions

Charitable giving has become such an important planning technique that a separate chapter is devoted to it—Chapter 19.

Shifting the Tax Burden to Others

Because of the progressive federal income tax structure, it may be attractive tax-wise to shift income or capital gains from persons in higher tax brackets to those in lower brackets. This is normally done within the family.

Outright Gifts of Income-Producing Property

One of the simplest ways of shifting income to others is the outright gift to them of income-producing property. Father gives stock to his adult children, Grandmother gives mutual fund shares to her grandchildren, Mother registers Series EE savings bonds in her children's names, and so on. In general, when a donor gives a donee property, future income from the property is taxable to the donee.

For capital gain purposes, the donee of an appreciated capital asset takes the donor's income tax basis in the property plus any gift tax paid by the donor attributable to the net appreciation in the gift property at the time of the gift. Thus, if Father paid $5,000 10 years ago for common stock that is now worth $20,000 and gives the stock to his son, the son's tax basis is $5,000 (assuming no gift tax resulted). If the son later sells the stock for $30,000, he will have a capital gain of $25,000. Thus, the donor (Father) can transfer a potential capital gain to his presumably lower-tax-bracket son, provided the kiddie tax does not apply.

For capital loss purposes, however, different rules apply. In this case, the donee's tax basis is either the donor's basis or the fair market value of the property at the date of the gift, whichever is lower. This means capital losses cannot be transferred to the donee. Therefore, property in which the owner has a sizable paper loss is not desirable gift property from an income tax–saving standpoint. Here, it would be better to sell the property, take the capital loss, and give away other assets.

Gifts of Income-Producing Property in Trust

Rather than being given outright, property can be given in trust—an irrevocable lifetime (inter vivos) trust. The income taxation of trusts was described in Chapter 10. As explained, depending on the terms of the trust and assuming it is not a grantor trust, trust income generally will be taxed to the beneficiaries if distributed to them, or to the trust itself if accumulated in the trust. Thus, income from property placed in the trust can be shifted in this way. For grantor trusts, income is taxed to the grantor, regardless of to whom it is distributed. Thus, grantor trusts are not income-shifting devices, but since the grantor pays the income tax that otherwise would be paid by the trust beneficiaries or the trust, in effect, this aspect of irrevocable grantor trusts results in additional tax-free gifts (the income tax) to the beneficiaries.

Gifts to Minors

Income shifting may be one reason for making gifts to minors. However, there usually are other reasons as well. Gifts to minors and the methods of making them are discussed in Chapter 27.

Allowing Wealth to Accumulate without Current Taxation and Postponing Taxation

Postponing taxes can be advantageous for several reasons. Taxpayers may be in a lower tax bracket in the future; their financial circumstances may be better known then; they may get investment returns on the postponed tax; they may not be in a financial position to pay the tax now; and, under some circumstances, the tax may never have to be paid.

Tax-Deferred Buildup of Qualified Retirement Plans and IRAs

Various kinds of qualified retirement plans provided by employers, traditional IRAs, executive compensation plans, and tax-sheltered annuity plans represent important ways by which people postpone taxation. These plans are discussed in Chapters 13, 14, and 15.

Postponing Income Taxation on U.S. Savings Bonds

Series EE and Series I U.S. savings bonds were described in Chapter 7. Owners of these bonds have a choice as to when they want to be taxed on the increase in value of their bonds. They may elect to report and pay tax on the increase in redemption value as interest each year, or they can take no action and thus postpone paying tax on the increase until the bonds mature or are redeemed. Thus, postponement is the automatic method.

Another possible tax advantage for Series EE and Series I bonds issued after December 31, 1989, is that the accrued interest on such bonds redeemed to finance qualified higher education expenses for the taxpayer, the taxpayer's spouse, or the taxpayer's dependents is excluded from the taxpayer's gross income for federal income tax purposes. Qualified higher education expenses include tuition and fees, and the exclusion also applies to redemption proceeds contributed to qualified tuition programs. To qualify, the bonds must be redeemed in the year the qualified higher education expenses are paid; the bonds must be issued in the taxpayer's or the taxpayer's and his or her spouse's name; the taxpayer must be age 24 or older when the bonds were issued; and the taxpayer's filing status must be single, married filing a joint return, head of household, or a qualifying surviving spouse with dependent child. This accrued interest exclusion is phased out between certain income levels (e.g., from $104,900 to $134,900 of modified adjusted gross income for married taxpayers filing a joint return and from $69,950 to $84,950 for individual taxpayers, indexed for inflation) in 2009.

Selecting the Particular Stock Certificates to Be Sold

The tax law permits investors to select the particular stock certificates they want to sell, assuming they are going to sell only part of their holdings of a stock. For example, suppose an investor owns 300 shares of a common stock with a present market value of $50 per share. The stock was acquired over the years as indicated here, and the investor now wishes to sell 100 shares:

Purchased 100 shares 10 years ago at $20 per share
Purchased 100 shares 3 years ago at $50 per share
Purchased 100 shares 2 years ago at $60 per share

Thus, depending on which certificates the investor elects to sell, he or she could have a capital gain, no gain or loss, or a capital loss. In the absence of identification as to which certificates are sold, the tax law assumes the first purchased are the first sold (a first-in, first-out concept). It often is good planning for investors to select shares that will minimize their capital gains or produce capital losses.

The same general principle applies to selecting which mutual fund shares are assumed to be redeemed. However, the rules are different and were described in Chapter 8.

Tax-Deferred ("Tax-Free") Buildup of Life Insurance and Deferred Annuity Policy Values

Life Insurance Cash Values These values are not subject to income taxation as they increase year by year but this "inside buildup" is taxed only when the policy or is surrendered for cash, is sold, or in some cases when partial withdrawals are made. Therefore, when planning to take distributions from life insurance cash values, one normally tries to do so without incurring income taxation. This is discussed in Chapter 29.

Deferred Annuity Cash Values Similarly, the growth in the policy value of nonqualified deferred annuity contracts is not taxed currently. The income tax is deferred until the owner begins receiving periodic payments from the annuity, surrenders it for cash, takes nonperiodic withdrawals from it, secures loans on it, or the value of the annuity is paid to a beneficiary upon the owner's death. Investment annuities are discussed in Chapter 17.

Installment Sales

For various kinds of property (other than publicly traded stocks or securities), when the selling price is paid in a tax year after the year of the sale (i.e., in installments), the seller generally pays tax on any gain arising from the sale as the installments are collected rather than in the year the sale is made, unless the seller elects otherwise. This is referred to as the *installment method.* It results in deferring the tax on the uncollected installments and was illustrated in Chapter 6.

Taking Returns as Capital Gains

As explained in Chapter 4, taking returns on directly owned property as capital gains offers distinct tax advantages.

Taxation and the Capital Gains Lock-In Problem

The capital gains tax can produce a situation in which investors feel locked in to a stock or other property because of their investment success. This involves a situation in which investors find themselves (happily, of course) with large paper gains in stocks or other appreciated property and are afraid to sell because they will have to pay sizeable taxes on the capital gains.

This kind of lock-in problem can have several unfortunate effects for investors. Investors' portfolios may become heavily concentrated in the locked-in stock or appreciated property, and diversification may be badly lacking. This may be a particularly severe problem in a declining market. In addition, there may be better investments now than the locked-in stock or property. Furthermore, while the investors' personal situations may have changed and they could use the money, they may be afraid to sell the stock and pay the tax for fear of depriving their children and other heirs of part of their inheritances. Assuming a lock-in problem with respect to directly owned assets, let us briefly review what investors' strategies might be.

Tax Avoidance Strategies

First, let us consider some strategies investors might use to avoid capital gains taxes altogether.

Step-Up in Basis at Death Investors could simply hold appreciated property—never sell it during their lifetime—and upon their death, it currently will get a stepped-up income tax basis equal to its fair market value on that date. Thus, investors could pass the appreciated property on to their heirs free of capital gains tax as of the date of death. However, this means the investor can't diversify if needed and must remain at risk for possible declines in the value of the appreciated property until his or her death.

Gifts to Charity As explained in Chapter 19, investors can give some or all of their appreciated property directly to charity, to charitable remainder trusts (CRTs), to pooled income funds, for charitable gift annuities, or in other ways and not realize a capital gain.

Use of Exclusion Provisions in Tax Law We have already noted one such exclusion for sales of principal residences. To encourage the formation of small businesses, another is that stockholders (other than C corporations as stockholders) of new, small corporations can exclude 50 percent of any gain on the sale or exchange of their stock. To qualify for this exclusion, the stock must be *qualified small business stock.* This means the stock must be newly issued when the taxpayer acquired it; the stock must be acquired after August 10, 1993; the corporation must have been engaged in an active business for substantially all the time the taxpayer held the stock; and the corporation's gross assets must not have exceeded $50 million when the stock was issued. Furthermore, the stockholder must have held the stock for more than five years before the sale or exchange. There also is an annual dollar limit per shareholder on the exclusion of $10 million or 10 times the amount the shareholder paid for the stock, whichever is larger. However, as noted in Chapter 10, 7 percent of the excluded gain is a tax preference item for individual AMT purposes.

Tax-Deferral Strategies (Possibly Until Death)

These are strategies that defer the realization or recognition of capital gains. If the deferral lasts long enough (until death), gain can be avoided entirely because the property gets a stepped-up basis at death (subject to the rules of EGTRRA).

Like-Kind Exchanges This nonrecognition provision (Section 1031 of the IRC) was explained in Chapters 6 and 10.

Tax-Free Corporate Reorganizations The effects of a tax-free reorganization are that neither the corporation nor its stockholders recognize gain or loss on the exchange (assuming no cash or other property, called *boot,* is received in the transaction) and the stockholders' bases in their old (surrendered) stock or securities are carried over to their new (exchanged for) stock or securities.[4]

[4] The IRC provides for seven types of tax-free reorganizations in Section 368. They are (1) statutory merger or consolidation, or Type A; (2) acquiring another corporation's stock, or Type B; (3) acquiring another corporation's property, or Type C; (4) transfer of assets to another corporation, or Type D; (5) recapitalization, or Type E; (6) change in identity, form, or place of organization of one corporation, or Type F; and (7) insolvency reorganization, or Type G. Each of these types has its own characteristics and requirements. Further discussion of them is beyond the scope of this book.

Thus, any gain or loss is deferred and will be recognized if the new stock or securities are later sold in a taxable transaction.

Of course, if the new stock or securities are held until death, they currently will receive a step-up (or step-down) in basis.

CASE EXAMPLE

Suppose Harry Martinez purchased 500 shares of ABC Technology common stock five years ago for $10 per share. ABC common has been publicly trading at around $50 per share. Recently, however, XYZ Technology merged with ABC in a tax-free reorganization and exchanged two of its common shares (with a market value of $76 for the two) for every share of ABC common. Thus, in this tax-free reorganization, Harry has surrendered his 500 shares of ABC common in exchange for 1,000 shares of XYZ common, has recognized no gain on the exchange, and has a basis of $5 per share in his new XYZ common (his former basis in ABC of $10 per share is carried over and allocated to the new stock—two for one in this case). If Harry later sells any of his XYZ common, his capital gain or loss will be the difference between the amount realized (market price minus selling costs) and his basis—$5 per share. His holding period for his former ABC common will be added (referred to as *tacked*) to that of the XYZ common to determine the holding period of the XYZ common for capital gain purposes.

ANOTHER CASE EXAMPLE

Assume that Heather Rosen started a new business, New Computer, six years ago with an initial investment of $100,000 to develop and market computer software. She organized New Computer as a C corporation, and 100 percent of the common stock (the only class of stock outstanding) was issued to her. She worked extremely hard, developed new products, the business prospered, and now it is valued by outside appraisers (there is no public market) as worth $10 million on a going-concern basis. However, now that she is wealthy, Heather would like to dispose of her corporation and devote herself entirely to organizing computer education and support programs for disadvantaged youth in her community.

Megacorp Computer Corporation, a large, profitable, publicly traded corporation that pays modest dividends, would like to acquire New Computer for $10 million. If this is done as a tax-free reorganization, Heather would surrender her 100 percent stock ownership in New Computer in exchange for $10 million worth of Megacorp common stock, she would recognize no gain on the exchange, and she would have an income tax basis in her Megacorp stock of $100,000. As a result, Heather would have exchanged her nonmarketable, closely held stock for publicly traded, dividend-paying stock in a major corporation. She can periodically sell part of her Megacorp stock if she needs funds (of course, then recognizing capital gains), or she could use other techniques to avoid the gain as described in this section.

On the other hand, referring back to tax avoidance strategies, it may be noted that Heather's stock in New Corporation is qualified small business stock. Therefore, if she simply sold the stock to Megacorp for cash, she could exclude 50 percent (75% for the stock acquired from 2009 until 2011) of her capital gain ($10,000,000 amount realized – $100,000 adjusted basis = $9,900,000 × 0.5 = $4,950,000 of excluded gain) for tax purposes. This means the effective tax rate for Heather on the total gain ($9,900,000) is 7.5 percent (15% × 0.5 = 7.5%). However, 7 percent of the amount excluded is a tax preference for AMT purposes.

Equity Collars with "Monetizing" the Hedged Stock This is a sophisticated technique designed to hedge against a decline in the value of appreciated stock, defer capital gain, and then "monetize" the stock by currently receiving cash or its practical equivalent equal to a reasonable percentage of the market value of the hedged stock for other investment.

CASE EXAMPLE

Suppose that Homer Kelly has been an executive of the Acme Corporation for 30 years. He now is a senior vice president. Over the years, Homer has invested primarily in his Acme stock through the exercise of stock options, participation in other stock plans, and direct purchases in the open market. The price of Acme stock has shown substantial growth over the years. As a result, the market value of Homer's directly owned Acme stock is now about $12 million and constitutes more than 90 percent of his assets. His basis in this stock is only $900,000.

However, Homer is concerned about the lack of diversification in his portfolio and the risk he is running if Acme stock should decline substantially in price. Therefore, he has entered into an *equity collar* around his Acme stock without actually selling the stock. Suppose the current market price of Acme stock is $70 per share. Homer can establish the equity collar by purchasing, say, a three-year cash-settled put option on Acme stock with a strike

> price (option price) of $63 per share and selling, say, a three-year cash-settled call option on Acme stock with a strike price (option price) of $77 per share.[5] The purpose of the put option is to protect (hedge) Homer against a fall in the market price of Acme stock below $63 per share. On the other hand, the purpose of selling the call option is to receive an income (premium) from the call to offset or perhaps more than offset the cost to Homer of buying the put. Collars can be renewed for successive periods.

Equity collars can be structured in several ways. A common approach is the *zero-outlay collar*. In this case, the premium received from the sale of the call just offsets the cost of the put. Other approaches are the *income-producing* (or *credit premium*) *collar* and the *debit collar*. The value of the underlying stock with an equity collar can be converted into a separate investment fund (monetized) in several ways. For example, the investor could borrow against the stock, subject to margin requirements, and invest the loan proceeds in a separate investment fund. Or, the investor might enter into an investment swap transaction with a securities firm involving a diversified portfolio.

These are complex transactions that may be entered into by persons with large positions in highly appreciated stock. Most of the other techniques that had been used to hedge such positions without actually selling the stock and realizing a large capital gain were eliminated by the constructive sale rules of the Taxpayer Relief Act of 1997. Equity collars are still a viable technique, but care should be taken not to run afoul of the broad language of the constructive sale rules.

Exchange Funds These are another sophisticated technique for deferring gain on highly appreciated stock. Here, an investor contributes his or her appreciated stock to a limited partnership (the exchange fund) in return for a limited partnership interest in the fund. This contribution to a partnership in exchange for a partnership interest is a tax-free exchange, provided not more than 80 percent of the partnership's gross assets are marketable securities. Other investors make similar exchanges, and the partnership builds its desired portfolio. Once established, the fund may be passively managed.

The investor carries over his or her basis in the appreciated stock to his or her partnership interest. If the investor-partner holds his or her partnership interest for at least seven years, the partnership can distribute, tax-free, a portion of its diversified portfolio to the partner (as a distribution in kind of partnership assets). The partnership's basis in those assets generally would be carried over to the distributed assets now in the investor's hands.

[5] The general nature of put options and call options was described in Chapter 6.

Thus, for example, upon liquidation of the investor's partnership interest or termination of the partnership, the investor can receive, tax-free, a diversified portfolio of securities with a carryover income tax basis.

On the other hand, if the investor-partner receives a distribution of partnership assets within seven years, he or she generally will incur a tax liability. Also, since the partnership is a pass-through entity, investment income and capital gains are taxed to the partners, whether distributed to them or not. This is one reason why exchange funds may be passively managed. Exchange funds may not be liquid investments. Investment selection and management are in the hands of fund management and not the individual limited partners. Exchange funds may have front-end loads and have annual management fees.

Other Investment Products Some investors use other products and strategies to deal with low-basis, highly appreciated stock. One is the issuance by the investor in a public offering of exchangeable equity-linked notes. This is available only for very large blocks of stock.

Another is the entering into with a securities firm of a prepaid variable forward contract (or variable delivery forward contract). However, the IRS has raised tax questions about these contracts, which has tended to curtail their use. A complete discussion of such strategies is beyond the scope of this book.

Sales of Stock to an ESOP Under certain circumstances, the owner of appreciated stock in a closely held corporation can sell part or all of the stock to the corporation's employee stock ownership plan (ESOP) and defer capital gain, possibly until the owner's death. An ESOP is a qualified retirement plan for employees that is normally structured either as a stock bonus plan or as a combination of stock bonus plan and money purchase pension plan.[6] Unlike other qualified retirement plans, ESOPs must invest primarily (meaning at least 50 percent of plan assets) in employer securities.

A *leveraged ESOP* may borrow funds from a bank, the employer, or other qualified lender with which to buy stock from existing stockholders or the corporation. The employer-corporation then makes tax-deductible contributions to the employee stock ownership plan (ESOP), and these contributions can be used by the ESOP to pay principal and interest on the loan. Annual tax-deductible contributions up to 25 percent of covered employee compensation can be made to repay loan principal, and unlimited contributions can be made to pay interest. In effect, the loan used by a leveraged ESOP to buy employer securities is financed with tax-deductible employer contributions.

[6] These kinds of qualified retirement plans are described more fully in Chapter 14.

In addition, there is a special nonrecognition provision applying to sales of qualified securities to ESOPs.[7] This provision permits a seller of closely held qualified securities[8] that have been held by the seller for at least three years prior to the sale to an ESOP to elect not to recognize any capital gain from the sale of such securities if, within a specified period (beginning three months before the sale and ending 12 months after such sale), the seller acquires an equivalent amount of qualified replacement property. In general, *qualified replacement property* means any equity or debt security of a domestic operating corporation. There can also be a partial nonrecognition of gain. The income tax basis of the seller in the replacement securities is the same as his or her basis in the securities sold to the ESOP. To qualify for this nonrecognition of capital gain, the ESOP must own at least 30 percent of the total value or number of shares of employer securities outstanding after the sale.

CASE EXAMPLE

We can illustrate this approach by referring back to the case of Heather Rosen. If Heather's corporation, New Computer, establishes a leveraged ESOP, she could sell 30 percent or more of her stock to the ESOP. Heather would not recognize any capital gain on the sale. She would invest the sale proceeds in marketable stocks or bonds of domestic operating companies (replacement securities), which could provide marketability and diversification for her portfolio. Furthermore, she would not necessarily have to sell all of her corporation stock (or even a controlling interest in it). The ESOP only needs to own 30 percent of the corporation's stock after the sale. However, there are restrictions on the ESOP's ability to dispose of the qualified securities for three years after the sale and on allocations of qualified securities by the ESOP to the selling shareholder or to a more than 25 percent shareholder who may be a participating employee in the ESOP.

Rollover of Gain from Qualified Small Business Stock In addition to the exclusion of one-half of the gain provision noted earlier, there is a nonrecognition of gain provision[9] under which gain realized from the sale or exchange of qualified small business stock held for more than six months by a taxpayer is not recognized (i.e., is rolled over) to the extent that the

[7] The provision is Section 1042 of the IRC.

[8] In general, qualified securities are employer securities that are issued by a domestic corporation that has no stock outstanding that is readily tradable on an established securities market and meets certain other conditions (i.e., is a closely held corporation).

[9] This is Section 1045 of the IRC.

taxpayer uses the proceeds of the sale to purchase other qualified small business stock within 60 days of the sale. The basis of the former stock is carried over to the new stock. This essentially allows any stockholder of a qualified small business (other than a C corporation as a stockholder) to sell one small business and buy another business tax deferred.

Selling Strategies

Assume that the owner of appreciated property decides to sell or exchange the property in a taxable transaction. A sale might be desired because the owner wants cash now for reinvestment or other needs. The owner may want to have control over how the sale proceeds are reinvested. Also, there may not be any acceptable exclusion or deferral strategies available to the owner. Furthermore, if the owner expects the whole market to fall (e.g., a bear market), a sale, rather than deferral, may be the preferred course. Finally, if an investor already has sizeable capital losses in a year or carried forward from prior years, these would be available to offset some or all of any capital gains from a taxable sale.

Favorable Capital Gains Tax Rates The tax rates applying to net capital gains are now significantly lower than the rates applying to ordinary income. The deferral strategies described earlier almost always involve requirements, limitations, or costs that are not present in outright sales. Therefore, the lower capital gains rates become, the more tempted taxpayers may be to sell their appreciated assets and pay the capital gains tax.

Installment Sales Any capital gain on installment sales is realized and recognized as payments are made. The part of each installment that is capital gain is determined by multiplying the payment by a gross profit percentage, which is the gross profit on the sale divided by the contract price. Also, installment sales have interest on the unpaid balance. The part of each installment that constitutes interest is taxable as ordinary income to the seller.

However, there may be reasons not to structure sales as installment sales. First, the seller may want the sales price in cash now. There also may be other tax factors to consider, such as existing capital losses, suspended passive activity losses, and depreciation recapture. In addition, in an installment sale, the seller takes an installment note from the buyer for future payments. Thus, the security (credit risk) of future payments could be a factor.

Finally, not all sales are eligible for installment treatment. For example, marketable stocks or securities are not eligible.

Other Sales for Periodic Payments Aside from straight installment sales, as just described, there are other sales where the purchase price is paid over time. An example would be self-canceling installment notes (SCINs). These arrangements are made within the family and normally are undertaken for estate planning reasons.

A Combination of Approaches

Of course, investors do not have to follow just one of these strategies. They often mix them. They might, for example, sell some of their appreciated stock and reinvest the proceeds, use some to make charitable donations, give some away within their family, and keep the rest. Furthermore, if they happen to have acquired the stock at different times with different tax bases, they can sell the stock with the highest bases and give away to charity or keep the stock with the lowest bases.

PART IV

Financing Education Expenses

12

Education Planning

Competence Objectives for This Chapter After reading this chapter, planners should understand:

- The nature and estimation of education costs
- Financial aid for education arrangements
- Income tax credits and deductions for education costs
- Strategies in planning for education costs
- Qualified Tuition Programs (Section 529 plans)
- Coverdell Education Savings Accounts
- Other arrangements for advance funding of education

This chapter deals with the various ways for financing the increasingly important and growing cost of education. Several of these ways have become increasingly attractive since passage of EGTRRA in 2001 and PPA in 2006.

Importance as a Financial Objective

Financing education expenses is a growing and important financial objective for many people. There are many reasons for this. Education costs are high and generally are rising faster than the rate of inflation. More people are attending colleges and universities, graduate schools, and other educational programs. Education costs are reasonably predictable, although what a particular person will do regarding his or her education is far from certain. Many plans are available for dealing in advance with education costs. Finally, education costs can create considerable strain on a family's financial situation, perhaps at the very time other significant financial needs are emerging.

Nature and Growth of Education Costs

The amount of education costs naturally depends on the circumstances. These include, among other things:

- The type of program involved—for example, undergraduate programs in colleges and universities, graduate schools (medicine, dental, law, graduate business, and so forth), community colleges, and technical and other schools
- How many years are involved
- Whether the person is a resident or nonresident student
- Whether it is a public or private school (for colleges)
- What scholarships and other financial aid are available
- Whether the student will be working and contributing to the cost while in school (during the summer or in co-op programs, for example)
- How many children or others are involved

For college and graduate school, the types of expenses can include tuition and fees, room and board, books and supplies, transportation, and other incidental expenses. These typically are considerably higher for private colleges than for public institutions. Depending on family circumstances and desires, education expenses also may include costs of private secondary schools and other private programs.

College and graduate school costs have been growing for many years. Their rate of growth has varied over the years, and it has been more rapid for private schools than for public ones, but as a rule of thumb for planning purposes, one probably can set the rate of growth somewhere between 4 and 5.5 percent.

Estimating Education Costs

This necessarily involves many unknowns and assumptions, and so general approximations of expected costs are in order. To even roughly estimate future costs and funding needs, one should make assumptions as to (1) the type of program planned for, its length in years, and its current net cost per year; (2) an estimated average annual compound rate of growth in costs; (3) the number of years until the program starts; and (4) an estimated average annual compound after-tax rate of return on assets set aside for education funding. Financial institutions, financial planning software, and other sources have systems for estimating education costs given certain input data.

CASE EXAMPLE

Just as an example of the principles involved, assume David and Mary Smith (both age 35 and working outside the home) have a child age 1, Hortense, who they hope will enter college in

17 years. At present, they would like to begin to prepare financially for a four-year undergraduate program for Hortense as a resident student at a private university. Assume typical annual expenses for full-time resident undergraduates at private colleges and universities are about $33,000 (although they could go as high as $50,000 or more at some private schools). Corresponding typical annual expenses for public colleges and universities are about $13,000. Therefore, in 17 years, David and Mary will need about $132,000 (4 × $33,000 per year) for Hortense in terms of current education costs. If they assume private undergraduate college costs will increase at a 5 percent average annual compound rate over the 17 years, this need becomes $302,546 in 17 years (or $132,000 present value at 5% average annual compound rate of increase for 17 years).[1] Further assuming that an investment funding for education expenses would have an after-tax or tax-free average annual compound rate of total return of 6 percent (assuming, for example, use of a Section 529 plan, which would be tax free), the Smith's would need to invest about $10,724 per year to reach their goal of about $302,546 in 17 years (or the annual payment at 6% average annual compound rate of return to reach $302,546 in 17 years).

Different assumptions, of course, might be made. For example, if it is assumed that Hortense will work in the summers (or perhaps have a work-study program while in college) and perhaps will earn, say, $5,000 after taxes per year in current dollars (or $20,000 for four years), the $132,000 goal could be reduced to $112,000 (both in current dollars) for planning purposes. Scholarships or other aid also might be assumed, but this is a bit of a stretch at age 1. Finally, costs will be increased dramatically if graduate school education is assumed.

Financial Aid Considerations

Many students attending colleges, universities, and other schools receive various forms of financial aid. These aid packages may include low-interest loans, grants and scholarships, and earnings from work-study programs.

Eligibility for need-based financial aid under standardized formulas depends on the student's and his or her parents' incomes and assets, and

[1] This figure can be determined on a handheld calculator, on a computer, or by using the future value of a sum table. See Chapter 3.

perhaps other factors (such as the number of children in school). Generally, a student's "need" for federal purposes is the difference between the cost of attendance at the educational institution and the student's expected family contribution (EFC). The EFC is what the student and his or her parents are expected to pay for the student's education under standardized formulas.[2]

Grants or scholarships (gift aid) genarally are based on need and do not have to be paid back. Some examples are the federal Pell Grants to students and Supplemental Educational Opportunity Grants (SEOGs) made to colleges, which then provide grants to students. There also may be state and state-federal grants, Reserve Officer Training Corps (ROTC) scholarships, and other grants.

Loans might include low-interest or subsidized loans, such as federal programs for Perkins loans and subsidized Stafford loans. These are need-based loan programs. Other loans may not be need based, such as unsubsidized Stafford loans, Parents' Loans for Undergraduate Students (PLUS), and various private loan programs. There also may be earnings from work-study programs. In addition to need-based financial aid, there can be merit aid not based on financial need.

Tax "Breaks" for Education Costs

Federal Income Tax Credits

These include the *Hope Scholarship credit* and the *Lifetime Learning credit.* The Hope credit is for college tuition (reduced by any scholarship and fellowship grants excluded from income) and certain fees incurred by the taxpayer, his or her spouse, and a qualified dependent of the taxpayer for each of the first two years of college [for four years from 2009 and 2010 under the American Recovery and Reinvestment Act of 2009 (ARRA)]. It also applies to tuition for a vocational school leading to a recognized post-secondary school degree or credential. The credit applies to each student in a taxpayer's family. For each student, the credit is 100 percent of the first $1,200 (indexed) and 50 percent of the next $1,200 (indexed) in qualified tuition and fees per year (with increased limits for 2009 and 2010 under ARRA). Eligible students must be enrolled at least on a half-time basis.

[2] For example, the EFC (based on the Free Application for Federal Student Aid) includes up to 50 percent of the student's income (minus certain allowances), 35 percent of the student's assets, up to 47 percent of the parents' income (minus certain allowances), and 5.6 percent of the parents' assets. However, equity in the parents' home and their retirement assets are excluded from the EFC.

The Lifetime Learning credit is for tuition and fees for undergraduate and graduate college and university courses, as well as for courses at eligible institutions to acquire and improve job skills incurred by the taxpayer, his or her spouse, and a qualified dependent of the taxpayer. This credit applies only once per year per taxpayer, but can be taken for an unlimited number of years and a student can be enrolled on less than a half-time basis. For each tax return per year, the credit is 20 percent of up to $10,000 of qualified tuition and fees.

Both the Hope Scholarship credit and the Lifetime Learning credit cannot be taken for the same student in a given year. However, each is available for a year in which tax-free distributions are made from a state qualified tuition program (QTP) or an Education Savings Account (Coverdell IRA) for the same student, as long as they do not cover the same eligible expenses. Each of these credits are phased out for higher income taxpayers.

Federal Income Tax Deductions

Student Loan Interest Deduction A deduction from gross income to arrive at adjusted gross income (i.e., "above the line") is allowed for interest paid on "qualified education loans." The maximum annual deduction is $2,500 and it is available for the entire duration of the loan. However, this deduction is phased out for taxpayers with adjusted gross incomes (AGIs) over certain limits.

Deduction for Higher Education Expenses There also is a deduction above the line for "qualified higher education expenses" (defined as the Hope credit discussed previously) up to $4,000 for taxpayers whose AGI does not exceed certain amounts.

This deduction cannot be taken in the same year as the Hope or Lifetime Learning credit for the same student. Also, no deduction can be taken for expenses that are used for amounts excludable from income due to distributions from an Education Savings Account or a QTP, or due to excludable interest from a U.S. savings bond.

Exclusions from Income, Gift, or Penalty Taxes for Federal Tax Purposes There are a variety of situations in which amounts used for eligible education expenses are excluded from a taxpayer's gross income (i.e., are tax free or have other tax advantages).

- Earnings from qualified tuition programs, as discussed later in this chapter.
- Earnings from Education Savings Accounts, as discussed later in this chapter.
- Interest on certain U.S. savings bonds are noted in Chapter 7.
- Amounts up to $5,250 per employee, per year, from employer-provided education assistance plans, as noted in Chapter 11.

- Amounts of scholarships and fellowship grants given to degree candidates at an educational institution and used for tuition, related fees, books, and supplies and equipment normally are excluded from the recipient's gross income. However, amounts used for room and board and other personal items, as well as amounts received for required services (e.g., teaching or researching as a condition of the grant) are not excluded.
- Distributions from regular IRAs before age 59½ for eligible education expenses are not subject to the 10 percent penalty tax on premature distributions, but such distributions are still taxed as ordinary income (i.e., they are not income tax–free), as explained in Chapter 15.
- An unlimited gift tax exclusion for payments of tuition directly to an educational organization, as explained in Chapter 27.

Strategies in Planning for Education Costs

Rely on Financial Aid and Tax Breaks

It will be good if these things materialize, but it does not seem prudent to rely primarily on them, particularly when the potential student is relatively young. Scholarships and grants are uncertain.

Some work-study may be fine for many students, and in some cases may even improve their performance by making them more responsible. Some schools have co-op programs involving full-time study for part of the year and full-time work for another part. Furthermore, students often have summer jobs or internships when they are not in school. All of this will be helpful in financing their educations, but too much work while in school will dilute the educational experience and may put undue pressure on students. However, it seems entirely reasonable to assume a student can earn some part of his or her education expenses with perhaps limited work-study and certainly through summer employment. This can be considered when estimating education costs, as illustrated earlier in this chapter. Loans as a part of financial aid are considered in the next section.

Tax "breaks" are always nice, but as a practiced matter, they can only be a partial answer. They generally are limited in amount, are subject to income eligibility requirements, or are otherwise limited. The most significant tax advantages in planning for education expenses would seem to be the exclusion from income of earnings from qualified tuition programs and Education IRAs when used for eligible education expenses, as explained later.

Rely Primarily on Borrowing

This has become an increasingly important strategy in recent years. The vast majority of loans (about 95 percent) come from federally supported programs.

However, there also are a number of private loan programs specifically for college expenses. Finally, there are the normal sources of loans for any purpose, such as mortgage refinancing, home equity loans, life insurance policy loans, loans from qualified retirement plans, and other sources.

The basic problem with borrowing is that the loans plus interest (even at favorable rates) must be paid back. Today, graduates commonly leave school burdened with student loans. Parents may find themselves in debt to finance their children's education at the very time they should be building capital for their own retirement. For the same reason, borrowing from retirement plan account balances may be self-defeating. Thus, while borrowing may be necessary if no advance preparation has been made, it normally is not the preferred solution.

Advance Funding for Education Costs

This approach has received increasing attention recently, particularly with the attractive education incentives contained in EGTRRA which have been made permanent by the PPA of 2006. In the opinion of the authors, it is the preferred primary strategy. A number of plans are available for funding education costs. Some are designed specifically for that purpose, while others are more general in nature. However, they all require time to be effective, so it is a good idea to start saving early.

Factors Affecting Choice of Plans

There can be many factors to consider when evaluating these plans. Some obviously are more important than others. A combination of plans can also be used. These factors include:

- Nature of the plan and how to set it up
- Eligibility requirements, income ceilings, and limits on contributions
- Kinds of educational expenses that can be funded
- Tax treatment of plan contributions
- Income tax treatment of plan earnings
- Income tax treatment of distributions from the plan
- Federal estate tax, GST tax, and possibly state death tax status of plan balances on death of the plan owner or beneficiary
- Forms in which contributions can be made
- Investment options and flexibility allowed by the plan
- Fees and expenses of the plan
- Ability to make changes in the plan
- Protecting the plan in the event of the death or disability of the contributor before the plan is completed

- Coordination with other plans, scholarships, and tax "breaks"
- Possible creditor protection
- Possible "freezing" of future education costs

Qualified Tuition Programs (Section 529 Plans)[3]

These are state programs that may be 529 saving accounts (or saving account programs) or prepaid tuition programs (also called tuition credit or tuition certificate programs).[4] They are both referred to as QTPs or 529 plans, but by far, the more popular are saving account programs.

General Characteristics Prepaid tuition programs are state-operated trusts to which U.S. citizens[5] can make cash contributions that are applied to purchase credits or certificates for a designated beneficiary for tuition and fees for a given number of academic periods or course units at the current tuition rates. The investment of prepaid tuition funds normally is handled by the state, and some states do not guarantee the arrangement. Usually, if a student attends a private college or university or an out-of-state school, the funds accumulated in the plan still can be used for eligible higher education expenses, except the amount of covered expenses may be limited (such as to in-state tuition) and there is no locking in of current tuition rates.

Savings account programs are state-operated plans to which U.S. citizens can make cash contributions that are accumulated in accounts owned by the contributor and for payment of qualified higher education expenses of a designated beneficiary. While these programs are state plans, they usually are administered and the account balances invested by private financial intermediaries. Most of the remainder of this discussion deals with savings account programs.

QTPs must comply with Section 529 of the IRC and corresponding tax rules to get the substantial benefits afforded under federal tax law. However, they also are creatures of the individual states, and so contributions must comply with the rules of the particular state plan as well. Thus, both federal and individual state rules must be considered when contributing to Section 529 plans.

[3] Section 529 was added to the IRC by the Small Business Job Protection Act of 1996 and has been amended and expanded several times since. A significant expansion was made by EGTRRA, and this expansion was made permanent (i.e., no "sunset") by the PPA of 2006.
[4] Under EGTRRA, prepaid tuition programs (but not savings account plans) can be established and maintained by eligible private institutions (e.g., colleges and universities) that meet the requirements of Section 529 of the IRC.
[5] Sometimes these programs are limited to state residents.

Eligibility and Limits on Contributions With the exception of a few plans that have state residency requirements, QTP accounts can be set up by any U.S. citizen for any beneficiary, with no residency requirement or income ceilings on the person's ability to establish or contribute to the plan. Thus, persons desiring to set up 529 plans should "shop around" among state plans to find the most attractive one or ones for them. State plans differ in a number of respects, and a potential contributor may want to consider the following factors, among others, in his or her selection:

- State income tax (if any) treatment of contributions and qualified distributions (in the case of contributors who are state residents)
- Available investment options
- Who the investment manager is
- Fees charged, particularly the annual expense ratio on the investment options
- Whether the plan is as flexible as Section 529 allows with respect to rollovers to other plans, changes of designated beneficiary, and perhaps other matters
- Maximum contributions (or account values) allowed
- Higher education expenses and schools covered
- Possible state creditor protection. The Bankruptcy Abuse Prevention and Consumer Protection Act of 2005 exempts those education accounts from creditors' claims under federal bankruptcy law with some conditions.

Section 529 requires that a QTP take measures to prevent contributions beyond those reasonably necessary to pay for a beneficiary's qualified higher education expenses. Therefore, the plans set maximum limits on the aggregate lifetime contributions (or sometimes account values) that can be made for a single designated beneficiary in the state.[6] These maximums vary by state and may range from around $100,000 to over $280,000. Sometimes, they vary with the age of the designated beneficiary.

Qualified Higher Education Expenses In essence, these expenses can be paid tax free from QTPs. They include tuition, fees, books, supplies, and equipment for the attendance of a designated beneficiary at an eligible educational institution. They also include room and board for a designated beneficiary who is enrolled in a program leading to a degree or a recognized educational credential and carrying at least half the normal full-time workload for the program involved.[7]

[6] The states often determine this maximum limit by taking four or five years of eligible expenses at the most expensive school in the state. This maximum may increase periodically with increased education costs.

[7] Prepaid tuition programs may not include room and board.

An eligible educational institution includes any accredited post-secondary educational institution offering credit toward bachelor's, associate's, graduate, or professional degrees and includes certain vocational institutions. Such an institution must be eligible to participate in the Department of Education's student aid programs.

Tax Treatment of Contributions Contributions to a QTP are not deductible for federal income tax purposes. Depending on state law, they may be deductible up to a limit for state income tax purposes for residents of the state.

With respect to federal gift taxation, contributions are considered completed gifts of a present interest from the account owner to the designated beneficiary. Thus, in 2009, contributions qualify for the $13,000 per donee annual exclusion for both gift tax and GST tax purposes.

Furthermore, to encourage early funding, Section 529 allows so-called front-loading for annual exclusion purposes. This means an account owner can elect to treat a single year's gift that exceeds the annual exclusion for that year as if were made pro rata over five years for the purpose of applying the annual exclusions for those years. Thus, one person could give up to $65,000 ($13,000 annual exclusion × 5) and a married person with gift splitting could give up to $130,000 ($65,000 for each spouse) for one designated beneficiary in a single year.

CASE EXAMPLE

Suppose Gary, who is married to Susan, wants to start a QTP, with his granddaughter, Traci, as designated beneficiary. Gary has a substantial estate and would like to make as large an initial contribution as possible to take advantage of tax-free compounding and still stay within the gift tax and GST tax (since Traci would be a skip person to Gary) annual exclusions. Assuming Susan is willing to split the gifts, he could contribute $130,000 to the QTP in the first year and make the five-year election just described (assuming this is within the state's maximum limit). Then, he would be treated as having made a $26,000 gift in the first year and in each of the next four years (i.e., over five years). With gift splitting, this would be considered an annual gift of $13,000 each by Gary and Susan and within the annual exclusions of each.

Tax Treatment of Plan Earnings The earnings from the assets in a QTP are not currently taxed for federal income tax purposes. They also will not be taxed upon distribution if they are used to pay for qualified higher education expenses (i.e., a qualified distribution). Otherwise, they will be taxed as ordinary income upon distribution.

Tax Treatment of Plan Distributions As just stated, plan withdrawals used for qualified higher education expenses of the designated beneficiary are not gross income, for federal income tax purposes, to the designated beneficiary or account owner. This means the investment earnings on plan assets are never taxed when so used. Depending on state law, they also may be exempt from any state income tax.

To be exempt from federal income taxation, the distributions must be made in one of the following ways: (1) distributed directly to an eligible educational institution; (2) distributed by a check payable to both the designated beneficiary and an eligible educational institution; (3) distributed as reimbursement to the designated beneficiary for qualified higher education expenses paid, with the beneficiary producing receipts; (4) distributed to the designated beneficiary, who certifies in writing that the distribution will be used for qualified higher education expenses within a reasonable time; or (5) distributed as necessary for a special-needs beneficiary at an eligible educational institution. Also, a qualified distribution must be taken in the same tax year as the qualified higher education expenses were paid.

In the case of withdrawals not used for qualified higher education expenses (nonqualified distributions), the earnings element will be taxable as ordinary income to the distributee. Thus, in effect, any part of the investment earnings that normally would be a long-term capital gain becomes ordinary income in a nonqualified distribution. Nonqualified distributions are taxed under the annuity rules of Section 72 of the IRC (see Chapter 16). To do so, first the earnings element in the account balance is determined by subtracting the investment element (the contributions to the plan) from the total account balance. Then, an earnings ratio is determined by dividing this earnings element at the end of the calendar year by the total account value at that time. The taxable portion of any nonqualified distribution is this earnings ratio times the total distribution.

Furthermore, there is an additional 10 percent federal penalty tax on any taxable (earnings) portion of a nonqualified distribution, with some exceptions. For example, the penalty tax does not apply when the nonqualified distribution is made to the beneficiary's estate after his or her death; is attributable to the beneficiary's disability; or is made on account of the beneficiary's receipt of a scholarship, allowance, or certain other payments to the extent the distribution does not exceed the scholarship, allowance, or payment. There also may be state penalties for nonqualified distributions.

Federal Estate, GST, and Gift Tax Status of Plan Balances The balance in a QTP is not included in a deceased account owner's gross estate for federal estate tax purposes. The only exception is if the account owner elected for five-year annual exclusion treatment and dies within the five-year period. In this case, the remaining pro rata amounts would be in the decedent's gross estate. For example, suppose Mary Eduski, who is unmarried, contributed $65,000 to a 529 savings account in 2009, with her nephew as designated beneficiary, and elected to treat it as if made pro rata over five years. Furthermore, suppose Mary dies in 2011. In this case, $26,000 (for 2012 and 2013) would be in her gross estate.

Interestingly, this exclusion from the account owner's gross estate applies even though the account owner can direct how and when distributions are to be made to the designated beneficiary (normally for qualified higher education expenses, but perhaps not), can change the designated beneficiary, and can even recover the savings account balance for himself or herself.[8] This is the only financial and estate planning vehicle that allows such flexibility and tax advantages in making lifetime transfers without gift, GST, or estate tax consequences. This can make 529 plans a powerful estate planning tool, as illustrated next.

CASE EXAMPLE

Suppose that Michael Edgalia, age 70, is a widower with a substantial estate and an annual income in the top income tax bracket. He has three adult children and nine minor grandchildren. Michael himself never went to college, but he believes in education and wants to provide all the educational opportunities that his grandchildren want. Michael already is making direct annual exclusion gifts each year to his children. He also has paid tuition for several of his grandchildren directly to certain preschool programs and private elementary and secondary schools, all of which are free of federal gift tax.

Now in 2009, Michael decides to open 529 saving accounts in a carefully selected state QTP, with each of his grandchildren as a designated beneficiary of one of the accounts. Michael is the owner of all the accounts. He decides to contribute $65,000 to each 529 account and elect the five-year annual exclusion treatment. This means his gift will be within the federal gift tax annual exclusion for the current year and for each of the next four years for each grandchild, and also will be within the GST tax annual exclusion for each grandchild for each of those years (since each grandchild is a skip person to Michael). This gift also will be out

[8] These rights are subject to the rules of individual state plans. Therefore, it is important to check and evaluate state plans with regard to their flexibility in allowing such actions.

of Michael's gross estate for federal estate tax purposes, assuming he survives five years.

Thus, Michael effectively has moved more than a half million dollars (9 × $65,000 = $585,000) to his grandchildren without any transfer taxation and with no current income taxation on plan earnings, while retaining substantial control over the account as the owner. For example, he can direct how, when, and to what eligible institutions income tax–free distributions for qualified higher education expenses will be made for the designated beneficiaries. Michael also can change the designated beneficiary.[9] Furthermore, an account owner—Michael in this example—normally can recover the funds in the 529 account for himself or herself for any reason. Such a refund to the account owner would be a nonqualified distribution, and thus the earnings portion will be subject to ordinary income tax and the 10 percent federal penalty tax. Even so, there still will be deferral of tax on the investment earnings until the nonqualified distribution is made. The real "price" to Michael of a nonqualified refund is the 10 percent penalty tax on the earnings and that all the earnings will be taxed as ordinary income, even though part or all of the account balance may be invested in capital gain–type assets (e.g., common stocks).

If a designated beneficiary dies, the 529 plan account balance will be included in the deceased beneficiary's gross estate. This is true, even though, in fact, beneficiaries have no control over these plans. However, designated beneficiaries normally will be considerably younger than account owners, and so this would not seem to be a major issue.

Form of Contributions Contributions to QTPs may be made only in cash. Thus, appreciated property cannot be placed in these plans.

Flexibility in the Plan The 529 plans offer considerable flexibility in their creation and operation. Generally, any adult U.S. citizen can open an account and be the account owner. There are no income limits on eligibility to participate. Furthermore, some states permit custodians of Uniform Transfers to Minors Act (UTMA) or Uniform Gifts to Minors Act (UGMA) accounts

[9] As will be covered later in this chapter, there are no tax consequences for a change of beneficiary, as long as the new beneficiary is a "member of the family" (as defined in the tax law) of the former beneficiary and is not in a younger generation from that of the former beneficiary.

to use cash in the account to open a 529 plan for the account beneficiary. In this case, the 529 plan will be subject to the state's UTMA or UGMA statute. However, this may involve liquidity UTMA or UEMA investments thus triggering capital gains tax. Some QTPs will allow trusts, partnerships (perhaps a family limited partnership [FLP]), corporations, or other entities to open 529 plans. The trustee of an existing trust, for example, might use cash in the trust to open a 529 plan, with the trust as the account owner and a trust beneficiary as the designated beneficiary. State plans permit the naming of a successor account owner in the event of the original owner's death. Also, some QTPs may permit naming a successor owner in the event of the original owner's incapacity.[10]

Naming and Changing the Designated Beneficiary The account owner can name and change the designated beneficiary. Any individual can be designated beneficiary, including the account owner.

If the account owner changes the designated beneficiary to an eligible "member of the family" of the former designated beneficiary, as defined in the tax law,[11] it is not considered a nonqualified distribution and is not subject to income taxation. However, if the new beneficiary is not a "member of the family" of the former beneficiary, the change is treated as a nonqualified distribution of the account balance to the account owner and taxed accordingly.

In addition, if the account owner names a new beneficiary who is one or more generations younger than the former beneficiary (such as changing to a child of the former beneficiary), it is viewed in the proposed IRS regulations as a gift for federal gift tax purposes by the former beneficiary to the new beneficiary. It could also be a GST tax transfer by the former beneficiary to the new beneficiary, if the new beneficiary is two or more generations younger than the former beneficiary (such as changing to a grandchild of the former beneficiary). However, if the change is to someone in the same or an older generation than the former beneficiary, no adverse tax result occurs.

Rollovers to Other Plans QTPs normally allow an account owner to transfer (roll over) an account from one state plan to another state plan. In effect,

[10] The incapacity issue also can be handled by giving the agent under a durable general power of attorney authority to deal with the account.

[11] For this purpose, the tax law defines a "member of the family" as a child or the child's descendants; a stepchild; a brother, sister, stepbrother, or stepsister; the father, mother, or an ancestor of either; a stepfather or stepmother; a first cousin; a child of a brother or sister (i.e., a niece or nephew); a brother or sister of the father or mother (i.e., uncle or aunt); a son-in-law, daughter-in-law, father-in-law, mother-in-law, brother-in-law, or sister-in-law; or a spouse of the designated beneficiary or of any of the family members just named. This is a reasonably broad list of potential new beneficiaries.

this means changing the plan (including its investment selection) to a new account. The change to a new account also may be in the same state plan, depending on state plan rules. If the beneficiary is not changed, there can be only one rollover in any one 12-month period. However, if the beneficiary is changed, the account can be rolled over at any time.

Investment Options and Investment Flexibility One of the requirements of Section 529 is that neither the account owner nor the beneficiary may directly or indirectly oversee the investments in the 529 account. However, the seeming inflexibility of this requirement can be mitigated in practice in several respects. First, many state plans permit donors (account owners), upon initially opening an account, to select from a range of broad investment options and allocate his or her contributions among one or more of these options. The plans often offer so-called age-based asset allocation options, under which the allocation in the option among, say, common stock, bond, and money market funds automatically changes as the beneficiary gets older. These investment options (age-based and non-age-based) often are in mutual funds that are managed by outside investment intermediaries for the state.

Second, the ability to roll over an account to an account in another plan effectively allows account owners to change the investment selection for the new account. Assuming the beneficiary is not changed, such a rollover can be made once every 12 months. This would seem to give an account owner reasonable flexibility to change investment strategies, if desired, after an account has been opened. If the beneficiary is changed (subject to the tax rules explained earlier), a rollover can be made at any time.

Finally, the IRS permits account owners to change investment options twice per calendar year or upon a beneficiary change within the same plan. Some plans allow this by permitting transfers of existing account balances to other investment options within the same plan upon a beneficiary change. This allows investment flexibility without having to roll over an account to another state plan. Also, QTPs often allow the directing of future contributions to different investment options.

Thus, while 529 savings account owners cannot select individual securities or other assets for their accounts (as they could, for example, for Education IRAs and UTMA or UGMA accounts), they have a reasonably broad choice among mutual funds and perhaps guaranteed principal accounts, depending on the particular state plan. State plans vary in the number and nature of the investment options offered and in their investment performance. Therefore, among the important factors to consider when choosing a state QTP are the investment options offered; the flexibility allowed in changing the investment strategy of an existing account; the financial intermediary, if any, managing the investment funds; and the performance record and expense ratios of the various funds and plans.

A QTP cannot allow the assets in an account to serve as security for any loan.

Fees and Expenses of the Plans Here again, state plans vary widely in their costs. Sometimes costs are lower for state residents than nonresidents. There may be application fees, annual fees to cover program expenses, and fees for other services. However, perhaps most important are the annual asset-based investment fund fees, which are a percentage of the value of the assets in the account.[12] These annual asset-based percentage charges are analogous to the expense ratios of mutual funds, and may vary with the investment choices made.[13] They also vary widely among different QTPs.

Coordination with Other Plans and Financial Aid Considerations As noted earlier, a person can contribute to a 529 plan and an Education IRA for the same beneficiary in the same year. Of course, to avoid a taxable gift, the combined contributions must be within the gift tax annual exclusion for the beneficiary for the year.

When qualified higher education expenses are incurred, they are first reduced by any scholarship or fellowship grants excluded from gross income and any other tax-free education benefits received by the beneficiary. Then they are reduced by any expenses taken into account in determining the Hope or Lifetime Learning credit. The remaining qualified expenses then can be paid tax free from a 529 plan. They could also be paid tax free from an Education IRA. If there should be total distributions from both a 529 plan and an Education IRA that exceed such reduced expenses, the expenses are allocated between the distributions.

For purposes of federal student financial aid, a 529 plan is considered an asset of the account owner. Therefore, if the student is the account owner, it will be his or her asset; but if a parent is the account owner, it will be the parent's asset for determining the EFC. If a grandparent or other relative is the account owner, the 529 account itself should not affect financial aid considerations.

Protecting the Plan in the Event of Death or Disability of Donor Only life insurance and disability insurance can perform this function. Therefore, the need for coverage to meet future education costs in the event of a contributor's early death or disability should be considered in the insurance plan, as illustrated in Chapter 21.

[12] This may be a "wrap fee" that covers program expenses and investment fund fees in one annual asset-based percentage charge.

[13] In fact, the various investment options offered by QTPs usually are invested in one or more mutual funds.

Possible "Freezing" of Future Education Costs This can only be done through prepaid tuition plans.

Education IRAs (Coverdell Education Savings Accounts) These also are tax-favored plans to accumulate funds to pay for education expenses that were liberalized by EGTRRA and made permanent by PPA. See Chapter 15 for more information.

As compared to 529 plans, Education IRAs have some advantages, but also some drawbacks. Tax-free distributions from Education IRAs can be used not only for qualified higher education expenses (as is true for 529 plans), but also for qualified elementary and secondary education expenses for grades K through 12 (which are not covered by 529 plans). Thus, in the case of beneficiaries for whom elementary and secondary education expenses may be incurred (e.g., attending private schools), an eligible contributor may want to consider an Education IRA to fund those expenses in a tax-free basis. This may be in addition to a 529 plan, which could be used for qualified higher education expenses. Furthermore, Education IRA account owners have greater investment latitude than with 529 plans. Finally, Education IRAs are not subject to individual state plan rules, as are 529 plans.

On the other hand, a major drawback for Education IRAs is the $2,000 annual limit per beneficiary that a person can contribute. Up to $13,000 (in 2009) gift tax–free per beneficiary–donee per year can be placed in a 529 plan, and contributions can be "front-loaded" for five years. Another drawback is the income limit on eligibility to contribute to Education IRAs. The required rollover or distribution when a beneficiary reaches age 30 is another constraining factor. There are no such distribution requirements for 529 plans. Finally, a significant advantage for most 529 plans, which is not available for any other plan, is the ability of the account owner to recover (withdraw) the account balance at any time for himself or herself. The only "cost" of such recovery is paying tax at ordinary income rates plus a 10 percent federal penalty tax on the earnings portion of such a withdrawal. This provides unusual financial planning latitude for 529 plan account owners.

Other Arrangements for Advance Funding

Other approaches can be used for funding education costs that are not specifically designed for that purpose. These are described in other chapters and so will only be briefly noted here.

Uniform Transfers and Uniform Gifts to Minors Acts These custodianships are discussed in Chapter 27. A custodian under these plans can make payments for the beneficiary's education expenses or can make distributions to the beneficiary, which he or she can then use for that purpose. Of course, payments for the benefit of and distributions to the beneficiary can be made for other purposes as well.

The advantages of these custodianships are that contributions to them can be made in kind (e.g., appreciated securities), so any capital gains can be taxed to the minor; the custodian has wide investment latitude; and the assets can be used for or by the minor (or adult at age 21) for any purpose (e.g., travel, buying a home, or starting a business). On the other hand, the earnings on the assets in the account will be taxed currently to the minor. They are not tax free, unless invested in municipal bonds or funds. Also, the account must go outright to the minor at the statutory age (usually 21) and then will be subject to the beneficiary's absolute control. Even if the custodian invests UTMA or UGMA funds in a Section 529 plan, the beneficiary will get control of the 529 account at the statutory age. And, of course, the original donor can never get the funds back.

Trusts for Minors These also are discussed in Chapter 27. The trustee can be given authority to use trust assets for educational expenses of trust beneficiaries, as well as for other purposes.

The advantages are that contributions can be made in kind; the trustee can be given broad investment powers; and trust assets can be used for or by the trust beneficiaries for any purpose, subject to the terms of the trust. On the other hand, the earnings on trust assets will be taxed currently to the trust if accumulated or to the beneficiary(ies) if paid out currently to them. Either way, the investment earnings are not tax free, unless trust assets are invested in municipal securities. Also, in the case of Section 2503(c) trusts, the assets must go outright to the beneficiary at age 21, unless the beneficiary consents to their remaining in trust. And, of course, the original grantor can never recover the trust assets for himself or herself if they are to be excluded from the grantor's gross estate and the income not taxed to the grantor.

As noted earlier, some QTPs allow trustees to open 529 plans for trust beneficiaries with cash from the trust. In this case, the trust is the account owner and a trust beneficiary is the designated beneficiary. The trustee then can direct qualified distributions for the beneficiary, change the beneficiary to another trust beneficiary, or direct a withdrawal (recovery) back into the trust corpus. A trustee has a fiduciary duty to the trust beneficiaries to impartially and properly administer the trust, and so there may be advantages to the beneficiaries in having a trust as owner of a 529 account. It also may be an attractive, tax-free (for qualified higher education expenses) investment of trust assets. On the other hand, since only cash can be contributed to a 529 plan, if the trustee must sell appreciated assets to raise the cash, this will result in capital gains for the trust. This same caveat can also be made for 529 plans held in UTMA or UGMA accounts.

United States Savings Bonds Redeemed for Education Expenses This was explained in Chapter 7 in the description of U.S. savings bonds. While this exclusion of interest may be helpful in some cases, it generally cannot be counted on as a complete advance funding technique in itself.

Cash-Value Life Insurance These policies normally cover a parent as the insured and the owner. They are intended to accumulate a cash value, which can be used for education expenses (usually through policy loans or withdrawals less than basis) if the insured survives, but if the insured should die or become disabled before the education is begun or completed, the death proceeds (or waiver of premium benefit) are there to complete the education plan. This approach effectively utilizes the income tax advantages of life insurance, as explained in Chapter 29. It also could be owned by an irrevocable life insurance trust for estate tax reasons if desired.

Use of Individually Owned Assets or Savings For many years, people simply have saved or accumulated assets—either separately in their own names or jointly with their spouses—in anticipation of using those assets to pay for their children's education. This certainly is a simple and flexible approach, and has certain advantages. The owner controls the assets and their use. If the education plans do not materialize or do not materialize to the parents' (or grandparents') satisfaction, they still own the assets. No outside intermediaries need to be used.

On the other hand, income and capital gains from these assets will be taxed currently to the owners (except for the interest exclusion for U.S. savings bonds just discussed and interest from municipal securities). The assets also will not have been removed from the owner's gross estate for federal estate tax purposes, if this is an issue. The owners will have the unlimited gift tax exclusion for direct payments of tuition, but need to be careful to stay within the per-donee annual exclusion for the remainder of any expenses paid.

The nature of the assets accumulated for this purpose depends on the investment strategy and overall asset allocation position of the person or couple. For a younger child or grandchild, the accumulation period will be relatively long, and so good-quality common stocks or stock mutual funds might be appropriate. To be more conservative, a balanced mutual fund might be considered. On the other hand, the person or couple may want more security and therefore choose bonds or guaranteed principal investments.

For tax-efficient investments for this purpose, one possibility would be investment-grade, zero coupon municipal bonds, with maturities corresponding to the prospective student's years in school. These would approach the attractions of a 529 plan invested in a fixed-income option, except that their respective yields would have to be compared. The bonds' investment income would be income tax–free in all cases; the yield would be locked in for the maturity of the bonds; and they would be available to the owner to pay any education expenses, to make other gifts (presumably within the annual exclusions), or simply to keep for his or her own use (without any 10 percent penalty tax). However, the munis would be in the owner's gross estate for federal estate tax purposes, if he or she should die before they were used for education expenses or other needs. The real point of comparison then would seem to be the locked-in yield of the zero coupon munis as compared with the yield on investment in a 529 plan or an Education IRA of comparable quality and maturities. Of course, if only equity investments (e.g., common stocks) are desired, munis would not be a viable alternative.

Overall Advantage of QTPs and Possible Diversification in Education Funding

With all factors considered, it seems hard to beat a well-selected 529 plan, with flexible plan provisions, a reasonable number of well-managed investment options, and a reasonable expense ratio and other costs, as a vehicle for funding education costs. Such a plan or plans probably should be a core part of most education funding strategies.

However, as with most areas of financial planning, there is much to be said for a diversified approach. For example, along with a 529 plan, a person might have an Education IRA (if eligible) and possibly a UTMA or UGMA or a trust for the minor. Directly owned assets might also be used. Finally, some life and disability insurance arrangements will be needed in case the donor should die or become disabled before the education plan can be completed.

On the other hand, it should be noted that some commentators argue that for relatively wealthy donors, 529 plans should not be used. Rather, annual exclusion gifts for donee's should be made in other ways. Then, when the donees are in colleges or universities, tuition could be paid directly to the institution within the unlimited gift tax exclusion for such tuition.

PART V

Retirement Planning, Stock Compensation, and Other Employee Benefits

13

Retirement Needs Analysis, Social Security, and Employer-Provided Qualified Retirement Plans

Competence Objectives for This Chapter After reading this chapter, planners should understand:

- Retirement needs and assumptions for retirement planning
- Uses of Monte Carlo simulations in retirement planning
- Alternatives to compensate for projected and actual retirement income shortfalls
- Features of the Social Security (OASDHI) system and its benefits
- Planning issues concerning when to begin taking Social Security retirement benefits
- Requirements for qualified retirement plans
- Advantages and limitations of qualified retirement plans
- Characteristics of defined-benefit and defined-contribution qualified plans
- Marital rights in qualified plans
- Loans from qualified plans
- Limitations on contributions and benefits for qualified plans
- Vesting under qualified plans
- Integration (permitted disparity) with Social Security
- Top-heavy retirement plans
- The nature and characteristics of pension plans, profit-sharing plans, and savings plans
- The structure of cash or deferred arrangements [Section 401(k) plans]
- The nature and characteristics of stock bonus plans and employee stock ownership plans (ESOPs)

- The nature of various hybrid qualified retirement plans
- The characteristics and uses of retirement plans for the self-employed (HR-10 plans)

Retirement Needs Analysis

Assumptions for Retirement Planning

The assumption is often made that people's financial needs decrease after retirement. To some extent, this assumption may be valid. However, the actual reduction in the financial needs of retired persons probably has been overstated. These people normally do not want any drastic change in their standards of living at retirement. Expenses for medical care, and perhaps custodial care (long-term care), probably will increase significantly during retirement. Also, retired persons may have travel plans or other recreational goals in mind.

In addition, depending on the circumstances, retirees may find themselves in the position of wanting (or needing) to help their adult children or grandchildren financially. They may help fund the education costs for grandchildren or even children and may provide down payments for first-time home purchases, for example. Individuals and their advisers should not forget what economic forces, such as inflation or deflation, can do to their carefully planned retirement income. While assumptions concerning inflation traditionally have been made in retirement planning, the possibility of deflation should not be ignored.

Another factor affecting planning is that some persons wish to retire at younger ages than the traditional age 65. Also, life expectancy has increased dramatically. Within the past 70 years, for example, life expectancy at birth has increased from around 47 years to 80 years or more. An assumption needs to be made concerning the potential retirement period of retirees. Also, in making this assumption it must be remembered that individual retirees may live well beyond their statistical life expectancies. Finally, persons near or in retirement often have family giving or bequest goals and charitable giving objectives. These may be carried out during the persons' lifetimes (lifetime gifts) or at death. Hence, many persons wish to have or retain assets for these purposes.

Steps in the Retirement Income Planning Process

There are many issues involved in planning for retirement, but certainly an important one is assuring adequate retirement income. The steps in the process for doing so can be outlined as follows:

1. Set desired retirement age.
2. Identify sources of retirement income.
3. Project estimated retirement income (by source) to desired retirement age.

4. Estimate income needed at desired retirement age in current dollars.
5. Adjust estimated retirement income needed and projected retirement income available at desired retirement age for estimated inflation, if any, from the present to the desired retirement age.
6. Compare retirement income needed with projected retirement income available both in current dollars and adjusted (where appropriate) for preretirement inflation as of the desired retirement age.
7. Compare projected postretirement income needs and projected postretirement income available (both adjusted for preretirement and postretirement inflation, if any) on a year-by-year basis to see how available income will meet expected needs during retirement.
8. Plan for meeting any deficiencies in projected retirement income as compared with retirement needs, as noted later in the section on alternatives, to compensate for projected cash-flow shortfalls.
9. Consider how and when benefits should be paid from the various sources of retirement income to the extent the person or couple has discretion in the matter.
10. Plan for the beneficiary designations in retirement plans when appropriate.
11. Review and revise the plan periodically as appropriate.

Sources of Retirement Income

The task of providing retirement income generally falls on people's ability to accumulate assets during their working years, government programs, and employer-provided plans. People frequently receive retirement benefits from all these sources.

Individually Provided Retirement Income Many people accumulate an investment fund, IRAs, individual nonqualified annuities, life insurance cash values, and other funds during their working years to help provide for their retirement. This seems only prudent.

Social Security Old-Age (Retirement) Benefits The essential purpose of Social Security is to provide a guaranteed income floor on which a more comfortable level of retirement income can be built by the individual and his or her employer. Unfortunately, however, in some cases, Social Security is expected (universally) to provide the main source of retirement income. Social Security is described in more detail later in this chapter.

Employer-Provided Retirement Plans Many employers have established tax-favored retirement plans. These are referred to in the tax law as "qualified retirement plans." The main types of these plans are described in this chapter.

Expected Total Returns Assumed During Retirement

This important assumption involves an estimate of the rate of return that can be expected on the person's or couple's retirement assets. Such an estimate depends on the characteristics of the retirement assets, whether capital is being liquidated to provide retirement income (as in a life annuity, for example), and on the asset allocation chosen for investments during retirement.

Straight-Line Returns versus Probability Analysis In making this estimate, one can determine the returns currently being received or estimate what those returns should be in the future (often based on historical studies) and then assume the estimated returns will continue into the future without significant variation. It then can be determined how these expected returns compare with expected outlays during retirement. These might be referred to as *straight-line returns* or average returns.

On the other hand, a *probabilistic analysis* would use computer programs to simulate thousands of market scenarios and various asset allocation strategies to develop probabilities of success for different investment and withdrawal strategies. Various assumptions are made concerning expected annual returns from different asset classes and their correlations. This approach is also referred to as a *Monte Carlo analysis.*

CASE EXAMPLE

Suppose Harry and Susan Wong, both age 70, are preparing to retire. They have a combined investment portfolio of about \$1,500,000 as well as pension and Social Security benefits. They would like to know how much of their investment portfolio they can safely withdraw each year without running out of money. Their financial adviser tells them that based on a Monte Carlo simulation, and assuming their investment portfolio is placed 40 percent in common stocks, 40 percent in investment grade bonds, and 20 percent in cash equivalents, there is a 99 percent probability that if they take 4 percent of the initial amount (increased each year by an assumed 3 percent inflation rate), or about \$60,000 per year (\$5,000 per month), for the next 25 years (or until they are 95), their investment portfolio will not be exhausted (i.e., they will not run out of money). On the other hand, using the same assumptions, if they increase their withdrawals to 5 percent of the initial amount, or about \$75,000 per year (\$6,250 per month), there is only an 80 percent probability that the Wongs will not run out of money over the 25 years.

This example illustrates what is often called the "*4% solution.*" This means that with a 4 percent withdrawal rate (plus an annual constant increase to reflect assumed inflation), many Monte Carlo simulations show there is a high probability (90 percent or better) that that retiree will not run out of money for a substantial period of time (e.g., 25 or 30 years), depending on the assumptions made.

However, it must be noted that these simulations are heavily dependent on the assumptions inherent in them. Also, taxes typically are not taken into account. Furthermore, extreme market movements or crises probably will seriously distort the model's results. Finally, there is no guarantee that the withdrawal results predicted by the model will hold true. They are not like life annuities sold by life insurance companies or guaranteed minimum withdrawal benefits (GMWBs) sold by some life insurers.

Life Annuity (Pure Annuity) versus Capital Preservation This is a basic tradeoff decision in retirement planning. Payment of retirement benefits as a *life annuity* involves payments for as long as one or two persons live (the annuitants) and ceases upon the person's death or the death of the last of the two annuitants (except for any survivors' benefits). This involves liquidating capital (i.e., liquidating the cost of the life annuity) over the annuitants' lifetimes. By doing so, the annuitants are guaranteed an income they cannot outlive. They also are increasing their retirement income (as compared with just investing their capital in securities of comparable risk) because annuitizing involves the systematic liquidation of the amount invested in the annuity (i.e., capital). Therefore, each annuity payment consists of investment income and a return of capital.

People can life-annuitize their wealth in a variety of ways. Probably the most common is to purchase an immediate life annuity from a life insurance company, as explained in Chapter 17. Also, the decision to take a life income, rather than a lump sum settlement if available, from a pension plan is a decision to life-annuitize. Furthermore, entering into a charitable gift annuity involves a life annuity.

On the other hand, retirees can simply live off their actual current investment income and *preserve their capital* (investment portfolio). Their capital then would remain intact for future investment opportunities, cash needs, emergencies, inheritances for their heirs (the bequest motive), and possibly charitable giving.

In many cases, it may be logical to follow a combination of approaches. For example, in the case situation of Harry and Susan Wong discussed earlier, when they retire at age 70, they could use $500,000 of their assets as the premium (annuity consideration) for an immediate joint and last survivor life annuity from a highly rated life insurance company. This might provide them with about an 8 percent return on the $500,000 ($40,000 per year) for their lifetimes. They then could preserve the $1,000,000 and live off its investment income (or perhaps employ the "4% solution" for this amount).

Still another combination approach might be for Harry and Susan to begin their retirement by preserving their capital (the $1,500,000 of assets) and using the investment income and perhaps some capital for living expenses. Then, some years later in their retirement, say, when they are 75 or 80, they can reevaluate the situation, and if they need more retirement income, they can purchase a joint and survivor life annuity with some of their capital. Because they are older, the rate of return on the annuity will be higher at this point.

Alternatives to Compensate for Projected Income (Cash-Flow) Shortfalls

After a retirement-needs analysis, people may find that there is a shortfall or gap between their needs (or desires) and their present or projected retirement income. Filling this shortfall can present some difficult choices.

If the person or couple has not yet retired, several strategies may be followed, such as:

- Increase saving for retirement. This may involve cutting current consumption expenditures. There is considerable evidence that in recent years, Americans in general have not been saving enough for retirement and other needs.
- Review investment planning and asset allocation to see if investment yield can be improved within acceptable risk levels. The degree of investment risk also should be evaluated, considering the time left before planned retirement.
- Consider contributing more to tax-advantaged retirement plans, if possible.
- Perhaps postpone the planned retirement date (i.e., work longer).
- If one spouse is not currently working outside the home but once had a career, perhaps he or she should consider returning to the workforce. In other words, become a two-earner family again.

However, if the person or couple is at retirement age or is retired, several strategies may present themselves to cover any shortfall, such as:

- Try to reduce current expenses in retirement. For example, it may be possible to postpone planned trips or vacations. It also may be desirable to reduce or postpone planned giving programs to children or grandchildren. Other reductions may be possible without severely affecting the retirees' lifestyle.
- Review investment planning and asset allocation, as just described.

- If possible, consider postponing the planned retirement date, or one or both spouses can return to active employment on a full- or part-time basis. This sometimes is referred to as "dynamic retirement planning." The problem is that at the very time the former retiree wants to return to work, the labor market may not be very receptive to the return of the older worker, particularly during a recession or depression.
- As discussed previously, a strategy for increasing retirement income without undue risk is to devote capital to the purchase of an immediate life annuity from a highly rated life insurance company. For those who are charitably inclined, the creating of a charitable gift annuity also fits this strategy. However, the problem with life annuitization is that capital is not preserved and any bequest motive is impeded.
- If the person or couple is eligible, they can take a reverse mortgage on their home, as described in Chapter 9. This, in effect, will convert the equity in their home into an income stream (analogous to a life annuity) but still leave the possibility of some of this equity going to their heirs after the last of their deaths. There are some limitations on reverse mortgages, however, as discussed in Chapter 9.

Social Security (OASDHI)

Before considering in more detail the private approaches to providing retirement income, death benefits, disability benefits, and health benefits, it will be helpful to describe briefly the social insurance system for providing such benefits in the United States: Social Security.

Overview of Social Security

While the bulk of Social Security benefits are paid as retirement benefits, the Social Security system (or old age, survivors, disability, and health insurance system, OASDHI) actually provides four distinct categories of benefits: *old-age* (retirement) benefits for covered workers and their eligible dependents, *survivors'* (death) benefits for eligible surviving dependents of covered workers, *disability* benefits for covered workers and their eligible dependents, and *health insurance* benefits (Medicare) for covered persons age 65 or older and certain other beneficiaries.

Coverage, Benefit Eligibility, and Social Security Taxes

Almost everyone will be covered under the Social Security system and is paying or will pay social security taxes during their working years.

Covered Persons All employees and self-employed persons working in the United States and certain possessions are covered, except for a few groups specifically excluded by law.

Insured Status In addition to being a covered worker, a person's eligibility for benefits depends on having the appropriate insured status at the time of his or her retirement, disability, or death. There are three types of insured status requirements: fully insured, currently insured, and disability insured.

A worker attains *fully insured status* if he or she has 40 quarters of coverage. If not, he or she still may be fully insured by having a specified minimum number of quarters. A minimum of 6 quarters is required in any event.

A worker meets the requirements for *currently insured status* if he or she has at least 6 quarters of coverage during the 13 quarters ending with his or her death, eligibility for old-age benefits, or disability.

Disability-insured status has the strictest requirements of all. Workers who are age 31 or older when they become disabled must be fully insured and have at least 20 quarters of coverage during the 40-quarter period ending when their disabilities begin.

Social Security Taxable Earnings Base (Covered Earnings) and Tax Rates Covered earnings are those to which social security tax rates (FICA taxes) are applied and that also generally serve as a maximum in calculating a worker's average monthly earnings for purposes of determining his or her primary insurance amount.

For employees, all their compensation (up to the maximum, if any) from employment is subject to FICA tax. For self-employed persons, taxable compensation includes income from self-employment, which essentially means net earnings from operating an unincorporated trade or business as determined for federal income tax purposes.

The amount of the Social Security taxable earnings base (and benefit base) has constantly increased over the years, from a low of $3,000 per year for 1937 through 1950 to $106,800 for 2009. For the hospital insurance (HI) tax under Medicare, all compensation is taxable.[1] This tax and benefit base will increase in the future in proportion to the increase in average annual wages in the United States.

[1] Beginning in 1994, the hospital insurance (HI) tax rate of 1.45 percent for employees and 2.90 percent for self-employed persons (which is included in the 7.65 percent and 15.30 percent totals here) is applied to a person's total taxable earnings or self-employment income. Thus, this HI tax effectively becomes an additional income tax on personal earnings (or self-employment income), with no maximum limit. It also effectively requires the annual valuation of amounts deferred under nonqualified deferred-compensation plans for highly compensated executives.

The total FICA tax rate for employees is 7.65 percent for 2009. There is an equal tax rate on employers. For self-employed persons, the FICA tax rate is 15.30 percent for 2009; however, one-half of this FICA tax is allowed as an income tax deduction from gross income, and self-employment income is reduced by 7.65 percent (without regard to the maximum earnings base) in determining taxable self-employment income.

Primary Insurance Amount and Family Maximum Benefit Social Security benefits (other than Medicare) are based on the worker's *primary insurance amount* (PIA). In turn, the *family maximum benefit* (FMB), which is the total amount of benefits that may be paid to a worker and his or her eligible dependents, also is determined based on the worker's PIA. A worker's PIA is calculated by applying a formula (which varies according to the year of eligibility for benefits) to the worker's average monthly earnings over a certain number of years.

Calculation of a person's or family's Social Security benefits is complicated. Fortunately, this complication is substantially diminished for planning purposes by personal earnings and benefit estimate statements (Social Security statements) available from the Social Security Administration. These statements are mailed each year to workers about three months before their birthday. (An additional copy can be secured from www.ssa.gov/mystatement). In addition, the Social Security Administration maintains a Web site to help individuals determine their benefit amount at www.ssa.gov/OACT/quickcalc.

Social Security Retirement Benefits

Retired Worker's Benefits To be eligible for old-age benefits, a worker must be age 62 or older and have attained fully insured status. At the full-benefit retirement age (also called the Social Security normal retirement age or SSNRA), the retirement benefit is equal to the worker's PIA. For workers born in 1937 and earlier, the SSNRA was age 65. However, starting with workers born in 1938 and thereafter, the full-benefit retirement age gradually increases until it reaches age 67 for workers born in 1960 and later. As of this writing, the full-benefit retirement age for persons just eligible for Social Security is age 66. A covered worker may elect to receive a retirement benefit as early as age 62; however, if such an early-retirement benefit is elected, the worker's retirement benefit will be permanently reduced. For example, for retirees with an SSNRA of 66, the early retirement benefit starting at age 62 would be 75 percent of the full benefit at age 66. Workers can also elect to delay retirement until age 70, with increased benefits. After age 70, benefits are no longer increased by delay.

Spouse of Retired Worker The spouse of a retired worker who is at least age 62 is eligible to receive a lifetime retirement benefit based on the worker's PIA. For an eligible spouse at full-benefit retirement age, the spouse's benefit is equal to 50 percent of the covered worker's PIA. However, a spouse may begin receiving reduced retirement benefits as early as age 62. A divorced spouse also may be eligible for retirement benefits under certain conditions.

A spouse may be entitled to receive a Social Security retirement benefit because of the spouse's own employment record. When this occurs, the spouse will receive the larger of his or her own benefit or the benefit as a spouse, but not both.

Other Dependents of Retired Workers Social Security retirement benefits also may be available for a spouse caring for a child and for each eligible child or grandchild of a retired worker.

Planning Issues Concerning When to Begin Taking Social Security Retirement Benefits This may be a significant retirement planning issue. As just noted, an eligible worker and his or her eligible spouse can begin receiving reduced retirement benefits as early as age 62 or can delay them (with increased benefits) until age 70.

A number of considerations will affect when these benefits should be taken. If the covered worker and his or her spouse want to retire early, say around age 62, and need the benefits to live on, they probably should begin taking Social Security payments early (e.g., at age 62), even if these payments are reduced. This would be another alternative to compensate for a shortfall in other retirement benefits. Also, if the person is in poor health (and thus has a reduced life expectancy), it normally is better to begin benefits early, although the spouse's benefits also must be considered in this decision.

On the other hand, if the retirees stop working and can afford to delay taking Social Security benefits, they need to evaluate the financial results of delaying at least until full benefit age and perhaps even to age 70. The factors that might be considered in such a decision include:

- The extent of the differences in benefits. For example, assuming the full benefit retirement age is 66 and the full benefit is $2,000 per month, the corresponding benefit at age 62 would be $1,500 per month (or 25 percent less), while the corresponding monthly benefit at age 70 would be $2,640 (or 32 percent more).
- The retiree's life expectancy.
- The expected investment earnings rate on the benefits and the tax rate on those earnings.
- The expected inflation rate.

Given such factors, a "break-even age" can be calculated, at which point the accumulated expected benefits for a person who delayed taking Social Security benefits (say, until SSNRA or age 70) will just equal and thereafter exceed the accumulated expected benefits for a person who began benefits early (say, at age 62). A government Web site at www.ssa.gov/retire2/delayret.htm deals with delayed retirement decisions. Also, at the Social Security Administration's Web site (www.ssa.gov), there is a "break-even calculator" that can determine break-even ages.

It should also be noted that a retiree and his or her spouse can file separately for their respective benefits. For example, one spouse can file for a worker's benefit early and then the other spouse can file for a spouse's benefit at SSNRA (based on his or her worker spouse's projected benefit at the worker spouse's SSNRA).

Personal Earnings While Receiving Social Security Retirement Benefits At present, personal earnings after SSNRA retirement age do not reduce an otherwise eligible person's Social Security retirement benefits. However, if an early-retirement benefit is elected, the worker's benefit can be reduced for personal earnings until normal retirement age is reached.

Cost-of-Living Increases in Social Security Benefits Social Security is one of the few retirement programs that automatically increases benefits in the face of cost-of-living increases. All Social Security benefits (old-age, survivors', and disability) are increased each year when there has been an increase in the average consumer price index (CPI).

Social Security Survivorship (Death) Benefits

These are benefits to certain survivors of deceased actively employed workers, disabled workers, or retired workers. They are based on the covered worker's primary insurance amount (PIA) and are paid in the form of monthly income to the eligible family member. In addition, there is a $255 lump-sum death benefit to a surviving spouse or, if there is no surviving spouse, to eligible children.

Surviving Spouse

The surviving spouse of a deceased worker who had a fully insured status can receive a survivor's benefit, provided the surviving spouse is age 60 or older, or is disabled, and at least 50. The amount of this benefit is 100 percent of the deceased worker's survivor PIA, if the surviving spouse has reached the full-benefit retirement age, and is reduced for younger surviving spouses.

Other Dependents

Unmarried children (and, in certain circumstances, unmarried grandchildren) of a deceased worker are entitled to a child's monthly survivor's benefit. This benefit is equal to 75 percent of the deceased parent's PIA, provided the child is under age 18, under age 19 and an elementary or secondary school student, or 18 or older but disabled before age 22.

In addition, the surviving spouse of a deceased worker is eligible for a *mother's or father's survivor's benefit* equal to 75 percent of the deceased worker's PIA as long as the surviving spouse is caring for an eligible child who is under age 16 or is older and disabled before reaching age 22. The surviving spouse is eligible for the benefit at any age. A surviving divorced spouse also may be eligible for this benefit. Further, a surviving *dependent parent* who is at least 62 years old may be entitled to a monthly survivor's benefit.

As is the case for other Social Security benefits, there is a family maximum benefit (FMB) that applies to the combined survivor's benefits from the PIA of a deceased worker.

Social Security Disability Benefits

There are two kinds of Social Security disability benefits: cash disability income benefits, payable to the disabled worker and his or her eligible dependents, and freezing of a disabled worker's wage position for purposes of determining his or her future retirement or survivorship benefits.

An eligible worker is considered disabled when he or she has a medically determinable physical or mental impairment that is so severe that the worker is unable to engage in any substantially gainful work or employment. This amounts to an "any occupation" definition of disability and is strict by health insurance standards. In addition, the disability must last 5 months before benefits can begin. After 5 months of disability, benefits are payable, if the impairment can be expected to last for at least 12 months or to result in death, or if it has actually lasted 12 months. This amounts to a 5-month waiting (elimination) period.

Taxation of Social Security Benefits

The Social Security Amendments of 1983 introduced a previously unthinkable concept: the taxing of Social Security benefits.

The first step is to determine whether any of a person's or couple's benefits will be subject to tax. This will occur if their so-called provisional income exceeds certain base amounts. Provisional income is the sum of (1) 50 percent of the Social Security benefit payable; (2) the person's or couple's adjusted gross income (AGI) for federal income tax purposes (with certain additions);

and (3) tax-exempt interest (from municipal bonds[2]). If this provisional income does not exceed $25,000 for a single taxpayer or $32,000 for a married couple filing a joint return, Social Security benefits remain tax-free.

In the second step, if provisional income exceeds the appropriate base amount but does not exceed $34,000 for a single taxpayer or $44,000 for married taxpayers filing a joint return, the amount of benefits includible in gross income is the smaller of one-half the Social Security benefits or one-half the excess of provisional income over the base amount.

Finally, in the third step, if provisional income exceeds $34,000 for a single taxpayer or $44,000 for married taxpayers filing a joint return, the amount includible in gross income is the smaller of 85 percent of Social Security benefits or the sum of (1) the smaller of the amount calculated in the second step or $4,500 for a single taxpayer or $6,000 for married taxpayers filing a joint return; and (2) 85 percent of the amount by which provisional income exceeds $34,000 for a single taxpayer or $44,000 for married taxpayers filing a joint return. Thus, higher-income taxpayers could be taxed on as much as 85 percent of their Social Security benefits. Fortunately, the IRS Forms and Instructions booklet contains a worksheet to help taxpayers determine the taxable amount, if any, of their Social Security benefits.

Characteristics of Employer-Provided Retirement Plans

Employer-provided retirement plans are part of the employer's overall employee benefits program. The most important are *qualified pension plans, profit-sharing plans,* and *savings plans.* However, employers also may have other plans that aid their employees or some of their employees in providing for retirement. Some of these include simplified employee pension plans (SEPs), tax-sheltered annuity (TSA) plans for nonprofit and certain other employers, qualified stock bonus plans, qualified employee stock ownership plans (ESOPs), savings incentive match plans for employees of small employers (SIMPLE) plans, nonqualified deferred-compensation plans, and supplemental executive retirement plans (SERPs).

Qualified Retirement Plans

The phrase *qualified retirement plan* is a tax term and refers to those kinds of retirement plans spelled out in the Internal Revenue Code (Section 401[a])

[2]The sum of a person's or couple's regular adjusted gross income, with certain additions, and their tax-exempt interest is referred to as their *modified adjusted gross income* (or modified AGI) in this calculation.

that are accorded special tax advantages if they meet certain nondiscrimination and other requirements of the law. Some of the important qualification requirements for these plans can be summarized as follows:

- There must be a legally binding arrangement that is in writing and communicated to the employees.
- The plan must be for the exclusive benefit of the employees or their beneficiaries.
- The principal or income of the plan must not be diverted from these benefits for any other purpose.
- The plan must benefit a broad class of employees and not discriminate in favor of highly compensated employees.
- The plan must meet certain minimum vesting requirements.
- Plans must meet minimum eligibility, coverage, and participation requirements.
- Plans must provide certain spousal rights in benefits.
- There must be certain minimum benefit distribution rules.
- Plans must meet minimum funding standards.

The qualified plans covered in this chapter include:

- Pension plans
- Profit-sharing plans
- Savings (or thrift) plans
- Cash or deferred arrangements (Section 401[k] options)
- Stock bonus plans
- Employee stock ownership plans (ESOPs)
- Retirement plans for the self-employed (HR-10 or Keogh plans)

Advantages and Limitations of Qualified Plans

Some commentators have referred to qualified retirement plans as the "perfect tax shelter." While there probably is no perfect tax shelter, qualified retirement plans do have significant tax and nontax advantages.

Tax Advantages of Qualified Plans These include the following:

- Employer contributions, within the limits of the tax law, are deductible for income tax purposes by the employer.
- Even though the employer receives a current income tax deduction, covered employees (called participants) do not receive taxable income from the plan due to employer contributions until benefits are actually distributed to the participants or their beneficiaries.
- Investment income or gains on assets within the plan are not subject to income taxation until paid out as benefits.

- Employees may be able to contribute to some plans with before-tax dollars (i.e., on a salary-reduction basis).
- Lump-sum distributions to participants (or their beneficiaries) may be given favorable income tax treatment under limited circumstances.
- Under a special grandfather provision, certain amounts payable upon the death of a plan participant may be entitled to either an unlimited or a $100,000 estate tax exclusion, depending on when the participant (decedent) separated from the employer's service. In general, however, there no longer is an estate tax exclusion for qualified plan death benefits as there once was.

Other Advantages of Qualified Plans In addition to these tax advantages, qualified plans may have the following nontax advantages for participants:

- The employer may pay the full cost of a plan (a noncontributory plan) or part of the cost (a contributory plan).
- Plans may have favorable investment options that are not available to persons outside the plan.
- If the plan is contributory, regular employee contributions by way of payroll deduction (on either a before-tax or after-tax basis) may be a convenient way for employees to save.
- Plans often have loan provisions that permit participants to borrow from the plan.

Limitations of Qualified Plans However, there may be drawbacks to these plans from the participants' point of view.

- The rights to benefits of participants who leave the employer before retirement are subject to the terms of the plan. Therefore, the particular plan's provisions will determine when and how a participant can receive benefits from the plan.
- Investment options under some plans may be limited.
- The rights of participants to benefits attributable to the employer's contributions are determined by the vesting provisions of the plan.
- A participant's rights to distributions from qualified retirement plans are subject to certain spousal (marital) rights under the Retirement Equity Act of 1984 (REA), as described in the section "Impact of Marital Rights on Qualified Retirement Plans."
- Since qualified retirement plans are intended to provide retirement income for participants, if premature distributions are taken from qualified plans (as well as from IRAs and certain other plans), the distributions will be subject to a 10 percent penalty tax in addition to the regular income tax on the distribution. Premature distributions are described in Chapter 16, but they generally are those prior to age 59½, subject to certain exceptions.

- Correspondingly, since these plans are intended to provide retirement income for participants and their spouses rather than income tax–deferred wealth transfers, benefits from these plans (as well as from traditional IRAs) must begin by a participant's required beginning date (RBD), which often is age 70½, and at least minimum distributions must be taken starting at the RBD. These minimum distribution rules are explained more fully in Chapter 16.
- Death benefits from these plans are included in a participant's gross estate for federal estate tax purposes (except for a few grandfathered cases) and are also income in respect of a decedent (IRD). Hence, they are heavily taxed at death.
- The structuring and administration of the plan and selection of funding agencies (e.g., banks or insurance companies) and other third-party service providers normally is up to the employer.
- Finally, the employer can modify or terminate the plan for the future, unless it is subject to collective bargaining.

On balance, however, the advantages of qualified retirement plans far outweigh possible drawbacks, so employees usually are well advised to participate fully in such plans.

Defined-Benefit and Defined-Contribution Plans

Qualified retirement plans can be classified as either defined-benefit plans or defined-contribution plans. This distinction can be important in planning for these plans.

A *defined-benefit (DB) plan* is one in which the retirement benefits are expressed as a specified benefit at retirement. The benefit may be a dollar amount or it may be determined by a formula specified in the plan. Thus, the essence of a DB plan is that the retirement benefits are specified or fixed, while the contributions necessary to fund those benefits vary. The type of DB plan with which most people are concerned is the *defined-benefit pension plan.*

A *defined-contribution (DC) plan,* on the other hand, is one that provides for an individual account for each participant and for specified or variable contributions being made to those accounts. These plans are sometimes called *individual account plans.* The accumulated account balance for a participant may be affected by such factors as contributions to the account (by the employer, the employee, or both), investment income, investment gains and losses from the assets in the account, and possible forfeitures by other plan participants that may be allocated to the account. A participant's retirement income from a DC plan, then, is based on the income or other distributions the participant's accumulated account balance will produce at his or her retirement age, depending on how benefits are taken from the plan. Some pension plans, called *money-purchase pension plans,* are DC plans. All the other types of qualified plans discussed in this chapter also are DC plans. Some people have both DB and DC plans from their employers. However, others will have only one type, usually a DC plan.

Impact of Marital Rights on Qualified Retirement Plans

There have been significant changes in the law concerning the rights of noncovered spouses (also called nonparticipant spouses or NPSs) in the retirement plan benefits of their covered spouses. These rights can significantly affect retirement and estate planning by married persons.

Retirement Equity Act of 1984 (REA) The purpose of REA is to give a noncovered spouse certain survivorship rights in the qualified retirement plan benefits of the covered spouse, unless those rights are waived by the covered spouse, with the proper witnessed consent in writing by the noncovered spouse. REA essentially mandates two forms of survivorship benefits to protect the noncovered spouse: a preretirement spouse's benefit, called a *qualified preretirement survivor annuity* (QPSA), and a postretirement spouse's benefit, called a *qualified joint and survivor annuity* (QJSA).

Plans Covered by REA Rules REA applies to qualified defined-benefit and money-purchase pension plans. It also covers qualified profit-sharing (including savings) and stock bonus plans, unless these plans meet certain requirements for exclusion from the rules. In general, to be excepted from REA, a participant's benefit arrangement under a profit-sharing, savings, or stock bonus plan must meet the following requirements: First, the participant's vested account balance must be payable in full upon the participant's death to his or her surviving spouse (unless the spouse consents in the proper form to another beneficiary designation, as noted subsequently). Second, the participant cannot elect for benefits to be payable in the form of a life annuity. And, third, the plan cannot have received a transfer from a pension plan. In effect, then, if an employee covered under a profit-sharing, savings, or stock bonus plan wishes to have the death benefit payable in any way other than outright to his or her spouse, the spouse must consent to the other beneficiary designation in the proper form, or else the spouse's REA rights will apply.

It may be noted that the REA rules do not apply to IRAs.

Qualified Preretirement Survivor Annuity (QPSA) A QPSA is a life annuity for the surviving spouse of a plan participant who had a vested benefit in the plan and who dies before his or her normal retirement benefits are to begin. If the participant dies after the earliest age at which retirement benefits could have been received under the plan, the surviving spouse's QPSA is the amount that would have been payable to the surviving spouse under an annuity form of a lifetime income for the employee, with a 50 percent survivorship annuity for the spouse, assuming the deceased employee had actually retired with such an annuity on the day before his or her death.

CASE EXAMPLE

Suppose Mary Warnaki is age 56, married, and participates in a pension plan that has a normal retirement age of 65 but permits early retirement as soon as age 55. Mary's husband is age 58. If Mary were to retire at her current age of 56, she and her husband would receive a joint and 50-percent-to-the-survivor pension benefit of $2,000 per month. Given these facts, if Mary (while actively employed) dies at age 56 with her husband surviving, her husband will receive a QPSA benefit of $1,000 per month ($2,000 × 50 percent) for his life.

If an employee dies before the earliest age at which he or she could have retired under the plan, the calculation is more complex but the principle is essentially the same. In this case, the surviving spouse must wait until when the deceased employee would have attained the plan's early retirement age to begin receiving his or her QPSA benefit.

REA permits an employer to charge the increased cost of QPSA rights against the retirement benefits that otherwise would be payable to the participant. However, an employer voluntarily may not reduce the benefits otherwise payable.

A participant may decide to waive these QPSA benefits. For QPSA rights only, this can be done at any time during an election period, which generally begins after a participant attains age 35. A waiver is not effective unless the participant's spouse consents in writing and the consent is witnessed by a plan representative or a notary public. A significant planning issue is whether a participant and his or her spouse should elect to waive these rights. This issue is considered further in the next section.

Qualified Joint and Survivor Annuity (QJSA) REA also requires that qualified plan retirement benefits payable to a married participant must be provided as a QJSA, unless the participant (with the consent of his or her spouse) elects to waive the QJSA form or unless a profit-sharing, savings, or stock bonus plan account meets the requirements for exclusion from the REA rules. The QJSA form is an annuity for the lifetime of the participant, with a survivorship annuity for the lifetime of his or her surviving spouse of not less than 50 percent, or more than 100 percent, of the annuity payable during their joint lives.

CASE EXAMPLE

Assume that Henry Sullivan is married, age 65, and about to retire under his employer's defined-benefit pension plan. His wife also is age 65. Assume further that Henry does not elect to waive the QJSA form and so retires with an annuity benefit payable under a 50-percent QJSA form of $6,000 per month. Given these facts, if Henry should predecease his wife, a survivorship annuity would continue to her of $3,000 per month for the remainder of her lifetime ($6,000 × 50 percent). On the other hand, if Henry's wife should predecease him, the original $6,000 per month would continue for his lifetime.

As with QPSA rights, REA permits a plan to charge the increased cost against the pension benefits otherwise payable. Just as an example, one pension plan applies a reduction factor of 10.7 percent from the life annuity for the participant alone (a straight life annuity) for a QJSA form, when both the participant and spouse are age 65. However, again, an employer may voluntarily subsidize the QJSA form.

A plan participant, with the consent in the proper form of his or her spouse, may elect to waive the QJSA form within an election period, which is the 90-day period before retirement benefits are to begin. As with the QPSA form, whether a married participant and his or her spouse should elect to waive the QJSA form is an important planning issue.

One reason for considering such a waiver is to avoid reduction of retirement benefits during the joint lifetimes of the husband and wife. Of course, if the forms are subsidized by the employer, this reason is gone and the plan probably will not allow for a waiver. The couple may also desire a retirement payment other than a QJSA, such as a lump-sum payment from a pension plan. Furthermore, there may be estate planning reasons for a waiver if it is desirable for a plan's death benefits to be payable other than outright to the surviving spouse, such as to a trust, for example.

Balanced against these factors, however, is the loss of the protection of the survivorship feature for the nonparticipant spouse in the event he or she survives the participant. This really is part of the broader planning issue of how to protect the surviving spouse.

A significant factor in dealing with this issue is the amount of life insurance on the retired employee's life that continues into retirement for the protection of the nonparticipant spouse.

Finally, if a waiver is to be used, the nonparticipant spouse may want to consider the terms and extent of the waiver and of his or her consent. For example, is the consent revocable or irrevocable? Is it general so that the participant can name any beneficiary he or she wishes or later change the beneficiary, or is it specific (limited) to the beneficiary named when the consent was given? And if a trust is named, can the participant later change the trust beneficiaries?

Other Marital Rights The domestic relations laws of most states recognize that a noncovered spouse may have certain marital property rights in retirement plan benefits and other employee benefits of a spouse in the event of separation or divorce. Under equitable distribution of property laws, retirement plan rights often are considered *marital property* and thus are subject to equitable division between the spouses upon separation or divorce.

These marital and child support rights may be enforced through presenting a *qualified domestic relations order* (QDRO) to the plan administrator. A QDRO is a domestic relations order, issued by a court or other appropriate authority, that recognizes the rights of alternative payees to part or all of a participant's benefits under a qualified retirement plan. Alternate payees may be a spouse, former spouse, child, or other dependent of the plan participant. Assuming the order meets the requirements for a valid QDRO, the plan administrator must make the proper payments of benefits to the alternative payee(s) when the benefits otherwise would have been payable to the participant.

Also, in states that have community property laws or similar laws, the rights that a covered spouse accumulates in various employer-provided plans during marriage become community property and hence each spouse owns half.

Loans from Qualified Plans

Many qualified retirement plans (particularly profit-sharing and savings plans) contain loan provisions that allow participants to borrow from the plan. Such plan loans are not considered taxable distributions from the plan as long as the requirements of the tax law are observed.

The law specifies that for loans not to be considered taxable distributions, the loan may not exceed the smaller of $50,000 or one-half the present value of the participant's vested benefits in the plan. However, loans of less than $10,000 are not treated as taxable distributions, regardless of these limits. The law also requires that a loan be repaid within five years in substantially level payments made at least quarterly. There is an exception to this rule for plan loans used to acquire a primary residence. They must be repaid only within a reasonable time. Loans must also bear a "reasonable" interest rate.

Limitations on Contributions and Benefits for Qualified Plans

Section 415 Limits Under these limits (found in Section 415 of the IRC), for 2009, annual employer-provided pension benefits under a defined-benefit pension plan may not exceed the lesser of $195,000 (adjusted for inflation in increments of $5,000) or 100 percent of the participant's average annual compensation for his or her three highest consecutive years of compensation in the plan. There is actuarial reduction of this dollar limit only if the participant retires before age 62. Furthermore, for 2009, annual additions for a participant under a defined-contribution plan may not exceed the lesser of $49,000 (adjusted for inflation in increments of $1,000) or 100 percent of the participant's annual compensation. Many employers provide that if an employee's benefits under the regular benefit formula exceed the Section 415 limits, the employer will pay the difference from an unfunded nonqualified retirement plan (called an *excess benefits plan*).

Limits for Section 401(k) Plans Special limitations applying to Section 401(k) plans. are described later in this chapter.

Limits on Tax-Deductible Employer Contributions The tax law also places limits on the amount an employer or a self-employed person can deduct in a given year for contributions to various types of qualified retirement plans.

Defined-Benefit Plans: The annual deductible limit for these plans is the amount needed to fund the benefits provided under the plan according to reasonable funding methods and actuarial assumptions adopted by the employer or self-employed person. Furthermore, an employer may deduct at least the amount needed to meet the minimum funding requirements for the current year.

The overall effect of these rules is that defined-benefit pension plans (particularly with permitted disparity, as described later) may generate relatively large tax-deductible contributions for an employer or self-employed person on behalf of older, more highly compensated participants. This can be attractive for owner–employees of closely held businesses or self-employed persons because they often are older, are more highly compensated, and have longer tenures of service than other employees of the business.

However, the tax law and ERISA specify certain minimum funding requirements for defined-benefit plans that an employer or a self-employed person must meet. This means an employer may have to make contributions to a DB plan in bad times as well as good. Thus, DB pension plans create *funding rigidity* for the employer or self-employed person that is not present for profit-sharing plans.

Money-Purchase Pension Plans: As DC plans, the maximum annual deductible employer contribution is 25 percent of aggregate compensation of participants under the plan. Also, since these are pension plans, the employer or self-employed person must make contributions each year, whether the firm is profitable or not.

Profit-Sharing and Stock Bonus Plans: For these DC plans, the maximum aggregate annual tax-deductible employer contributions also cannot exceed 25 percent of total compensation paid to participants for the year. Furthermore, contributions to profit-sharing plans normally are discretionary on the part of the employer, and hence, can be made when the employer feels financially able to do so, but cannot be made when the reverse is true. Thus, the employer has greater funding flexibility under profit-sharing plans as compared with money-purchase pension plans. Since the same 25 percent aggregate limit on tax-deductible employer contributions now applies to both types of plans, most commentators believe few employers will adopt money-purchase pension plans.

Other Plans: There are a number of other types of retirement plans for which there may be limits on contributions. They include Section 401(k) plans, SIMPLE plans, ESOPs, target benefit plans, SEPs, and various kinds of IRAs. The limits on contributions to these plans are covered in this and subsequent chapters.

Limit on Includible Compensation There is a limit (indexed for inflation in $5,000 increments) for qualified retirement plans on the amount of a participant's annual compensation that can be taken into account in determining contributions to or benefits from the plan.[3] This is referred to as the *compensation cap*. As of 2009, the limit stands at $245,000.

Vesting Under Qualified Plans

Vesting means that a participant has a nonforfeitable right in his or her account balance under a defined-contribution plan or to an accrued benefit under a defined-benefit plan that results from employer contributions to the plan. A participant has a right to his or her vested benefits, regardless of whether or not the participant stays with the employer.

[3] This maximum annual compensation limit also applies to simplified employee pensions (SEPs), tax-sheltered annuities (TSAs), and voluntary employee beneficiary associations (VEBAs), as well as to qualified retirement plans.

Vesting can take several forms. Immediate and 100 percent vesting is, of course, the most liberal from the participating employee's standpoint. However, most private plans do not provide immediate and 100 percent vesting. The other form is deferred vesting, which is the most common.

Qualified retirement plans are required to meet certain minimum vesting standards. For defined-benefit plans, vesting must be at least as rapid as under one of two alternative minimum vesting schedules: (1)100 percent vesting upon the participant's completion of five years of service (referred to as *cliff vesting*); or (2) graded or graduated vesting at the rate of 20 percent after three years of service, 40 percent after four years, 60 percent after five years, 80 percent after six years, and 100 percent after seven years or more of service. For defined-contribution plans, there are more rapid minimum vesting schedules for employer contributions, which are 100 percent after three years of service for cliff vesting; or graded vesting at the rate of 20 percent after two years of service, 40 percent after three years, 60 percent after four years, 80 percent after five years, and 100 percent after six or more years of service.

Vesting, particularly cliff vesting, will eliminate benefits for short-service employees. This may be beneficial for plans covering owner-employers of closely held businesses.

Naturally, under contributory plans where employees pay part of the cost, participants are always entitled to a refund (or the right to a deferred benefit) of their own contributions to the plan upon termination of employment.

Integration (Permitted Disparity) with Social Security

General Considerations An *integrated plan* is one in which either benefits or contributions under Social Security are taken into account in establishing the benefits or contributions under the plan. This concept is now referred to in the tax law as *permitted disparity*.

The permitted disparity (integration) rules set limits on the extent to which a qualified plan's benefits or contributions on employee compensation above a compensation level assumed for Social Security purposes (called the *integration level*) can exceed plan benefits or contributions for compensation at or below that level. These limits differ for DB plans and DC plans. However, integration may result in larger relative benefits for higher paid employees (like owner–employees of closely held businesses, for example). Of course, a plan does not have to be integrated with Social Security at all. Some qualified plans are not so integrated. In this case, the permitted disparity rules are not relevant.

Integration of Defined-Benefit Plans There are two basic methods used to integrate DB plans: the excess method and the offset method. An *excess plan* is one under which there is a smaller benefit payable on earnings up to the Social Security integration level than on earnings above that level. An *offset plan* is one under which a pension benefit is calculated without regard to Social Security benefits, and then a percentage of the Social Security benefit is usually deducted from the pension benefit.

Integration of Defined-Contribution Plans DC plans are integrated based on contribution percentages to the plan. A plan will meet the integration rules if the plan's excess contribution percentage (the contribution percentage applying to compensation in excess of the plan's Social Security integration level) does not exceed the lesser of (1) 200 percent of the contribution percentage on compensation not in excess of the plan's integration level (base contribution percentage) or, (2) the greater of the base contribution percentage plus 5.7 percent or the base contribution percentage plus the portion of the employer-paid social security tax attributable to the old-age benefit.

CASE EXAMPLE

As an example of how integration might work in the context of a small employer, suppose that Aysha Ahmed is the 100 percent stockholder and CEO of a small C corporation—AA Corporation, Inc. Aysha receives an annual salary of $260,000. The corporation has three other employees with annual compensations of $60,000, $35,000, and $25,000. AA has a discretionary qualified profit-sharing plan covering the four employees, with an integrated contribution formula of 10 percent of each covered employee's compensation, up to the Social Security wage base (the integration level in this case), and 15.7 percent of each covered employee's compensation over that amount, up to the compensation cap for qualified plans. The contributions under this formula for a given year are shown in Table 13.1.

Top-Heavy Retirement Plans

Some qualified retirement plans are defined as top-heavy and must meet special requirements for qualification. The idea behind these requirements is to try to avoid discrimination in favor of certain employees and to protect lower-paid employees in plans in which a high proportion of benefits or contributions is actually being allocated to participants defined as *key employees.*[4]

[4]A *key employee* for this purpose is any participant who is an officer of the employer with annual compensation greater than 50 percent of the Section 415 dollar limit for DB plans, a more than 5 percent owner of the employer, or a more than 1 percent owner of the employer who has annual compensation from the employer of more than $160,000 in 2009.

Table 13.1. Example of Integration of Profit-Sharing Plan with Social Security

Col. 1 Employee	Col. 2 Compensation (as counted for plan purposes*)	Col. 3 Base Contribution (base contribution percentage [10%] × compensation up to the $106,800 integration level†)	Col. 4 Excess Contribution (excess contribution percentage [15.7%] × compensation [in excess of the integration level] up to compensation cap*)	Col. 5 Total Contribution (column 3 + column 4)
Aysha	$245,000	$10,680	$21,697	$32,377
A	$60,000	$6,000	—	$6,000
B	$35,000	$3,500	—	$3,500
C	$25,000	$2,500	—	$2,500

*The limit on includible compensation (compensation cap) in 2009 was $245,000 per year. Therefore, this is all that can be counted for Aysha for plan contribution (or benefit) purposes.

†This was the Social Security taxable wage base for 2009.

A plan is considered top-heavy with respect to any plan year if, in the case of a DB plan, the present value of the cumulative accrued benefits for key employees exceeds 60 percent of the corresponding value for all employees or, in the case of a DC plan, the aggregate accounts of the key employees exceed 60 percent of the aggregate accounts of all employees. Thus, for example, the integrated profit-sharing plan in the preceding example would be top-heavy for the year, assuming the contributions shown in Table 13.1 represent the account balances for all covered employees. Aysha is a key employee, while the others are not. Her $32,377 account balance is more than 60 percent of the aggregate accounts of all covered employees. The additional requirements that must be met by a plan classified as top-heavy include a minimum vesting schedule and minimum employer contributions or benefits for nonkey employees for top-heavy plan years.

Regulation of Qualified Retirement Plans

The main federal statute regulating employee benefit plans is the *Employee Retirement Income Security Act of 1974 (ERISA)*. It covers many areas, including reporting, disclosure, participation, and vesting requirements, funding standards, fiduciary responsibility and prohibited transactions, antidiscrimination rules, limitations on contributions and benefits, benefit accruals, limitations on distributions, spousal annuities, and others. The federal regulatory agency for part of ERISA (the so-called labor title—Title I) is the Department of Labor (DOL). However, since retirement plans must meet the requirements of the tax law to be qualified plans, they are also regulated under the IRC. (These tax provisions are also Title II of ERISA.) Thus, there is concurrent jurisdiction over qualified plan regulation by the IRS and the DOL.

Another important piece of federal legislation regulating retirement plans and other employee benefits is the *Pension Protection Act of 2006 (PPA)*. This law covers a number of subjects, including minimum funding requirements, investment and fiduciary rules, vesting requirements, plan distribution and rollover rules, automatic enrollment in 401(k) plans, and others.

In addition, many other federal laws regulate or affect retirement plans. For example, the *Retirement Equity Act of 1984 (REA)* deals with spousal rights in qualified retirement plans, as explained earlier in this chapter.

These federal statutes preempt state regulation related to these aspects of employee benefits.

Fiduciary Liability Issue

ERISA sets standards of conduct for certain individuals who manage employee benefit plans and their investments (fiduciary responsibility rules). Such persons are known as *ERISA fiduciaries*, and they have discretion in administering or managing some or all of a plan's operations or controlling its assets. A plan must have at least one fiduciary named in the plan, but also may have other fiduciaries who exercise discretion over the plan's affairs. These other fiduciaries may include members of a plan's administrative committee (if any), human resources department employees, or third-party service providers who manage the plan's day-to-day operations; plan trustees; investment advisers; and other individuals exercising discretion over the plan's operations.

On the other hand, professionals like attorneys, accountants, and actuaries normally are not fiduciaries when acting solely within their professional capacities. Also, employers making business decisions about the plan are not acting in a fiduciary capacity. Such business decisions might include, for example, whether to establish the plan, the nature of the benefit package, amending the plan, and whether to terminate the plan.

Fiduciaries have certain responsibilities to the plan, its participants, and their beneficiaries, including:

- To act solely in the interest of the plan participants and their beneficiaries
- To carry out their duties prudently
- To follow the plan documents so long as they are consistent with ERISA
- To diversify plan investments
- To pay only reasonable plan expenses

Fiduciaries who do not prudently conform to these responsibility standards may be personally liable to the plan. They may have to personally reimburse the plan for any losses due to their actions and may have to restore to the plan any profits made through improper use of plan assets due to their actions.

However, fiduciaries can take certain actions to protect themselves from potential liability. One is to carefully document the processes they employ to prudently carry out their fiduciary responsibilities. Another is to follow DOL regulations with respect to providing investment options (at least three), so employees can diversify their investments under participant-directed accounts, such as in 401(k) plans. If the DOL regulations are followed, a fiduciary's liability will be avoided for the investment decisions made by participants. However, fiduciaries still have the responsibility (and potential liability) for prudently selecting the investment options themselves, their providers, and for monitoring their performance. In addition, a fiduciary can hire third-party service providers to perform fiduciary functions and provide in their agreement that the service providers will assume liability for those functions. Of course, the fiduciary remains responsible for the prudent selection and monitoring of the third-party providers. Finally, there is liability insurance coverage, called fiduciary liability insurance or ERISA liability insurance, that employers can purchase to reimburse their fiduciaries for potential liability.

Prohibited Transactions

Certain ERISA-specific actions are prohibited for fiduciaries and others connected to a plan. Certain parties, called *parties-in-interest,* who include the employer; the union (if any); plan fiduciaries; service providers; and specified owners, officers, and relatives of parties-in-interest, are prohibited from doing business with the plan, unless an exemption applies. Specifically, some of these prohibited transactions include:

- A sale, exchange, or lease between the plan and a party-in-interest
- Lending money or another extension of credit between the plan and a party-in-interest
- Furnishing goods, services, or facilities between the plan and a party-in-interest

In addition, there are other prohibited transactions relating solely to fiduciaries. For example, fiduciaries are prohibited from using plan assets in their own interests, from acting on both sides of a transaction involving the plan, and from receiving money or other consideration from any party doing business with the plan related to that business.

ERISA spells out a number of exemptions to these prohibited transaction rules. One exemption allows plans to hire service providers for the plan so long as the services are necessary and the contract terms and compensation paid for them are reasonable. Another important exemption allows qualified plans to provide plan loans to participants (who normally would include some parties-in-interest). However, such loans must be available to all participants and meet certain other requirements, as noted previously. Still another exemption covers investment advice provided to participants by fiduciary advisers, as described later in this chapter.

Reporting Requirements

ERISA requires plan administrators to provide certain documents and reports to plan participants, beneficiaries, and the government. For plan participants and beneficiaries, the law requires:

- A summary plan description (SPD), which basically describes the plan and explains to participants their rights and responsibilities under it.
- A summary of material modification (SMM), which informs participants and beneficiaries of significant changes to the plan.
- An individual benefit statement that provides participants with information concerning their vested benefits and account balances. For single employer plans, such statements must be provided upon written request and upon termination of employment. However, some employers voluntarily provide such statements periodically to employee-participants.
- A summary annual report (SAR), which outlines financial information from the plan's Annual Report (Form 5500) and is furnished annually to participants.
- A blackout period notice informing participants when the plan is temporarily closed to participant transactions (such as when the plan changes record keepers or investment options).

ERISA requires plan administrators to file Form 5500 Annual Reports providing specified information about the plan and its operations to the appropriate federal agencies. These include the DOL, IRS, and the PBGC.

Investment Considerations for Retirement Plans

The assets of retirement plans are frequently held in trust funds. Retirement benefits can also be funded through insurance contracts. The regulatory standards for the investment of qualified retirement plan assets are provided by ERISA.

Suitability and Diversification

ERISA requires *prudent investing* of qualified plan assets. It also requires diversification of plan investments. Retirement plans generally are long-term undertakings, so a long *time horizon* can be assumed in their investment policies.

The so-called prudence norm for retirement plan investing has become the *prudent investor standard*. Court decisions and DOL regulations have recognized this standard for retirement plan investing. The prudent investor standard applies modern portfolio theory (MPT) by considering the risk-return characteristics and correlations of an entire portfolio rather than the riskiness of individual investments taken alone, as explained in Chapter 4.

As noted earlier, prudent investing and diversification may be fiduciary responsibilities of ERISA fiduciaries.

Individual Account [404(c)] Regulations

Many individual account plans, such as 401(k) plans and profit-sharing plans, allow participants or beneficiaries to make investment decisions (exercise control) regarding their account balances among a group of investment alternatives provided by the plan. These are referred to as "participant-directed plans" or "ERISA Section 404(c) plans."

As noted earlier, ERISA provides in Section 404(c) that no plan fiduciary will be liable for investment losses due to this participant control, provided the individual account plan complies with DOL regulations, referred to as the individual account regulations or 404(c) regulations. These regulations require that the plan provide a minimum of three diversified investment alternatives, with materially different risk-return characteristics, so the participant can achieve an appropriate portfolio for himself or herself. If the plan permits investment in employer securities, this must be an additional alternative; it cannot be one of the minimum three because employer securities are not diversified. Also, participants must be allowed to change among the alternatives at least quarterly.

Investment Advice Provided to Participants by Fiduciary Advisers

A significant provision of the Pension Protection Act of 2006 (PPA) provides a new prohibited transaction exemption allowing certain qualified "fiduciary advisers" to provide investment advice to plan participants and beneficiaries of 401(k) and other defined-contribution plans and to beneficiaries of IRAs. The investment advice may be specifically tailored to such participants and may be offered through "eligible investment advice arrangements" (i.e., generated from an unbiased computer model or provided for a flat fee that does not vary depending on the investment options chosen). Thus, through such an arrangement, an employer can offer individualized professional investment advice to its employees covered by these plans.

Employer Securities in Qualified Plans

Under certain conditions, qualified plans can invest in the securities of the employer sponsoring the plan. Employer securities include stock and debt obligations of the employer, but such investments normally involve common stock.

Employer stock often is an investment option under participant-directed plans [e.g., 401(k) plans]. Also, employers may place their matching contributions to 401(k) plans in their own stock. Thus, part of an employee's account balance in such plans may be invested in his or her employer's stock. In some cases, this investment in employer stock is substantial.

For defined-benefit pension plans (and money-purchase plans), ERISA generally prohibits the plan from holding more than 10 percent of its assets in employer securities. However, in the case of other defined-contribution plans, such as 401(k) plans and profit-sharing plans, there generally is no such limit, provided the plan document allows such investments. Stock bonus plans and ESOPs are intended to be invested in employer securities, as noted later in this chapter.

The PPA of 2006 includes certain diversification requirements for plan investments in employer securities in defined-contribution plans, such as 401(k) plans. In the case of employee contributions and elective deferrals invested in employer securities, participants and beneficiaries with accounts under the plan must be allowed to direct the plan to divest the employer securities from their accounts and reinvest the proceeds in other investment options as they choose. With respect to employer contributions (e.g., employer-matching contributions) invested in employer securities, participants with at least three years of service or beneficiaries similarly must be allowed to direct the plan to divest employer securities and reinvest the proceeds in other options.

These ERISA and IRC diversification requirements, added by PPA, are valuable for participants and beneficiaries to allow them to balance (diversify) their overall investment portfolios and not become unduly concentrated in their employer's stock. Such overconcentration may be a problem in some cases due to stock option plans, restricted stock, employee stock purchase plans, and other employer stock plans, as well as the natural tendency of many employees to be loyal to their company's stock and think of it as a "good investment." On the other hand, it should be remembered that there may be tax advantages in taking a lump-sum distribution in one taxable year of an entire account balance containing appreciated employer securities from a qualified plan. This is discussed in Chapter 16. However, in most cases, it is questionable whether such possible tax advantages will justify investment overconcentration (including retirement plans) in employer securities.

Unrelated Business Taxable Income (UBTI)

It was noted earlier that the investment earnings inside a qualified retirement plan are not currently taxable. This is also true for IRAs. An exception to this important general tax advantage is that if the IRA (both traditional and Roth IRAs) or the qualified plan has investments that produce *unrelated business taxable income (UBTI)*, the UBTI will be taxable income.

UBTI can result from net earnings from the conduct of an unrelated trade or business regularly carried on by the exempt trust or organization and from income from debt-financed property. Thus, if an IRA or qualified plan carries on an unrelated trade or business, receives certain passive income from a business entity it controls, or invests in a pass-through entity (such as a partnership or LLC) that conducts such a trade or business (including limited partnership interests, as described in Chapter 6), it will produce UBTI. Similarly, if a plan borrows money to acquire property to produce income, it will be debt-financed property and the income from such property will be UBTI. Some examples of such debt-financed property are margin accounts (as described in Chapter 5), real estate mortgages only for IRAs, and life insurance policy loans used to finance other property in the case of qualified plans (IRAs cannot invest in life insurance policies). UBTI under $1,000 is tax deductible.

Naturally, UBTI should be avoided when structuring the investments of qualified plans and IRAs. UBTI essentially results in income being taxed twice—once to the plan and again to plan participants or beneficiaries when it is paid out to them as distributions (except for distributions from Roth IRAs).

It should also be noted that the UBTI concept applies not only to qualified plans and IRAs, but to other kinds of tax-exempt entities as well. Such other entities include charities and charitable remainder trusts (CRTs), discussed in Chapter 19.

Life Insurance Owned by the Plan

Some qualified retirement plans may be funded, at least in part, with life insurance contracts (called individual policy plans), and others may purchase life insurance policies (or health insurance) on the lives of participants as an investment of the plan. (IRAs may not purchase life insurance as a plan asset.) The IRS *in Treasury* regulations has provided that such life and health insurance benefits must be incidental to the primary purpose of the plans. The primary purpose of a pension plan is to provide retirement income; the primary purpose of a profit-sharing plan is to provide deferred compensation.

The main way the IRS determines whether life and health insurance are "incidental" is by requiring that the cost of providing current insurance protection (i.e., the term cost for life insurance) be less than 25 percent of the cost of providing all benefits under the plan. This basic requirement is applied in different ways, depending on the type of plan involved and the insurance contracts used. For profit-sharing plans where ordinary life insurance (whole life) policies are purchased on participants' lives, the annual policy premiums must be less than 50 percent of the annual amount allocated to each participant's account (on the theory that about one-half of ordinary life premiums during an employee's working years go for the cost of current life insurance protection, i.e., the term cost). Profit-sharing plans purchasing term insurance and some other types of insurance must meet the 25 percent test. For pension plans, the incidental death benefit requirement is satisfied if the death benefit does not exceed that which would be paid if all benefits under the plan were funded by retirement income type life insurance policies, which provide a death benefit of $1,000 (or the policy reserve, if greater) for each $10 of monthly lifetime retirement income guaranteed by the policy at a designated retirement age (referred to as the 100-to-1 rule), or the death benefit satisfies the less-than-50-percent test for ordinary life policies described earlier.

In connection with the 100-to-1 rule, defined-benefit pension plans that are entirely funded with life insurance or annuity contracts are referred to as *412(i) plans.* They are named after the IRC provision that exempts such plans meeting certain requirements from the minimum funding requirements otherwise applying to defined-benefit plans.

The use of life insurance in qualified plans and some planning issues concerning such life insurance are covered further in Chapter 21.

Nonqualified Retirement Plans

These are plans that do not meet the requirements for qualification set by the tax law. Nonqualified plans, for example, can be structured to favor highly compensated employees (i.e., to be discriminatory). The compensation cap and other limits on contributions or benefits for qualified plans have increasingly caused employers to adopt nonqualified plans for their higher-paid employees. These plans are described in Chapter 14.

Pension Plans

Basic Characteristics

A pension plan is a qualified retirement plan maintained by an employer primarily to provide *definitely determinable benefits* to employees or their beneficiaries at and after retirement. A plan may provide definitely determinable benefits either by providing fixed benefits at retirement (a defined-benefit plan) or by having fixed employer contributions (a money-purchase plan) that normally are a set percentage of employees' compensation.

Pension plans cannot permit the withdrawal of employer contributions or the investment earnings thereon before the employee's retirement, death, disability, severance of employment, or termination of the plan. Contributions to fund a pension plan are not discretionary for an employer. The employer must make annual contributions necessary to fund the benefits provided by the plan.

When Are Retirement Benefits Payable?

Normal Retirement Age The normal retirement age in a DB plan is the earliest age at which participants can retire with full benefits. For example, the normal retirement age may be 65, usually assuming some minimum period of service. An employee usually is not required to retire at this age; it is simply the age at which full pension benefits are payable.

Early Retirement Provisions Many DB plans provide reduced benefits when employees retire at specified ages that are earlier than normal retirement age, often subject to certain conditions. Sometimes, when employers want to encourage early retirement by offering employees a temporary early retirement plan (a so-called early retirement window), a part of the program will be to eliminate or reduce any regular early retirement reduction factors. This is one of the factors to consider when deciding whether to accept such an early retirement option.

In the case of DC plans, the benefit available at early retirement is the account balance accumulated when the employee actually retires. There is no formal early retirement reduction factor, but, of course, no further contributions would be made to the employee's account after retirement.

Deferred Retirement Employers no longer can require employees to retire at any mandatory age, except for certain executive employees. Thus, most employees can continue working past normal retirement age if they wish and are able to do so. In this case, qualified DB plans must continue to accrue their benefits and DC plans must make contributions and allocations on their behalf for work past normal retirement age.

Kinds of Pension Plan Benefits

Retirement Benefits Pension plans traditionally have been designed to provide a life annuity (life income) for the covered employee or the covered employee and a joint annuitant. For married employees, the retirement benefit (annuity form) must be payable in accordance with the REA requirements described earlier.

Benefits may be payable in forms other than a life income. An increasing number of plans give employees the option of having their benefits actuarially converted (commuted) into a lump-sum payment at retirement. Whether this is desirable from the participant's (and perhaps his or her spouse's) viewpoint depends on the circumstances and how liberal the lump-sum payment is. However, it may be noted that in many cases, a lifetime income that the participant (or the participant and his or her spouse) cannot outlive provides a sound basis (with Social Security) upon which to plan a financially secure retirement. This issue is discussed further in Chapter 16. The ability to choose forms of retirement benefits is, of course, subject to the REA rules.

Benefits upon Termination of Employment These depend on the plan's vesting provisions and were discussed earlier.

Death Benefits Pension plans can provide death benefits in several ways. One is when an employee receives retirement income in the form of a *joint and survivor life annuity* or a *refund life annuity.* For example, if a married retiring employee provides for a joint life and full benefit to the survivor form of annuity for the employee and his or her spouse, the pension plan, in effect, is providing death protection equal to the full periodic pension benefit for the spouse in the event the employee dies first.[5]

Pension plans also may include *preretirement death benefits.* Such benefits may be from life insurance proceeds, in the case of plans funded with life insurance policies, but they mainly come from the QPSA required by REA.

Disability Income Benefits In some plans, a form of disability protection is afforded by allowing disabled workers to retire early. Other pension plans provide for a separate disability income benefit unrelated to retirement benefits.

Medical Expense Benefits Sometimes assets accumulated in pension plans may be used to provide medical benefits for retired employees, their spouses, and their dependents.

[5]Note that REA requires at least a joint life and 50 percent to the survivor annuity form (a QJSA). However, the parties can choose a more liberal survivor benefit (up to 100 percent), as shown in this example.

Pension Plan Benefit Formulas

Defined-Benefit Formulas A *flat-amount formula* sometimes is used. In this case, all participants upon retirement are given the same benefit. A formula that relates benefits to earnings is the *flat-percentage formula.* Under this formula, a pension equal to a given percentage of an employee's average annual compensation is paid at retirement to all employees completing a minimum number of years of credited service. Employees who fail to meet the minimum service requirement may be given a proportionately reduced pension. The average compensation to which the percentage applies may be the employees' average earnings over the full period of their participation in the plan (a career average approach) or the average of their earnings over the final few years of their participation (a final average approach).

A formula that relates benefits to years of service but not to earnings is the *flat-amount-unit-benefit formula.* Here, an employee is given a flat amount of benefit per month for each year of credited service.

A widely used formula is the *percentage-unit-benefit formula.* An employee may be given, say, a life annuity of 1.5 percent of earnings for each year of credited service starting at a given age (normal retirement age). Again, the earnings to which the percentage is applied may be the earnings during each year (career average) or the average annual earnings during, say, the last 5 or 10 years before retirement (final average).

Pension Benefit Guaranty Corporation (PBGC)

A part of ERISA was establishment of the Pension Benefit Guaranty Corporation (PBGC). This corporation sets up an insurance program for employees and pensioners of companies that have gone out of business, have become insolvent, or can no longer maintain their plan. The PBGC insures vested benefits of defined-benefit pension plans up to a certain amount. In 2009, this maximum amount was $4,500 per month for persons retiring at age 65, with a straight life annuity form. This maximum is adjusted for other eligible retirees.

This program provides an additional element of safety for covered active plan participants, former employees, and retirees. However, there is no comparable insolvency protection for pension benefits in excess of the maximum amount insured by the PBGC.

The PBGC is financed by premiums paid per covered employee by employers who maintain defined-benefit qualified plans. It is expected by many that if the PBGC's losses (say during difficult economic times) should exceed its resources, the government would provide additional financing. This is not guaranteed, however.

Profit-Sharing Plans

Basic Characteristics

Unlike pension plans, profit-sharing plans usually base their contributions for employees on the employer's profits and hence do not provide definitely determinable benefits. However, the existence of current or accumulated profits is not required for contributions to these plans.

Profit-sharing plans are DC plans under which contributions are allocated to individual accounts for participants. These individual accounts are credited with investment earnings and may be credited with nonvested forfeitures from other accounts that may be reallocated due to employee turnover.

Annual contributions usually are discretionary with the employer (a discretionary contribution formula); however, once made, they must be allocated among participants according to a definite, predetermined formula (a fixed allocation formula).

Distributions from profit-sharing plans are legally permitted after a certain number of years; after reaching a certain age; after retirement; after other termination of employment; or upon the occurrence of some event such as death, illness, disability, or layoff. The terms of a particular plan, however, may limit such withdrawals.

Regular Profit-Sharing Plans

Many profit-sharing plans base their allocation formula only on participant compensation. This results in a uniform proportionate contribution for each covered employee, regardless of age. This approach tends to favor younger employees.

Age-Weighted Profit-Sharing Plans

These are more complicated plans and may be based on the concept of cross-testing for nondiscrimination purposes.[6] Cross-testing is allowed under IRS regulations and essentially involves testing defined-contribution plans for nondiscrimination based on projected benefits (like a defined-benefit plan) and testing defined-benefit plans for nondiscrimination based on contributions. However, cross-testing normally is applied to defined-contribution plans.

[6] There can also be age-weighted money-purchase pension plans, but age-weighted plans generally are structured as profit-sharing plans. Also, age-weighted plans may not be based on cross-testing under an IRS "safe harbor" formula.

An age-weighted profit-sharing plan is one that bases its allocation formula on both the age and the compensation of participants.[7] These plans tend to favor older employees with higher earnings (who are often the owner–employees of closely held businesses). However, total profit-sharing contributions in any year cannot exceed 25 percent of overall covered compensation, and allocations to any participant cannot exceed the Section 415 limits described earlier. As with profit-sharing plans generally, contributions usually are discretionary with the employer.

New Comparability Profit-Sharing Plans

These also are cross-tested plans. They are DC plans, but they are tested for nondiscrimination purposes like a DB plan. Current profit-sharing allocations can vary not only by each participant's covered compensation and age, but also by his or her job classification. The annual limits on tax-deductible employer contributions are the same as for age-weighted plans. Contributions can also be discretionary with the employer.

The effect of new comparability plans is that there can be considerable disparity between the proportionate allocations for older, more highly compensated employees than for younger, lower-compensated employees. However, the IRS now has minimum allocation standards for cross-tested plans.

Savings (Thrift) Plans

General Characteristics

Savings plans are qualified DC plans that have become popular over the years as a way for employees to accumulate capital in a tax-advantageous way. These plans permit employees to make voluntary contributions of a percentage of their compensation, and then may provide for the employer to contribute a specified percentage of the employee's contribution (called a *matching contribution*), up to a certain limit. Employees also may have the option of making additional unmatched contributions.

As an example, a savings plan might permit employees to contribute from 1 to 6 percent of their compensation each year and then provide that the employer will contribute at the end of the year an amount equal to 50 percent of the employee's contribution. In addition, employees might be permitted to contribute up to an additional 10 percent of their pay, which

[7] IRS regulations permit allocations under cross-tested profit-sharing plans to be weighted for age or service as well as compensation. This discussion assumes weighting by age and compensation.

would not be matched by the employer. Technically, savings plans are a form of profit-sharing plan. Larger employers often have a pension plan and a separate savings plan (usually with a Section 401(k) option), but some have only a savings plan with a Section 401(k) option.

Participant-Directed Accounts

Contributions on behalf of participants and the investment earnings thereon go into individual accounts for each participant. As noted earlier under "Investment Considerations for Retirement Plans," it has become increasingly common for savings plans (and perhaps other kinds of plans) to permit participants to decide how their account balances will be invested within the investment funds provided by the employer under the plan.

The number and kinds of separate funds vary among plans, but, as noted previously, they must include a reasonable breadth of investment products for different investment objectives. Employees may be given investment choices for all contributions, but often will initially will have choices only with respect to their own contributions. Employers may direct that their own matching contributions go into an employer stock fund.

Before-Tax and After-Tax Contributions

Employee contributions may be made from their pay after the withholding of income taxes (after-tax contributions) or through salary reduction arrangements before income taxes are withheld (before-tax contributions). When employee contributions are made on a before-tax basis, the plans are referred to as *cash or deferred arrangements* (CODAs) or more commonly as Section 401(k) plans (named after the section of the IRC that deals with cash or deferred arrangements). Today, most employee contributions are on a before-tax basis. Thus, to many people, the terms *savings plans* and *Section 401(k) plans* are almost synonymous.

Cash or Deferred Arrangements [Section 401(k) Plans]

General Characteristics

Section 401(k) permits covered employees to authorize their employer to reduce their salary and contribute the salary reduction to a qualified savings plan, profit-sharing plan, stock bonus plan, or money-purchase pension plan. No income tax is paid currently on the salary reduction.

The amounts participants elect to defer are called the employee's elective contributions, elective deferrals, or before-tax elective contributions, and special restrictions apply to them.

Limits on Contributions to 401(k) Plans

There are at least four separate limits on employee and employer contributions to qualified plans with a Section 401(k) option, as follows:

- There is an annual dollar cap on before-tax elective contributions from an employee to all CODAs covering the employee. This annual cap (base amount) is $16,500 for 2009 (with indexing for inflation in $500 increments).

  In addition to the annual cap just noted, participants age 50 and older can make additional annual catch-up contributions of $5,500 for 2009 (with indexing for inflation in $500 increments). Thus, in 2009, a participant age 50 or older could have elective contributions of $22,000 ($16,500 base amount plus $5,500 catch-up contribution).
- There is an actual deferral percentage (ADP) nondiscrimination test for elective contributions, which, depending on the relative average contributions of highly compensated employees (HCEs) compared to those of non–highly compensated employees, may result in a limit for HCEs for a given year that is lower than the annual dollar cap just noted. However, for plans where the employer makes certain minimum contributions for non–highly compensated employees and provides full and immediate vesting for these contributions [referred to as "traditional" safe-harbor 401(k) plans], the ADP and actual contribution percentage (ACP) nondiscrimination tests are not applied, and the annual dollar cap (plus any catch-up contribution) would be the limit for HCEs.
- There also is an actual contribution percentage (ACP nondiscrimination test for combined after-tax employee contributions and employer-matching contributions.
- The regular Section 415 limits also apply to these plans.

Restrictions on Distributions from 401(k) Plans

There are special restrictions on distributions from plans with 401(k) options. In general, amounts attributable to before-tax elective contributions may not be distributed to a participant or his or her beneficiary(ies) earlier than either attainment of age 59½, separation from employment, death, or disability, or in the event of hardship for the employee (as defined in IRS regulations).

Roth 401(k) Accounts (DRACs)

Since 2006, participants in 401(k) plans [and Section 403(b) plans] have been allowed to elect to have all or part of their employee elective contributions (salary reductions) contributed to a *designated Roth account (DRAC)* within the plan, provided the plan so permits. These are also called *Roth 401(k) accounts.* The maximum that can be contributed to a DRAC each year is the annual dollar cap on employee elective contributions, plus any allowed make-up contribution, noted previously. Amounts so contributed are not tax-deferred like regular 401(k) employee elective contributions, but are taxed currently as gross income to the employees. However, DRACs, like Roth IRAs, which are described in Chapter 15, have tax-free growth of investment earnings in the account and tax-free distributions of account balances to participants and their beneficiaries. There also are no income or age limits on who can contribute to a DRAC.

Thus, participants can choose to place all their 401(k) elective contributions in a regular 401(k) salary reduction account (with no tax at contribution, but taxed as ordinary income at distribution); or, if the plan permits, place all their elective contributions in a DRAC (with tax initially on the contributed amount but no tax on a "qualified distribution"); or place part of their elective contributions in each. A DRAC can be an attractive option for higher-income employees who otherwise would not be eligible for a regular Roth IRA.

The provision for DRACs and certain other pension and retirement plan benefit provisions were part of EGTRRA of 2001, whose provisions were scheduled to "sunset" in 2011. However, PPA of 2006 made DRACs and the other pension and retirement provisions of EGTRRA permanent, and so they will not sunset.

Automatic Enrollment in 401(k) Plans

PPA of 2006 provides another safe harbor from the nondiscrimination rules for 401(k) plans. If a 401(k) plan contains an "automatic contribution arrangement" (also called an automatic enrollment arrangement) that meets certain requirements, it is treated as meeting the nondiscrimination rules for deferrals and for matching employer contributions (the ADP and ACP tests) and also is not subject to the top-heavy rules.

Under this automatic arrangement, employees who are eligible to participate are assumed to have elected to have the employer make specific elective (salary reduction) contributions to the plan on their behalf, unless they affirmatively elect not to have such contributions made or to be made at a different level. This arrangement (including the additional safe harbor) is expected to encourage increased participation by employees in plans containing such an automatic contribution arrangement.

Advantages of 401(k) Plans

Tax Advantages Employee contributions are made on a before-tax basis, and savings plans afford the other tax advantages of qualified plans described earlier.

Systematic Savings and Investment Another appeal of savings plans is the opportunity they afford employees for systematic investment through payroll deductions on a comparatively low-cost basis.

Employer-Matching Contributions For savings plans with matching employer contributions, participants' accounts are credited with the matching contributions as well as the employees' own contributions and the investment earnings on both.

Employee Investment Choice Participants normally are given a choice among a prescribed number of investment options for their contributions and possibly their employers' matching contributions. Thus, employees can integrate the investment of their plan accounts with their general asset allocation strategy.

Tax-Efficient Changes in Asset Allocation Strategy Account balances present participants with an inherent tax advantage, in that asset allocation changes among available investment options within the plan can be made without there being a sale or exchange for capital gains tax purposes.

Limitations on 401(k) Plans

The advantages of Section 401(k) plans are impressive indeed. However, as with any planning tool, these plans also have some drawbacks.

Limits on Contributions As just explained, there are special limitations on contributions to Section 401(k) arrangements in addition to the regular limits on qualified plans in general.

Restrictions on Distributions There also are limits on distributions, as just described. However, these may not be that onerous because plan loans and hardship distributions usually are available.

Participants Must Be Able to Afford Their Contributions Savings plans with Section 401(k) options normally condition employer-matching contributions on initial employee contributions. This means participants must take a reduction in current wages or salary. Some cannot or will not do this.

Distributions Are Ordinary Income and Income in Respect of a Decedent (IRD) In many cases, participants will have no income tax basis in qualified retirement plans with Section 401(k) options.[8] This is because all funds have gone into the plan without any income taxes being paid on them. Therefore, when distributions come out of the plan (as they eventually must), they generally will be taxable as ordinary income, either when the participant receives them or as IRD after the participant's death.[9] This tax treatment is, of course, true for qualified retirement plans in general. Nevertheless, despite this significant taxation at distribution, the tax-deferred results of these plans normally far outweigh the results of after-tax investing in currently taxable assets. This *power of deferral* is shown in the illustrations presented next.

In general, tax-deferral strategies are an effective approach to building wealth. A number of such strategies are discussed in this book. For the remainder of this chapter, however, we shall discuss deferral through traditional 401(k) plans.

Illustration of Before-Tax Contributions (Investing) Compared with After-Tax Investing (or the Power of Deferral)

Assuming a Traditional Section 401(k) Plan with Employer Match

CASE EXAMPLE

To illustrate the principles just discussed, assume an employee, Lynn Rose, age 35, earns $200,000 per year and can participate in a qualified savings plan with a Section 401(k) option or can make similar investments (after-tax) in directly owned assets. The plan allows her to elect to have up to 6 percent of her salary contributed to the savings plan before tax, and then her employer will match her elective contribution 50 cents on the dollar. Assuming Lynn elects the full 6 percent salary reduction (and ignoring for the sake of simplicity the likelihood that the plan will permit her to make additional elective contributions beyond what the

[8] See Chapter 16 for an explanation of how participants can acquire an income tax basis in their qualified retirement plans.

[9] Exceptions to this statement are when there is net unrealized appreciation (NUA) on employer securities in the plan and a lump-sum distribution is taken (as described in Chapter 16) and for the income tax deduction for estate taxes paid on IRD items (as described in Chapter 10).

employer will match), her salary and contribution picture would be as follows:

Salary:	$200,000
Elective employee contribution (6%)	–12,000
Taxable salary	$188,000

Contributions going into the 401(k) plan for the Employee:

Elective employee contribution	$ 12,000
Employer matching contribution (0.50 × $12,000)	6,000
Total annual contributions available for investment in the plan (before-tax)	$ 18,000

Assume instead that Lynn decides not to participate in the plan and that she wants to invest the 6 percent of salary, after tax, outside the plan in directly owned assets, and that she is in the 33 percent top marginal federal income tax bracket.[10] Under these assumptions, her salary and investment picture would be:

Salary	$200,000
Taxable salary	200,000
Comparable amount available for investment (after-tax) in directly owned assets ($12,000 × 0.67 = $8,040)	$ 8,040

Further assume that Lynn can earn 6 percent (all taxable as ordinary income) on her directly owned assets and 6 percent in her 401(k) plan account. Thus, her after-tax rate of return on the directly owned assets would be 4.02 percent (6% × 0.67 = 4.02%). Now, just for the sake of this illustration, let us say Lynn takes the entire balance in her 401(k) account at age 65 (or in 30 years).[11] Thus, at age 65 (30 years later), the after-tax situation under both approaches would be as follows:[12]

Direct investment:	
$8,040 at 4.02% for 30 years	$452,433

[10] State and local income taxes are ignored in this illustration for the sake of convenience. Also, some states tax salary reduction amounts under 401(k) and other plans.

[11] As we shall see in Chapter 16, she normally would not do this. Rather, she would continue to defer for a much longer time. Thus, deferral in practice would be more favorable than shown here.

[12] This assumes, just for illustrative purposes, that Lynn's salary remains at $200,000 for this period and that her top marginal federal income tax rate remains at 33 percent.

Savings plan with Section 401(k) option:

$18,000 at 6% for 30 years	$1,423,048
Less Lynn's basis in the plan	0
Amount taxable as ordinary income	$1,423,048
Income tax payable (at 33%)	469,606
After-tax balance	$ 953,442

Bases for Superior Results

These rather spectacular results come from the following three factors:[13]

- Tax-deferred compounding on a larger periodic payment—$12,000 before tax versus $8,040 after tax. (This represents deferral of the tax on the initial investments.)
- Tax-deferred compounding on the full yield, i.e., 6 percent before tax compounded versus 4.02 percent after tax. (This represents deferral of the tax on the investment return.)
- The employer match.

The first two factors represent the pure power of tax deferral on the employee's money. The third is extra employer money with tax deferral.

Modifying the Assumptions

However, it may be argued that an employer's matching contribution is extra and really does not represent the power of deferral. It also may be argued that most investors will not invest a directly owned portfolio entirely in assets producing currently taxed ordinary income. They will include common stock (or other hopefully appreciating assets) in their asset allocations. Therefore, let us change our assumptions as follows:

- There is no employer match.
- The employee invests 50 percent of her directly owned portfolio in common stocks (with a 10 percent total return—6 percent capital gains and 4 percent qualified dividend income) and 50 percent in currently taxable assets (such as taxable bonds or CDs) earning 6 percent.
- The tax rate is 15 percent on realized capital gains (with gains realized each year), 15 percent on qualified dividends, and 33 percent on ordinary income.

[13] Identifying these factors is important because while they all may apply to 401(k) arrangements, only some of them apply to other tax-deferred arrangements. Therefore, other arrangements will not be as attractive as the typical qualified savings plan with a Section 401(k) option.

- One half of the capital gains on the directly owned portfolio is never taxed because there is a step-up in basis at death or for other reasons.
- The Section 401(k) account has the same asset allocation and average return, 8 percent, as the directly owned portfolio.

Given these new assumptions, which are generous in favor of the after-tax directly owned portfolio, the before-tax 401(k) approach still produces markedly better results, as the following calculation shown.

Direct investment:	
$8,040 at 6.49%* for 30 years	$ 693,219
Savings plan (with no employer match)	
with Section 401(k) option:	
$12,000 at 8% for 30 years	$1,359,399
Minus Lynn's basis in the plan	0
Amount taxable as ordinary income	$1,359,399
Minus income tax payable (at 33%)	448,602
After-tax balance	$ 910,797

*This is the after-tax total yield on the directly owned portfolio under the assumptions just given.

Thus, assuming a reasonably long period of deferral and consistent assumptions, the power of tax deferral alone in this example produces an after-tax retirement fund about 32 percent greater for the participants in the 401(k) plan despite the relatively heavy taxation on distributions.

Appropriate Assets for Tax-Advantaged versus Taxable Accounts

The extent of the power of tax deferral [e.g., in tax-advantaged accounts such as 401(k) plans] as compared with the investment results in taxable accounts depends on several factors. They include:

- *The length of the period of deferral.* The longer this period, the greater the power of deferral for tax-advantaged accounts. For relatively short periods, there may be no advantage, or taxable accounts may be favored, depending on the circumstances.
- *Tax rates.* The higher the marginal tax rate, the greater the advantage of tax deferral.
- *Investment returns.* The greater the investment returns assumed, the more effective tax deferral will be.
- *The nature of the asset classes in each kind of account.* This factor was illustrated in the modified assumptions for the case example just cited.

In actual asset allocation planning, however, it often is desirable to hold different asset classes in tax-advantaged accounts than in taxable accounts. This is referred to as *location analysis* and was discussed in Chapter 9.

Stock Bonus Plans and Employee Stock Ownership Plans (ESOPs)

Stock Bonus Plans

These are qualified retirement plans that are similar to profit-sharing plans, except that employer contributions do not necessarily depend on profit, and benefits may be distributable in the form of the employer's stock. Employers may make contributions to stock bonus plans in cash or in their own stock. Their annual contributions are limited to 25 percent of payroll.

Employee Stock Ownership Plans (ESOPs)

General Characteristics An ESOP is a qualified retirement plan that is structured either as a stock bonus plan or as a combination of a stock bonus plan and a money-purchase pension plan. An ESOP differs from traditional stock bonus plans in that the ESOP is designed to invest primarily in employer stock. A traditional stock bonus plan may invest in employer stock, but it is not required to do so other than to make distributions in employer stock to participants. Perhaps the most important difference, however, is that an employer establishing an ESOP may guarantee or make loans to the ESOP to enable the ESOP to acquire employer stock, whereas traditional stock bonus plans generally may not do this, since it would be a prohibited transaction under ERISA. ESOPs involving such debt are called *leveraged ESOPs.*

Several special provisions apply to ESOPs. For example, when a participant is entitled to a distribution, the plan normally is required to make the distribution in employer stock, although the distribution can be in cash if the participant is entitled to elect that it be in employer stock. However, if a participant receives a distribution of employer stock that is not readily tradable on an established market, the participant must have the right to sell the stock back to the employer for its fair market value. The law also has a provision with regard to the timing of distributions, unless a participant elects otherwise. In addition, there are special diversification elections for participants who have attained age 55 and have 10 or more years of participation.

Sale of Appreciated Stock to an ESOP In certain circumstances, an ESOP can provide a market for closely held stock through the purchase of such stock from a stockholder while he or she is alive, or from the stockholder's estate at the time of death. This technique is illustrated in Chapter 11.

Hybrid Qualified Retirement Plans

These are qualified plans that exhibit some characteristics of DB plans and some characteristics of DC plans.

Cash Balance Plans

These technically are DB plans, but are structured to look like DC plans. The employer typically contributes a percentage of each employee's compensation, which is actuarially determined so that there will be funds in the plan to pay the defined benefits. The contributions are pooled for all participants so there are no real individual accounts for each participant as there would be in a DC plan. However, a hypothetical account is maintained for each participant to which a fixed percentage of the participant's compensation (such as 4 or 5 percent) and an interest rate specified in the plan are credited each year. But this interest rate is not the rate of return actually earned on plan assets.

The retirement benefit is the annuity income that the hypothetical account balance would purchase using mortality and interest assumptions provided by the plan. Since these are DB plans, they are subject to ERISA's minimum funding requirements and to PBGC rules and premiums.

Cash balance plans have been adopted by some larger employers and often result from conversions of traditional DB plans. They generally result in relatively greater benefits for younger and shorter-service employees, relatively lower benefits for older and longer-service employees, and lower overall costs for the employer than traditional DB plans. Benefits generally may be paid to participants as a lump sum or in periodic payments.

Pension Equity Plans

Another type of hybrid DB plan is the pension equity plan. For that plan, benefits are normally expressed as a percentage of final average pay, with the percentage based on points received for each year of service. The points may be greater for older or longer service participants.

In the past, cash balance and pension equity plans have faced age discrimination challenges by participants in the courts. However, PPA of 2006 provides that these plans do not violate the age discrimination or minimum present value rules provided they meet certain requirements.

Target Benefit Plans

Target benefit plans technically are DC plans. However, an employer's annual contributions to the plan are based on a target benefit formula, with given actuarial assumptions, that is the same kind of formula that would be used in a DB plan. However, employer contributions are allocated to actual individual accounts for participants whose retirement benefits will be based on the balances actually accumulated in each participant's account at retirement.

Floor Offset Plans

This is another hybrid arrangement that involves an employer having both a DB plan and a DC plan. In essence, participants receive the larger of the retirement benefits produced by each of these plans, but not the benefits from both. In practice, the benefits produced by the DB plan are reduced by a participant's account balance in the DC plan.

Retirement Plans for the Self-Employed (HR-10 or Keogh Plans)

General Considerations

Before 1963, sole proprietors and partners could have qualified retirement plans covering their employees, but they, as owners of their businesses (i.e., principals), could not get the tax advantages of these plans because technically they were not employees even though they were actively engaged in the operation of the business. However, the Self-Employed Individuals Tax Retirement Act of 1962 (also called HR-10 or the Keogh Act), with its subsequent amendments, has made it possible for owners of unincorporated businesses and other self-employed persons to be covered under qualified retirement plans. An HR-10 plan, therefore, is a formal arrangement whereby self-employed persons may establish a program to provide tax-favored retirement benefits for themselves and their eligible employees.

The tax law allows self-employed persons to be considered employees for purposes of establishing and contributing to qualified retirement plans in any year in which they have earned income. *Earned income* for this purpose means a person's net earnings from self-employment in a trade or business (including a profession) in which the person's personal services are a material income-producing factor. (Note that capital may also be a material income-producing factor and the net earnings still will qualify for HR-10 purposes.) Net earnings from self-employment generally are determined by deducting business expenses (including contributions to the HR-10 plan and contributions to other tax-deductible employee benefit plans for the regular [nonowner] employees of the firm)[14] from the net revenues of the business. In essence, they are the net profits of the business.

Earned income is the basis for determining contributions to an HR-10 plan on behalf of self-employed persons. However, in calculating earned income, one-half of the person's self-employment tax (social security tax) and the contributions made to the HR-10 plan on his or her behalf must be deducted from otherwise determined net earnings to arrive at earned income.[15]

CASE EXAMPLE

As an illustration, suppose that Homer Stone, age 45, is a sole proprietor who employs two common-law employees in his business. Homer is self-employed and materially participates in managing the business. The business's annual gross income is $600,000 and it has business expenses (aside from any contributions to a qualified retirement plan) of $451,000. Assume Homer decides to adopt a qualified discretionary profit-sharing (HR-10) plan covering himself and his two employees. Homer further decides this year to contribute 15 percent of covered compensation to this plan. One of Homer's employees is paid $35,000 per year and the other is paid $25,000 per year. The situation with respect to this HR-10 plan at the end of a year would be as follows:

Gross income of business	$600,000
Business expenses (other than retirement plan contributions)	–451,000
Retirement plan contributions for common-law employees ($60,000 × 0.15)	–9,000
Net profit of business	$140,000

The amount that Homer can contribute to the HR-10 plan for himself would be determined as follows:

$$\frac{\text{Profit} - \frac{1}{2}\text{of self-employment (Social Security) tax}}{1 + \text{plan contribution percentage as a decimal}} = \text{earned income}$$

[14] These regular employees are referred to as the *common-law employees* of the business. They are not the owners of the business and are in the same position as any employees of an employer with regard to employee benefits and other employment matters. A self-employed person may or may not have common-law employees.

[15] This involves a rather complicated and circular calculation, as shown in the following example. It results in maximum limits on tax-deductible contributions to HR-10 plans on behalf of self-employed persons that, in effect, are lower than the 25 percent of compensation for profit-sharing, stock bonus, and money-purchase pension plans.

Which in this example would be:

$$\frac{\$140{,}000-\$8{,}496}{1+0.15(\text{or } 1.15)}=\$114{,}351 \text{ (Homer's earned income for the year)}$$

Then, the *contribution amount* to the plan for the year for Homer would be:

$$\$114{,}351 \times 0.15\ (15\%) = \$17{,}153$$

While this contribution amount is 15 percent of Homer's earned income as just calculated, it equals only 12.25 percent of his net earnings from self-employment ($17,153 ÷ $140,000 = 0.1225 or 12.25 percent).

Deductible Contributions

The contributions to an HR-10 plan on behalf of self-employed persons are deductible by the self-employed persons on their own individual tax returns from their gross income to arrive at their adjusted gross income.[16] The contributions are not deductible by the business itself in determining its net profit. Thus, in the illustration just given, Homer would report $140,000 net profit from his business as part of his gross income, but then he would deduct the $17,153 contribution to the HR-10 plan from his gross income to arrive at his adjusted gross income. This would result in a net amount of business income subject to income tax of $122,847 ($140,000 – $17,153).

While not involving HR-10 plans, it may also be noted that self-employed persons may deduct 100 percent of the health insurance premiums paid for themselves, their spouses, and their dependents from their gross income to arrive at their adjusted gross income. This applies the same principle to health insurance premiums that HR-10 applies to retirement benefits. However, the costs of other kinds of employee benefits (such as group term life insurance and disability income insurance) on behalf of self-employed persons (and more than 5 percent owners of S corporations) are not deductible by either the business or the self-employed person. This is a disadvantage of self-employed and S corporation ownership status.

Who May Establish HR-10 Plans?

Sole proprietors with earned income can establish their own HR-10 plans. They may have common-law employees covered by the plan as well.

[16] Thus, they are deductible whether or not the taxpayer itemizes his or her deductions. In tax terms, they are deductible *above the line.*

On the other hand, they may not have any employees and be the only covered person.

A self-employed person may have an HR-10 plan with respect to his or her earned income from self-employment, and at the same time, he or she may be a common-law employee for another employer and also be covered under that employer's qualified retirement plan or plans.

A partnership can establish an HR-10 plan for its partners as well as for any covered common-law employees. However, in order for a partner to participate in a firm's plan, he or she must have earned income from the partnership's trade or business in which his or her personal services were a material income-producing factor. Thus, a purely investment interest in a partnership (like most limited partners, for example), with respect to which no personal services are rendered, will not suffice for HR-10 participation.

A partner's earned income normally is his or her share of the partnership's net income, including any guaranteed payments to the partner. The members of an LLC normally are treated like partners for tax purposes, assuming they elect to be taxed like a partnership under the check-the-box regulations.

The stockholder–employees of corporations (either C corporations or S corporations) are not self-employed persons and are not eligible for HR-10 plans. They can be covered as regular employees under qualified retirement plans established by their corporation.

Finally, some self-employed persons are classified as owner–employees for HR-10 purposes. Owner–employees are persons who own 100 percent of an unincorporated trade or business (sole proprietors) or partners who own more than 10 percent of either a capital interest or a profit interest in a partnership.

Kinds of HR-10 Plans

Self-employed persons can adopt a variety of HR-10 plans. For example, they may have a defined-benefit pension plan, a money purchase pension plan, a profit-sharing plan, or a 401(k) plan. Keogh plans may also be integrated with Social Security.

Self-employed persons also can adopt SEP plans and SIMPLE plans. However, they cannot have one of these plans and another type of retirement plan (such as an HR-10 plan). SEP and SIMPLE plans are covered in Chapter 14.

Parity with Corporate Retirement Plans

Prior to 1982, HR-10 plans were subject to a number of special restrictions and limits that did not apply to qualified corporate retirement plans.

However, the Tax Equity and Fiscal Responsibility Act of 1982 (TEFRA) eliminated almost all of these special requirements for HR-10 plans.

Therefore, HR-10 plans generally have the same eligibility and coverage requirements, contribution limits (except as just noted), vesting requirements, rules for integration with Social Security, and other plan requirements as for qualified retirement plans covering corporate employees.

14

Other Employer-Provided Retirement Plans and Employee Benefits

Competence Objectives for This Chapter After reading this chapter, planners should understand:

- The characteristics of some other employer-provided retirement plans
- The nature, tax status, and planning for nonqualified deferred compensation
- The types of nontaxable fringe benefits and tax status of other benefits

Other Employer-Provided Retirement Plans

Simplified Employee Pension (SEP) Plans

Basic Characteristics Employers can establish SEPs for their employees utilizing individual retirement accounts or annuities[1] that are owned by the individual employees and that effectively may accept a rate of contribution from the employer up to the lesser of 25 percent of each participant's compensation or $49,000 in 2009 (indexed for inflation in $1,000 increments). Self-employed persons also can establish SEPs for themselves and their employees, if any. Employer's contributions are deductible by the employer and not currently taxable to employees. For self-employed persons, contributions on their behalf are deductible by the self-employed person on his or her tax return in the same manner as contributions to HR-10 plans.

SEPs are intended to reduce the paperwork and regulations required for HR-10 and qualified corporate retirement plans and, as a result, be easier for employers and self-employed persons to adopt. Like profit-sharing plans,

[1] IRAs are described in detail in Chapter 15.

SEPs allow for discretionary contributions by employers. These streamlined plans tend to appeal mainly to smaller employers, although there is no employer size limit in the law.[2]

Technically, SEPs are not classified as qualified retirement plans. Rather, they are defined as regular (traditional) IRAs that meet the requirements of the tax law to be a SEP. SEP contributions cannot be made to a Roth IRA.

Participation Requirements For an IRA to be a SEP, the employer must contribute for each employee who has performed services for the employer during the year, attained age 21, performed services for the employer in at least three of the immediately preceding five calendar years, and received at least $550 as of 2009 (indexed for inflation) in compensation from the employer for that year. All such eligible employees must be covered by the SEP.

Nondiscrimination Requirements An employer's contributions to a SEP may not discriminate in favor of highly compensated employees or self-employed persons. In general, this means contributions must bear a uniform relationship to the total compensation of each employee maintaining a SEP. The top-heavy rules also apply. SEPs may be integrated with Social Security.

Nonforfeitable Contributions (Immediate Vesting) SEPs must provide immediate and 100 percent vesting of employer contributions. In addition, employees must be permitted to withdraw amounts in their SEP-IRA accounts at any time. The individual employees own and control their own IRAs.

Distributions In general, as with traditional IRAs, distributions are taxed to the employee as ordinary income. In addition, premature distributions are subject to the 10 percent penalty tax, and a participant must begin receiving distributions by the required beginning date and according to the minimum distribution rules, as described in Chapter 16. Finally, loans by employees are not permitted from SEPs.

Savings Incentive Match Plans for Employees (SIMPLE Plans)

Another approach to encouraging smaller employers and self-employed persons to adopt retirement plans for themselves and their employees is the SIMPLE plan concept, which was adopted in 1997. This concept actually refers to two separate kinds of plans: SIMPLE-IRA plans and SIMPLE 401(k) plans.

SIMPLE-IRA Plans These plans allow eligible employees and self-employed persons to elect to receive compensation or earned income in cash or to

[2] Prior to 1997, employers with 25 or fewer employees could establish salary-reduction SEPs called SAR-SEPs. However, the law has been changed and no new SAR-SEPs could be established after 1996.

contribute to a SIMPLE-IRA under a qualified salary-reduction agreement. The employer must make either certain matching contributions or nonelective contributions for all eligible employees, regardless of whether they elect to contribute. An employer's contributions are deductible by the employer and not currently taxable to employees. For self-employed persons, contributions on their behalf are deductible on their own tax returns.

These plans are regular (traditional) IRAs that meet the requirements of the tax law to be SIMPLE-IRAs. Each participant owns his or her own SIMPLE-IRA.

Eligible Employers: An employer eligible to establish a SIMPLE-IRA plan is one that employs no more than 100 employees earning at least $5,000 from the employer during the preceding year.

Contribution Requirements: Eligible employees (and self-employed persons) must be allowed to make an elective (salary reduction) contribution, which may be expressed as a percentage of compensation or a fixed dollar amount. These elective contributions may not exceed $11,500 in 2009 (indexed for inflation). Also, participants age 50 and over can make additional annual catch-up contributions of up to $2,500 in 2009 (indexed for inflation).

Employers are required to make either matching contributions or nonelective contributions. Employer-matching contributions are required to match employee elective contributions dollar for dollar, generally up to an amount not exceeding 3 percent of the employee's compensation. Employer-matching contributions also may not exceed the dollar limits on elective contributions just noted. Alternatively, employers can choose to make nonelective contributions of 2 percent of compensation per year on behalf of all eligible employees, whether or not they make elective contributions.

Unlike SEPs, an employer does not have discretion in deciding whether to contribute to a SIMPLE-IRA plan in a given year. Employee elective contributions are at the option of eligible employees, and the employer then must make either employer-matching contributions or employer nonelective contributions.

Participation Requirements: All employees (except for limited groups of excludable employees) who received at least $5,000 in compensation from the employer during any two preceding years and who are reasonably expected to receive $5,000 in compensation in the current year must be eligible to participate. However, unlike SEPs, no nondiscrimination or top-heavy rules apply to SIMPLE-IRAs.

Nonforfeitable Contributions (Immediate Vesting): Like SEPs, employer contributions to a SIMPLE-IRA must be immediately and 100 percent vested in the participants' SIMPLE-IRAs. Also, participants must be permitted to withdraw the amounts in their SIMPLE-IRAs at any time.

Exclusive Plan Requirement: A plan will not be treated as a SIMPLE-IRA plan in any year the employer also had a qualified retirement plan, tax-sheltered annuity plan, SEP, or governmental plan (other than a Section 457 plan) under which contributions were made or benefits were accrued. This is different from SEPs, where an employer may also have these other plans.

Distributions: As in the case of traditional IRAs, in general, distributions from an employee's SIMPLE-IRA are taxed to the employee as ordinary income. Also, premature distributions are subject to the normal 10 percent penalty tax and loans are not permitted from the plan. However, for SIMPLE-IRAs, premature distributions within the first two years of an employee's participation in the plan carry a 25 percent premature distributions tax. After this two-year period, the penalty tax drops down to the normal 10 percent. The minimum distribution rules also apply.

Rollovers: For participants who have been in the plan for less than two years, rollovers and transfers can only be made from one SIMPLE-IRA to another SIMPLE-IRA. However, after an employee participates in the plan for two years or more, rollovers can be made from a SIMPLE-IRA to another SIMPLE plan, a qualified retirement plan, a tax-sheltered annuity (TSA), a traditional IRA, or a Section 457 plan.

SIMPLE 401(k) Plans This is a Section 401(k) plan for an eligible employer (defined the same way as for SIMPLE-IRAs) that is allowed to meet the ADP nondiscrimination test (see Chapter 13) by satisfying the requirements to be a SIMPLE 401(k) plan. These requirements include a contribution requirement, a nonforfeitable (immediate vesting) requirement, and an exclusive plan requirement, like those for SIMPLE-IRAs. However, SIMPLE 401(k) plans are subject to the other qualification and distribution requirements that apply to Section 401(k) plans generally.

Tax-Sheltered Annuity (TSA) Plans

A TSA plan, or Section 403(b) annuity, is an arrangement whereby an employee of a qualified organization can enter into an agreement with his or her employer to have part of the employee's earnings set aside for retirement on a before-tax basis.

Who Is Eligible? Any employee who works for a public school system or a tax-exempt organization established and operating exclusively for charitable, religious, scientific, or educational purposes is eligible.

How Much Can an Eligible Employee Contribute Each Year? There are two ways of approaching contributions to a TSA plan: an additional contribution by the employer (salary increase) for the employee or a salary reduction agreement (elective deferral) between the employee and his or her employer. Salary reduction is the most common approach. For salary reduction agreements, there is an annual elective deferral limit of $16,500 (indexed for inflation). Further, the Section 415 limits for defined contributions plans, noted previously, also apply to Section 403(b) annuities. In addition, for participants age 50 and over, the annual limit on elective deferrals can be increased by catch-up contributions of $5,500 for 2009.

Taxation of Distributions Benefits are taxed as ordinary income when received by a participant. However, tax-free transfers and rollovers are allowed between TSA plans and traditional IRAs, qualified plans, Section 457 plans, and other TSAs. TSA plans also are subject to the minimum distribution rules and the 10 percent excise tax on premature distributions. They must be nondiscriminatory.

Nonqualified Deferred Compensation

A deferred-compensation arrangement is an agreement whereby an employer promises to pay an employee in the future for services rendered today. The plan usually is set up to provide for the payment of deferred amounts into an account for the employee, which may be paid out under specified conditions in the future. Plans also may be in the form of salary continuation over a period of years following retirement or other termination of employment. These plans are called *nonqualified* because they do not meet the tax law requirements for qualified retirement plans. They normally are available only to a selected group of executives.

Why Nonqualified Deferred Compensation? Some businesses do not have qualified retirement plans, and so they may provide nonqualified plans for selected employees. However, in many cases, employers do have qualified plans covering the bulk of their employees but want additional benefits for certain key people. This is particularly true because of the limits on benefits under qualified plans (e.g., the compensation cap, Section 415 limits, and so forth). Furthermore, executives often want to defer income to get the advantages of before-tax deferral.

Types of Plans Either the employer or the employee may initiate these plans. When requested by an employee, it sometimes is known as a *deferred-oriented* or *savings-type* plan. In these plans, employees voluntarily agree that a portion of their income should be deferred. Many plans are of this type. On the other hand, plans initiated by an employer may be called *benefit-oriented* or *inducement-to-stay* plans.

Plans may also be classified as *deferral-type plans,* as just described, or as *supplemental plans,* which are provided and paid for by employers to supplement qualified retirement plans for highly paid employees. There also are *death-benefit-only plans,* which provide benefits, usually in the form of annual installments, to survivors of a deceased participant. Finally, there are *Section 457 nonqualified deferred-compensation plans* for employees of state and local governments and nonprofit organizations.

Taxation of Nonqualified Deferred-Compensation Plans Two doctrines or theories of tax law may particularly affect nonqualified plans. These are the *constructive receipt* doctrine and the *economic benefit* theory. Under the doctrine of constructive receipt, as explained in Chapter 10, a taxpayer may be taxed on income not actually received if it is considered received constructively. For example, say an employer deposits funds with a trustee and that an employee has a right to the funds and may withdraw them or receive benefits from them at any time without substantial limitation. In this case, the funds placed with the trustee will be considered constructively received by the employee—not when they are actually withdrawn, but when they are placed with the trustee. Under the economic benefit theory, a person may be taxed whenever a monetary value can be attached to compensation or benefits. To successfully defer income taxation, a nonqualified deferred-compensation plan must not come under either of these doctrines.

In analyzing the tax status of these plans, it makes a difference whether the plan is considered funded for tax purposes. A *funded* plan is one in which specific assets have been set aside and in which the employee is given a current beneficial interest in the assets. Plans without such assets securing the benefits are *unfunded.* If a plan is unfunded, income taxation on the benefits can be postponed until they are actually received by the employee or his or her beneficiary. Thus, if an employer merely promises to pay deferred amounts (and the accumulated before-tax investment income on such amounts) upon the occurrence of certain events (such as the passage of time, termination of employment, retirement, death, or disability), the plan normally is not hampered by the constructive receipt doctrine because the delay is a substantial limitation on the receipt of the benefits. Moreover, if the plan is not secured so as to be protected from the employer's creditors, most authorities feel the employee should not be considered to have received an economic benefit. Thus, an *unfunded deferred-compensation plan* normally can provide an employee with a postponed accumulated account balance, and the employee's rights to the account balance can be nonforfeitable, unconditional, and vested, with the income tax on the deferred compensation and investment earnings being deferred until actual receipt. The employee (or his or her beneficiaries) is taxed when the deferred benefits are actually received.

Due to some perceived abuses regarding nonqualified deferred compensation and other plans, Section 409A was added to the tax code in 2004 by the American Jobs Creation Act. Section 409A provides for the inclusion in the gross income of certain participants in nonqualified deferred compensation plans of all amounts deferred under the plans when the plans fail to meet specified requirements of the provision. Such requirements deal with when distributions can be made from the plans, acceleration of benefits, employee elections for deferral, changes in the time and form of deferral, some rules regarding funding, and so forth. Thus, it is important for plans covered by Section 409A to comply with its terms to avoid immediate taxation on deferred amounts.

With a funded plan, in which an employee is given rights to specific assets, the employee will be taxed currently on the value of the assets added to the fund each year, unless the employee's rights to the benefits are subject to a *substantial risk of forfeiture.* This means there must be a risk that the employee will never receive the benefits. Most nonqualified plans are unfunded.

Security Arrangements and Informal Funding for Nonqualified Plans Employers sometimes have informal funding arrangements to provide themselves with assets to discharge their obligations under these plans. These arrangements (often involving the purchase of life insurance on the participating executives' lives) are owned by, controlled by, and made payable to the employer, and hence, do not provide any direct security to the executives covered by the agreements. The employer's commitments remain unsecured promises to pay, which covered executives can enforce only as general creditors of the employer. For tax purposes, such "informally funded plans" are still regarded as unfunded plans.

In recent years, there has been heightened interest in finding ways to provide greater security to executives with regard to unfunded nonqualified plans. One such security arrangement is the so-called rabbi trust.[3] A rabbi trust is an irrevocable trust set up by an employer to provide various kinds of nonqualified retirement benefits to selected employees. The trust provides that its assets will be paid out to meet the employer's obligations under certain circumstances, but that the trust assets remain subject to the claims of the employer's general creditors in the event of the employer's bankruptcy or insolvency. This means that even though the employer places assets in these trusts, they do not result in current taxable income to the covered employees. Thus, rabbi trusts can provide at least limited security for covered executives without losing the income tax advantages of an unfunded plan. For funded

[3] These trusts are called *rabbi trusts* because the first case involving their use, upon which the IRS ruled, involved such a trust set up by a synagogue for its rabbi.

plans, some arrangements to secure benefits are employee-owned trusts (sometimes called *secular trusts*) and employee-owned annuities.

Planning Issues for Nonqualified Deferred Compensation These plans can be attractive for selected executives and corporate directors. The executives often do not need the current income and they may be in a lower tax bracket when the deferred benefits are paid out. Investment earnings on the deferred amounts also are tax deferred, and some employers provide attractive investment outlets for deferred amounts. On the other hand, the security issue is there for unfunded plans. Its importance would seem to vary with the circumstances and be more important during difficult economic times.

In a different area, nonqualified deferred compensation may be used in connection with the sale of closely held business interests. Part of the purchase price (for a closely held C corporation, for example) effectively might be in the form of a nonqualified deferred-compensation agreement with the selling owner–employee. The deferred payments would be tax deductible to the corporation (and indirectly to the buyer), and thus part of the purchase price would be in tax-deductible dollars. On the other hand, these payments would be taxable as ordinary income to the selling owner–employee. Such arrangements are complex and require advance planning.

Supplemental Executive Retirement Plans

Supplemental nonqualified plans in the forms of ERISA excess benefit plans and supplemental executive retirement plans (SERPs) are also established for executives. ERISA excess benefits plans pay the difference between the maximum permitted limits under qualified retirement plans (e.g., the Section 415 limits) and the employee's full benefit, as determined by a regular plan's benefit formula. In addition, SERPs may be set up to increase the level of retirement income for executives beyond that contemplated under the basic retirement plan benefit formula.

Other Employee Benefits

Dependent Care Assistance

This benefit typically provides day care for specified dependents of employees, including dependent children, parents, or spouses. The IRC provides that employees do not have to include in their gross income amounts not exceeding $5,000 per year paid or incurred by their employer for dependent care assistance, if the assistance is provided under a program meeting certain requirements. Eligible expenses include the expense of a child or senior daycare center, a babysitter while the employee is working, a nursery school, a day camp, and a nurse at home. Such expenses are only eligible if they permit the employee or the employee and his or her spouse to work or to attend school full-time. These expenses frequently are also covered under flexible spending accounts (FSAs) on a pretax basis.

Educational Assistance

The gross income of employees does not include amounts paid or incurred by an employer for educational assistance to employees under a program that meets certain requirements, up to a maximum of $5,250 per employee per year.

Financial and Other Counseling Services

Many companies provide financial planning services on an individual basis for their executives as an executive benefit. In some cases, employers may provide such financial planning services for a broader range of employees. Employers may also provide their employees with other types of counseling; one popular area is retirement planning and counseling.

Cafeteria Compensation (Flexible Benefits)

Basic Characteristics The nature of these plans is described in Chapter 22 and so will not be repeated here.

Tax Status of Cafeteria Plans Section 125 of the IRC allows employees to choose among certain nontaxable benefits and taxable compensation without having the choice itself be a taxable event under the constructive receipt doctrine. Section 125 plans must be nondiscriminatory and meet certain other tax law requirements. In effect, this means the constructive receipt doctrine will not apply to otherwise nontaxable benefits elected by employees, even though they could have elected taxable benefits (cash) as well. Of course, to the extent employees actually elect cash compensation, it will constitute gross income to them.

Nontaxable Fringe Benefits

Employers can provide employees with a variety of benefits and services, which the tax law specifically provides are not gross income to the employees.[4] The term *fringe benefits* sometimes is used loosely to mean any kind of

[4]Section 132 of the IRC provides that "certain fringe benefits" are excluded from gross income. Prior to Section 132, there was uncertainty about the tax status of many of these items.

employee benefit other than retirement benefits. However, in the context of nontaxable fringe benefits under Section 132, it refers only to certain benefits specified in the law, as described next.

Types of Nontaxable Fringes The specific benefits include the following:

No-Additional-Cost Services: These are the same services employers sell to the general public that are provided free or at reduced cost to employees.

Qualified Employee Discounts: These generally are discounts up to 20 percent on the prices of goods and services.

Working Condition Fringes: These are a variety of expenses paid for by employers that otherwise would be deductible by employees as business expenses on their own tax returns. They may include items such as professional dues; subscriptions to business periodicals; cars, aircraft, and the like (for business purposes); club dues; outplacement assistance; and home computers.

De Minimus Fringes: In general, these are items that are so small and infrequently received that it is not practical for employers to account for them. However, it does include meals available at employer-provided eating facilities and certain employer-provided dependent group life insurance.

Qualified Transportation Fringes: These include employer-paid commuter highway vehicle transportation (e.g., a van pool with at least six passengers), transit passes, and qualified parking, up to limited amounts per month. These fringes also include any cash reimbursements by employers for such expenses, and allow employees a choice between these fringes and cash without constructive receipt if the nontaxable fringes are elected.

Qualified Moving Expense Reimbursements: These are employer-reimbursed or paid moving expenses for an employee to relocate to a new place of work, provided they otherwise would have been deductible by the employee as moving expenses.

On-Premises Athletic Facilities: The use of on-premises athletic facilities is a nontaxable fringe benefit if substantially all the use of such facilities is by employees, their spouses, and their dependent children.

Other Benefits If an employer provides other benefits to employees, aside from these specified nontaxable fringe benefits and the previously discussed employee benefits excluded from income by other sections of the tax code, the value of the benefit normally will be taxable to employees as compensation.

15

Individual Retirement Accounts and Annuities (IRAs)

Competence Objectives for This Chapter After reading this chapter, planners should understand:

- The types of individual retirement accounts or annuities
- IRA rollovers and direct transfers
- Making the decision to establish different kinds of IRAs
- The tax factors and economics in deciding whether to convert a traditional IRA to a Roth IRA
- Rollover of Roth 401(k) account balance to a Roth IRA
- Making gifts to family members so they can contribute to IRA's early
- Deciding whether to use IRAs for qualified first-time home buyer distributions or higher education expenses

IRAs have become important and advantageous retirement and financial planning tools for many people. At the same time, however, as a result of numerous changes in the tax law, they have become quite complex. The following kinds of IRAs are now available to individuals:

- Regular (earnings-related) traditional IRA
- Rollover traditional IRA
- Nondeductible traditional IRA
- Roth IRA (earnings-related)
- Roth IRA (conversion from traditional IRA)
- Spousal IRA
- Coverdell Education Savings Account (Education IRA)

- SEP-IRA
- SIMPLE-IRA

The SEP- and SIMPLE-IRAs were described in Chapter 14. The other kinds of IRAs are covered in this chapter.

Basic Concepts

IRAs afford individuals an opportunity to set up their own tax-favored retirement plans, subject to certain conditions and limitations. An IRA can be an individual retirement account or individual retirement annuity. An *individual retirement account* can be set up under the terms of a written trust (in which case it may be called a "trusteed IRA") or as a custodial account with a fiduciary institution that meets the requirements of the IRS. The bulk of IRAs are in custodial accounts. An *individual retirement annuity* is a flexible premium annuity contract and may be a fixed-dollar annuity or a variable annuity.

For IRAs generally, the interest of the IRA owner must be nonforfeitable. Also, if an IRA is used as security for a loan or is assigned to another (other than a transfer incident to divorce), there will be a deemed distribution to the extent of the loan or transfer. Thus, IRAs generally cannot be borrowed against or given away to others.

Types of IRAs

There is now an almost bewildering array of IRA plans with different rules or limits applying to each.

Regular (Earnings-Related) Traditional IRAs

These plans may be called traditional IRAs, regular IRAs, or front-end IRAs. Only cash can be contributed to these plans.

Nature and Limits of Contributions Individuals may make income tax–deductible contributions (from gross income to arrive at adjusted gross income) to these IRAs based on their earnings, marital status, and whether they (and their spouse) are covered under certain employer-provided retirement plans. First, in situations where a person and his or her spouse (if any) are *not* covered by an employer retirement plan (i.e., are not "active participants"), each income earner can make tax-deductible contributions each year, up to the smaller of 100 percent of compensation or $5,000 for 2009 (with indexing for future inflation in $500 increments). In addition, for IRA owners ages 50 and over, this annual limit is increased by $1,000 for 2009 (indexed).

For this purpose, employer retirement plans include qualified retirement plans; federal, state, and local government plans; tax-sheltered annuity plans; SEPs; SIMPLE plans; and certain other plans. Also for this purpose, *compensation* means earned income as an employee, income from self-employment, or alimony.

In situations where a person is covered under an employer retirement plan, the income earner still may be able to make deductible contributions to a traditional IRA, subject to certain income limits. For married taxpayers filing a joint return (and for qualifying widows or widowers), for the year 2009, their modified adjusted gross income (MAGI[1]) for federal income tax purposes must not exceed $89,000 for a full deduction. The deduction then is phased out for MAGI between $89,000 and $109,000. For single taxpayers and heads of households, the MAGI limit is $55,000 for a full IRA deduction, and the deduction then is phased out between $55,000 and $65,000.

Finally, in situations where married persons are filing jointly and one of them is covered by an employer retirement plan but the other is not, the spouse covered by the plan can make deductible IRA contributions subject to the income limits just described. However, the noncovered spouse may make deductible IRA contributions subject to an MAGI phase-out range for their combined income of $166,000 to $176,000 in 2009 (all indexed).

CASE EXAMPLE

First, let us assume Warren Williams, age 35, is a single taxpayer who works for a large corporation and is covered under the corporation's qualified pension plan. In the year 2009, Warren earns a salary of $50,000 per year (which is also his MAGI). Warren can make a tax-deductible contribution to a traditional IRA, up to the full $5,000 for the year, because, while he is covered by an employer retirement plan, his MAGI is less than $55,000 for the year. However, if Warren's salary had been $75,000, he could not have made any tax-deductible contribution to the IRA.[2]

[1] Modified adjusted gross income for traditional IRAs is adjusted gross income (AGI) plus any IRA deduction and certain other items. Thus, it is essentially the person's or couple's AGI.

[2] As will be explained in the later section on Roth IRAs, Warren could, however, have made a $5,000 contribution to a non-tax-deductible but tax-free Roth IRA for the year because the phase-out range for single taxpayers for Roth IRAs is $105,000 to $120,000 in 2009. He could also have contributed to a nondeductible regular IRA.

On the other hand, if Warren's salary (and MAGI) for 2009 were $60,000, he would be in the phase-out range for that year and could make a partial contribution to a tax-deductible IRA.[3] Thus, Warren could deduct a $2,500 contribution in 2009.[4]

Finally, if Warren's salary (and MAGI) for 2009 were $125,000, he could not make any tax-deductible contribution to an IRA since he would be well beyond the phase-out range. He also could not make any contribution to a Roth IRA because he would be beyond its phase-out range as well.[5]

CASE EXAMPLE

As another example, let us assume Peter and Mary Schmidt are married and file a joint income tax return. Peter, age 42, works for a corporation that covers him under its qualified 401(k) plan and receives a salary of $100,000 in 2009. Mary works for a small employer with no retirement plan and receives a salary of $60,000 in 2009. Assume their MAGI is $160,000 for 2009. In this case, Peter could not make any deductible contribution to a traditional IRA since he is an active participant under an employer retirement plan and their MAGI exceeds the phase-out range for married persons for 2009. However, Mary could make a $5,000 deductible contribution to a traditional IRA since she is not covered by an employer plan and their MAGI is below the phase-out range for a married person who is not covered by an employer plan but whose spouse is.[6]

[3] The formula for this calculation is:

$$\text{Percentage of Reduction} = \frac{\text{MAGI} - \text{applicable dollar amount (the lower limit of the phase-out range)}}{\$10{,}000 \text{ (or other difference in the phase-out range)}}$$

[4] He could also make a $2,500 contribution to a Roth IRA since a Roth permits contributions of the lesser of 100 percent of compensation or $5,000, reduced by any contributions made for the year to a traditional IRA on the person's behalf, and the Roth phase-out limits would be $105,000 to $120,000.

[5] As will be noted later, in this situation, Warren still could have made a $5,000 nondeductible contribution to a traditional IRA.

[6] It may also be noted that Peter as well as Mary (as an alternative to her deductible IRA) each could make $5,000 cash contributions ($10,000 total for the two) to Roth IRAs since coverage under employer retirement plans does not affect Roth eligibility and their MAGI is below the phase-out range for Roths ($166,000 to $176,000 for married persons filing jointly in 2009). Mary could also split her $5,000 contribution between a deductible traditional IRA and a Roth IRA.

Eligibility Requirements Any individual who has compensation and has not attained age 70½ may be eligible to contribute to a deductible traditional IRA. Of course, if a person (or his or her spouse) is covered by an employer retirement plan, this may limit or eliminate his or her deductible IRA contribution, as just described. Also, employers in their qualified plans may allow employees to make voluntary contributions to a separate account or annuity that meets the requirements of a traditional or Roth IRA. These are referred to as *deemed IRAs* under employer plans.

Tax Status When making deductible contributions to a traditional IRA, the person or couple receives a current income tax deduction for the contribution, up to the previously described limits. Furthermore, investment earnings in the IRA grow without current taxation. But with respect to withdrawals, all amounts distributed are fully taxable as ordinary income.

In addition, distributions made prior to a traditional IRA owner's reaching age 59½ are considered premature distributions and are subject to an additional 10 percent penalty tax on the taxable amount, unless an exception applies. The exceptions include distributions due to the owner's death or disability; for deductible medical care; by unemployed persons to pay for health insurance premiums; to pay for qualified higher education expenses for the owner, the owner's spouse, or a child or grandchild of the owner or his or her spouse;[7] as qualified first-time home buyer distributions (subject to a lifetime $10,000 limit[8]); and as part of a series of substantially equal periodic payments made at least annually for the life or the life expectancy of the IRA owner or the joint lives or life expectancies of the owner and his or her designated beneficiary of the IRA. It should be noted, however, that even if one of these exceptions applies, a distribution is still taxed as ordinary income.

When an IRA owner dies, any account balance in the IRA will be included in his or her gross estate for federal estate tax purposes. The account balance will be payable on death to the beneficiary or beneficiaries named in the IRA. The nature of this beneficiary designation will affect the estate tax status of the IRA, as explained in Chapter 26. This is true for all types of IRAs. However, for deductible traditional IRAs, the account balance is also

[7] Qualified higher education expenses include postsecondary school tuition, books, student supplies, and minimum room and board. These allowable expenses are reduced by nontaxable scholarships, fellowship grants, and educational assistance allowances.

[8] These are distributions received and used by the individual for qualified acquisition costs for a principal residence for a first-time home buyer, who may be the individual; his or her spouse; or any child, grandchild, or ancestor of the individual or his or her spouse. For this purpose, a first-time home buyer is an individual who did not have an ownership interest in a principal residence during the two-year period before the principal residence was acquired.

IRD to the beneficiary, as explained in Chapter 10. Planning for these issues is covered in Chapter 16.

Required Distributions The owner of a traditional IRA must begin taking taxable distributions no later than April 1 of the calendar year following the calendar year in which the owner attains age 70½. This is called the *required beginning date* (RBD). After this date, certain minimum annual distributions must be taken. The calculation of and planning for these minimum distributions are covered in Chapter 16. People often have more than one traditional IRA, which may include earnings-related IRAs, discussed here, and rollover IRAs, covered next. The IRS requires that minimum distributions be calculated separately for each IRA, but then they may be totaled and can be taken from any one or more of the IRAs. There also are minimum distributions required for IRA account balances after an owner's death. Naturally, an IRA owner can take distributions before the RBD and larger distributions than the minimum.

Rollover Traditional IRAs

These are traditional IRAs that receive *eligible rollover distributions* (defined in Chapter 16) from qualified retirement plans, TSAs, and Section 457 governmental deferred-compensation plans. These rollover distributions can be in the form of cash or property (such as employer stock from a qualified profit-sharing or savings plan). There also may be rollovers from an IRA to a qualified plan, a TSA, and a Section 457 plan.

Eligibility Requirements Any individuals, regardless of whether they currently have compensation (earnings), their income, or whether they are covered by an employer retirement plan, can establish a rollover IRA to receive an eligible rollover distribution.

Tax Status There is no current income taxation on the amount of an eligible rollover distribution to a rollover IRA. Thus, as an example, suppose that Mary Levy, age 40, has a $400,000 account balance in her employer's qualified savings plan with a Section 401(k) option (i.e., the entire $400,000 will eventually be taxable). She is leaving her current employer to join a new firm. She can elect to roll over all or part of the $400,000 account balance (an eligible rollover distribution) into her own rollover IRA without any current income taxation on the transaction.[9] Like other traditional IRAs, rollover IRAs are subject to taxation of distributions as ordinary income, the

[9] She also could elect to roll this amount over, tax-free, into her new employer's qualified retirement plan, if permitted by the new employer, or to a TSA or Section 457 plan.

10 percent penalty tax on premature distributions with the same rules and exceptions, inclusion in the gross estate for federal estate tax purposes, and being treated as IRD.

Required Distributions Like other traditional IRAs, rollover IRAs are subject to the minimum distribution rules just described.

Nondeductible Contributions to Traditional IRAs

Since there are income limits on deductible IRA contributions when a person (or his or her spouse) is covered under an employer's retirement plan (as well as income limits on contributions to Roth IRAs, considered next), it is possible to make nondeductible contributions to traditional IRAs equal to the difference between what could have been contributed had there been no income limits and the amounts (if any) of deductible IRA contributions and Roth IRA contributions. When distributions are made, nondeductible (after-tax) contributions are the IRA owner's investment in the contract, which will be recovered income tax–free. However, for this purpose, all traditional IRAs owned by a person are treated as contract and any distributions in one year are treated as one distribution. Therefore, any nondeductible (nontaxable) portion of this hypothetical contract is considered to come pro rata from any distribution from any of the traditional IRAs owned even if the IRA from which the distribution is actually taken has most or all of the nondeductible contributions. This has been called the "cream in the coffee rule" (i.e., the contributions are all mixed up) and may result in reduced tax-free distributions from traditional IRAs with nondeductible contributions when the owner also has IRAs with no or few nondeductible contributions. These after-tax contributions can be rolled over to another IRA but not to an employer plan.

The only real tax advantage of making nondeductible IRA contributions is that investment income and capital gains accumulate in the IRA without current income taxation. However, when distributed, such income and capital gains are taxed as ordinary income.

Roth IRAs (Earnings-Related)

A newer IRA concept is the non-tax-deductible but distribution tax–free Roth IRA.

Nature and Limits of Contributions Individuals may make contributions to Roth IRAs based on their earnings and marital status. It does not matter whether they are covered under an employer retirement plan. An individual income earner can make a contribution to a Roth IRA up to the smaller of

100 percent of compensation or the same dollar limits described previously for earnings-related traditional IRAs. There are also the same catch-up limits for owners age 50 or over. All these Roth dollar limits are indexed for inflation starting in 2010.

The income limits (phase-out ranges) for Roth IRAs are $105,000 to $120,000 of MAGI[10] for single persons and heads of households and $166,000 to $176,000 of MAGI for married persons filing jointly in 2009 (indexed). The annual dollar limits also are reduced by any contributions to traditional IRAs for the same person during the year.

Eligibility Requirements Any individual who has compensation (earned income or taxable alimony) and whose MAGI does not exceed or is within the income limits is eligible to contribute to a Roth IRA. Roth contributions can be made after age 70½. Neither SEP- nor SIMPLE-IRA contributions can be made to a Roth IRA. However, once these contributions are in a traditional IRA, it can be converted to a Roth IRA under the rules for such conversions.

As explained in Chapter 13, Section 401(k) plans and Section 403(b) annuities can permit employees to elect to have all or part of their own elective deferrals designated as after-tax "Roth contributions" (DRACs). In this case, the employees must pay income tax currently on these Roth deferrals, but they will grow and be distributed tax-free. Any 401(k) or 403(b) plan participant can make DRAC contributions, regardless of income. These Roth 401(k) or 403(b) accounts can be rolled over tax-free to a Roth IRA under the rules for such rollover.

Tax Status Contributions to a Roth IRA are not deductible for income tax purposes, but investment earnings and capital gains in the IRA grow tax-free. Distributions from a Roth IRA (either earnings-related or a conversion from a traditional IRA) are not included in gross income for federal income tax purposes, provided they are qualified distributions. A *qualified distribution* is one made at least five years after the tax year in which a person made the first contribution to any Roth IRA or in which a rollover (conversion) was made to the Roth IRA, *and* the distribution is taken on or after the person attains age 59½, on account of the person's death or disability, or is a qualified first-time home buyer distribution.[11] Thus, a qualified Roth distribution must meet both a five-year test and a triggering events test. If a distribution does not meet these requirements, it is a nonqualified distribution and the

[10] This is MAGI for traditional IRA purposes minus any deductible IRA contributions and any income resulting from the conversion of a traditional IRA to a Roth IRA (considered next).

[11] Defined in the same way as in Footnote 8.

previously untaxed investment income will be taxable. Even in this situation, however, the non-tax-deductible contributions are assumed to come out first, so no tax is imposed until total nonqualifying distributions (from all Roth IRAs) exceed total contributions. (This really is the opposite of the "cream-in-the-coffee" rule.) If a distribution is taxable, the 10 percent penalty tax on premature distributions also may apply.

DRAC accounts also have similar qualifying (nontaxable) and nonqualifying (taxable) distributions. However, for DRACs there is no first-time home buyer triggering event and the five-year period begins when the participant makes the first contribution to that particular DRAC.

As a planning matter, it would seem unwise to take nonqualifying distributions that exceed total contributions. In fact, as an overall planning strategy, it seems prudent to keep assets in Roth IRAs and traditional IRAs for as long as possible to get the most advantage from tax-free growth of investment earnings for Roths and tax-deferred growth of earnings for traditional IRAs. This is the "stretch IRA" concept discussed in Chapter 16.

As in the case of traditional IRAs, when a Roth IRA owner dies, any account balance in the IRA is included in his or her gross estate for federal estate tax purposes. The account balance will be payable on death to the beneficiary or beneficiaries named in the IRA, and this will affect the estate tax status of the IRA. However, unlike traditional IRAs, the account balance is not taxable income as IRD to the beneficiary.

Required Distributions During the lifetime of a Roth IRA owner, there are no mandatory distributions. There is no required beginning date, and there are no required minimum distributions. This is a major advantage for the Roth IRA over traditional IRAs and qualified retirement plans, both of which are subject to mandatory distribution rules starting at age 70½. At the death of a Roth IRA owner, the minimum distribution rules applying to traditional IRA beneficiaries also apply to Roth IRA beneficiaries (see Chapter 16).

The situation is different for DRAC participants. Since DRACs are part of a qualified retirement plan, the required minimum distribution rules (which are required for plan qualification) must apply to DRAC participants. However, a DRAC participant can avoid them by rolling over his or her DRAC to a Roth IRA when eligible to do so.

Roth IRAs (Conversion from Traditional IRAs)

Nature and Limits of Conversions A traditional IRA account balance may be converted into a Roth IRA by the owner, provided the owner's MAGI (as either a single person or a married person filing a joint return) does not exceed $100,000 for the year of conversion.[12] However, beginning in 2010 this $100,000 limitation will be repealed and any traditional IRA owner, regardless of income, can convert a traditional IRA to a Roth IRA. Any amount can be converted and conversions can be spread out to avoid bunching of ordinary income in only one or a few years.

A conversion can be affected by the traditional IRA owner's taking a distribution and then rolling over the amount to be converted into the Roth IRA within 60 days of the distribution or having a transfer of the amount converted from the trustee or custodian of the traditional IRA to the trustee or custodian of the Roth IRA without the owner actually receiving a distribution (a trustee-to-trustee transfer).[13] Under either of these methods, the amount converted is taxable as ordinary income.

Eligibility Requirements The $100,000 MAGI limit has already been noted. This limit will no longer apply after 2009. A SEP can be converted to a Roth. A SIMPLE-IRA can be converted after two years from the date the owner first participated in any SIMPLE-IRA plan of the employer. A qualified retirement plan now can be directly converted to a Roth IRA under PPA of 2006.

Tax Status The taxable portion of a traditional IRA that is converted to a Roth IRA is gross income for federal income tax purposes in the year of conversion. It normally is preferable to pay this tax from other, non-tax-advantaged assets so the full amount in the IRA can grow on a tax-free basis. While the taxable portion on conversion is subject to regular federal income taxation, it is not subject to the 10 percent tax on premature distributions.

> **CASE EXAMPLE**
>
> Let us continue the example of Mary Levy. Ten years (in 2010) after she directly transferred the $400,000 account balance from her qualified savings plan into her traditional rollover IRA, the account balance is now $700,000. At this time (because the $100,000 limit no longer applies), she decides to convert her traditional IRA to a Roth IRA. Thus, the $700,000 would be

[12] As stated in Footnote 11, MAGI, for this purpose, does not include income resulting from the conversion itself. Also, MAGI, for purposes of conversion eligibility, does not include minimum required distributions from traditional IRAs. This may be helpful for older persons, who may not have other income in excess of $100,000 in a year, to make such conversions, perhaps for estate planning reasons.

[13] It may be noted that these are the same general methods as those used for rollovers and transfers from qualified retirement plans and TSAs to traditional IRAs. However, the tax withholding rules are different, as will be explained in Chapter 16.

added to her gross income in that year. If her tax rate on this amount of added income were, say, 35 percent, her added tax would be $245,000 ($700,000 × 0.35). Assuming this tax comes from other sources (so the full $700,000 can grow tax-free in her Roth IRA), she effectively would lose the after-tax return on the $245,000 tax payment for the future. This must be considered in analyzing a conversion. When Mary dies, any account balance will be in her gross estate, but it is not IRD.

Required Distributions The rules for required distributions from Roth IRAs have already been noted.

Spousal IRAs

For married persons filing a joint return, when one of the spouses has no compensation (or compensation less than that of the other spouse) during a tax year, the working spouse may make contributions to an IRA for the nonworking spouse (a spousal IRA), as well as to the working spouse's own IRA. The maximum contribution to each of the IRAs for the year is the lesser of 100 percent of the working spouse's compensation (less certain items) or the dollar limits on contributions described previously. The spousal IRA can be a traditional IRA or a Roth IRA. No more than the applicable limit can be contributed to each spouse's IRA, and each spouse must have his or her own separate IRA or subaccount in a plan.

CASE EXAMPLE

Suppose that Sam and Martha Johnson, 52 and 48, respectively, are married and file a joint return and that Sam earns $150,000 per year. He is an active participant under his employer's qualified savings plan. Martha works in their home and has no compensation for IRA purposes. In this case, Sam could make a $6,000 contribution ($5,000 regular and $1,000 catch-up since he is over 50) in 2009 to his Roth IRA and another $5,000 contribution to Martha's spousal Roth IRA for the year. This is because their MAGI is less than the Roth IRA phase-out range for married couples. As an alternative for Martha, Sam could contribute $5,000 to a traditional deductible spousal IRA for her since their MAGI is less than the phase-out range when one spouse (Sam) is covered by an employer retirement plan but the other (Martha) is not. Sam cannot contribute to a deductible IRA for himself because he is covered by an employer plan and their MAGI exceeds the phase-out range for that situation.

Coverdell Education Savings Accounts (Education IRAs)[14]

Nature and Limits of Contributions Individuals (whether they have earnings or not) can contribute up to $2,000 per year per beneficiary to Coverdell Education Savings Accounts, subject to certain income limits. The income limits are a MAGI of $95,000 to $110,000 for single persons and $190,000 to $220,000 for married persons filing jointly. The phase-out operates in the same way as for Roth IRAs. The $2,000-per-year limit is in addition to the limits for other IRAs discussed previously.

Eligibility Requirements In addition to eligible individuals, corporations and other entities also may make contributions to Education Savings Accounts, and in this case, the income limits just noted do not apply.

Tax Status Contributions to Education IRAs are not tax deductible and, correspondingly, withdrawals that meet the requirements of the tax law are not taxable. Investment earnings accumulate tax-free. To be eligible for tax-free withdrawals, the amounts withdrawn by the beneficiary must not exceed qualified education expenses.[15] To the extent they do, a pro rata share of the untaxed investment earnings will be taxable to the beneficiary and a 10 percent penalty tax also will be applicable.

Rollovers and Required Distributions When the beneficiary of an Education IRA reaches age 30, he or she may roll over any unwithdrawn amounts (within 60 days of distribution) to an Education IRA for another member of the beneficiary's family. Such a rollover also can be done before age 30. If such actions have not been taken by age 30, any remaining funds must be distributed to the beneficiary, and the untaxed investment earnings will be taxable as ordinary income (including the 10 percent penalty tax).

Contributions to Education Savings Accounts are subject to gift tax, but are eligible for the $13,000 ($26,000 for married couples splitting gifts) in 2009, indexed for inflation, per donee per year gift tax annual exclusion.[16] In a beneficiary-to-beneficiary rollover, as long as the beneficiaries are of the

[14] These are different in concept from the IRAs discussed previously in that they are designed for the funding of education expenses rather than for retirement. They originally were called "Education IRAs," but their official name now is "Coverdell Education Savings Accounts." In this book, we shall refer to them either as Education Savings Accounts or Education IRAs.

[15] These include qualified elementary and secondary education expenses (grades 1 through 12) and qualified higher education expenses, such as for tuition, books, supplies, equipment, room and board, and other items. They are reduced by nontaxable scholarships, fellowship grants, and educational assistance allowances.

[16] The gift tax annual exclusion is described in Chapter 27.

same generation (brothers and sisters, for example), there will be no taxable gift. However, when a new beneficiary is in the generation after that of the former beneficiary (a child of the former beneficiary, for example), there is a gift tax, but the annual exclusion applies.

Education IRAs serve the same general purpose as Section 529 plans–advance funding of education costs. (Section 529 plans are covered in Chapter 12.) However, they are less flexible than 529 plans, have lower contribution limits, have income phase-out limits, and require distribution when the beneficiary reaches age 30. Qualified education expenses for these IRAs are more extensive in that they include qualified elementary and secondary school expenses as well as qualified higher education expenses (which are the only expenses covered by 529 plans). Therefore, depending on the circumstances, a person might combine these two approaches and contribute annually $2,000 to an Education IRA and $11,000 to a 529 plan (in 2009) as a $13,000 annual exclusion gift for a beneficiary. Then, the Education IRA could be used tax-free for elementary and secondary private schools (if desired) and, if necessary, for higher education expenses, while the 529 plan would be available tax-free for qualified higher education expenses.

IRA Rollovers and Direct Transfers

Another kind of rollover to an IRA occurs when part or all of the assets received from one IRA are rolled over within 60 days to another IRA of the same type. There is no current income tax on such a rollover. This is called an *IRA-to-IRA rollover.* Part or all of the IRA assets are distributed to the owner, and then the owner rolls over those assets into another IRA. Such a rollover can be made only once a year, and the same property must be rolled over to the new IRA.

The other approach is a *direct IRA transfer.* Here, the assets of an IRA are transferred directly from one plan sponsor to another without passing into the hands of the IRA owner. In this case, there is no limit on the number of transfers that can be made in a year.

Financial Institutions That Offer IRAs

Many financial institutions offer IRAs to the public. Some of these institutions offer *self-directed IRAs.* These are IRAs in which the owner has virtually complete control over the selection of a broad range of investments. On the other hand, under these self-directed plans, the full burden of investment decision making falls on the IRA owner.

IRA Investments

IRAs can be invested in a wide range of assets. These investments can be made through financial intermediaries or in individual assets through self-directed IRAs. However, life insurance policies and certain collectibles are not eligible investments for IRAs.

Planning Issues for IRAs

Deciding Whether to Establish an IRA

The threshold issue is whether to contribute to an IRA at all. If a person is eligible to make deductible contributions to a traditional IRA or nondeductible contributions to a Roth IRA, there appear to be many advantages in doing so.

For deductible traditional IRAs, both the contributions and the investment earnings are before-tax, so the owner gets the power of deferral on both.

For Roth IRAs, the advantages of tax-free growth of investment earnings and longer time for tax-free growth make this plan just as attractive as, and possibly more so than, the traditional IRA. Which one is to be preferred in a given situation is a complicated issue that is considered in the next section.

With respect to nondeductible contributions to a traditional IRA, however, the case is not so clear. The only real advantage is tax deferral on investment earnings.

Deciding between Traditional and Roth IRAs and Whether to Convert to a Roth IRA

Of course, if a person is eligible for only one type, that settles the question. But many people will be eligible for both. Unfortunately, there is no sure answer to this question.

It can be divided into two subissues. The first issue is whether an eligible person should contribute to an earnings-related traditional IRA or Roth IRA. The second issue is whether an eligible person who has a traditional IRA should convert to a Roth IRA.

Basic Equality between Deductible and Tax-Free Growth In analyzing these issues, it may be helpful at the outset to note that if one takes a sum of money or a series of contributions, accumulates them tax-deferred, and then pays tax on the balance after a specified period (as in a traditional IRA), the result is the same as paying tax on the sum or series of contributions up front, deducting the tax, and accumulating the balance tax-free for the same period (as in a Roth IRA), provided the interest rates and tax rates assumed in both cases are the same. This may be somewhat counterintuitive, so let us take an example using a conversion situation.

CASE EXAMPLE

Assume that Henry Petrofski, age 50, is in the 33 percent federal income tax bracket, owns a traditional IRA with a $100,000 account balance, and plans to convert to a Roth IRA. Furthermore, assume he can earn a before-tax investment return of 8 percent and an after-tax return of 5.36 percent (8 percent × 0.67 = 5.36 percent). First, we shall assume Henry leaves the funds in his traditional IRA at an 8 percent average annual compound rate of return and withdraws all of them 20 years later at age 70.[17] He then pays income tax on the entire $466,096 accumulated balance at 33 percent.[18] As a result, his after-tax return on the IRA at the end of the 20 years would be $466,096 × 0.67 = $312,284 (after tax). On the other hand, if we assume Henry converts his traditional IRA to a Roth, pays the income tax on the conversion from the IRA proceeds,[19] allows the balance ($67,000) to accumulate tax-free in the Roth at the 8 percent average annual compound rate of return, and then withdraws the entire balance tax-free in 20 years at age 70, Henry's after-tax return at the end of 20 years would be the same ($100,000 × 0.67 = $67,000 in the Roth IRA, which accumulates at 8 percent over 20 years to the same $312, 284). But note that the fundamental assumptions in reaching this equality are that the investment earnings, tax rate, and the period of tax-deferred or tax-free growth must be the same for both scenarios at the beginning and end of the period.

However, as was stated in Footnote 19 and earlier, it is not good planning to take the tax on conversion from the IRA proceeds.[20] Therefore, let us change the previous example to

[17] As a planning matter, he normally would withdraw them over time to preserve tax deferral for as long as possible. We make this assumption here only for purposes of illustration.

[18] Again, as a practical matter, if he took this amount into income in one year, his tax bracket would increase to the maximum marginal rate. But we are making this tax rate assumption for purposes of comparison.

[19] As noted previously, it is not desirable to take the tax from the traditional IRA proceeds. It is better to use other non-tax-advantaged assets to pay the tax (or even to borrow to do so) so that the entire amount ($100,000 in this illustration) can continue to grow tax-free. The opposite assumption is used here to make the analysis comparable.

[20] Correspondingly, one normally should contribute the full amount possible to an earnings-related Roth IRA even though it is not deductible. The money to cover the foregone tax deduction must come from other non-tax-advantaged sources. The principle is the same.

assume that Henry converts the entire $100,000 traditional IRA to the Roth IRA and uses other non-tax-advantaged assets to pay the $33,000 tax due. In this case, the Roth would grow tax-free at 8 percent to $466,096 in 20 years. However, the $33,000 of assets used to pay the tax on conversion also would have grown during this period, but at an after-tax average annual rate of 5.36 percent. This $33,000 at 5.36 percent would have equaled $93,762 in 20 years. Thus, if we subtract this amount from the Roth balance, we have $466,096 – $93,762 (accumulated after-tax value of tax) = $372,334 value of the Roth.

This analysis shows an inherent advantage of the Roth IRA, either converted or earnings related. The foregone tax payment (or deduction) in effect grows tax-free inside the Roth IRA (at 8 percent here), while it would have grown at an after-tax rate (5.36 percent here) outside the Roth. This will always favor the Roth as long as the assumptions are held constant.

However, an even greater inherent advantage of the Roth is that the mandatory distribution rules do not apply to Roth IRAs during the owner's lifetime, but they do apply to traditional IRAs. Thus, in the previous example, Henry would have to start taking distributions from the traditional IRA—and paying tax on them—at age 70½. From that point on, the funds would be out of the IRA and, assuming they were reinvested, could earn only the assumed after-tax return of 5.36 percent.[21] On the other hand, the funds in the Roth IRA could remain intact and continue to earn a tax-free return of 8 percent until Henry's death (at which time the minimum distribution rules relating to beneficiaries would apply).

Factors in Choosing Which IRA Given the inherent advantages of Roth IRAs just described, a number of other factors might be considered in this choice. First, let us consider the choice of making earnings-related contributions to a Roth IRA or to a traditional IRA.

Relationship of Tax Rates at Time of Contribution and (Assumed) Rates at Distribution: The same rates cause a wash, as just illustrated, except that the inherent advantages of Roth IRAs tilt the decision in their favor. Lower rates at time of contribution than assumed at time of distribution favor the Roth. The reverse favors the traditional. One may well wonder, however,

[21] The minimum distribution rules for qualified plans and IRAs are described in Chapter 16.

how anyone can predict with any degree of confidence what tax rates will be 10, 20, 30, 40, or even more years from now. The authors certainly cannot. It is even difficult to say that income tax rates during retirement many years in the future will be lower than rates during active employment.

Length of Time until Distribution from IRA: As far as the basic equality described previously is concerned, it does not make any difference. However, the longer this period, the greater is the inherent deferral advantage of Roth IRAs.

Rate of Investment Return on IRA Assets: Again, as far as the basic equality is concerned, this factor is neutral as long as the same investment returns and tax rates are assumed for both types of IRAs. However, higher rates increase the inherent tax-free advantages of Roth IRAs.

Need for IRA Assets for Retirement Income (or Before Death): This shortens the deferral period and so lessens the inherent advantages of Roths.

Qualifying for and Financing the IRA: The eligibility and contribution rules differ for these two types of IRAs. Also, it is easier from a cash flow point of view to make a full contribution each year to a traditional IRA than to a Roth IRA because of the current income tax deduction for contributions to a traditional IRA.

With respect to converting from a traditional IRA to a Roth IRA, the decision factors just noted are essentially the same, except their relative importance may vary. There also are some other factors affecting whether to convert.

Financing a Conversion: This involves paying the income tax on the traditional IRA. The entire tax is due for the amount converted in the year of conversion. This may pose a cash drain problem for taxpayers.

Owner's Tax Rate Due to Conversion: The additional income from the conversion may push the owner-taxpayer into a higher income tax bracket. This may raise tax rates at the time of conversion relative to the time of distribution which may favor keeping the traditional IRA. However, the amounts converted can be spread out over several years to mitigate this factor. Also, in some cases IRA owners may be able to do time conversions for years in which they have relatively low taxable incomes and tax rates.

Making Gifts So Family Members Can Contribute to IRAs Parents or others may wish to make gifts to their children or other family members who have earned income to enable them to contribute to their own IRAs. This probably would be to Roth IRAs, since a tax deduction would be relatively insignificant for lower-income taxpayers. These gifts normally would fall within the $13,000 (indexed) per year, per donee gift tax annual exclusion (in 2009), and hence no taxable gift would result.

Investing IRA Funds

Another planning issue is how to invest IRA money. First, IRA investments should fit into the overall asset allocation strategy. Second, from a tax point of view, the factors presented in Chapter 9 concerning the ways investments should be held are applicable to this planning issue, at least with respect to traditional IRAs.

The main difference may lie with respect to Roth IRAs. Since distributions from Roth IRAs are tax-free, all investment returns inside a Roth come out income tax–free during the owner's lifetime or to his or her beneficiary after the owner's death. The effect of this is much like the step-up in basis rule for directly owned capital assets at the owner's death. Hence, assets that may produce long-term capital gains on this basis would be more attractive in a Roth than in a traditional IRA. However, from a tax perspective, it still may be preferable to hold long-term capital gain assets directly.

Use of IRAs for Qualified First-Time Home Buyer Distributions or Qualified Higher Education Expenses

As noted earlier, distributions for these purposes from a traditional IRA will not be subject to the 10 percent tax on premature distributions. However, they will be subject to regular tax as ordinary income. Also, a first-time home buyer distribution is a qualified tax-free distribution from a Roth IRA. However, such distributions take otherwise tax-deferred or tax-free funds from the IRA and result in current taxation for traditional IRAs. Hence, it seems better to finance these needs from other sources, if possible.

Naming the IRA Beneficiary or Beneficiaries

There is a more extensive discussion of this issue for IRAs and qualified retirement plans in the next chapter.

Planning Distributions from IRAs

Planning for distributions from IRAs and qualified retirement plans also is discussed in Chapter 16.

16

Planning for Taking Distributions from Retirement Plans

Competence Objectives for This Chapter After reading this chapter, planners should understand:

- Factors affecting planning for retirement plan benefits
- Federal income taxation of retirement plan benefits
- Planning for lump-sum distributions
- Planning for rollovers to an IRA or another qualified plan
- Penalty taxes on premature distributions and insufficient distributions
- Required beginning date (RBD) and minimum distribution rules
- Planning for naming plan beneficiaries and designated beneficiaries
- Minimum distribution rules after a participant's or owner's death
- Planning for spousal rollover
- Planning for nonspousal inherited IRAs
- Federal estate taxation of retirement plan benefits
- Planning for taking distributions in various circumstances, such as while in service, on separation from services prior to retirement, at retirement, and at participant's or owner's death
- How to utilize the "stretch IRA" approach
- Advantages and limitations of taking retirement benefits as a lifetime annuity income

Chapters 13 and 14 described the various kinds of qualified retirement plans and other plans provided by employers, and Chapter 15 dealt with IRAs. This chapter discusses how and when benefits should be taken from these plans.

A person or a couple may need to plan for taking benefits from these plans in one or more of the following circumstances:

- While a participant-employee is still employed (i.e., is in service)
- If a participant separates from an employer's service prior to retirement
- At retirement
- At the time of a participant's or IRA owner's death

General Considerations Affecting Planning

Objectives for Plan Benefits

These may include the following:

- Provide a secure lifetime retirement income for the person and his or her spouse (if any) or others
- Provide capital for investment
- Accumulate capital on a tax-deferred or tax-free basis for as long as possible in order to pass it on to one's heirs
- Accumulate capital on a tax-deferred or tax-free basis to allow maximum future flexibility in the use of the funds as retirement income or for estate planning purposes as future conditions may dictate
- Avoid penalty taxes and reduce other taxes to the greatest extent feasible, consistent with other objectives
- Keep funds in qualified retirement plans (and perhaps in IRAs) for creditor protection

What the Plan Allows

Persons and their advisers must look to the provisions of their particular plan to determine their rights and benefits under it. In some cases, a participant or IRA owner might want to take a particular action, but if the plan documents do not permit it, that may be that.

Available Resources and Need for Income

If benefits are needed to provide current retirement income, they must be taken in a fashion that will produce adequate income. On the other hand, if there are other substantial resources or income, planning horizons are broader.

Health Status

This may affect planning in several ways. For example, a person in poor health would not want to take retirement benefits as a life annuity if alternatives are available, or might elect an annuity form with substantial survivors benefits.

Money Management Considerations

People vary in the extent to which they want or are able to manage the funds behind their retirement benefits. Some methods of distribution imply active management by the recipient (such as a transfer to a self-directed IRA or a lump-sum distribution), while others do not (such as taking a life annuity). Another aspect of this consideration may be concern over the solvency of financial institutions (funding agencies) holding retirement plan assets. If a person or couple is concerned on this score, they may want to transfer their retirement funds into a rollover IRA with a more secure institution.

Income Tax Deferral

As a general principle, participants and IRA owners want to keep their retirement assets inside a qualified retirement plan or IRA as long as possible to take advantage of the deferral of income taxes (or tax-free growth, in the case of Roth IRAs). This normally makes good tax sense, but it may run counter to other considerations, such as a need for current retirement income.

Avoiding Penalty Taxes

Two penalty taxes may apply to distributions from qualified and other retirement plans or IRAs: a 10 percent tax on premature distributions and a 50 percent tax on insufficient distributions (i.e., that do not conform to the minimum distribution rules). These penalty taxes are described later in this chapter. When considering retirement plan distributions, the 50 percent tax should always be avoided, while the 10 percent tax should be avoided (or reduced) if possible.

Meeting Retirement Equity Act of 1984 (REA) Rules

As explained in Chapter 13, a married participant in a qualified pension plan must have his or her plan benefits payable in accordance with the REA rules, unless they are waived by the participant with the informed consent of his or her spouse. Furthermore, a married participant in a qualified profit-sharing plan, savings plan, or stock bonus plan must either meet the REA requirements for an exemption or have the benefits payable in accordance with the REA rules, unless waived with the spouse's consent. The REA rules do not apply to IRAs.

Estate Planning Considerations

In some cases, estate planning considerations become quite important in determining how qualified plan and IRA death benefits are to be arranged.

Creditor Protection

Participants and owners of retirement plans may find themselves in bankruptcy or with creditors' claims against them. This is particularly true during difficult economic times such as exist as of this writing. In this case, there are two levels of concern for the debtor. One is whether his or her assets are included in the bankruptcy estate under federal bankruptcy law and the other is whether the assets may be subject to attachment or garnishment under state law.

The federal Bankruptcy Abuse and Prevention and Consumer Protection Act of 2005 (BAPCPA) clarified and expanded in some areas the creditor protection available for retirement plan assets. Qualified retirement plans (such as pension, profit-sharing, 401(k), and stock bonus plans) are completely exempt from creditors' claims under federal and state law. When qualified retirement plan benefits are rolled over to an IRA, BAPCPA provides unlimited creditor protection for the rollover IRA assets in federal bankruptcy proceedings. This federal unlimited exemption also applies to SEP-IRAs and SIMPLE-IRAs.

Under BAPCPA, regular traditional and Roth IRAs (i.e., those created and funded by the owner) are exempt in federal bankruptcy proceedings up to an aggregate limit of $1,000,000 (unless the bankruptcy judge allows more if "the interests of justice so require"). However, creditor protection for IRAs with respect to state insolvency, attachment, or garnishment actions depends on state law. Many states have enacted laws protecting IRA assets from creditors' claims, but they vary in the extent of such protection.

Taxation of Benefits from Qualified Plans and IRAs

The taxation of benefits from qualified retirement plans and IRAs is a complex subject. Only the general principles will be covered here.

Federal Income Tax on Distributions

The general principle underlying federal income taxation of payments from qualified retirement plans and traditional IRAs is that, to the extent such payments come from money in the plan that was not previously taxed (i.e., employer contributions, before-tax employee contributions, deductible IRA contributions, and investment earnings on plan assets), the payments should be taxed to the participant (or owner), or to his or her beneficiary, when they are finally paid out from the plan. However, to the extent that payments come from money that has already been taxed (generally after-tax employee contributions and nondeductible IRA contributions), they should be excluded from gross income when finally paid out as benefits. On the other hand, qualified distributions from Roth IRAs are entirely income tax–free.

Periodic Income from Qualified Plans Employees frequently take benefits at retirement from death-benefit (DB) pension plans in the form of a periodic lifetime income for themselves or for themselves and their spouses. They sometimes also use their account balances under defined-contribution (DC) plans to similarly provide lifetime incomes or to be paid out in periodic installments of a fixed amount or over a fixed period of years. As a general principle, periodic distributions are subject to the rules governing taxation of annuities (in Section 72 of the IRC). However, special provisions are applicable to qualified retirement plans.

Under the *general annuity rule,* the taxable part of any annuity or installment payment is determined by excluding the part of the payment that is attributable to the employee's own net investment in the plan (cost basis), if any. This is done by calculating an *exclusion ratio* as of the annuity starting date and then multiplying this exclusion ratio by the periodic distribution. This determines the nontaxable or excluded amount. The exclusion ratio is the annuitant's net investment in the plan (cost basis) divided by his or her expected return from the plan.

However, for life annuity and installment payments from qualified retirement plans and TSAs, special rules apply, depending on when annuity payments started or will start. Under the most recent rule, which sometimes is referred to as the *modified simplified general rule,* when the annuity starting date is after December 31, 1997,[1] the nontaxable portion of each annuity payment is determined by dividing the annuitant's investment in the contract (if any) by a factor from federal tables that is based only on a single annuitant's age, or on the combined ages if the annuity is payable over two or more lives. For a fixed number of installment payments, the number of monthly payments is used as the divisor.

CASE EXAMPLE

Suppose Mary Riley is a participant in a DB pension plan to which she has made after-tax contributions of $32,500 over the years. She is age 65 and her husband is 68. Mary is retiring this year and will receive a joint and 50 percent survivor life annuity for herself and her husband of $3,000 per month while she is alive and, if her

[1] Other rules apply in each case when the annuity starting date was after November 18, 1996, but before January 1, 1998, or was after July 1, 1986, but before November 19, 1996, or was on or before July 1, 1986. There have been numerous changes in this area, and these are transition rules. Also, this simplified rule does not apply when the annuitant is age 75 or older on the annuity starting date, unless there are fewer than five years of guaranteed payments.

husband should survive her, reducing to $1,500 per month for her husband's remaining lifetime (i.e., a QJSA annuity form). Under these assumptions, Mary can exclude $125 per month from her pension income. This is determined by dividing her net investment in the contract ($32,500) by 260 from the federal tables.[2] The remainder ($2,875 per month) will be taxable as ordinary income.

Under the annuity rules (both the general annuity rule and the special rules for qualified plans), an annuitant generally can recover only his or her net investment in the contract tax free. After that, all future payments are fully taxable. Thus, in the previous example, after Mary recovers her $32,500 basis tax-free, the entire $3,000 monthly pension will be gross income to her. However, if Mary and her husband should die before the $32,500 basis is recovered tax-free, the unrecovered amount will be deductible on the final income tax return of the last of them to die.

Distributions from IRAs As in the case of qualified plans, traditional IRA owners can recover any investment in the contract (nondeductible contributions) tax-free, while other distributions are taxable as ordinary income. In taxing partial distributions from traditional IRAs, the general annuity rules of Section 72 generally apply. All traditional IRAs owned by a person are treated as one contract for this purpose. Any excludible portion of a distribution is determined by dividing the owner's net investment in the contracts by the expected return from the contracts (the IRA account balances plus certain adjustments), and then multiplying this fraction (if any) by the amount of the distribution. The remainder is gross income. As with qualified plans, an owner can recover tax free only the amount of his or her basis. Qualified distributions from Roth IRAs are income tax–free.

Net Investment (Basis) in the Plan or Contract An employee's net investment in a qualified retirement plan may include the following:

- Any after-tax employee contributions to the plan
- The total term cost of any pure life insurance protection on the employee's life provided by the plan that had been previously taxed to the employee
- The amount of any plan loans that were repaid by the employee but had been previously taxed to the employee (e.g., loans that did not meet the requirements for nontaxable plan loans)
- Any employer contributions that, for some reason, had been previously taxed to the employee

[2] This is the factor to be used when the combined ages of the annuitants is between 130 and 140; in this case, the ages are 65 + 68 = 133.

Then, from this amount an employee must subtract any nontaxable distributions previously received from the plan and any unrepaid plan loans. The result is the employee's net investment in the plan.

A traditional IRA owner's investment in the contract is any nondeductible contributions.

Plans Where Participants and Owners Have No Basis In many cases, participants and traditional IRA owners will have no investment (basis) in the plan or contract. Thus, as a practical matter, distributions from many plans will be taxable as ordinary income.

Lump-Sum Distributions Many pension plans and virtually all profit-sharing, savings, and stock bonus plans permit participants or their beneficiaries to take their benefits as a lump-sum distribution.

Definition of a Lump-Sum Distribution: A *lump-sum distribution* is a distribution made to a participant or his or her beneficiary from a qualified retirement plan of the employee's entire account balance or interest in the plan within one taxable year of the recipient. The distribution must be made because of certain triggering events, which are, the employee attains age 59½; the employee's severance from employment, including retirement; or the employee dies. (For self-employed persons, these triggering events are attaining age 59½, death, or becoming disabled.)

In determining whether there has been a distribution of the entire account balance or interest in the plan, all qualified plans of the same type maintained by the employer for the employee must be considered together as one plan. For this purpose, all pension plans are one type of plan, all profit-sharing plans are another type of plan, and all stock bonus plans are still another type. Thus, for example, suppose an employer maintains a DB pension plan and a savings plan for its employees, and John Jones is covered by both plans. John is retiring. He could decide to receive a life annuity from the pension plan and still take his entire account balance under the savings plan as a lump-sum distribution.

Taxable Amount of a Lump-Sum Distribution: To determine the taxable amount of a lump-sum distribution, certain items are subtracted from the total distribution. These items may include:

- The employee's own after-tax contributions (minus any previous nontaxable distributions).
- The net unrealized appreciation (NUA) on any employer securities included in the lump-sum distribution (i.e., the difference between the fair market value of the securities at distribution and their cost or other basis to the plan). A number of qualified retirement plans, particularly

profit-sharing, savings, stock bonus, and employee stock ownership plans, may invest at least part of plan assets in employer securities (e.g., common stock of the employer) and may distribute such securities to employees or their beneficiaries as part of a lump-sum distribution. When this is done, the employee or beneficiary can deduct the amount by which the employer securities have appreciated in value in the hands of the plan;[3] however, the income tax basis of the employer securities in the hands of the distributee is their value when they were contributed to or purchased by the plan (a carryover basis).[4]

- The term cost of any life insurance protection the employee previously included in his or her income.
- Repayments of any plan loans that previously were included in the employee's gross income.
- The actuarial value of any annuity contracts that are included in the lump-sum distribution.

Decision Factors Concerning Lump-Sum Distributions: If a participant decides to take a lump-sum distribution, he or she still has to decide whether to pay the income tax currently on the taxable amount (perhaps with some favorable tax features) or to directly transfer (rollover) part or all of the distribution into a traditional IRA, a Roth IRA (with current taxation), or into another qualified plan that will accept such transfers.

Many people opt to defer the tax on the lump sum further through a rollover. This option is discussed later in this chapter. However, there may be circumstances favoring taking a lump-sum distribution and paying tax currently. These might include when the distribution is relatively small, when 10-year forward averaging and capital gain treatment applies under a transition rule for persons who were age 50 or older on January 1, 1986,[5] or when a substantial portion of a distribution consists of highly appreciated employer securities (containing NUA). In the case of employer securities with NUA, a partial rollover of plan assets other than employer securities also may be done, as explained later in this chapter. It must be remembered, however, that the 10 percent penalty tax on premature distributions also may apply to taxable lump-sum distributions.

[3] The NUA on employer securities attributable to employer contributions and the earnings on employer and any employee contributions generally is excludible only in the case of a lump-sum distribution. The NUA on employer securities attributable to any employee contributions is excludible from any distribution.

[4] A recipient of employer securities may elect to waive this exclusion of NUA.

[5] There also had been a five-year forward averaging rule available in certain circumstances. However, five-year forward averaging has been repealed for tax years after 1999.

Options for Taxing Lump-Sum Distributions for Employees Age 50 or Older on January 1, 1986: These choices include (1) pay tax on the entire taxable amount as ordinary income at current income tax rates, (2) use a one-time 10-year averaging method using 1986 ordinary income tax rates, or (3) pay a flat capital gains tax on the pre-1974 portion of the taxable amount and use 10-year averaging for the remainder.

Lump-Sum Distributions Containing Employer Securities: As already explained, the NUA on employer securities in a lump-sum distribution is not taxed currently to the recipient. A participant's basis in the distributed securities is the same as their basis in the plan. Thus, when the participant subsequently sells the securities, the NUA and any subsequent gain or loss is subject to capital gains taxation. The NUA is considered long-term capital gain, while any subsequent gain or loss is either short-term or long-term, depending on how long the participant has held the securities since distribution. Upon a participant's death, the NUA does not get a stepped-up income tax basis. Instead, it is treated as income in respect of a decedent (IRD) to a plan beneficiary, who receives the securities in a lump-sum distribution, or to the recipient of the securities under the participant's will. The IRD is realized and recognized as long-term capital gain when the securities are sold by the beneficiary or heir.

Thus, the advantages of taking employer securities in a lump-sum distribution are that the tax on the NUA is deferred until the securities are finally sold (either by the participant or his or her heirs) and that the NUA is converted from ordinary income to a long-term capital gain. But the price for these advantages is that some tax, at ordinary income rates, must be paid immediately on part of the distribution.

Whether a lump-sum distribution or, alternatively, a direct transfer (rollover) to a traditional IRA is best depends on the circumstances. The factors determining which will provide the greatest after-tax results are as follows:

- The proportion of employer securities in the distribution
- The extent of NUA
- Taxable assets in the distribution and whether a partial rollover of assets other than the employer securities is done
- How and at what after-tax rate of return the securities and possibly the other assets will be invested once they are outside the plan
- The after-tax opportunity cost for tax currently paid
- An assumption about how long the employer securities will be held before they are sold and the capital gains tax rate at sale
- The period of deferral for the traditional IRA
- Whether any of the plan benefits are placed in a Roth IRA
- Whether the 10 percent tax on premature distributions will apply to the taxable part of the lump-sum distribution

This clearly is a complex analysis. Advisers may use computer programs to help in this decision.

CASE EXAMPLE

Suppose that Mary Johnson, age 60, has been employed by a rapidly growing corporation, the XYZ Company, for many years. She is a participant in the company's savings plan with a Section 401(k) option. Her total account balance in the plan is $685,000 and she has no investment (basis) in the plan. All of her employer's matching contributions have been invested in XYZ common stock (employer securities). Mary's elective contributions have been divided equally between XYZ stock and a bond fund. XYZ stock is publicly traded and has grown rapidly in value over the years. The current value of XYZ stock in Mary's account balance is $575,000 and it has a total basis to the plan (purchase price by the plan or value when contributed to the plan) of $120,000. The other $110,000 is in the bond fund.

Mary is retiring this year. If she takes a lump-sum distribution of the entire account balance in the savings plan (the only profit-sharing type plan provided by XYZ) and is in the 35 percent tax bracket, her potential taxable amount on the distribution will be as follows:

Total Lump-Sum Distribution	$685,000
Minus:	
Employee's investment (basis) in plan	0
NUA on employer securities	
($575,000 – $120,000)	–455,000
Potential taxable amount	$230,000

Assume Mary plans to rollover the potentially taxable amount of the distribution that is not in employer securities (i.e., the $110,000 in the bond fund) to her own traditional IRA and further defer the tax on this amount (a partial rollover). Thus, she must pay tax as ordinary income only on $120,000 (which is the basis of the XYZ stock to the plan). She plans to take this tax from other non-tax-advantaged assets. Thus, when the dust clears, Mary will have $575,000 of directly owned XYZ stock, with an income tax basis to her of $120,000 (the plan's basis on which she paid tax) and a traditional IRA with a $110,000 account balance. She will have paid $42,000 in tax ($120,000 × 0.35) from other assets. The XYZ stock may, of course, either increase or decrease in value. Mary may sell or otherwise dispose of the stock during her lifetime or hold it until her death and pass it to her heirs by will. At death, however, the NUA does not get a step-up in basis.

Alternatively, Mary could rollover the $685,000 account balance to a traditional IRA with no current tax liability. She then could withdraw from the IRA as she needs funds or continue to defer until her RBD (age 70½). However, all distributions from the IRA will be taxed as ordinary income. Mary might also rollover part or all of the account balance directly to a Roth IRA and pay tax on the amount rolled over.

Direct Transfers or 60-Day Rollovers to an IRA or Another Qualified Plan This may be done by either having the participant's employer transfer directly all or part of an eligible rollover distribution to a traditional IRA (or Roth IRA with current taxation) or to another qualified retirement plan (or TSA) that will accept such transfers; or having the distribution paid to the participating employee, who then rolls over all or part of the distribution to an IRA or to another qualified plan (or TSA) within 60 days of receipt of the distribution.

For this purpose, an *eligible rollover distribution* is any distribution of all or any portion of the balance to the credit of the employee in a qualified retirement plan (or tax-sheltered annuity); except that it does not include distributions made as substantially equal periodic payments over the lifetime (or life expectancy) of the employee or the lifetimes (or life expectancies) of the employee and his or her designated beneficiary, or distributions for a specified period of 10 years or more, or distributions required to satisfy the minimum distribution rules. Direct transfers and rollovers can be made regardless of an employee's age, are available for any number of eligible distributions, and are not subject to any dollar limit on the amount that can be transferred or rolled over. There also is no triggering-event requirement. Any part or all of an employee's balance in the plan can be an eligible rollover distribution. The entire amount of an eligible distribution may be transferred to a traditional IRA, a Roth IRA (subject to current taxation), or a qualified plan or TSA, or qualified plan, including any employee after-tax contributions, if the qualified plan agrees to separately track the after-tax contributions and their earnings.

To the extent that an otherwise taxable distribution is directly transferred or rolled over, it is not currently taxable (except to rollovers to a Roth IRA) and will be taxed only when paid out to the employee or his or her beneficiary from the traditional IRA or other plan. However, there is a mandatory 20 percent income tax withholding requirement applicable to eligible rollover distributions, except when the distributee elects to have the distribution directly transferred. Thus, a 60-day rollover is subject to mandatory 20 percent withholding, while a direct transfer is not. This distinction strongly favors direct transfers over 60-day rollovers.

In the event a surviving spouse of a deceased participant in a qualified retirement plan, 403(b), or other eligible plan receives an eligible rollover distribution from the plan, as beneficiary, the spouse also may directly transfer or roll the distribution over to the spouse's own IRA or to another qualified retirement plan, TSA, or Section 457 plan in which the spouse participates. Aside from a surviving spouse, no other beneficiary of the plan's death benefits can avail themselves of this rollover treatment.

However, PPA of 2006 provided a different, but important, rollover provision for nonspouse beneficiaries of deceased participants in qualified plans, TSAs, and Section 457 plans. These beneficiaries (including the trustees of trusts named as plan beneficiaries for the benefit of nonspouse beneficiaries) can directly transfer (a trustee-to-trustee transfer) the plan's death benefits to an IRA established by the beneficiary to receive them on behalf of the nonspouse beneficiary. This IRA is in the deceased participant's name but is for the benefit of the nonspouse beneficiary (an inherited IRA). Thus, the nonspouse beneficiary does not own this IRA in the same way that a surviving spouse does in the case of a spousal rollover. However, once the plan's death benefit is in the inherited IRA account, the IRA custodian or trustee will allow the distribution to be paid out over the life expectancy of the non-spouse beneficiary or the remaining life expectancy of the decedent under the minimum distribution rules explained later in this chapter.

Penalty Tax on Premature Distributions In an effort to discourage withdrawals from tax-advantaged retirement plans prior to retirement, the tax law imposes an additional 10 percent excise tax on the taxable portion of distributions from such plans made prior to age 59½, subject to certain exceptions. This 10 percent penalty tax is in addition to the regular income tax paid.

For qualified retirement plans, aside from reaching age 59½, the other exceptions to the imposition of this tax include:

- Distributions made on or after the employee's death
- Distributions due to an employee's disability
- Payments made as substantially equal periodic benefits for the lifetime or life expectancy of the employee (or for the joint lives or expectancies of the employee and his or her beneficiary)
- Distributions to an employee after attaining age 55 upon separation from service

- Distributions to an employee for deductible medical expenses
- Distributions to persons (alternate payees) under QDROs
- Certain other distributions

This 10 percent tax applies to qualified retirement plans, TSA plans, and IRAs. Note that the exceptions for IRAs are somewhat different from those just outlined. TSAs also have some differences in their exceptions.

Required Beginning Date (RBD) and Minimum Distribution Rules The tax law requires that persons participating in qualified retirement plans, traditional IRAs, TSAs, and Section 457 plans must meet certain minimum distribution rules. There are three elements in determining the minimum amounts that must be distributed: the required beginning date, the amount of the IRA owner's or plan participant's benefit in the plan as of the valuation date, and the minimum required distribution periods (or divisors) for employees' or owners' ages according to the IRS's Uniform Lifetime Table. There also are special rules when an owner's or participant's spouse is the plan beneficiary. It is important to comply with these rules, because there is a 50 percent penalty tax on the difference between what was actually distributed in a given year and what should have been distributed under the minimum distribution rules. This is called the *penalty tax on insufficient distributions.*

Required Beginning Date (RBD): Distributions from qualified retirement plans to participants generally must begin by either April 1 of the calendar year following the calendar year in which the person attains age 70½ or April 1 of the calendar year following the calendar year in which the person retires (but this retirement date applies only if the participant is not more than a 5 percent owner of the sponsoring employer), whichever is later. Distributions from traditional IRAs to owners must begin no later than April 1 of the calendar year following the calendar year in which the owner attains age 70½.

Distributions Before the RBD: Before the RBD, distributions can or cannot be taken at the discretion of the participant or IRA owner.

Benefit Amount and Valuation Date: For *qualified individual account plans* (e.g., profit-sharing plans and 401(k) plans), the benefit for calculating the minimum distribution is the plan's account balance as of the plan's last valuation date in the calendar year preceding the calendar year of the distribution (with certain adjustments). For *traditional IRAs,* the benefit amount is the plan's account balance on December 31 of the calendar year preceding the calendar year of the distribution.

Minimum Distribution Rules for Distributions at and After the RBD and Before Death: Once an IRA owner or plan participant reaches the RBD, he or she must begin taking a minimum distribution each year from the plans just noted.[6]

The minimum amount that must be distributed from a plan (whose benefits are not paid as a life annuity) for the first required distribution year is determined by dividing the owner's or participant's benefit in the plan by the distribution period (or applicable divisor) from the Uniform Lifetime Table for the owner's or participant's age at the end of each distribution year. For example, this period (divisor) is 27.4 for age 70 and 26.5 for age 71.[7] This is referred to as *recalculation.* It is used for the participant or owner of a plan and a surviving spouse as direct beneficiary. Its importance lies in the fact that while the divisor declines each year as the person gets older, it does not decline by one full year. Thus, there is always some divisor and so the plan balance is never completely exhausted. This slows distributions and enhances deferral.

For years after the first distribution year, the minimum distribution is determined by dividing the owner's or participant's benefit in the plan, as of the prior year, by the applicable period (divisor) for the owner's or participant's age at the end of the current year. A distribution period is given in the IRS Uniform Lifetime Table for each age up to 115 and over.[8] These periods gradually diminish with age. For example, the period for age 75 is 22.9 and for age 85 is 14.8. Aside from the exception to be noted next, the periods (divisors) to be used for minimum distribution calculations during the IRA owner's or plan participant's lifetime are not affected by the plan's

[6] As of this writing, the minimum distribution requirements have been suspended for 2009 as part of the government's economic stimulus program.

[7] As just noted, the first distribution must be made by April 1 of the calendar year following the calendar year in which the IRA owner or retired qualified plan participant becomes age 70½ (the RBD). Then, distributions must be made by December 31 for each year after the 70½ year. This means there will be a doubling up of distributions in the calendar year following the 70½ year if the participant delays taking his or her first distribution until the year (by April 1) following the 70½ year. For example, assume that Howard Schwartz became age 70 on February 2, 2006, and is the owner of a traditional IRA. If he takes his first distribution on April 1, 2007 (for the first required distribution year of 2006), he also must take a distribution by December 31, 2007 (for 2007). Then, at a minimum, he must take a distribution by December 31 of each succeeding year. This may require some planning because such doubling up of distributions and hence taxable income in the calendar year following the 70½ year may be undesirable in some cases due to higher income tax rates and taxes. Thus, in these cases, it may be better income tax–wise to take the first required distribution in the 70½ year and spread the taxable income more. This decision depends on the person's circumstances, tax rates, and expected income in the two years.

[8] This "Uniform Lifetime Table" is based on joint life expectancies (on a gender neutral basis) starting at age 70 for an employee or owner and a hypothetical individual beneficiary who is 10 years younger than the employee or owner.

beneficiary designation. On the other hand, after an IRA owner's or plan participant's death, the minimum required distributions of any remaining account balances are determined by the beneficiary designation.

The exception just noted is when the owner or participant names his or her spouse, who is *more than* 10 years younger than the owner or participant, as the sole primary plan beneficiary. In this case, their actual joint life expectancies each year can be used to calculate the minimum required distributions as long as both are alive. This will produce lower required minimum distributions than the IRS Uniform Table.

Defined-Benefit Plans and the Minimum Distribution Rules: For *defined-benefit plans* with their benefits payable as a *life income*, the minimum distribution rules will be met by level payments made at least annually, commencing on or before the RBD, over the life of the participant or the joint and survivor lives of the participant and his or her spouse as designated beneficiary.[9]

CASE EXAMPLE

It may be helpful at this point to illustrate these rules with a common situation. Suppose Martin and Sara Wilson are married, and Martin retired eight years ago when he was age 62 and Sara was age 57. Sara is a self-employed consulting engineer, and Martin had been an executive for a large corporation. Since Martin retired, they have had more-than-adequate income from Social Security, a joint and 50 percent to the survivor life income from Martin's defined-benefit pension plan, current returns from their investment portfolios, and consulting work that Sara still does. Martin also was a participant in a qualified savings plan with a Section 401(k) option (in which he has no cost basis), with an account balance at his retirement of $280,000. Sara and Martin have one son and three grandchildren to whom they would like to leave as much of their assets as possible after their deaths.

At his retirement, Martin rolled over the entire $280,000 savings plan balance to a traditional IRA and named Sara as designated beneficiary.[10] The IRA has had an average annual total rate

[9] If the designated beneficiary is someone other than the spouse, certain minimum distribution incidental death benefit (MDIB) rules must be met. There also are special rules for period-certain guarantees.

[10] Note that, unlike the situation for the qualified savings plan, the REA does not apply to an IRA; therefore, Martin could name anyone he wishes as beneficiary of his IRA. In this situation, however, he decided to name his spouse. This has many advantages for both qualified plans and IRAs. However, it also means the spouse will have complete control over the funds after the owner's (Martin's) death. This is something to consider in planning. Its importance depends on the circumstances (state of the marriage, children from prior marriages, and so forth).

of return of about 8 percent per year over the last eight years. The account balance as of December 31, 2005 (the valuation date), was $518,260 (we will round down to $518,000 for this example).

Martin turned 70 on February 1, 2006, and Sara was age 65 on March 5, 2006. Martin's RBD is April 1, 2007, and his first required distribution year (70½ year) is 2006. The first required minimum distribution for 2006 would be determined by dividing the IRA account balance as of the valuation date (December 31 of the preceding year) of $518,000 by the Uniform Table divisor for age 70 (Martin's age at the end of 2006), which is 27.4. Note that Sara's age does not affect the divisor because she is not more than 10 years younger than Martin.[11] Thus, the minimum distribution for 2006 is $18,905 ($518,000 ÷ 27.4) and the account balance on December 31, 2006 (assuming an 8 percent total return for all of 2006), would be $540,535 ($518,000 + $41,440 investment return – $18,905 minimum distribution). The minimum distribution for the next year (2007) would be $20,398 ($540,535 ÷ 26.5) and the account balance on December 31, 2007, would be $563,380 ($540,535 + $43,243 investment return – $20,398 minimum distribution).[12]

This procedure will continue over Martin's lifetime. Computer programs are available to show this under various assumptions. Financial institutions (e.g., the custodian for Martin's IRA) normally will perform these calculations for their customers. Depending on investment yields, the value of the account normally will continue to grow for a number of years after the RBD, until it begins to decline because of the constantly declining divisors and hence increasing minimum distributions required.

Designated Beneficiaries: A *designated beneficiary* is any identifiable individual designated by a participant or owner to receive any remaining plan benefits after the participant's or owner's death. The beneficiary may be any person or persons. But if a participant is married and names anyone other than his or her spouse, the proper waiver and spousal consent requirements of REA must be observed if REA applies to the plan.

[11] But if we were to change the facts and say that Sara is age 50 in 2006, then the divisor would be based on their actual joint life expectancies each year from the IRS Joint and Last Survivor Table. This divisor for a person age 70 and another person age 50 is 35.1. This divisor would be recalculated each year Martin and Sara are alive.

[12] Under the minimum distribution rules, Martin could defer taking the first distribution until April 1, 2007, but for the reasons given in Footnote 6, let us assume he takes his minimum distribution for each year as of December 31 of that year.

If a participant or owner designates *multiple beneficiaries*, the person with the shortest life expectancy is considered the designated beneficiary. A participant or owner also can name a designated beneficiary or beneficiaries by an identifiable status or class, such as children of the participant, provided the beneficiary or beneficiaries themselves are identifiable.

Because of the rules concerning multiple beneficiaries, a useful planning technique when there are to be several beneficiaries of an IRA is to request the IRA custodian or trustee to divide the IRA account into subaccounts or sub-IRAs (within the original IRA), with one subaccount for each beneficiary. Then each beneficiary is the designated beneficiary of his or her subaccount, and his or her own life expectancy will govern minimum distributions. This planning approach is discussed later in the chapter.

A trust can be named as beneficiary to receive any remaining plan benefits after a participant's or owner's death. In that event, the individuals who are beneficiaries of the trust can be considered as designated beneficiaries for purposes of the minimum distribution rules, provided the trust meets certain requirements. These are called *see-through trusts* and:

- They must be valid under applicable state law.
- They must be irrevocable, or by their terms will become irrevocable at the participant's or owner's death.
- The trust beneficiaries must be individuals and be identifiable from the trust instrument.
- A copy of the trust instrument must be provided to the plan administrator or IRA custodian, or a list of beneficiaries with a description of the conditions of their entitlement must be provided.

Another kind of trust where the individual trust beneficiaries can be considered designated beneficiaries is called a *conduit trust.* A conduit trust is the same as a see-through trust except that the trustee must distribute to an individual trust beneficiary any distribution the trustee receives from the retirement plan. This means the trustee cannot accumulate plan distributions in the trust as is possible for a see-through trust.

The significance of being a "designated beneficiary" is that the life expectancy of a designated beneficiary, whether named directly or as a beneficiary of a see-through trust, may be used to determine the required minimum distributions after a participant's or owner's death. The rules regarding minimum distributions after death are discussed in the next section.

There can be plan beneficiaries who are not "designated beneficiaries," such as charities, a trust that is not a see-through trust, or the participant's or owner's estate. In this case, no life expectancy is used and any remaining account balance must be paid out within five years after the year of the participant's or owner's death (the "five-year rule"). Furthermore, if there are multiple beneficiaries and some are designated beneficiaries but one or more are not, then none will be considered designated beneficiaries. For example, if an IRA owner with a $1,300,000 account balance names a charity as a beneficiary to receive $100,000 and names her three children as equal beneficiaries to receive the balance, since the charity is not a designated beneficiary (even though the children are), at the owner's death none will be considered designated beneficiaries and the five-year rule will apply.

However, a helpful rule is that the identity of a designated beneficiary does not need to be finally determined until September 30 of the calendar year following the year in which the participant or owner dies. The importance of this is that planning actions can be taken after the owner's or participant's death and before this September 30 date) to produce the most appropriate designated beneficiary or beneficiaries for tax-deferral purposes. Such actions may include disclaimers by one or more beneficiaries (disclaimers are covered in Chapter 26); total distributions ("cash-outs") to some beneficiaries (such as charities); and account divisions in the case of multiple individual designated beneficiaries. For example, in the case situation in the previous paragraph, the $100,000 could be paid to the charity before the September 30 date (i.e., it could be "cashed out"). Then, on the September 30 date there would be only individual designated beneficiaries and their life expectancies could be used for minimum distribution planning.

However, this does not mean that, for example, a deceased owner's or participant's executor can name one or more new designated beneficiaries after the owner's or participant's death. The owner or participant should name the beneficiary or beneficiaries he or she wants prior to his or her death. It is just that these planning actions can deal with an existing beneficiary designation.

Minimum Distribution Rules After an Owner's or Participant's Death Before the RBD: In this event, the required minimum distributions depend on whether a surviving spouse is the sole primary designated beneficiary (either directly or as the sole designated beneficiary of a trust),[13] an individual other than the spouse is the designated beneficiary, or there is no designated beneficiary (e.g., a charity or the decedent's estate is named as beneficiary).

When a *surviving spouse* is sole primary designated beneficiary, the required minimum distributions may begin either by December 31 of the calendar year following the year of the owner's or participant's death, or by

[13] A spouse is the sole designated beneficiary of a trust when he or she can withdraw all distributions to the trust from the IRA or plan.

December 31 of the year in which the decedent would have reached age 70½, whichever is later. The decedent's interest in the plan or IRA may be paid out in annual amounts over the life expectancy of the spouse, determined each year from the Uniform Lifetime Table with recalculation. Upon the spouse's subsequent death, any remaining balance may be paid out in annual amounts to the spouse's estate or to a subsequent designated beneficiary over the deceased spouse's life expectancy as of the date of his or her death and subtracting one year for each year thereafter.

When *someone other than the spouse* is the designated beneficiary (children, for example), the required minimum distributions must begin no later than December 31 of the calendar year following the owner's or participant's death. Then, the decedent's interest in the plan or IRA may be paid out in annual amounts over the life expectancy of the designated beneficiary as of the year after the owner's or participant's death using the Single Life Table and subtracting one year for each year thereafter.

The rules just stated for spousal designated beneficiaries and nonspousal designated beneficiaries involve the *life expectancy distribution option.* This option requires minimum annual distributions over a beneficiary's life expectancy (i.e., the account balance at the end of the previous year divided by the life expectancy number for the distribution year). This can be a relatively long time and result in considerable income tax deferral. For example, under the IRS Single Life Table, life expectancies are 43.6 years for age 40, 34.2 years for age 50, and 25.2 years for age 60.

On the other hand, when the beneficiary is *not a designated beneficiary,* a different rule applies. In this case, the decedent's entire interest in the plan must be distributed to the beneficiary by the end of the fifth year following the year of death. This is known as the *five-year rule.* It clearly provides much less opportunity for tax deferral than the life expectancy option.

Minimum Distribution Rules After an Owner's or Participant's Death After the RBD: These are similar to the rules just described, but with some differences. When a *surviving spouse* is the sole primary designated beneficiary, the required minimum distributions must begin by December 31 of the calendar year following the year of the owner's or participant's death. The decedent's remaining interest in the plan or IRA then may be paid out in annual amounts over the spouse's life expectancy, determined each year from the Uniform Lifetime Table with recalculation. Upon the spouse's death, the treatment is the same as described previously for death before the RBD.

When *someone other than the spouse* is the designated beneficiary, minimum distributions must begin by December 31 of the calendar year following the year of the owner's or participant's death, and the plan balance may be paid out in annual amounts over the life expectancy of the designated beneficiary as of the year after the owner's or participant's death using the Single Life Table and subtracting one year for each year thereafter.

When the beneficiary is not classified as a designated beneficiary, distributions must begin by December 31 of the year following the year of death. But in this case, the plan balance may be paid out in annual amounts over the life expectancy of someone the age of the deceased owner or participant as of the year of the owner's or participant's death using the Single Life Table and subtracting one year for each year thereafter.

With regard to the previously discussed minimum distribution rules, it should be noted that an IRA agreement or the provisions of a qualified plan can specify whether the five-year rule or the life expectancy option is to apply, or the plan terms can permit either the participant or owner, or the beneficiary, to choose which rule applies. As a practiced matter, qualified retirement plans usually require that the decedent's plan balance be paid out to the beneficiary immediately or within the five-year rule allowing little or no deferral. IRA agreements, on the other hand, normally allow the life expectancy option. Therefore, if a participant in a qualified plan dies and deferral is desired for the designated beneficiary (as it usually is), it is desirable to roll the decedent's account balance over into an IRA for the beneficiary. This could always be done if the designated beneficiary were the participant-decedent's surviving spouse who could roll the account balance over into his or her own IRA. Fortunately, PPA of 2006 now also allows a nonspouse designated beneficiary to directly transfer the qualified plan account balance to an inherited IRA for the beneficiary and thus be able to utilize the beneficiary's life expectancy.

A designated beneficiary can be named directly or indirectly as an identifiable beneficiary of a see-through trust meeting the requirements noted earlier. If a trust does not meet these requirements, the five-year rule or the owner or participant age life expectancy rule applies. But if a trust for the spouse is named as beneficiary (even if the spouse is designated beneficiary of the trust), the spouse in most cases cannot transfer (roll over) plan benefits to his or her own IRA or treat an IRA as his or her own, as a surviving spouse could if named as the individual designated beneficiary.

Rollover Option for Surviving Spouse Only: When a surviving spouse is the sole primary designated beneficiary of a qualified plan or IRA, an alternative to taking distributions under the rules just described is to rollover the account balance to the spouse's own traditional IRA or to treat the decedent's IRA as the spouse's IRA. In this case, the minimum distribution rules apply to the IRA as the spouse's own IRA and hence distributions would not have to begin until the spouse's own RBD (spouse's age 70½). This may be an attractive alternative, particularly if the spouse is younger than the participant.

The spouse also could convert or rollover to a Roth IRA (if eligible) and then delay distributions from the Roth IRA until the spouse's death.

Then, we assume that the spouse names, for example, a child or children as the designated beneficiary or beneficiaries of the spouse's IRA (either traditional or Roth), the IRA balance could be paid annually over the life expectancy of the designated beneficiary or beneficiaries (the children) using the Single Life Table and subtracting one year for each year thereafter after the spouse's death. This could allow a long period of tax deferral or tax-free growth. This is the concept of the "stretch IRA."

Also, if the designated beneficiary of an IRA is the spouse of a deceased owner, the surviving spouse may elect to assume the IRA and treat it as if it were his or her own, or roll it over into another IRA as if the surviving spouse had originally established it. In either event, the minimum distribution rules for IRAs would apply just as for the spouse's own IRA. Thus, the RBD for a traditional IRA would be the surviving spouse's age 70½. Distributions from a Roth IRA would not have to start until the surviving spouse's death and then would be payable to a designated beneficiary or beneficiaries, as just noted.

Rollover (Direct Transfer) Option for Nonspouse Beneficiaries: As already explained, PPA of 2006 now allows a nonspouse designated beneficiary to directly transfer the account balance of a deceased participant in a qualified retirement plan, TSA, or Section 457 plan to an inherited IRA for the beneficiary. A nonspouse beneficiary of a deceased IRA owner's IRA can also treat it as an inherited IRA.

Federal Estate Taxation

The full value of any death benefits payable under a qualified retirement plan, TSA, traditional or Roth IRA, or similar plan are includible in the decedent's gross estate for federal estate tax purposes. To the extent that such death benefits are payable to a decedent's surviving spouse (either directly or through a qualifying trust), they will qualify for the marital deduction and be deductible from the gross estate in arriving at the taxable estate. (See Chapter 26.)

Married persons with estates large enough to need federal estate tax planning may want to have qualified plan and IRA death benefits qualify for the marital deduction. It can be argued that these often are good kinds of property interests to qualify because they generally are *wasting assets.* That is, they are burdened with an inherent income tax liability at the time of any distribution (except for Roth IRAs) to the surviving spouse, which will further reduce the surviving spouse's own estate at his or her subsequent death. This planning idea really is true of any IRD item in the gross estate.

There are several ways these death benefits can be made to qualify for the marital deduction, including by being payable:

- In a lump sum to the surviving spouse as beneficiary[14]
- As a joint life and last survivor annuity for the participant and his or her spouse if no person other than the participant and his or her spouse can receive any payments prior to the death of the last spouse to die
- To a trust that will qualify for the marital deduction

The planning issues involving these methods are discussed in the final section of this chapter.

Generation-Skipping Transfer (GST) Taxation

In some cases, a GST tax might apply to qualified plan or IRA death benefits. The GST tax is described more fully in Chapter 26.

Planning for Distributions from Qualified Retirement Plans and IRAs

Planning for these benefits is an extensive subject. Only the salient issues are presented here. In doing so, we have divided the issues into those applying while a participant (or owner) is still in service, at separation from service before retirement (as when the person changes jobs or is laid off), at retirement, and at death.

While in Service

Plan participants may face several issues while in service. Some of these have already been discussed. With regard to getting cash from qualified plans while still in service, the choices may be:

- Use of plan loans.
- Possible in-service withdrawals. While such withdrawals may be permitted in some cases, they have lost much of their attraction.

[14]Another approach to this issue is to name the spouse as beneficiary and then, after the participant's or owner's death, the spouse at his or her option can *disclaim* (meeting the tax requirements for a valid disclaimer) part or all of the plan benefits, with those benefits then going into a nonmarital trust or other trust. This, in effect, allows the surviving spouse to fund a nonmarital trust or gift if he or she wishes to do so for estate planning reasons. This approach may be particularly useful after EGTRRA.

At Separation from Service Prior to Retirement

With regard to vested qualified plan benefits, the choices may be as follows:

- Leave vested benefits in the former employer's plan if permitted. However, the person's rights to the benefits then will depend on the plan's terms.
- Take a lump-sum distribution. This will be discussed more fully in the next section.
- Elect a direct transfer to an IRA, to a new employer's qualified plan (if that plan accepts such transfers), or to another eligible plan. This also is covered more fully in the next section.

At Retirement

Again, many planning issues face the former employee (and his or her spouse, if any). With regard to qualified plan and IRA benefits at retirement, there may be the choices discussed in the following sections.

Receiving Periodic Annuity Income (and What Annuity Form to Select)

Some plans contemplate the taking of retirement benefits as a life annuity or a joint life and last survivor annuity. There are two basic planning issues in this area: whether to take benefits as a life income or as a lump sum (if available) and if a life income is desired, selecting the annuity form.

Advantages of Lifetime Annuity Income:

- Security of income for life. This is one of the basic purposes of a pension plan. Also, if a joint life and last survivor annuity form is chosen, a lifetime income can be guaranteed for the retiring employee or IRA owner and his or her spouse. It gives them an income they cannot outlive.
- The retiree may be able to secure relatively generous life annuity rates from a pension plan or perhaps even under a defined-contribution plan. On the other hand, the reverse also may be true. This factor simply must be evaluated in each case based on the annuity income from the plan compared with what can be received or earned on a lump sum outside the plan after taxes.
- For married retirees, this is the form of pension plan benefit mandated by the REA (a QJSA), unless the employee waives it and his or her spouse consents in the proper form.
- Some employers may make voluntary increases for inflation in lifetime pension benefits. If benefits are taken as a lump sum, such adjustments will be lost in the future.

- The retiree may need the largest available current income to make retirement financially feasible.
- The retiree and his or her spouse are relieved of the need to make investment decisions concerning lump-sum distributions.

Limitations of Lifetime Annuity Income: On the other hand, there may be disadvantages of a life annuity.

- The *annuity risk* or *mortality risk* is perhaps the most important, since there is a loss of capital at the retired employee's or spouse's death. Therefore, a person or couple, in making this decision, might want to evaluate what kind of after-tax investment yield they can conservatively secure on the capital that would result from any available lump-sum distribution. Alternatively, they might evaluate the return while they are alive and what would remain for their beneficiaries after their deaths from a rollover IRA.
- Loss of flexibility (investment, withdrawal, etc.) inherent in taking a lifetime annuity income.
- Loss of possible tax advantages of a lump-sum distribution, particularly if the distribution contains appreciated employer securities (NUA).
- The retiree and his or her spouse will be dependent on the financial soundness of the funding agency (a pension trust or life insurance company) for a long time. On the other hand, with their own investments (from a lump-sum distribution) or their own IRA (from a rollover IRA), they can change investments or financial intermediaries quite easily. They may also be able to convert a rollover traditional IRA to a Roth IRA. However, the PBGC does cover defined-benefit pension income from insolvent plans up to a limit.
- A life annuity is not a good choice if the retiree is in poor health.

Deciding What Annuity Form to Use: Assuming a retiring employee and his or her spouse, if married, have decided to take some or all of their retirement benefits as a life annuity (or in installments), they now must decide what kind of annuity among those offered by the plan to use. This is known as selecting the *annuity form.* The following are various kinds of annuity forms that could be available under qualified retirement plans. They are described more fully in Chapters 17 and 21.

- Single (or straight) life annuity.
- Joint life annuity with a 50 percent survivor's benefit to the second annuitant. This is the minimum QJSA form described previously.
- Other joint life and last survivor annuity forms.
- Life annuities with various refund features.
- Payments for a fixed period or in a fixed amount.

An important planning issue in selecting the annuity form is how much, if any, benefit is to be provided for a survivor. A factor in this decision is how much, if any, a straight life annuity will be reduced for the QJSA (or other survivorship) protection for a surviving spouse. This actuarial reduction, if any, varies among plans, but is normally less when the parties are younger. The following are some sample reduction factors for one corporate pension plan.

Ages at Retirement		Percentage by Which Single Life Annuity Will Be Reduced for QJSA Form
Plan Participant	**Spouse**	
55	55	7.5%
60	60	9.0%
65	65	10.7%

In general, unless there are other resources or existing life insurance to protect a surviving spouse, it probably is logical to accept the QJSA form or even to use a larger survivor's percentage to protect a surviving spouse if a life annuity is being taken. Of course, if a QJSA form is subsidized by a particular employer, there really is no choice.

Taking a Lump-Sum Distribution and Paying Some Tax Currently Following are some of the reasons to take this approach:

- The main reason would be if there is favorable income tax treatment, such as NUA on employer securities (as illustrated earlier) and possible transitional tax rules.
- After the distribution, the participant gains complete investment and other control over the funds (after taxes).
- The participant and his or her spouse may feel that income tax rates are relatively low currently, compared to what they might be in the future. However, this kind of guesstimate can be uncertain.
- In some cases, defined-benefit pension plans may offer relatively liberal lump-sum options.
- It may be convenient to take smaller benefits as a lump-sum distribution.

Making a Direct Transfer to a Rollover IRA Such transfers to an IRA can be quite advantageous.

- There is no current income tax for traditional IRAs.
- The investment income and realized and unrealized capital gains on the amount transferred continue to accumulate income tax–deferred or –free.
- The IRA owner generally can decide when to take money from the IRA. However, the owner must comply with the minimum distribution rules.

- A traditional IRA owner (or his or her surviving spouse) can convert a traditional IRA to a Roth IRA over time (i.e., to spread out the tax payments).
- The owner has control over the IRA and, if the owner chooses, can direct its investments over a broad range of investment instruments. Furthermore, if the owner wishes a life annuity, he or she can place originally, transfer, or roll over the IRA to a life insurance company individual retirement annuity.
- A surviving spouse as beneficiary can assume the IRA and treat it as his or her own with no current income taxation.
- The REA rules do not apply to IRAs. Therefore, from the viewpoint of the plan participant, to the extent the REA rules may cause estate planning complications, being free of them may be an advantage. On the other hand, from the viewpoint of the participant's spouse, the reverse may be true, and REA protection may be lost. In reality, this may or may not be a controversial issue, depending on the circumstances.
- A rollover now can also be made from a qualified plan or TSA directly to a Roth IRA.
- In some cases, defined-benefit pension plans may offer relatively liberal rollover eligible distributions.

Leaving Benefits in a Former Employer's Plan This may be done if the plan's terms permit it. It may be attractive if the plan has especially favorable investment options or other features. Depending on state law, there also may be more favorable creditor protection for assets in a qualified plan than in an IRA. On the other hand, the terms of the plan will continue to apply to the retiree's account, and the REA rules will apply.

General Considerations on Taking Plan Benefits at Retirement Unfortunately, there are no pat answers for this important decision. It depends largely on the facts and circumstances of each case. However, the following general principles may be helpful:

- With respect to many retirees, it probably is wise to provide at least a base level of guaranteed lifetime income for the person or couple.
- If the special tax advantages of a lump-sum distribution (e.g., a large amount of highly appreciated employer securities with substantial NUA) are especially significant in a particular case, the participant might consider taking a lump-sum distribution and paying some tax currently.
- If a retiree wants flexibility, control, and yet continued income tax deferral, often little would seem to be lost by transferring to a rollover traditional IRA and then making withdrawal or conversion decisions later.

- If a traditional IRA owner wants long-term tax-free deferral and wealth growth for himself or herself, or his or her heirs, a conversion or direct rollover to a Roth IRA should be considered, provided the owner can afford (or can finance) the tax on conversion or rollover.
- There may well be merit in following a diversified approach to taking retirement plan benefits. For example, a person or couple may take a lifetime retirement income from a defined-benefit pension plan and then directly transfer the account balance from a defined-contribution plan to an IRA.

Death Benefits Under Qualified Plans and IRAs

Kinds of Death Benefits There may be significant death benefits prior to retirement as well as after retirement.

Preretirement death benefits may include:

- QPSA (under REA)
- Account balances under DC plans and IRAs
- Incidental life insurance as part of a qualified plan

Postretirement death benefits may include:

- QJSA (under REA) or other survivors' benefits
- Any remaining account balances under DC plans and IRAs

Strategies for Naming Beneficiaries of Death Benefits This choice really is part of the owner's or participant's estate planning. If the primary beneficiary is an individual, a contingent beneficiary or beneficiaries normally should be named to take the benefits in the event the primary beneficiary predeceases the owner or participant. Details on beneficiaries is given in the following sections.

The Owner's or Participant's Spouse Directly (Outright): This is a common choice and offers many advantages. These include the ability to rollover qualified plan's death benefits to his or her own traditional IRA, or to assume a deceased spouse's IRA as his or her own, and hence, defer income taxation; the ability to qualify for the federal estate tax marital deduction, and hence, defer estate taxation; and exemption from the REA rules for qualified plans other than pension plans. On the other hand, this gives the surviving spouse complete control over the death benefits after the owner's or participant's death. For personal, family (e.g., a second marriage), or estate planning reasons, this may not be acceptable in some cases.

A planning technique that may be used in some cases is to name the spouse as primary beneficiary with a trust (that can skip the spouse's estate for estate tax purposes—a nonmarital or credit-shelter trust as described in

Chapter 28) named as contingent beneficiary. Then, after the owner's or participant's death, the surviving spouse can decide whether to take the death benefit as the designated beneficiary or transfer it to his or her own IRA, or disclaim[15] part or all of the death benefit within nine months after the owner's or participant's death and have the disclaimed part pass to the trust, which would avoid overqualifying the decedent's estate for the marital deductions and reduce estate taxes. This decision will depend on the circumstances after the owner's or participant's death. Of course, this technique also gives the surviving spouse complete control after death.

An Individual or Individuals Other Than the Spouse Directly (e.g., a Child or Children): As indicated earlier, if multiple beneficiaries are to be named, a useful planning technique to attain maximum income tax deferral after death is to divide an IRA into separate IRAs or to request the IRA custodian or trustee to divide the IRA account into subaccounts or sub-IRAs, with one for each beneficiary. Then, each beneficiary's life expectancy will govern minimum distributions from his or her IRA or subaccount.

CASE EXAMPLE

Assume Helen Smith died, leaving her husband, Frank, as primary beneficiary of her $1,100,000 401(k) account. After Helen's death, Frank decides to roll over the account balance to his own traditional IRA. The Smiths have three children: Tom, Susan, and Mary. Frank wants to name his (and Helen's) three children as equal beneficiaries of his IRA. Assume further that Frank tragically is killed in an automobile accident two years later, when the account balance in his IRA is $1,200,000, and in the year after his death, the children's ages are as follows: Tom, age 55; Susan, age 52; and Mary, age 38.

If Frank simply named the children as equal multiple beneficiaries of his one IRA, Tom, age 55, who has the shortest life expectancy, would be considered the designated beneficiary and the entire IRA account balance would have to be paid out in annual amounts to the beneficiaries over Tom's life expectancy of 29.6 years (based on the Single Life Table and reduced by one year for each subsequent year). This means the entire account balance would have to be distributed to all beneficiaries within about 30 years since the 29.6 life expectancy number is reduced by one each year thereafter. On the other hand, if Frank had provided for the division of his IRA into a separate IRA (or subaccount)

[15] Qualified disclaimers are described in Chapter 26.

for each beneficiary (of about $400,000 each), each child's own life expectancy (as designated beneficiary) would govern the minimum distributions to him or her starting the year after their father's death. This would be expectancies of 29.6 years for Tom, 32.3 years for Susan, and 45.6 years for Mary. The result would be substantially longer tax deferral (about 16 years, or 56 percent longer for the youngest beneficiary in this example).[16]

A Trust That Qualifies for the Federal Estate Tax Marital Deduction (a Marital Trust): This would be a trust for the surviving spouse's benefit during his or her lifetime, and then the corpus would pass to others at the surviving spouse's death. The benefits (trust corpus) would qualify for the federal estate tax marital deduction, so estate taxation would be deferred. Furthermore, if the trust meets the requirements described earlier, the surviving spouse, as beneficiary of the trust, will be considered the designated beneficiary for purposes of the minimum distribution rules, and plan or IRA benefits could be paid out in annual amounts over the spouse's life expectancy, determined by his or her age in each distribution year (i.e., recalculated). However, the rules for both minimum distributions and qualifying for the marital deduction must be met. Also, rollover of qualified plan balances to IRAs or treating IRAs as his or her own generally would not be available to a surviving spouse since he or she would not be the outright beneficiary. In addition, there would be no exemption from the REA and so the spouse would have to consent in the proper form for qualified plans.

A Trust That Does Not Qualify for the Federal Estate Tax Marital Deduction (a Nonmarital, Credit Shelter, or Bypass Trust): In essence, the corpus of these trusts is intended to be subject to federal estate taxation in the decedent's estate, but the estate tax is absorbed by the applicable credit amount (unified credit). Plan benefits might have to be paid to such a trust for estate planning reasons, usually because there are not enough other assets in the estate to fund such a trust at death. In general, however, use of qualified plan, TSA, or traditional IRA death benefits to fund nonmarital trusts is not attractive because they are IRD items. (See Chapter 28 for a more complete discussion of marital deduction planning.) Also note the use of such nonmarital trusts as contingent beneficiaries discussed previously.

[16] It may be noted that these principles and results would be substantially the same after Frank's death if this had been a Roth IRA (converted by Frank from his traditional IRA), except that Frank would not have had to take any minimum distributions during his lifetime, and so the balance would have been greater at his death and the distributions after his death would be tax free to the beneficiaries. Roth IRAs are subject to the minimum distribution rules after the owner's death.

A Charity or a Charitable Remainder Trust (CRT): When a participant or IRA owner is charitably inclined, this can be an interesting possibility. A charity named as beneficiary avoids income taxation, since a charity is tax-exempt, and also avoids federal estate taxation because of the charitable estate tax deduction. Hence, the normal heavy taxation at death of these IRD items is avoided. CRTs are described in Chapter 19.

If a CRT is named as beneficiary, a surviving spouse could be the non-charitable income beneficiary and thus receive an income (either a unitrust or an annuity trust amount) for his or her lifetime. This income would be taxable. At the spouse's death, the corpus would go to the charity. As with any CRT, life insurance in an estate tax–protected irrevocable life insurance trust might be used to recoup the amount of the charitable gift for the family.

As noted earlier, the tax regulations have facilitated the naming of charities for at least part of a plan's death benefits. This is because the final designated beneficiary does not have to be determined until September 30 of the year following the year of the owner's or participant's death. Thus, when a charity and an individual(s) or trust are named, the charity's interest can be paid ("cashed out") before that date, leaving only the individual or individual trust benefcicaries as designated beneficiaries over whose life expectancy minimum distributions can be made. Of course, the same result could be achieved by the owner's dividing an IRA into separate IRAs or subaccounts during the owner's lifetime: one for the owner with the charity as beneficiary and one for the owner with the individual as beneficiary.

Other Trusts: Participants or owners (who perhaps are not married) may want to name other trusts as beneficiaries in particular circumstances.

The Participant's or Owner's Estate: This designation seems to have few planning advantages.

17

Individual Investment Annuity Contracts

Competence Objectives for This Chapter After reading this chapter, planners should understand:

- The fundamental purposes of annuities
- The types of individual annuity contracts
- Methods of paying annuity premiums
- Parties to the annuity contract
- The accumulation phase and distribution phase of annuities
- Investment returns on annuities
- Expense charges on annuities
- Withdrawals from annuities
- Exchanges of annuities
- Annuity payout options
- Guaranteed minimum benefits and benefit riders on nonqualified annuities
- Annuity death benefits
- Federal income taxation of nonqualified annuities
- Federal estate taxation of nonqualified annuities
- Using life insurance cash values to provide retirement income

This chapter covers individual annuities sold to the public as investments. They have become a major financial product for many people. These contracts are called nonqualified annuities to contrast them with the qualified retirement plans provided by employers to their employers and covered in Chapter 13.

Fundamental Purposes of Annuities

Traditionally, in its payout phase, a *life annuity* (or an *immediate life annuity*) involves an individual paying an insurance company a specified sum (called the *annuity consideration,* or *premium*) in exchange for a promise that the insurer will make a series of periodic payments to the individual (called the *annuitant*) for as long as he or she lives. Thus, the basic purpose of any life annuity is to assure the annuitant an income he or she cannot outlive.

However, modern individual annuity contracts permit the payout of accumulated funds (cash value) in a variety of ways. In fact, relatively few individual annuities today are taken as a life income. For tax purposes, then, another purpose of nonqualified annuities is to provide an investment vehicle whose earnings grow inside the annuity, income tax-deferred, until they are taken as distributions from the annuity.

Conceptually, the income from a life annuity should be relatively large compared with other investment returns because the annuity principle involves the gradual liquidation of the purchase price (principal) of the annuity over the annuitant's lifetime. Thus, each life annuity payment consists partly of liquidation of principal and partly of investment income. When the life annuitant or annuitants die, the annuity consideration is entirely liquidated (except possibly for minor refund features), and nothing (or little) remains for their heirs. This sometimes is called the mortality risk or annuity risk in life annuities. It exists for all life annuities.

Types of Individual Annuities

Investment annuities can be classified in several ways.

Who Determines Investments and Bears Investment Risks

A fundamental issue is whether the annuity owner or the insurance company makes investment decisions and bears investment risks.

Fixed-Dollar Annuities In these annuities, the cash-value accumulation is a stated dollar amount that is guaranteed by the insurance company and on which the insurer pays a specified or determinable rate of interest. Investment authority and investment risks are borne by the insurance company. The assets behind these annuities are invested in the general assets of the insurance company; hence, they are referred to as *portfolio products.* In the unlikely case the insurer should become insolvent, fixed-dollar annuity owners would become general creditors of the insurer.

Variable Annuities (VAs) Under this type, the annuity owner can choose from among a number of different investment funds or subaccounts into which he or she wishes to place the annuity premiums. The owner also has the option of moving his or her annuity contributions and the cash values among the various subaccounts at reasonable intervals.

These subaccounts are managed by or for the insurance company. They are not part of the general assets of the insurer, but are part of one or more separate accounts maintained by the insurer. The separate accounts are organized as investment companies (normally as unit investment trusts as described in Chapter 8). Their investment results stand on their own. Therefore, the cash values of VAs depend on the investment experience of the particular subaccount or accounts into which the cash values have been allocated by the annuity owner. Thus, investment risks reside with the annuity owner.

The separate accounts also are not subject to the claims of the insurance company's creditors. Thus, they are not subject to any insolvency risk of the insurance company. The available subaccounts depend on the particular contract involved. However, annuity owners generally have a wide range of investment options.

This variable annuity concept also applies when accumulated values are taken as variable retirement benefits. At this time, the current value of the investment fund is converted into units of retirement income (often called *annuity units*), and the annuitant receives an income of so many annuity units per month. The value of these annuity units depends on the investment experience of the fund in which the annuity accumulation is invested. This may be one of the payout options under an annuity.

Combination Plans Individual annuities may give annuity owners the choice of putting their annuity values in a fixed-dollar fund (stable value fund), in one or more variable funds, or in a combination of fixed and variable accounts.

Equity Indexed Annuities (EIAs) These technically are fixed-dollar annuities. They combine minimum insurance company guarantees with linking of interest earnings on the cash value to a stock market index.

CASE EXAMPLE

As an example of an EIA, a person might pay a premium of $100,000 for a single-premium deferred EIA. The policy guarantees a minimum value of, say, 90 percent of this principal amount ($90,000) increased by a guaranteed interest rate of, say, 3 percent each year. The value of the EIA will not fall below this minimum guarantee. In addition, if it is higher, the policy will pay a percentage (which varies among policies, but let us say 85 percent here) of the increase in an equity index (say the S&P 500) over a period, which might be five years. This percentage of the index increase is called the *participation rate.* Thus, if the increase in the S&P 500 over the five years were, for example, 80 percent (or a 12.47 percent average annual compound rate of return), the interest credited for this index increase would be $68,000 (80 percent index increase × 85 percent participation rate × $100,000 = $68,000), and the accumulated value of the EIA would be $168,000 (which, of course, is greater than the guaranteed value for this period). The annuity then could continue for additional periods. However, if the S&P 500 stock index were to decline, the EIA owner still would have the minimum guaranteed cash value at the minimum guaranteed interest rate. This is only an example to illustrate the principles involved. The design features in EIAs being sold can differ markedly and cause considerable differences in total returns.[1]

Insurance company EIAs were patterned after bank-offered market-linked CDs, which were described in Chapter 7. However, EIAs are annuities, so the inside buildup is not currently taxed. This is not true for bank CDs. However, the CDs normally are covered by FDIC insurance, while the EIAs are not.

Methods of Paying Premiums

Flexible-Premium Annuities These contracts allow the annuity owner the discretion of when to pay periodic premiums. Premiums can be discontinued or changed at the owner's option. This approach may be referred to as *flexible-premium deferred annuities.*

Single-Premium Annuities Here, the contract is purchased with a single lump-sum payment. The single premium may be paid well in advance of when benefits are to be taken from the annuity (a *single-premium deferred annuity,* or SPDA), or it may be paid just before annuity payments are to begin (a *single-premium immediate annuity*).

[1] The insurance companies themselves may finance these products by using the premiums they receive to purchase a portfolio of fixed bonds to cover the guaranteed part of the EIA and then purchase options on stock indexes or other option arrangements to cover the equity index part.

When Annuity Payments Begin

Deferred Annuities As just noted, a *deferred annuity* is one under which the benefits will not be payable until some years in the future. They essentially involve the tax-deferred growth of capital over time.

Immediate Annuities On the other hand, an *immediate annuity* is one in which the benefits begin as soon as the purchase price is paid. An immediate annuity might be purchased at retirement by someone ready to start receiving lifetime retirement benefits at that time.

Annuity Starting Date As its name implies, this is when annuity payments begin. Under the tax law, it is the first day of the first period (e.g., month) for which an amount is received as an annuity.

Parties to the Annuity Contract

These are the annuity owner, the annuitant, the beneficiary, and the issuing insurance company. In most instances, the annuity owner and the annuitant are the same person. The *annuity owner* is the person or entity who owns the rights under an annuity contract. The *annuitant* is the person whose life generally determines the timing and amount of any payout affected by life expectancy. In other words, the annuitant's life is used in determining any life income payments. The *beneficiary* is the person or entity named in the contract to receive the death benefit in the event the owner or annuitant dies before the benefits are paid from the annuity. In the event that the beneficiary is the deceased owner's surviving spouse, he or she is allowed by the tax law to treat the annuity as his or her own and to continue it as the new owner. The *insurance company* is the life insurance company issuing the contract.

Phases of Annuities

Individual annuities have an accumulation phase and a distribution phase. During the *accumulation phase,* contributions are made to the annuity and it is a capital-accumulation device. There is no legal or tax limit on the amount of annual contributions (or single premiums) that an annuity owner can make. However, contributions are made after taxes.

The *distribution phase* is when the owner receives benefits or payouts from the annuity. Distributions generally can be made at the owner's option, except for certain limiting factors. First, most annuities have reducing surrender charges if distributions are taken during the early years of the contract. Surrender charges are completely eliminated after a certain period, such as

10 years or even younger. However, annuities often allow the annuity owner to withdraw, say, up to 10 percent of the cash value during the period without a charge. Second, individual annuities are subject to the 10 percent penalty tax on premature distributions (before age 59½), with certain exceptions. Finally, annuity contracts generally specify a maximum age by which benefits must commence. However, this age may be quite advanced, such as age 85 or even 95. There is no tax law RBD for nonqualified annuities.

Investment Returns on Annuities

Important considerations in deciding whether to purchase an annuity or in deciding which one(s) to purchase are the rate of annual investment return that may be expected (in relation to investment risk) and the expense charges (direct and indirect) that are levied by insurers. Investment returns are discussed here; expense charges are discussed in the next section.

Returns on Fixed-Dollar Annuities

For this type of annuity, the insurance company specifies an *initial credited interest rate* that it will pay on the cash accumulation under the contract. This rate (or perhaps several alternative rates) often is guaranteed by the insurer for a specified period. This may be called the *yield guarantee.* This period can vary among insurers and annuity contracts from as little as 1 year to as long as 10 years. After any yield guarantee period ends, the insurer can set monthly or annually the interest rate it will pay in the future on the cash accumulation. This is the *current yield* or *current credited interest rate.* It can be increased or decreased by the insurer and often is less than the initial credited rate. However, fixed-dollar annuities also have a *minimum guaranteed interest rate,* below which the insurer cannot set its current rate. Also, some annuities have what is referred to as a *bailout escape rate* or *bailout provision* under which, if the current rate declared by the insurer falls below a certain level, the annuity owner can withdraw all funds in the annuity or exchange the annuity for another without a surrender charge. Thus, the minimum guaranteed rate and possibly a bailout rate provide some protection to annuity owners against declines in current interest rates. However, in recent years guaranteed rate on new policies have been lowered by many insurers or based on an index.

The current rate usually applies to all monies received for the annuity, regardless of when they were paid or received. In other words, there is one current rate set by the insurer based on the insurer's return on its own general investment portfolio. These may be called *portfolio-rated products.* A few insurers base their current rates on some outside market interest rate (such as a U.S. Treasury securities rate), so it changes with market conditions. These sometimes are called *interest-indexed annuities* (IIAs). At least one insurer uses a *new money approach* where the current rate depends on when the annuity considerations were paid to the insurer.

When it comes to fixed-dollar annuities, it may be helpful for consumers to review some current interest rate history for the annuity or annuities being considered. However, the general reputation and financial ratings of the insurer are very important, since it is the insurer's financial strength that stands behind its contracts and their returns. Purchasers should not be unduly attracted by an unusually high initial interest rate (possibly a *teaser rate*). First, the insurer normally lowers this rate after the yield guarantee period ends (which may be comparatively short, such as one year). Furthermore, it may not be financially sound for the insurer to offer rates that are too much out of line with market conditions, and this may financially weaken the insurer.

Fixed-dollar annuities are a guaranteed principal product and will be attractive during periods of rising interest rates. This is because their cash value is fixed and thus generally will not decline with rising interest rates, as will bond prices. Except that, in recent years some insurers have added *market value adjustments* (MVAs) to new annuity contracts which will reduce annuity values when market interest rates rise and increase them when market rates fall. In addition, current crediting rates will rise because insurers will be earning more on their general portfolios, and competition will force them to raise their current rates to maintain their annuity business.

On the other hand, during periods of low or declining interest rates in the economy, the reverse will be true. Current rates on annuities will decline, but their cash value will remain fixed. Bonds, on the other hand, will rise in price in the face of declining interest rates, unless they are called. Again, since no one knows what the future will bring, a diversified asset allocation strategy seems best for most people.

Returns on Variable Annuities

Here, investment returns depend on the performance of the subaccount or accounts to which the annuity funds are allocated. Therefore, a prospective purchaser should evaluate the past investment performance of the insurer (or other investment manager) over a reasonably long time (such as 10 or even 20 years) with respect to those separate accounts, much as should be done when buying investment company shares or variable life insurance. Consumers also may evaluate the variety of the subaccounts included in the investment options under the contract. Some annuities have more and better options than others.

Returns on EIAs

EIAs vary considerably in their design characteristics. This can have a significant impact on their returns. Some of the features that can affect results are the equity index used, the participation rate, any caps on the gain in the equity index that is credited to the annuity value, how the interest based on the equity index is calculated (the calculation method), the minimum cash-value guarantee (sometimes called the *guaranteed minimum account value*—GMAV), the minimum guaranteed interest rate, and a possible account charge. A number of equity indexes are used. The one used in the particular EIA selected involves at least some degree of investment strategy. For example, use of a broad index, like the commonly used S&P 500 stock index, implies an index investing strategy. Participation rates vary widely. In the previous example, we assumed an 85 percent participation rate, but these rates can range from 55 percent to more than 100 percent. There are a number of calculation methods. In the previous example, the point-to-point method was used. Other methods include a ladder method, high water/low water method, and ratchet designs.

For asset allocation purposes, EIAs perhaps should be considered equity investments, since the expectation normally is that the equity indexed interest will outpace the GMAV. However, returns on EIAs may be lower than those on other equity investments, such as directly owned stocks and stock mutual funds, because of possible participation rates below 100 percent, possible caps on interest credits, and the fact that equity indexes (like the S&P 500) do not include dividends paid on the common stocks in the index. They are indexes of the market prices of stocks.

Expense Charges on Annuities

There are two broad categories of charges: sales or surrender charges (loads) and other, usually annual, charges.

Sales Charges

Sometimes a sales charge is deducted from the premiums when an annuity is purchased; this is called a *front-end load.* The trend in the insurance industry, however, is not to impose front-end loads on individual annuities, but rather to levy a *surrender charge* if more than a certain amount (often, more than 10 percent of the annuity value per year) is withdrawn or surrendered within a specified period after purchase (such as 7 or 10 years). Technically, this is a contingent-deferred sales charge, but it is popularly known as a *back-end load.* Back-end loads normally are a diminishing percentage of the annuity value and, while they vary among insurers, might start at 7 or 8 percent of the annuity value in the first year and then decline year by year to become zero by, say, the tenth year. Back-end loads tend to discourage annuity owners from exchanging or surrendering their annuities during the period in which such surrender charges may be imposed. However, some variable annuities do not levy any sales load or surrender charge or impose reduced loads or charges. These may be called no-load or low-load contracts. They are analogous to no-load or low-load mutual funds.

Periodic Expense Charges

In the case of *fixed-dollar annuities,* there often are no separately stated annual fees (other than possibly a small maintenance fee). Rather, the insurer recovers its costs from the spread between the current interest rate it pays on the annuity value and the rate it can earn on its own investment portfolio. Thus, for fixed-dollar annuities, there usually are no front-end sales loads and no separately charged annual fees. However, there generally is a surrender charge (back-end load).

For *variable annuities,* the situation is different. There always are annual charges levied against the contract's accumulated value, whether or not there are any sales or surrender charges. These annual charges fall into two general categories: *contract charges (policy-level expenses)*, which do not vary with the particular subaccount or accounts selected, and fund or *portfolio operating expenses (fund-level expenses)*, which do vary with the subaccount or accounts selected. Contract charges are insurance-type charges and administrative expenses. They are the mortality and expense (M&E) risk charge, which may include elements for administrative expenses, sales expenses, a risk charge for standard death benefits, and insurer profits. Fund-level charges are investment management fees and administrative expenses for managing the particular subaccounts. They are somewhat analogous to expense ratios for mutual funds. Both of these kinds of charges are customarily expressed as percentages of a fund's average net assets. In addition, there are charges for any guaranteed minimum benefit riders the annuity owner may have purchased. Guaranteed minimum benefits are discussed later in this chapter.

These annual charges can be significant in affecting total returns under variable annuities. Annual policy-level M&E charges can vary from 0.50 to 1.65 percent (or more) of assets, while annual fund-level charges vary according to particular subaccounts, typically being lower for money market and domestic bond funds and higher for growth stock, specialty, and international funds. On average, however, total combined annual charges might run 2.10 percent of assets or more. However, as just noted, these combined annual expenses can vary considerably among different variable annuities. This is an important factor to consider for purchasers of variable annuities.

Withdrawals and Loans

Individual annuities normally permit withdrawals from the cash value at any time, but they may be subject to a surrender charge during the surrender period. Some also permit loans against the cash value, but loans against annuities are rare because loans are considered taxable distributions. For annuity contracts issued after January 18, 1985, any amount withdrawn (or taken as a loan) prior to age 59½ will be subject to the 10 percent penalty tax on premature distributions, with some exceptions. In addition to reaching age 59½, other exceptions are the person's disability or death, when payments are made in substantially equal periodic payments for the life or life expectancy of the annuitant or the joint lives or life expectancies of the annuitant and his or her beneficiary, and for the purchase of an immediate annuity.

Exchanges of Annuities

Annuity contracts can be exchanged tax free for other annuity contracts under the terms of Section 1035 of the IRC. Thus, if an annuity owner is dissatisfied with the service, yield, or security of his or her individual deferred annuity, the owner can exchange the contract for another annuity contract without current income tax consequences. However, such exchanges of annuity contracts may give rise to back-end loads.

Fixed or Variable Annuity (Payout) Options

Depending on the policy involved, annuity benefits can be payable in a stated number of dollars or as variable annuity units in a separate subaccount. Fixed-dollar annuities normally provide stated dollar payouts, while variable annuities may provide either variable payouts or fixed payouts at the option of the annuity owner.

Annuity Payment Options

These options vary somewhat from one annuity contract to another, but some common ones include cash surrender of all or part of the accumulated value, installment payments over a fixed period or in a fixed amount, straight life annuity, joint life and survivor annuity, and various life annuities with refund features.

Annuity Death Benefits

While individual annuities are primarily capital accumulation and liquidation vehicles, the owner does name a beneficiary or beneficiaries to receive the accumulated value in the event of the owner's death before this value is paid out. It should be noted, however, that there are no life insurance proceeds involved in such an annuity death benefit. Individual annuity contracts normally allow the annuity owner or the beneficiary to select one or more payout options for the death benefit.

In connection with variable annuities, the *standard death benefit* is the larger of the amount the owner invested in the policy (minus any withdrawals) or the policy's cash value. This means that if the cash value in a subaccount or accounts (such as a common stock account) should decline below the owner's investment in the contract (net premiums paid), there would be a mortality risk element equal to the difference. This can be important in declining markets. Some variable annuity contracts have other, *enhanced death benefit*, provisions. One of these is the stepped-up death benefit. Here, the death benefit is reset at periodic intervals (such as every five years) at the then-current cash value. From then on, it will not be less than this amount, or, in some annuities, the highest reset amount (high-point death benefit). Another provision increases the death benefit by a stated percentage (such as 5 percent) each year. There normally are additional asset-based percentage charges for enhanced death benefits. The consumer should evaluate whether these additional charges are worth the death protection, compared with just buying life insurance. Also, it should be noted that the difference between the annuity owner's basis in the contract (normally the premium paid) and the death benefit (standard or enhanced) is taxable IRD to the beneficiary. On the other hand, life insurance death proceeds are income tax–free to the beneficiary. Once annuity payments have commenced, any death benefit will depend on the payout option selected.

The IRC requires that for contracts issued after January 18, 1985, to be considered annuities for tax purposes (i.e., to be taxed under Section 72 of the IRC), the contracts must meet certain distribution rules in the event of an annuity owner's death. If the owner's death occurs before the annuity starting date, his or her entire interest in the contract must be distributed within five years after the owner's death. But if the owner's death occurs on or after the annuity starting date and before his or her entire interest has been distributed, the remaining interest must be distributed at least as rapidly as under the distribution method being used at the owner's death. However, under both of these rules, if part or all of an owner's interest is to be distributed to a beneficiary over the life of the beneficiary, or over a period that does not exceed the life expectancy of the beneficiary, and if such distribution begins within one year of the owner's death, that portion will be treated as if it had been distributed on the day the distribution began. Furthermore, if a deceased owner's spouse is the beneficiary, these requirements treat the surviving spouse as the annuity owner for the future.

Guaranteed Minimum Benefits Under Variable Annuities (VAs)

There are a number of guaranteed minimum benefits riders that can be added to nonqualified VAs. Many insurance companies offer them and they have been very popular with VA owners. The terms and costs of these riders vary considerably among insurers and there had been considerable competition among insurers in their sale to the public. Insurers make a separate annual percentage charge against the VA's accumulated value for these riders. However, as of this writing, insurance companies are cutting back on these guaranteed benefits and increasing their asset-based charges for them due to the difficult stock market and economic climate.[2]

Guaranteed Minimum Death Benefits (GMDBs)

For VAs, they are represented by the standard death benefit (financed by a portion of the M&E risk charge) and enhanced death benefits for which a separate asset based charge may be levied.

Guaranteed Minimum Living Benefits (GMLBs)

In contrast to GMDBs, these guarantee retirement benefits in various forms during the annuitant's lifetime. They can be classified as guaranteed minimum accumulation benefits (GMABs), guaranteed minimum income benefits (GMIBs), guaranteed minimum withdrawal benefits (GMWBs), or some combination of these guarantees.

[2] Insurers generally use financial hedging techniques to attempt to protect themselves against stock market declines with respect to these products.

Guaranteed Minimum Accumulation Benefits (GMABs) These are provisions usually guaranteeing that the value of a benefit base in the VA will increase at a certain rate regardless of how the subaccount or accounts in which the VA owner actually invested perform. This may take the form of periodically (e.g., quarterly) locking in the investment gains in a benefit base if the owner does not take withdrawals. Thus, the benefit base will hold its gains (i.e., they are locked in) even if the subaccount values should decline. Another form is to guarantee that purchase payments (annuity considerations) will increase a benefit base at a guaranteed rate, such as 5 percent or even 7 percent, for a period of time, such as 10 years. The same result can be achieved by guaranteeing that the benefit base will double in a certain number of years. The effect of these guarantees is that the VA contract has an *actual accumulation value (cash value)*. These are determined by the actual performance of the investment subaccounts the owner selects, the annuity's expense charges (as well as other transactions), and one or more benefit bases which will be determined by the contract guarantees just mentioned and will normally be different (more or less) than the actual cash value.

Guaranteed Minimum Income Benefits (GMIBs) These benefits often guarantee a future lifetime annuity income based on a guaranteed benefit base. GMIBs normally apply after the VA has been in force for a given period, such as 10 years, and require life annuitization. Thus, the life annuity principle applies once the GMIB starts.

Guaranteed Minimum Withdrawal Benefits (GMWBs) In this case, the insurer guarantees that the annuitant can withdraw up to a specified percentage (such as 5 percent at age 55) of the accumulated value as long as the annuitant lives. The percentage guaranteed increases with the annuitant's age. However, the remaining accumulated value (after the guaranteed withdrawals) remains available to the annuitant or his or her heirs after the annuitant's death. In other words, GMWBs do not require annuitization and may be available immediately on purchase of an immediate annuity.

Long-Term Care (LTC) Riders to Annuity Contracts

These insurance coverages may be added as riders (endorsements) to an annuity or life insurance contract. LTC insurance is covered in Chapter 23.

This approach likely will attain increased importance starting in 2010, because PPA of 2006 provides significant tax advantages for such *combination contracts* (annuities or life insurance and LTC contracts) starting after December 31, 2009. PPA of 2006 provides that charges against the cash value of such a combination contract for qualified LTC coverage will not be considered gross income for federal income tax purposes. This means the tax-deferred inside buildup of an annuity policy (or life insurance policy) can be used tax free to pay for LTC coverage. In this case, the income tax basis of the annuity contract (or life insurance policy) will be reduced by such nontaxed charges. However, the effect of this basis adjustment will be to defer, probably for a long time, the tax on the LTC charges because the lower basis will result in a larger untaxed buildup in the annuity contract which will be taxed upon distribution at some point in the future.

Underwriting of Individual Annuities

Unlike life insurance (discussed in Chapter 21), individual annuity contracts generally are not subject to any medical underwriting (selection) by the insurance company issuing them. The early death of a life annuitant actually will be financially beneficial to the insurer.

However, some insurance companies write medically underwritten immediate life annuities. In this case, the insurers do consider the medical condition of the prospective annuitant and will offer better life annuity rates to persons in poorer health (referred to as "impaired lives").

Taxation of Nonqualified Annuities

Taxation of nonqualified annuities can be complex. Only the basic principles are presented here.

Federal Income Taxation

An annuity owner's *investment in the contract* (income tax basis in the contract) is the owner's premiums paid minus any nontaxed distributions. Since this amount has been paid with after-tax dollars, the owner (or his or her beneficiary at death) is entitled to this amount back tax free when benefits are taken from the annuity.

Accumulation Phase (Inside Buildup) The investment earnings of an annuity contract increase or decrease without current income taxation or losses. This is the famous *tax-deferred inside buildup of annuity cash values,* and is one of the main advantages of individual (nonqualified) deferred annuities. For variable annuities, the owner can also move the cash value between or among the subaccounts within the annuity without this being considered a sale or exchange for capital gains tax purposes.

Annuities Held Other Than by Natural Persons The previous tax-deferral principle does not apply when contributions have been made after February 28,

1986, for a deferred annuity that is not held by a natural person. This would include deferred annuity contracts held by corporations, charitable remainder trusts, and certain other entities. When a contract is held by a non-natural person, it is not treated as an annuity under Section 72 of the IRC, and income earned by the contract (the inside buildup) will be taxed as ordinary income to the owner for that year. However, this provision does not apply to annuities held by an estate because of the owner's death; annuities held by qualified retirement plans, TSAs, and IRAs; immediate annuities; and annuities held by trusts or other entities as agents for natural persons.

Annuity Payments (Periodic Distributions) These payments are taxed under the general annuity rules of Section 72 of the IRC.[3] Under these rules, an owner of a fixed-dollar annuity determines the ratio of his or her investment in the contract to the expected return (the annual payment times the annuitant's life expectancy in years) from the contract and excludes a similar proportion of each annuity payment from his or her gross income. This ratio is the exclusion ratio. For variable annuities, the excluded amount is determined by dividing the owner's investment in the contract by the annuitant's life expectancy in years.

For annuity starting dates after December 31, 1986, the exclusion continues until the owner's investment in the contract is recovered, and then the annuity payments are fully taxable. For prior annuity starting dates, the exclusion goes on even after the owner's investment in the contract is recovered. If an owner-annuitant should die before recovering the premiums tax free, the remainder would be deductible on his or her final income tax return.

Amounts Not Received as an Annuity Section 72 also deals with distributions that are not received as an annuity. These include nonperiodic distributions before the annuity starting date, such as cash withdrawals, loans, and surrenders.

Surrenders: If an annuity contract is entirely surrendered for cash, the difference between the cash surrender value and the investment in the contract is taxed as ordinary income in the year of the surrender. This normally is not a desirable strategy unless there are special circumstances.

Cash Withdrawals: If there are partial withdrawals on annuities issued after August 13, 1982, they are viewed for tax purposes as coming first from any untaxed investment earnings in the contract and are taxed as

[3] This is the same general concept as discussed in Chapter 16 for periodic distributions from qualified retirement plans, except there are special exceptions for qualified plans that do not apply to nonqualified annuities. Nonqualified annuities are taxed only under the general annuity rules.

ordinary income until such investment earnings are exhausted. Once the inside buildup is exhausted, further withdrawals are viewed as a return of the investment in the contract and are income tax–free. This can be termed an *interest first* concept of taxation and is the opposite from that generally employed for partial withdrawals from life insurance contracts that are not modified endowment contracts (MECs). For nonqualified annuities issued on or before August 13, 1982, partial surrenders are considered to come first (untaxed) from the investment in the contract like life insurance.

Loans: For income tax purposes, these are considered distributions from the contract and hence, are taxable the same as just described for partial withdrawals. This also is the opposite from the treatment of policy loans from life insurance policies that are not MECs and loans from qualified retirement plans.

Gifts of Annuities: For annuity contracts issued after April 22, 1987, the transfer of an annuity for less than full and adequate consideration (i.e., gift of the annuity) will be treated for income tax purposes as if the owner-transferor had received an amount not received as an annuity equal to the difference between the cash value at the time of the gift and the investment in the contract. This amount is taxable to the owner-transferor at that time as ordinary income. Thus, gifts of annuities generally will trigger taxation to the donor of the untaxed inside buildup. Therefore, while gifts of life insurance often are attractive for estate planning reasons, the same is not true for gifts of deferred annuities. This rule does not apply to gifts of annuities between spouses or incident to divorce.

Death: At the death of an annuity owner, the difference between the annuity's accumulated value and the decedent's investment in the contract is IRD to the beneficiary, according to the principles explained in Chapter 10. The ordinary income is received as payments are made from the annuity. Therefore, it may be desirable to spread out the tax impact over a period of years to the extent allowed by the distribution rules described previously.

As a result of these rules, it can be seen that the inside buildup in deferred annuities will always be taxed as ordinary income at some point: on receiving periodic income, on surrender of the contract, as partial distributions, as loans, upon gift of the contract, or at death. Also, except for death, tax on the buildup cannot be shifted to someone else.

Penalty Tax on Premature Distributions For nonqualified annuity contracts issued after January 18, 1985, any taxable amount withdrawn prior to age 59½ generally will be subject to the 10 percent excise tax on premature distributions. There are, however, certain exceptions as described earlier in this chapter.

Federal Estate Taxation

The total death benefit of a deferred annuity will be included in the deceased owner's gross estate for federal estate tax purposes. However, the beneficiary gets an income tax deduction for any federal estate tax paid by the decedent's estate that is attributable to this IRD item.

Other Individual Annuity Arrangements

Charitable Gift Annuities

These are part charitable contribution and part annuity arrangements provided by some charities. They are described in Chapter 19.

Using Life Insurance Values to Provide Retirement Income

As explained in Chapter 21, most life insurance companies make available by contract, or as a matter of practice, settlement options for the policyowner as well as for death beneficiaries. Policyowners at or near retirement may choose to use some or all of their life insurance cash values in this way, assuming they feel they no longer need some or all of the life insurance protection. Life insurance cash values (or death proceeds) placed under such options are taxed under the general annuity rules of Section 72 of the IRC.

On the other hand, policyowners may choose not to surrender their policies, but to keep them in force while taking cash from them in other ways, as described in Chapters 21 and 29. Still another alternative is to keep life insurance fully in force to meet various needs. For example, it may be needed to provide protection for a surviving spouse or others.

Finally, life insurance contracts can be exchanged tax free for annuity contracts under Section 1035 of the IRC.

18

Employee Stock Compensation Plans

Competence Objectives for This Chapter After reading this chapter, planners should understand:

- The types of employee stock compensation plans
- The requirements for and tax treatment of incentive stock options (ISOs)
- The requirements for and tax treatment of employee stock purchase plans
- Qualified retirement plans invested in employer securities
- The general tax law provisions relating to employee stock compensation and the requirements for a Section 83(b) election
- The nature and tax treatment of nonqualified stock options (NQSOs)
- The nature and tax treatment of restricted stock
- The nature of other stock-based compensation plans
- Various provisions of stock option plans
- How stock options can be exercised and their valuation, including option pricing models (such as the Black-Scholes model)
- Various planning issues concerning employee stock options and other stock plans

Employee stock options and other stock plans have been used for many years, and the tax law has had various provisions concerning them.[1] But for most of this time, stock options were granted only, or mainly, to senior executives. However, in recent years, some corporations have adopted more

[1] At various times, tax-favored stock options were called *restricted stock options* and *qualified stock options*. These particular plans have been discontinued. The present tax-favored stock option is called an ISO.

broadly based plans covering more levels of management, or even most of their full-time employees. Of course, many companies also have employee stock purchase plans that are designed to cover virtually all employees.

Types of Plans

In the classification that follows, we have divided employer stock plans into *statutory plans* and *nonstatutory plans.* Statutory plans are those to which the tax law accords special tax advantages but which also must meet certain requirements to be eligible for the advantages. On the other hand, nonstatutory plans are not based on any special tax provisions, but rather, are governed by general tax principles.

Statutory Plans

Incentive Stock Options These options were created by the Economic Recovery Tax Act of 1981 (ERTA) in Section 422 of the IRC. They can be made available at the employer's discretion to only some employees, normally certain highly compensated executives, and hence, can be discriminatory in nature.

Requirements for ISOs: A number of requirements must be met before a plan can qualify as an ISO plan. For example, the term of an option cannot exceed 10 years; the option price must equal or exceed the value of the stock when the option was granted; no disposition can be made of the stock by the person within 2 years from granting the option and within 1 year of the transfer of the stock to him or her (i.e., after exercise of the option); the option must be nontransferable (except by will or inheritance at death); and the maximum value of stock for which an employee can exercise ISOs for the first time in a calendar year generally cannot exceed $100,000 (valued as of the date of grant).

Tax Treatment to Employees: The main tax advantage of ISOs is that there is no regular income tax levied at the grant or at the exercise of the option by the employee. However, as noted in Chapter 10, the bargain element upon exercise of an ISO (i.e., the difference between the fair market value of the stock at exercise and the option price) is an adjustment item for individual AMT purposes. Aside from this AMT issue, the employee is taxed only when he or she sells the stock purchased under the option plan, and then any gain realized is taxed as a capital gain. The capital gain would be the difference between the option price (the income tax basis of the stock) and the stock's fair market value on the date of sale.

CASE EXAMPLE

Assume that in 2003, Laura Johnson was granted an ISO to purchase 1,000 shares of her employer's (Acme Corporation) common stock at an option price (*strike price*) of $20 per share, which was its fair market value at the time. The ISO's term was 10 years. Laura had no gross income for federal income tax purposes at the grant of this option. Assume further that in 2007 Laura exercised the option with cash and purchased 1,000 shares of Acme common from her employer for $20,000 (1,000 shares × $20 per share = $20,000). At that time (2007), the stock's fair market value was $50 per share and the bargain element was $30,000 ($50 – $20 = $30 × 1,000 shares = $30,000). Laura had no regular gross income at exercise of the ISO, but she did have an AMT adjustment item of $30,000. Note, however, that if this adjustment item produces an AMT, the AMT may be recouped in future years because of the minimum tax credit (MTC) described in Chapter 10. Laura's regular income tax basis for the 1,000 shares is her cost (purchase price) of $20,000, or $20 per share.

Now assume that in 2009 Laura sells the 1,000 shares for $80 per share. At this point, Laura realizes long-term capital gain of $60 per share, or $60,000 ($80 – $20 = $60 per share × 1,000 shares = $60,000).[2] Furthermore, if Laura does not sell during her lifetime but holds the Acme stock until her death, it would get a stepped-up income tax basis and the gain to that point would never be taxed.

Tax Treatment for the Employer: The general principle is that an employer gets a corporate income tax deduction for compensation expenses at the same time and in the same amount as the employee realizes gross compensation income from the stock plan. In the case of an ISO, an employee never realizes compensation income, and so the employer never gets a corporate tax deduction.

Employee Stock Purchase Plans

Basic Characteristics: These are option arrangements under which all full-time employees meeting certain eligibility requirements are allowed to

[2] Note that in this example the holding requirements for an ISO have been met (i.e., two years from grant and one year from exercise). However, if the requirements for an ISO had been violated, the option would be treated as a nonqualified stock option (NQSO), described later in this chapter.

buy stock in their employer corporation, usually at a discount. The option price cannot be less than the lower of 85 percent of the stock's fair market value when the option was granted or 85 percent of the stock's fair market value when the option was exercised. Many employers use these maximum discounts as the option (strike) prices under their plans.

Employees who participate agree to have an estimated amount withheld from their pay to provide the funds with which to exercise their options at the end of an option period. If an employee decides not to exercise an option, the plan will return the amounts withheld to the employee, usually with interest.

Employee stock purchase plans are nondiscriminatory in that they cannot favor the highly paid executives of a corporation. In fact, no employee who owns 5 percent or more of the stock of a corporation can be granted such an option, and the maximum annual value of stock subject to these plans (determined as of the grant of the option) is $25,000.

Tax Treatment to Employees: If the requirements of Section 423 of the IRC are met, there is no gross income for participating employees at the grant or exercise of options under employee stock purchase plans. However, to get this favorable tax treatment, no disposition can be made of the stock by the employee within two years from grant of the option and within one year from its exercise. If such a disqualifying disposition were to occur, the employee would be taxed as ordinary compensation income in the year of disposition on the difference between the fair market value of the stock and the option strike price when the option was exercised.

For dispositions (sales) of the stock after the two-year and one-year holding periods (or upon death, whenever occurring), when the option price was between 85 percent and 100 percent of the stock's fair market value at grant, the employee (or his or her estate) will be taxed as ordinary compensation income on the lesser of the difference between the fair market value of the stock and the option price at the time of disposition or death, or the difference between the fair market value of the stock and the option price as of the time the option was granted. The remainder of any gain at sale during the employee's lifetime would be capital gain. At the employee's death, his or her estate or heirs currently would get a stepped-up basis for the remainder of any gain and it would never be taxed.

Many corporations have adopted employee stock purchase plans. While a company's plan may not necessarily be as liberal as permitted by the tax law, a great many are. Therefore, eligible employees normally would be well advised to participate in these plans if they are at all financially able to do so. If an employee really does not want to hold the stock, he or she can simply sell it at a profit (assuming the stock price was such that the employee should have exercised the option in the first place).

Tax Treatment for the Employer: The employer does not get a corporate income tax deduction at grant or exercise of options under employee stock purchase plans.

Qualified Retirement Plans Invested in Employer Securities These plans were discussed in Chapters 13 and 14. Stock bonus plans permit investment in employer stock and allow distribution of that stock to participants. ESOPs must invest primarily in employer stock. Qualified savings plans with Section 401(k) options often allow significant portions of employee account balances to be invested in employer stock. The planning issue of possible lump-sum distributions of employer securities was explored in Chapter 16.

Nonstatutory Plans

General Tax Law Principles Governing Stock Compensation Plans

General Provisions Since there are no special provisions governing these plans, they are interpreted under provisions of the code related to income—Section 61 in general and Section 83 in particular. Section 61 is simply the all-inclusive definition of gross income for federal income tax purposes. The more significant provision is Section 83, which deals with taxation of property transferred in connection with the performance of services.

Section 83, in essence, provides that the fair market value of property (minus any amount paid for the property) transferred to a person for the performance of services shall be included in that person's gross income in the first taxable year in which the person's rights in the property become transferable or are not subject to a substantial risk of forfeiture, whichever is applicable. A substantial risk of forfeiture might exist, for example, if an employee has to remain with the employer for a certain number of years to receive unfettered ownership or rights to the property. In effect, the property (minus any amount paid for it) is taxable to the person rendering the services as soon as all substantial conditions on his or her having it are removed.

Section 83(b) Election However, an important subsection, Section 83(b), provides that a person performing services (e.g., an employee) may elect within 30 days of a transfer to include the fair market value of the transferred property (minus any amount paid for the property) in his or her gross income, even though the property then was subject to a substantial risk of forfeiture or was not transferable and hence, under Section 83, normally would not have been taxable at that point. This is called a *Section 83(b) election.* It can be an important planning tool.

However, if one makes a Section 83(b) election, and the value of transferred property is included in the person's gross income, but the property subsequently is forfeited (because, say, the employee did not remain with the employer for the required period), no tax deduction is allowed for the forfeiture. The election also cannot be revoked without the consent of the Secretary of the Treasury. On the other hand, when the substantial risk of forfeiture expires, there is no tax. Normally, of course, one does not want to pay taxes any sooner than necessary.

On the other hand, a person receiving property for the performance of services (e.g., an executive receiving restricted employer stock) might want to make a Section 83(b) election and be taxed on the current value of the stock if the current value is relatively low, the person expects it to rise significantly in the future, and he or she expects to remain with the employer at least through the forfeiture period. These, of course, may be big "ifs." Much depends on the circumstances. But if the stock price currently is low and is expected to do well (as in some start-up situations, for example), the only real risk the person would seem to be taking is the possible loss of his or her current tax payment.

If an employee makes a Section 83(b) election and is currently taxed, the employer gets a corporate income tax deduction for compensation paid in the amount taxable to the employee. The effects of a Section 83(b) election will be illustrated later in connection with the discussion of restricted stock.

Current Stock Bonus

Some employers pay part of employees' current compensation in unrestricted stock. In this case, the employees receive current compensation equal to the fair market value of the stock. On the other hand, employers often pay part of a current bonus in cash and part in restricted stock (i.e., subject to the condition that the employee stays with the employer for a minimum period). In this case, the rules for restricted stock apply.

Nonqualified Stock Options (NQSOs)

Basic Characteristics These are stock options that do not meet the requirements for ISOs and so are taxed on the basis of the general principles just discussed. Correspondingly, NQSOs can have terms decided upon by the parties and are not limited in the amount of stock subject to such options exercisable by an employee in any one year (as are ISOs). Hence, NQSOs can be considerably more flexible for employers and employees. Like ISOs, they can be granted only to certain employees, and hence, may be discriminatory. NQSOs generally have become more popular than ISOs as a compensation technique. While there are no statutory requirements to do so, NQSOs are often granted with an option price equal to 100 percent of the fair market value of the stock on the date of grant and for option terms of around 10 years.

Tax Treatment to Employees There normally is no taxable event (gross income) at grant because the tax regulations view their value then as not being readily ascertainable.[3] On the other hand, upon exercise of an option (and transfer of the stock to the employee), the employee will receive ordinary compensation income for regular federal income tax purposes equal to the difference between the fair market value of the stock at exercise and the option price (the bargain element). The employee's income tax basis in the stock is its fair market value at exercise. This is because the employee paid the option price to the employer (a cost basis) and included the remainder of the stock's value (bargain element) in his or her gross income as compensation (basis under the tax benefit principle). Thus, an immediate sale of the stock by the employee (there are no two-year and one-year holding periods for NQSOs) will produce zero capital gain or loss, since the amount realized would equal the adjusted basis for the stock.

CASE EXAMPLE

Let us illustrate these principles by returning to our example involving Laura Johnson. If we assume the same facts, except that Laura was granted an NQSO instead of an ISO in 2003, the tax results would be as follows. Laura would have no gross income at grant of the option. However, when Laura exercised her NQSO in 2007, she would have had ordinary compensation income of $30,000 in that year.[4] Laura's income tax basis for the 1,000 shares is $50,000, or $50 per share ($20 per share of cost basis and $30 per share of basis due to that amount having already been taxed).

Now when Laura sells her 1,000 shares of Acme common in 2009 at a price of $80 per share, she will realize long-term capital gain of $30 per share, or $30,000 ($80 – $50 = $30 per share × 1,000 shares = $30,000). Thus, for the NQSO, the total gain on the option stock would still be $60,000, except that $30,000 would be ordinary compensation income and $30,000 would be long-term capital gain taxable at a maximum 15 percent rate.

[3] Employee stock options, of course, are not traded on organized or over-the-counter markets, may not be transferable, and normally are not vested at grant.

[4] Note that the AMT is not involved here because the $30,000 bargain element is taxable for regular income tax purposes.

Tax Treatment for the Employer The employer gets a corporate income tax deduction for the amount of compensation income the employee realizes at exercise of the option.

Restricted Stock

Basic Characteristics *Restricted stock plans* are arrangements whereby a corporation grants stock or stock options to an employee (or someone rendering services to the corporation), but where ownership of the stock is subject to a substantial risk of forfeiture, such as the employee's not remaining with the employer for a certain number of years or the corporation's not meeting certain profit goals. Such stock may be provided to employees in a variety of circumstances. It can be part of a general compensation package, perhaps to entice the person to go with the employer. It can be part of a bonus plan, as noted earlier. And in some cases, stock issued on exercise of an NQSO can be restricted stock in order to further postpone taxation.

Tax Treatment to Employees and the Section 83(b) Election As explained earlier, an employee receives ordinary compensation income in the year the employee's rights to the stock are first not subject to the substantial risk of forfeiture or are transferable. The gross income is measured by the fair market value of the stock at that time minus any cost to the employee. However, depending on the circumstances, a Section 83(b) election (described earlier) may be considered. A person receiving restricted stock must make a planning decision regarding this election.

CASE EXAMPLES

To illustrate these principles, let us assume that John Venturesome is a young information technology executive with a large corporation. Recently, a former college classmate invited him to join a newer start-up company (XYZ.com) that has some exciting new products in information technology. The offer is for less salary, but XYZ.com, which recently went public, will give John a compensation package that includes NQSOs and 10,000 shares of restricted stock (which is conditioned on John's staying with the company for at least three years). John does not have to pay anything for the 10,000 shares. XYZ.com common stock was selling at $2 per share when the offer was made.

Assume that John accepted the offer in 2006 and made no Section 83(b) election. First, John had no gross income from receipt of the 10,000 shares of restricted stock, since it is subject to a substantial risk of forfeiture. Let us further assume that at the end of three years (in 2009), John is still with XYZ.com and that its stock has done well. Its price in 2009 is $20 per share. When the substantial risk of forfeiture ends in 2009, John will have ordinary compensation income of $200,000 (10,000 shares × $20 per share = $200,000). His income tax basis in the 10,000 shares also will be $200,000, or $20 per share.

Now let us change our facts and assume John made the Section 83(b) election in 2006 within 30 days of when the 10,000 shares were transferred to him. He then would have be taxed on $20,000 in year 2006 ($2 per share × 10,000 shares = $20,000) as ordinary compensation income and his basis in the 10,000 shares also would be $20,000, or $2 per share. If John is still with XYZ.com at the end of the three years in 2009, the substantial risk of forfeiture would end and he would have unrestricted rights to the stock. He would incur no further gross income. On the other hand, if John had left XYZ.com after, say, two years, he would forfeit the 10,000 shares and could have taken no tax deduction for that. In effect, he would lose the tax he paid in 2006 on the $20,000 of ordinary income.

Let us now assume that John stayed with XYZ.com until 2009 and that two years later (in 2011) John sells the 10,000 shares for $30 per share. If he had not made the Section 83(b) election in 2006, he would have $100,000 of long-term capital gain ($300,000 amount realized – $200,000 adjusted basis = $100,000 gain realized). In effect, he would have had $300,000 of total gain on the 10,000 shares of restricted stock ($200,000 of ordinary compensation income and $100,000 of long-term capital gain). On the other hand, if John had made the Section 83(b) election in 2006, he would have $280,000 of long-term capital gain ($300,000 amount realized – $20,000 adjusted basis = $280,000 gain realized). In this situation, he also would have had $300,000 of total gain on the 10,000 shares of restricted stock, but now it is divided as $20,000 of ordinary compensation income and $280,000 of long-term capital gain. Furthermore, if John does not sell the 10,000 shares (or all of them) during his lifetime, he can still consider the techniques described in Chapter 11 for possibly avoiding capital gains taxation. Finally, if he does not sell or otherwise dispose of his stock, it currently will get a stepped-up basis at death. But if the market price of the stock falls or it becomes worthless, John would have been better off not making the Section 83(b) election.

Tax Treatment for the Employer Again, the employer gets a corporate income tax deduction when the employee receives gross compensation income. This is either when the substantial risk of forfeiture ends or the Section 83(b) election is made.

Other Stock-Based Plans

This is a complex field, and only a brief description of some of these plans will be given here.

Stock Appreciation Rights (SARs) These are accounts, maintained for selected employees, that reflect the appreciation in the employer's stock over a certain period. When an executive's rights to an SAR become final, it normally is paid out to him or her in cash and is taxable then.

Phantom Stock These also are accounts maintained for selected employees, but they normally reflect the full value of a certain amount of employer stock. The account value varies with the stock's value and normally is paid to the executive in cash at some point. However, there is no actual stock in the account.

Performance Shares or Performance-Based Stock Options In this case, selected employees are granted stock or stock options whose vesting is contingent on certain corporate or other performance measures being met.

Provisions of Stock Option Plans

Vesting of Options

This is the period of continuous employment that must elapse after an option is granted and before the employee can exercise the option. There generally are vesting requirements in stock option plans. The periods required for vesting vary, but often range from two to four years.

Transferability of Options

Traditionally, employee stock options have not been transferable by the employees receiving the options other than at death. They could not be sold or given away. One of the requirements to be an ISO is that the option by its terms must not be transferable (other than by will or intestate distribution) and must be exercisable during the employee's lifetime only by him or her.

There is no corresponding prohibition for NQSOs. But in the past, corporations in practice have not allowed their NQSOs to be transferable. Recently, however, some corporations have amended their stock option plans to allow NQSOs to be transferred by the holder to members of his or her family, trusts for such members, or possibly family limited partnerships with such members as partners, with the consent of the corporation.

Effect of Certain Contingencies on Options

Stock option plans normally have certain forfeiture provisions in the event of termination of employment for various reasons. The option holder (or his or her estate or heirs) usually has a limited period to exercise the option after he or she retires (such as three to five years), becomes disabled on a long-term basis (such as three to five years), dies (such as one or two years), voluntarily terminates employment (such as three months), or for other reasons. Some plans also provide that options will be forfeited automatically if the holder becomes employed by or associated with a competitor of his or her former employer. In such a case, if an option holder is planning to change jobs and go with a competing firm, he or she should exercise favorable (i.e., "in the money") vested options before terminating employment.

Exercise of Options

Stock options generally can be exercised in several ways.

Cash Exercise An option holder can make a *cash exercise* by paying the option price to the employer and having the stock transferred to him or her. In the case of NQSOs, the employer also will require withholding of federal, state, and local income taxes and FICA taxes on the taxable amount. The option holder must lay out the option price (and any withholding) in cash.

Stock-for-Stock Exercise A plan may allow payment of the exercise price by delivering previously owned shares of stock of the employer that are equal in value to the option price to the employer and having the option stock transferred to the option holder.

> **CASE EXAMPLE**
> Suppose that Ahmed Bastor exercises NQSOs to buy 1,000 shares of ABC Corporation common stock at an option price of $20 per share at a time when the fair market value of the stock is $50 per share. Ahmed already owns ABC common through previous stock option exercises. In a stock-for-stock exercise, Ahmed could deliver 400 shares of his previously owned ABC common to the corporation in payment of the $20,000 exercise price (1,000 shares × $20 per share = $20,000 exercise price ÷ $50 per share = 400 shares of stock to deliver). Assume the 400 shares of

previously owned stock had an income tax basis to Ahmed of $10 per share. There is no gain recognized on the exchange of the 400 previously owned shares for 400 of the new option shares, and the new shares will have the same holding period for capital gain purposes as the previously owned shares. This is because this is a tax-free exchange of common stock in a corporation for common stock in the same corporation, as provided in Section 1036 of the IRC.[5]

The income tax basis of the exchanged shares ($10 per share) will be carried over to 400 of the new option shares. The remainder of the new option shares will be as if it were a cash exercise. The difference between the fair market value of the stock received (600 shares × $50 per share = $30,000) minus any cash paid for the stock (0 in this example) would be ordinary compensation income to Ahmed, and his income tax basis in these 600 shares would be $50 per share (or $30,000), which is the amount taken into his gross income for them. The corporation may require cash withholding or allow withholding in the form of stock otherwise issuable to the option holder. In this case, the option holder is paying for some of the new option stock with existing stock in the same corporation. This reduces the option holder's overall stock position in the company, as compared with a cash exercise, and is the reason reload options (discussed later) may be granted in this situation.

Cashless Exercise This type of exercise involves working through a stockbroker, who can buy the option stock from the corporation at the exercise price, sell enough stock in the open market to cover the purchase price plus broker's commissions and a small amount of margin interest, and then deliver the remaining stock to the option holder.

Reload Options These are additional options that may be granted to employees when they pay the exercise price for stock with previously owned stock of the corporation (a stock-for-stock exercise). The reload option normally is for the same number of shares used to pay the exercise price (plus, perhaps, shares used for federal, state, and local income taxes and FICA taxes for withholding tax purposes) and is for the remainder of the option period of the underlying option that was exercised.

A stock-for-stock exercise of an underlying option when there is a reload option can be attractive for an option holder. Using our previous example of

[5] See Chapter 10 for an explanation of this and other nonrecognition provisions in the tax code.

Ahmed Bastor, assume that ABC's plan provides for reload options. In this case, if the underlying option Ahmed exercised originally had a term of 10 years and Ahmed engaged in the stock-for-stock exercise described previously 4 years after the grant date, he might be granted a reload option for 400 shares (ignoring, for the sake of simplicity, any stock used for tax withholding purposes) at an option price of $50 per share (the current fair market value of the stock) for a term of 6 years (the remaining term of the exercised underlying option).

Compared with a cash exercise and a stock-for-stock exercise with no reload option, Ahmed now is in a better position. Under a cash exercise, he would have an exposure to ABC Corporation stock of 1,400 directly owned shares (400 previously owned and 1,000 option shares), but he would have had to come up with the $20,000 needed to exercise the underlying option. Under a stock-for-stock exercise with no reload feature, Ahmed's exposure to ABC stock would be reduced to 1,000 directly owned shares (the option shares). However, under the stock-for-stock exercise with a reload feature, his exposure to ABC stock remains at 1,400 shares (1,000 directly owned option shares and 400 reload option shares), but he would not have needed to disturb his other assets or cash reserves to exercise the underlying option. This occurs because Ahmed has been given a new option (the reload option), which itself has value.

Valuation of Stock Options

This is a complex subject. It is made even more so by the fact that employee stock options are different in many ways from publicly traded stock and other options discussed in Chapter 5. In essence, however, employee stock options are really call options for the employees on employer stock.

People may be concerned about the valuation of employee stock options for many reasons. Employees want to know what these options are really worth, since they have become an important part of many compensation arrangements. They also need to be valued for purposes of an employee's asset allocation planning, as noted in Chapter 9. In some cases, employees may give up cash compensation in exchange for stock options and so they want to have an idea of what the options are worth to evaluate the exchange. Finally, employee stock options may need to be valued for estate planning purposes.

Traded Options

The market prices of publicly traded options are readily available in the financial press and from other sources. Employee stock options, of course, are not publicly traded and have no readily ascertainable market value.

Most traded options are for relatively short durations, such as a few months. However, just to get an idea of how the market values longer-term options relative to the prices of the underlying stocks, it may be instructive to note the market premiums (prices) for leaps. *Leaps* are longer-term publicly traded options. For example, at one point, the price of a 30-month call option on one major company's stock with a strike price of $115 when the underlying stock's current market price was $94 1/16 (i.e., this call option was out of the money) was $40 per share, or about 42.5 percent of the underlying stock's market price.

Naturally, the prices of such publicly traded long-term options will vary with the characteristics of the underlying stocks and market conditions. The only point we are making here is that the market itself sets a considerable value on longer-term options, even when they have no intrinsic value. Clearly then, the market value (as well as the economic value) of long-term options can be substantial.

Intrinsic Value

As noted in Chapters 9 and 10, the intrinsic value of a stock option is the difference between the underlying stock's current market price and the option's strike price. For example, if an employee is granted a 10-year NQSO with an option price of $25 per share when the underlying stock's market price also is $25 per share, the intrinsic value of the option is $0 at grant. As we have just seen for traded options, the intrinsic value does not reflect the fair value or economic worth of an option. In fact, as will be shown in the next section, the economic worth of a long-term option, such as that previously cited, can be quite substantial.

Option Pricing Models

A number of models (mathematical systems of analysis) have been developed to compute the fair value or economic worth of options. Probably the best known is the Black-Scholes option pricing model. This model is based on the following six factors to determine the economic value of an option.[6] (Let us say for the following illustration of these factors that we are valuing an employee stock option.)

[6] The concept behind these option pricing models is that the fair value of an option (which, in general, is an instrument that allows but does not require a person to buy or sell an asset at a prearranged price during a set period) consists of two elements: the intrinsic value and a time value, arising because the option holder may benefit from favorable future price movements (volatility) in the asset without having the downside risk of actual ownership of the asset.

- Option exercise price (strike price).
- Current market price of the underlying stock.
- Risk-free interest rate during the expected term of the option.
- Expected dividend yield on the stock.
- Expected life of the option. The expected life is the time period the employee is actually expected to hold the option before exercising it. It may be shorter than the maximum option period in the plan.
- Expected volatility of the underlying stock's market price. This normally is the most important factor in the model. The greater the expected volatility, the more likely there will be time value gains (see Footnote 6) and the greater the option value will be. Volatility can be estimated from the historical standard deviation of the stock's price changes over past periods.

CASE EXAMPLE

To illustrate the *fair value* of an option, let us continue our fact pattern for the NQSO noted earlier with respect to intrinsic value. Using the factors just listed, we assume that this NQSO has an option exercise price of $25 per share, a current market price of the underlying stock of $25 per share, an assumed risk-free interest rate of 5 percent, an expected dividend yield of 0, an assumed expected life of the option of 10 years, and an expected volatility of the underlying stock's price of 20 percent per month. Under these assumptions, the Black-Scholes model would produce a fair value of $19.75 per option. This equals 79 percent of the underlying stock's current price. Of course, if the assumed expected life of the option were reduced, the fair value would decline. For example, if the expected life were one year, the fair value would be $7.24 per option. Most employee stock options have an expected life of considerably more than one year. Software is available for calculating the fair value of options under option pricing models.

It is clear from this discussion that the *economic value* (fair value) of stock options granted to employees can be substantial. However, it must also be recognized that the *actual value* of such options may never reach the fair value at grant (from an option pricing model) and may even be zero if the actual market price of the underlying stock should decline or fail to rise from the option price.

Sometimes when a stock's price falls and many executive stock options are "under water" (i.e., the stock's market price is below the option price and the option is out of the money), the employer will *reprice the options* to be equal to the stock's current market price (i.e., cancel the old out-of-the-money options and issue new ones at the stock's current market value). However, this is a controversial tactic.

Some Caveats Concerning Stock Options and Other Plans

While employee stock options and other stock compensation plans have been a boon for many employees and a bonanza for some, some caveats concerning them are in order.

What Goes Up Can Come Down!

It seems almost trite to say that while employee stock plans can be attractive when the price of a company's stock is rising, the reverse will be true when the price is falling. However, some employees may not truly understand this. They can overcommit themselves financially on the basis of paper gains in their stock options and other plans.

Some Employees May Not Realize the True Economic Worth of Options

The other side of the coin is that some employees may not truly understand, or may have difficulty in analyzing, the economic value of options or other stock rights granted to them.

Risk of Excessive Concentration in Employer Stock

While employees usually are well advised to take advantage of these plans when such plans are attractive to them, they also should deal with any overconcentration issue, assuming they want a reasonably diversified investment portfolio.

Planning Issues Regarding Stock Options and Other Stock Plans

Some of these issues may be summarized as follows:

- Whether to participate in employee stock purchase plan offerings. This depends on the terms of the plan and the employer stock. In general, these plans are advantageous for employees and are flexible as to whether participating employees will take the stock.
- When to exercise stock options. This can be a complicated issue. An employee can simply hold a vested, unexercised option for as long as possible before exercising it. In this case, he or she can benefit from the underlying stock's possible increase in price over the options' exercise price without actually committing any funds, and delaying income taxation in

the case of NQSOs until exercise. This is attractive if the stock's price does increase during the remaining option period. It also can be attractive if income tax rates on ordinary compensation income (such as will arise from exercising NQSOs) are expected to decline in the future. But if the concern is that the stock's price may fall and not really ever recover during the remaining option period, it is better to exercise now and sell the stock as soon as possible. Also, if overconcentration in employer stock is an issue, as it often is, the exercise of NQSOs and immediate sale of the stock can be a tax-efficient remedy, since compensation income must be realized at some point anyway and there is no capital gain on immediate sale because the basis is equal to fair market value at exercise.

- Whether, in effect, to change an ISO into an NQSO by breaking an ISO requirement (i.e., making a disqualifying disposition by sale of the stock within one year of exercise). This may be done to avoid an AMT problem or if the stock's price is expected to fall dramatically. A planning technique that may be used in this situation is *AMT neutralization*. In AMT neutralization, the employee sells enough ISO shares (after exercise) in disqualifying dispositions so that his or her regular tax for the year becomes equal to his or her AMT. Then there is no AMT to pay.
- How to exercise options (including possible availability of reload options).
- Whether to make a Section 83(b) election with regard to restricted stock or other plans.
- Whether to take option stock as restricted stock, if available under the plan. This is done to further delay recognition of income on exercise of NQSOs.
- Whether to take bonuses or other compensation in the form of stock options, if available.
- How to maintain investment diversification in light of possible favorable terms for acquiring more employer stock.
- Any estate planning actions with regard to stock plans. This might include making gifts of NQSOs if allowed by the plan. However, such gifts should be analyzed carefully. It also may include the exercise of any in-the-money unexercised NQSOs before death (e.g., a "death bed exercise") for estate tax reasons.

PART VI

Charitable Giving

19

Charitable Giving Techniques

Competence Objectives for This Chapter After reading this chapter, planners should understand:

- The basic tax principles concerning charitable giving
- The advantages of giving appreciated property
- The nature of split (remainder) gifts to charity
- The types and tax treatment of charitable remainder trusts (CRTs)
- Uses of life insurance in relation to CRTs
- The nature of pooled income funds
- The characteristics and tax treatment of charitable gift annuities
- Partial interest charitable gifts
- Gifts of qualified conservation contributions or easements
- Bargain sales to charity
- Gifts of closely held stock to charity
- Naming charities as beneficiaries of qualified retirement plans and traditional IRAs
- Gifts of life insurance to charities
- Planning for when to make charitable contributions

Charitable giving has become an important part of financial and estate planning. Most charitable gifts are straightforward gifts of money. However, many times, appreciated property is given. On the other hand, a number of more sophisticated techniques may give the charitably inclined substantial tax and other benefits in addition to the satisfaction of knowing they have helped others.

Basic Tax Principles

Income Tax Deduction

Contributions to eligible charities can be taken as an itemized deduction (subject to certain annual limits explained next and the phase-out rules described in Chapter 10) for federal income tax purposes.

Annual Limits on Income Tax Deduction

There are complicated rules that determine the amount of deduction that can be taken each year.[1] This amount depends on the type of property given, the type of charity involved, the contribution base of the taxpayer, and ordering rules for applying the percentage limits. The rules are only briefly described here.

Contribution Base A taxpayer's *contribution base* is his or her AGI without allowance for any net operating loss carryback.

Cash Contributions For cash contributions to charities generally defined as *public charities* (e.g., churches, educational organizations, hospital and medical research organizations, governmental units, and publicly supported organizations),[2] the annual limit is 50 percent of the contribution base. For cash contributions to other eligible charities, the limit is 30 percent of the contribution base (or what is left of the 50 percent limit if less).

Long-Term Capital Gain Property For gifts of *intangible personal property* (e.g., stocks and bonds) or *real property* (real estate), which, if sold, would produce long-term capital gain, to public charities, the full fair market value of the property at the time of the gift can be deducted, but the annual limit is 30 percent of the contribution base (or what is left of the 50 percent limit if less).[3] For gifts of long-term capital gain property to other eligible charities, the full fair market value can be deducted, but the annual limit is 20 percent of the contribution base (or what is left of the 30 percent limit if less).

[1] While there are annual limits on the deductibility of charitable contributions for federal income tax purposes, there are no such limits on federal gift tax and federal estate tax charitable deductions. For these taxes, gifts to any eligible charities are deductible in full.

[2] Certain private operating foundations and nonoperating "feeder foundations" also are included. These are organizations described in Section 170(b)(1)(A) of the IRC.

[3] As an alternative, a taxpayer can elect to limit his or her deduction to the income tax basis (not the fair market value) of the donated long-term capital gain property. If this election were made, the annual limit would be 50 percent of the contribution base. Normally, however, such an election would be of limited usefulness.

Private Foundations For gifts of appreciated property to private foundations (other than certain private operating foundations and nonoperating feeder foundations), in general, the deduction allowed is limited to the donor's income tax basis in the property. However, an exception to this general rule allows taxpayers to deduct the full fair market value (up to 20 percent of the contribution base) of appreciated publicly traded stock (qualified appreciated stock) given to private foundations.

Short-Term Capital Gain Property For gifts of appreciated property, which, if sold, would not produce long-term capital gain (e.g., capital assets held for 12 months or less and inventory held for sale) to public charities, the deduction is limited to the taxpayer's basis in the property and the annual limit is 50 percent of the contribution base.

Tangible Personal Property Finally, if appreciated tangible personal property (e.g., artwork), which, if sold, would produce long-term capital gain, are given to public charities whose function is related to the use of the property (e.g., a public art museum), the amount deductible is the full fair market value of the property and the annual limit is 30 percent of the contribution base. On the other hand, if the function of the public charity is unrelated to the use of the tangible personal property, the deduction is limited to the donor's basis in the property, but the annual limit is 50 percent of the contribution base.

Carryover of Excess Charitable Deductions Any unused charitable deduction for a given year that exceeds the annual limitation can be carried over for up to five additional years. The deductions during this five-year carryover period are subject to certain ordering provisions in the tax law.

Nonrecognition of Capital Gains on Donated Property

No capital gain is realized and recognized by a donor when he or she gives appreciated property to charity. Correspondingly, if the donor can deduct the full fair market value of the appreciated property, in effect, the potential capital gain escapes taxation entirely. Furthermore, when a charity or a charitable remainder trust (CRT) sells appreciated property given to it, the donor does not realize any gain. The charity or CRT also does not realize gain because it is tax exempt.

Gift and Estate Tax Deductions for Transfers to Charity

Eligible transfers to charity are deductible in full for federal gift tax purposes (for lifetime transfers) and for federal estate tax purposes (for transfers at death). They are also deductible for GST tax purposes.

Reporting and Valuation Requirements

Contributions to a charity in excess of $250 must be acknowledged by the charity in writing. The donor may also have to keep other records for contributions over $250 and over $500. Furthermore, if the claimed charitable deduction for an item of property or a group of similar items of property (other than money or publicly traded securities) exceeds $5,000, the donor-taxpayer must get a qualified appraisal of the property from a qualified appraiser and attach a summary to his or her tax return.

Planning Techniques

Giving Appreciated Property

One interesting technique that may be available to many persons is giving appreciated long-term capital gain property, such as common stock. Here the gift generally is deductible at its fair market value and no capital gain would be realized by the donor.

CASE EXAMPLE

Suppose that Mary Whitcomb has owned common stock in a growth company for a long time and it has appreciated considerably. She would like to dispose of some of this stock to diversify her portfolio but has no offsetting losses. She also customarily gives about $3,000 per year to her church. If she were to give $3,000 worth of this stock (rather than her customary cash donation) to the church, she would be better off tax-wise and the church would get the same dollar donation (minus any selling expenses on the stock).

Let us see why. Assume that Mary's cost basis in the donated stock is $300 and she and her husband are in a 33 percent federal income tax bracket. We shall compare the tax results of a gift to charity of the stock itself with the results of a sale of the stock, retaining the after-tax proceeds of the sale and making the investor's customary $3,000 cash contribution to charity.

The net effect is a tax saving equal to the capital gains tax on the sale of the appreciated property. But this works only if the taxpayer is going to make a charitable contribution anyway.

	Sale of Stock and Gift of Cash		Gift of Stock	
Market value of stock (fair market value)	$3,000		$3,000	
Cost basis	–$300		—	
Capital gain	$2,700			
Charitable contribution	$3,000	(cash)	$3,000	(stock)
Tax deduction	–$990		–$990	
	$2,010		$2,010	
Capital gains tax (on above at the 15% rate)	$405		—	
After-tax cost of transaction to taxpayer	$2,415	(the $3,000 gift + $405 capital gains tax – $990 charitable deduction)	$2,010	(the $3,000 gift – $990 charitable deduction)

Capital Loss Property On the other hand, if a person is holding property on which he or she has an unrealized capital loss, the reverse is true. The contributor is better off tax-wise first to sell the property and take the tax loss, and then to give the proceeds to charity in cash. That way, the contributor gets both the capital loss on the sale and the charitable deduction.

Making Split (Remainder) Gifts to Charity

An increasingly popular approach to more sophisticated charitable giving is to make a gift now of a future interest in property to charity while retaining a present interest in the property for the donor and/or the donor's family. This is commonly done by giving a remainder interest in property to a charity. This involves the donor's retaining an intervening interest in the property for a period of years, or for one or more persons' lifetimes, and then when this interest ends, the property goes to the charity (i.e., the remainder interest to charity).[4] This approach can be attractive in retirement or estate planning. However, the tax law permits this to be done only in certain ways: these are gift of a remainder interest in a personal residence or farm, use of a charitable remainder unitrust, use of a charitable remainder annuity trust, and use of pooled income funds.

[4] There also are other kinds of split gifts to charity. These are charitable lead trusts, where the charity receives the initial income interest and then a noncharitable beneficiary gets the remainder interest and joint ownership with a charity. These approaches are described later in this chapter.

Gift of Remainder Interest in Personal Residence or Farm A donor may give these types of real property to charity but reserve the right to live in or use the property for the remaining lifetime of the donor or the donor and his or her spouse. The donor gets a current income tax charitable deduction for the present value of the charity's remainder interest in the *depreciated value* of the residence or farm. This type of future gift to charity does not require a formal trust. However, since improvements on the land (e.g., buildings) must be depreciated in calculating the charitable deduction, this approach may not be as attractive as it might first appear.

Charitable Remainder Unitrust (CRUT) A *charitable remainder trust (CRT),* in general, involves the creation of a formal irrevocable trust into which the donor (as grantor of the trust) places property that is the subject of the charitable gift. There are two types of CRTs: the *charitable remainder unitrust* (CRUT) and the *charitable remainder annuity trust* (CRAT). We shall describe the CRUT in this section and the CRAT in the next.

Straight Charitable Remainder Unitrust: In this approach to a CRUT, the donor creates and places highly appreciated property into an irrevocable charitable trust under which the donor (or perhaps the donor and another beneficiary or beneficiaries after the donor's death) will receive a specified percentage (but no less than 5 percent or no more than 50 percent) of each year's current value of the trust assets for the beneficiary's lifetime or for a fixed period of years not exceeding 20 years. If trust income is not sufficient to pay the specified unitrust amount, trust corpus must be used to do so.

Net Income with Makeup Charitable Remainder Unitrust (NIMCRUT): A variation on the payout under a straight CRUT is the *net income with makeup charitable remainder unitrust* (NIMCRUT). In this case, the noncharitable income beneficiaries will receive the *lesser* of the stated unitrust amount (say, 5 percent of the trust corpus each year) or that year's actual accounting income of the trust. The trust also provides that to the extent its accounting income in any year is less than the stated unitrust amount, the difference is accumulated as trust principal and can be paid out to the income beneficiary(ies) in any future year to the extent that trust accounting income exceeds the stated unitrust amount. This is the makeup provision. A NIMCRUT, for example, can be useful in providing a deferred retirement plan for the donor and perhaps his or her spouse.

CASE EXAMPLE

As an illustration, suppose Harry Blum and his wife Amy are both age 55, in good health, work outside the home, and would like to retire at age 60 (in five years). Over the years, Harry has invested in several publicly traded growth common stocks that now have a combined market value of $1,000,000, an income tax basis to Harry of $400,000, and a current yield of about 1 percent. Harry and Amy have other assets and retirement plans as well. They feel they will need more income when they retire, but they do not need current income now. Harry and Amy are also charitably inclined.

Therefore, Harry decides to establish a NIMCRUT and place the $1,000,000 of growth common stocks in it. The NIMCRUT provides that the lesser of the trust's accounting income or the unitrust amount—say, 5 percent of trust corpus—will be paid to Harry and Amy while both are alive and then to the survivor for the remainder of his or her lifetime. Upon the death of the last of them to die, the trust corpus will pass to their synagogue (a public charity) as remainderperson. The trust has a makeup provision.

In the year this trust is established, assume Harry and Amy are entitled to a charitable income tax deduction of about $250,000,[5] which is the present value at that time of the remainder interest that ultimately will go to the charity. Note that they probably will not be able to take the full amount of this deduction in the year the trust is established because of the annual limit on such deductions.

Table 19.1 shows how the payments to Harry and Amy and the makeup provision of this NIMCRUT would work in this situation. It is assumed the trust retains the growth stocks (or sells some or all of them and invests in similar growth stocks) for the first five years and then sells the growth stocks and invests in higher-yielding income-producing assets.[6] No gain is realized by the trust on the sale because it is tax exempt. There also is no gain realized by Harry and Amy. The result is a substantial deferral of income until the noncharitable beneficiaries (Harry and Amy) retire. Under these assumptions, their annual income from the NIMCRUT will rise from $15,735 to $110,146 when they reach their planned retirement age of 60.

[5] This value depends on the actuarial value of Harry and Amy's unitrust life income interests, which, in turn, is based on an assumed mortality table and an interest rate. The mortality table is promulgated by the IRS and is revised every 10 years. The interest rate is the Section 7529 rate for the appropriate month.

[6] However, there can be no restrictions in the trust document as to how the trustee can invest trust assets. It is anticipated that the trustee will understand the nature of the transaction and the intentions of the parties.

Table 19.1. Operation of a Hypothetical Net Income with Makeup Charitable Remainder Unitrust

1 Year	2 Value of Trust Assets (Beginning of Year)*	3 Stated Unitrust Amount (5% in This Example)	4 Actual Trust Accounting Income*	5 Deficiency to Be Made Up Later	6 Income Paid to Beneficiary
1	$1,000,000	$50,000	$10,000	$40,000	$10,000
2	$1,120,000	$56,000	$11,200	$84,800	$11,200
3	$1,254,400	$70,246	$12,544	$134,976	$12,544
4	$1,404,928	$78,676	$14,049	$191,173	$14,049
5	$1,573,519	$78,676	$15,735	$254,114	$15,735
6†	$1,573,519	$78,676	$110,146	$222,644	$110,146
7	$1,573,519	$78,676	$110,146	$191,174	$110,146
8	$1,573,519	$78,676	$110,146	$159,704	$110,146
9	$1,573,519	$78,676	$110,146	$128,234	$110,146
10	$1,573,519	$78,676	$110,146	$96,764	$110,146
11	$1,573,519	$78,676	$110,146	$65,294	$110,146
12	$1,573,519	$78,676	$110,146	$33,824	$110,146
13	$1,573,519	$78,676	$110,146	$2,354	$110,146
14	$1,573,519	$78,676	$110,146	0	$81,030
15	$1,602,635	$80,132	$112,184	0	$80,132

*The assumptions underlying these figures are that for the first five years the trust invests in growth common stocks, with a 1 percent current yield and 12 percent annual capital growth. For the sixth and subsequent years, the trust invests in a diversified portfolio of bonds (U.S. Treasury bonds, investment-grade corporates, and some high-yield corporates) with diversified maturities (laddered). This bond portfolio has a 7 percent current yield and zero capital growth. Naturally, other investment assumptions can be, and often are, made.

†It is assumed that in this year the trust sells the common stock and buys the bonds. There is no gain to the trust because it is tax exempt, nor is there gain to Harry and Amy.

Clearly, the investment strategy for this kind of trust is critical. There is, of course, no assurance that the expected returns from growth stocks will actually be realized. Also, after the sale of the growth stocks, the trustee could follow a more diversified asset allocation strategy, such as using a combination of bonds and income-oriented common stocks, which would produce income but also more capital growth for the trust. A possible problem here, depending on the investment climate at the time, may be in achieving high enough current accounting income in the trust so the makeup provision can apply. Some advisers have suggested devices such as deferred annuities and partnerships, where permitted, in these trusts. Another possible approach, where allowed, is for the trust instrument to consider capital gains as accounting income.

Net Income Charitable Remainder Unitrust: Here the noncharitable beneficiaries receive the lesser of the stated unitrust amount or that year's actual accounting income of the trust. However, there is no makeup provision.

Flip Unitrust: This is another variation from the straight CRUT. In this case, a donor often contributes highly appreciated, nonliquid assets (such as closely held business interests or real estate) to a CRT. The CRT begins as a NIMCRUT (or a net income unitrust), but when the trustee later sells the appreciated asset, the CRT converts (flips) by its terms to be a straight CRUT. The advantage of this approach is that before the sale, the unitrust only has to pay the noncharitable beneficiary the accounting income, if any, from the trust. On the other hand, after the sale, the beneficiary is assured of receiving the unitrust amount even if the accounting income might be less.[7] By its regulations, the IRS allows flip unitrusts. The flip must be based on some objective event, such as a beneficiary's reaching a certain age or the sale of an unmarketable asset. Also, after the flip, the trustee must pay at least annually the unitrust amount without any makeup payments that may have accrued before the flip.

Charitable Remainder Annuity Trust (CRAT) The CRAT uses essentially the same general concept as the charitable remainder unitrust, except that the return to the noncharitable income beneficiary must be a fixed or determined amount (again, no less than 5 percent or no more than 50 percent), calculated on the basis of the initial value of the property originally transferred to the trust. The CRAT does not have the variations in income payout that have just been described for the CRUT.

Amount of Charitable Deduction The current income tax deduction received by a donor to a CRT is equal to the actuarial present value of the remainder interest that ultimately will pass to the charity, valued as of the time the donor makes the gift to the CRT. This present value may depend on the type of CRT; the specified payment to the noncharitable beneficiary(ies); the term of the payments to the noncharitable beneficiary(ies), which may depend on the age(s) of the beneficiary(ies) and the mortality table assumed; and the Section 7520 interest rate for the month the gift is made (or for either of the two preceding months at the option of the taxpayer).

As explained in Chapter 3, the *Section 7520 rate*[8] is the interest rate to be used in valuing annuities, life interests or interests for a term of years, and remainder and reversionary interests for federal tax purposes. It is determined and published monthly by the government, and is 120 percent of the federal

[7] This is the difference between a flip unitrust and a regular NIMCRUT. In a regular NIMCRUT, if the accounting income is less than the percentage unitrust amount, only the accounting income will be paid to the noncharitable beneficiary.

[8] This rate is defined in Section 7520(a) of the IRC and is described in Chapter 3.

midterm rate for the month.[9] The Section 7520 rate, in effect, is the rate the IRS assumes can be earned on assets. Other valuation factors also are prescribed in government tables. Computer software is available to aid advisers in calculating values needed in planning for CRTs, other charitable giving techniques, and other estate planning techniques.

Taxation of Noncharitable Income Beneficiaries The payouts received by noncharitable income beneficiaries of CRTs are taxed on a four-tier system for income tax purposes. To the extent that a CRT has present or accumulated income of the various types, distributions are first deemed to be ordinary income, second as capital gains, next as other income (such as tax-exempt income), and finally as a return of principal.

This means that if a CRT receives any ordinary income from its assets or any capital gains (such as from the sale of appreciated assets), the CRT itself will not have any taxable income because it is tax exempt, but as distributions are made to the noncharitable beneficiary(ies), they are considered to receive income under this system. Thus, if a CRT sells highly appreciated assets contributed to it, the capital gain ultimately will be taxed to the noncharitable beneficiaries as distributions are made to them. This is why a CRT can sometimes be said to act as an installment sales substitute.

Minimum Remainders to Charity The tax law requires that certain minimum remainder values must go to the charity under CRTs. First, the actuarial present value of the charitable remainder interest must equal at least 10 percent of a property's value when it is contributed to a CRT (the 10 percent test). Second, for CRATs, there cannot be greater than a 5 percent probability that the trust's corpus will be exhausted before the charity is supposed to receive something (the 5 percent test). Both tests must be met when applicable. In effect, this means that CRTs cannot be used when the charity's interests are negligible at their creation. Fortunately, the law permits CRTs to be reformed when their terms fail to meet the 10 percent test (or certain other requirements).

Life Insurance and CRTs Life insurance can be used to replace all or part of the value passing to charity after the death of the noncharitable income beneficiary(ies). When the donor is the income beneficiary, the life insurance would be on his or her life. When the donor and his or her spouse are income beneficiaries, the life insurance can be a second-to-die policy on both lives. The life insurance often is purchased and owned by an *irrevocable life insurance trust* (ILIT). (These trusts are described in Chapter 29.) The amount

[9] The *federal midterm rate* is the applicable federal rate determined on the basis of the average market yield on outstanding marketable obligations of the United States with remaining maturities of three to nine years for each calendar month.

of life insurance needed depends on the circumstances. For example, it can be based on what the family otherwise might lose (after taxes) but for the creation of the CRT.

Comparing CRUT to CRAT As noted earlier, these are two distinct types of CRT. Each has advantages, depending on the circumstances.

CASE EXAMPLE

Suppose that John Silver, age 65, is an executive of Growth Corporation, is planning to retire soon, and has a large part of his investment portfolio in highly appreciated Growth Corporation common stock (with a 1 percent current yield). John is married, and his wife, Lynn, also is age 65. John and Lynn have three adult children and six grandchildren. John would like to make a meaningful contribution to the university from which he graduated many years ago, mainly with the help of scholarship money.

One possibility is that John could transfer, say, $600,000 of his highly appreciated Growth Corporation stock (which has an income tax basis to him of $100,000) to a CRAT, with a 7 percent payout rate to John and his wife for as long as either of them lives. As a result, Mr. and Mrs. Silver would receive a fixed annual distribution of $42,000 from the trust ($600,000 × 0.07), and this amount will not change even if the corpus of the trust should rise or fall in value. If trust income is not sufficient to pay this amount, trust principal will have to be used to make up the difference. Then, upon the last of their deaths, the value at that time of the trust corpus will go outright to the university. The Silvers will get a current income tax deduction for the actuarial value of the charity's remainder interest. Finally, the Silvers will realize no capital gain from the appreciated stock transferred to the CRAT, and, of course, neither would the CRAT because it is tax exempt.

On the other hand, if John had used a CRUT with the same general terms, he and his wife would receive an annual distribution from the trust for their lifetimes of 7 percent of each year's value of the trust assets. Thus, if trust assets grow in value, their annual income correspondingly will grow, but if trust assets decline in value, the reverse will be true. Thus, to make an admittedly overly simplistic comparison, a unitrust may be better for donors and their families in the event of capital growth, while the annuity trust may provide donors and their families with a stable income in the face of declines in asset values (e.g., during recessions or depressions). There, of course, are other differences, such as possible use of NIMCRUTs to build greater future income and flip unitrusts. Also, after the trust is established, additional contributions can be made to a unitrust but not to an annuity trust.

A Further Illustration with an Irrevocable Life Insurance Trust

Suppose now that Mr. and Mrs. Silver decide to contribute the $600,000 of Growth Corporation stock to a 7 percent straight CRUT. Also assume they would be entitled to a current income tax deduction of $155,382, which will be spread over several years because of the 30 percent of AGI annual limit. If the Silvers are in the 35 percent federal income tax bracket (ignoring any state or local income taxes for the sake of simplicity), their tax saving can be estimated as $54,384 (0.35 × $155,382).

Let us assume further that the trust sells the Growth Corporation stock for $600,000 and invests the proceeds in a diversified portfolio of 50 percent of income-oriented common stocks and 50 percent of diversified, mostly investment grade, corporate bonds. Assume this portfolio yields a return of 5 percent from common stock dividends, 7 percent in taxable interest from the corporate bonds, and 3 percent in long-term capital growth from the common stocks (ignoring expenses of the trust). However, when the CRUT pays the annual 7 percent unitrust amount to Mr. and Mrs. Silver (which initially would be $42,000, assuming the CRUT corpus is $600,000); under the four-tier system for taxing the noncharitable beneficiaries, first to be taxed would be the interest on the corporate bonds as ordinary income and dividends from the common stocks as qualified dividends. Then the remainder would be taxed as capital gains because the CRUT realized those gains in the sale of the growth company stock. The remaining gains would constitute unrealized appreciation in the trust corpus, which would serve to increase future 7 percent payouts from the Thus, the after-tax annual return for the Silvers in the first year would be 5.25 percent or $31,500 (0.0525 × $600,000). This annual payout will grow if the CRUT corpus grows, but correspondingly, it will decline if the CRUT corpus declines. At the last of their deaths, the existing trust corpus will go to the university as remainderperson.

On the other hand, suppose that the Silvers do not contribute this stock to a CRUT as just described, but rather they either retain it or sell it and invest the proceeds to provide retirement income for themselves until the last of their deaths. At that time, the survivor would leave it to their children. Let us further suppose

Mr. and Mrs. Silver decide to sell the $600,000 of Growth stock and reinvest the net proceeds (after capital gains tax) in the same kind of diversified portfolio described previously for the CRUT.

They made this decision, despite having to pay a sizeable capital gains tax of $75,000 ($600,000 amount realized – $100,000 adjusted basis = $500,000 gain realized and recognized × 0.15 = $75,000 tax), because their investable assets are far too concentrated in Growth Corporation stock, they want a more income-oriented asset allocation strategy during retirement, and John still will have Growth Corporation common in his portfolio from other sources even after the sale.

After the sale, the Silvers will have $525,000 of net proceeds (ignoring expenses of the sale) to invest. Assuming the same asset allocation and returns as previously, and that all investment income and gains are paid out currently to the Silvers, their corresponding after-tax annual return would be 5.67 percent of $525,000, or $29,767.

Now, assuming their joint life expectancies are about 20 years (or to age 85), the $525,000 investment fund would be about $525,000 after the last of their deaths (assuming all investment returns are paid out currently for retirement expenses). However, this amount would be in the gross estate for federal estate tax purposes of the last spouse to die, assuming adoption of a marital deduction strategy that results in no estate tax due at the first death. If we further assume that the surviving spouse's estate will be in the 45 percent federal estate tax bracket, the federal estate tax alone (ignoring any state death taxes and other estate settlement costs) will diminish this amount for their children to an estimated $288,750. This is the estimated amount that might be lost to their family if the CRUT were used instead of retaining the property until the last death.

Therefore, at this point, the Silvers' annual retirement income situation from these two possibilities can be compared as follows:

Contribution to the 7% CRUT	
After-tax annual income from CRUT	$31,500
After-tax annual income from tax savings from current charitable deduction on creating the CRUT ($54,384 × 0.0567 = $3,084)[10]	$3,084
Total retirement income	$34,584

[10] This assumes the same after-tax total return as from the retained net assets.

Sale of appreciated stock and reinvestment of net proceeds
After-tax annual income $29,767

Clearly, the CRUT results in more after-tax retirement income for Mr. and Mrs. Silver. It also enables them to make a substantial and meaningful gift to their university. However, the issue of the loss of the otherwise retained property's value to their children and grandchildren remains.

It may be that Mr. and Mrs. Silver will feel that their other assets constitute a sufficient inheritance for their children and grandchildren. However, the Silvers may feel they do not want to reduce what their children and grandchildren will receive after both of them are gone. In this event, Mr. or Mrs. Silver can establish an ILIT to purchase, own, and be the beneficiary of a second-to-die life insurance policy on both their lives in an amount of approximately $288,750 (or more, if desired). The level of premium needed to carry such a policy (on a male and a female, both age 65 and in good health) might be $3,000 to $4,000 per year. Mr. or Mrs. Silver could give approximately this amount each year to the trustee of the ILIT so the trustee could pay the premiums. Their children (and perhaps grandchildren) would be the beneficiaries of this trust.

General Considerations Regarding CRTs It can be seen that establishment of a charitable remainder unitrust or annuity trust is a complicated legal and financial transaction that requires the aid of the donor's professional advisers. These arrangements normally are practical only for larger gifts. It is possible for the donor-grantor to serve as trustee or co-trustee of the charitable trust. However, in this case, the donor must act in a fiduciary capacity. The trust may also contain a provision allowing the donor to change the charitable beneficiary to another eligible charity.

Pooled Income Fund The final way to make remainder gifts to charity is through pooled income funds maintained by many larger charities. These are funds in which the contributions of a number of donors are combined for investment purposes. In this sense, they are like mutual funds run by charities. Some larger charities maintain several pooled income funds with different investment objectives to meet the needs of their donors.

Like the previously described charitable remainder unitrusts and annuity trusts, a donor can make a gift of appreciated property and escape capital gains tax on the appreciation, get an immediate income tax deduction for the actuarial value of the charity's remainder interest, and receive an income from the fund for life or for a period of years. In the case of pooled income funds, however, the donor receives a certain number of units (the number depending on their current value and the amount contributed) in a particular pooled income fund. In addition, the donor gets the advantage of investment diversification through a well-managed fund or funds.

The annual income received by the donor or others is determined each year by the pooled income fund's investment return. Thus, before contributing to such a fund, a potential donor, or his or her advisers, should check into the fund's current and past investment returns as well as its investment objectives, much like one would before investing in a mutual fund or other financial intermediary.

To contribute to a pooled income fund, a donor does not have to create an individual trust. Thus, carefully selected pooled income funds can be a practical technique even for donors making smaller gifts. Of course, after the noncharitable income interest or interests expire, the property will go to the charity. Again, the donor (if insurable) can use life insurance to make up the loss to his or her family.

Other Forms of Charitable Contributions

Charitable Gift Annuity This is a different kind of arrangement from those discussed in the preceding sections. The *charitable gift annuity* is the sale of an annuity by a charity to a donor-annuitant for a price in excess of what would be charged for the same annuity by a commercial insurance company. This determines the income tax charitable deduction for the donor-annuitant which is the projected remainder value going to the charity after the annuitant's death. The annuity income received by the donor-annuitant, and possibly other annuitants, varies with the annuitant's age and among charities. Many charities follow the annuity rate recommendations (called the Suggested Charitable Gift Annuity Rates) adopted by the American Council on Gift Annuities.[11] Normally, a donor-annuitant would not consider such an annuity absent his or her charitable motive.

A gift annuity is a contract guaranteed by the charity. Therefore, a donor-annuitant should consider the financial soundness of the charity, just as

[11] The council is an organization sponsored by a large number of charitable organizations. Use of its recommended rates is voluntary on the part of charities selling gift annuities. These annuity rates are designed to result in approximately a 50 percent return to the charity once the annuitant dies. However, some charities use gift annuity rates that are designed to produce greater returns for the charity (and thus less for the annuitants). This may be a point for potential donor-annuitants to check before purchasing a gift annuity from a charity.

an annuitant should evaluate the financial soundness of a life insurance company issuing a commercial annuity contract.

Charitable gift annuities are taxed under the general annuity rules. Therefore a portion of each annuity payment is an income tax–free return of investment in the contract, while the remainder is taxable investment income. Gift annuities can be purchased with appropriated assets. In this case, a portion of the gain (on the projected amount going to charity) is not taxed. This remainder is taxed pro-rata as the annuity payments are received. In effect, the tax on this portion of the capital gain is deferred.

Gift of Undivided Portion of an Owner's Entire Interest in Property This involves making the charity a co-owner of property. For example, a charity might be given one-half of a piece of artwork, with the donor retaining the other half. A current income tax deduction could be taken for the value of the charity's interest. However, the PPA of 2006 put substantial new requirements on donation of fractional interests in tangible personal property (such as art to an art museum) that limited the attractiveness of this strategy.

Gift of Qualified Conservation Contributions or Easements These contributions often involve the granting of conservation easements with respect to real estate to qualified charities or governments. An easement in gross (i.e., one not derived from the ownership of adjacent or other lands) is a personal interest in, or the right to use, the land of another. The tax law allows rather generous income tax deductions as well as estate and gift tax exclusions for qualified conservation contributions or easements.

A *qualified conservation contribution* is a contribution of a qualified real property interest to a qualified organization (governments and publicly supported charities) exclusively for conservation purposes. For purposes of this definition, *a qualified real property interest* includes a restriction (such as an easement) that is granted in perpetuity on the use of real property.[12]

Income Tax Deduction: A charitable deduction can be taken for the value of a qualified conservation contribution made during the donor's lifetime. The value of a contribution (such as a conservation easement) may be determined as the difference between the fair market value of the real property before the easement was granted and the fair market value after the easement was granted.[13]

[12] Other qualified real property interests are the entire interest of a donor other than a qualified mineral interest and a remainder interest.

[13] If there should happen to be substantial records of sales of similar easements, the value would be based on this. However, such sales or records may not be available.

Estate Tax Exclusion: An executor can exclude from a decedent's gross estate for federal estate tax purposes an applicable percentage (up to 40 percent) of the value of land subject to a qualified conservation easement up to a dollar exclusion limitation and subject to certain other requirements. The applicable percentage is 40 percent reduced by two percentage points for each one percentage point by which the value of the qualified conservation easement is less than 30 percent of the value of the land without regard to the value of the easement and reduced by the value of any retained development right. The dollar exclusion limitation is $500,000. The easement may be made during the owner's lifetime or after his or her death.

On the other hand, a qualified conservation easement must be granted in perpetuity. It thus may lessen the future uses to which real property can be put and its future sales value.

Bargain Sales to Charity Sometimes donors do not want to give the full value of property to charity. Thus, the donor may sell the property to a charity for less than its fair market value—a bargain sale. However, such a bargain sale of appreciated property will be classified for tax purposes into two parts: a contribution portion (which is deductible) and a sale portion (which is taxable). The tax is determined by allocating the property's tax basis between the contribution portion and the sale portion based on the ratio of the sales price to the fair market value.

Gifts of Closely Held Stock to Charity with a Redemption Donors may own appreciated, closely held, corporate stock for which there is no ready market. Sometimes, an owner will give such stock to a charity with the informal understanding, but not a legally binding obligation on the part of the charity, that the stock will be redeemed by the corporation from the charity after the gift. The result is that the donor-stockholder has made a charitable contribution; he or she can take an income tax deduction for the fair market value of the stock (without realizing capital gain); the closely held corporation uses its cash to make the redemption from the charity without any tax effect on the donor-stockholder; and the charity ends up with cash, which is normally what it wants, rather than with closely held stock. This technique sometimes is called a *charity bailout.*

Naming Charities as Death Beneficiaries of Qualified Retirement Plans and Traditional IRAs If a person wants to make a charitable contribution at death in any event, a favorable way to do so from a tax point of view is to name the charity as beneficiary of part or all of the person's remaining account balances under defined contribution retirement plans or traditional IRAs. Death benefits payable to noncharitable beneficiaries under these plans are heavily taxed—first in the participant's or IRA owner's gross estate for federal estate tax (and perhaps state death tax) purposes, and then as IRD (with a deduction for any estate taxes paid on the IRD item) to the beneficiary for federal income tax purposes.[14] These taxes are avoided when IRD items are made payable to (or are left to) charitable beneficiaries at death. Thus, a person can plan to use IRD items to fulfill charitable-giving objectives at death and then use non-IRD items, along with the remainder of any IRD items, for noncharitable gifts and bequests.[15]

Gifts of Life Insurance to Charity Sometimes, donors give life insurance policies on their lives to charity. When a donor absolutely assigns (i.e., gives array) all incidents of ownership in a policy to a charity, the donor-insured has made a deductible charitable contribution equal to the value of the policy at the time of the gift, plus additional deductible contributions if the donor-insured makes future premium payments on the policy.

Charitable Lead Trusts Charitable lead trusts, also called *charitable income trusts* or *front trusts,* are the reverse of the CRAT and CRUT described previously. In a lead trust, the charity receives an annuity interest based on the initial value of the trust's corpus (a charitable lead annuity trust, CLAT) or a unitrust interest based on the value of the trust's corpus each year (a charitable lead unitrust, CLUT) for a fixed period, after which the remainder interest goes to noncharitable beneficiaries, such as the donor's family. These trusts can be created during a donor's lifetime as a living trust or under his or her will as a testamentary trust.

Charitable lead trusts can be attractive when a donor wants to make a meaningful charitable contribution, his or her family does not need current income from the property, and the donor wants to get a significant gift or estate tax deduction for the present value (using Section 7520 rates) of the charity's income interest.

For example, suppose Harry Carter would like to make lifetime gifts of about $1,000,000 each to his two adult children from a previous marriage. The children are successful in their careers and do not need current income. Harry also would like to make a meaningful charitable gift to a local hospital. Furthermore, assume that Harry has more than enough other assets for himself, his present wife, and the children of his second marriage. In this situation, Harry might create a living charitable lead annuity trust with $2,000,000 of his assets that will pay a 7 percent annuity interest ($140,000 per year) to the hospital for 10 years and then pay the remainder to Harry's

[14] The nature of such IRD treatment was explained in Chapter 10.

[15] Planning for taking distributions from retirement plans in general is discussed in Chapter 16.

two children in equal shares. The present value of the hospital's annuity interest for 10 years (using a 6 percent Section 7520 interest rate) would be $1,030,412. Harry can take a gift tax charitable deduction for this amount, and so the taxable gift for federal gift tax purposes would be the present value of the remainder interest to his two children after 10 years, or $969,588 ($2,000,000 – $1,030,412).[16] It may be noted that if the actual investment returns on the assets in the charitable lead trust exceed the Section 7520 interest rate, such as by investing the CLAT's assets for growth, the taxable remainder interest will be undervalued for gift tax purposes and the donor's family will benefit (i.e., each adult child will receive more than one-half of $969,588 in 10 years). On the other hand, if the trust earns less than the Section 7520 rate, the reverse will be true. Also, as explained in Footnote 16, no gift tax actually would be paid by Harry.

When to Make Charitable Contributions

Charitable contributions can be made during a donor's lifetime or at death under his or her will. From a tax perspective, it normally is better to make charitable gifts during life, because the donor gets an income tax deduction for the value of the gift, and, effectively, the gift amount (minus the income tax saving) is removed from his or her gross estate for federal estate tax purposes. Gifts at death get only a federal estate-tax charitable deduction. Of course, tax factors are not the only consideration in this decision.

[16] Harry would have to file a gift tax return, but assuming he has not made any previous taxable gifts, his applicable exclusion amount of $1,000,000 for gift tax purposes (based on a unified credit of $345,800) will more than offset the gift tax due on this transfer. Thus, no gift tax will actually be payable at this time. However, Harry will have used up most of his applicable exclusion amount, which will not be available for future lifetime gifts or at his death for estate tax purposes.

PART

VII

Insurance Planning and Risk Management

20

Basic Insurance Principles and Selecting Insurers

Competence Objectives for This Chapter After reading this chapter, planners should understand:

- The nature of personal risk management
- The nature of insurance and the pooling of risk
- The large loss principle in buying insurance
- The use of deductibles and other cost-sharing features to help control the cost of insurance
- Considerations in selecting an insurer
- Considerations in choosing an agent or broker
- Knowledge about financial advisers in general

Insurance provides an important means of meeting the financial objectives of most people. This chapter deals with some important concepts about the nature of insurance and the evaluation and selection of insurance companies.

Personal Risk Management

The term *risk management* normally means identifying risk exposures and consideration of alternative methods for dealing with risk. Business firms commonly use this approach in managing their exposures to risk. It also can be used by individuals in managing their personal exposures, in which case, it sometimes is called *personal risk management.*

The logical start of any risk management program is the recognition of one's exposures. This may not be as easy as it seems. For example, if a person hires a domestic worker in his or her home, what liability for worker's compensation or employment practices liability may exist? If the person serves on the board of directors or trustees of a corporation or local organization, could he or she be personally liable for actions taken by the organization under directors' and officers' liability? What about a person's potential liability for libel, slander, invasion of privacy, and other "intentional" torts? What about any business or professional liability exposure a person may have? These and other personal risk exposures should be identified and evaluated in personal risk management.

The basic risk management techniques are avoidance of risk, loss prevention and reduction (loss control), retention (planned assumption) of risk, and transfer of risk. *Insurance* is the most important transfer device. Part VII of the book discusses the various kinds of insurance that can be used for this purpose.

Basic Insurance Principles

Pooling of Exposures

Not all risks are insurable. However, many potentially serious events can be insured against by transferring them through insurance contracts to insurers who combine the risks of many so that accurate insurance premiums can be calculated and applied. This results from the law of large numbers as noted in Chapter 2. In essence, insurance is a means of eliminating or reducing the financial burden of such events by dividing the losses they produce among many individuals or firms exposed to the events. This is the concept of *pooling,* which lies at the heart of insurance.

Large-Loss Principle

Another basic principle is that in buying insurance, the buyer should place primary emphasis on those risks that potentially could wipe out or substantially deplete the person's or family's net worth. This sometimes is called the *large-loss principle.* Note that the severity of a potential loss, not its frequency, should be the determining factor.

Use of Deductibles and Other Cost-Sharing Devices

Whenever feasible, use of deductibles should be considered in insurance planning. A deductible requires the insured to pay the first portion, such as the first $500, of a covered loss before the insurance comes into play. An elimination (or waiting) period used in some forms of insurance has the same effect. Use of deductibles often benefits the insured because they normally make insurance considerably less expensive. Deductibles eliminate small losses and, hence, the disproportionately high administrative expenses of settling such claims.

Considerations in Choosing an Insurer

Selection of insurers is one of the practical problems faced in buying insurance. In some cases, this problem may be resolved either by the selection of an agent or broker, who then determines the insurer to be used, or by the use of insurance-buying facilities (such as the Internet). However, despite these factors, insureds should take responsibility for selecting sound insurers. Also, wealth management professionals should take care to exercise due diligence in this important area, particularly considering the economic environment existing as of this writing.

It should be noted at the outset that no generalization should be made concerning choice of a particular insurer solely on the basis of its legal form of organization—that is, whether the insurer is a stock company, a mutual company, or a reciprocal, as described in Chapter 2. Instead, an insurer should be evaluated on such grounds as its financial soundness, the extent and quality of the service it renders, the types of coverage and policies the insurer offers, and the price it charges for a particular coverage.

Financial Soundness

General Considerations The financial soundness of an insurer is of paramount importance to potential insureds and their wealth management advisers. Unfortunately, it may be difficult for the average person to assess the financial status of an insurer.

Buyers of insurance may receive some assurance about the strength and stability of insurers through the regulatory procedures of the various states. While the financial requirements that insurers must meet vary among the states, there nevertheless may be some indication that an insurer is stable and financially sound if it is authorized to sell insurance in states with effective insurance regulation. People often cite the state of New York as an example in this regard.

Financial Ratings of Insurers Perhaps the most widely used and readily available measure of financial soundness or claims-paying ability of insurance companies is the financial ratings given to many insurance companies, particularly the larger ones, by several independent insurance rating services. While there are several such services, some of the most widely followed are A.M. Best, Moody's, and Standard & Poor's. Two other frequently mentioned services are Fitch and Weiss Research. Each of these services differs at least to some degree from the others, and their rating grades and standards are not uniform. This has created a situation in which a given insurer may have several ratings from different rating services.

Nevertheless, as a practical matter, the rating services' gradings are probably the main, or perhaps the only, measures that most consumers will have of the financial soundness or claims-paying ability of particular insurance companies. Before purchasing insurance from an insurer, consumers should check into whether the company has been rated by one or more of the rating services and, if so, what its financial strength ratings are by each of the services that rated the insurer. Consumers also should inquire into whether the company's rating or ratings have recently been downgraded by any of the services and, if so, why.

Naturally, wealth management advisers should carefully evaluate these ratings, as well as other factors, before recommending an insurer.

While the ratings of the different services do not exactly correspond to each other, it will be helpful at least to list here the hierarchy of insurance company financial strength ratings for the three most widely followed rating services. These hierarchies of ratings, listed from highest to lowest, are as follows (the ratings of these services are not necessarily consistent with each other just because they are placed parallel in this listing):

Moody's	Standard & Poor's	A.M. Best
Aaa	AAA	A++
Aa1	AA+	A+
Aa2	AA	A
Aa3	AA–	A–
A1	A+	
A2	A	B++
A3	A–	B+
Baa1	BBB+	
Baa2	BBB	B
Baa3	BBB–	B–
Ba1	BB+	
Ba2	BB	C++
Ba3	BB–	C+
B1	B+	
B2	B	C
B3	B–	C–
Caa	CCC	D
Ca	CC	E
C	D	F

State Insurance Guaranty Funds Some protection is provided to consumers by state guaranty funds, which may reimburse insureds and claimants for certain losses they may suffer due to the insolvency of insurance companies in the state. All states now have such guaranty funds that separately cover life insurance companies and property and liability insurance companies.

While these funds offer valuable protection to policyholders and claimants in the event of insurer insolvencies, there are limits to the amount of protection they provide, and the funds may not be available to cover all losses or in all circumstances. Therefore, it does not seem prudent for buyers of insurance to place primary reliance on state guaranty funds to protect them against insurer insolvencies. These funds are further described in Chapter 2.

General Observations on Insurer Financial Soundness Unfortunately, there are no hard-and-fast rules to guide consumers only to financially secure insurers. All that really can be offered are some general observations that may prove helpful.

- It is very helpful for the insurer to be rated by at least two of the independent rating services and for their ratings to be consistent, stable, and on the high side of the hierarchy of ratings. What the minimum acceptable ratings might be is difficult to say, but an example might be that an insurer should be at least within the top three grades of at least two rating services, unless there is an adequate explanation of why this is not the case.
- It is also helpful for the insurer to do business in and be subject to the regulation of one or more states with capable, effective insurance regulation, such as the state of New York.
- Consumers should watch the general financial press for both unfavorable and positive news items about the insurer.
- If the insurer's products or rates seem too good to be true, they probably are. Thus, if an insurer's product terms, prices, or rates of return are way out of line with those of comparable products generally available from other insurance companies, watch out!
- From the viewpoint of financial strength, there may be advantages in dealing with insurers with proven records of financial soundness and stability over a reasonably long period. However, it must be stated that this comment has not held true in a few cases of well-established, formerly highly regarded insurers that unexpectedly (at least to their policyholders) ran into financial problems.
- If an insurer does weaken financially, the insured or policyowner should evaluate whether to secure other coverage and then cancel the coverage with the weakened insurer (in the case of property and liability insurance), or whether to exchange a life insurance policy or an annuity contract in the weaker insurer for a comparable contract in a stronger insurer, which would be a tax-free exchange under Section 1035 of the Internal Revenue Code, provided the tax law requirements for such exchanges are met.

Service

There are many facets to the service an insurer might be expected to offer its customers. Naturally, *claims service*—the expeditiousness and fairness with which claims are settled—is a major consideration.

Other services also may be important to insureds. For example, life and health insurance needs analyses and other estate analysis services in life insurance, and risk analysis and insurance surveys for property and liability insurance, may be of considerable importance.

Types of Coverage

The types of contracts an insurer offers are a consideration. Some insurers have a broader portfolio of policies than others have. Some insurers may offer policies that are more attractive in terms of coverage, price, or both in some areas, while others may have better contracts in other areas.

Price

It is self-evident that the price charged for insurance is of significance to buyers. However, price considerations should never be placed above financial safety, since protection in an unstable organization is a questionable buy at any price. If a particular policy is available at a lower cost because the insurer provides less service, customers should evaluate how important the service is to them.

Considerations in Choosing an Agent or Broker

How does an individual go about finding a good insurance agent or broker? (The distinction between an agent and a broker was noted in Chapter 2.) Some pertinent factors might be: What is the experience of the agent or broker in terms of years and extent of practice? Are they noted specialists in any certain line? Do they do business mostly with individual households, with business firms, or on a general across-the-board basis? Do they engage in survey selling or estate analysis? Do they present a unified program of coverage based on a careful analysis of exposures or needs? Do they represent a sound company or companies? Do they hold professional designations in insurance, as explained next?

Information about Financial Advisers

Obtaining information about financial advisers probably is more difficult than investigating insurers. One positive indication of a financial planner's knowledge and basic professional commitment to his or her career is whether the person has earned the Certified Financial Planner (CFP) designation, the Chartered Life Underwriter (CLU) and Chartered Financial Consultant (ChFC) designations, the Certified Employee Benefit Specialist (CEBS) designation, the Chartered Property Casualty Underwriter (CPCU) designation, and other corresponding professional degrees or designations. Depending on the particular program to obtain these designations, a practitioner must have passed a series of examinations covering such diverse fields as insurance and risk management, law, economics, social legislation, finance, investments, accounting, taxation, estate planning, employee benefits, and management. Although many competent practitioners do not have these designations and such designations do not always indicate competence, the consumer should be aware of the existence and meaning of CFP, CLU, ChFC, CEBS, and CPCU.

21

Life Insurance and Social Security

Competence Objectives for This Chapter After reading this chapter, planners should understand:

- The sources of life insurance protection
- Social Security survivorship benefits
- The types of individual life insurance
- The nature and uses of term life insurance
- The nature and uses of guaranteed-dollar (fixed dollar) permanent (cash-value) life insurance policies
- Universal life (UL) and variable universal life (VUL) policies
- No-lapse guarantees (secondary guarantees) for universal life and variable universal life policies
- Second-to-die and other joint life insurance policies
- Diversification in buying life insurance
- Tax law definitions of life insurance
- Single-premium life insurance
- Important life insurance policy provisions
- Cash values and nonforfeiture options
- Life insurance policy dividends and their uses (options)
- Life insurance policy settlement options
- Supplementary benefits or provisions added to individual life insurance contracts
- The nature of life insurance premiums and dividends
- Life insurance beneficiary designations
- Financed life insurance policies
- Private placement variable universal life policies

- Cash-value life insurance as an asset class in asset allocation planning and internal rate of return (IRR) calculations
- Life insurance underwriting
- Group life insurance
- Consideration of how much life insurance is needed
- The nature of life settlement transactions

This chapter deals with various forms of life insurance protection and the decision factors involved in life insurance planning.

Sources of Life Insurance Protection

These sources can conveniently be broken down into individually purchased policies, employer-sponsored benefits, and government-sponsored coverages.

Individually Purchased Life Insurance

In this case, the individual applies for and, if found insurable, is issued an individual contract of life insurance. This is the main area in which life insurance planning occurs. In recent years, the average size of individual life insurance policies sold has increased considerably as the uses for life insurance have become more varied and sophisticated and life insurance has been viewed as an efficient wealth transfer vehicle.

Employer-Sponsored Life Insurance

This coverage is provided through the employer-employee relationship. Most of it is group term life insurance under the employer's benefit plan.

Group Life Insurance Group life insurance generally is available with part or all of the cost paid by the employer and generally is issued without individual evidence of insurability. The amount of insurance on individual employees normally is determined by some type of benefit formula.

Wholesale Life Insurance This is a hybrid between individual and group life insurance and normally is used for groups too small to qualify for group coverage. An individual policy is issued to each covered person in the group, and there may be some individual underwriting.

Group Universal Life Insurance This is a group, employee-pay-all version of individual UL or individual VUL insurance.[1]

[1] Individual UL and VUL insurance are described in greater detail later in this chapter.

Federal Government Life Programs

Although not normally thought of as life insurance, Social Security provides survivorship benefits, which, in essence, represent significant death benefits. These survivorship benefits are described next. At various times, the federal government has issued or arranged for life insurance for persons serving in the armed forces.

Social Security Survivorship (Death) Benefits

The overall structure of Social Security benefits and the Social Security system was described in Chapter 13 in connection with retirement planning. The focus of this chapter is on the survivorship (death) benefits to certain survivors of deceased actively employed workers, disabled workers, or retired workers. These survivorship benefits are based on the covered worker's PIA and are paid in the form of monthly income to the eligible family member.

Surviving Spouse The surviving spouse of fully insured worker can receive a survivor's benefit, provided the surviving spouse is age 60 or older or is disabled and at least age 50. The amount of this benefit is 100 percent of the deceased worker's survivor PIA, if the surviving spouse has reached the full-benefit retirement age. The benefit is reduced for eligible younger widows or widowers. Furthermore, a surviving divorced spouse who had been married to the deceased worker for at least 10 consecutive years, or who has an eligible child in his or her care, may be eligible for a survivor's benefit in generally the same manner as a surviving spouse.

Other Dependents An *unmarried child* (and, in certain circumstances, an unmarried grandchild) of a deceased worker (who might have been actively employed, disabled, or retired at the time of his or her death) is entitled to a child's monthly survivor's benefit. This benefit is equal to 75 percent of the deceased parent's PIA, provided the child is under age 18, or is under age 19 and an elementary or secondary school student, or is 18 or older but became disabled before age 22.

In addition, the surviving spouse of a deceased worker is eligible for a *mother's or father's survivor's benefit* equal to 75 percent of the deceased worker's PIA as long as the surviving spouse is caring for an eligible child who is under age 16, or is age 16 or older if the child was disabled before reaching age 22. The surviving spouse is eligible for this benefit at any age. A surviving divorced spouse also may be eligible for this benefit. Furthermore, a surviving *dependent parent* who is at least 62 years old may be entitled to a monthly survivor's benefit.

As is the case for other Social Security benefits, there is a family maximum benefit (FMB) that applies to the combined survivors' benefits from the PIA of a deceased worker.

Types of Individual Life Insurance Contracts

In the past, there were three traditional types of individual life insurance contracts: term, whole life, and endowment. However, in recent years, a number of newer types have been developed and they have increased greatly in their complexity.

Assuming a person needs individual life insurance, one of the fundamental issues that must be decided is what type or types of contracts to purchase and from which insurance company or companies to purchase them. However, in making this choice, the consumer really has to make decisions on several underlying issues.

The first is whether to rely largely or entirely on term life insurance for his or her insurance needs. If so, presumably the person will look to non–life insurance investment media for his or her investment or savings needs and may not purchase much, if any, life insurance that accumulates a cash value. A problem with this approach is that the cost of term insurance will increase with age (and rapidly at the older ages) and so at some point the policyowner may be tempted to discontinue (lapse) the term insurance. Of course, the person by then may have accumulated an investment fund outside of the life insurance. In any event, term insurance probably is best thought of as a way of meeting *temporary* needs for life insurance, rather than providing life insurance over the insured's entire lifetime.

On the other hand, if the person wants a more or less level premium for the life insurance and thus is interested in developing a cash value (in effect, an investment element) as part of the life insurance contract, he or she should consider one or more of the various types of cash-value or permanent life insurance for part or all of his or her insurance portfolio. This is the long-standing "term or cash-value" debate. Actually, many people resolve this issue by using term insurance for shorter-term protection needs and also cash-value contracts to meet their long-term life insurance needs. This is a more diversified approach.

Assuming at least some cash-value life insurance is to be purchased, the next underlying issue is to decide who is to make the investment decisions and bear the investment risks with regard to the cash value. In this regard, one choice would be to buy life insurance in which the cash value is guaranteed as to a principal amount and a minimum rate of return by the insurance company (which might be termed a *guaranteed-dollar* or *fixed-dollar* policy) and for which the investment decisions and risks fall on the insurance company. The other choice would be life insurance in which the investment of the cash value is decided upon by the policyowner from among the subaccounts (investment funds) available under the policy (variable life insurance), and thus where the investment decisions and risks inherent in the accounts fall on the policyowner.

Again assuming cash-value life insurance is to be purchased, a separate issue is whether the insurance should be on a fixed-premium basis or a flexible-premium basis: In *fixed-premium contracts,* the periodic premiums are set in advance by the insurer based on the insured's age, gender, smoker or nonsmoker status, and underwriting status (class). Under *flexible-premium* contracts, the policyowner can decide, within limits, what, if any, premium will be paid in any given year, provided enough is paid to keep the policy from lapsing.

Thus, the consumer is faced with the following choices:

I. Term insurance
II. Cash-value or permanent life insurance
  a. Guaranteed-dollar policies
    i. Traditional (fixed-premium) cash-value life insurance
    ii. Flexible-premium policies (universal life [UL] insurance)
  b. Variable policies
    i. Variable life insurance (VL)
    ii. Variable universal life insurance (VUL)

Term Insurance

Term life insurance provides protection for a specified period. If death occurs during the period, the face amount of the policy is paid, with nothing being paid in the event that the insured survives the period. Term policies generally have no cash or loan values. Since term insurance provides only a death benefit without also building up a cash value, as of a given age at purchase, it will have a lower premium per $1,000 of insurance than comparable whole life policies.

Considerations in Buying Term Insurance While term insurance is rather simple in concept, there are a number of different contracts on the market that the consumer might consider. The prices charged for term insurance vary considerably among life insurance companies, and so some shopping by the consumer (on the Internet, for example), or by an agent or broker representing the consumer, may produce premium savings in this area.

Annually Renewable Term (ART) For this term product, which is also called *yearly renewable term* (YRT), the premium charged per $1,000 of insurance increases for each successive year as the insured's attained age increases. As a result, the cost of a level amount of term insurance will continually increase year by year as the insured grows older. It will be quite low when the insured is younger (say, under age 50), but it will increase dramatically as the insured gets older.

Level Term Here, the premium remains fixed, or level, for a stated period of coverage, such as 10, 15, or even 20 or 30 years, after which the premium increases to that of an insured at that attained age. Many level term policies allow renewal for additional similar level term periods, but usually at greatly higher premium rates.

Reentry Term This type of policy provides that after a certain number of years of coverage, often 10 years, insureds who pass a new physical examination are permitted to continue their term coverage at a given set of increased term rates (usually the same rates as a new buyer of term insurance at the same age would have to pay), but if the insured does not submit to the new medical examination or fails to pass the new physical, the renewal rates for continued coverage will be substantially higher. Because of this repricing feature, reentry term may carry a lower premium rate per $1,000 of insurance than other term products, but it also carries greater risks for the policyowner.

Decreasing Term This form provides a declining amount of insurance over the period of the contract. A good example is mortgage protection insurance designed to cover for an amount that will pay off an amortizing home mortgage. Sometimes it also may be used to meet the current protection needs for a family when it is perceived that the need for life insurance will decrease over time as children become self-supporting or as a separate investment fund may grow.

Renewable and Convertible Term Many term policies are *renewable* for successive periods at the policyowner's option without having to show any evidence of insurability at renewal. The age to which such policies may be renewed usually is limited.

Term policies also generally are *convertible.* This means the policyowner has the right during the conversion period to change the term policy into a whole life or other permanent policy of a like or lesser amount of insurance without having to show any evidence of insurability at the time of conversion. Again, the age up to which a term policy may be converted usually is limited. The renewable and convertible features of term policies can be particularly valuable for insureds who later become uninsurable or insurable only on a substandard basis.

Term Premium Structures Term policies may have guaranteed rate structures or may be indeterminate-premium policies.

When there is a *guaranteed rate structure,* the premium rates for each age are set when the policy is issued and cannot be increased in the future. Naturally, as the insured grows older, the premium rate applied will increase; however, the whole rate schedule by age is guaranteed once the policy is issued. *Indeterminate-premium policies,* on the other hand, have a lower current rate structure, which can be increased or decreased by the insurance company according to its actuarial experience, but cannot be increased beyond a higher maximum guaranteed level of rates. Some term policies are participating (i.e., they pay policy dividends), while others are not.

Term with Whole Life Insurance Insurance companies often offer life insurance contracts that are combinations of term insurance and whole life insurance. These policies are sometimes called *hybrids* or *blended policies.* They are intended to lower the initial premiums for the policyowner while still providing some cash value in the policy. The term element in blended policies usually will gradually decline over the policy's duration. Furthermore, some policies that nominally are whole life policies are structured so that the cash value develops so slowly that they are essentially term policies. These are sometimes called *term-like* policies.

Cash-Value or Permanent Life Insurance

This broad classification embraces those policies that are designed to develop a cash value inside the life insurance contract. Traditionally, this cash value developed because of the level-premium approach to paying for this kind of life insurance, in contrast to the increasing premiums with attained age for term insurance. Periodic growth in the cash values of life insurance contracts is often referred to as the *inside buildup* in permanent life insurance policies.

Guaranteed-Dollar Cash-Value Policies

There are a variety of policies in the guaranteed-dollar category. Because the cash values of these policies are invested by the insurance company and thus constitute part of its overall assets or general portfolio, these policies are sometimes called *portfolio products.* Because the cash values of these policies are included in the general assets of the insurance company, they are subject to the claims of creditors of the insurer in the event of its insolvency.

Traditional (Fixed-Premium) Cash-Value Life Insurance

These policies have a *fixed premium* that is determined primarily by the insured's age at issue, gender, and whether the insured is a smoker or a nonsmoker.[2] Premiums per $1,000 of life insurance may also be lower for policies with larger face amounts of insurance.

These traditional forms can be *participating* (pay policy dividends based on the actuarial experience of the insurer) or *nonparticipating* (pay no policy dividends). If they are participating, it is the gross premium (before dividends) that is fixed, and the final cost and financial results of the policy often will be substantially affected by the policy dividends (which are *not* guaranteed) that are declared on the policy in the future by the insurance company. These future and uncertain policy dividends on participating life insurance are a major reason why it is so difficult to compare policies.

Gross premiums for these policies are set when the policy is issued, and their guaranteed cash values increase according to a schedule contained in the policy. Thus, the cost elements (mortality cost for death claims, charges for expenses, and the interest rate credited by the insurer on policy values) are not shown to the policyowner separately; hence, these policies may be referred to as *bundled* contracts.[3]

These policies, in effect, are front-end loaded for expenses. This is because for the first several years a policy is in force, normally there either is no cash value or the cash value is significantly less than the premiums paid. While there is no separately stated expense charge for traditional cash-value policies, the reason for this reduced cash-value pattern is to reflect the expenses of the insurance company in writing the policy. Therefore, the policyowner will lose money if such a policy is surrendered after it has been in force for only a few years.

The following are various kinds of traditional, fixed-premium life insurance contracts. By far, the most common is whole life insurance.

Whole Life Insurance This policy furnishes protection for the entire life. Premiums may be paid throughout the insured's lifetime, over a limited period, such as 10, 20, or 30 years, or to a specified age. The premium also may be

[2] The premium for any life insurance policy also may be affected by the insured's health and other individual underwriting factors. Thus, so-called substandard policies that do not meet the insurer's underwriting requirements for standard policies normally are "rated" in that they have a higher premium per $1,000 of insurance than do comparable policies issued at standard rates. In addition, so-called preferred policies also may have lower rates than non-preferred standard policies.

[3] This is in contrast to policies that are *unbundled,* such as universal life, as discussed later in this section.

paid in one lump sum at the inception of the policy, in which case the policy is referred to as a *single-premium whole life* (SPWL) policy. When the insured is to pay premiums throughout his or her lifetime, the policy is commonly referred to as *ordinary life* or *straight life.* When the insured is to pay premiums over a specified period, it is referred to as *limited-payment life insurance.*

Endowment Insurance Endowment life insurance offers insurance protection against death for a specified period, such as 10, 20, or 30 years, to age 65, and so forth; then, if the insured lives to the end of the period, the contract pays the face amount. Endowment insurance does not meet the tax law definition of life insurance and so is of no significance in the United States today.

Modified Life Insurance Here, the premiums normally are smaller for the first few years than for the remainder of the contract.

Graded-Premium Whole Life These contracts are somewhat similar in concept to modified life, except that the initially lower premiums increase annually for a longer period (such as from 5 to 40 years) until they level off. During this annually increasing premium period, there are no or low cash values in these policies.

Family Income Riders or Policies Under this type of contract, if the insured dies during a specified family income period, income payments (which might be $10, $15, or even $20 per month for each $1,000 of face amount) are paid to the beneficiary until the end of the family income period, at which time the face amount of insurance is paid.

Family Maintenance Riders or Policies This is similar to the family income policy or rider, except that the income period is for a stated number of years after the insured's death.

Family Policy This policy includes coverage on all family members in one contract.

Current Assumption or Interest-Sensitive Whole Life

This is a cross between the traditional whole life policy and UL insurance, which will be discussed next. The policy normally has an initial premium, which can be *redetermined* (recalculated by the insurance company) periodically, based on new actuarial assumptions and the level of the policy's current accumulation account. The policy does provide some guarantees as to minimum interest rates and perhaps maximum mortality and expense charges in setting any new actuarial assumptions.

The policy's current *accumulation account* (cash value) is determined by using the current experience of the insurance company. From the periodic premium as currently set by the insurer, an expense charge may be deducted and the net amount added to the previous year's accumulation account. Then, interest is credited at the current rate being assumed, and a mortality charge calculated on the pure life insurance protection (the policy face minus the accumulation account) is deducted. The balance is the policy's accumulation account at the end of the year.

Universal Life (UL)

General Features The key aspects of UL insurance are flexibility for the policyowner and identifiable cost elements. The policy cash value is set up as a cash-value fund (or accumulation fund) to which is credited any net premium payments by the policyowner and a current interest rate, and from which is taken the cost of term insurance (as a mortality charge) at the insured's attained age and any annual expense charges. This separation of the cash value from the death benefit has been referred to as *unbundling* the traditional life insurance product, or as an *open architectural* product.

Premium Payments For UL, these are at the discretion of the policyowner, except that there must be a minimum initial premium to start coverage, and then there must be at least enough cash value in the policy each month to cover the mortality and any expense charges so the policy will not lapse. Insurers also set maximum premium payments.

Death Benefits There are two general types of death benefit systems under UL: option A and option B. Under option A, there is a level death benefit, and so if the cash value increases, the net amount of pure (or term) death protection (also referred to as the *net amount at risk*) declines. Under option B, the death benefit is equal to a specified face amount selected by the policyowner when the policy is purchased, plus the policy's current cash value. Thus, under this option, the death benefit will increase if the cash value increases. Which of these options the policyowner should purchase depends on how much insurance protection is desired relative to the investment element in the policy. Option B provides more death protection relative to cash value than option A. Finally, insurers often allow policyowners to increase or decrease their policies' death benefits as they desire, except that if the death benefit is increased, the insured generally must show individual evidence of insurability.

Interest Credits The cash value under UL is credited with an interest rate (usually monthly). There is a guaranteed minimum interest rate specified in the policy, and then the insurer may pay a higher current crediting rate. The interest rates actually paid by an insurer on its UL policies may be determined in several ways. One is a *portfolio rate,* which is one rate set by the insurer and generally based on the investment performance of the insurer's whole investment portfolio. This is the most common approach. A second option is a *new money approach,* where the insurer sets more than one rate depending on when the policy premiums were paid. Third, some UL policies credit interest rates that are indexed to some outside interest rate measure, such as a percentage of average long-term corporate bond rates. This is known as *interest-indexed life* (IIL) *insurance.* Finally, a few policies base the current return on some outside equity index, such as the S&P 500 stock index. This is called *equity-indexed universal life* (EIUL).

UL policies often are sold based on certain assumptions (projections) of the interest rates that will be paid on cash values far into the future. The same kind of thing also is done for other kinds of life insurance policies. The consumer should be careful of these long-term projections because no one can know what interest rates (or the other cost elements of life insurance) will be 10, 20, 30, or more years from now. Instead, the consumer should note the current interest rate on any policy being considered, what the history of the insurer has been with regard to interest rates paid, and the minimum guaranteed rate in the policy. Naturally, the financial strength and general reputation of the insurer are of paramount importance.

Mortality Charges A *cost of insurance (COI)* charge is the mortality cost that is deducted each month from the cash value based on the insured's attained age and the policy's current net amount at risk. The net amount at risk is the policy's death benefit minus its cash value. UL policies typically have a schedule of guaranteed maximum mortality charges, but the insurer often charges less than the guaranteed maximum as the current COI. However, the insurer can increase (up to the maximum) or decrease the current mortality charges.

Expense Charges Insurers also may levy expense charges against premiums or cash values. Some UL policies have *front-end loads,* whereby an expense charge is made for the first policy year and perhaps lower charges in subsequent years. Others do not charge any front-end load. UL policies also may have *back-end loads,* which are charges levied on the surrender or exchange of the policy. Such back-end loads normally diminish year by year as the policy remains in force, reaching zero at a certain point (say, after 10 to 15 years). Some policies have both front-end and back-end loads.

In any event, insurers can recover their sales and administrative costs from the spread between what the insurer earns on his or her own investment portfolio and the interest rate credited to the policy. This is one of the things that makes comparing UL policies with traditional whole life policies difficult. Traditional whole life policies charge initial costs to the first few premiums (in effect, they have a front-end load) and hence have no or reduced early cash values. However, once there is a cash value, they may credit it with higher interest rates. UL policies, on the other hand, may have no front-end load and hence no or little reduction in cash values, but they may credit lower interest rates.

Cash Withdrawals Since UL policies are unbundled, they normally allow the policyowner to make cash withdrawals (partial surrenders) from the cash value while the policy is in force. This can be an attractive feature. However, any such withdrawals often reduce the policy's death benefit dollar for dollar. UL policies also have policy loan provisions like other permanent life insurance policies. On the other hand, traditional whole life policies do not permit such partial withdrawals.

Target Premiums UL policies usually have target premium amounts, which are suggested annual level premiums that will keep the policy in force, given certain actuarial and interest assumptions. These are not guaranteed or required premiums, but only projections based on assumed levels of credited interest.

However, insurers do offer riders to UL policies that provide guarantees that the policy will not lapse if specified premiums are paid. These are referred to as no-lapse guarantee universal life policies (NLGUL policies) and are discussed later in this chapter.

The UL policies of different insurance companies can vary considerably as to the current interest rate being credited, the guaranteed interest rate, the method used to credit interest, mortality charges, and the nature and amount of any expense charges. Consumers need to consider all of these factors.

Variable Policies

General Features As opposed to the guaranteed- or fixed-principal approach just discussed, variable policies allow the policyowner to allocate his or her premium payments to or among one or more investment subaccounts (mutual funds) offered by the insurance company and also to shift cash values among the subaccounts. The amount of the policy cash value, and perhaps the death benefit, depend on the values (investment performance) of the subaccount or accounts to which the policyowner has allocated the funds under the policy. Hence, the investment decisions and the corresponding investment risks fall on the policyowner rather than on the insurer.

Investment Accounts The subaccounts offered under variable life policies (and under variable annuities, as described in Chapter 17) essentially are mutual funds held by the insurance company in a separate account that is distinct from the insurer's general investment portfolio. Insurers may offer a significant number of subaccounts with a wide range of investment objectives in their variable products. Policyowners also may be given the option of having their funds invested in the general investment portfolio of the insurance company (a fixed-principal account). These subaccounts are much like a group (or *family*) of mutual funds; in fact, in many cases the same investment management firms that manage groups of mutual funds also provide subaccounts to insurers for their separate accounts.[4]

One important reason for the development of variable life insurance was to allow policyowners to invest their policy cash values in whole or in part in common stock funds or balanced funds that would be more competitive with other kinds of investment media (such as mutual funds) and that would maintain—or even enhance—the purchasing power of policy values in the face of inflation. However, the investment performance of subaccounts can vary considerably among life insurance companies. Also, like other investment companies, an analysis of insurance company subaccount performance should be over a considerable time—such as 5, 10, 15, or even 20 years, if available—rather than for only one or a few good years. Policyowners may follow other investment strategies in these accounts as well, such as in bond or other subaccounts.

Changes in Asset Allocation A significant investment/tax advantage of variable insurance products (either variable life insurance or variable annuities) lies in the ability of the policyowner to move the policy cash value among the subaccounts inside the policy without any current income tax liability. In effect, this allows the policyowner to make changes in his or her asset allocation strategy within the policy without adverse tax consequences.

CASE EXAMPLE

Assume Norman Lee purchased a VUL insurance policy (described next) a number of years ago and has paid a total of $150,000 in premiums for the policy, which has a $1,000,000 (type A) face amount. He has elected to have the policy's cash value placed in a common stock subaccount, which is now worth $400,000. However, Norman has become concerned that he has too much of his overall investment portfolio in common stocks. Therefore, he has decided to change the VUL policy's cash value from the policy's common stock account to its investment-grade bond account. This change is not deemed a sale or exchange of a capital asset for capital gains tax purposes. Furthermore, if Norman should become dissatisfied with the investment management of the

[4] However, for tax reasons, the subaccounts under variable life insurance and variable annuities cannot be the same as the mutual funds offered by these firms to the public.

subaccounts in his VUL policy, he could exchange his policy, income tax–free under the provisions of IRC Section 1035, for another life insurance policy with a different insurer. Of course, any surrender charge (back-end load) applicable to his VUL policy would apply to such a tax-free exchange. Thus, the policyowner can have considerable flexibility when changing the asset allocation under a variable life (or variable annuity) policy.[5]

Variable policies are of two general types: *variable life (VL) insurance* and *variable universal life (VUL) insurance.*

VL Insurance This is a fixed-premium contract that is similar in some ways to traditional fixed-premium (nonvariable) whole life insurance. In VL, however, the cash values and death benefits vary with the investment experience of the subaccounts to which premiums are allocated. However, VL policies have a guaranteed minimum death benefit. They were the original contracts sold as variable insurance and are not common today.

VUL Insurance This is the more common form of variable life insurance. It is universal life combined with the variable life concept. The policyowner can decide into which subaccount or accounts his or her flexible premiums will go. The cash value then will be determined by the investment experience of the subaccount or accounts chosen. The death benefit will depend on whether the policyowner selects UL option A (level death benefit) or option B (face amount plus the cash value at death). Thus, under VUL, the policyowner has the greatest flexibility of all—flexibility with regard to both investment of cash values and payment of premiums.

Expense Charges in VUL There are expense loadings in VUL products, which can be significant. First, VUL policies often have initial sales charges

[5] By way of comparison, if instead these investment funds had not been in subaccounts under a variable life policy (or variable annuity), but rather had been mutual funds in a family of mutual funds (as explained in Chapter 8), then the exchanging of one mutual fund (say, a common stock fund) for another mutual fund (say, an investment-grade bond fund), as in this illustration, would result in an exchange of a capital asset for another for capital gains tax purposes and hence, a currently taxable gain or a loss. In this illustration, there would have been a currently recognized $250,000 capital gain ($400,000 value [amount realized] – $150,000 adjusted basis = $250,000 capital gain). There would, of course, have been the same gain if Norman had held the stocks and then the bonds directly rather than through a family of mutual funds. On the other hand, if there had been a capital loss on this transaction, it would have been better tax-wise to have held the assets in a mutual fund or directly, because then Norman could have taken the loss currently against any capital gains he might have had that year and then against ordinary income to the extent of $3,000 per year. See Chapters 10 and 11 for a more complete discussion of these tax concepts.

(front-end loads) based on the premiums paid. Furthermore, they may have back-end loads upon surrender—referred to as *surrender charges* or *contingent deferred sales charges.* Like UL policies, these back-end loads decline with policy duration and after 10 to 15 years, usually reach zero.

Second, there are annual (or periodic) *investment management fees* levied against the net assets of the particular subaccounts. The amount of these fees varies, depending on the nature of the subaccount. For example, an investment management fee might be 1.2 percent for a growth common stock account, 0.8 percent for a bond account, and 0.5 percent for a money market account. These fees are to cover the expenses of investing the subaccounts and are referred to as *fund-* or *account-level fees.*

Third, there are annual (or periodic) *mortality and expense* (M&E) *risk charges* levied against the assets of each policy. M&E charges are to cover administrative expenses and provide a margin for the insurer. M&E risk charges vary among insurers, but might range from 0.6 percent to 1.0 percent or more. They sometimes are referred to as *policy-* or *contract-level fees.*

Fourth, there may be periodic *administrative charges.* These may be a fixed amount per policy or a percentage of premiums or values. There may be a further charge for premium taxes.

The total of these annual expense loadings vary considerably among insurers, but may range, say, from 1 percent or less to 2.5 percent or more per year of the assets standing behind a VUL policy.[6] Since these expense loadings can be significant, the consumer should evaluate them in relation to those of other VUL policies.

Mortality Costs in VUL In addition to the expense loadings just described, VUL policies also charge a *cost of insurance* (COI) for the mortality cost or term cost of the pure life insurance protection they are providing. This is a periodic mortality charge that varies with the insured's attained age and is applied to the net amount at risk under the policy, as was described earlier for UL policies.

No-Lapse Guarantees for UL and VUL Policies

It can be seen from the preceding discussion that a traditional whole life policy with its fixed premium *will not* lapse (terminate) as long as the

[6] This percentage of assets is somewhat analogous to the expense ratio of mutual funds, which is discussed in Chapter 8. The comparison is not completely appropriate, however, because mutual funds themselves do not provide life insurance protection, and some of the periodic expense loadings of variable policies are for the creation or administration of the life insurance coverage (although not for the actual term cost). Recognizing that there are limitations on the comparison, the expense ratios of comparable mutual funds are generally lower than the expense loadings as a percentage of plan assets for variable life insurance.

policyowner continues to pay the premium or the policy otherwise becomes paid up. The guaranteed cash value in the policy also will continue to increase. Furthermore, if the policy is participating, the insurer may continue to pay policy dividends.

However, in the case of UL and VUL policies, with their flexible premiums, policies *may lapse* before the insured's death. This will depend on the premium payments actually made by the policyowner, the investment performance of the cash value (i.e., the interest credited for UL and the subaccount performance for VUL), the monthly charges against the cash value (e.g., COI for UL and COI, M&E risk, and account level charges for VUL), and any partial withdrawals from the cash value.

Therefore, insurance companies now may offer no-lapse riders for UL and VUL policies to protect policyowners against lapse as long as they meet certain conditions. These are also called *secondary guarantees.*

Many insurers offer no-lapse guarantee riders for UL policies (referred to as NLGUL policies). These riders guarantee against lapse as long as the policyowner pays a stated annual premium. The *guarantee period* varies, but may be until the insured reaches age 100, 121, or for the insured's lifetime. The stated premium also varies among insurers and will have to be paid until the insured reaches a specified age (such as age 100 or 121) or dies. Insurers charge additional premiums for no-lapse guarantee riders.

The original no-lapse guarantee feature had a strict requirement that the stated premium had to be paid on time. If the policyowner failed to do so, the no-lapse guarantee would be void. However, later UL no-lapse guarantee structures contained what is called a "shadow account design." The shadow account is a hypothetical account (not the real cash value), and as long as this shadow account showed a value, the secondary guarantee would not be voided even if the policyowner failed to pay a stated premium when due.

The stated premiums for NLGUL policies typically are considerably less than the guaranteed fixed gross premiums for comparable traditional whole life insurance. However, the cash values of NLGUL policies are not guaranteed, while they are for traditional whole life policies.

Some insurers also sell no-lapse riders for VUL policies, often regardless of the subaccounts in which policy values are invested. These are referred to as NLGVUL policies. Like NLGUL policies, these contracts have stated annual premiums, guarantee periods, and periods of time the stated premiums must be paid.

Under NLGUL and NLGVUL policies, the cash values can increase or decline, depending on the policy's investment returns, stated premiums paid, and the annual COI and expense charges taken from the cash value. In fact, it is possible that the cash value could fall to the point where it would not cover the annual charges levied by the insurer against the policy, and even fall to zero. Even if that occurred, however, the policy would not lapse because of the secondary guarantee. In that event, the insurer would have to carry the policy (pay its costs) out of its own assets.

CASE EXAMPLE

Harry Shapiro, age 55, is a real estate investor with a potentially sizeable estate that will attract federal estate taxation. Since his real estate holdings are not liquid or readily marketable, Harry is interested in buying an additional $2,000,000 of life insurance for estate liquidity and conservation purposes (as described in Chapter 29). Harry is in good health and his insurance adviser has told him that he can secure a $2,000,000 NLGUL policy, nonsmoker, best underwriting class, with a lifetime guarantee period, and premiums payable until age 100, from an excellently rated insurer for an annual stated premium of $25,000. Harry decides to buy this policy because he is primarily concerned with death protection for the whole of his life at a level premium in a sound insurer. Cash-value accumulation is of secondary importance to him.

Second-to-Die or Survivorship Life Insurance

All the previously discussed forms of life insurance cover only one person's life as the insured. Second-to-die life insurance (also called *survivorship* or *joint and last survivor* life insurance) normally insures two lives in the same policy and the policy proceeds are payable at the death of the second insured to die. The two lives insured are usually a husband and wife.

Premiums on second-to-die policies normally are considerably less than the premiums for comparable policies on single lives of the same ages, sex, and amount. This is because two lives are insured and the proceeds are not payable until the second death.

One thing to consider when purchasing second-to-die life insurance is whether the policy allows the owners to split it into two single-life plans, one for each life insured, in amounts on each equal to the second-to-die policy benefit or some other amount, or to change it into a single-life plan on only one of the insureds. Most policies allow such a split. This right may be valuable for spouses in the event of divorce or other family discord, possible changes in the estate tax law, or changes in their estate situation or plans.

First-to-Die or Joint Life Insurance

Under this form, two or more lives are insured in the same policy and the policy proceeds are payable to the beneficiary at the death of the first insured to die. The lives insured may be a husband and wife, or they may be others, such as the owners of a closely held business pursuant to a buy–sell agreement. For example, both spouses may be working outside the home and both their incomes may be needed to support their family. Hence, insurance is needed at either of their deaths, and a joint life policy might be purchased. Furthermore, suppose there are three stockholders of a closely held corporation who have agreed to buy each other out in the event one of them dies (a buy–sell agreement). The agreement could be funded with a joint life policy insuring all three of them. Joint life policies often allow the policy to be split into two or more single-life plans. Since a joint life policy usually terminates after the first death, the policies may contain an option for a surviving insured to continue insurance under a separate single life policy or, if there is more than one survivor, under a new joint life policy.

Private Placement Life Insurance

The courts have held that variable insurance products (variable life and variable annuities) are securities and so must meet the requirements of the securities laws when sold to the public. As noted in Chapter 2, this involves registration with the SEC and meeting the requirements of federal and state securities laws, as well as state insurance laws. However, an exception to these registration requirements is when securities are sold as a private placement.

Private placement life insurance is variable universal life insurance (PPVUL) that typically is customized and sold to a limited group of high-net-worth purchasers (such as accredited investors and qualified purchasers for domestic sales). It is not registered with the SEC or state securities regulators. It may be sold as a domestic private placement or an offshore private placement. There may be considerable flexibility in the subaccounts allowed in such policies, such as alternative investments like hedge funds, private equity, commodity funds and the like. There may be pricing flexibility as well.

Internal Rates of Return (IRRs) for Life Insurance Values

It is clear from the previous discussion that there are a wide variety of life insurance contracts available to the public with different cash flow patterns (i.e., premiums, dividends, cash values, and death proceeds). It is difficult to compare the returns for these policies. Also, it has been suggested here and in

Chapter 9 that life insurance should be considered as an asset class for asset allocation purposes. In this case, it is valuable to have an idea of how efficient life insurance is as a way to transfer wealth to the insured's family and heirs. An analysis of an insurance policy's projected values and their resulting internal rates of return, assuming surrender for cash and death at an advanced age (i.e., after a long period in force), will be helpful in considering these issues.

CASE EXAMPLE

John Roma is age 40, in good health, a nonsmoker, and a successful business owner. He is interested in including life insurance in his asset allocation planning as a way to transfer wealth to trusts in his family after his death, and to provide a guaranteed cash value, if he needs it, for retirement puposes or possibly business needs (through policy loans). It has been suggested that John purchase a $1,000,000 participating whole life policy from a top-rated insurer and use policy dividends to purchase paid-up additional amounts of insurance.

However, John would like some idea of how efficient this policy may be for these purposes. His insurance adviser has furnished John with a projection of potential future policy values (called a ledger statement) based on its current premium and guaranteed cash values (which are guaranteed) and its current dividend scale (which is not guaranteed). This projection estimates that if John surrenders the policy for cash at age 65, its internal rate of return (IRR) on the surrender value will have been almost 4.0 percent, and if he surrenders it at age 80, the IRR is estimated at about 5.6 percent (ignoring income tax on the untaxed buildup). On the other hand, if John continues the policy until he dies, say at age 80, the IRR in the death proceeds is estimated to be about 7.5 percent (with death benefits being income tax–free).

It can be suggested to John, then, that an IRR on surrender of say, 4.0 percent or 5.6 percent on a stable value asset is quite reasonable considering that John's family will have had the life insurance protection for 25 or 40 years. However, depending on whether its policyowner needs the cash value for retirement or other purposes, it generally is better not to surrender life insurance policies for cash, but rather to retain them until the insured's death. Other policies will have different results. For example, NLGUL policies normally will show better results at death than on surrender. Also, it must be remembered that these results are based on projections over long periods of time.

A Diversification Strategy in Purchasing Life Insurance

With the sometimes bewildering growth in different kinds of life insurance policies and the current emphasis on insurer financial soundness, insurance advisers may recommend that persons buying life insurance, particularly if the amounts are substantial, diversify their purchases by kind of policy and also among different financially sound insurance companies. This is simply transferring to insurance purchases the diversification concepts we routinely employ in the investment area.

> **CASE EXAMPLE**
> As an illustration, assume that Jane Olson is the divorced mother of two young children. Jane earns a good salary and her future career prospects are bright, but she works for a smaller company that provides her with only $50,000 of noncontributory group term life insurance. To protect her children and provide for their education if she should die prematurely, Jane feels she needs at least $1,500,000 of life insurance. To satisfy the need for an additional $1,450,000 of life insurance, Jane might purchase $650,000 of preferred term (she is in excellent health) from one insurance company to get immediate, low-cost protection. This term should be renewable and convertible. She also might purchase $400,000 of participating traditional whole life insurance from another company to get guaranteed premiums and to start building a guaranteed cash value. Policy dividends (if the policy is participating) can be used to purchase paid-up additions to increase gradually her life insurance protection and cash values. Finally, Jane might purchase $400,000 of VUL insurance in a third company. She could allocate the cash value of this policy to one or more of its subaccounts (including common stock accounts), if desired, but in making this decision, she should consider her overall asset allocation strategy.

This example is only meant to illustrate the diversification concept. There is no correct diversification model for everyone. Different combinations of policies could be recommended, depending on a person's or couple's needs, current premium-paying ability, tolerance for risk, relative desire for flexibility and guarantees, investment philosophy, and other factors.

There are some downsides to diversification. The first is complexity. Furthermore, sometimes life insurance is less expensive when purchased in larger policies. Finally, sometimes consumers have a single insurance-buying philosophy that they wish to follow. However, as in asset allocation in general, for people buying significant amounts of life insurance, diversification often seems the better strategy.

Definitions of Life Insurance for Income Tax Purposes

Tax Advantages of Life Insurance: An Overview

Life insurance contracts have a number of income tax advantages for the policyowner and beneficiary. First, life insurance proceeds paid by reason of the insured's death normally are received income tax–free by the beneficiary. Second, the periodic increase, or changes in subaccounts in variable products, of policy cash values are not taxed currently as income. Third, loans secured by life insurance policies are treated for tax purposes as loans and not as taxable distributions. Fourth, there is no 10 percent penalty tax on premature distributions (generally, distributions before age 59½) from life insurance policies. Fifth, partial surrenders (withdrawals), where permitted by the policy, are viewed as coming first tax free from the policyowner's investment in the contract (income tax basis) and then, when that tax basis is recovered, from potentially taxable investment earnings inside the policy.[7] Finally, one life insurance policy can be exchanged tax-free for another life insurance policy or for an annuity contract under Section 1035 of the IRC.

General Tax Definition of Life Insurance (IRC Section 7702)

In order to get these rather substantial tax advantages, a policy issued after December 31, 1984, must be a life insurance contract under state law and must meet one of two alternative tests under Section 7702 of the IRC. These tests are a cash-value accumulation test or a guideline premium and corridor test.

Modified Endowment Contracts (MECs)

An MEC is a policy that meets the general tax law definition of life insurance, was entered into on or after June 21, 1988, and does not meet a special seven-pay test given in the law. A policy will not meet this seven-pay test if the accumulated premiums at any time during the first seven years of the policy are more than what would have been the sum of the net level premiums for a paid-up policy at the end of seven years. In essence, this rather

[7] The income tax status of life insurance policies is discussed further in Chapter 29. Also, as noted next, some of these tax advantages do not apply to modified endowment contracts.

complicated definition means that if premiums are paid faster than those for a hypothetical seven-pay life policy, it is an MEC.

The significance of being an MEC is that such a policy loses some, but not all, of the income tax benefits from being a life insurance contract. Loans secured by an MEC are treated as taxable distributions, there is a 10 percent penalty tax on premature distributions, and distributions from MECs are viewed as first coming from the investment earnings inside the policy (and hence are taxable) and then as a tax-free return of the policyowner's investment in the contract.[8]

A policy that otherwise would be an MEC entered into before June 21, 1988, generally is "grandfathered" and the regular tax rules applying to life insurance apply to it, unless the policy is materially changed. Of course, life insurance contracts whose premium-payment patterns meet the seven-pay test are not MECs, regardless of when they were entered into. Most life insurance policies are not MECs.

Single-Premium Life Insurance

This represents primarily an investment-type life insurance product. The policyowner pays a single premium and receives a fully paid-up life insurance contract. Single-premium policies are written as whole life (SPWL), variable life, universal life, and variable universal life policies. As just explained, they now are taxed as MECs (unless grandfathered).

The Life Insurance Contract

Several features of individual policies may be useful in planning. They are explained next.

Some Important Policy Provisions

Assignment Life insurance contracts are freely transferable (assignable) by the owner. There are two types of assignments. One is the *absolute assignment,* under which all ownership rights are transferred to another. An absolute assignment may be used, for example, when a policy is given to another person or to an irrevocable trust to avoid federal estate taxation (see Chapter 29).

[8] These income tax rules also apply to regular (nonqualified) annuity contracts, as explained in Chapter 17. Thus, in effect, the tax writers applied some of the nonqualified annuity income tax rules to life insurance contracts *when they are MECs.*

The second type is the *collateral assignment,* whereby only certain rights are transferred to another when the policy is to serve as security for a loan.

Grace Period The grace period, commonly 31 days, is a period, after the premium for a life insurance policy is due, during which the policy remains in full force even though the premium has not yet been paid.

Incontestability This provision states that after a life insurance contract has been in force a certain length of time (called the *contestable period*), which normally is two years, the insurer agrees not to deny a claim because of any error, concealment, or misstatement by the applicant.

Suicide Life insurance contracts contain a suicide provision stating that if the insured commits suicide during a certain period after the policy is issued, generally two years, the insurer is liable only to return the premiums paid. After the two-year period, suicide is a covered cause of death.

Reinstatement This clause usually gives the insured the right to reinstate the policy within a specified period, usually three years of any default in premium payment, subject to furnishing evidence of insurability and payment of back premiums.

Policy Loan Provision This provision allows the policyowner to take a loan (technically an *advance,* because it does not have to be repaid) up to an amount that, with interest on the loan, will not exceed the cash (loan) value of the policy. The rate of interest may be stated in the contract or may vary periodically according to some standard. Policy loans on older policies may have a 5 or 6 percent guaranteed interest rate, and on more recent policies an 8 percent guaranteed rate. Some policies allow for lower loan rates after the policy has been in force for a certain time and on loans below a certain percentage of the cash value. Loan rates may also be expressed on a net interest basis (such as 1 or 2 percent over the rate of return in the policy).

The policy loan provision enables the policyowner to draw on policy cash values to meet financial needs without surrendering the contract. It also enables the policyowner to take money out of his or her life insurance policy (except for an MEC) without any income tax liability.

On the other hand, an important disadvantage of policy loans is that death proceeds will be reduced by any outstanding policy loans at that insured's death. Furthermore, interest paid by individuals on policy loans generally is not deductible for federal income tax purposes.

Finally, many insurance companies include in their policies a *direct recognition provision* under which policy dividends or credited interest rates are less for policies with policy loans against them than for comparable policies without such loans.

Automatic Premium Loan Provision This provision operates when a policyowner fails to pay a premium when due. In this event, the premium is paid as a policy loan and the policy does not lapse, as long as there is enough loan value in the contract.

Beneficiary Designation A life insurance contract allows the policyowner to select the person or persons who will receive the proceeds of the contract in the event of the insured's death. When the owner reserves the right to change the beneficiary, the beneficiary designation is called *revocable.* When the owner does not reserve this right, the designation is called *irrevocable.* An irrevocable beneficiary in effect becomes a joint owner of the policy rights. Revocable beneficiary designations are used in most cases. It also usually is advisable to name a second or contingent beneficiary to receive the proceeds in case the first (primary) beneficiary predeceases the insured.

Policyownership Life insurance policies generally state on the front of the contract who owns the policy. This is the person, persons, or entity who legally owns the right to exercise all rights and powers under the contract, which are technically called *incidents of ownership.* The policyowner may be the same person as the one whose life is insured, or it may be someone else or another entity (such as the trustee of a trust, a corporation, a partnership, or other business entity). Ownership of a life insurance contract may be transferred to another by gift or by sale during the insured's lifetime.

Cash Values and Nonforfeiture Options

Life insurance contracts are required to include certain nonforfeiture provisions (options). These options normally include a cash surrender value, reduced paid-up life insurance, or extended term life insurance.

Cash Surrender Value Under state nonforfeiture laws, a cash value generally is required, at the latest, after premiums have been paid for three years and the policy produces a nonforfeiture value. Many traditional whole life policies today, however, provide for some cash value at the end of the second (or even first) year. For UL, VUL, and interest-sensitive whole life, there may be a cash value the first year.

When the cash-value option is elected by a policyowner, the policy is surrendered to the insurance company for cash, the life insurance protection ceases, and the insurer has no further obligation under the policy. Furthermore, surrender of a life insurance contract will produce ordinary income for the policyowner to the extent the cash surrender value received exceeds the net premiums paid for the contract. Hence, in general, surrendering life insurance policies for cash may be a questionable financial and tax strategy. Some strategies for taking cash out of life insurance contracts without surrendering them are discussed in Chapter 29.

Reduced Paid-Up Insurance This option permits the policyowner to use the cash value to produce paid-up insurance of the same type as the original policy but for a reduced face amount. This option might be appropriate when a smaller amount of permanent insurance is satisfactory and it is desirable to discontinue premium payments. Furthermore, if the policy is participating, policy dividends will continue to be paid.

Extended Term Insurance This nonforfeiture option allows the policyowner to exchange the cash value for paid-up term insurance for the full face amount of the policy for a limited period.

Uses of Policy Dividends

Policyowners who have participating life insurance contracts may use the policy dividends in various ways, called dividend options.

Types of Dividend Options These options usually allow dividends to be taken in cash, applied toward payment of future premiums, left with the insurance company to accumulate interest, used to buy additional amounts of paid-up insurance (called *paid-up additions*), or used to purchase one-year term insurance.

Cash dividends frequently are taken when a policy is paid up. This may be done, for example, during retirement to provide an additional source of retirement income. The use of dividends toward the payment of future premiums may be a convenient and simple way to handle dividends.

A popular dividend option is *paid-up additions.* These have cash values of their own and are themselves participating. Furthermore, the growth in the cash values of paid-up additions is not subject to current income taxation. One-year term insurance, generally equal to the cash value of the policy, is offered by many insurance companies.

Vanishing-Premium Insurance (Quick-Pay Plans) This idea for participating life insurance policies is to use policy dividends, and possibly cash values of surrendered paid-up additions, to pay the current policy premiums. The concept is that when a policy has been in force long enough, the premium can be paid by the current year's policy dividend and, in case that dividend is not sufficient to pay the whole premium, by the cash value from the surrender of just enough previously purchased paid-up additions to make up the difference. The policy duration at which this can be done depends on the insurance company's dividend scale and is not guaranteed.

It must be emphasized, however, that quick-pay is not the same as paid-up life insurance. When a life insurance policy is paid up, it means that the accumulated values in the policy are equal to the net single premium for the face amount of insurance, and so it is guaranteed that no further premiums are required to keep the policy in force. Both participating and nonparticipating policies can become paid up.

Settlement Options

Life insurance policies provide that when the proceeds become payable, the insured or the beneficiary may elect to have such proceeds paid in some form other than a lump sum. These forms are called *settlement options.* They include interest options, fixed-amount options, fixed-period options, and life income options. One of the planning decisions a policyowner must make is whether to have his or her life insurance payable on the insured's death in a lump sum, under one or more policy settlement options, or to a trust. This issue is discussed further in Chapter 29.

Interest Option The proceeds of a life insurance policy may be left with the insurer at a guaranteed rate of interest, such as 3 or 4 percent. In addition, most life insurers pay an additional, nonguaranteed rate of interest consistent with the earnings on their investments (called *excess interest*). Proceeds left under the interest option may carry a limited or unlimited right of withdrawal by the beneficiary. The beneficiary also may be given the right to change to another option or options.

Fixed-Amount Option This option provides a stated amount of income each month until the proceeds are exhausted. Each payment is partly interest and partly a return of principal. Again, the insurer usually guarantees a minimum rate of interest, but actually pays a rate closer to that being earned on its investments.

Fixed-Period Option This option is similar to the fixed-amount option, except that the time over which payments are made is fixed and the amount of each monthly installment varies accordingly.

Life Income Options Under this option, the insured or beneficiary elects to have the proceeds paid for the rest of his or her life, or for the life of one or more beneficiaries. This amounts to using the proceeds to buy a life annuity or a life annuity with a survivorship feature.

Supplementary Benefits Added to Individual Life Insurance Contracts

Supplementary benefits or riders are a way of adding additional amounts and/or types of benefits to a basic life insurance contract.

Guaranteed Insurability For an additional premium, this option permits the policyowner to purchase additional amounts of insurance at stated intervals without further proof of insurability.

Double Indemnity This clause or rider, often referred to as an *accidental death benefit,* provides that double (or sometimes triple or more) the face amount of life insurance is payable if the insured's death is caused by accidental means. From an economic standpoint, there seems little justification for double indemnity.

Waiver of Premium This benefit may be added for an extra premium or it may be included in the basic rates. It provides that, in the event the insured becomes totally disabled before a certain age, typically 60 or 65, premiums on the life insurance policy will be waived during the continuance of disability. The values in the policy continue just as if the disabled insured actually were paying the premiums.

Disability Income Riders Some life insurance companies allow disability income benefits to be added to permanent life insurance policies for an extra premium.

Long-Term Care (LTC) Riders For an additional premium, life insurers may offer riders to individual life insurance contracts that provide long-term care (LTC) benefits for skilled or intermediate nursing home care, custodial care, and home health care. LTC coverage is described in greater detail in Chapter 23. As noted previously in Chapter 17, PPA of 2006 provides that in 2010 and thereafter for combination contracts (i.e., those combining life insurance or annuities and LTC coverage), charges for LTC insurance taken from the life insurance or annuity cash values will not be gross income for tax purposes. However, the policy basis will be reduced by such charges.

Accelerated Death Benefit Provisions Many life insurance contracts provide that the discounted value of all or a portion of the policy death benefit will be paid to the policyowner in the event the insured contracts a dread disease, at the onset of a terminal illness, or perhaps in specified other events (such as permanent residence in a nursing home). Such accelerated benefits reduce the cash value and death benefits of the underlying policy. There may be no initial premium charged for this benefit.

Other Riders There can be a variety of other riders or options on life insurance contracts. These might include options to provide additional amounts of life insurance and cash values through increased premiums, options to make one-time payments (dump-ins) into life policies, children's insurance riders, payor's benefit riders, term insurance riders, options to change premium patterns, and transfer-of-insureds riders.

Planning and Using Life Insurance

Life Insurance Premiums and Dividends

Premiums Graded (Reduced) by Size of Policy Most life insurers follow the practice of grading premium rates by size of policy issued. That is, the larger the face amount of the policy, the lower the premium rate will be per $1,000 of insurance. As a practical matter, another way of doing this is by offering certain policies only in minimum face amounts.

Lower Cost for Women Women have lower mortality rates than men. Today, life insurance companies have lower premium rates for women than for men, and sometimes the difference can be substantial.

Life Insurance Policy Dividends *Participating* whole life insurance refunds a portion of the gross premium to the policyowner in the form of policy dividends that are based on the insurer's actual mortality experience, investment earnings, and administrative expenses. Such policy dividends cannot be guaranteed by the insurer and depend on the insurer's actual experience. Policy dividends do not constitute gross income for income tax purposes to the policyowner, but they may reduce a policy's income tax basis.

For most participating whole life insurance plans, a given dividend scale will produce dividends that generally increase with policy duration. However, an insurer may increase or decrease its whole dividend scale depending on its experience.

Beneficiary Designations

The right to name a beneficiary is vested in the policyowner. Most policyowners also reserve the right to change the beneficiary. Consider this beneficiary designation: "Sue Smith, wife of the insured, if living at the death of the insured, otherwise equally to such of the lawful children of the insured as may be living at the death of the insured." Here, Sue Smith is the primary beneficiary and the children are contingent beneficiaries. Second contingent beneficiaries may be designated in the event that none of the primary or contingent beneficiaries survive the insured. On the other hand, if a policy is owned by someone other than the insured (a trust, for example), the policyowner also should be named as beneficiary.

An insured who is also the owner of the policy may wish to have the death proceeds paid to a trustee as beneficiary, with the trust to be administered for his or her family, rather than to individual beneficiaries. Such a trust may be established under an agreement signed by the insured during his or her lifetime or under the insured's will. Sometimes, insureds name an individual (e.g., wife or husband) as primary beneficiary and a trustee as contingent beneficiary. This is referred to as a *contingent life insurance trust.*

How Should Life Insurance Be Arranged in the Financial Plan?

The issues of how life insurance should be owned, who or what entity should be the beneficiary, how it should be arranged for tax purposes, how life insurance can provide liquidity for an estate or business, and similar matters, are important and can be complex. They are considered in greater depth in Chapter 29.

Financed Life Insurance

This involves borrowing some or all of the premiums for general account life insurance policies (also referred to as leveraged life insurance). It is usually done by irrevocable life insurance trusts (ILITs) involving high-net-worth individuals as grantors and insureds. The grantors may make gifts to the ILITs to pay the interest.

There are several types of premium financing plans. They are usually fully collateralized and the policy's cash value is pledged as security for the loan. The borrower also may have to post additional collateral with the lender and/or personally guarantee the loan.

The interest on such loans is considered personal interest and is not deductible for federal income tax purposes. Thus, this strategy may be effective when the funds can be borrowed at an interest rate that is lower than the rate being earned on the cash value inside the policy. This may be questionable, particularly when interest rates increase significantly in the economy. These loans usually are short-term and so may have to be renegotiated with the lender. Thus, as with any short-term loans taken to finance long-term investment assets, this can be a risky strategy.

Substandard Risks

Most applicants who cannot qualify for individual life insurance at standard rates can still obtain insurance on a so-called substandard (rated) basis. Life insurance underwriting has been refined and improved over the years so that increasing numbers of previously uninsurable applicants can now be afforded coverage on some reasonable basis. Furthermore, an insured who has been issued insurance on a substandard basis may subsequently learn that he or she is eligible for new insurance at standard rates or at least under better terms. Such an insured should appeal to the insurer for reconsideration of the original substandard rating.

If an applicant has been told he or she can get insurance only on a rated basis, the applicant or his or her advisers may want to check with other companies to see what kind of insurance coverage may be available from them. Reputable life insurance companies can differ in their underwriting of certain conditions, and so a lower rating or perhaps even none at all may be secured by shopping around a little.

Nonmedical Life Insurance

Nonmedical insurance typically refers to regular life insurance issued without requiring the applicant to submit to a medical examination. The amounts of insurance that will be issued on a nonmedical basis vary by age groups, with the largest amounts being permitted at younger ages. There may be an age limit beyond which nonmedical insurance is not available.

What Actions Can an Uninsurable Person Take?

First, they can see if it is possible to remove or reduce the reason for the uninsurability. Second, as just noted, they should check with several different insurers. Third, look for sources of insurance that do not require the showing of individual evidence of insurability. Group insurance, for example, may be available through the place of employment. Other groups or associations to which the person belongs may be checked to see if he or she can get association group insurance through them. However, association group coverage often requires at least some individual underwriting. Nonmedical insurance also may be available on an individual basis. Remember, though, that nonmedical insurance does involve individual underwriting. Finally, persons can sometimes qualify for life insurance on a so-called guaranteed-issue basis, where members of a group cannot be denied coverage by the insurer.

Group Life Insurance

Most people who are eligible for group life insurance obtain such coverage through their place of employment. This coverage normally is term insurance.

Group Term Life Insurance

This insurance provides covered employees with pure insurance protection (with no cash values) while they are working for the employer. If an employee leaves the employer, group term coverage normally terminates 31 days after employment ceases, subject to the right of the employee to convert the group insurance to an individual permanent life insurance contract. This conversion privilege is discussed later. Group term coverage may also continue during retirement in reduced amounts and in certain other situations.

Elective Group Coverages

Employers may make several group life plans available to their employees. Such arrangements may specify that an employee must sign up for a basic plan to be eligible to elect coverage under one or more other group plans. Such *elective plans* often include additional levels of group term insurance. Additional levels of group term insurance also usually are available under flexible-benefits (cafeteria compensation) employee benefit plans.

Other Group Plans

Group Universal Life Plans (GULPs) These plans are made available to employees on a voluntary basis, with the employees able to decide, within limits, how much life insurance they wish to purchase and how much in premiums they wish to contribute to the savings element of the plan. Participating employees may withdraw their cash values from the plan, take policy loans against them, and upon termination of employment, continue the coverage by making premium payments directly to the insurance company. The insured employees pay the full cost of a GULP from their after-tax pay (on a salary withholding basis).

Survivor Income Plans Another type of employer-employee group plan is one designed to provide a monthly income that becomes payable to surviving dependents specified in the plan upon the death of an employee.

Conversion Rights

An insured employee has the right to convert, up to the face amount of his or her group term life insurance, to an individual policy of permanent insurance under certain conditions. Typically, the employee can convert within 31 days after termination of employment to one of the insurer's regular permanent forms at standard rates for his or her attained age without evidence of insurability. For employees who are in poor health or even uninsurable, this can be a valuable provision.

Coverage After Retirement

Today, some group life plans continue at least some coverage after retirement.

How Much Life Insurance Is Needed?

This question often perplexes consumers. Unfortunately, there is no one answer. It obviously depends on the purpose or purposes for which the insurance is intended.

Estate Planning and Business Insurance Needs For estate liquidity and conservation purposes, the amount of life insurance needed depends on the size of the estate or estates involved, the potential estate shrinkage, any other liquid assets or arrangements available, and the person's overall estate plan, as explained in Chapter 29. The person or couple also may have other estate-planning goals involving life insurance, such as the possible establishment of a dynasty trust, replacement of family wealth going to charity under charitable remainder trusts, or other charitable giving needs. These possible needs are covered throughout the book.

For business life insurance needs, it depends on the owners' goals for their business, on the business values involved, and on the particular business plans adopted, as explained in Chapter 31. Life insurance also is commonly used in business compensation planning. The amounts needed for this depend on compensation levels, the plans involved, and other factors.

Family Protection Needs The traditional function of life insurance has been to protect a person's loved ones in the event of his or her death. For this purpose, most people with an earned income and family or personal responsibilities need life insurance protection. A number of approaches are used, or have been used, to estimate the amount of life insurance needed for family protection.[9] The main ones are described next.

A Justification for Approximation: Before discussing specific approaches, it may be noted that in determining these amounts, approximation is quite acceptable for several reasons. First, family needs, available resources, and other factors are estimated far into the future, and who knows what the future will bring? Second, with our mobile society, family structures and needs will change in many cases. Third, investment returns may be used in these calculations, and who knows what these will be in the future? Fourth, inflation (or deflation) may also affect future needs, and that is another imponderable. Finally, the cost of term life insurance, particularly for younger persons who normally have the greatest family protection needs, is quite low today, so it often doesn't cost too much to be a little conservative in estimating the amount of life insurance needed.

[9] An excellent discussion of this subject can be found in *McGill's Life Insurance*, Edward E. Graves, ed. (The American College, 1994).

Just Buying an Arbitrary Amount of Insurance: Sometimes consumers are presented with proposals to buy a stated amount of insurance without really evaluating their needs. This is not a logical approach from a planning perspective. Of course, it probably is better than nothing if the coverage is otherwise needed.

A Multiple of Gross Earnings: This is a rough approximation of needs. The person is asked to buy, say, from 6 to 10 times his or her annual earnings. The multiple can be roughly estimated from the person's family situation and perceived needs. This approach is easy to use, but is only a general approximation.

An Earnings Replacement and Cash Needs Approach: This is a more complete but more complicated approach. The goal is to estimate the amount of capital needed to replace each spouse's or person's personal earnings if he or she were to die today. This process starts with each person's gross annual earnings from their personal efforts.

Then, taking each person separately when they are both working outside the home, estimate what percentage of gross earnings should be continued to survivors if the person were to die. This percentage often is around 70 to 80 percent. The concept behind this is that some annual outlays will not continue after the person's death, but others (like child-care expenses) may increase.

The third step is to estimate what existing sources of income will be available after the person's death. These sources may include annual earnings of a surviving spouse, Social Security survivorship benefits, investment income, pension survivorship benefits, and other income sources.

The fourth step is to subtract the existing sources of income to the survivors from the gross income desired for the survivors to arrive at any deficit in the amount of annual income desired.

The fifth step is to convert this deficit into a lump-sum amount of capital needed to meet the earnings replacement need. This is a difficult step, and advisers differ on the technique to be used. Some argue that only enough capital is needed to take care of the deficit until the youngest child finishes college or graduate school. Others argue that this capital fund should be used up (liquidated) over the surviving spouse's life expectancy or some other period. However, the technique favored by the authors is a simple capitalization-of-income approach using a conservative interest rate that may reflect assumed inflation. This approach assumes the capital fund is to remain intact over the surviving spouse's lifetime and then be passed on to the children or others at the surviving spouse's death. This approach is more conservative and will produce a need for more life insurance, but it is defended on the grounds that the future is uncertain and unexpected needs may arise.

Next, the cash needs that will exist after the person's death are considered. These may include an emergency fund, a mortgage and other debt liquidation fund, and an education fund, depending on the circumstances.

Finally, the lump-sum personal earnings replacement need and the cash needs are combined, and then the person's other assets and present life insurance coverage are subtracted from the total need for coverage to determine the amount of new life insurance (if any) the person needs.

The same analysis should be repeated for each person involved. Each person should be considered separately because they will have different earnings, resources, and perhaps needs.

If one spouse works in the home while the other works outside the home, this analysis can be done for the spouse working outside the home. Then the need for a child-care fund and the other expenses that will be necessary in the event of the death of the spouse working in the home can be determined. This will provide the basis for estimating the amount of life insurance needed on that spouse's life.

Fortunately, it normally is not necessary for consumers to perform these calculations for themselves. Life insurance agents, brokers, insurance companies, and other advisers often have computer programs that will use this approach (or one like it) or the programming approach described next to make recommendations to consumers as to how much life insurance they need.

Programming or Needs Approach: For many years, this approach was the main method used in the marketplace for determining how much life insurance a person should have. It is more detailed than the method just described because it takes into consideration changes in the income stream for the family over the years.[10] However, in recent years, the programming approach has not been used nearly as much as it once was.[11]

Human Life Value Approach: This approach attempts to measure the economic worth of an individual to his or her family. It was popularized many years ago (1924) in the writings of Dr. Solomon S. Huebner, who was a pioneer in insurance education. However, it has not been used in practice for many years and so will not be described here.[12]

[10] For example, Social Security survivorship benefits will cease when the youngest child reaches age 18 or 19 and will not begin again until the surviving spouse reaches age 60 (or the full benefit age for full benefits). This is commonly called the Social Security *gap* or *blackout period.*

[11] For a complete discussion of this and related methods, see *Life and Health Insurance,* 13th ed., by Kenneth Black, Jr., and Harold D. Skipper, Jr. (Prentice-Hall, 2000). The fifth edition of this book may also be helpful.

[12] For an illustration of how this method was used, see the fifth edition of Black and Skipper (the full citation is in Footnote 11).

Life Settlement Transactions

These are transactions involving the sale of a life insurance policy to a third-party purchaser for an amount normally significantly larger than the policy's cash value. Such sales are economically feasible for the third-party purchaser because the insured is determined to be in poor health and normally is expected to die in 7 to 8 years.

The life settlement companies typically originate the transactions but then generally pool the purchased policies and sell interests in the pooled contracts to investors. Thus, it is argued that the investors (who stand to profit from the early deaths of the insureds whose policies were purchased) do not know who these insureds are.

For policies to be eligible for a life settlement purchase, the insured normally must be over age 60 or 65, be in poor health, and the policy must be in force in a sound insurance company. The life settlement company normally requests medical information from a prospective seller to evaluate how much, if anything, it will offer for the policy. In effect, it is underwriting in reverse of what a life insurance company does when it is deciding whether to issue a policy on an applicant for life insurance. If the situation meets their standards, life settlement companies then offer the policyowner a purchase price that well exceeds the policy's cash value. If the company purchases a policy, it will continue to pay the premiums necessary to keep the policy in force until the issue dies when it will collect the death proceeds from the insurer for its investors.

Such a policy purchase is a transfer for a valuable consideration for federal income tax purposes. Therefore, the policy's death proceeds are not income tax–free [under Section 101(a) of the IRC], but rather the death proceeds less the life settlement company's basis in the policy (its purchase price plus the premiums it has paid) is ordinary taxable income to the company. This is an example of the transfer for value rule described further in Chapter 29.

For the policyowner-seller, the difference between the amount he or she received from the sale less his or her basis in its contract (net premium paid) is taxable income. Thus, the seller receives the price paid by the life settlement company less the tax payable due to the sale. Of course, if the policyowner had surrendered the policy for cash to the insurer, he or she similarly would have received ordinary income equal to the difference between the cash value (a lower figure) and his or her basis in the contract. On the other hand, if the policyowner-insured retained the policy until death (perhaps financing the premium payments), his or her beneficiary would receive the entire policy proceeds (face amount) income tax–free. Thus, in a potential life settlement situation, the real choice would seem to be whether to sell the policy or retain it until death. This is a rather controversial issue. Most life settlement transactions involve UL or term policies.

CASE EXAMPLE

Peter Impaired, age 65, has recently retired as an executive from Able Corporation, because of poor health. He owns a $5,000,000 UL policy with a $600,000 cash value. Peter has paid $500,000 in premiums for this policy. He feels he needs additional retirement income, does not want to pay future premiums, and so wants to terminate the UL policy. After reviewing the situation, Peter's financial adviser has contacted a number of life settlement companies and, after submitting medical information on Peter's health situation to them, has received several life settlement offers ranging from $700,000 to $1,100,000. Peter decides to accept the $1,100,000 offer and so sells his UL policy to that company. This is a sale of life insurance for a valuable consideration so the difference between the amount Peter receives ($1,100,000) and his basis in the policy (the $500,000 of net premiums paid), or $600,000, is taxable to Peter.

22

Health and Disability Income Insurance

Competence Objectives for This Chapter After reading this chapter, planners should understand:

- The sources of health insurance protection
- The features of individual disability income insurance policies
- Social Security disability benefits
- The features of employer-provided group disability income insurance
- The income tax treatment of employer-provided and individually provided disability income insurance
- Kinds of medical expense benefits
- Medicare benefits
- The nature of employer-provided medical expense benefits
- COBRA continuation rights
- Strategies for planning for terminated health insurance coverage
- Individual health insurance policy provisions
- Health Savings Accounts (HSAs) and Health Reimbursement Arrangements (HRAs)

There are two traditional types of health losses against which people should protect themselves and their families: *disability income losses* and *medical care expenses.* They are covered in this chapter. Another type of related loss—*custodial care expenses*—is the subject of Chapter 23.

Sources of Health Insurance Protection

Social Insurance

The main social insurance programs that provide health benefits are the disability portion of the federal Social Security system; the Medicare portion of the federal Social Security system; state and federal worker's compensation laws; nonoccupational temporary disability benefits laws of some states; and, while not social insurance as such, the Medicaid program.

Group Coverages

Group coverages are the predominant way of providing private health benefits in the United States. Group health coverage generally is a benefits arrangement made by an employer for its employees.

Individual Coverages

Individual health policies are contracts with an insurer made by individuals to cover themselves and perhaps members of their family.

Franchise and Association Group Insurance

Franchise health insurance is a mixture of the individual and group approaches. It involves issuance of individual policies to employees or to members of other groups under an arrangement with the employer or other entity. Association group insurance is similar to franchise insurance, except that it is typically issued to members of professional or trade association groups.

Disability Income (Loss-of-Time) Coverages

Features Affecting Disability Income Coverage

Maximum Benefit Period This is the maximum period that disability benefits will be paid to a disabled person. It may be expressed in weeks or months, or extending to a specified age or even for life. Generally speaking, the longer the maximum benefit period, the better is the coverage for the insured.

Perils Insured Against These perils normally are either *accident alone* or *accident and sickness.* Coverage of disability caused by accident only is limited in scope and normally should be avoided. Coverage generally should be purchased for both accident and sickness.

Waiting (Elimination) Period This is the time that must elapse after a covered disability starts before disability income benefits begin. Suppose, for example, a plan has a 30-day elimination period for accident and sickness. If an insured person becomes disabled as defined by the plan, he or she must wait 30 days after the start of disability before beginning to collect benefits.

Definition of Disability This important provision describes when a person is considered disabled for purposes of collecting benefits. Definitions can be structured in terms of the inability to perform occupational duties, or in terms of loss of earned income, or both.

When the definition is structured in terms of the insured's inability to perform occupational duties, there are essentially three varieties of definitions of disability in use today—the "any occupation" type, the "own occupation" type, and the so-called split definition.

As it was originally conceived, the "any occupation" type defines disability as the complete inability of the covered person to engage in any occupation whatsoever. This is a strict approach. The modern tendency is to phrase an "any occupation" definition in a way that will consider total disability as the "complete inability of the insured to engage in any gainful occupation for which he (or she) is or becomes reasonably fitted by education, training, or experience," or some similar wording. The "any occupation" approach is the least liberal from the consumer's viewpoint.

The "own occupation" type defines disability as when the covered person is "prevented from performing any and every duty pertaining to the employee's (or insured's) occupation." In some policies, this may be phrased as the insured's inability to engage in the substantial and material duties of his or her regular occupation or specialty, or some similar broader wording. This "own occupation" (or "own occ") approach is the most liberal from the consumer's viewpoint.

The split definition is a combination of these two approaches. An example is as follows:

> "Total disability" means complete inability of the insured to engage in *any* [emphasis added] gainful occupation for which he (or she) is reasonably fitted by education, training, or experience; however, during the first 60 months of any period of disability, the Company (insurer) will deem the insured to be totally disabled if he (or she) is completely unable to engage in *his* (or *her*) [emphasis added] regular occupation and is not engaged in any form of gainful occupation.

This definition, in effect, applies an "own occ" definition for a specified period—60 months in this example—and then applies an "any occupation for which the insured is reasonably fitted" definition for the remainder of the benefit period.

The other general method for defining disability is in terms of loss of a certain percentage of the insured's earned income due to accident or sickness. It may be used as the sole definition of disability, or an occupational approach may be used for a policy's basic disability benefit, and then a loss-of-income approach employed for the policy's residual disability benefit.

Social Security Disability Benefits

Benefits Provided There are two basic kinds of Social Security disability benefits: cash disability income benefits and freezing of a disabled worker's wage position for purposes of determining his or her future retirement or survivorship benefits.

An eligible worker is considered disabled when he or she has a medically determinable physical or mental impairment that is so severe the worker is unable to engage in any substantially gainful work or employment. This amounts to an "any occupation" definition of disability and is strict by health insurance standards. In addition, the disability must last five months before benefits can begin. After five months of disability, benefits are payable if the impairment can be expected to last for at least 12 months, or to result in death, or if it has actually lasted 12 months. This amounts to a five-month waiting (elimination) period.

The amount of monthly Social Security cash disability benefits payable to a disabled worker and his or her dependents is based on the worker's covered wages.

Workers' Compensation Disability Benefits

These laws are intended to provide benefits only for work injuries and diseases, and so they really cannot be relied upon in health insurance planning.

Employer-Provided Group Disability Income Benefits

Group coverages as part of employee benefit plans may provide two basic kinds of disability benefits: short-term benefits and long-term benefits.

Benefits Provided *Short-term plans* are characterized by a schedule of weekly benefits based on earnings categories but with relatively low maximum benefits; short elimination periods; and short maximum benefit periods of, for example, 13, 26, or 52 weeks.

Long-term plans (commonly called *LTD coverage*) are designed to take care of more serious, long-term disabilities. They are characterized by benefits stated as a percentage of earnings (such as 60 percent of base salary); a relatively high maximum monthly benefit of $3,000, $5,000, or more; a longer elimination period, such as 90 days or 5 months; a split definition of disability; and longer maximum benefit periods, such as 5 years, 10 years, or to a certain age, such as 65 or 70.

Coordination of Benefits Most group LTD plans have *coordination-of-benefits* provisions that indicate how other disability income benefits will affect the benefits payable under the group plan. Such provisions are important in planning disability protection. They are not uniform, but they generally reduce group LTD benefits by Social Security benefits, state disability benefits, or benefits or salary otherwise provided by the employer. The important point for planning is that group plans normally do not reduce their benefits because of individual disability income insurance that is not provided by the employer.

CASE EXAMPLE

Assume Harry Smart is covered by his employer's noncontributory group LTD plan providing a benefit of 60 percent of salary, up to $5,000 per month, after a five-month elimination period, up to age 65. Tragically, Harry becomes ill and is totally disabled under the plan's definition of disability. Harry's base salary is $125,000 per year, or about $10,416 per month. Sixty percent of $10,416 is $6,250 per month, which is more than the plan's maximum monthly benefit. Therefore, after the five-month elimination period, Harry potentially could recover up to $5,000 per month from the group plan. However, under the plan's coordination-of-benefits provision. Harry's family Social Security disability benefit of $2,800 per month would be deducted from the benefit otherwise payable by the group plan. Therefore, the group plan benefit would become $2,200 per month ($5,000 – $2,800). Note that if Harry had purchased a personally owned disability income policy to supplement his group benefits, its benefits would not reduce his group benefit.

Termination of Coverage A covered employee's group disability income coverage typically terminates when the employee leaves his or her employment, the employee retires, the group policy is terminated by the employer, or the employer fails to pay the premium for the employee. Also, contrary to the case with group life insurance, a terminating employee often does not have the right to convert the group coverage to an individual disability income policy.

Taxation of Benefits The tax code provides that amounts received through accident or health insurance for personal injuries or sickness are not considered gross income for federal income tax purposes, *except* for amounts received as an employee to the extent such amounts are attributable to employer contributions that were not includible in the employee's gross income.

Thus, disability benefits from personally purchased disability income insurance are not gross income, nor are benefits received as an employee from an employment-related plan to the extent the employee contributed to the cost of the benefits. However, to the extent that disability income benefits for an employee are attributable to employer contributions that are not includible in the employee's gross income (as normally would be the situation for employer-provided disability income benefits), they constitute gross income to the disabled employee. Thus, in the case of Harry Smart, the group LTD benefits would be gross income to Harry, since his employer paid the full cost of the plan. However, if Harry had paid for an individual disability income policy, its benefits would not be taxable.

Individual Disability Income Insurance

Need for Coverage There are several reasons why people might need individual coverage despite the growth of group benefits. They may not be members of groups that provide such coverage, or they may not yet be eligible to participate in a group plan. Group benefits may be inadequate, either in amount or in duration. Some people may not want to rely entirely on their employer's group benefits. Finally, individual policies may be used where business health insurance is needed.

Benefits Provided Individual policies provide monthly benefits for a specified period (maximum benefit period) during the continuance of the insured's total (and sometimes partial) disability. Individual disability income insurance should be analyzed mainly in terms of the perils covered, maximum benefit period, definition of disability, elimination period, and amount of coverage. Any individual health insurance should also be analyzed in terms of its renewal or continuance provision. Naturally, cost also is an important consideration. Premiums can vary among insurers.

Individual policies may cover disability either resulting from accidental bodily injury or resulting from accidental bodily injury or from sickness. As we said before, it is important to protect against both accident and sickness, as opposed to accident only.

Today, there is a wide choice of maximum benefit periods, ranging from as short as six months to as long as the insured's reaching age 65 or 70, or for the insured's lifetime. The period selected should depend on the person's needs. However, assuming that permanent protection is needed, consider buying or recommending coverage with longer maximum benefit periods, such as to age 65 or 70, or for life, for both accident and sickness. To buy shorter benefit periods (usually to reduce the cost) may result in benefits running out before the person reaches retirement age (when, presumably, his or her retirement benefits will start).

When insurers use a split definition of disability, in general, the longer the "own occupation" period, the better for the consumer. Of course, an "own occupation" definition for the entire maximum benefit period is better yet for the consumer.

There is a wide choice of elimination periods. They may range, for example, from none for accident and seven days for sickness up to one year or more for accident and sickness. Several factors may be considered when choosing an appropriate elimination period.

- *Coordination with other disability coverage.* Other disability benefits may be available during an initial period of a disability, such as an employer's noninsured salary-continuation (sick-pay) plan.
- *Other resources.* For example, an emergency fund could be maintained to take care of short periods of disability, among other purposes.
- *Cost savings.* A relatively small increase in the elimination period will normally produce considerable savings in premium.

Amount of Coverage Within limits, applicants can choose the amount of coverage for which they want to apply. This, of course, depends on the amount of benefits they need, want, and can afford. It also may depend on the amount of insurance insurers are willing to write on a given individual.

When underwriting individual disability income insurance, insurers have issue and participation limits. An *issue limit* is the maximum amount of monthly benefit an insurer will write on any one individual. A *participation limit* is the maximum amount of monthly benefits from all sources in which an insurer will participate (i.e., write a portion of the coverage). In addition—to try to avoid overinsurance—insurers limit the amount of disability income insurance they will issue to a person so that monthly benefits from all sources will not exceed a specified percentage of the person's earned income.

These underwriting rules may limit the amount of coverage available to a consumer. However, since they vary among insurers, consumers or their advisers may be able to get the amount of coverage they want by shopping around a little.

Supplementary Benefits Some of the more important benefits include the following:

- *Waiver of Premium.* This provision is included automatically in most individual policies and is comparable to the similar benefit in life insurance.
- *Residual Disability (Partial Disability) Benefit.* This benefit may be an integral part of the disability contract, but is often written as an optional rider for an extra premium. The residual disability benefit normally pays a proportionate part of the total disability benefit when the insured suffers at least a specified percentage reduction in his or her earned income (such

as at least a 20 percent reduction). Loss of income often is the coverage trigger for this benefit. Many policies will pay this benefit only after a period of total disability.

- *Guaranteed Insurability.* This commonly provides that on stated policy anniversary dates, the insured may purchase specified additional amounts of disability income benefits with no evidence of insurability.
- *Cost-of-Living Adjustment (COLA).* This benefit provides specified cost-of living increases in disability benefits after a total disability has lasted a certain period, such as one year. COLA coverage that applies to disability income benefit limits prior to a disability also may be purchased.
- *Social Security Supplement Coverage.* This provides additional benefits when the insured is disabled and receives no Social Security benefits. This may be helpful because the Social Security definition of disability generally is considerably stricter than the definition in most individual policies, and so benefits may be payable under an individual policy but not by Social Security.
- *Accidental Death or Accidental Death and Dismemberment (AD&D) Coverage.* This is similar to double indemnity in life insurance. And, as with life insurance, the logic of buying this kind of coverage is highly questionable.
- *Accident Medical Reimbursement, Hospital Income, or Other Medical Expense Benefits.* These types of benefits usually can be added to disability income policies.
- *Benefits That Increase the Amount of the Basic Disability Income Coverage.* One such benefit is a *family income-type benefit* that provides for a decreasing amount of disability income insurance. Another is a variable benefit that allows the amount of monthly income to vary during an initial period of disability to coordinate with other disability benefits.

Coordination of Benefits In general, individual disability income policies pay their benefits, regardless of other disability benefits. However, insurers may place certain provisions relating to other insurance in their contracts, but they usually do not do so today. Also, most individual policies are written on a "24-hour basis." This means they pay for both occupational and nonoccupational disabilities.

Termination of Coverage As explained later, policies that are noncancelable or guaranteed renewable typically provide that coverage will continue, provided the insured continues to pay the premiums, until a specified age, such as age 65. Some policies allow the insured to continue coverage beyond age 65 on a guaranteed renewable basis, on a conditionally renewable basis, or at the option of the insurer, usually provided the insured continues to be gainfully employed. Policies may have a terminal age, such as 70 or older, beyond which the coverage cannot be continued in any event.

Taxation of Benefits As noted earlier, benefits paid from personally purchased disability income insurance are not gross income for federal income tax purposes.

Other Disability Benefits

Group Life Insurance Disability Benefits Several types of disability provisions may be used in group term life insurance plans. However, the most common is a *waiver-of-premium type* that provides for the continuation of a disabled employee's group term life coverage after termination of employment during continuation of disability.

Disability Benefits Under Pension Plans Pension plans may contain some disability benefits, such as the following:

- A number of plans allow an employee who has become totally and permanently disabled to take early retirement under certain conditions.
- Some pension plans provide a separate disability benefit for a totally and permanently disabled employee who has met specified requirements.
- Many plans allow full vesting of an employee's pension benefits in the event of total and permanent disability.
- Some plans provide a disability benefit akin to waiver of premium or the disability freeze in the Social Security system. This benefit allows a disabled employee's pension credits to continue to accumulate during his or her disability.

Medical Expense Coverages

Managed Care versus Fee-for-Service (Indemnity) Benefits

A basic choice for many people today is whether they will have their medical expense coverage under a traditional fee-for-service (FFS; also called an *indemnity*) type plan or under a managed care type plan. They also may have several choices within each category.

Fee-for-Service (Indemnity) Plans These are primarily reimbursement mechanisms that pay for covered health care within the limits of the plan. They allow covered persons to decide when, from whom, and how much health care to use, and then they usually pay the "reasonable and customary" (or some similar term) fees or charges for that care, subject to the limits of the plan. They do not attempt to control access to care or utilization of care.

Today, most fee-for-service plans are major medical plans, but some plans are more limited.

Managed Care Plans This term can embrace a number of health-care arrangements. However, the basic idea is that the plan not only finances health care, but also organizes the care and, to some degree, controls access to care. Thus, providers of care (doctors, hospitals, pharmacies, and so forth) have contracted with or are employed by the managed care plan and are, in varying degrees, controlled by the plan.

Types of Managed Care Plans There is considerable diversity among managed care plans, but the main types are as follows.

Traditional Health Maintenance Organizations (HMOs): These are the original managed care plans. A covered person selects a primary care physician from among those participating in the HMO. This physician then manages the person's medical care and may refer the person to specialists, hospital care, and other medical services, again generally from among those participating in the HMO.

There are several types of HMOs, but they generally have the following characteristics:

- Comprehensive benefits, including emphasis on preventive care, such as routine physical examinations, well-baby care, and inoculations
- Little or no cost sharing (deductibles and coinsurance) by covered persons
- Few or no claim forms to fill out
- Generally only paying for services rendered in-network
- Providing care in limited geographic areas
- Often being low-cost plans for the coverage provided

Preferred Provider Organizations (PPOs): PPOs contract with certain providers to form a network. The providers agree to render health care to persons covered by the PPO (such as employees) and to be paid according to a negotiated fee schedule, which is usually discounted from their regular fees. Covered persons may elect to secure medical care from providers within the PPO (in-network) or outside the PPO (out-of-network) under an indemnity plan. But when they use the indemnity plan, they are penalized financially by greater cost sharing or perhaps lower benefits.

Point-of-Service (POS) Plans: These can be viewed as a combination of the traditional HMO and a traditional fee-for-service plan. Covered persons select a primary care physician, who manages the person's medical care and who may refer the person to network specialists and other in-network forms of care. However, at the time medical services are to be rendered (i.e., at the point of service), the covered person may choose to receive care in-network (with little or no cost sharing and perhaps broader benefits) or to go out of network under the indemnity plan but with significantly higher cost sharing, perhaps lesser benefits, and the necessity of claim forms.

Availability of Consumer Choice Many consumers can choose from among one or more managed care plans and one or more indemnity plans. Employee benefit plans often allow employees to choose from among one or more HMOs, a PPO, and one or more indemnity plans. There may be different levels of employee contributions, depending on which plan is chosen.

Consumers also may purchase HMO or indemnity coverage on an individual basis. Furthermore, persons on Medicare (which generally has been a fee-for-service program) may be able to choose coverage under the Medicare + Choice program (described later in this chapter).

Decision Factors in Making the Choice The choice between fee-for-service and managed care may not be easy for many people. Following are some factors consumers may consider in making this choice:

- Extent of benefits provided (including for preventive care)
- Cost sharing required
- Extent of controls over access to care
- Size and reputation of managed care networks
- Whether the consumer's present physicians are already in the managed care network
- Relative desire for uncontrolled access to care
- Cost of plans
- Geographic limits of plans
- Flexibility allowed in plans (e.g., availability of POS approach)

Kinds of Medical Expense Benefits

Although there are many kinds of medical expense benefits, the following are the most common. These may be provided under fee-for-service or managed care plans.

- Hospital expense benefits
- Surgical benefits
- Regular medical (doctors' expense) benefits
- Laboratory and diagnostic expense benefits
- Prescription drug benefits
- Dental plans
- Preventive services
- Other basic benefits

Major Medical Plans

Major medical and comprehensive medical coverages represent the backbone of protection against medical expenses on a fee-for-service basis today.

Covered Expenses These plans cover most kinds of medical expenses, whether or not the covered person is confined in a hospital. They specify that only reasonable and customary (R&C) or usual, customary, and reasonable (UCR) charges will be paid. Thus, on this basis, insurers may reduce covered charges that they feel do not fall within the prevailing pattern of charges in a community.

Maximum Limit Plans usually contain an overall maximum limit of liability that may range from as low as $10,000 to $1,000,000 or more. Some plans have no maximum limit at all. Maximum limits can usually be reinstated after a specified amount of benefits, such as $1,000, have been paid and the covered person submits evidence of insurability or returns to work for a specified period. Some policies, however, provide for automatic restoration of the maximum.

Deductibles Major medical deductibles are applied to the first $200, $300, $500, or more of covered medical expenses before benefits are paid.

Coinsurance After the deductible is satisfied, major medical policies normally require the covered person to bear a certain portion, commonly 20 or 25 percent, of covered expenses, with the insurer paying the remainder. This is referred to as a *coinsurance provision.* However, most plans today have *stop-loss provisions,* which limit the unreimbursed, covered expenses for a person to a maximum amount, such as $1,500 per year. After this unreimbursed stop-loss limit is reached in a year, the plan pays 100 percent of covered expenses up to a maximum limit.

Excess Major Medical Some insurance companies write excess major medical coverage on an association group basis or as an individual policy. Excess major medical applies after other medical expense coverage has paid its limits or a large deductible has been satisfied by the insured.

Medicare

Persons age 65 and over who are not currently employed may rely primarily on Medicare for their medical expense protection, although they may also have retiree health coverage from their former employer, use individual plans to supplement Medicare, or be covered by so-called Medicare HMOs. Private plans are generally coordinated with Medicare so their benefits will not overlap.[1] The original Medicare program comprised two major plans: Part A–Hospital Insurance (HI) and Part B Supplementary Medical Insurance (SMI). These original plans are on a free-for-service basis and are described in the next sections.

Subsequent legislation has increased the options available to covered persons through a new Medicare Part C (called Medicare + Choice) and a later Medicare Part D (a Medicare prescription drug coverage). These plans also are described later in this chapter.

Hospital Insurance (HI) Nearly everyone age 65 or over is eligible for HI, which provides the following main benefits (as of 2009):

- HI covers up to 90 days of inpatient care in any participating hospital for each benefit period. For the first 60 days, HI pays for all covered services except for a $1,068 deductible. For the 61st through the 90th days, it pays for all covered services except for a deductible of $267 per day.
- There is an additional lifetime reserve of 60 hospital days. For each of these days used, HI pays for all covered services except for a $534-per-day deductible.
- After hospital confinement, HI covers up to 100 days of care in a participating extended-care facility (nursing home). It pays for all covered services for the first 20 days and all but a $133.50-per-day deductible for up to 80 additional days.[2]
- HI covers unlimited home health visits by a participating home health agency (e.g., a participating visiting nurse service) on a part-time, intermittent basis.
- HI also covers certain hospice care services.

Supplementary Medical Insurance (SMI) This portion of Medicare is voluntary, although persons eligible for HI are covered automatically unless they decline SMI coverage. SMI is financed by individuals age 65 and over who participate and by contributions from the federal government. It generally pays 80 percent of the reasonable charges for covered medical services

[1] Under federal law, for active workers and their spouses over age 65, their employer's health plan is primary over Medicare. For retired workers and their spouses, Medicare can be made primary, and usually is so, by any employer's health plan.

[2] All of these deductibles or cost-sharing provisions are adjusted periodically to reflect changes in hospital costs. Some of what we have called deductions (because that is their effect) are technically called *coinsurance* by Social Security.

after a $135 deductible in each calendar year. The following are some of the major services covered by SMI:

- Physicians' and surgeons' services and supplies
- Home health services on an unlimited basis
- Other medical and health services, such as diagnostic tests
- Outpatient physical and occupational therapy services
- All outpatient services of participating hospitals

Expenses Not Covered by Medicare (Medicare Gaps) These noncovered expenses give rise to the planning issue of whether and how Medicare should be supplemented to cover these gaps. Following are some of the main gaps in Medicare coverage:

- Custodial care intended primarily to meet the daily living needs of persons who can no longer be self-sufficient
- Cost-sharing provisions under HI and SMI (e.g., deductibles and coinsurance)
- Periods of hospitalization and skilled nursing home services beyond the HI limits on numbers of days
- Routine physical examinations and immunizations
- Eyeglasses and regular eye examinations
- Hearing aids and regular audiological examinations
- Cosmetic surgery (except where immediately required due to accidental injury)
- Routine foot care and orthopedic shoes
- Ordinary dentures and dental work
- Doctors' charges and other charges above what Medicare will pay as reasonable charges
- Private-duty nursing in a hospital or skilled nursing facility
- Private room in a hospital or skilled nursing facility (unless medically necessary)
- Medical care outside the United States

Medicare Supplements People may seek to supplement Medicare with individual or association group policies.[3] The policies sold by insurance companies to supplement Medicare—called *Medicare supplement policies* or

[3] An employer may provide continuing medical expense coverage for its retired, former employees and often their spouses (retiree health coverage). When the retired, former employees and their spouses (if covered) are age 65 or over and hence are covered by Medicare, this retiree health coverage is secondary to Medicare and thus supplements Medicare. Whether a retired, former employee and his or her spouse with reasonable retiree health coverage needs to supplement Medicare further with individual coverage is questionable, depending, as always, on the circumstances.

Medigap policies—essentially are standardized. There now are 10 approved Medigap policies that can be sold to the public. In effect, if insurers are in the Medicare supplement market, these are the plans (with some exceptions) they can offer.

All these standard plans contain a basic core of benefits, which include the 20 percent SMI coinsurance, the HI daily copayment for the 61st through the 90th days of hospitalization, coverage for 365 additional days of hospitalization beyond the 90 days provided by HI, and coverage of the patient's charges for the first three pints of blood each year. One standard plan provides only these core benefits. The other nine plans provide these core benefits and one or more additional optional benefits.

In addition to the standard policy requirements just described, persons enrolling in Medicare Part B (SMI) after November 1, 1991, are given a six-month open enrollment period during which insurers may not deny the person a Medigap policy nor discriminate against them in pricing such coverage due to the person's health status, claims experience, or medical condition. This open-window enrollment period can provide protection for Medicare enrollees who are in poor health and desire Medigap coverage.

Medicare HMOs Some HMOs have contractual arrangements with Medicare (the Health Care Financing Agency) under which eligible HMO subscribers receive their Medicare benefits through the HMO and the HMO also may provide additional services that supplement Medicare.

Medicare Premiums Charged to Covered Persons Social Security beneficiaries do not pay any additional premium for Part A (HI). They do, however, pay a monthly premium for Part B (SMI), which has increased dramatically over the years. Also, the Part B premium now increases with the person's or married couple's income for tax purposes. Nevertheless, eligible persons generally should enroll in Part B because the coverage is well worth the cost.

The relatively few persons who are age 65 and over but who are not otherwise eligible for Medicare can enroll voluntarily in Part A (HI) and Part B (SMI) and pay a rather substantial monthly cost for both, or enroll only in Part B and pay a lesser monthly cost.

Medicare + Choice The Balanced Budget Act of 1997 created Medicare Part C (Medicare + Choice), effective January 1, 1999. Under this program, each year, Medicare beneficiaries have the opportunity to choose the Medicare plan in which they wish to participate. First, Medicare beneficiaries who are already enrolled in the original Medicare plan (HI and SMI), the original plan with supplemental insurance, or a Medicare HMO may remain with their plan if they wish. However, Medicare beneficiaries who are entitled to Part A and enrolled in Part B and those newly eligible for Parts A and B may choose to enroll in the Medicare + Choice option under Part C, rather than in Parts A and B.

There are two options under Medicare + Choice. One is termed coordinated care plans (or Medicare-managed care plans) and is a managed-care option. The plans available under this option include traditional HMOs; provider-sponsored organizations (PSOs), which are like HMOs but are organized by health-care providers; HMOs with point-of-service options; and PPOs. These plans may provide additional benefits, but some may also charge an additional premium.

A second option is a private fee-for-service (PFFS) plan. Under this option, beneficiaries can choose their own providers of care, but providers may charge beneficiaries more than the amount allowed for their services by the plan, up to a limit. In this case, the beneficiary must pay the difference to the provider. This is referred to as *balance billing.* Balance billing is not permitted under the original Medicare plan if the provider accepts assignment of Medicare benefits. Even if a provider does not accept assignment, there still generally is a limit on the amount doctors and other providers can charge over the Medicare-approved amount (called the limiting charge). If the PFFS option is chosen, Medicare pays the PFFS plan a premium and the PFFS plan provides all Medicare benefits and perhaps additional benefits to the beneficiary. The beneficiary may have to pay an additional premium.

Planning Issues Under Medicare + Choice Some of the factors involved in making selections between the original Medicare plan and Medicare + Choice (and, if Medicare + Choice, which option to choose) include:

- Control over access to care (choice of providers)
- Services covered and availability of extra benefits, such as outpatient prescription drugs, vision care, hearing aids, and routine physical exams
- Cost sharing by beneficiaries
- Ability of providers to bill beneficiaries for more than plan benefits (balance billing)
- Additional premium for beneficiaries
- Geographic limitations on coverage

Medicare Prescription Drug Coverage This is Part D of Medicare and offers prescription drug coverage for everyone with other Medicare coverage. Eligible persons can enroll in Medicare prescription drug programs provided by many insurance companies and others. They can also get drug coverage through Medicare Advantage Plans that offer such coverage.

Persons can enroll in Medicare prescription drug programs when they first become eligible for Medicare or, if later, between November 15 and December 31 of each year. However, persons who do not enroll when first eligible will have to pay a late enrollment penalty which will increase their monthly fee from then on. There are some exceptions to this late enrollment fee. The monthly fee and drugs covered depend on the particular plan that covered persons select.

For each year, there is a deductible that must be met before the plan will begin to pay for covered drugs. This deductible is $295. Then there is a copayment or coinsurance that the covered person must pay for covered drugs with the plan paying the balance. The coverage continues until the total amount paid for drugs by both the plan and covered person equals $2,700. Then the covered person must pay all the cost of covered drugs until he or she has spent $4,350. This is the coverage gap (or "doughnut"). After this $4,350 has been spent, almost all the remaining costs for the year are covered under what is called the catastrophic coverage.

Workers' Compensation

Workers' compensation laws provide unlimited medical benefits to employees injured on the job. Other plans normally exclude expenses for which a covered person is entitled to workers' compensation benefits.

Employer-Provided Medical Expense Benefits (Group Benefits)

The lion's share of private medical expense benefits in the United States is provided under group coverages established by employers for their employees. Therefore, the beginning point in medical expense coverage planning is to determine what, if any, group protection applies.

Who Is Covered? Group plans cover employees and their dependents. The definition of *dependents* is important and perhaps will indicate some dependents for whom other arrangements may need to be made.

Plans may allow employees to waive coverage for certain dependents (such as spouses working outside the home), provided they have other coverage. They also may offer employees financial incentives to do so. This may be something for employees to consider (when applicable) as a cost-saving measure.

Benefits Provided Group plans can provide any of the benefits previously described. The group technique generally makes possible the provision of broader benefits at lower cost than can be provided under individual policies.

Coordination of Benefits Most group plans include a coordination-of-benefits (COB) provision, which has the effect of setting a priority of payment among plans and limiting the total amount recoverable from group plans (and certain other coverages) in effect for a person to 100 percent (or some other percentage, such as 80 percent) of the expenses covered under any of the plans. This serves to avoid duplication of benefits when a person is covered under more than one group plan. In most cases, however, group plans do not coordinate with individual policies.

Termination of Coverage An employee's group coverage may terminate when the employee terminates his or her employment. Dependents' coverage may terminate when the employee's coverage terminates or when their dependency status changes.

COBRA Continuation Rights The *Consolidated Omnibus Budget Reconciliation Act of 1985* (popularly called *COBRA*) requires most employers to provide continued coverage under group health plans to covered employees and other qualified beneficiaries (spouse and dependent children) in case of certain qualifying events, such as termination of employment or reduction of hours, death of the employee, divorce or legal separation, and a child's reaching the maximum age for coverage, without the qualified beneficiary's needing to show any evidence of insurability.

The continued coverage is the same as under the group health plan and must be available for 18 or 36 months, depending on the nature of the qualifying event. The qualified person must elect this continuation, and a premium may be charged to the qualified person for it up to 102 percent of the cost of the coverage to the plan.[4] Such continuation generally is not available when there is coverage under another group plan or Medicare. When a qualified beneficiary's continuation coverage expires, the beneficiary must be given the option of enrolling in the conversion health plan that otherwise is available under the group plan.

Health Insurance Portability Another federal measure broadening the rights of employees and their dependents under group health plans is the *Health Insurance Portability and Accountability Act of 1996* (HIPAA). For most group health plans, this law regulates the terms of any preexisting-conditions exclusion and requires group plans to give credit for prior coverage under a wide variety of other health plans in meeting the requirements of any preexisting-conditions exclusion.

[4] Under the American Recovery and Reinvesment Act of 2009 (the federal stimulus program), a temporary 65 percent reduction in this premium is granted to eligible individuals who are involuntarily terminated. An eligible individual is a qualified beneficiary who became eligible for COBRA from September 1, 2008, through December 31, 2009, and is not a high-income person. Employees are given a refundable tax credit for their premium reductions. Thus, the federal government really pays the tax for them.

Suppose, for example, that Maria Hernandez has been covered for five years as an employee under the group health plan of the ABC Corporation and that her 12-year-old son is covered as a dependent. Unfortunately, her son has a congenital heart condition that is treated regularly. Maria has just received an attractive job offer from XYZ Corporation. XYZ also has a group health plan, but it has a 12-month preexisting-conditions exclusion. Maria is worried that if she changes jobs, her son will lose health coverage for 12 months under her new employer's plan. She need not worry! HIPAA requires XYZ's plan to count her prior coverage under ABC's plan toward its 12-month exclusion period, and so, in her case, there will be no preexisting-conditions exclusion applying to her son under XYZ's plan.

HIPAA also does not permit group health plans to discriminate as to eligibility or premiums for coverage based solely on health status, medical condition, claims experience, medical history, genetic information, evidence of insurability, and certain other factors. Thus, XYZ's plan could not impose stricter eligibility requirements or higher premiums on Maria's son because of his health impairment.

Retiree Health Coverage Employers may continue medical expense coverage for their retirees and often the retirees' dependents. When these benefits are provided, there normally are some age and/or service requirements to qualify. Thus, one factor employees should consider in deciding on their retirement age (or whether to accept an early retirement offer) is how it will affect their eligibility for retiree benefits.

Once retired, former employees and their spouses age 65 and over are eligible for Medicare. Retiree health coverage is coordinated with Medicare so there is no duplicate coverage, with Medicare being the primary coverage. In effect, these plans supplement Medicare.

One point for retirees and employees to consider is whether an employer that now has retiree health coverage may in the future attempt to modify or terminate those benefits. Employers normally reserve the right to modify or terminate retiree health coverage (as well as other employee benefits, for that matter) in the future. However, many employers, particularly larger employers, have maintained retiree health coverage for many years.

Strategies in Planning for Terminated Coverage There are several possibilities for a person whose group coverage has terminated.

- The person may be eligible immediately for other group insurance.
- The person may be eligible for Medicare upon reaching age 65. In this case, the person (and possibly his or her spouse) may also be fortunate enough to have retiree health coverage.

- The person may elect continuation of group coverage under COBRA. In this case, he or she also will have conversion rights at the end of the COBRA period.
- The person (and covered dependents) may have the right to convert the terminating group insurance to an individual policy without evidence of insurability. As just noted, conversion rights must also be made available at the end of a COBRA continuation period (through election during the preceding 180 days).
- The person may purchase new individual insurance to replace terminated group coverage. HIPAA requires insurers to offer such coverage without individual evidence of insurability under certain conditions.

Employer-Provided Cafeteria Compensation or Flexible Benefits Programs A number of employers have organized their employee benefit plans so that employees can choose at least part of their benefit package from among several types and levels of benefits. This is referred to as *cafeteria compensation* or *flexible benefits.*[5]

Employees frequently are given a set number of dollar credits, which they can spend on a menu of benefit choices. These choices may include one or more medical expense plans, group term life insurance, dependent group life insurance, and disability income benefits. If an employee spends more than his or her allotted credits, his or her salary is reduced *before tax* to pay for the extra cost. On the other hand, if the employee spends less, his or her salary may be increased by the difference or it may be placed in certain retirement plans. When employees are offered a wide choice of benefits, such as just described, it is sometimes referred to as *full flex.* Employers also may offer flexible benefits plans that are more limited.

Another more limited kind of flexible benefits program is the health-care *flexible spending account* (FSA). An employee may elect to have his or her salary reduced by a certain amount (up to a limit specified in the plan), and this amount then is placed *before tax* in a separate account from which medical expenses that are not otherwise covered by the employer's plan can be paid. However, employees should take care not to place more in an FSA than will be covered by it in a given year. If the amount in an FSA at the end of a year exceeds the benefits paid from it during the year, the employee will forfeit the balance. This is referred to as the "use it or lose it" rule. The attraction of FSAs is that otherwise-noncovered medical expenses can be paid on a

[5] Since these plans are permitted by Section 125 of the Internal Revenue Code, they also are called Section 125 plans.

before-tax basis. There also may be FSAs for dependent care expenses. FSAs may be part of a full-flex program or may stand alone.

Individual Health Insurance

A great many different individual and family medical expense policies are available to the public from many different insurers. These policies may offer consumers broad coverage, but some provide only limited coverage. Therefore, such policies should be evaluated carefully.

Who Is Covered? Individual medical expense insurance can be written to cover the insured person, the insured's spouse, and other dependents.

Benefits Provided The same kinds of medical expense benefits can be provided under individual policies as under group coverages, except that individual policies often offer less liberal benefits.

Coordination of Benefits Since people are free to buy individual medical expense policies from a number of insurers, may have group coverage, and also may be covered by other medical expense benefits, they may find themselves with several sources of recovery for medical expenses. This is not necessarily bad, but it is an area that can be analyzed to see if premium dollars can be saved by dropping any unnecessary coverage. Individual policies usually do not contain provisions that would coordinate or prorate their benefits with other coverage. Insurers generally try to avoid overinsurance by their underwriting requirements.

Termination of Coverage Individual policies may terminate the insured's or spouse's coverage when he or she reaches age 65 or first becomes eligible for Medicare. Of course, Medicare supplement policies are not terminated.

Individual Health Insurance Policy Provisions

Several kinds of policy provisions may be important in making policy purchase decisions.

Renewal or Continuance Provisions

Renewal or continuance provisions relate to the insured's rights to continue his or her individual coverage from one policy period to another. They generally can be classified as given here. Policies have been issued that were renewable at the option of the insurer (or optionally renewable). This approach generally is not used today. Another approach that sometimes is used is that policies may be conditionally renewable (or nonrenewable for stated reasons only), in that there are restrictions on the insurer's right of nonrenewal. An example is in franchise or association group coverages, where the insurer may not be able to refuse renewal unless the insured ceases to be a member of the association, the insured ceases to be actively engaged in the occupation, or the insurer refuses to renew all policies issued to members of the particular group.

A common approach is for individual policies to be *guaranteed renewable.* In this case, the policy provides that the insured has the right to renew coverage for a specified period, such as to age 65, or in some cases for life. During this period, the insurer cannot by itself make any change in the policy, except that the insurer retains the right to make changes in premium rates for whole classes of policies. This means the insurer cannot change the premium or classification for an individual policy by itself, but may change the rates for whole rating classifications.

For policies issued after June 30, 1997, HIPAA requires most individual medical expense contracts to be guaranteed renewable at the option of the policyholder. It would seem desirable for policyholders to make this election, even if the cost is somewhat higher. Nonrenewal is allowed only in limited circumstances. Insurers also may write disability income coverages on a guaranteed renewable basis.

The final category is the *noncancelable and guaranteed renewable* (or noncancelable) type. When the term *noncancelable,* or *noncan,* is used alone to describe a renewal provision, it means the noncancelable and guaranteed renewable type. This provision gives the insured the right to continue the policy in force by the timely payment of premiums as specified in the policy, usually for a specified period, such as to age 65. The insurer retains no right by itself to make any change in any policy provision during this period. The distinction between this and a guaranteed renewable policy is that the insurer guarantees the premium rates for noncancelable contracts but reserves the right to change premiums for whole classes of insureds under guaranteed renewable contracts.

Not surprisingly, the greater the renewal guarantees contained in a policy, the higher the premium will tend to be. Thus, assuming the consumer has a choice among renewal provisions, the question becomes: How much is he or she willing to pay for renewal protection? In general, it probably is better to try to purchase noncancelable coverage if it is available; otherwise, he or she should purchase guaranteed renewable coverage.

Preexisting Conditions

Individual health insurance policies normally limit coverage for conditions existing prior to the effective date of coverage. Group health plans, on the other hand, may cover preexisting conditions on the same basis as other conditions or may use a preexisting-conditions exclusion that meets the requirements of HIPAA.

However, a section of the "time limit on certain defenses" provision, which is a required provision in individual health insurance policies, in effect provides that after a policy has been in force for two or three years, coverage cannot be denied by the insurer on the ground that a loss was caused by a preexisting condition, unless the condition is specifically excluded in the policy. Many states have further restricted the application of preexisting-conditions exclusions.

General Provisions

Time Limit on Certain Defenses In addition to the part of this provision dealing with preexisting conditions, another aspect specifies that after a policy has been in force for two or three years, no misstatements, except fraudulent misstatements, made by the applicant in securing the policy can be used to void the policy or to deny liability for a loss commencing after the two- or three-year period. It is similar in concept to the incontestable clause used in life insurance.

Grace Period Like life insurance policies, individual health contracts allow a grace period for the payment of premiums.

Notice and Proof Requirements The policy indicates certain time limits for the insured to give written notice of a claim and furnish the insurer with completed proofs of loss.

Health Savings Accounts and Health Reimbursement Arrangements

These are included in the general category of consumer driven health plans (CDHPs) that aim to give consumers the power to direct their health-care spending in an efficient manner for them. The concept is that it will encourage consumers to spend carefully and thus help control health-care costs. Consumers are provided with accounts (sums of money) to use for their health-care spending. In essence, they are health-care defined-contribution plans.

One form of this approach is the *health flexible spending account* (FSA) that has already been discussed in this chapter.

Another development in this concept was the *Archer medical savings account* (MSA) that was launched in 1977 and tested again later. However, no new Archer MSAs may be established since December 31, 2003.

Health Savings Accounts (HSAs)

General Considerations The successor to the Archer MSA is the health savings account (HSA). HSAs were adopted starting in 2004 by the Medicare Prescription Drug, Improvement, and Modernization Act of 2003. The concept behind the HSA is to enable persons, or employers on behalf of their employees, to set aside annual contributions in a tax-exempt trust or custodial account to pay for or reimburse qualifying medical expenses.

Eligible Individuals To be eligible for an HSA, an individual must be covered under a high deductible health plan, have no other health coverage (with some exceptions), not be enrolled in Medicare, and not be a dependent on another's tax return. For married persons, each eligible spouse must open his or her own HSA.

High Deductible Health Plans A required *high deductible health plan* (HDHP) has a high annual deductible and places limits on annual out-of-pocket expenses. For 2009, the annual deductible must be at least $2,000 and not more than $3,000 for self-only coverage and at least $4,000 but not over $6,050 for family coverage. Correspondingly, the annual out-of-pocket expenses (other than for premiums) for covered expenses cannot exceed $4,000 for self-only coverage and $7,350 for family coverage. These amounts are indexed for inflation.

Permitted Contribution Annual contributions now are limited by a statutory maximum (regardless of HDHP deductibles) which in 2009 is $3,000 for self-only coverage and $5,950 for family coverage. There also are catch-up contributions for taxpayers age 55 or over of $1,000 as of 2009. These limits also are indexed for inflations. Contributions can be made by the eligible individual, his or her employer on behalf of the individual, or family members for the individual. All contributions must be in cash.

Tax Treatment of HSAs The tax treatment of HSAs is quite favorable. Contributions (within certain limits) are deductible from the person's gross income, and if made by the individual's employer, are excluded from his or her gross income. Investment earnings on the assets in an HSA are not currently taxable income to the individual owner. Distributions from an HSA to pay qualified medical expenses for the individual, his or her spouse, or his or her dependents are excluded from the individual's gross income. Distributions for any other purpose are taxable. They are also subject to a 10 percent penalty, unless the individual is disabled, becomes eligible for Medicare, or is deceased.

HSA Rollovers At present, there can be one-time rollovers from a health reimbursement arrangement (HRA), considered next, and an FSA to the person's HSA. These rollovers do not count as contributions and so are not subject to the HSA contribution limits. These HRA and FSA rollover provisions are scheduled to sunset on December 31, 2011.

A one-time rollover also is permitted from an IRA owned by the individual. However, this rollover does count as a contribution and so is subject to the HSA contribution limits.

Distributions Income tax–free distributions can be made from an HSA for qualified medical expenses, which generally are those that would be deductible for federal income tax purposes. However, this generally does not include health insurance premiums, except in some cases such as premiums for COBRA continuation coverage and for qualified LTC insurance. Also, any health insurance premiums (other than for Medigap coverage) are qualified expenses once the person attains Medicare coverage. In effect then, these health premiums can be paid with before-tax dollars from the HSA. As noted earlier, other distributions are taxable as ordinary income and may be subject to a 10 percent penalty tax.

At Death If the deceased owner's spouse is the designated beneficiary, the spouse becomes the owner of the HSA and may treat it as his or her own HSA. On the other hand, if anyone else is the beneficiary, it will be paid to that person, but its value at death will be included in the beneficiary's gross income for federal income tax purposes.

Its value at death will be included in the deceased owner's gross estate for federal estate tax purposes. But if the benefit is ordinary income (i.e., to a non-spouse beneficiary), it will also be IRD to that beneficiary.

Planning Issues Under the right circumstances, HSAs can be attractive health coverage and wealth accumulation vehicles. If the owner and his or her family are in reasonably good health and thus medical expenses are reasonable, the account value with its tax-deferred or tax-free investment earnings can grow substantially over time. When the person becomes eligible for Medicare, he or she can no longer contribute to the HSA, but the account balance will be available to pay non-Medicare-covered medical expenses on a before-tax basis. It can also be used to pay LTC premiums before-tax.

Of course, the HSA owner must pay for the required HDHP. However, this plan will be available to cover unexpected or catastrophic expenses over the deductible and an annual out-of-pocket limit.

However, if an employee has good employer-financial health coverage, he or she would not be eligible for an HSA.

Health Reimbursement Arrangements (HRAs)

These are employer-paid plans that create an account or fund for employees to use to pay for qualified medical expenses. In essence, HRAs are defined contribution health plans. Neither the employer contributions to the HRA nor the distributions made to cover qualified medical expenses are taxable to the covered employees. Also, like other employee benefits, reasonable employer contributions are deductible as ordinary and necessary business expenses by the employer.

Unlike FSAs (which involve elective employee deferrals), unused accounts in an employee's HRA at the end of a year are not lost to the employee (i.e., the use it or lose it FSA feature). Instead, such unused amounts can be carried forward in the HRA to future years and used for medical expenses even after the employee leaves the employer. The balances in these accounts may not be taken in cash. However, as noted earlier, HRAs may be rolled over one time before December 31, 2011, to a person's HSA.

23

Long-Term Care Insurance and Medicaid Planning

Competence Objectives for This Chapter After reading this chapter, planners should understand:

- The nature of the custodial care exposure
- The elements of long-term care (LTC) insurance
- Long-term care benefits under life insurance policies
- The tax treatment of LTC benefits
- Lack of coverage under Medicare and private health insurance for long-term care exposure
- The nature and eligibility requirements for Medicaid
- Medicaid as a source of custodial care coverage
- Asset transfers and Medicaid eligibility
- Other Medicaid planning techniques

The nature of the long-term care or custodial care exposure was outlined in Chapter 1. It has attracted increasing attention and concern over the years.

Nature of Exposure

Long-term care can be financially devastating. If, for example, a loved one requires skilled nursing facility care, an average cost might be around $200 (or more) per day, or $73,000 per year, for nursing home care alone. This amount normally will be deductible for federal income tax purposes, by the person paying the cost, as an itemized medical expense.[1] However, even with a tax deduction, this level of expense can be a financial disaster for most families. Of course, different levels of care may cost less, but it still will be significant.

The persons who may be at financial risk for such care, of course, include the person who needs the care and his or her spouse. However, they also may include children, grandchildren, other family members, and their spouses who may be faced with parents, grandparents, or other loved ones who need custodial or long-term care.

Several possible levels of long-term care services may be utilized, depending on the situation and the desires of the parties. These include the following and are listed from the highest level of care to the lowest:

- *Skilled nursing care facilitie.* These facilities have the staff and equipment necessary to provide skilled nursing or rehabilitative services on a daily basis.
- *Intermediate-care facilitie.* These provide primarily custodial care, but also have skilled nursing and rehabilitative services available if needed.
- *Custodial care facilitie.* Such facilities are residential facilities designed to provide primarily custodial care and are not equipped to provide skilled nursing services.
- *Adult day care.* These facilities provide care on a nonresidential basis.
- *Home health care.* Facilities like these may cover services provided by a qualified home health-care agency or others.

Basic Planning Approaches

The following planning approaches are being used to meet this exposure:

- Purchase of long-term care (LTC) insurance. This involves advance planning and funding for this expense.
- Planning to become eligible for government benefits, essentially Medicaid.
- Other estate planning decisions made with long-term care needs in mind.

[1] Medical and dental expenses paid by a taxpayer for the taxpayer, his or her spouse, or his or her dependents are considered an itemized deduction (i.e., from adjusted gross income to arrive at taxable income, if the taxpayer itemizes his or her deductions) to the extent that the expenses exceed 7.5 percent of the taxpayer's adjusted gross income for the year.

Under the Health Insurance Portability and Accountability Act (HIPAA) of 1996, unreimbursed expenses for qualified long-term care services are considered to be for medical care and are deductible under the medical expense provision of the IRC. Qualified long-term care services generally are services or care given to provide assistance to a chronically ill or disabled individual. They are explained further in this chapter.

Long-Term Care (LTC) Insurance and Other Arrangements

LTC insurance is the main source of advance insurance funding for the long-term care exposure.

Sources of LTC Insurance

- Individual LTC insurance purchased by consumers
- LTC insurance purchased by individuals through association group plans
- LTC riders added to life insurance and annuity contracts
- Group LTC insurance purchased by employees through their employers
- Coverage available through continuing care retirement community (CCRC) plans

General Nature of Coverage

LTC insurance customarily provides a specified reimbursement or an indemnity benefit per day (a per diem benefit) for covered care after an initial waiting period of a stated number of days, up to certain maximum benefits. Under present contracts, there usually are multiple definitions of when coverage begins, but benefits generally are payable when the insured person becomes unable to perform a certain number (usually two or three) of *activities of daily living* (ADLs) that are stated in the policy. Examples of ADLs are eating, bathing, dressing, taking medication, toileting, and transferring and walking.

Insured persons normally can select from a range of elimination (waiting) periods, maximum daily benefits, and maximum lifetime benefits. LTC policies often provide optional inflation protection, guaranteed insurability, and other optional benefits. They usually have waiver-of-premium provisions. When LTC benefits are offered on a group basis as an employee benefit, coverage normally is voluntary and employees generally must pay the full cost. When LTC coverage is purchased as a rider to a life insurance contract, the benefits may or may not be a function of the face amount of life insurance.

Covered Services (Levels of Care)

The kinds of services that may be covered under LTC policies include skilled nursing facility care, intermediate nursing facility care, custodial nursing facility care, other custodial facility care, home health care, home care, adult day care, respite care, and hospice care. Many commentators have suggested that consumers are better protected by purchasing coverage with a relatively broad range of services that includes not only nursing home care, but also custodial facility care, home health care, home care, and probably adult day care. This is because many people will want to receive custodial care other than in an institutional format when possible.

Benefit Amounts Provided

LTC policies provide a specified dollar amount per day for the covered levels of care. The insured often has a choice among a range of daily benefit amounts (such as from $50 to $300 or more per day), with the premium naturally increasing as the daily benefit increases.

The daily benefit may vary with the level of care used. On the other hand, many LTC policies today provide the same daily benefit for all covered levels of care. This is preferable for the consumer.

In choosing the benefit amount, the consumer must balance adequate protection against premium cost. Of course, other resources (such as an investment fund) may affect this decision. However, many people prefer not to deplete their other resources unduly, especially since they do not know how long they might need custodial care in the future. They often want to preserve their estates for their spouses, children, or other heirs.

There are two ways the daily benefit amount can be structured. The first is to pay actual charges incurred up to the policy's daily benefit amount. This is referred to as an *expense reimbursement policy.* The other is to pay the policy's daily benefit, regardless of the actual charges incurred. This is called a *per diem policy.* The tax treatment of an LTC policy depends on which form is involved.

Maximum Benefits

LTC plans normally have maximum lifetime benefit limits. This is the maximum aggregate time period (number of days or months) or dollar amount of benefits the insurer will pay during the lifetime of an insured. In addition, some plans impose a maximum limit for each period of confinement, each period of care, or each illness. This is less desirable for the insured. A few policies have an unlimited benefit period.

The insured often is given a choice among several maximum limits. In general, it seems better to select the longest (or largest) maximum benefit available, even though the cost will be greater. The insured has no way of knowing how long he or she may need long-term care in the future.

Elimination Period (Waiting Period)

The waiting period is the number of days of continuous confinement or care that must be incurred before LTC benefits will commence. Most LTC insurance has such a waiting period, ranging from 15 to 100 days or more. LTC policies often give the purchaser a choice of several waiting periods, with premium reductions for longer waiting periods. One way to reduce cost is to purchase coverage with a longer waiting period. On the other hand, the consumer needs to consider whether the premium savings are worth the potential loss of benefits.

Coverage (or Benefit) Triggers

Modern LTC policies commonly have several definitions of when a covered person can qualify for benefits. These are called *definitions of disability* or *coverage triggers*. The following are possible alternative coverage triggers:

- The covered person is unable to perform a specified number (usually two or three) of a list of activities of daily living (ADLs).
- The covered person has a *cognitive impairment*, which generally means the deterioration in or loss of the person's intellectual capacity, and can be measured by clinical evidence and standardized tests. Examples would be organic brain disorders like Alzheimer's disease and Parkinson's disease.[2]
- A physician certifies that the covered person needs long-term care services as a medical necessity. This alternative definition may be liberal for the insured since his or her own physician may be able to certify the need for benefits.

Most policies allow coverage if one of the first two alternative benefit triggers exists, but some use all three. All three would be more liberal for the insured.

Continuance (or Renewal) Provisions

The consumer should seek to buy individual LTC coverage that is at least guaranteed renewable, as was explained in Chapter 22. LTC insurance normally is not available on a noncancelable basis. When LTC insurance is purchased as association group coverage, check to see what rights, if any, the insured person has to continue the coverage directly with the insurance company in the event the group policy is terminated.

[2]The National Association of Insurance Commissioners (NAIC) in its Model Act on LTC insurance requires that LTC policies cover Alzheimer's disease, Parkinson's disease, and other organic brain disorders that occur after the LTC policy has been issued. Individual state insurance laws (which are controlling) may or may not follow this Model Act.

Issue Ages

Insurance companies often limit the persons to whom they will sell LTC coverage to those within certain age ranges, commonly ages 50 to 80. Once issued, LTC policies usually can be continued for life.

Extent of Individual Underwriting

Individual and association group plans almost always require some measure of individual underwriting for each applicant. Larger group plans may allow coverage on a guaranteed issue basis without individual selection.

Premiums and Nonforfeiture Values

The premiums for LTC insurance normally depend on such factors as the insured's age, gender, maximum benefit period, waiting period, daily benefit amount, any inflation protection or other optional benefits, and perhaps the state where the policy is issued. Premium rates normally are level, based on the insured's age when the policy was originally issued. That is, the premium (as of the original issue age) remains level as the insured gets older, except for possible rate increases applied to whole classes of insureds under guaranteed renewable policies. Obtaining lower, level premiums for the rest of the insured's life is one advantage of buying LTC coverage early. In addition, the person may become uninsurable for LTC coverage as he or she gets older.

LTC policies may contain nonforfeiture benefits, which provide continuing benefits for the policyowner if he or she should stop paying premiums after the policy has been in force for a reasonable period. The nonforfeiture benefit may take the form of a paid-up policy for a reduced daily benefit or extended term coverage for the same daily benefit for a given period. LTC policies normally do not provide cash values.

Benefits under Life Insurance and Annuity Policies

These LTC riders provide essentially the same kinds of benefits as the LTC policies just discussed. They are combination contracts and provide the tax advantages discussed in Chapters 17 and 21 for such contracts starting in 2010.

Tax Treatment of LTC and Accelerated Death Benefits

Accelerated death benefits paid under life insurance contracts are excluded from gross income for federal income tax purposes if the insured is *terminally ill.* For this purpose, a terminally ill person has an illness or physical condition that has been certified to be reasonably expected to result in death within 24 months. Also excluded from gross income are life insurance accelerated death benefits on insureds who are *chronically ill*, as defined in the next paragraph.

With respect to the federal income tax status of LTC insurance contracts, the tax law treats qualified long-term care insurance contracts as accident and health insurance for tax purposes. *Qualified long-term care insurance contracts* are insurance contracts (either LTC riders on life insurance or annuity policies or other LTC policies) that provide coverage only for "qualified long-term care services" and meet certain other requirements.[3] *Qualified long-term care services* include necessary diagnostic, preventive, therapeutic, curing, treating, mitigating, rehabilitative, maintenance, and personal care services for a "chronically ill individual" that are provided pursuant to a plan of care prescribed by a licensed health-care practitioner. A *chronically ill individual* is a person who is unable to perform at least two activities of daily living[4] due to loss of functional capacity or a similar level of disability, or who requires substantial supervision because of severe cognitive impairment. In essence, then, a qualified long-term care insurance contract for tax purposes provides benefits for personal care and services to maintain and care for a chronically ill individual, defined in terms of the inability to perform at least two activities of daily living or a severe cognitive impairment.[5]

The tax benefits from a qualified LTC insurance contract are as follows:

- Benefits received are excluded (or partially excluded) from gross income for federal income tax purposes. Periodic payments (e.g., daily benefits) that do not exceed the actual costs incurred are entirely tax free. When benefits do exceed the actual costs incurred (as they might, for example, under a per diem–type LTC contract), they are excluded from gross income only up to a maximum of $280 per day in 2009.[6]

CASE EXAMPLE

Suppose that Mary Donnelly is insured under a per diem–type qualified LTC contract providing a daily benefit of $300. Furthermore, assume that she becomes unable to perform two

[3] For example, the contract must be guaranteed renewable, not have a cash surrender value, not duplicate Medicare benefits, and satisfy various consumer protection provisions of the long-term care insurance Model Act and regulations promulgated by the NAIC.

[4] The activities of daily living included are eating, toileting, transferring, bathing, dressing, and continence. At least five of these activities must be used in the contract before it will be treated as a qualified long-term care insurance contract.

[5] Note that for tax purposes, a terminally ill individual is not considered chronically ill.

[6] This excluded amount is indexed for inflation based on changes in the medical care component of the consumer price index in $10 multiples.

out of six ADLs (a benefit trigger under her policy) and is confined in a covered nursing home where she incurs actual costs for qualified long-term care services of $200 per day. In this case, $280 (in 2009) of the $300 per diem benefit she receives will be excluded from Mary's gross income for federal tax purposes and the other $20 per day will be gross income to her. Thus, benefits from per diem–type qualified LTC contracts will be income tax–free to the extent just described. On the other hand, benefits received from expense reimbursement–type qualified LTC contracts will be entirely tax-free since they are payable only to the extent of actual costs incurred.

- Premiums paid by employers for employer-provided qualified LTC insurance generally are excluded from a covered employee's gross income.
- Finally, as cited in Footnote 1 of this chapter, unreimbursed amounts paid for qualified long-term care services provided to a taxpayer or the taxpayer's spouse or dependents may be deductible as medical care for individuals. In addition, premiums paid for qualified LTC insurance, up to specified limits based on the insured's attained age,[7] similarly may be deductible as medical expenses. It must be remembered, however, that medical expenses (including LTC expenses and premiums) are deductible only if the taxpayer itemizes his or her deductions and only to the extent that total medical expenses in a year exceed 7.5 percent of the taxpayer's AGI.

Medicaid Planning for Long-Term (Custodial) Care

Assuming a person has not made adequate advance preparation for the long-term care exposure through LTC insurance, another strategy is to seek coverage for this exposure through government programs—mainly the Medicaid program. Various techniques and possible pitfalls are involved in this approach, which will be explored in this section. Planning in this area has been significantly affected by the Deficit Reduction Act of 2005 (DRA). This law generally made it more difficult for persons to qualify for Medicaid to meet the custodial care exposure.

[7] This annual dollar limit ranges from $320 for persons not more than 40 years old to $3,980 for persons over age 70 as of 2009.

Medicare and Private Health Insurance and the Long-Term Care Exposure

Medicare and private health insurance (other than LTC insurance) really cannot be counted on to meet the long-term care exposure. The Medicare benefits most likely to respond to the long-term care exposure—coverage of skilled nursing home care and home health care—are limited. For example, Medicare nursing home coverage applies only to skilled nursing care or skilled rehabilitative care, after medically necessary hospitalization for at least three consecutive days, to admission to the skilled nursing facility within 30 days after the hospital discharge, and only after a physician certifies the need for skilled care. Many custodial care facilities and levels of care would be precluded by these requirements. Furthermore, Medicare covers only a maximum of 100 days of skilled nursing facility care, with a copayment for the 21st through the 100th days. Medicare home health-care coverage applies only to part-time or intermittent care, to housebound patients, under a physician's care who certifies the need for care.

In general, Medicare is designed to provide coverage for acute medical conditions rather than custodial care. However, limited coverage still may be available from Medicare, and it certainly should be investigated when faced with an actual need.

Private health insurance, aside from LTC insurance, normally specifically excludes expenses incurred for custodial care. This includes Medigap policies, which only fill the gaps in Medicare, rather than broadening that coverage to include LTC benefits. However, as in the case of Medicare, all forms of available private health insurance should be used to the extent feasible.

Medicaid

Medicaid is a federal-state public assistance (welfare) program aimed at providing broad medical expense benefits to certain categories of the needy. The overall standards for the program are established by the federal government, but the specific eligibility requirements and benefits provided vary among the states. Therefore, the specific requirements of a person's own state must be consulted in Medicaid planning.

Eligibility Requirements in General To be eligible for Medicaid, persons must be in an eligible category and must meet certain financial requirements of need. These financial requirements include resource (asset) limits and income limits. Some states place limits on both the assets a person may have and the income he or she may receive. Other states only limit assets for eligibility. However, even in states with no eligibility cap on income, a

Medicaid recipient will be required to pay (spend down) virtually all of his or her privately available income for any nursing home care received before Medicaid will pay for the remaining cost. Federal regulations define such income broadly as ". . . anything you receive in cash or in kind that you can use to meet your needs for food, clothing, or shelter." The resource limit varies by state, but generally is from $2,000 to $3,000 in nonexempt assets.

Benefits Provided The services covered by Medicaid are broad and, with a few exceptions, do not require any copayments, deductibles, or coinsurance by eligible recipients. They embrace not only comprehensive coverage for acute care, but also substantial coverage for long-term care, such as unlimited nursing home care and home health-care services.

What Assets and Income Are Considered in Determining Medicaid Eligibility?

Both Spouses Considered The nonexempt assets of both spouses are considered in determining the eligibility of one or both spouses for Medicaid. One spouse, for example, may be entering a nursing home for custodial care, while the other still may be living independently in the outside community. The spouse in the nursing home may be referred to as the *institutionalized spouse* (who may be seeking eligibility for Medicaid), while the other may be referred to as the *community spouse* (or *healthy spouse*), who is still living independently in the general community. In such a case, the nonexempt assets of both spouses will be counted in determining whether the resource limitation has been exceeded at the time of application for Medicaid by the institutionalized spouse. This is referred to as the "spousal unity rule."

There are, however, several exceptions to this general statement that may offer planning opportunities. First, this counting of the community spouse's assets is made only once at the time of application for Medicaid by the institutionalized spouse. It is like a snapshot picture of the community spouse's assets at that time. Therefore, nonexempt assets the community spouse may acquire after that date do not count toward the resource limit of the institutionalized spouse.

Second, the community spouse is allowed to keep (without it being considered a resource) the greater of a minimum amount or one-half the couple's total nonexempt assets, up to a maximum dollar amount. Furthermore, states can increase this minimum up to the maximum amount.[8] Thus, the

[8] The minimum and maximum that the community spouse can keep in his or her name without disqualifying the other spouse for Medicaid are indexed for inflation. The healthy spouse also may be able to keep additional assets, depending on the couple's income and expenses.

community spouse does not have to be impoverished in order for the institutionalized spouse to be eligible for Medicaid.

Third, the community spouse can keep all of his or her own income without affecting the other spouse's eligibility. Thus, it may be desirable to shift income to the community spouse, such as through the purchase of an annuity (subject to certain conditions).

Finally, the community spouse may be able to keep a portion of the Medicaid recipient's income, depending on the community spouse's expenses and the federal poverty rate of income for a two-person household.

Trust Assets or Income as a Resource of a Trust Beneficiary With regard to *living (inter vivos) trusts*[9] created by anyone other than the Medicaid applicant or the applicant's spouse, and with regard to *testamentary trusts*[10] created by anyone, any trust assets or income that are required to be paid to a beneficiary or any trust assets or income that a beneficiary has the power to withdraw will be counted as a resource or as income for purposes of the beneficiary's eligibility for Medicaid. Hence, a planning technique may be to use *discretionary trusts* created by someone other than a potential Medicaid applicant or his or her spouse or *discretionary testamentary trusts.*

With regard to living trusts created by a Medicaid applicant or the applicant's spouse (as grantor) for the benefit of either of them, any trust assets or income that the trustee may pay out to the Medicaid applicant or the applicant's spouse, assuming full use of the trustee's discretion in favor of the Medicaid applicant or his or her spouse, will be counted as a resource or as income for purposes of determining the grantor-beneficiary's eligibility for Medicaid. Under this rule, the applicable trust assets or income are deemed available to the applicant or his or her spouse, whether they are actually paid to him or her by the trustee or not. These are referred to as *Medicaid qualifying trusts* (MQTs), and such trusts cannot be used to facilitate eligibility for Medicaid. However, discretianory testamentary trusts created by anyone and supplementary needs trusts created by others are not MQTs and will not cause their assets or income to be counted as resources or income for a beneficiary's Medicaid eligibility.

Qualified Retirement Plans and IRAs as Available Resources Qualified retirement plans, such as Section 401(k) plans, often are not counted as available resources for Medicaid eligibility and often are not required to be

[9] These are trusts created while the grantor or creator of the trust is alive. They are normally created by a deed of trust.

[10] These are trusts created after the grantor's or creator's death under the terms of the grantor's or creator's will.

liquidated by a Medicaid applicant, even when he or she is able to do so. On the other hand, IRAs and retirement plans for the self-employed (HR-10 plans) may be considered available resources and, hence, must be liquidated and spent down before their owners can seek Medicaid nursing home coverage. Therefore, as a planning matter, it may not be desirable for someone who is likely to become a Medicaid applicant to roll over his or her qualified retirement plan balance into an IRA if it can be kept in a former employer's qualified retirement plan.

Exempt Assets Various assets belonging to a Medicaid applicant (or his or her spouse) will not be counted in determining Medicaid eligibility. For example, an exempt asset may be an applicant's principal residence (with home equity limited to $500,000 or $750,000), subject to certain conditions and the possibility that the government may place a lien on the home to recover nursing home costs, which generally is exercisable at death or on the sale of the home. There are other exempt assets as well. Owning exempt assets and possibly converting nonexempt assets into exempt assets can present Medicaid planning possibilities.

Transferred Assets Certain gratuitous transfers of assets (gifts) by the applicant or the applicant's spouse will cause the value of those assets to be considered resources of the applicant and may result in the applicant's being ineligible for Medicaid for a period. Thus, transfers of assets to family members or others (other than the applicant's spouse, since their assets are considered together anyway) to get below the resource limit for Medicaid eligibility must be done within certain rules for proper planning. These rules are discussed separately in the next section.

Asset Transfers and Medicaid Eligibility

Persons (or their families) who are faced with the need for long-term nursing home care may want to transfer as much of their assets as possible to family members and then qualify for Medicaid. The alternative (assuming there is no LTC insurance) would be for the person to exhaust (spend down) almost all of his or her nonexempt assets in paying for the care before he or she could reach the resource limit to qualify for Medicaid. In this case, there probably would be little left after the person's death. However, the government has placed rules and possibly roadblocks in the way of such planning.

The Lookback Rule and Planning Techniques Transfers of assets for less than fair market value (gifts) by a potential Medicaid applicant or his or her spouse within the so-called lookback period will be attributed back to the applicant as available resources and may cause the applicant to be temporarily ineligible. The lookback period under the Deficit Reduction Act of 2005 is now 60 months prior to the date of application for Medicaid. The period of ineligibility for Medicaid that results from transfers of nonexempt assets within the lookback period (other than exempt transfers, described next) is the period in months measured by the value of the gratuitous transfer divided by the particular state's average monthly cost for private-pay nursing home care. Under the DRA of 2005, any such period of ineligibility begins to run from the date on which the Medicaid applicant would have been eligible except for the transfer penalty (i.e., when the applicant's resources are depleted below the resource limit).

Medicaid planning involving asset transfers may be used when there are enough assets (or insurance) so that application for Medicaid can be delayed until after the 60-month lookback period has ended.

CASE EXAMPLE

Suppose that John Wilson, who is age 72 and divorced, owns $500,000 of nonexempt assets in his own name and needs to enter a nursing home for custodial care. He does not have LTC insurance. The nursing home cost is $150 per day, or about $4,500 per month. At the urging of his children, John transfers about $230,000 of his nonexempt assets to his children or others and retains around $270,000 to pay (spend down) for nursing home care for the 60-month lookback period ($4,500 per month × 60 months = $270,000). After the end of the lookback period, John applies for Medicaid. The transfer to his children would not be counted as a resource because it was made before the lookback period began (60 months before applying for Medicaid). He would have virtually no nonexempt assets because he had already spent them down for nursing home care and other expenses over the past 60 months. Thus, he would at that point be eligible for Medicaid, which would pay for nursing home care from then on.[11]

Exempt Transfers Certain transfers are excluded from the previously described rules. These exempt transfers sometimes can present planning opportunities.

[11] If John had income during this period, he might have to spend down the income before Medicaid would pay or, depending on state law, he might be ineligible for Medicaid. Also, if John had a noninstitutionalized (community) spouse at the time he applied for Medicaid, her nonexempt assets (over the allowance discussed previously) would also be considered as available resources in determining John's eligibility.

Cautions in Transferring Assets to Attain Medicaid Eligibility

There are disadvantages as well as advantages in transferring assets to attain Medicaid eligibility. To qualify for Medicaid, an applicant must virtually impoverish himself or herself (with the exception of exempt assets and other techniques discussed here). This has several implications. It may cause intergenerational conflicts. The aged parent who seeks nursing home care may resist giving away virtually all of his or her life's savings, while the children may want to preserve at least some of those assets for themselves or future generations. Furthermore, if the institutionalized person's condition should improve sufficiently to return to the community, what then? Some have suggested that there may be less favorable treatment in nursing homes for Medicaid patients than for private-paying patients. Such discrimination against Medicaid patients is illegal, but the perception still may be that it exists. Finally, the coverage for persons on Medicaid, while broad, does have some limits.

Furthermore, to the extent that lifetime giving is employed to attain Medicaid eligibility, the general cautions about making lifetime gifts (discussed more fully in Chapter 27) apply here. In particular, if an aged person gives away assets with a low income tax basis (say, to children) and then dies, the assets do not get a stepped-up income tax basis in the hands of the donee-children as they would if the children had inherited them from their parent at death. On the other hand, the general advantages of lifetime giving apply. Much depends on the facts of the particular situation.

Finally, it is clear that government policy does not favor transfers of resources to qualify for Medicaid. This is clear from the DRA of 2005.

Thus, for persons or families who are in a position to make advance preparation for the custodial care exposure, such as through the purchase of adequate LTC insurance, these cautioning factors should be carefully considered. It normally is better to insure against the LTC exposure. Of course, if a person is already advanced in years or is uninsurable and is in need of nursing home care, Medicaid planning may be the only viable alternative.

Overview of Medicaid Planning Techniques

We have seen that a number of techniques can aid a person in becoming eligible for Medicaid and conserving assets for the family. One possibility is to convert nonexempt assets into exempt assets to the extent feasible. For example, cash and marketable assets (e.g., securities) could be used to pay off a mortgage on a residence or even to purchase a residence. Other exempt assets could also be purchased. Also, nonexempt assets could be transferred to a community spouse (an exempt transfer) so that the community spouse can have the maximum amount of assets allowed by law without having those assets considered in determining the institutionalized spouse's eligibility.

Another technique might be for a residence (or other exempt assets) to be transferred to a community spouse before application for Medicaid by the other spouse. Once the institutionalized spouse has qualified for Medicaid, the community spouse will be free to sell the residence or other exempt assets without disqualifying the institutionalized spouse.

Furthermore, income can be provided for a community spouse because that spouse's income is not counted in determining Medicaid eligibility of the institutionalized spouse. One way to do this is for the community spouse to purchase an annuity contract, with the income payments not to extend beyond the life expectancy of the community spouse. Such an annuity may not be considered a resource for Medicaid eligibility purposes, but rather as a source of income for the community spouse. A potential Medicaid applicant may also use exempt transfers of his or her nonexempt assets to the extent possible to shift these assets to other eligible family members.

As explained earlier, a common planning technique is to transfer part of a potential Medicaid applicant's nonexempt assets to family members (other than the applicant's spouse) before the 60-month lookback period begins.

Finally, in their estate planning, others may consider the Medicaid eligibility status of family members. For example, suppose a potential community spouse has assets that he or she would like to leave at death for the benefit of a spouse who may be institutionalized. Instead of leaving the assets outright to the spouse (which might later disqualify that spouse for Medicaid), the propertied spouse might leave the assets under a testamentary trust, with the other spouse being a discretionary beneficiary only. Other family members also may use trusts that give broad discretionary powers to the trustee for the benefit of persons who may need to qualify for government assistance benefits.

24

Property and Liability Insurance

Competence Objectives for This Chapter After reading this chapter, planners should understand:

- The nature of property and personal liability exposures
- Comprehensive personal liability (CPL) coverage
- The types of homeowners' insurance policies and a sample of homeowners coverage
- Replacement cost property coverage
- Internal property insurance limits
- Homeowners insurance liability exclusions
- Automobile insurance coverage
- Persons insured under automobile insurance
- The features of personal excess (umbrella) liability policies
- Directors and officers (D&O) liability coverage
- Professional liability
- Business liability coverages
- Worker's compensation and other employment liability
- Flood exposures and insurance
- Insuring investment properties
- Covering property held in trust or in other entities

Buying appropriate property and liability insurance is important in planning for personal financial security. This is particularly true for liability insurance, because people in general have become so litigious and claims-conscious.

Property Insurance

There are two basic approaches to insuring property: specified perils coverage and "any risk of loss" coverage (or risks of direct physical loss coverage). *Specified perils coverage* protects against the specific perils (causes of loss) named in the policy. Some common examples include homeowners policies 2, 3 (for personal property), 6, and 8, and certain dwelling forms (such as DP-1 and DP-2).

Any risk (also called *open risk*) coverage protects against all the risks or perils that may cause loss to the covered property, except those specifically excluded in the policy. Thus, the exclusions are important in determining the real extent of open risk coverage. This coverage frequently is broader than specified perils coverage, but it also usually costs more. Some common examples of open risk–type coverage are homeowners policy 3, personal articles floater coverage (e.g., on furs, jewels, fine arts, stamp collections, and cameras), and automobile comprehensive physical damage insurance.

Which Coverage and in What Amount?

The question then becomes, which policies or coverages should be purchased? This often can be decided through an insurance survey of needs conducted by a qualified insurance professional.

Once decisions have been made about types of coverage, the amounts of insurance must be determined. Insureds normally want policy limits (including sublimits) that are adequate to cover losses likely to occur from covered damage to the various kinds of property at risk, including adequate limits to meet any replacement cost provisions in homeowners policies.

Personal Liability

A potentially greater risk is the loss of assets or earnings through the judicial process as a result of one's negligence or other legal liability. Large liability judgments and settlements are commonplace today. When consumers look at their personal liability exposures, the following general categories of exposures come to mind:

- Ownership, rental, and/or use of automobiles
- Ownership and/or rental of premises
- Professional or business activities
- Directorships or officerships in corporations, credit unions, school boards, and other organizations
- Employment of others
- Ownership, rental, or use of watercraft or aircraft
- Other personal activities

These exposures can be covered by a variety of liability insurance coverages. We shall consider first the comprehensive personal liability coverage, which can be purchased separately, but usually is bought as a part of a homeowners policy.

Comprehensive Personal Liability (CPL) Coverage

Daily nonbusiness activities include a host of exposures to loss through legal liability. A person's dog bites a neighbor, a visitor trips and falls on the front walk, or a tee shot on the eighth hole slices and hits another golfer—all these accidents could result in liability losses.

CPL insurance (using Liability Coverages–Section II of the homeowners policy for illustrative purposes) agrees to pay on behalf of an insured[1] all sums up to the policy limit that the insured becomes legally obligated to pay as damages because of bodily injury and property damage. The insurance company also agrees to defend the insured in any suit that would be covered by the policy, even if the suit is groundless, false, or fraudulent. However, the insurer's duty to defend ends when the amount the insurer pays for a settlement or judgement from an occurrence equals the policy's limit of liability. This is an important reason to carry adequate limits of liability.

The previously stated insuring agreement is limited by certain important exclusions.

Coverage, for example, does not apply to:

- Business or professional pursuits. (Separate liability insurance is available for such exposures, and some insurers endorse limited coverage on their homeowners forms.)
- Ownership, maintenance, or use of automobiles, larger watercraft, and aircraft. (Separate policies are used to cover each of these exposures.)
- Injury or damage caused intentionally by the insured. (Some forms of intentional torts can be covered by personal injury coverage that can be purchased through umbrella liability policies discussed elsewhere in this chapter.)
- Benefits payable under any worker's compensation law.
- Liability assumed by the insured under any unwritten contract or agreement, or under any business contract or agreement.
- Damage to property rented to, used by, or in the care of the insured, except for property damage caused by fire, smoke, or explosion; or property owned by an insured; or bodily injury to an insured.
- Bodily injury or property damage arising from controlled substances, criminal activities, communicable diseases, and certain other activities of insureds.

[1] The word *insured* includes the named insured and, if residents of his or her household, his or her relatives, and other persons under the age of 21 in their care, and certain students.

In addition to basic liability coverage, CPL insurance covers medical payments and damage to property of others. Medical payments coverage agrees to pay reasonable expenses incurred by persons other than insureds within three years from the date of an accident for necessary medical, surgical, dental, and similar services for each person who sustains bodily injury caused by an accident both while on the insured's premises with permission and elsewhere, if the accident is caused by an insured, a resident employee, or an animal owned by the insured. Note that this provision is not based on the insured's legal liability. Damage to property of others promises to pay under certain conditions for loss of property belonging to others caused by an insured up to a policy limit, again without regard to the legal liability of the insured.

Limits of Liability

CPL insurance provides bodily injury liability and property damage liability coverage on a single-limit basis—which means that one limit of liability, such as $100,000, $300,000, or more, applies to each occurrence, regardless of the number of persons injured or the amount of separate property damage. Medical payments coverage is written subject to a per-person limit for each accident.

Homeowners Insurance

When basic property coverage and CPL coverage are added to some other coverages (such as personal theft insurance), or in some cases written on an open perils basis, the resulting package is called a *homeowners policy.*

Types of Policies

There are basically six variations of homeowners policies, as follows.

Homeowners 2 (HO-2)	Provides broad specified perils property coverage.
Homeowners 3 (HO-3)	Open perils on buildings and broad form on personal property.
Homeowners 4 (HO-4)	Personal property coverage only (broad form); for tenants.
Homeowners 5 (HO-5)	Comprehensive form providing open perils coverage on all covered property.
Homeowners 6 (HO-6)	Personal property and loss-of-use coverage (broad form), and certain dwelling coverage within the unit and for which the unit owner may have insurance responsibility under an association agreement, for condominium and cooperative unit owners.

Homeowners 8 (HO-8)	Coverage on buildings and personal property that is more limited than HO-2; used to provide coverage on homes that may not meet the insurer's underwriting requirements for other homeowners forms.

Homeowners policies contain a set of standard coverages that may be altered by endorsements, which can increase the amount of insurance, broaden the coverage, or modify conditions or restrictions. An example of coverages and limits under an HO-3 is as follows.[2]

Section I Property Coverages		
Coverage A	Dwelling	$500,000 (selected by the insured or recommended by the insurer)
Coverage B	Other structures	$50,000 (10% of dwelling amount, but may be increased)
Coverage C	Personal property (unscheduled[3]) that is anywhere in the world	$250,000 (50% of dwelling amount, but may be increased, or reduced to 40%)
	Personal property, usually at a residence of an insured other than the residence premises described in the policy	$25,000 (10% of the Coverage C limit, but no less than $1,000)
Coverage D	Loss of use (including additional living expenses)	$100,000 (20% of dwelling amount)
Section II Liability Coverages		
Coverage E	Personal liability	$300,000 each occurrence
Coverage F	Medical payments to others	$1,000 each person

Replacement Cost Provision

The replacement cost provision that applies to Coverages A and B (the dwelling and other structures) is advantageous to the insured because if the proper amount of insurance is maintained, the insured can recover any loss to the

[2] Homeowners policies generally follow this basic pattern, but variations exist in certain states and under the forms used by some insurers.

[3] *Unscheduled* means property owned or used by an insured that is not specifically named or listed in a schedule in the policy. As we shall see later, a person sometimes needs to list certain valuable property in a separate schedule for full coverage.

dwelling and private structures (but not personal property, unless the insured purchases additional coverage providing replacement cost coverage on replaceable personal contents) on the basis of the full cost to repair or replace the damaged property *without any deduction for depreciation.* Without such a provision, the homeowners policy would pay only the actual cash value at the time of the loss of lost or damaged property. Actual cash value (ACV) normally means new replacement cost minus the amount the property has physically depreciated since it was built or was new. Note that property still physically depreciates even though its market value may rise or fall.

However, the insured must carry enough insurance in relation to the value of the dwelling to get the benefit of this replacement cost provision. Specifically, the homeowners policy provides that if the insured carries insurance on a building equal to at least 80 percent of its replacement cost new, any covered loss to the building will be paid to the extent of the full cost to repair or replace the damage without deducting depreciation, up to the policy limit. The policy provides for a lesser recovery if the insurance is less than 80 percent of replacement cost. Therefore, it is important to maintain enough insurance to meet the 80 percent requirement.

Instead of this standard replacement cost provision, however, some homeowners policies may have added to them a replacement or repair cost protection endorsement under which, if the insured allows the insurance company to adjust the coverage A dwelling limit (and the premium) in accordance with a property evaluation the insurer makes, the form will automatically increase the limit of liability on the dwelling to its current replacement cost if there is a loss that exceeds the limit stated in the policy. (There are also corresponding proportionate increases in the limits for Coverages B, C, and D.) In addition, if the insured conforms to the terms of the endorsement, losses to the dwelling and other structures will be paid on a replacement cost basis. This endorsement is valuable since it relieves the insured from estimating the right amount of insurance to meet the standard replacement cost requirements. There is also an additional limit of liability endorsement.

Furthermore, in most states, the insured can buy an inflation guard endorsement on homeowners policies that automatically increases coverage limits periodically by small percentage amounts. Finally, insureds may be able to purchase for an additional premium a personal property replacement cost endorsement that extends replacement cost coverage to personal property (Coverage C) under certain conditions.

Internal Limits (Sublimits)

Another thing to consider in property and liability insurance planning is the smaller internal limits (called *sublimits*) that apply to certain kinds of property under homeowners policies. Following are some of the more important of these sublimits:

- $200 aggregate limit on money, bank notes, bullion, gold other than goldware, silver other than silverware, platinum, coins, and medals
- $1,500 aggregate limit on securities, accounts, deeds and similar property, or stamps, including philatelic property (stamp collections)
- $1,500 aggregate limit on watercraft, including their trailers, furnishings, equipment, and outboard motors
- $1,500 aggregate limit on trailers not used with watercraft
- $1,500 aggregate limit for loss by theft of jewelry, watches, precious and semiprecious stones, and furs
- $2,500 aggregate limit for loss by theft of firearms
- $2,500 aggregate limit for loss by theft of silverware, silver-plated ware, goldware, gold-plated ware, and pewterware
- $2,500 aggregate limit on property on the residence premises used primarily for business purposes

The effect of these internal limits may be to make it necessary to schedule additional amounts of insurance on certain property items. This can be done under a *scheduled personal property endorsement* added to the homeowners policy or under a separate *personal articles floater.* Kinds of property that often are separately scheduled and insured include jewelry, furs, cameras, musical instruments, silverware, golfers' equipment, guns, fine arts, stamps, and coins.

Liability Exclusions

Proper planning for personal liability requires analyzing the liability exclusions under homeowners policies and making sure that there are no uncovered exposures. Following are some excluded potential liability exposures that should be reviewed and evaluated:

- Motor vehicle liability (for which automobile liability insurance should be purchased).
- Watercraft liability with certain exceptions for smaller cratfs. For excluded watercraft, boat or yacht insurance may be needed.
- Aircraft or aircraft exposures.
- Rendering or failing to render professional services.
- Most business pursuits of an insured.
- Any premises, other than insured premises, owned by or rented to any insured.
- Cases where the insured is liable to provide worker's compensation benefits or does provide such benefits.

- Bodily injury or property damage that is expected or intended by the insured.
- Bodily injury or property damage arising out of controlled substances.

Eligibility

Form 4 is designed for tenants, while form 6 is for condominium unit owners. Homeowner forms 2, 3, 5, and 8 are intended to cover owner-occupied dwellings. Seasonal dwellings not rented to others are considered owner-occupied.

Cost

Homeowners premiums reflect many factors and can vary among insurers. The policies usually have a deductible applying to losses under property damage coverages, which can be increased for a reduced premium.

Automobile Insurance

Coverages Provided

Personal auto policies typically may provide the following coverages.

Part A	Liability coverage (including bodily injury and property damage liability)
Part B	Medical payments coverage
Part C	Uninsured motorists coverage (or uninsured/underinsured motorists coverage)
Part D	Damage to covered autos (including comprehensive, collision, towing and labor, and transportation expenses)

About half the states have enacted some form of no-fault auto insurance, which may remove some auto accidents from the realm of negligence liability. Auto policies issued to residents of these states contain the appropriate no-fault endorsement or coverage for that state. These no-fault benefits may be called *personal injury protection* (PIP), *basic reparations benefits,* or other names. They basically are payable to injured, covered persons by their own insurance company without the covered persons having to show that anyone was negligent in causing their injuries. Depending on state law, the injured persons then may or may not have restrictions placed on their right to sue the negligent motorists who caused their injuries. Some states have adopted what are called choice-type no-fault plans. Under these plans, insured persons can voluntarily relinquish a part of their right to sue in return for reduced auto insurance premiums. This is something to consider as a cost-saving measure for these insureds.

The insuring agreement of the automobile liability policy covers the insured's liability arising out of the ownership, maintenance, or use of owned and nonowned automobiles. Commonly used policies, such as the *personal auto policy* (PAP), have a single limit of liability that applies to all covered liability arising out of an accident, regardless of the number of persons injured or the amount of separate property damage.

For example, some sample limits for a PAP might be as follows:

$300,000 each occurrence	Liability (bodily injury and property damage)
$5,000 each person in any one accident	Medical payments
$30,000 each occurrence	Uninsured motorists
Actual cash value	Collision and/or other than collision (subject to a $100 deductible)
Personal injury protection per endorsement	Statutory

Uninsured motorist coverage generally provides a minimum limit for bodily injury from uninsured and hit-and-run motorists. An insured may also purchase underinsured motorists coverage, which provides coverage in the event another motorist has valid liability insurance but the limits are not sufficient to pay the full amount of the insured's legally recoverable damages against the other motorist up to the underinsured coverage limit.

The next coverages are property insurance (technically called *physical damage* coverage) on the insured's own car. *Other than collision* (or comprehensive) provides broad open perils coverage except for collision. Recovery is made on an actual cash-value basis. *Collision* also is written on an actual cash-value basis. A deductible(s) normally applies to both collision and comprehensive coverages. Finally, in the illustrative limits cited here, the policy contains a mandatory state no-fault endorsement. This would not be so in states that do not have automobile no-fault laws (although they might provide out-of-state no-fault coverage).

Persons Insured

Under the PAP, the following are considered to be a "covered person" as far as liability coverage is concerned:

- The "named insured" (i.e., the person named in the policy declarations), his or her spouse if a resident of the same household, and any family member (i.e., a person related to the named insured or spouse by blood, marriage, or adoption and a resident of the insured's household) with respect to the ownership, maintenance, or use of any auto or trailer

- Any person using the insured's covered auto
- Any other person or organization with regard to the insured's covered auto, but only for their legal responsibility for the acts or omissions of a person for whom coverage otherwise is provided under the liability part of the policy
- Any other person or organization with regard to any auto other than the insured's covered auto, but only for their legal responsibility for the acts or omissions of the named insured, his or her spouse, and any family member covered under the liability part of the policy

This can be generally summed up by saying that the auto insurance follows the insured and a covered auto.

As always, exclusions are important in defining the coverage of an insurance contract. The following are some of the important liability exclusions of the PAP:

- Damage to property owned or being transported by a covered person.
- Damage to property rented to, used by, or in the care of a covered person.
- Bodily injury to an employee of a covered person during the course of employment; however, this exclusion does not apply to a domestic employee, unless worker's compensation benefits are required for or made available for that employee.
- Liability arising out of the ownership or operation of a vehicle while it is being used to carry persons or property for a fee; however, this exclusion does not apply to normal share-the-expense carpools.
- The ownership, maintenance, or use of a motorcycle or other self-propelled vehicle having fewer than four wheels. (Additional liability coverage is needed for this kind of exposure.)
- The ownership, maintenance, or use of any vehicle, other than the insured's covered autos, that is owned by or furnished or available for the regular use of the named insured or his or her spouse.
- The ownership, maintenance, or use of any vehicle, other than the insured's covered autos, that is owned by or furnished or available for the regular use of any family member; however, this exclusion does not apply to the named insured or his or her spouse.
- Any person using a vehicle without a reasonable belief that the person is entitled to do so.

Cost

The rating of automobile liability insurance generally is based on four factors: age and perhaps sex of drivers, use of the auto, territory where the car is garaged, and the operators' driving records. Auto physical damage rates generally are affected by such factors as the cost (new) of the car and its age. As the years go by, the actual cash value of a car diminishes through depreciation, and thus the physical damage premium also declines. However, at some point in the life of a car, it normally is economical for the insured to consider dropping his or her collision (and perhaps comprehensive) coverage. The value left to insure simply is not worth even a reduced premium.

It generally costs relatively little to increase auto liability limits to a more adequate level. There is no simple formula to determine the "correct" limit of liability an insured should carry. The problem, however, generally is best solved by incurring the small cost differential for the higher limits. Of course, the problem also can be solved by carrying an adequate excess or umbrella liability policy, described later in this chapter.

The cost of automobile insurance can vary considerably among insurance companies. Thus, consumers or their advisers may secure significant savings by shopping around for their automobile insurance. Of course, as explained in Chapter 20, cost is not the only factor that should be considered. In the area of physical damage insurance, one major cost-cutting technique that often is not utilized fully is the use of higher deductibles.

Variations in Policies

Up to this point, we have been talking about the PAP. Many individuals and families are covered by the PAP. However, some insurers (including some large ones) use their own forms of automobile insurance policies.

In addition, other kinds of automobile policies are used, each serving its own purpose. For example, a *business auto coverage form* is the most widely used form to insure commercial vehicles.

Other Property and Liability Policies to Consider

Personal Excess (Umbrella) Liability

The desire of individuals for higher liability limits and broader protection inspired the creation of the personal excess liability, catastrophe liability, or umbrella contract. It is "excess" insurance, and so underlying liability policies, such as automobile and homeowners policies, are required. Many personal umbrella policies are issued with a minimum limit of $1 million, but higher limits are available. In fact, some insurers are willing to write very high limits for persons of high net worth.

Personal umbrella policies are issued by many insurers, but they are not standardized. The umbrella policy is designed to pay and defend liability claims after the limits of underlying liability policies are exhausted. For example, suppose John Doe is involved in an auto accident and, as the result of his negligence, Richard Roe is seriously injured. A jury finds John liable to Richard for damages of $500,000. John's automobile policy, written with a single limit of $300,000, which John thought was "more than adequate," pays its limit of $300,000. Unfortunately, John remains personally liable for the remaining $200,000. However, if John had purchased a personal umbrella policy with, say, a $1 million limit, this excess policy would have paid the $200,000 on his behalf.

In addition, personal umbrella policies are written on a broad coverage basis. This results in some important extensions of coverage, such as:

- Property damage liability for loss of property of others in the insured's care, custody, or control
- Worldwide coverage (no territorial restriction)
- Coverage of specified personal injury claims, which might include libel, slander, false arrest, wrongful entry, invasion of privacy, malicious prosecution, and the like

Such extensions, which are not covered by the underlying liability policies, are subject to a deductible (called a *self-insured retention* or SIR) that might be $250 or more.

Most people, whether they think of themselves as well off or not, should consider buying personal umbrella liability insurance. While the likelihood of a catastrophic liability loss is small, if it did happen, it would financially destroy the person involved. That is not a risk people can afford to take. Furthermore, the premium is not burdensome. Also, a personal umbrella policy may require underlying liability insurance with lower limits than the insured now is carrying. Thus, the insured may be able to reduce some present liability limits and save some premium there.

Directors and Officers Liability

A trend by the courts of imposing liability on officers and directors of corporations and other organizations in connection with the performance of their duties therein has increased the need for insurance to meet this risk. The Directors and Officers Liability (D&O) policy covers any "wrongful act," which generally is defined as a breach of duty, neglect, error, misstatement, misleading statement, or omission.

For persons serving on various kinds of boards of directors or otherwise subject to this exposure, there is the potential for catastrophic financial loss. This has been particularly true in recent years, with the increased concern over corporate governance. Thus, persons so exposed or invited to serve on boards should inquire into what protection they are afforded by the corporations or organizations involved. Sometimes, the organization agrees to indemnify its directors and then it carries D&O coverage to protect itself; other times, the organization carries D&O coverage that directly covers its directors.

Furthermore, some personal excess (umbrella) liability policies cover insured persons against personal liability for personal injury or property damage arising from their volunteer participation on the board for a not-for-profit corporation or organization.

Professional Liability

Many professionals and businesspeople need liability coverage to protect themselves against claims and suits arising out of possible or alleged negligence or errors or omissions in the practice of their professions or business pursuits. Such claims and suits are not covered under other personal liability coverages.

Specialized professional liability forms for the various professions and businesses are needed to cover this exposure. Such professional liability policies often are written on a *claims-made* basis. This normally means the event or incident covered must occur after a retroactive date stated in the policy, and a claim arising out of the event or incident must be made and reported to the insurance company during the policy period.

The other kinds of liability insurance policies discussed in this chapter are *occurrence* forms. This means the covered injury or event must occur during the policy period, but claim can be made for it and reported to the insurance company after the policy period ends, as well as during the policy period. Occurrence forms generally are more favorable from the insured's viewpoint than claims-made forms.

Coverage under Business Liability Policies

Sometimes, executive officers or employees can be sued personally for their activities on behalf of their employer (say, a corporation). It may be alleged that they caused bodily injury, property damage, or personal injury to others. Business liability policies (such as the commercial general liability form) normally broadly define who is insured so as to include executive officers and employees so long as they are acting within the limits of their employment or duties with the employer. If a person feels that he or she may have a business liability exposure, the person or his or her advisers may want to check into the employer's liability coverage.

Worker's Compensation and Other Employment Liability

All 50 states, the District of Columbia, and the federal government have worker's compensation laws, which set forth the benefits payable to employees who suffer on-the-job injuries and occupational diseases. This risk may seem somewhat remote in the context of personal risk management, but certain states include domestic and/or casual employees under their worker's compensation acts. Therefore, depending on the particular state law, a person may need or may voluntarily carry worker's compensation insurance for such employees.

Another area of liability that some individuals, particularly persons of high net worth, possibly could face is employment practices liability. This would involve claims by their employees that they suffered various forms of employment discrimination. Some insurers include employment practices liability coverage in the personal umbrella forms for some insureds.

Investment Properties

Investment properties a person may own or manage present similar risks of loss to those discussed previously. Because homeowners policies generally are limited to owner-occupants, commercial policies may be used to provide the necessary property and liability protection.

Coverage of Property and Liability Exposures for Properties Held in Trust or by Other Entities

In the case of high-net-worth clients, it is not unusual for them to have an interest in residences or other properties that are held in trusts, family limited partnerships, or family limited liability companies. A qualified personal residence trust (QPRT), which is discussed in Chapter 27, is an example. In this case, several insurable interests may be involved and should be protected with adequate property and liability insurance. For example, an entity (e.g., a trust) may own the property, but it may be occupied by others with their own contents who may or may not be beneficiaries of the entity. Personal risk management should take care that additional insured endorsements or coverage is provided so that all insurable interests in the property are covered for both property and liability exposures.

Flood Exposure

Homeowners policies exclude property damage caused by flood or mudslide. In many areas, these can be important exposures. In most cases, the only source of flood and mudslide coverage for individuals is through the National Flood Insurance Program (NFIP). This is a federal program, but the insurance is sold through private insurance agents, brokers, and some insurance companies.

Types of Property and Liability Insurers

Property and liability insurers sell their products in different ways, and these approaches may have cost implications. In this sense, insurers are independent agency companies (distribution through independent insurance agents or brokers who represent several insurance companies), exclusive agency companies (which distribute their products through agents representing only the one company), and direct writers (distribution through company-employed salespeople or the mails). In addition, insurers can be classified on the basis of their organizational form as stock insurers, mutual insurers, reciprocal exchanges, and so forth.

PART VIII

Estate Planning

25

Estate Planning Principles

Competence Objectives for This Chapter After reading this chapter, planners should understand:

- The objectives of estate planning
- The various forms of property ownership
- The nature of marital rights in property
- Prenuptial agreements and other planning considerations regarding marital rights
- Nature of the probate estate
- The meaning of the gross estate for federal estate tax purposes
- Principles and steps involved in settling an estate
- The nature and kinds of trusts in estate planning
- The reasons for creating trusts
- The nature of trustees' fees
- Selecting the trustee(s) and situs of a trust
- How to achieve flexibility or changes in irrevocable trusts
- Duration of trusts, rules against perpetuities, and modern dynasty trusts
- The principles involved in the investment of trust assets
- The Uniform Prudent Investor rule
- Various trust payout options

Estate planning can be defined as arranging for the transfer of a person's property from one generation to another so as to achieve, as much as possible, the person's objectives for his or her family and perhaps others. In our tax-oriented economy, tax minimization often is an important motivator for estate planning. Tax saving, however, is not the only goal of estate planning and should not be overemphasized.

Objectives of Estate Planning

The following are a number of specific estate planning objectives, some or all of which apply to most people:

- Determining who will be the estate owner's heirs or beneficiaries and how much each will receive.
- Planning adequate financial support for the estate owner's dependents.
- Reducing estate transfer costs (death taxes, expenses of administration, and the like) to a minimum, consistent with the estate owner's other objectives.
- Planning for the way in which the estate owner's heirs or beneficiaries are to receive the assets passing to them. This often involves the question of whether they are to receive assets outright or in trust, and if a trust is to be used, what its terms, conditions, and duration should be, as well as who should be the trustee or trustees.
- Providing sufficient liquid assets for the estate to meet its obligations.
- Planning for possible arrangements (such as irrevocable life insurance trusts) that will conserve the estate for the owner's heirs and beneficiaries in the face of inevitable shrinkage due to taxes and expenses.
- Deciding who is to settle the estate. This involves selecting the executor or coexecutors.
- Planning how the estate owner's property is to be distributed. The methods of property disposition are outlined in the next section.
- Planning for the disposition of any closely held business interests.
- Planning for any charitable giving.

Methods of Property Disposition

These methods are outlined briefly here to give an overview of how wealth may be moved to others.

I. Lifetime transfers
    A. Lifetime gifts
        1. Outright
        2. In irrevocable trusts (inter vivos trusts)
        3. In custodianships
    B. Exercise of powers of appointment
    C. Exercise of powers of attorney
    D. As noncharitable beneficiary of split gifts to charity
    E. Sales within the family
II. Transfers at death

A. By will
   1. Outright
   2. In trust (testamentary trust)
B. Intestate distribution (not desirable)
C. Life insurance beneficiary designations
   1. Individuals
      a. Outright
      b. Under settlement options
   2. To trusts
D. Qualified retirement plan, TSA, and IRA beneficiary designations
   1. To surviving spouse
   2. To other individuals
   3. To trusts
   4. To charity
E. Other beneficiary designations (such as nonqualified annuities and nonqualified deferred compensation)
F. Revocable living trusts
G. Joint tenancy with right of survivorship
H. Other arrangements (such as transfers on death [TOD] in states that have adopted the Uniform Transfer on Death Act)

Property and Property Interests

In general, *property* is anything that can be owned. Basically, there are two kinds of property: real property and personal property. *Real property* (or real estate) is land and everything attached to the land with the intention that it be part of the land. *Personal property* is all other kinds of property. Personal property can be *tangible*—property that has physical substance, such as a car, jewelry, art, or antiques—or it can be *intangible*—property that does not have physical substance, such as a stock certificate, bond, bank deposit, or life insurance policy.

Forms of Property Ownership

Outright Ownership Outright or sole owners hold property in their own names and can deal with it during their lifetimes. They can sell it, use it as collateral, or give it away. They can also pass it on to their heirs by will as they wish, within some broad limits.

Joint Ownership (or Concurrent Interests in Property) This exists when two or more persons have ownership rights in the same property at the same time. The more important kinds of joint ownership are as follows.

Joint Tenancy with Right of Survivorship: The outstanding characteristic of joint tenancy with right of survivorship (WROS) is that if one of the joint owners dies, all ownership in the property passes automatically, by operation of law, to the other joint owner(s). This is the meaning of "with right of survivorship." Thus, if John and his wife Mary own their residence as joint tenants WROS and John dies, Mary automatically owns the residence (now in her own name) by right of survivorship. The same would be true if John and his daughter Susan owned some investment real estate as joint tenants WROS. Joint tenancy WROS can exist between anyone. However, it often exists between husband and wife, and sometimes between parents and children. During the lifetime of the joint tenants, the survivorship aspect can be destroyed by one of the joint tenants through a sale of his or her interest, attachment by his or her creditors, or a court action for partition. The parties then own the property as tenants in common.

Tenancy by the Entirety: In some states, this form of ownership exists when property is held jointly by a husband and wife. It is similar to a joint tenancy, but there are some differences. Tenancy by the entirety exists only between husband and wife. Also, in many states, the survivorship rights in it cannot be terminated except with the consent of both parties.

Property held as tenants by the entirety generally is protected against the claims of creditors of one of the parties, with some exceptions such as tax claims of the U.S. government. This creditor protection may vary in some states that allow this form of joint ownership. Thus, holding property as tenants by the entireties can be an aspect of asset protection planning.

The fact that property is held as joint tenants or tenants by the entirety does not mean it has to stay that way. The joint owners can agree to split up their interests. Also, as just noted in the case of joint tenancy (but not tenancy by the entirety), one joint tenant acting alone can sever (partition) the joint ownership into tenants in common. The advantages and disadvantages of joint ownership are discussed in Chapter 30.

Other Joint Interests: There are some other forms of joint ownership that involve the right of survivorship. These include joint bank accounts, some joint brokerage accounts, and jointly owned government savings bonds.

Tenancy in Common: The main difference between this and the previous kinds of joint ownership is that tenants in common do not have the right of survivorship.

CASE EXAMPLE

Suppose John and his brother Frank own investment real estate equally as tenants in common. If John dies, his half of the real estate goes to his heirs under his will. Frank, of course, retains his half interest. Tenants in common can have different proportionate interests in the property. For example, John and Frank could have 75 and 25 percent interests, respectively. Joint tenants WROS and tenants by the entirety always have equal interests.

Community Property Eight states (Arizona, California, Idaho, Louisiana, Nevada, New Mexico, Texas, and Washington) are community property states. In addition, the Uniform Marital Property Act (UMPA) provides each spouse owns one-half of property acquired during marriage, with certain exceptions. This is called *marital property*. Wisconsin has adopted the UMPA. While there are some technical differences, marital property is essentially the same as community property. Finally, Alaska allows married couples to elect to treat some assets as marital property.

The other states are referred to as *common-law states*. In these states, the forms of property ownership described previously apply. However, in the nine community property or marital property states, the situation is quite different with respect to property owned by husbands and wives.

General Principles: In community property states, husbands and wives can own separate property and community property. While the laws of community property states are not uniform, *separate property* generally consists of property that a husband or wife owned before marriage, property that each individually inherits or receives as a gift, separate property before the couple became domiciled in a community property state, and property purchased with separate property funds. This property remains separate, and the owner-spouse can deal with it as he or she chooses. Income from separate property may remain separate property or become community property, depending on the community property state involved.

Community property, on the other hand, generally consists of property that either spouse acquires during marriage from his or her earnings while domiciled in a community property or marital property state. Each spouse has an undivided one-half interest in community property. While the husband and wife are both alive, the applicable community property law determines who has the rights of management and control over the community property. However, upon his or her death, each spouse can dispose of only his or her half of the community property by will.

However, even those living in noncommunity property states can have community property. This can happen if spouses once lived in a community property state and acquired community property there. Such property remains community property even after the owners move to a common-law state. Also, property acquired by spouses while domiciled in a common-law state does not become community property when they move to a community property state.

Community property laws generally presume that all property owned by a married couple domiciled in the state is community property or marital property, regardless of how it is actually titled, unless there is an agreement between the parties about the status of the property that provides otherwise or there is proof that the property is separate property. Thus, if community property and separate property are commingled, and if adequate records are not kept so that the separate property can be traced, this presumption normally will cause all the commingled property to become community property. How community property is titled (as solely owned by one spouse, for example) does not matter. It will be treated as community property if that is what it is.

Spouses or prospective spouses can enter into agreements about the community property or separate property status of property they own or will acquire in the future. Such prenuptial or postnuptial agreements are recognized in all community property and marital property states. These agreements must, of course, conform to the requirements of state law. (Marital agreements in general are discussed later in this chapter.)

Planning Issues: Planning for community property can be complicated and generally is beyond the scope of this book. However, it may be noted that holding property as community property even after the parties have moved to a common-law state may have several advantages. Perhaps foremost is that for federal income tax purposes, all of community or marital property currently gets a stepped-up income tax basis at death, even though only half its value is included in the gross estate of a deceased spouse. By contrast, for other property interests, only property included in a decedent's gross estate gets a stepped-up basis. For federal estate tax purposes, community property automatically is divided equally between the spouses. There also may be fractional interest valuation discounts in the case of community property because each spouse owns only an undivided one-half interest.

Other Property Interests

There are other interests in property that are commonly involved in estate planning. An example can help illustrate these interests.

CASE EXAMPLE

Suppose that by his will, A leaves property to the XYZ Bank *in trust* to keep it invested and to distribute the net income from it to his wife, B, if she survives him, during her lifetime. At B's death, or at A's death if B does not survive him, the property is to go outright in equal shares to C and D (A's adult children) or their issue.

Legal Interests and Equitable Interests In this example, upon A's death, the XYZ Bank technically becomes legal owner of the property that passes into the trust. However, the bank must exercise ownership rights as trustee according to the terms of the trust agreement. The trustee acts in a *fiduciary capacity* with respect to the trust. B, C, and D have equitable (or beneficial) interests in the property, since it is held for their benefit.

Life Interests, Term Interests, and Remainder Interests A *life interest* in property entitles the holder to the income from or the use of the property, or a portion of the property, for his or her lifetime. A *term interest* entitles the holder to the income or the use of the property, or a portion of the property, for a term of years. The *remainder interest* (or remainderperson) is entitled to the property itself after a life interest or term interest has ended. In the example just given, B has a life interest in the trust property. C and D (or their issue—for example, children—if they are deceased) have remainder interests and are remainderpersons. Life interests usually are created by trusts, but there can also be legal life estates without a trust.

Furthermore, trusts may give the *grantor* (the creator of a trust) an income or use interest, an annuity interest, or a unitrust interest in the trust for a term of years, followed by a remainder interest in someone else. These are called grantor-retained income trusts (GRITs), grantor-retained annuity trusts (GRATs), and grantor-retained unitrusts (GRUTs).[1]

Present Interests and Future Interests A *present interest* exists in property when the holder has a present and immediate right to the use, possession, or enjoyment of the property. With a *future interest,* the right to use or enjoy the property is postponed to some future time or is in the control of someone other than the holder. In the previous example, upon A's death, B has a present interest in the trust income because she has the immediate right to it for her lifetime. C and D have future interests because their rights to the property are postponed until B's death. As we shall see later in Chapter 27, the concepts of present and future interests are important in connection with gift tax planning.

Powers of Appointment A *power of appointment* is a power or right given to a person (called the *donee of the power*) that enables the donee to designate,

[1]Note that the terms *annuity trust* and *unitrust* are the same as were used in Chapter 19 to describe CRATs and CRUTs. The ideas are essentially the same, except that the remainderperson in the case of GRATs and GRUTs is a noncharitable entity (e.g., a family member), while for CRATs and CRUTs, the remainderperson is a charity.

sometimes within certain limits, who is to get property that is subject to the power (called the *objects of the power*). The basic nontax purposes of powers of appointment are to postpone and delegate the decision about who is to get property until a later time when the circumstances can be better known. Powers also are used for estate tax and GST tax reasons, as will be explained later. There are several kinds of powers of appointment, as explained next.

General Powers: A *general power* is a power to appoint property to the person with the power (the donee), the donee's estate, the donee's creditors, or creditors of the donee's estate. It is close to owning the property. For federal estate tax purposes, property will be included in the gross estate of someone who has a general power over it.

Special or Limited Powers (Nongeneral Powers): These powers allow donees to appoint property only to certain persons who are not the donees themselves, their estate, their creditors, or the creditors of their estate. The possession of a special or limited power over property at a person's death does not result in the property's being included in the donee's gross estate.

How Property Is Appointed: When donees of either a general or nongeneral power can appoint the property only at their death, it is referred to as a power exercisable *by will*, or a *testamentary power*. A power exercisable *by deed* is one where donees can appoint the property only during their lifetime. The broadest power in this respect is one exercisable *by deed or will*, which is exercisable both ways.

Powers Subject to an Ascertainable Standard: When the exercise of a power by a person is subject to an *ascertainable standard* (such as for the person's health, education, maintenance, or support), it is not considered a general power for tax purposes; hence, the property subject to the power will not be included in the powerholder's gross estate. This point can be important in structuring trusts.

Marital Rights in Property

This has become an increasingly important subject because of societal changes and other factors. The REA of 1984, which granted QPSA and QJSA rights to nonparticipant spouses in qualified retirement plans, has been covered in Chapter 13 and will not be repeated here.

Spouse's Elective Share With certain exceptions, people can leave their property by will to whomever they like. One important exception, however, is that in most common law (separate property) states, a husband or wife cannot deprive his or her surviving spouse of the spouse's statutory elective share of the estate. This is referred to as the *spouse's right to elect against the will*.

Taking against the will does not deny the will's validity, but simply involves the spouse's taking his or her elective share (forced share) allowed by law rather than what is left to him or her under the will.

Originally, elective share statutes only gave a surviving spouse rights to part of a deceased spouse's probate estate (which will be defined next). However, the *Uniform Probate Code* (UPC) modified this traditional approach by allowing a surviving spouse to elect to take part of his or her deceased spouse's *augmented estate.* The augmented estate includes probate and some nonprobate assets. Some states have adopted this approach. Then, in 1990, the UPC was revised and significant changes were made in its elective share provisions. These included expanding the augmented estate to include other assets and a surviving spouse's own property, and to base the percentage elective share on the length of the marriage (from 5 percent to 50 percent). A number of states have adopted this approach. Thus, there is considerable variation among state laws regarding the elective share.

To avoid a surviving spouse's electing to take against the will, persons with property may enter into prenuptial agreements (or postnuptial agreements after marriage) under which each party relinquishes in whole or in part his or her statutory rights to the other's property at death. Finally, it should be noted that, except in one state, children do not have any comparable right to a spouse's elective share in their parents' estates.

Marital Rights upon Divorce The states have adopted equitable-distribution statutes applying to so-called marital property in the event of divorce. Under these statutes, the appropriate court can divide a divorcing couple's marital property between the parties in an "equitable manner" according to certain factors specified in state domestic relations law, regardless of how title to the marital property is actually held.

What is considered marital property can vary among the states, but it may include all property acquired during marriage from the earnings of either spouse, with certain exceptions. Thus, it may not include, for example, property owned by a person before marriage or property acquired by a spouse by gift or inheritance. However, if this exempt property is commingled with marital property, and if adequate records are not kept so that nonmarital property can be traced, all the property may be considered marital property. Thus, if gift property is placed in an irrevocable trust (by a parent or grandparent, for example) for a trust beneficiary (child or grandchild), the corpus of the trust normally would clearly be identified as exempt property (gift property) in the event of the beneficiary's divorce (i.e., it would be "divorce-proof"). The same would be true for property placed in FLPs for gifts of limited partnership interests. Also, to avoid the effects of equitable distribution statutes or other divorce laws, persons who are about to marry are increasingly entering into prenuptial agreements that specify how their property is to be divided in the event of divorce.

Prenuptial Agreements For a variety of reasons, prenuptial (or antenuptial) agreements are becoming increasingly common. They are now recognized in virtually all states. However, the rules regarding these agreements vary among the states. There is a Uniform Prenuptial Agreement Act (UPAA), which has been adopted in about half the states. The UPAA requires such agreements be in writing and signed by both parties, and provides that the agreement can cover many issues, including the disposition of any property of either or both parties upon separation, marital dissolution, death, or the occurrence or nonoccurrence of any event. A prenuptial agreement becomes effective with the marriage. The general rule is that spousal consent to an REA waiver in a prenuptial agreement is not effective. Consent must be given when the nonparticipant is a spouse. It is often necessary that there be full, fair, and reasonable disclosure of the property and obligations of the parties.

Planning Considerations We have seen in this chapter and elsewhere that marriage can create certain rights in the property of each spouse. However, for estate planning, retirement planning, or other reasons, spouses may want to relinquish or modify some of these marital rights. To review, the kinds of marital agreements that have been covered in this book are:

- Waiver of REA rights in qualified retirement plans by the participant spouse and written consent to the waiver in the proper form by the nonparticipant spouse
- Prenuptial and postnuptial agreements concerning spousal rights in property at death
- Prenuptial and postnuptial agreements concerning spousal rights in property incident to divorce
- Prenuptial and postnuptial agreements concerning community and separate property

What Is Meant by the "Estate"?

Probate Estate

The *probate estate* is the property that is handled and distributed by the personal representative (executor if there is a will; administrator if there is not) upon a person's death. Thus, probate property is the property disposed of by the decedent's will, including:

- Property owned outright in the person's own name
- Interests in property held as tenants in common

- Proceeds or benefits payable to a person's estate at death
- A person's half of community property

It is sometimes argued that having property pass through a decedent's probate estate is bad. This is not necessarily true—it depends on the circumstances. There are, however, some disadvantages in leaving property so that it will be part of a person's probate estate, such as:

- There may be delay in settling the estate.
- The costs of administering an estate (executor's fees, attorney's fees, etc.) may be based largely on the probate estate.
- Assets in the probate estate are subject to creditor's claims.
- The probate estate can be made public knowledge.
- Disgruntled heirs may seek to contest a will and obtain probate assets.
- Sometimes, state death taxes can be increased, depending on the property and the state involved.

On the other hand, having property bypass the probate estate is not an estate planning panacea. Cost savings from avoiding probate depend on the circumstances and may not be that significant. Furthermore, some commonly advocated methods for avoiding probate, such as the revocable living trust, have costs of their own (see Chapter 30). Other arrangements (such as jointly owned property) also may have problems (see Chapter 30). Therefore, avoiding probate is not an open-and-shut issue and should be evaluated carefully.

Most people have a probate estate. First, property owned outright at death must pass through the probate estate. Many people will hold property in a variety of ways during their lifetimes—some in the probate estate and some not. Furthermore, estate owners want their executors to have adequate assets to pay the claims, expenses, and taxes that their estates will owe and so will need to have property (especially liquid or marketable assets) in their probate estate.

Gross Estate for Federal Estate Tax Purposes

The gross estate is defined by the tax law and is the starting point for calculating how much, if any, federal estate tax is due. While the calculation of the gross estate is illustrated here, it is explained more fully in Chapter 26.

State Death Tax Value

Most states have some form of death tax. Some have *inheritance taxes,* which are levied on the right to receive property by inheritance; many have *estate taxes,* which are levied on the right to give property at death; and some have both.

The Net Estate to One's Heirs

The *net estate to one's heirs* is perhaps what is significant to most people. This estate consists of the assets that will go to one's heirs after the payment of the costs of dying (debts, claims, administration expenses, and taxes).

CASE EXAMPLE

To illustrate these ideas, let us take the case of a successful executive, George Able, and his wife, Mary. They have three children, ages 22, 18, and 14. George's asset picture may be summarized as follows. He owns in his own name about $1,500,000 worth of his employer's stock, which he acquired under the company's employee stock purchase plan and by exercising some NQSOs. He also owns in his own name about $40,000 worth of other listed common stocks, $100,000 worth of mutual fund shares, $40,000 in a money market fund, and $30,000 worth of tangible personal property. George and Mary own jointly (WROS) their main home, worth about $680,000 and with a $180,000 mortgage still due; their summer home, valued at about $500,000 and with a $30,000 mortgage still due; and savings and checking accounts of $100,000. In addition to these mortgages, George has a $40,000 bank loan outstanding and about $10,000 of other personal debts.

Through his employer, George has group term life insurance of $500,000, which is payable to Mary as primary beneficiary; a qualified profit-sharing plan, with $600,000 credited to George's account; and a qualified savings plan with a Section 401(k) option, with $1,000,000 credited to his account. The benefits of the profit-sharing and savings plans also are payable to Mary at George's death. Finally, George owns individually purchased life insurance policies on his life with total death benefits of $800,000. This insurance is payable to George's estate as beneficiary.

George has a will that leaves everything outright to Mary if she survives him; otherwise, everything is left outright to his children in equal shares. George and Mary have always lived in common-law states. Thus, George's property interests can be summarized as follows:

Property George owns outright in his own name:	
His employer's common stock	$1,500,000
Other listed common stock	$40,000
Mutual fund shares	$100,000
Money market fund	$40,000

Tangible personal property	$30,000
	$1,710,000
Property George and Mary own jointly (WROS):	
Principal residence	$680,000
Summer home	$500,000
Bank accounts	$100,000
	$1,280,000
Life insurance George owns on his life:	
Group term life insurance, payable to Mary in a lump sum	$500,000
Individual life insurance, payable to George's estate in a lump sum	$800,000
	$1,300,000
Retirement plan benefits:	
Profit-sharing plan death benefit, payable to Mary	$600,000
Savings plan death benefit, payable to Mary	$1,000,000
	$1,600,000

Given these facts, if George were to die today, his *probate estate* would be $2,510,000. This includes the $1,710,000 of property George owns in his own name and the $800,000 of life insurance proceeds payable to his estate. The rest of the assets pass to Mary outside of George's probate estate.

Again assuming if George were to die today, his *gross estate for federal estate tax purposes* would be calculated as follows. (The items included in the gross estate are described more fully in Chapter 26.)

Property owned in the decedent's own name	$1,710,000
One-half of property owned jointly (WROS) by him and Mary ($1,280,000 ÷ 2 = $640,000)[2]	$640,000
Life insurance on George's life that he owned (i.e., in which he had incidents of ownership) at the time of his death or was payable to his estate	$1,300,000
Retirement plan death benefits	$1,600,000
Gross estate	$5,250,000

[2] One-half of jointly owned property (WROS) held by husband and wife is included in the gross estate of the first spouse to die. This is referred to as the *fractional interest rule.*

In this case, because of the unlimited federal estate tax marital deduction, there would be no federal estate tax payable at George's death as his estate now stands. However, as will be explained more fully in Chapter 28, it would be a better planning strategy if all of George's estate were not qualified (eligible) for the marital deduction. Only the proper amount should be qualified. This is because, as matters now stand, a greater-than-necessary tax burden probably will fall on Mary's estate when she subsequently dies. Let us also assume there would be no state death tax payable at George's death. Now, let us see what George can transmit to his family—his *net estate.* This is estimated as follows:

Total asset and death benefits (including jointly owned property and retirement assets)[3]	$5,890,000
Minus:	
George's debts (including the full amount of mortgages on homes)	$260,000
Estimated funeral and estate administration expenses	$55,000
Estimated federal estate tax payable	—0—
Estimated state death tax payable	—0—
Total estate shrinkage	–$315,000
Net estate to George's family	$5,575,000

Settling the Estate

When a person dies, what happens to his or her property? This depends on whether the person died *intestate*—that is, without having made a valid will—or whether a valid will was made. People should make a valid will.

Intestate Distribution

If someone dies intestate, his or her probate estate is distributed according to the applicable state intestate law. An administrator, who is appointed by a court, handles the estate settlement. The estate owner has no voice in who will receive the property or who will be administrator. This should be avoided. The laws of intestate distribution vary among the states. A surviving

[3] The retirement assets would produce income (IRD) for the beneficiary (Mary, in this case) and hence result in an income tax liability for her (see Chapter 10). However, depending on her age, this tax liability can be deferred and so is not counted as "shrinkage" here.

spouse first is entitled to his or her statutory share of the estate.[4] Then, there is a statutory order of distribution to persons other than a surviving spouse.

Problems with Intestate Distribution

We noted that people normally should make a will. A number of problems can arise when a person dies intestate.

- Perhaps most important is that intestate distribution is not chosen by the estate owner. It is dictated by the applicable state statute.
- Beneficiaries receive their inheritances outright, without regard to their individual capacities to manage property. Guardians must be appointed for minor beneficiaries. Trusts cannot be used for the heirs.
- The estate owner cannot select his or her executor.
- Estate taxes may be increased because the surviving spouse's share may not be large enough to take full advantage of the marital deduction or, on the other hand, may be too large for efficient tax planning.

Distribution by Will

A *will* is a legally enforceable declaration of what people want done with their probate property and their instructions about other matters when they die. A will does not take effect until the person's (testator's) death, and may be changed or revoked at any time until death. Thus, a will is referred to as being *ambulatory* until the maker's death. To be effective, a will must be executed in accordance with the legal requirements of the state for a valid will. It is important for both husband and wife to have valid wills for a complete estate plan.

Steps in Estate Settlement

What does a deceased's personal representative (executor under a will or administrator of a person dying intestate) do in settling the estate? After the executor's or administrator's appointment, the following basic functions are performed. The time required to settle an estate can vary greatly—from a year or less to many years.

- Assembling the property belonging to the estate (probate property).
- Safekeeping, safeguarding, and insuring estate property during estate administration.
- Temporary management of estate property.

[4] Note that this is not the same as a spouse's right to elect to take against the will. In that case, there is a valid will.

- Payment of estate debts, expenses, and taxes. A will normally contains a *tax clause* indicating what interest or interests will bear death taxes.
- Accounting for the estate administration.
- Making distribution of the net estate to the proper heirs.

For performing these functions, the executor is entitled to reasonable compensation, which is deducted from the estate. Sometimes, individual executors will consider waiving this compensation, as explained next.

Selecting the Executor or Coexecutors

An executor can be an individual (e.g., the testator's spouse, brother or sister, an adult son or daughter, a trusted friend, etc.), a professional executor (e.g., a bank or trust company or an attorney), or coexecutors (such as the testator's spouse and a bank). An estate owner may consider naming an individual executor or executors, who also may be family members and heirs under the will. However, an executor's duties can be complex, time-consuming, and technical, and the executor can be held personally liable for mistakes or omissions. Therefore, many people decide to name a professional executor or a professional executor and one or more family members as coexecutors and pay the fee involved. Executors' fees are deductible from any federal estate tax due or on the decedent's final income tax return, whichever the executor elects.

When an individual (e.g., a family member) is named executor or coexecutor with a professional executor, he or she may consider waiving his or her executor's commission if the individual is an heir under the will anyway. Any commission will be ordinary income to the individual, but will be deductible by the estate. However, the individual executor may not be the only heir under the will. While this decision depends on the circumstances, it would seem an individual executor should think carefully before waiving his or her executor's commissions.

An executor normally has an attorney to provide advice regarding administering and settling the estate. The attorney's fees are charged to and may be deductible by the estate or on the income tax return. The attorney for the estate generally is considered to represent the executor and not the heirs under the will. Thus, under some circumstances, heirs may need to secure their own legal counsel.

Trusts in Estate Planning

The famous jurist Oliver Wendell Holmes once said, "Don't put your trust in money; put your money in trust." Trusts have an important place in tax and estate planning. We have already been introduced to the income taxation of trusts in Chapter 10. As noted, a trust is a fiduciary arrangement[5] set up by someone, called the *grantor, creator,* or *settlor* of the trust, whereby a person, corporation, or organization, called the *trustee,* has legal title to property placed in the trust by the grantor. The trustee holds and manages this property, which technically is called the trust *corpus* or *principal,* for the benefit of someone, called the *beneficiary* of the trust. The beneficiary has equitable title to the trust property.

Kinds of Trusts

There are various kinds of trusts, but as far as how and when they are created are concerned, the most important are living (*inter vivos*) trusts, trusts under will (testamentary trusts), and insurance trusts. A *living trust* is created during the grantor's lifetime to benefit the grantor or someone else. The terms of a living trust are contained in a deed of trust executed during the grantor's lifetime. A *testamentary trust* is created under a person's will that, like the will, does not become effective until the grantor's death. The terms of a testamentary trust are part of the grantor's will. An *insurance trust* is a particular kind of living trust whose corpus consists partly or wholly of life insurance policies during the insured's lifetime and life insurance proceeds after the insured's death.

Living trusts can be revocable or irrevocable. A *revocable trust* is one in which the grantor reserves the right to revoke or amend the trust. In an *irrevocable trust,* the creator does not reserve the right to revoke or alter it. Most trusts are created by one person as grantor. In some cases, however, two or more persons will create *joint trusts.*

Reasons for Creating Trusts

Trusts have become important in financial and estate planning. Some of the common reasons or purposes for the trusts are as follows:

- To allow the trustee to use his, her, or its discretion (as a fiduciary) in handling trust property for the benefit of the creator, his or her family, or others within the terms of the trust.
- To provide a vehicle for holding family wealth as it passes from one generation to the next and perhaps over a number of generations.
- To protect the creator's family or dependents against demands and entreaties from well-meaning, or perhaps not so well-meaning, family members, friends, spouses, ex-spouses, spouses-to-be, and the like.

[5] A fiduciary is an individual or corporation that acts in good faith for the benefit of another with respect to things falling within the scope of the fiduciary relationship.

- To provide a way for giving or leaving property to minors so that the trustee can manage it for them until they are old enough to handle the property themselves.
- In some cases, to protect trust beneficiaries from themselves when they are physically, mentally, or emotionally unable to manage property.
- Trusts also can protect beneficiaries from their creditors. If an irrevocable trust contains a spendthrift clause that normally prohibits the beneficiary from alienating, assigning, or encumbering trust assets, the beneficiary's creditors generally can have no claim against trust assets. Correspondingly, trust assets can remain free from marital claims by present or future spouses of trust beneficiaries as gift property. These can be important reasons for giving property in trust rather than outright.
- As a corollary to the previous two reasons, creators sometimes include conditions or requirements in trust documents, especially for longer-term trusts, that are intended to produce or encourage productive or socially useful behavior on the part of trust beneficiaries. These might include, for example, educational requirements, work requirements, matching trust distributions with the beneficiary's own earned income, pursuing socially useful (but perhaps lower-paid) occupations or activities, caring for other family members, distributions on marriage, and combinations of these or others. Such provisions are intended to try to avoid having the trust itself allow beneficiaries simply to live off the trust and do nothing productive with their lives. Trusts with such provisions are often called *incentive trusts.*
- To create *special-needs trusts* for beneficiaries with disabilities who need to maintain eligibility for various government benefits, like Medicaid (see Chapter 23). Special-needs trusts limit the use of their assets and income to supplemental needs of the beneficiary that are not covered by government programs and that are not primary care, so the beneficiary will not be disqualified from receiving government benefits.
- To provide professional investment and property management for other beneficiaries or for the creator himself or herself during his or her lifetime. Investment diversification also can be provided through mutual funds under the prudent investor rule.
- To manage a business interest after the owner's death until it can be sold or one of his or her heirs can take over.
- To provide a vehicle for setting up tax-saving plans.
- As a recent development, in some states, grantors can protect themselves from their own future creditors by placing assets in irrevocable trusts created in those states. When established in one of the states permitting them in the United States, they are commonly called *asset protection trusts (APTs)*

or "onshore trusts." When established in a foreign country (some of which tailor their laws to attract such business), they often are called *offshore asset protection trusts (OAPTs).* Such creditor protection from the grantor's own creditors is discussed further in the material on dynasty trusts.

Trustees' Fees

Trustees, like executors, may receive compensation for their work. The fees charged by professional trustees vary; however, they usually are based on the value of the trust corpus, with a minimum annual fee. Trustees also may charge payout commissions on principal distributed from a trust. The following is an example of an annual commission schedule for personal trusts.

Account Value Trust Corpus	Managed Account Individually Managed Portfolio	Managed Account 100% Invested in Trustees' Own Mutual Funds*
First $500,000	.90%	.55%
$500,001–$1,000,000	.90%	.45%
$1,000,001–$2,000,000	.70%	.35%
$2,000,001–$4,000,000	.60%	.25%
Over $4,000,000	.50%	.25%
Minimum Annual Fee	$3,000	$1,500

*Investment of trust assets in mutual funds now is permitted because the Uniform Prudent Investor Act or rule allows trustees to prudently delegate trust investment activities. The percentage fee is reduced because there also is a charge for investment management included in the mutual fund's expense ratio (see Chapter 8 and further in this chapter).

Thus, if we assume an individually managed trust with $500,000 of principal (corpus) and earnings of $25,000 per year in investment income, the trustee's annual fee under this schedule would be $4,500 ($500,000 × .009). This equals 0.90 percent of the principal and 18 percent of the income.

Who Should Be the Trustee and What Should the Trust's Situs Be?

A trustee can be an individual, a corporation, or any other group or organization legally capable of owning property. There can be one trustee or two or more cotrustees. Cotrustees, for example, can be two or more individuals, or a corporate trustee and one or more individual trustees. The creator of a trust or a beneficiary of the trust can be a trustee, but care must be taken to avoid tax problems when the creator (or the creator's spouse) or a beneficiary is trustee or a cotrustee.

The selection of a trustee is an important decision, and the choice often boils down to an individual or a corporate trustee. An individual trustee (or trustees) may be the creator, a member of the family, a trusted friend, an attorney, or someone else. The creator may want to continue to administer the property as trustee, making investment decisions, for example. In this case, however, care must be taken in drafting the trust so that there are no unintended tax results. An individual trustee might decide not to charge any fee. It also can be argued that an individual trustee may be closer to the trust beneficiaries and, hence, more likely to be responsive to their needs than a corporate trustee. Finally, individual trustees can get professional help from attorneys, investment advisers, financial planners, and the like in administering the trust.

On the other hand, arguments can be made for the use of corporate trustees. Corporate trustees are professional money and property managers and, hence, can provide technical expertise in this area. Also, individual trustees may die, resign, or otherwise become incapacitated, while corporate trustees provide continuity of management. Correspondingly, corporate trustees are unbiased and independent of family pressures. Corporate trustees also are financially able to respond to damages in the event of trust mismanagement. Furthermore, if an individual trustee is given full discretionary powers over trust income or corpus and he or she is a trust beneficiary, the trustee may be considered the owner of the trust corpus for federal estate and income tax purposes. This would not be true of a corporate trustee. On the other hand, properly drafted powers for individual trustees or beneficiaries (such as being subject to an ascertainable standard) normally will not give rise to these tax problems. Finally, a corporate trustee can serve as cotrustee with one or more individual trustees, thus combining at least some of the advantages of both.

It also is possible to provide in a trust agreement that a corporate trustee can be removed and another independent corporate trustee substituted upon the demand of trust beneficiaries, the grantor, or someone else. Thus, if one corporate trustee (or another independent trustee) should prove unsatisfactory, a mechanism can be provided in the trust instrument to replace that trustee with another corporate (or other independent) trustee.

The *situs* of a trust generally is the state or country where it is located. The law of the trust situs normally governs its construction and administration. Most trusts are located in the state where the grantor lives (the grantor's domicile). However, there has been an increasing tendency to establish trusts or to move existing trusts to states or countries other than the grantor's home state to take advantage of more favorable laws in certain jurisdictions. Such laws may allow dynasty trusts (so-called "dynasty trust jurisdictions" that do not have a rule against perpetuities), have stronger creditor protection (often called "domestic APT jurisdictions"), and have no or low state income taxes or trust income.

Achieving Flexibility or Changes in Irrevocable Trusts

An irrevocable trust is one that normally cannot be revoked or amended by the grantor. However, it is possible to give others the power to change an irrevocable trust or its administration if circumstances make it desirable.

One approach is to provide for a *directed trust* which authorizes the trustee to follow the direction of an adviser in such matters as investment decision (investment advisers) or making trust distributions (distribution advisers). Another concept is to name someone who is not a trust beneficiary as a *trust protector* with powers to change the trust's terms. These powers can be limited, such as the power to make administrative changes, or broader, such as allowing the trust protector to make substantive changes in the provisions of the trust, replace the trustee or others, move the trust to another jurisdiction, terminate the trust, or other powers. Such powers can be conditioned on certain factual events, such as actual repeal of the federal estate tax or imposition of carryover basis, or can arise in the event of the grantor's disability. Of course, the grantor himself or herself could change the terms of a testamentary trust by changing his or her will, or change the terms of a revocable living trust, assuming the grantor remains legally competent to do so. State laws differ in their treatement of directed trusts and trust protectors.

Still another approach is to give an independent trustee broad powers to make changes. For example, a trust document could give such a trustee power to make distributions of trust assets to another trust for the beneficiaries, effectively terminating the existing trust. An independent trustee also could be given power to change the situs of a trust. A practical problem with such planning for flexibility, however, is who should be named trust protector or independent trustee with broad powers. This can be a difficult and perhaps delicate choice, since this person or institution might have a considerable impact on the results for the grantor's family or other beneficiaries.

How Long Should Trusts Last?

Some trusts are intended to be in place for only a relatively short duration, such as until a minor reaches a certain age, like 35 or 40. Other trusts are for the beneficiary's lifetime, providing a life interest or life estate. Recently, however, the concept has emerged in some states of creating trusts that have unlimited duration and theoretically can last forever. These are commonly called *dynasty trusts* or *unlimited duration generation-skipping trusts.*

The old common law set a limit on the duration of trusts for public policy reasons. This is called the *rule against perpetuities.* It provides that an interest in property must vest (e.g., a trust must terminate) no later than the end of a period measured by a life or lives in being at the creation of the interest (the lives usually being the beneficiaries identified in the trust document) plus 21 years, plus the period of gestation. This common-law rule has been incorporated into the statutory law of some states. Thus, it still serves to limit the permissible duration of trusts established in those states.

In recent years, however, states have adopted the Uniform Statutory Rule Against Perpetuities (USRAP), promulgated in 1993. In these states, the maximum duration effectively is the longer of the traditional limit or 90 years, with the ability to reform interests that do not comply with this rule.

The most dramatic development in this area, however, has been that states have recently amended their statutes generally to permit trusts created in those states to have unlimited duration (to be *dynasty trusts*). They have effectively repealed the rule against perpetuities in whole or in part and, in essence, allow trusts to last forever. Some of these states also exempt trusts from state income and capital gains taxation. Also, some of them give trust assets that may be used for the grantor's benefit creditor protection against claims by the grantor's own future creditors. The nature of this protection against the grantor's own creditors varies somewhat among these states and, depending on state law, does not apply in certain situations. Dynasty trusts also may avoid all future estate taxes and GST taxes since the trust never terminates.[6] They also can provide creditor protection against the beneficiaries' creditors and protection from marital claims against beneficiaries (i.e., can be creditor-proof and divorce-proof) for an unlimited time. These trusts sometimes are referred to as *family banks.*

On the other hand, others may argue that keeping property tied up in a trust indefinitely may not be a good idea. Future generations should be able to direct their own destinies, even at the cost of higher wealth-transfer taxes. Also, laws permitting dynasty trusts, and particularly those allowing protection against the grantor's own creditors, are quite new and have not yet been fully tested. These trusts also result in long-term trust administration and trustees' fees. Finally, due to the nature and complexity of dynasty trusts, they probably are mainly for wealthy families.

[6] There might, of course, be tax on the creation of the trust—a gift tax if created during the grantor's lifetime or an estate tax if created under the grantor's will. It may also be that the grantor has applied part or all of his or her GST tax exemption to the trust so it will be exempt from the GST tax in the future. If not, the GST tax may apply to taxable distributions. See Chapter 26 for an explanation of the GST tax.

Investment of Trust Assets

Trust instruments can direct how trust assets are to be invested. The grantor can put directions concerning investment policy in the terms of the trust, which the trustee generally must follow. However, trusts frequently give trustees investment discretion under the terms of the law of the state where the trust is to be administered.

Uniform Prudent Investor Act Many states have adopted the Uniform Prudent Investor Act or some modification of it, which was first promulgated in 1994. This law applies to trust investments. It adopts the *prudent investor rule,*[7] which holds that a trustee should make trust investments by exercising reasonable care, skill, and caution given the circumstances and objectives of the trust and considering the trust's investment portfolio as a whole. The act applies modern portfolio theory to trust investments, in that it is the overall risk/return relationships of the whole portfolio that must be evaluated rather than each asset class taken alone. No particular class (or classes) of investment by itself, is prohibited, but investment media are to be evaluated in terms of their relationship to the overall portfolio's risk structure (e.g., their degree of correlation with other assets in the portfolio).

The act generally requires diversification of investments, but there may be circumstances that will justify a lack of diversification. Trustees also are allowed to prudently delegate investment activities and so they can invest in properly selected mutual funds. As noted earlier, when trust institutions invest in their own mutual funds, they may charge lower trustees' fees because of the funds' own expense ratios. The Uniform Prudent Investor Act generally applies, unless the grantor provides otherwise in the trust instrument.

Total Return Trusts Normally when a trust specifies that income may or must be paid to a beneficiary, the income means interest, dividends, rents or other income from trust assets, but it does not include realized capital gains (unless the trust terms so provide) or distributions from principal (corpus). The practical problem with this system is that over the years, dividend yields on common stocks have declined substantially. Thus, if a trust is invested for greatest reasonable total returns (e.g., with a substantial asset allocation to common stocks), the annual income to an income beneficiary will suffer, and this beneficiary will be unhappy. On the other hand, if the trust is invested primarily for income (e.g., mainly in bonds), principal (corpus) growth will be inhibited and the remainderperson will be equally unhappy.

[7] The prudent investor rule was first announced in 1992 in Section 227 of the American Law Institute's *Restatement (Third) of Trusts.*

It is argued that the solution to this dilemma is the *total return trust,* in which a part of the annual payment to an income beneficiary may consist of principal. This allows the trustee to invest for total returns without being unfair to either group of beneficiaries. To help accomplish this, one approach has been to enact legislation granting trustees the discretionary power to adjust distributions by transferring principal to an income beneficiary (or the reverse—income to principal) to the extent the trustee believes is needed for equity among income and remainder beneficiaries. This *power to adjust* ("equitable adjustment") concept was adopted in the 1997 revision of the Uniform Principal and Income Act, which, as of this writing, has been adopted in many of the states.

Another approach is legislation allowing trustees to convert *an income providing trust to a unitrust.* Such a unitrust requires or permits a trustee to distribute a fixed percentage (between 3 and 5 percent) of the current trust corpus (recalculated each year) to the current income beneficiary. The IRS has ruled that such "equitable adjustment trusts and unitrusts" under these laws providing unitrust payments of between 3 and 5 percent meet the requirements for marital deduction and certain GST trusts.

26

The Transfer Tax System

Competence Objectives for This Chapter After reading this chapter, planners should understand:

- The impact of the Economic Growth and Tax Relief Reconciliation Act (EGTRRA) on gift, estate and generation-skipping transfer (GST) taxes
- The operation of the applicable credit amount (unified credit) and applicable exclusion amount on gift and estate taxes
- The meaning of taxable transfers for federal gift tax purposes
- Ways of making gifts
- Gift tax exclusions and deductions
- Gift tax marital deduction
- Gift splitting by married persons
- When gift tax returns must be filed
- Valuation of gift property and some valuation discounts
- The effect of Chapter 14 of the IRC on valuation
- The structure of the federal estate tax
- What is included in the gross estate
- Federal estate tax marital deduction
- Federal estate tax charitable deduction
- Valuation of property in the gross estate and special use valuation
- When estate tax returns must be filed and payment of the estate tax (including payment in installments under IRC Section 6166)
- The structure of the federal GST tax
- GST tax exemptions and exclusions
- The types of GST taxable transfers
- Possible future changes in the federal transfer tax system

This chapter gives an overview of the federal transfer tax system as it stands as of this writing—the federal gift tax, estate tax, and generation-skipping transfer (GST) tax. This system generally was designed so that wealth would be subject to a transfer tax in each generation. This includes lifetime transfers by gift, transfers at death, and transfers designed to skip generations. Thus, it has been referred to as a *unified transfer tax system.*

Impact of Economic Growth and Tax Relief Reconciliation Act (EGTRRA)

As noted in Chapter 2, the *Economic Growth and Tax Relief Reconciliation Act* (EGTRRA) of 2001 may dramatically change this system. The three transfer taxes will remain, with some changes, through 2009. Then, in 2010, the federal estate tax and GST tax will be repealed entirely for that year, but the gift tax will be retained. However, in 2011, the unified transfer tax system as it stood in 2001 will be reinstated for the future under the sunset provision. Most commentators think there will be new tax legislation before 2011 (probably in 2009) that will change this scenario, but no one can be sure at this time.

At the end of this chapter, there is a discussion on some likely changes in the system that probably will be made before 2011. They include: no repeal of the estate tax, retention of this present exclusion amount of $3,500,000, retention of the present tax rate of 45 percent, and allowing the transfer (probability) of a deceased spouse's unused unified credit to a surviving spouse.

Applicable Credit Amount (Unified Credit) and Applicable Exclusion Amount

The tax law provides for each person a one-time *applicable credit amount (unified credit)*[1] of $1,455,800 in 2009. This credit can be applied to reduce or eliminate any federal estate tax payable at the person's death. The unified credit will allow a person to pass a substantial amount of wealth to others free of federal estate tax. This amount is called the *applicable exclusion amount.*

The operation of this system can be seen if we say, for example, that in the year 2009, a decedent has a taxable estate of $3,500,000. Applying the unified transfer tax rate schedule (not shown here), we can calculate a tentative tax on this amount of $1,455,800. An applicable credit amount of

[1] The terms *applicable credit amount* and *unified credit* mean the same thing. In practice, they tend to be used interchangeably and are so used in this book.

$1,455,800 will exactly offset this tentative tax, so that is the applicable credit amount which produces an applicable exclusion amount of $3,500,000. This excluded amount will return to $1,000,000 in 2011 unless there is new tax legislation changing it. As we shall see in Chapter 28, a great deal of marital deduction planning is aimed at using effectively the applicable credit amounts of both spouses. The unified credit and applicable exclusion amounts are not indexed for inflation.

The unified credit-applicable exclusion amount system also applies to gift taxation. For 2009, the applicable exclusion amount for federal gift tax purposes is $1,000,000 and remains so in subsequent years. The gift tax is not repealed in 2010. However, under EGTRRA's sunset provision, all transfer tax rules, including for gift taxes, return to their 2001 form. The gift tax excluded amount is not indexed for inflation.

Federal Gift Tax

It comes as a surprise to many people that there is a federal gift tax. It applies to transferring ownership rights in property during a lifetime and is levied against the donor, who must file a gift tax return when required by law.

What Are Taxable Transfers for Gift Tax Purposes?

The gift tax is on the transfer of property by any individual. Only individuals are subject to gift taxation. The term *gift* is not expressly defined in the IRC, but it is construed to mean the transfer of property for less than full and adequate consideration. To be a taxable gift, the transfer must be *complete.* This means the donor must have relinquished enough dominion and control over the property so that it no longer is subject to his or her will and the donor no longer can control its disposition. For example, if a donor alone deposits funds in a joint bank account or a joint brokerage account with his or her child, with either having the power unilaterally to withdraw the full amount, there has been no completed gift because the donor could simply withdraw the whole amount and recover the property. On the other hand, if the child in fact did withdraw his or her half (or more), there would be a completed gift of that amount at that time.

Methods of Making Gifts

Some common methods are as follows:

- *Outright gifts.* Here, the donee has immediate possession, use, and enjoyment of the gift property.

- *Gifts to irrevocable inter vivos (living) trusts.* In this case, the donee(s) are the beneficiaries of the trust.
- *Gifts to custodianship arrangements.* Here, the donee(s) are minor recipients of property held by a custodian under a Uniform Transfers to Minors Act or Uniform Gifts to Minors Act. (These acts are discussed in Chapter 27.)
- *Receiving property as joint owners with the donor.* In this situation, the donor places property or funds that he or she formerly owned outright in joint names with the donee.
- *The exercise, release, or lapse during the lifetime of a general power of appointment in favor of someone other than the holder of the power.*[2] Here, the gift is from the possessor of the power to the other party or parties. However, the tax law provides that the lapse of a power during the possessor's lifetime will only be considered a release of that power (and hence a taxable transfer) to the extent that the property that could have been appointed exceeds the larger of $5,000 or 5 percent of the aggregate value of the assets out of which the power could have been satisfied. This means, for example, that if a trust beneficiary is given a power of withdrawal (a general power) each year over trust assets that is limited to the greater of $5,000 or 5 percent of the trust corpus, and the power for each year expires (lapses) at the end of that year, a lapse of this withdrawal right will not result in a taxable gift by its possessor (the trust beneficiary) to the other trust beneficiaries. This is referred to as a *5 and 5 power.* It is an important concept in estate planning.
- *Other gifts.*

Exclusions and Deductions

The gifts most people make will not be subject to gift taxation. This is because of exclusions and deductions applying to the federal gift tax.

Per-Donee Annual Exclusion Every donor can make tax-free gifts each year up to $13,000, in 2009 (indexed for inflation in increments of $1,000), each to however many persons the donor wishes. Gifts within the annual exclusion do not reduce the donor's unified credit. Rather sizeable amounts

[2] As explained in Chapter 25, a general power of appointment exists when the holder of the power can exercise it in favor of himself or herself, his or her creditors, his or her estate, or the creditors of his or her estate. The aforementioned rule applies to general powers of appointment created after October 21, 1942. For general powers created on or before that date, the exercise of the power results in a transfer (gift) by the holder, but the failure to exercise (lapse) or release of such a power is not considered an exercise of the power and, hence, is not a taxable event. Thus, in the relatively few cases of these pre–October 21, 1942, general powers, the holder generally should not exercise the power and thus would avoid transfer taxation on property subject to the power.

often can be given away each year under the annual exclusion. To take a rather extreme example, in 2009, a donor might give $13,000 in money or securities outright to each of, say, 12 persons (perhaps his or her children and grandchildren), or total gifts of $156,000 in the year, without reducing his or her unified credit at all. For this reason, spacing out gifts to one or more donees over a period of years often can keep the amounts within the annual exclusion. It must be remembered, however, that the annual exclusion applies to all gifts made by a donor to a donee during a year. Therefore, if a donor already has made several smaller gifts to a donee in a year, the donor cannot make the full $13,000 (indexed) gift to the same donee during the year and stay within the annual exclusion.

Present Interest Requirement for Annual Exclusion The annual exclusion applies only to gifts of a *present interest* in property (i.e., where the donee has the immediate possession, use, or enjoyment of the gift); it does not apply to gifts of future interests (i.e., where the donee's possession, use, or enjoyment is deferred). For example, an outright gift is a gift of a present interest of the full value of the property because the donee has the unrestricted immediate use, possession, and enjoyment of all the gift property by virtue of sole ownership. However, when gifts are made in trust, this issue becomes more complicated. It depends on the terms of the trust.

CASE EXAMPLE

Assume, for example, an irrevocable trust provides that income must be paid annually to a beneficiary for a term of 15 years (mandatory right to income), and at the end of that time the corpus will be paid outright to the beneficiary or his or her issue (as remainderperson).[3] Further assume that Amy (as grantor) transfers $13,000 worth of common stock into this trust. The present value of the mandatory right to income from the gift property is a gift of a present interest to the beneficiary since he or she has the immediate possession, use, and enjoyment of the income stream for 15 years. This value qualifies for the per-donee annual exclusion. On the other hand, the present value of the remainder interest is a future interest (since its possession, use, and enjoyment is delayed for 15 years) and does not qualify for the annual exclusion. Assuming a 7.2 percent interest rate (the Section 7520 rate

[3]Assume for the sake of this illustration that this trust does not qualify for any special annual exclusion treatment. In other words, it is what may be referred to as a Section 2503(b) income interest trust. Other ways for qualifying periodic gifts for the annual exclusion (such as for minors) are discussed in Chapter 27.

explained in Chapter 3), the present value of an income interest for 15 years is 0.647566 (64.7566 percent) and the corresponding present value of a remainder interest at the end of 15 years is 0.352434 (35.2434 percent) of the amount transferred to the trust. Therefore, in this example, $8,418 ($13,000 × 0.647566) is a gift of a present interest and qualifies for the annual exclusion, while $4,582 ($10,000 × 0.352434) is a gift of a future interest, does not qualify for the annual exclusion, and would be a taxable gift this year for Amy.

However, if we change this example to say the trust provides that the trustee may accumulate income in the trust or pay it out to the beneficiary in the trustee's discretion during the 15-year term (a discretionary income provision), none of the transfer would be a gift of a present interest because the beneficiary does not have unrestricted immediate possession, use, or enjoyment of the income stream (it can be changed at the trustee's discretion) or of the principal (payment of the remainder interest is delayed 15 years). Therefore, Amy does not have any annual exclusion and the full $13,000 transfer this year is a taxable gift by Amy to the trust beneficiary.[4]

Unlimited Exclusion for Transfers for Educational and Medical Expenses This important exclusion is in addition to the per-donee annual exclusion. It excludes from gift taxation any amount paid on behalf of an individual (no particular relationship to the donor is required) to an educational organization[5] as tuition (books, room and board, etc., are not included) for the education or training of such individual. It also excludes any amount paid on behalf of an individual to any person or entity that provides medical care with respect to such individual. These can be valuable exclusions for planning purposes.

[4] As we shall see in the next chapter, an important way of making a transfer of property to a trust a gift of a present interest is to give the beneficiary or beneficiaries a power of withdrawal over the transferred property. Such a presently exercisable power allows the holder (beneficiary or beneficiaries) to get the transferred property outright and hence makes the gift one of a present interest eligible for the annual exclusion. This is the principle behind the use of *Crummey powers.* Donors normally want to make gifts that will qualify for the per-donee annual exclusion if possible.

[5] An educational organization for this purpose is one that normally maintains a regular faculty and curriculum and has a regularly enrolled body of students who are in attendance at the place where its educational activities are carried on. It can be seen that this definition can embrace a relatively wide range of organizations. Whether it would go as far as nursery school or other preschool programs depends on the facts of the case.

CASE EXAMPLE

Suppose, for example, that Gary would like to help his 21-year-old granddaughter through medical school. Gary can pay the $40,000-per-year medical school tuition directly to the school and also give his granddaughter $13,000 (indexed)[6] each year under the per-donee annual exclusion. He can also pay his granddaughter's medical expenses (including health insurance premiums) directly to the providers.[7] None of these gifts will be subject to gift taxation since they are under the exclusion for transfers for educational and medical expenses and the per-donee annual exclusion.

It may also be useful at this point to relate these gift tax exclusions to the GST tax, which will be covered later in this chapter. In this situation, Gary's granddaughter is a *skip person* for GST purposes (i.e., she is two or more generations younger than the transferor—Gary) and Gary's gifts to her are *direct skips* for GST tax purposes. However, since these direct skips are nontaxable outright gifts under the annual exclusion and the exclusion for transfers for educational and medical expenses, they are not taxable for GST tax purposes as well. However, with regard to annual exclusion gifts in trust, the situation is more complex. The GST tax imposes special conditions on such gifts, which are described later.

Federal Gift Tax Marital Deduction When married persons make gifts to each other, an unlimited federal gift tax marital deduction normally applies. This generally parallels the unlimited federal estate tax marital deduction that is explained elsewhere in this chapter and in Chapter 28. It operates as a deduction from a donor's taxable transfers to arrive at taxable gifts and hence allows gifts between spouses to be free of federal gift tax.

Gifts to U.S. Citizen Spouses: Before a deduction is allowed, gifts to a U.S. citizen spouse must be made in a way that qualifies for the marital deduction. The methods for qualifying property for the marital deduction are described in Chapter 28.

[6]As we shall see later in this chapter, if Gary is married at the time he makes the gift, he can split the annual gift with his wife, and effectively they both can give up to $26,000 per year to each donee (their granddaughter in this case) in cash outright or in appreciated securities, since their granddaughter probably will be in a lower capital gains tax bracket than Gary and his wife.

[7]In fact, he could make similar gifts to his son, daughter-in-law, and other persons.

Gifts to Non–U.S. Citizen Spouses: These gifts are treated differently. For gifts made after July 13, 1988, the gift tax marital deduction does not apply. Instead, there is a special $133,000 (in 2009) gift tax annual exclusion for such transfers. This exclusion applies each year to transfers of a present interest to noncitizen spouses, provided the transfers would have qualified for the marital deduction had the spouse been a U.S. citizen. This annual exclusion is indexed for inflation.

Federal Gift Tax Charitable Deduction As noted in Chapter 19, there is an unlimited charitable deduction for gifts to eligible charities.

Gift Splitting by Married Persons

Married persons can split any gifts that either spouse makes while they are married. Thus, if either spouse makes a gift to a third person, it can be treated for tax purposes as if made one-half by the donor-spouse and one-half by the other spouse, provided the other spouse consents to the gift on a gift tax return filed by the donor. Suppose, for example, that Husband wants to give outright $26,000 of common stock he owns in his own name to his adult daughter in one year. If Wife consents to the gift, the $26,000 gift is treated as a $13,000 gift by Husband and a $13,000 gift by Wife. Both these gifts would be within their $13,000 (indexed) annual exclusions and hence not taxable.

To elect gift splitting, both spouses must be U.S. citizens or permanent residents. Also, if gift splitting is elected in a particular year, all gifts made in that year by either spouse must be split. However, for the next year and each subsequent year, they can decide whether or not to split their gifts.

Who Owes the Gift Tax and Who Must File a Return?

The donor owes any gift tax payable. Sometimes, a gift is made on condition that the donee will pay the gift tax. This is called a *net gift,* and the gift tax paid by the donee is deducted from the value of the gift property to determine the taxable gift. A donor must file a gift tax return[8] when his or her transfers of present interests exceed the annual exclusion and the other exclusions. A donor also must file a gift tax return for all transfers of future interests and in cases where gift splitting by spouses is involved.[9]

[8] This is IRS Form 709 entitled United States Gift (and Generation-Skipping Transfer) Tax Return.

[9] When split gifts are not taxable because they are within the annual exclusions, a short-form return may be filed.

Valuation of Gift Property

General Principles The general principles of valuing interests for federal gift and estate tax purposes are reasonably straightforward. The value of a transfer is equal to the fair market value of the gift property (minus any payment made by the donee) as of the date a completed transfer takes place. This *fair market value* generally is the price at which the property would change hands between a willing buyer and a willing seller, with neither being under any compulsion to buy or to sell, and with both having reasonable knowledge of the relevant facts. This is referred to as the *willing buyer/willing seller test.* When property has a ready market, such as for stocks, bonds, and commodities traded on organized exchanges, or for mutual fund shares, this value can be determined easily.[10] On the other hand, for property with limited marketability, such as closely held business interests, family limited partnership (FLP) interests, real estate, and art or antiques, there may be valuation disputes and negotiations between donor-taxpayers and the IRS.

Valuation Discounts and Premiums The values of certain property interests under this willing buyer/willing seller test may be less than (discounted from) the underlying value of property in the interest because of the legal and economic nature of the interests. This may be true, for example, because of lack of control by or lack of marketability of the interest. Correspondingly, the values of other property interests may be more than the underlying value of property in the interest. This may occur, for example, because of the going-concern value of a business (goodwill factor) or because the holder of the interest is in control of a business or property (control premium).

Valuation in this context is a complex issue. However, valuation discounts may be important in estate planning and underlie such planning techniques as giving interests in FLPs, as covered in Chapter 27. There also may be differences of opinion on such discounts between donors (and their advisers) and the IRS. In some cases, disputes, compromises, and even litigation result. Some common discounts and premium and other valuation concepts are outlined next.

Discount for Lack of Marketability This discount from otherwise calculated value reflects the fact that interests in closely held entities have no ready market and hence are difficult to sell. This makes them much less attractive to a willing buyer than would be publicly traded securities. Also, closely held

[10] For publicly traded stocks and bonds, it is the average of the high and low selling prices on the valuation date. For mutual funds, it is the bid or redemption price on the valuation date.

entities may place restrictions on an owner's ability to sell his or her interest to outsiders. This discount may be applied first in the valuation process.

Discount for Lack of Control (Minority Interest Discount) The owner of a minority interest cannot control the operations of an entity. This makes such interests much less attractive to a willing buyer. This may be applied after the lack of marketability discount in the valuation process.

Control Premium On the other hand, an interest that represents control of an entity may be valued at a premium over an otherwise calculated value.

Fractional Interest Discount This discount may arise because only a partial interest in property (usually real estate) is transferred, and hence the owner of the fractional interest normally must act with the other owner or owners to deal with the property or must pay the expense to partition it. Thus, a willing buyer normally will pay less for a fractional interest than its pro rata share of the property's value.

Blockage Discounts These are discounts that may be applied to transfers of large blocks of publicly traded securities. The reason for such a discount is that the sale of such a large block may depress the normal market price for the securities.

Valuation of Life Estates, Term Interests, Remainders, Reversions, and Certain Annuities As noted in Chapter 3, transfers of such interests are valued according to factors corresponding to interest rates (Section 7520 rates) that the federal government publishes monthly.

Effect of Chapter 14 of the IRC on Valuation

This chapter of the Internal Revenue Code was enacted to redress certain perceived valuation abuses involving transfers between family members. Nevertheless, there are planning techniques for making gifts within the rules of Chapter 14 that may yield significant estate planning benefits.

To give a brief overview of Chapter 14, Section 2701 applies to the valuation freeze techniques that were used with respect to gifts of corporate stock (such as common stock) or comparable partnership interests to younger family members with the retention of senior stock (such as preferred stock) or comparable partnership interests by older family members. Unless the retained senior interests meet certain requirements, Chapter 14 values them at zero for transfer tax purposes. Thus, as a practical matter, this has essentially ended this valuation freeze approach purely for tax purposes.

Section 2702 applies to transfers in trust when the grantor retains an interest in the trust and then transfers the remainder interest to a family member. Unless certain exceptions apply, the grantor's retained interest is valued at zero and the full value of the trust corpus is assigned to the gift of the remainder interest. Thus, the exceptions are important for planning purposes. They are PRTs, QPRTs, GRATs, GRUTs, and retained term interests in certain tangible, nondepreciable property. When one of these exceptions applies, the grantor's retained interest is valued using IRS tables, and only the difference between the value of the property placed in the trust and the value of the grantor's retained interest is a taxable transfer (gift) to the family member. The planning possibilities inherent in these exceptions are considered in Chapter 27.

Section 2703 imposes certain conditions on option agreements, rights to acquire property, or restrictions on the sale or use of property between family members to assure that they are bona fide agreements. These conditions apply to business buy–sell agreements and are covered in Chapter 31.

Finally, Section 2704 deals with the effect on value of certain lapsing voting rights or liquidation rights in a corporation or partnership when the person holding the rights and members of his or her family control the corporation or partnership before and after the lapse.

Federal Estate Tax

It is said that nothing is certain except death and taxes. Here we are dealing with both. The federal estate tax is an excise tax imposed on the passing of property to others at death. At this point, we shall describe the nature of the federal estate tax. Planning to reduce or defer the estate tax is covered in Chapters 27 through 29.

Structure of the Federal Estate Tax

Gross estate (Items included are listed next)

Minus: Certain estate settlement deductions (i.e., estate administration expenses; funeral expenses; claims against the estate; unpaid mortgages or other indebtedness on property whose value, undiminished by the mortgages or indebtedness, is included in the gross estate; and casualty losses incurred during the settlement of the estate).[11]

Note: The gross estate minus these deductions equals what has been called the adjusted gross estate. This figure still is used to determine such things as eligibility for a Section 303 redemption of corporate stock and installment

[11] Estate administration expenses can be taken either on the estate's income tax return or on the estate tax return. If the executor elects to take them on the income tax return, they cannot be deducted from the gross estate.

payment of the estate tax under Section 6166. Modifications of it also may be used for other purposes.

Minus: Marital deduction (which may be up to the full amount, that is, 100 percent, of property included in the gross estate that passes to a surviving spouse so as to qualify for the marital deduction).

Minus: Charitable deduction.

Equals—

Taxable estate

Plus: Adjusted taxable gifts (post-1976 taxable gifts other than those included in the gross estate)

Equals—

Tentative tax base, to which the unified transfer tax rates are applied to produce—

Federal estate tax on the tentative tax base

Minus: Credit for gift taxes payable (at current rates) on post-1976 taxable gifts

Equals—

Federal estate tax before application of other credits

Minus: Applicable credit amount (unified credit)

Minus: Other credits

Equals—

Federal estate tax payable

It may be noted that the purpose of adding any post-1976 taxable gifts to the taxable estate to arrive at the tentative tax base (to which the unified transfer tax rates are applied) and then deducting a credit equal to any post-1976 gift taxes payable is to have the amount of any previous lifetime gifts serve to increase the unified transfer tax brackets applicable to estate assets that pass at death. At present, however, effectively the estate tax rate is a flat 45 percent of the amount over the applicable exclusion amount.

What Is in the Gross Estate?

The gross estate is the starting point for determining how much estate tax an estate must pay. In general, it includes the following items.

Property Owned at Death All property a decedent owned in his or her own name or had an interest in (such as the decedent's share of tenancies in common or community property) at the time of death will be in the decedent's gross estate.

Life Insurance on the Decedent's Life The gross estate includes proceeds of life insurance policies on a decedent's life if he or she had ownership rights in the policy (incidents of ownership) at the time of death or if the policy was payable to the estate. It also includes the proceeds of life insurance policies given away within three years of death.

Joint Tenancies (WROS) In this case, the gross estate of the first joint owner to die includes one-half the value of property held jointly (WROS) by a husband and wife (fractional interest rule) or the full value of property held jointly (WROS) with other than a husband or wife, except to the extent it can be shown the surviving owner contributed to the purchase price of the property (consideration furnished rule) from property never received by gift from the deceased owner.

General Powers of Appointment Property over which a person held a general power of appointment at his or her death will be in the decedent's gross estate. On the other hand, possession of a special or limited power will not cause inclusion in the holder's gross estate.

Annuities This item includes in a decedent's gross estate the actuarial value of payments a surviving joint annuitant may receive after the decedent's death. These might be from a joint and last survivor annuity form, for example. It also includes a beneficiary's rights to the value of annuity payments (account balances) a decedent has not yet received as of his or her death. These survivors' benefits might come from the various qualified retirement plans, traditional and Roth IRAs,[12] nonqualified annuities, TSAs, and nonqualified deferred-compensation plans. These benefits, other than from Roth IRAs, also are IRD. On the other hand, if annuity payments cease at a person's death and nothing is payable to a survivor or beneficiary thereafter (as from a straight life annuity, for example), nothing will be in the decedent's gross estate.

Revocable Transfers If a person transfers property but has the right to alter, amend, revoke, or terminate the enjoyment of the property as of the date of death, the value of the property will be included in his or her gross estate. It also will be in the gross estate if the decedent relinquished such right within three years of death. The inclusion applies regardless of the capacity in which the person is acting (e.g., as a trustee) and regardless of whether the person

[12]While benefits from Roth IRAs are free from federal income tax, they are included in a deceased owner's gross estate for federal estate tax purposes.

must act alone or in conjunction with any other person.[13] This means, for example, that if a grantor of an irrevocable trust has the right to change a trust beneficiary, the amount received by a beneficiary, or the timing of benefits to a beneficiary, this provision will apply and the corpus will be in his or her gross estate. It also will apply, of course, to revocable living trusts at the grantor's death.

Grantors of irrevocable *inter vivos* (living) trusts often want to retain at least some control over the trust, usually by being a trustee. A grantor can be a trustee, and as trustee can exercise certain powers over trust investments and other matters of trust administration without adverse estate tax consequences. However, care must be taken that a grantor or grantor-trustee does not have such powers over the beneficial enjoyment of trust corpus that it will cause the property to be in the grantor's gross estate at his or her death. On the other hand, unrestricted discretionary powers over distribution of principal and income to trust beneficiaries and other matters can be placed in the hands of an independent trustee or cotrustee (who is neither related to nor subordinate to the grantor). Also, a grantor-trustee of an irrevocable trust can have the power to invade trust corpus for or control income flows to trust beneficiaries, provided the power is limited by an ascertainable standard (i.e., for the health, education, support, or maintenance of the beneficiaries), without having the trust property included in the grantor's gross estate. Furthermore, a grantor can have the power to remove one trustee and appoint another individual or corporate trustee in its place, provided the new trustee is not the grantor and is not related or subordinate to the grantor. This can be done without causing the trust property to be included in the grantor's gross estate.

Transfers with Retained Life Estate This is another provision that may result in lifetime transfers being included in a decedent's gross estate.[14] The gross estate includes the value of all property a decedent transferred by trust or otherwise if the decedent retained for his or her lifetime, or for any period not ascertainable without reference to the decedent's death, or for any period that does not in fact end before his or her death, the possession or enjoyment of, or the right to the income from, the transferred property. This inclusion provision [IRC Section 2036(a)] also applies if the decedent retained the right, alone or in conjunction with any other person, to designate the persons who will possess or enjoy the property or the income from the property. In effect, when a transferor (e.g., a grantor of a trust) transfers property but retains a life income from the property or a lifetime power to determine

[13] Section 2038 of the IRC deals with revocable and similar transfers.

[14] Transfers with retained life estates are covered in Section 2036 of the IRC.

who will enjoy the property, the value of the property at the date of death will be in the transferor's gross estate. This is also true when a transferor retains a lifetime right to vote the shares of transferred stock in a controlled corporation.

CASE EXAMPLE

Assume that Susan Smith, age 65 and in good health, transfers $1 million of stocks and bonds to an irrevocable trust with the income payable to herself for her lifetime, and at her death the trust corpus would go in equal shares to her two children or their issue as remainderpersons. Susan dies 20 years later at age 85 when the trust corpus is worth $3 million. Since Susan retained a life income (life estate) in the transferred property, the value of this trust at her death, $3 million, will be in Susan's gross estate.

Transfers Taking Effect at Death The gross estate also includes the value of property transferred by a decedent during his or her life, when the possession or enjoyment of the property as owner can be obtained only by surviving the decedent and the decedent retained a reversionary interest in the property with a value immediately before death of more than 5 percent of the property's value.

Transfers within Three Years of Death In general, property given away during life is not in the donor's gross estate at death. This applies regardless of how close in time the date of death was to the date of the gift. However, there are several exceptions to this general rule. We have already seen that if there has been a lifetime transfer and the transferor retains or has certain rights or interests in the transferred property (e.g., transfers with retained life estates, transfers taking effect at death, and revocable transfers) as of his or her death, the value of the transferred property as of the date of death will be included in the gross estate. In addition, transfers of life insurance policies by a person on his or her life within three years of death will cause the full life insurance proceeds to be in the insured's gross estate. Furthermore, relinquishment of retained rights or powers in transferred property that otherwise would cause its inclusion in the gross estate, as just noted, within three years of death will result in the property being included in the gross estate. Finally, the gross estate includes the amount of any gift tax paid on gifts made by the decedent or his or her spouse within three years of the decedent's death. This is referred to as the *gift tax gross-up.*

Marital Deduction Property in a Q-TIP Trust One way to qualify property for the federal estate tax marital deduction is to leave it to a surviving spouse in a qualified terminable interest property (Q-TIP) trust. When this is done, the property in the Q-TIP trust will be in the surviving spouse's gross estate at his or her death. However, the surviving spouse may require reimbursement for the estate tax payable on the Q-TIP property from the Q-TIP trust.

Property Not in the Gross Estate

The property included in the gross estate consists of all property and property interests, as just described, of a decedent who was a U.S. citizen or resident wherever the property is situated. In other words, only the categories of property specifically enumerated in the IRC are in the gross estate; other property interests are not.

For planning purposes, we often are concerned with keeping property out of the gross estate, as well as with using estate tax deductions and credits wisely. Planners are interested in ways of giving persons economic advantages in property without having it included in their gross estates when they die. In this regard, when property is placed in irrevocable trusts for beneficiaries (either *inter vivos* or testamentary trusts), substantial rights and powers can be given to the beneficiaries or exercised on their behalf over the trust corpus and income without having the corpus included in the beneficiaries' gross estates upon their death. These have been referred to as *almost-owner powers* or *nontaxable ownership equivalents.* These nontaxable interests and powers are as follows:

- The right to trust income for the beneficiary's lifetime (or a term of years).
- The beneficiary's being a permissible distributee of trust corpus at the discretion of an independent trustee.
- The beneficiary's possession of a special power of appointment over trust corpus.
- The beneficiary's possession of a power to withdraw or invade trust corpus for himself or herself subject to an ascertainable standard related to the beneficiary's health, education, support, or maintenance.
- The right in the beneficiary's discretion to withdraw up to the larger of $5,000 or 5 percent of the corpus each year. At the beneficiary's death, at most, only the amount that could have been withdrawn in the year of death can be included in the beneficiary's gross estate. There can be complications with such 5 and 5 powers, but they are available for beneficiaries if desired.

Naturally, not all of these non-estate-taxable interests and powers need be given by a grantor to trust beneficiaries. However, they are available to the extent they are desired or needed.

Federal Estate Tax Marital Deduction

This often is an important tax-deferring device for married estate owners. Planning for its use will be considered in Chapter 28.

Transfers to U.S. Citizen Spouses The marital deduction operates as a deduction from a decedent's gross estate to arrive at the taxable estate and allows unlimited transfers between spouses free of federal estate taxation. However, property in a decedent's gross estate must pass to his or her surviving spouse in a way that qualifies for the marital deduction, as explained in Chapter 28.

Transfers to Non–U.S. Citizen Spouses Property passing to spouses who are not U.S. citizens is treated differently. A transfer can be made to a *qualified domestic trust* (QDOT), which is a trust for a noncitizen surviving spouse who has elected QDOT treatment, meets certain other requirements, and qualifies for the marital deduction. At the first spouse's death (the U.S. citizen or resident), it operates as a deduction from the gross estate to arrive at the taxable estate. It applies to distributions of principal during the surviving spouse's lifetime as well as the value of the trust principal at his or her death. The estate tax is calculated as if the taxable assets from the QDOT were in the first spouse's gross estate.

Federal Estate Tax Charitable Deduction

This deduction parallels the gift tax charitable deduction. It is unlimited and operates as a deduction from the gross estate to arrive at the taxable estate.

Federal Estate Tax Deduction for State Death Taxes

This is a deduction for any state death taxes actually paid on property included in the gross estate.

Applicable Credit Amount (Unified Credit)

This credit was described previously.[15]

[15] Note again the difference between a deduction and a credit. A *deduction* is taken from a potentially taxable amount to arrive at a tax base to which the tax rates are applied (such as the marital deduction and charitable deduction from the gross estate to arrive at the taxable estate). A *credit* is a dollar-for-dollar reduction in the tax itself (such as the applicable credit amount from the federal estate tax). Obviously, a credit is more valuable than a deduction.

Other Credits

There can be several other credits to reduce the federal estate tax otherwise payable. They come after the unified credit in the following order of priority.

Credit for Gift Taxes This credit is for gift taxes on taxable gifts made before 1977 that are included in the gross estate at death.

Credit for Foreign Death Taxes This is a credit for death taxes paid to foreign governments or to a possession of the United States when a U.S. citizen or resident decedent has property in the countries or possessions.

Credit for Tax on Prior Transfers (TPT Credit) When the heirs or beneficiaries of a decedent die within 10 years after or 2 years before the decedent's death, there is a decreasing credit against the estate tax payable by the heir's or beneficiary's estate for property received from the decedent that was also taxable in the decedent's estate. This credit is intended to redress or ameliorate the effect of property being taxed several times within a relatively short period. The amount of the credit depends on the time elapsing between the two deaths.

Valuation of Property in the Gross Estate

General Principles The general principles of valuing property and property interests for federal estate tax purposes are generally the same as for gift tax purposes, with some special rules. The value generally is the fair market value of property in the gross estate, either at the date of death or as of an alternate valuation date six months after the date of death at the executor's election. Fair market value is determined under the willing buyer/willing seller test described previously.

Alternate Valuation Date An executor might elect this date if the value of the estate has declined since the date of death.[16] If elected, all assets must be valued at the alternate valuation date. The election can be made only if it actually will decrease the size of the gross estate and the estate tax payable. The present step-up in income tax basis at death rule applies to the valuation date actually used. Therefore, the basis of assets will be lower if the alternate valuation date is elected. If the alternate valuation date is elected and property is disposed of during the six months after death, it is valued as of the date of disposition.

[16] For historical interest, the reason an alternative valuation date is in the tax code is that at the beginning of the Great Depression of the 1930s, many estate assets declined so precipitously in value from the date of death until the tax was due that, in some cases, they actually were worth less than the estate tax due.

Valuation Discounts and Premium The valuation discounts and premium applying to some types of assets, discussed earlier with respect to gift taxation, also may apply to the federal estate tax values of those assets.

Special Use Valuation This special valuation provision (contained in Section 2032A of the IRC) applies to real property located in the United States (qualified real property) used in farming or in a closely held business conducted by the decedent or a family member. The provision allows a decedent's executor to elect to value such property according to its current use (e.g., as a farm or part of a closely held business) rather than according to its possible *highest and best use* (e.g., as land for a housing development or industrial park). Normally, fair market value of real property is based on its highest and best use. The reduction in value from highest-and-best-use value cannot exceed $1,000,000 in 2009 (indexed for inflation in $10,000 increments). A number of requirements must be met to qualify for special-use valuation. However, under the proper circumstances, it can be a valuable provision for reducing estate taxes.

Filing the Tax Return and Payment of the Tax

General Principles When a federal estate tax return[17] is required (generally when the gross estate of a decedent who is a U.S. citizen or resident exceeds the applicable exclusion amount), the basic rule is that it must be filed and the tax paid within 9 months after the decedent's death. However, the IRS normally will grant a 6-month extension for filing the return, so as a practical matter, the executor may have up to 15 months after death to file the estate tax return. The IRS also may grant an extension of time to pay the tax due, but this requires the executor to show reasonable cause why the tax cannot be paid when due.

Election to Pay Tax on Closely Held Businesses in Installments Section 6166 of the IRC allows an executor to elect to pay the estate tax attributable to certain closely held business interests in 10 equal annual installments, beginning 5 years after the date the tax is otherwise due. This effectively allows payment over a 14-year period. Only interest need be paid for the first four years. However, the interest rate on the estate tax deferred on the first $1,330,000, in 2009 (indexed for inflation in $10,000 increments), of business value is only 2 percent, and the rate on the balance is 45 percent of the IRS underpayment rate. This interest is not deductible as an estate

[17] The estate tax return is IRS Form 706.

administration expense.[18] There are a number of requirements to qualify for this installment payment option, but Section 6166 can be attractive for the estates of closely held business owners if they are eligible.

Tax Apportionment and Tax Provisions The IRC places the burden of paying the federal estate tax on the executor of a decedent's estate. However, federal and state apportionment statutes may allow the executor to recover some of the tax from interests includible in the gross estate but not in the probate estate.

The estate owner in his or her will or other document can override these apportionment statutes and indicate from what interest or interests in his or her gross estate any death taxes are to be paid. This is referred to as a *tax clause or provision.* Otherwise, death taxes may reduce interests the estate owner may prefer not to be reduced by them. For example, it normally is not desirable for death taxes to be paid from interests that are going to qualify for the marital deduction. If they are, it will correspondingly reduce the marital deduction and increase estate taxes in a circular fashion.[19] It also may not be desirable for death taxes to be paid from qualified retirement plan or IRA account balances because it would reduce future income tax deferral (or tax-free growth). A tax clause, for example, might specify that death taxes are to be paid from the residuary probate estate that does not qualify for the marital deduction. Of course, there must be enough liquid assets in, or available to, the probate estate to do this; otherwise, the tax will be apportioned elsewhere. This is a matter of providing adequate estate liquidity.

Federal Generation-Skipping Transfer (GST) Tax

Basic Concepts

The rationale behind this tax is that a federal transfer tax should be imposed on the transfer of wealth by each generation to the next. The GST tax may apply to a direct skip, a taxable termination, or a taxable distribution from a transferor to a skip person. These are referred to as *taxable transfers.* In essence, the tax applies, with certain exceptions, when a transfer of property misses, or *skips,* a generation in terms of the property not being subject to gift or estate tax in that generation.

[18] Note that other interest paid or payable on debt incurred to finance payment of federal estate taxes may be deductible as an estate administration expense, depending on the circumstances. This, in itself, may offer planning possibilities.

[19] Under equitable apportionment principles, there should be no tax apportioned to marital deduction property because it does not generate any of the estate tax.

As a planning matter, payment of a GST tax normally should be avoided. This is because the GST tax rate effectively is equal to the maximum federal estate tax rate and a gift tax or an estate tax also will be paid on the original transfer. Planning to avoid GST tax may involve making transfers that are exempt or otherwise not subject to GST tax, as explained later in this section, or not having transfers actually skip an intervening generation's estate.

Skip Person

A skip person is a natural person assigned to a generation two or more generations younger than that of the transferor of property. Thus, a transferor's grandchildren or great-grandchildren are examples of skip persons.[20] A skip person can also be a trust, in which all interests are held by a skip person or persons (or no person holds an interest in the trust and at no time can a distribution be made to a non-skip person). In essence, this means the trust is exclusively for one or more skip persons (e.g., a grandchild or a grandchild and his or her issue).

Transferor

The transferor is the person originally subject to transfer taxation. It is the donor for transfers subject to gift taxation and the decedent in the case of transfers subject to estate taxation. It is necessary to identify the transferor so generations can be counted in determining whether there has been a taxable transfer to a skip person.

If a transfer is made by an original transferor in trust and the corpus of the trust is included in a beneficiary's gross estate for federal estate tax purposes (such as if the beneficiary had a general power of appointment over the trust corpus at his or her death), the transferor for GST tax purposes changes and the beneficiary becomes the new transferor. This is because the transfer did not skip the beneficiary's estate. This can be important in planning to avoid the GST tax.

However, a special election is permitted when property is given or left by one spouse to the other in a Q-TIP trust to qualify for the marital deduction. In this case, the executor of the first spouse to die can elect to have that spouse continue to be treated as the transferor of the trust corpus for GST tax purposes. This is called a reverse Q-TIP election. However, since under EGTRRA, the GST tax lifetime exemption will be equal to the estate tax

[20] Generations are assigned according to lineal descendants (parents, children, grandchildren, etc.), starting from the grandparents of the transferor, or if the person is not a lineal descendent, by the number of years younger than the transferor. Under this non-lineal-descendent rule, if a person is more than 37½ years younger than the transferor, he or she is a skip person.

applicable exclusion amount for 2004 and thereafter, the reverse Q-TIP election has substantially diminished in importance for planning purposes.

Generation-Skipping Transfers Not Subject to GST Tax

Since the GST tax normally is to be avoided, it is important to know which GSTs will escape taxation.

GST Exemption Each person making generation-skipping transfers (a transferor) is allowed an aggregate exemption, which can be allocated to otherwise taxable transfers made during the transferor's lifetime or at his or her death. Under EGTRRA, for 2004 and thereafter, the GST exemption will be equal to the federal estate tax applicable exclusion amount and will not be indexed for inflation. The GST tax rate also is equal to the maximum federal estate tax rate.

The effect of allocating part or all of an individual's exemption to an otherwise taxable transfer is that it becomes partially or totally free of GST tax. Proper planning calls for allocating one's exemption to make a transfer totally free of GST tax (i.e., to allocate exemption equal to the value of the transfer), rather than make a transfer only partially exempt. For example, suppose in 2009, Grandmother gives $500,000 in an irrevocable trust that provides a life income to her adult grandson and then the remainder to his issue. Grandmother is the transferor and the trust is a skip person. It is a direct skip (i.e., a direct transfer to a skip person) because the transfer is subject to gift taxation (with Grandmother as donor) and the trust is a skip person. If $500,000 of Grandmother's $3,500,000 exemption is allocated to this trust, it will be completely exempt for GST tax purposes.[21]

In the case of lifetime direct skips (such as just illustrated) and "indirect skips" as defined in the law, the tax law automatically allocates enough

[21] The calculation of any GST tax is complicated. Technically, the GST tax rate applied to taxable amounts (e.g., the $500,000 direct skip here), called the *applicable rate,* is the maximum federal estate tax rate times an inclusion ratio. The *inclusion ratio* is 1 minus an applicable fraction. The *applicable fraction* is determined by dividing the value of the property transferred minus any federal or state death taxes and any charitable deduction (or $500,000 in this example) by the amount of the GST tax exemption allocated to the taxable transfer (again, $500,000 in this example). In this illustration, the applicable fraction is 1 ($500,000 ÷ $500,000 = 1) and the inclusion ratio is 0 (1 – 1 [the applicable fraction] = 0). The maximum estate tax rate times zero equals a zero applicable rate, and $500,000 times zero equals zero GST tax. Of course, if no exemption amount is allocated to a taxable transfer, the applicable rate is the maximum federal estate tax rate; if less than the value of the property transferred is allocated, the applicable rate will be greater than zero but less than the maximum rate, depending on the percentage of value transferred that was allocated. However, as noted in the text, it is not good planning to have an inclusion ratio at a rate greater than zero (i.e., to pay a GST tax).

(if available) of the transferor's exemption to make the transfer totally exempt, unless the transferor affirmatively elects otherwise. For certain transfers, exemption also can be retroactively allocated. However, a transferor can determine the allocation pattern by making an allocation on a tax return. An allocation also can be expressed as a formula. Such a formula might provide, for example, that the maximum amount or share is to be allocated to a generation-skipping trust, say, for grandchildren, so that the inclusion ratio (see Footnote 21) does not exceed zero. After EGTRRA (with its increasing GST exemptions), such formula provisions should be reviewed to see that they will not result in funding a generation-skipping trust to a greater extent than the transferor may have originally intended.

Per-Donee Annual Exclusion Direct skips (i.e., direct transfers to a skip person) made outright to a donee that are exempt from gift taxation because of the per-donee annual exclusion are also exempt from the GST tax. Thus, for example, if Grandfather gives $26,000 outright to each of his three adult grandchildren in 2009 (or $78,000 in total), and Grandmother (his wife) agrees to split the gifts, all the gifts would fall under the gift tax annual exclusion and would also be exempt from the GST tax.

However, the situation is more complicated when gifts are made in trust. For direct skip transfers made after March 31, 1988, in trust, even though they qualify for the gift tax annual exclusion (such as through use of Crummey powers, as described in Chapter 27), they will not be exempt from the GST tax unless the trust provides that a single skip person as beneficiary is the only permissible recipient of trust income or corpus during his or her lifetime and has an interest in the trust so that the corpus will be included in the beneficiary's gross estate at his or her death (if the trust does not terminate before his or her death). In effect, this means that for a trust that qualifies for the gift tax annual exclusion also to be exempt on this basis from the GST tax, the trust can have only one skip person beneficiary and can skip only once (normally only one generation), because the corpus (and income) must either be paid to the beneficiary during his or her lifetime or be included in his or her gross estate at death. If more than one skip is desired, the transferor would have to allocate part of his or her exemption to the trust.

Unlimited Exclusion for Transfers for Educational and Medical Expenses In similar fashion, unlimited transfers made directly to educational organizations for tuition or directly to providers for medical expenses for skip persons, which if made during the person's lifetime would be excluded from gift taxation, also are not subject to GST tax. This exclusion applies to taxable distributions from trusts (to be defined next), as well as to outright transfers during the transferor's lifetime.

Grandfathered Trusts When the GST tax system was substantially revised in 1986, certain existing trusts were grandfathered and made exempt from GST taxation. These are irrevocable trusts created on or before September 25, 1985, and certain revocable trusts or testamentary trusts, if the person died before 1987.

Types of Generation-Skipping Transfers (Taxable Transfers)

Direct Skips These are transfers of an interest in property directly to a skip person (a natural person or a trust meeting the requirements to be a skip person) that are subject to either gift tax or estate tax. The taxable amount is the value of the property received by the transferee (the skip person), and any GST tax must be paid by the transferor.[22]

Taxable Terminations These are terminations by death, lapse of time, release of a power, or otherwise of an interest in property held in trust, unless immediately after such termination a non-skip person has an interest in the property or at no time after such termination can a distribution, including distributions on termination, be made from such trust to a skip person. The taxable amount is the value of the property with respect to which the taxable termination occurred, reduced by certain allowable expenses. Any GST tax payable must be paid by the trustee.

> **CASE EXAMPLE**
>
> Suppose that Mrs. Johnson, a widow with a sizeable estate, has two adult children, a son and a daughter, each of whom also has two children. Both the son and daughter are successful in their careers, and they and their spouses are accumulating good-sized estates on their own. Therefore, Mrs. Johnson has decided that in her will, she will leave her residuary estate (net estate) in equal trusts, for each of her children. The terms of these trusts provide that trust income is to be paid to or among the child, the child's children, or their issue, or accumulated in the trust at an independent trustee's sole discretion (i.e., a sprinkle or spray power over income). At each child's death, the corpus of his or her trust will pass outright to that child's children (Mrs. Johnson's grandchildren) or their issue in equal shares. These would be generation-skipping trusts (assuming Mrs. Johnson's son

[22] Except for direct skips from trusts, in which case, the tax is paid by the trustee.

and daughter are alive when the transfer is made, i.e., when Mrs. Johnson dies), and the grandchildren would be skip persons.

Assume now that Mrs. Johnson dies, leaving a residuary estate (after debts, expenses, and federal estate and other death taxes on her estate) of $8,000,000, so that $4,000,000 funds the trusts for each child. Furthermore, suppose that after 20 years, her son dies, when the corpus of his trusts have grown to $9,000,000. Upon the son's death, there would be a taxable termination of his interest in the trusts, and this would cause the then-fair market value of the corpus to be a generation-skipping transfer.

In this situation, as a planning matter, it normally would have been better for Mrs. Johnson's executor after her death to have divided the children's trusts into two or more trusts (under authority in the will to do so) and then allocate enough of Mrs. Johnson's GST exemption to one or more trusts to make the trusts completely exempt from GST tax. Then, each child might have been given a general power of appointment over the corpus of the other (nonexempt) trusts or given the property outright.

Taxable Distributions These are any distributions from a trust to a skip person. The taxable amount is the value of the property received by the transferee (skip person), minus certain expenses. The transferee is liable for any GST tax. If, for example, the trusts created after Mrs. Johnson's death in the previous example had made distributions to one of her grandchildren other than for educational or medical expenses, it would have been a taxable distribution.

Estate Tax Inclusion Period (ETIP)

When an individual makes a lifetime transfer and retains an interest in the property such that it would be included in his or her gross estate if the individual died immediately, no allocation of the GST exemption can be made until the earlier of the end of the period during which the property could be included in the individual's gross estate if he or she died (the estate tax inclusion period) or the individual's death. This rule can affect use of the GST exemption in connection with gifts with a retained income or use interest. For example, if Grandfather sets up a 10-year QPRT, as described in Chapter 27, and designates his granddaughter as the remainderperson to receive the residence after the 10-year period, he generally cannot allocate any of his exemption to the trust until the earlier of his death or the end of the 10-year period.

Possible Estate Tax Changes

As stated earlier in this chapter, many commentators believe changes will be made in the estate tax system before 2010 to avoid estate tax repeal, the consequences of EGTRRA's sunset provision, and for other reasons. Of course, as of this writing no one can be certain of such changes, particularly in the area of tax legislation, but the following are considered likely to occur. Naturally, other changes also may be made.

No Estate Tax Repeal, Applicable Exclusion, and Tax Rate

The estate tax (and GST tax) will not be repealed in 2010, the applicable exclusion amount probably willl remain at the present $3,500,000 (with the corresponding unified credit at $1,455,800), and the estate tax top rate probably will remain at 45 persent.

Transferability (Portability) of Unused Unified Credit Between Spouses

To simplify estate planning, it is very possible that the law will be changed to allow any unused unified credit at the death of the first spouse to die to be transferred to the surviving spouse and added to his or her own unified credit. This effectively would presently give married couples a combined $7,000,000 applicable exclusion amount, no matter who dies first. This would avoid the need, purely for estate tax reasons, for credit-shelter trusts and gifts between spouses so each spouse's estate can use his or her full unified credit as described in Chapter 28.

27

Lifetime Giving and Other Intrafamily Techniques

Competence Objectives for This Chapter After reading this chapter, planners should understand:

- The advantages and limitations of making lifetime gifts
- Methods of making gifts to minors
- The tax treatment of gifts between spouses and the gift tax marital deduction
- The uses of gifts of remainder interests with retained use or income interests
- The nature and uses of qualified personal residence trusts (QPRTs)
- The nature and uses of grantor retained annuity trusts (GRATs)
- The nature of family limited partnerships (FLPs) and the uses of FLPs and other entities in making gifts
- The idea of sales within the family as an estate planning technique
- Sales to defective grantor trusts
- Sales paid for by self-canceling installment notes (SCINs)
- Loans within the family as an estate planning technique

Making lifetime gifts is an important estate planning strategy. There are tax and nontax advantages for doing so. However, lifetime giving is not an unmixed blessing, and there are limitations and caveats that should be considered. Certain methods of selling property to family members and loans to family members also are described in this chapter.

Making Lifetime (*Inter Vivos*) Gifts to Noncharitable Donees

Advantages of Lifetime Gifts

Lifetime gifts can be an attractive estate tax-saving (and GST tax-saving) technique under the right conditions. They can have the following advantages over bequeathing property at death.

No Tax on Annual Exclusion Gifts Amounts within the per-donee gift tax annual exclusion and unlimited exclusion for direct payments of tuition and medical expenses will escape gift taxation and will not be in the donor's gross estate. Similar outright transfers also will avoid the GST tax; transfers in trust may do so if they meet the requirements for such trusts. Much property can escape all transfer taxation this way.

Post-Gift Appreciation Escapes Taxation Future appreciation in the value of gift property will escape taxation in the donor's estate.

Shifting Income from Gift Property Taxable income and realized and recognized capital gains from gift property will be transferred to the donee for income tax purposes.

Reduced Probate Costs Estate administration expenses, which generally are based on the probate estate, will be reduced.

Reduced State Death Taxes Similarly, state death taxes can be saved.

Any Gift Taxes Paid Are Removed from the Gross Estate For gifts made more than three years before death, gift taxes paid by the donor are not in the donor's gross estate at death. On the other hand, if the estate and GST taxes should be repealed, or if the estate should be less than the exemption amounts at death any gift taxes paid would not reduce any estate or GST taxes. In effect, any gift taxes actually paid would be a loss to the estate owner and his or her heirs in these unlikely situations.

Gift Taxes Are Tax-Exclusive, While Estate Taxes Are Tax-Inclusive This is really another way of making the previous point. The idea is that the gift tax is paid by the donor and the full gift goes to the donee (tax-exclusive), while the estate tax is paid by the executor on the full taxable estate, with only the balance going to the heirs (tax-inclusive). In effect, estate tax is paid on the tax itself, while this is not so with the gift tax.

Valuation Discounts May Be Taken in Certain Cases The valuation discounts described in Chapter 26 may be available, depending on the circumstances.

Of course, valuation discounts also can be taken for federal estate tax purposes, but they are commonly associated with lifetime gifts.

Nontax Personal Advantages Finally, donors can enjoy all the personal and family advantages of their generosity during their lifetimes. Also, donees can receive the gift property now when it might be needed the most. The importance of such nontax factors depends on individual circumstances. These might include the age and health of the donor; the size of the estate; the ages, educational and other needs, and marital statuses of potential donees; and other personal considerations.

Limitations and Caveats Concerning Lifetime Gifts

No One Knows What the Future May Hold Donors should be careful that they can do without the gift property, particularly during retirement. What if their health deteriorates? What if they find themselves in an expensive custodial care situation without adequate LTC insurance? What if the stock market plummets? What if interest rates decline or rise precipitously? What if some present source or sources of income should dry up in the event of career difficulties or economic recession, or even depression?

Uncertainties Created by EGTRRA and Potential Transfer Tax Reform Given the uncertain future structure of the transfer tax system, longer applicable exclusion amounts for the estate tax but a level $1,000,000 excluded amount for the gift tax, and uncertain maximum transfer tax rates in general, it can be argued that it is better planning to "pay no tax before its time."

Marital Situations If donors are considering giving assets to their spouses, what would happen if they separated, divorced, or stayed together and had marital difficulties? In some cases, this may be an issue; in others, not. Similarly, the marital situation of other potential donees (e.g., children) may affect how and when gifts may be made to them. For example, one normally would not want a portion of gift property to end up in the hands of a donee's ex-spouse (such as, for example, in the form of commingled marital property).

Liquidity Considerations Donors should be careful about giving away liquid assets if their estates may have liquidity problems. On the other hand, there are various planning techniques for providing liquidity to an estate. In addition, owners of closely held business interests who are planning to have their estates take advantage of tax provisions, such as Section 6166 or Section 303, should take care that they do not give away so much of their closely held stock or other business interest that their estates cannot qualify for these favorable provisions.

Control Considerations Owners of closely held corporation stock (or other business interests) should consider whether they are impairing their control over the corporation by gifts of stock. Sometimes, a controlling owner wants to relinquish control to family members during his or her lifetime; however, often he or she does not.

Personal Impact on Donees Some family members actually may be harmed by having control over too much property too soon—or even ever. This is an individual matter and depends on the personalities and characters of the people involved. Also, in making gifts to minors, it is difficult to know what kind of people they will grow up to be or whom they may marry.

Gift Taxes May Have to Be Paid Now This may be true for larger gifts that exceed available exclusions and use up the gift tax unified credit. Actual payment of gift taxes not only involves the uncertainties already mentioned, but also results in loss of the time value of money on the gift tax paid.

Postgift Depreciation May Enhance Taxation Obviously, the advantage of removal of postgift appreciation from the gross estate applies only if there is appreciation. If the value of gifted property declines, gift tax will have been paid or unified credit used at a value greater than was removed from the gross estate.

No Step-up in Basis at Death for Gift Property Hence, the donee loses the present step-up in basis at death and may face larger capital gains (or lower capital losses) on a subsequent sale or exchange of the property. However, the impact of this issue may depend on many factors, including what the donee does with the gift property, the age of the donor, and the relationship between estate tax and capital gains tax rates.

Some Observations on Lifetime Gifts

Commentators have suggested that in this uncertain tax environment people who normally would be making lifetime gifts for all the reasons previously noted should continue to do so. However, this generally should be done without actually incurring gift taxes. Thus, gifts within the annual exclusion and tuition and medical exclusions can be made. Transfer techniques that do not result in any taxable gifts at all also are possibilities. These include "zeroed out" GRATs, sales to defective grantor trusts, intrafamily loans, and self-canceling installment notes, and are discussed later in this chapter. Finally, gifts made at a "discount," hopefully within the gift tax applicable exclusion amount, such as QPRTs, and also gifts of FLPs, may be logical strategies.

Gifts to Minors—General Considerations

People frequently want to make gifts to minors—children or grandchildren, for example. Because the donees are minors and, hence, usually cannot deal with the property during their minority (generally until age 18), special arrangements often are made for such gifts. Donors also may want to defer control over gift property until younger donees reach an age when it is presumed they will be more mature and experienced in managing money. Finally, some donors want to skip generations with such gifts.

Methods for Making Gifts to Minors

Outright Gifts Some kinds of property may conveniently be given outright to minors, such as savings accounts, U.S. series EE savings bonds, and life insurance on the minor's life. However, outright gifts of other kinds of property may cause problems because outsiders normally are not willing to deal with minors in managing the property, since minors generally are not legally competent to contract. Of course, a legal guardian could be appointed for minors, but guardianship tends to be inflexible and expensive, and donors generally prefer other methods. Therefore, outright gifts are not really a practical method for structuring substantial, long-term giving programs for minors.

Uniform Transfers (Gifts) to Minors Act The UTMA or the original UGMA is a popular way to make gifts of securities and other property to minors. Laws of this type have been enacted in all states and the District of Columbia. In general, they provide for the registration of securities and brokerage accounts, life insurance policies, annuity contracts, mutual funds, money market accounts, and other investments a "prudent person" would make[1] in the name of an adult to act as custodian of the property for the minor. As an example, a father might give stock to his minor son, with the boy's adult aunt named as custodian for the minor-donee under the particular state's UTMA.

This arrangement technically creates a custodianship, not a trust. The custodianship operates according to the terms of the state law under which it was created, and the donor cannot change those terms. The gift property is held by the custodian, who manages, invests, and reinvests it for the minor's benefit. The custodian can apply the property or the income from it for the benefit of the minor (including for educational expenses) or accumulate it in the custodian's sole discretion. To the extent that the property and income

[1] The former UGMA limited eligible assets to a specific list, such as securities, life insurance and annuity contracts, and money.

are not expended for the minor's benefit, they must be delivered or paid over to the minor when he or she reaches majority, which generally is specified in the law to be age 21. If the minor dies before attaining majority, the property and income must go to his or her estate. Thus, a possible disadvantage of this method is the forced distribution of the property and accumulated income to the former minor at majority.

The UTMA simplifies making gifts to minors. No formal trust agreement is required. Income and capital gains are taxable to the minor, unless the income is used to satisfy a legal obligation to support the minor. Also, the donor gets full use of the gift tax annual exclusion, even though the custodian may accumulate income for the minor. Thus, to continue the previous example, if a father gave $13,000 worth of stock to his son in 2009 under his state's UTMA, all $13,000 would qualify for the gift tax annual exclusion and no taxable gift would result. Also, the gift property would be removed from the donor's gross estate. However, if the donor acts as custodian and dies before the minor reaches majority, the property will be in the donor's gross estate because the donor-custodian will have made a transfer with a retained power to alter or amend the enjoyment of the transferred property (see Chapter 26).

Trusts for Minors Under Section 2503(c) Under this section of the code, a donor can have full use of the annual exclusion for gifts to a minor in trust. Thus, if a father transfers $13,000 of stock in 2009 to an irrevocable trust with his minor son as beneficiary and the trust meets the requirements of Section 2503(c), the full $13,000 will qualify for the annual exclusion.

To receive this treatment, Section 2503(c) requires that trust income and principal may be expended by the trustee for or on behalf of the beneficiary until the minor reaches age 21. Second, any amounts remaining in the trust when the beneficiary becomes 21 must be distributed or made available to the beneficiary at that time. This may be a disadvantage because donors may prefer to postpone distribution until after age 21 or perhaps in installments, such as one-third at 25, one-third at 30, and the final third at 35.

It is permissible for the trust itself to continue beyond age 21, provided the beneficiary has the power (even for only a limited period) to obtain outright the property and any accumulated income in the trust at majority. The trust terms might give the beneficiary such a right for a brief period after the beneficiary turns age 21, in the hope that he or she may not exercise it, and then the irrevocable trust can continue for whatever period the original grantor specified in the terms of the trust. (This is not possible for UTMA gifts.) Third, if the beneficiary dies prior to age 21, the trust property must go to the beneficiary's estate or as the beneficiary designates. The gift property normally will be removed from the donor's gross estate.

Again, however, the grantor (donor) should not be a trustee because the same estate tax principle applies here as under UTMA gifts, since the trustee must have discretionary power to expend trust corpus or income for the minor's benefit before age 21. After age 21, the trust terms may be different if the trust continues. Income and capital gains from these trusts are taxable to the trust for federal income tax purposes, if accumulated, and to the beneficiary, if distributed to him or her.[2]

Use of Regular Trusts Gifts can be made to minors through regular irrevocable trusts, sometimes called Section 2503(b) trusts, the same as they can to anyone else. Trusts enable the grantor-donor to set the terms of the gift within the rules of the state's trust law. A trust other than a Section 2503(c) trust does not have to make the corpus available when a beneficiary reaches majority or even, in many cases, for many years (or even generations) thereafter. Donors often want to use long-term (or even generation-skipping) trusts when planning for a substantial lifetime giving program.

The practical problems are that a formal trust must be established and, depending on the size of the gift and terms of the trust, the donor may not be able to take full advantage of the gift tax annual exclusion. This is because, without a so-called Crummey power (described next), only a part or none of each gift to the trust will be considered a gift of a present interest to the donee (the trust beneficiary or beneficiaries), and only a present interest will qualify for the annual exclusion.

If the terms of a trust call for the accumulation of trust income or for discretion by the trustee in paying trust income to or for one or more beneficiaries (e.g., a sprinkle or spray power), no part of a gift to the trust would be a present interest to any specific beneficiary. If a trust requires the current distribution of its income to a trust beneficiary or beneficiaries, only a part of each gift would be a gift of a present interest (measured by the part representing the mandatory income interest), and the remainder would be a future interest. This was illustrated in Chapter 25. However, a mandatory income requirement may not be suitable for long-term trusts for minors. Also, it means that the $13,000 in 2009 (indexed for inflation) annual exclusion will never be able to shelter the entire annual gifts to the trust.

[2] If trust income is accumulated and taxable to the trust, the kiddie tax on unearned income of minors age 18 or under, or of students under age 24 will not apply. The kiddie tax would apply to UTMA gifts for minors since custodianship income is taxed to the minor. Note also that trust income used to discharge a legal obligation to support a minor may be taxed to the person with that obligation.

Regular (Section 2503[b]) Trusts with Crummey Powers The famous Crummey case[3] and its eventual acceptance by the IRS gave estate planners a possible solution to the problems of making gifts in trust so that the whole gift (up to certain limits) will be a gift of a present interest and hence qualify for the annual exclusion. This solution involves having a *Crummey power* in these trusts.

The terms of an irrevocable trust may give the trust beneficiary or each beneficiary (no matter how young) the noncumulative right each year to withdraw his or her pro rata share of that year's gift to the trust up to an amount equal to the annual exclusion; or an amount equal to twice the annual exclusion if gift splitting is contemplated. This right to withdraw normally is available for only a brief period during the year, such as 30 days.

This withdrawal right is a Crummey power and is intended to assure an annual exclusion for each year's gift to the trust up to the limit for each beneficiary with a Crummey power. This is because each beneficiary can get the immediate possession, use, or enjoyment of his or her share of the gift by withdrawing it. However, even though the purpose of a Crummey power is to get the annual exclusion for the grantor, it must be a real power and not just illusory. Thus, the powerholder(s)—trust beneficiary or beneficiaries—must actually possess the withdrawal right for a reasonable period (often 30 days), must be notified of it, and there must be assets in the trust with which to satisfy the power if it were to be exercised.

Technically, Crummey withdrawal rights are general powers of appointment over the property subject to withdrawal. If these rights are not exercised during the limited withdrawal period and are noncumulative, it represents the lapse in that year of a general power of appointment over the property subject to withdrawal. These might be called *annually lapsing powers.* The tax code provides that lapses of general powers each year for each beneficiary that do not exceed the larger of $5,000 or 5 percent of the value of the property from which the powers could have been exercised are not a *release* of the powers, which might be a taxable event. The amount covered by this so-called 5 and 5 power is often referred to as the *lapse protected amount,* and lapses within this amount will not give rise to any gift or estate tax consequences for the powerholder. However, lapses in a year for a powerholder (e.g., beneficiary) that exceed the larger of $5,000 or 5 percent of corpus are considered *releases* of a general power of appointment, and may give rise to

[3] Since Crummey powers are so commonly used and widely discussed in estate planning, the citation for the Crummey case is *Crummey v. Commissioner,* 397 F.2d 82 (9th Cir. 1968), rev 'g 25 T.C.M. 772 (1966).

taxable gifts by the powerholder to other trust beneficiaries and inclusion of corpus in the powerholder's gross estate upon his or her death, depending on the terms of the trust.

One planning approach to this issue is to limit the annual amount of the Crummey power to the $5,000 or 5 percent of corpus lapse potential amount even though it may be less than the annual exclusion. Another approach is not to limit the Crummey power (thus getting the full annual exclusion), but with the gift and estate tax issues just noted. The gift tax issue can be solved by giving the powerholder a testimentory power of appointment over the excess lapsed amount, but he estate tax issue remains. Also, if the withdrawal rights are cumulative over the duration of the trust and do not lapse if not exercised within the limited withdrawal period (other than lapsing to the extent of the greater of $5,000 or 5 percent of corpus each year), they are called *hanging powers.* Here the full annual exclusion will also be available each year, but the excess withdrawal right will remain with the beneficiaries. Such powers may be suggested by some planners.

Thus, regular irrevocable trusts with Crummey powers may produce some attractive results. They can result in shifting or accumulating trust income for income tax purposes, in removing trust property from the donor's gross estate for estate tax purposes, and normally in no taxable gifts being made because of the gift tax annual exclusion. The trustee also can be given discretionary power to distribute income and corpus to the beneficiaries, subject to an ascertainable standard or at an independent trustee's sole discretion. Thus, funds could be provided for the beneficiaries' educational needs or other needs. Finally, such trusts can continue for many years after the beneficiaries reach majority—or even for the beneficiaries' lifetimes, depending on the desires of the creator of the trust. Thus, they could be generation-skipping trusts if a trust meets the requirements for a GST annual exclusion trust or if the grantor allocates enough of his or her GST exemption to the trust to make it exempt.

Income Tax Considerations Trust income or income from property held for a minor under a UTMA that is used to discharge a parent's legal obligation to support the minor will be taxed to the parent. What a parent's support obligation is in a given case depends on the law of the state in which they live and may vary with the circumstances of the parents.

Gifts Between Spouses

There is an unlimited federal gift tax marital deduction for qualifying gifts between spouses (when the donee spouse is a U.S. citizen). Thus, gifts between spouses are gift tax–free.

Gifts of Remainder Interests with Retained Use or Income Interests

We saw in Chapter 26 that Chapter 14 of the IRC effectively restricts gifts in trust of remainder interests to family members, with the retention of interests in the trust by the transferor (donor) to the following types of transfers.

Personal Residence Trusts (PRTs) These are irrevocable trusts under which the grantor transfers one personal residence to the trust and retains the right to use and occupy the residence for a period of years, and at the end of this period the residence goes to a remainderperson. In the case of a PRT, the trust cannot hold any other assets and the residence cannot be sold during the term. As a result, PRTs are inflexible and normally QPRTs are used.

Qualified Personal Residence Trusts (QPRTs) These are irrevocable trusts under which the grantor transfers one personal residence per trust (either a principal residence or one other residence of the grantor) to the trust, retains a term interest in the trust (i.e., the right to use or occupy the residence for a period of years), and grants a remainder interest in the trust to a family member or members at the end of the term period. In effect, the grantor is giving away his or her personal residence to family members but retaining the right to live in it for a fixed period of years.

The purpose is to give away the residence and hopefully get it out of the grantor's gross estate at a reduced gift tax value. The gift tax value is the fair market value of the residence minus both the value of the retained-use interest for the term of years selected, calculated according to the Section 7520 rates, and the actuarial value of a contingent reversionary interest in the event the grantor dies during the term of years that is usually retained by the grantor. Also, any postgift appreciation in the value of the residence is removed from the grantor's gross estate. The result is a substantially reduced transfer tax cost of moving the residence to family members (e.g., children), but still allowing the grantor to use the residence for the term period (and even beyond, with proper planning).

The grantor retains the right to use and occupy the personal residence for a period of years (the term interest), such as 10 or 15 years. The longer the period selected, the greater will be the value of the retained term interest and the smaller will be the taxable gift remainder interest. However, if the grantor dies during the term period, the full value of the property will be in his or her gross estate as a transfer with a retained interest that did not in fact end before his or her death. Therefore, the period selected normally is one that the grantor reasonably expects to survive. This, of course, can never be known for sure. Grantors often also retain the power in their will to direct how the QPRT property will be distributed (or it may revert to his or her probate estate) in the event of the grantor's death before the end of the term period. This is a contingent reversionary interest, which has an actuarial value that also reduces the value of the taxable gift.[4] To get the full tax benefits of a QPRT, the grantor must survive the term period. However, even if he or she does not, the grantor would appear to be in no worse position than he or she would have been had no QPRT been created in the first place and the homeowner had simply lived in the residence until his or her death.

Assuming the grantor survives the term period, the residence will pass to the QPRT's remainder beneficiary or beneficiaries or continue in trust for them. If the grantor wants to continue to live in the residence after the term period ends, the grantor can negotiate a lease for the residence from the remainderperson, or from the trustee of a continuing trust for the remainderperson, at a fair market rental. As a planning matter, it usually is an attractive technique to provide that the residence will remain in a continuing irrevocable grantor trust for the remainderperson after the term period ends. This way, lease payments by the grantor will not be taxable income to the remainderperson (since it is a grantor trust for income tax purposes), will not be gifts (assuming they reflect fair market rental value), and in effect will be removed from the grantor's gross estate at his or her death.[5]

The main disadvantage of QPRTs is that the family member remainderperson(s) does not get a stepped-up income tax basis in the residence at the grantor's death.

An Illustration of a QPRT Assume that Alexia Lee-Smith, age 65, owns in her name a condominium apartment as her principal residence worth $500,000 and a second residence in the country with a value of $300,000. Alexia has paid off the mortgages on both residences. Her basis in the apartment is $100,000 and in the country home is $125,000. Over the years, these properties have increased in value at an average annual compound rate of about 5 percent. Alexia is married and she has a 30-year-old daughter, D. Alexia and her husband are estimated to be in the top federal estate tax bracket, and

[4]Technically, such a contingent reversionary interest also reduces the value of a fixed-term interest (say, for 10 years), since now the interest is for the shorter of the grantor's life or the fixed period. However, the combined value of the term interest and the contingent reversion will be substantially larger than the value of a fixed-term interest alone. Retention of contingent reversionary interests is permitted for QPRTs and PRTs, but not for qualified interests (e.g., GRATs).

[5]As explained in Chapter 10, such a *defective grantor trust* is an irrevocable trust where the grantor is treated as owner of the trust corpus for income tax purposes, but not for estate tax purposes.

neither has made any prior taxable gifts. They would like to continue to use the residences until they die.

Assume, Alexia places each of these residences in a separate QPRT with the irrevocable grantor trusts continuing for D as remainderpersons. Under these QPRTs, Alexia retains the right to use the residences for 10 years (or until her prior death) and further retains the right to direct in her will how the residences will pass in the event of her death during the 10-year period. Alexia further agrees with the trustee that she will be able to lease either or both of the residences at fair market rental value following the 10-year term. During the 10-year period, Alexia will make additional cash contributions to the QPRTs to pay expenses of the properties (real estate taxes, insurance, maintenance expenses, etc.).

Under these facts, and assuming the applicable Section 7520 rate and actuarial value, Alexia will have has made the following combined taxable gifts of the remainder interests:

Value of the residences	$800,000
Value of 10-year retained term interests	–351,520
Value of contingent reversions	–148,880
Taxable transfer and gift (value of remainder interests)	$299,600
Tentative gift tax	$87,664
Applicable credit amount (unified credit) used (out of a total of $345,800	–87,664
Federal gift tax payable	$0

On the other hand, if Alexia simply retains ownership of these residences until her death (say, at age 80) and the properties continue to appreciate at an average annual compound rate of 5 percent, they will be valued in her gross estate at about $1,663,000.[6]

Grantor-Retained Annuity Trusts (GRATs) A GRAT is an irrevocable trust that pays a fixed amount (either a dollar amount or a fixed percentage of the initial fair market value of the property transferred to the GRAT) to the grantor for a specified period (the annuity period). Then the remaining trust corpus is distributed to designated trust beneficiaries (normally family members) or to trusts for them as remainderperson(s). The annuity period normally is for a specified term of years. If the grantor dies during the annuity period, any remaining payments are made to his or her estate or possibly to his or her spouse. Since GRATs are qualified interests under Section 2702, the value of the annuity payments is determined by using Section 7520 rates, rather than being valued at zero. GRATs can be funded with any kind of

[6] Of course, if Alexia's husband survives her, her estate can take a marital deduction, but then the value ultimately will be in her husband's taxable estate.

property, often with marketable securities, real estate, closely held stock, and partnership interests, among others. GRATs normally are grantor trusts.

When a GRAT is created, the taxable gift, if any, is measured by the fair market value of the property placed in the trust minus the value of the grantor's retained annuity interest. Thus, the greater the annuity payout selected, the higher will be the value of the retained interest, and the lower the gift tax value. In fact, it is possible today to set the annuity payments high enough so that at the creation of the GRAT, the actuarial value of the remainder interest, and hence the gift tax value, would be zero or, to be conservative, very low. This is referred to as "zeroing-out a GRAT." Such GRATs are often called "Walton GRATs" after the case that allowed it.

However, the annuity payments come back to the grantor and potentially add to his or her gross estate. If the grantor survives the annuity period, any remaining property in the GRAT is removed from his or her gross estate at no gift tax cost. On the other hand, if the grantor dies during the annuity period, the GRAT corpus will be partly or wholly in his or her gross estate. Thus, as in the case of the QPRT, the annuity period normally is selected with the expectation that the grantor will survive it. Since GRATs normally are wholly grantor trusts for income tax purposes, the grantor is taxed on the income of the trust, but is not taxed on the annuity payments.

The economics of GRATs are largely an investment play. If the total return on the assets in a GRAT exceeds the Section 7520 rate used in calculating the annuity interests (sometimes called the "hurdle rate"), the GRAT will benefit the grantor's family (remainderpersons). Thus, GRATs often are funded with hopefully rapidly appreciating or high-yielding assets. If total return of the GRAT is about the same or less than the Section 7520 rate, it will be essentially a wash. Thus, assuming a "zeroed-out GRAT," even if the total return should fall below the Section 7520 rate (or be negative), the annuity payments will simply exhaust the GRAT corpus and nothing will pass to the remainderpersons. However, even in this case, little (i.e., the costs of setting up and administering the GRAT) would be lost, since the grantor would simply get his or her property back without having made a taxable gift.[7] Thus, "zeroed-out GRATs" can be attractive, particularly considering the current transfer-tax uncertainties.

[7] In the Walton case, in 1993, Mrs. Audrey Walton transferred more than $100 million of Wal-Mart stock to each of two GRATs (more than $200 million in all). The GRATs were for a two-year term, with annuity payments to Mrs. Walton of 49.35 percent of the initial trust corpus the first year and 59.22 percent in the second. At the end of the two-year term, any assets in the GRATs would go to Mrs. Walton's daughters. If Mrs. Walton died during the two-year term, any remaining annuity payments would be made to her estate. These annuity payments were intended to "zero-out" these GRATs. The IRS contended the GRATs could not be "zeroed-out" and that a taxable gift was made by Mrs. Walton. The tax court

An Illustration of a Zeroed-out GRAT Suppose John Markowitz, age 65 and in good health, has a sizable estate and owns a large amount of his employer's stock, which has had good growth over the years. John decides to transfer $750,000 of this stock to an irrevocable trust (a GRAT) that will pay him an annuity of $106,783 per year for 10 years. If John should die during the 10-year term, the remaining annuity payments would go to his estate. At the end of this annuity period, the trust corpus is required to be paid to his son, Harry. Furthermore, assume the total return on the common stock averages 10 percent per year over the 10-year period and the Section 7520 rate ("hurdle rate") was 7 percent when the trust was created.

Given the Section 7520 rate of 7 percent, the $106,783 annuity payment will be just enough to cause the actuarial value of the remainder interest (to Harry) at creation of the GRAT to equal zero (or be "zeroed-out"). Therefore, there will be no taxable gift at creation of the GRAT. However, the GRAT's corpus (the common stock) actually produces a 10 percent total return (3 percentage points over the theoretical Section 7520 rate).[8] Therefore, when the 10-year annuity period ends, there actually will be about $243,463 in the GRAT to go to Harry without any transfer tax cost.

Grantor-Retained Unitrusts (GRUTs) These are like GRATs, except that the periodic amount to the grantor is expressed as a fixed percentage of the fair market value of the trust assets valued annually.

Retained Term Interest in Certain Tangible Property A grantor can retain an interest for a period of years in nondepreciable tangible property (such as paintings, other art objects, and bare land) with the remainder going to a family member. The value of the term interest reduces the value of the gift.

Use of FLPs or Other Entities in Making Gifts For many years, property owners have placed assets in various types of entities, such as partnerships, closely held corporations, and, more recently, LLCs, so the assets could be managed in the interest of family members. Various family members may be given ownership interests in the entity, but often, only certain family members control the entity. Limited partnerships (LPs)[9], which are controlled by

unanimously held to the contrary and said that the GRATs effectively could be "zeroed-out." *Est. of Walton v. Comm.*, 115 TC No. 41 (2000). In the actual Walton situation, however, the annuity payments to Mrs. Walton exhausted the GRATs and nothing actually went to her daughters.

[8] As indicated in Chapter 3, in valuing remainder interests, term interests, life estates, and other interests, the IRS in effect assumes the assets behind these interests will earn the Section 7520 rate. In fact, however, they actually may earn more or less than this rate.

[9] Limited partnerships (LPs) are partnerships with at least one general partner (who has management control over partnership affairs and unlimited liability for partnership debts) and one

one or a few family members and where substantially all the limited partners are family members, commonly called *family limited partnerships* (FLPs), often are employed as such an entity and will be used as the basis of this discussion. However, LLCs[10] also are used for this purpose.

Basic Concepts FLPs can be used in a number of ways. However, a traditional idea often has been for a senior family member or members (e.g., mother, father, or both) to set up a limited partnership (LP) to which the senior member contributes property (e.g., real estate, closely held business interests, or marketable securities) in return for a general partnership interest and a limited partnership interest. Younger family members may contribute small amounts (e.g., cash) to the LP in return for a small limited partnership interest.[11] Thus, once the LP is formed, the senior member (let us say, mother) has a general partnership interest and also a substantial limited partnership interest, while the other partners (let us say, children) have small limited partnership interests. Mother and children in this example own the partnership and are the partners, while the partnership owns the property contributed to it.[12] Mother, as general partner, controls the management of the LP. The limited partners lack control and their interests lack marketability because of the nature of limited partnership interests in an LP.

The general partner has unlimited liability for partnership debts, including tort liability. However, while one or more individuals can be the general partner (mother in our example), the general partner also could be another flow-through entity (such as an S corporation or a limited liability company)

or more limited partners (who do not have management control but have limited for partnership debts) and which are established under state law and registered as such. These and other forms of business organization are described in Chapter 31.

[10] Limited liability companies (LLCs) are a newer form of business organization created under state law. All states now have LLC statutes. These are a cross between corporations and partnerships. They are pass-through entities for income tax purposes (like partnerships), but give their members (owners) limited liability and management control (if desired) like corporations. They have become popular as a form of business entity.

[11] To be a partnership, an entity must have at least two partners; in an LP, at least one must be a general partner.

[12] Thus, the partners (mother and children in this example) own partnership interests that have values, and the partnership itself owns the assets inside the partnership, which also have values. The value of a partner's partnership interest is affected not only by his or her pro rata share of the net fair market value of the assets inside the partnership (i.e., liquidation value), but also by the partner's rights and obligations under the partnership agreement. These rights and obligations determine the ability of partners to reap the benefits of the partnership's assets and operations. Thus, the value of the partnership interests of limited partners in an FLP normally will be considerably less than their pro rata share of the net fair market value of partnership assets because of restrictions or limits on the ability of limited partners to control partnership affairs and to dispose of their interests.

owned by an individual (or individuals) or a combination of individuals and a flow-through entity so that no one person would have a controlling interest.[13] Such flow-through entities (see Chapter 31) generally will protect an individual owner of the entity from personal liability beyond his or her investment in the entity.

If the partners—usually senior family members—contribute appreciated property to the partnership, there is no capital gain on the exchange of the property for partnership interests. Instead, the contributing partner gets a carryover basis in his or her partnership interest.

After an FLP is formed, the senior family members normally make gifts of some or all of their limited partnership interest to younger family members or to trusts for their benefit. The value of these gift LP interests generally is substantially discounted from the pro rata value of the partnership assets underlying those interests.

Purposes of FLPs FLPs can have a number of tax and nontax purposes, such as the following.

Management of Family Assets: The general partner (or managing member of an LLC) has control over the management of partnership assets and thus can centralize and effectively manage family wealth.

Instruct Younger Family Members in Financial Affairs: A related purpose may be to provide an opportunity for more experienced family members to involve and educate less experienced family members in business and financial matters.

Secure Substantial Valuation Discounts for Tax Purposes: As has been explained in this chapter and in Chapter 26, substantial valuation discounts normally can be taken for gift tax and perhaps estate tax purposes. The discounts are based on lack of control and lack of marketability of limited partnership interests.

Creditor Protection: The FLP agreement may restrict the ability of limited partners to assign or pledge their interests as collateral. Also, even if a limited partner's creditors do levy against his or her partnership interest, under the Revised Uniform Limited Partnership Act (RULPA) (see Chapter 31), generally all a creditor can get is a charging order against the interest. This essentially allows the creditor the right to receive whatever partnership distributions are made to the limited partner (distributions that normally are controlled by the general partner).

[13] There can be 100 percent owned single-stockholder S corporations. Also, many state laws permit single-member LLCs.

Protection Against Marital Claims: In a similar vein, if a limited partner has marital difficulties, normally all the former spouse could receive in a divorce settlement or equitable distribution would be an assignee's interest in the limited partner's interest (or possibly a limited partner's interest), which again would be subject to the general partner's control. Also, an LP interest normally can be easily identified as nonmarital gift property.

Limitations of FLPs These arrangements can be complex, with commensurate cost of setting them up. They normally are used for substantial property interests. Also, care should be taken in planning and drafting these agreements so that they do not run afoul of various tax law provisions, thereby causing unwanted tax consequences. Competent legal counsel should be used in drafting them. Finally, it must be recognized that the IRS and others are watching FLPs closely. Hence, care should be taken in establishing these arrangements.

An Illustration Let us assume Henry Chang, age 60, owns a profitable apartment house with a net fair market value of $4 million and an adjusted basis of $800,000 in his own name. Henry is married to Tracy, age 56, and together they have sizeable gross estates. Neither Henry nor Tracy has made any prior taxable gifts. Henry and Tracy have two adult children and four grandchildren. Henry has decided to make substantial lifetime gifts to his children to help them financially now and to teach them the real estate business, but he would like to keep control of the management of his property. He also wants to keep any sizeable gifts within his and Tracy's applicable exclusion amounts. Tracy is willing to split any lifetime gifts. Therefore, Henry decides to transfer the apartment house to a family limited partnership in exchange for a 1 percent general partnership interest and a 97 percent limited partnership interest. Each of the children contributes a small amount of cash or securities for 1 percent limited partnership interests each.

After the FLP is formed, Henry makes gifts in of 42.08 percent limited partnership interests outright to each of his two children. The value of these gifts is determined by assuming a 20 percent discount for lack of marketability and a 25 percent discount for lack of control taken sequentially. An independent appraisal is secured to determine these discounts.[14]

[14] The amounts of these discounts may be affected by a variety of factors, such as the terms of the FLP agreement, underlying assets in the FLP (e.g., more for nonliquid assets; less for marketable securities), distribution history of the FLP, and others. Data from published studies and public markets often are used as starting points in determining these discounts.

$4,000,000	Fair market value of apartment house (without regard for the small amount of cash and marketable securities)
–40,000	Value of 1% general partnership interest at pro rata share of value of underlying partnership assets ($4,000,000 × 0.01)
$3,960,000	
×0.80	For 20% lack of marketability discount
$3,168,000	Value after lack of marketability discount
×0.4208	LP interest given to each child during the year (42.08%)
$1,333,094	Value before lack of control (minority) discount
×0.75	For 25% lack of control discount
$999,821	Value of LP interest given to each child
$2,000,000	Combined applicable exclusion amounts (assuming Henry and Tracy split gifts)

Therefore, no gift tax is payable, but use of Henry's and Tracy's current gift tax applicable credit amounts ($345,800 each) have been used.

After these gifts, Henry has a 1 percent general partnership interest and a 15.84 percent limited partnership interest. Thus, due to these substantial valuation discounts, Henry has transferred the underlying value of limited partnership assets of $1,683,200 (0.4208 × $4,000,000) to each of his children while staying within his and Tracy's current applicable credit amounts for gift tax purposes. Henry also remains in control of the FLP through his 1 percent general partnership interest.

Sales within the Family

The previous sections in this chapter were concerned with gifts—gratuitous transfers. This section deals with planning techniques where there are sales for full and adequate consideration between family members or between family members and trusts for other family members.

Sales to a Defective Grantor Trust

Basic Concept This technique is different in form from a zeroed-out GRAT, but the objective is much the same. In a typical situation, a senior family member sets up (is the grantor of) a so-called defective grantor trust (see Chapter 10), which is a grantor trust for federal income tax purposes (i.e., the corpus is treated as owned by the grantor), but which will not be included in the grantor's gross estate for federal estate tax purposes if the grantor dies during its term. The grantor then sells appreciated property to the trust in return for an interest-bearing promissory note that is due at the end of the trust term. At this time, any remaining corpus in the trust (after the principal and interest due on the note is paid to the grantor) will be paid to the trust beneficiaries (normally family members of the grantor).

If the interest rate on the promissory note is at least equal to the appropriate applicable federal rate (AFR),[15] and the principal (face) of the note is equal to the value of the property sold to the trust, there is no taxable gift by the grantor from the transaction. It is a sale, not a gift. Also, since the sale is to a grantor trust, there is no gain realized or recognized on the sale of the appreciated property because income tax–wise it is as if the grantor is selling the property to himself or herself. If the grantor should die during the term of the trust, the corpus of the irrevocable trust would not be included in his or her gross estate for federal estate tax purposes, since the grantor has made no gift with a retained interest (as would be true for a GRAT, for example) or kept any other power or right that would cause inclusion. As a practical matter, some planners suggest also having additional property in trusts to avoid possible estate tax issues. However, the value of the promissory note would be in the grantor's gross estate at death.

As with GRATs, sales to defective grantor trusts essentially are an investment play. If the total return on the property sold to the trust exceeds the interest on the promissory note to the grantor (the appropriate AFR), some assets will remain in the trust after the loan and interest are paid, and the trust will benefit the trust beneficiaries without any transfer tax cost. If the total return is equal to or less than the appropriate AFR, nothing will remain in the trust at the end of its term and nothing will go to the grantor's family. But even in this event, nothing really will have been lost by the grantor.

An Illustration Assume Paul Olson, age 65 and in good health, has a sizeable estate and would like to benefit his adult son and daughter during his lifetime. However, he does not wish to make any taxable gifts and already is making annual exclusion gifts to them. Paul decides to create an

[15] The AFRs are defined in Section 1274(d) of the IRC. As noted in chapter 3, there are three: the short-term rate for obligations with terms of less than three years, the midterm rate for obligations with terms from three to nine years, and the long-term rate for obligations whose terms exceed nine years. Recall that the Section 7520 rate (used for GRATs and other valuations) is 120 percent of the mid-term AFR. Thus, the AFR used in this situation probably will be less than the Section 7520 rate. (They both are sometimes referred to as "hurdle rates" in the context used here.) This can be an advantage for a sale to a defective grantor trust, as compared with a zeroed-out GRAT.

irrevocable defective grantor trust for a term of 10 years with his two children as beneficiaries. He then sells $1,200,000 of common stock (for which he paid $200,000 many years ago) to the trust in return for a $1,200,000 promissory note bearing 6 percent interest (the long-term AFR) paid annually (or $72,000 in interest per year to Paul). The principal and any accrued interest on the note are payable to Paul at the end of the trust's 10-year term. Paul has noted that the average annual compound rate of total return on this stock over the last 15 years has been more then 12 percent.

In this transaction, Paul has not realized and recognized any capital gain on the sale, has not made any taxable gift, and the trust corpus will not be in his gross estate if he should die during the 10-year term, all for the reasons just stated. If we assume the stock sold to the trust actually has an average annual compound rate of total return during the 10-year term of 10 percent (i.e., 4 percentage points over the 6 percent "hurdle rate"), approximately $764,996 worth of stock will remain in the trust after the loan principal and interest have been paid to Paul, and this amount will be distributed to his children at the end of the 10-year term without any transfer tax cost. On the other hand, if the total return is equal to or less than the 6 percent "hurdle rate," nothing will remain in the trust and nothing will go to Paul's children.

Installment Sales

In this case, the seller disposes of his or her entire interest in eligible property in return for annual payments for a stated period. This is essentially the same as any installment sale (as described in Chapter 10), except it is to a family member. The buyer is obligated to pay the installments when due, whether the seller survives the installment period or not.

Self-Canceling Installment Notes (SCINs)

In this installment arrangement, the seller disposes of his or her entire interest in eligible property in return for annual payments for the shorter of the installment period or the seller's lifetime. In other words, if the seller dies during the installment period, the note is cancelled and no further payments are due to the seller's estate. This eventuality would benefit the buyer, who would be a family member. Also, there would be no value for the note in a deceased seller's gross estate. However, to be considered an installment transaction, the payment term must be less than the seller's life expectancy at the time of sale. Also, to avoid a taxable gift, an adequate premium must be charged for the cancellation feature, usually in the form of a higher sales price, higher interest on the installments, or both.

Private Annuity Sales

Here, the seller disposes of his or her entire interest in the property in return for the buyer's unsecured promise to pay an annual income for the seller's lifetime—hence, the term *private annuity*. It is like a commercial life annuity, except it is provided by a family member rather than an insurance company. Thus, when the seller dies, the annuity payments cease and nothing (except for the previous annuity payments) is his or her gross estate. However, a recent proposed IRS regulation requires taxation of any gain on the property at the time of the sale for the private annuity. Hence, there will be no deferral of gain in the private annuities. This is expected to substantially reduce the use of this strategy.

Other Sale Arrangements

These may include sales of remainder interests for cash, sales of remainder interests for SCINs, and split purchases of property.

Loans to Family Members

This can be another approach to transferring significant wealth to family members without making taxable gifts. In this case, a senior family member might create a defective grantor trust for the benefit of other family members (e.g., children or grandchildren), lend money to the trust, and receive a promissory note from the trust for the loan. The face of the note would equal the amount of the loan, and it would bear interest at the appropriate AFR, so there should be no gift by the grantor. The note is due at the end of the trust's term. If the grantor should die during the term of the trust, the value of the note will be in his or her gross estate, but the corpus of the trust should not be.

As with GRATs and sales to defective grantor trusts, such loan arrangements are an investment play. If the total return on the assets in which the trustee invests the loan proceeds exceeds the "hurdle rate" (the interest rate on the note or AFR rate), some assets will remain in the trust after the loan and interest are paid, and they will go to the trust beneficiaries at the end of the trust's term without any transfer tax cost. However, if the total return is equal to or less than the appropriate AFR rate, nothing will remain in the trust at the end of its term and nothing will go to the beneficiaries. For example, instead of a sale, if Paul Olson in the previous illustration had loaned $1,200,000 to the defective grantor trust for 10 years at the 6 percent long-term AFR, and the trust assets had earned the assumed 10 percent average annual compound rate of total return, the economic results for his children would be the same as shown in the previous illustration.

Loans also can be made directly to other family members in the hope that their returns on the loan proceeds will exceed the interest they pay. Such loans also can be forgiven (which will be gifts) within the annual exclusion each year or possibly in greater amounts.

28

Marital Deduction Planning, Postmortem Planning, and Estate Liquidity

Competence Objectives for This Chapter After reading this chapter, planners should understand:

- The nature of the federal estate tax marital deduction in estate planning
- The components of a marital deduction strategy including planning for how much of the marital deduction should be used—the "optimal marital" deduction
- Planning so that each spouse can use the unified credit
- How property can be qualified for the marital deduction
- Methods of funding the marital deduction
- The concept of postmortem estate planning
- Planning for making a Q-TIP election
- Uses of qualified disclaimers
- Allocation of GST lifetime exemption
- Choosing where to deduct estate administration expenses
- Electing the alternate valuation date
- The need for adequate estate liquidity
- Estimating an estate's liquidity needs
- Methods of providing estate liquidity

Marital Deduction Planning

For persons or couples with potential estates large enough to attract federal estate taxation, proper use of the unlimited federal estate tax marital deduction is a critical decision issue in estate planning.

Using the Marital Deduction to Save Federal Estate Taxes

The basic idea of the marital deduction is to allow married estate owners to leave as much of their estates as they wish to their surviving spouse free of federal estate tax.[1] But this "marital" part must be left to a surviving spouse in such a way that it potentially would be included in the survivor's gross estate at his or her subsequent death. In tax language, these are referred to as transfers that *qualify* for the marital deduction. Thus, the marital deduction is essentially a tax-deferral technique.

Aside from tax deferral, another essential part of saving taxes through marital deduction planning is making sure that the applicable credit amount (unified credit) is fully used in *both* spouses' estates or lifetime gifts. This means the applicable exclusion amount will escape federal estate taxation in both spouses' estates and can pass tax free to their children or other family members. Thus, this exclusion amount, often in trust, bypasses the surviving spouse's gross estate and goes to the children or others. However, a surviving spouse can be given some or all of the so-called almost-owner powers (described in Chapter 26) in this bypass (nonmarital) trust. On the other hand, for tax or other reasons, the surviving spouse's rights in a bypass trust may be more limited.

Furthermore, it often is anticipated that a surviving spouse will consume, make lifetime gifts within the exclusions,[2] make charitable gifts, or take other planning actions so that the marital deduction share he or she received from the deceased spouse will not actually end up in the surviving spouse's gross estate. These actions will be influenced in part by how the marital share is left to the surviving spouse.

Essential Components of a Marital Deduction Strategy

These include deciding how much (if any) of the marital deduction should be used; making sure each spouse can utilize his or her applicable credit amount, regardless of which spouse dies first; deciding how (i.e., through what vehicles or in what ways) property is to qualify for the marital deduction; and deciding how the marital share should be funded. These issues can be complex, so only their basic elements are covered here. The illustrations used in this chapter are for explanatory purposes only.

[1] The marital deduction was originally placed in the tax code in 1948 with the goal of generally equalizing the tax situation of married persons in common-law states and community-property states. The maximum deduction then was one-half the adjusted gross estate. It became unlimited in 1981 under the Economic Recovery Tax Act.

[2] An attractive plan here may be for the surviving spouse to directly pay tuitions and/or medical expenses for, say, children or grandchildren, as well as make annual exclusion gifts out of his or her marital deduction share.

Overall Goals of Marital Deduction Planning

In many cases, spouses want first to assure the financial security of the surviving spouse for his or her remaining lifetime (sometimes called the surviving spouse's "overlife") and then plan for maximum wealth transfer for other generations. But if both spouses have significant assets and adequate income, they may give more weight to wealth transfer to future generations. In some cases, such as second marriages where both spouses have children or grandchildren from prior marriages, both spouses may be thinking primarily of leaving their wealth (or much of it) to their own children and grandchildren. Naturally, the spouses' objectives should guide their marital deduction strategies.

How Much (If Any) of the Marital Deduction Should Be Used?

Since the marital deduction is unlimited, at first blush, married estate owners may be tempted to plan on leaving all their assets outright to their spouse. These are sometimes dubbed "I love you wills." However, for tax reasons, the maximum deduction normally should not be used in situations where a federal estate tax may be payable. This will result in the estate being overqualified for the marital deduction, which may result in higher overall taxes. The following illustrations[3] point out some common issues in deciding how much property to qualify.

Estates Less Than the Applicable Exclusion Amount In situations where the gross estates of both spouses combined are expected to be less than the applicable exclusion amount, property can be left in full (or in lesser amounts) to either spouse with no adverse estate tax effects. In Example 1, assume that Harry Carter has an adjusted gross estate (gross estate minus debts and expenses) of $2,000,000 and his wife Martha has an adjusted gross estate (AGE) of $1,500,000. They each have wills leaving everything outright to the other (reciprocal wills). If Harry dies in 2009, his estate situation will be as follows.

Example 1

Adjusted gross estate	$2,000,000	
Marital deduction	–$2,000,000	(to Martha under Harry's will)
Taxable estate	$0	
Federal estate tax payable	$0	

[3] In all these illustrations, state death taxes and the federal estate tax deduction for state death taxes paid are ignored for the sake of simplicity. It is also assumed that administration expenses are taken as deductions on the estate tax return.

Now, if Martha dies later with the same unified credit, her estate situation will be[4]:

Adjusted gross estate	$1,500,000 (in her own name)
	$2,000,000 (from Harry's will)
	$3,500,000
Marital deduction	$0
Taxable estate	$3,500,000
Tentative estate tax	$1,455,800
Applicable credit amount	–$1,455,800
Federal estate tax payable	$0

The estate tax situation would not change if Martha dies first.

Avoid Overqualifying for Marital Deduction Once the combined estates of husband and wife exceed the applicable exclusion amount, it is better tax-wise to qualify less than the maximum allowable deduction. This is because there is no tax advantage in an estate owner qualifying that part of his or her estate that will be shielded from estate tax by the unified credit. However, when the surviving spouse dies, there is a tax disadvantage if the first spouse to die qualified all of his or her estate for the deduction. This is because all the property that passes to the surviving spouse in a qualifying manner will be included in that spouse's gross estate at death, unless he or she consumes it or makes nontaxable gifts while alive. As just noted, when all or "too much" property is qualified, it is referred to as an estate being *overqualified* for the marital deduction. This can occur in a variety of ways.

All Property to Spouse: Let us use the same facts as in Example 1, except Harry's adjusted gross estate is $4,500,000 and Martha's is $2,500,000. They have reciprocal wills as before. In this case (Example 2), if Harry dies in 2009, his estate situation will be as follows.

Example 2

Adjusted gross estate	$4,500,000
Marital deduction	–$4,500,000 (to Martha under Harry's will)
Taxable estate	$0
Federal estate tax payable	$0

[4] In all these illustrations, appreciation or depreciation in assets between the deaths is ignored for the sake of simplicity. It is also assumed that the surviving spouse does not remarry and no specific bequests to others are made. Furthermore, it is assumed that the federal estate tax is not repealed and the applicable credit amount (unified credit) remains at $1, 455, 800 in the future. These assumptions are in line with the likely changes in the estate tax law noted in Chapter 26

But if Martha dies later, her estate situation will be:

Adjusted gross estate	$2,500,000 (in her own name)
	$4,500,000 (from Harry's will)
	$7,000,000
Marital deduction	$0
Taxable estate	$7,000,000
Tentative estate tax	$3,030,800
Applicable credit amount	–$1,455,800
Federal estate tax payable	$1,575,000

Note that this tax occurs because an applicable credit amount is used in only one of the two estates (in the survivor's estate). This tax situation would be the same if Martha had predeceased Harry. It may be observed, however, that the estate tax would have been substantially eliminated if the unused unified credit at Harry's death could have been transferred to Martha's estate. This is the possible change of "portability" of unified credits between spouses as noted in Chapter 26.

Too Much Jointly Owned Property: Now suppose that Harry and Martha Carter own all of their $7,000,000 adjusted gross estate as joint tenants with right of survivorship.[5] In this situation (Example 3), if Harry dies in 2009, his estate situation will be as follows:

Example 3

Adjusted gross estate (0.5 × $7,000,000)	$3,500,000
Marital deduction	–$3,500,000
Taxable estate	$0
Federal estate tax payable	$0

If Martha dies later, her estate situation will be:

Adjusted gross estate ($7,000,000 by operation of law)	$7,000,000
Marital deduction	$0
Taxable estate	$7,000,000
Tentative estate tax	$3,030,800
Applicable credit amount	–$1,455,800
Federal estate tax payable	$1,575,000

The result would be the same if Martha had predeceased Harry.

Estate Consisting of Qualified Retirement Plan or IRA Death Benefits: The same kind of overqualification can occur in situations where people have the bulk of their estates in qualified retirement plans or IRAs

[5] This, of course, is unlikely as a practical matter. However, this assumption helps illustrate the problem of owning too much property as joint tenants with right of survivorship.

naming their spouse as beneficiary. In this event, the plan's death benefits will be in the participant's gross estate but will qualify for the marital deduction. Thus, the participant's estate may be overqualified.

Reduce-to-Zero (Zero-Tax) Formula Provision This type of provision in a will or revocable living trust[6] is designed to pass to the surviving spouse just enough of the estate to eliminate (or reduce to the lowest possible figure) the federal estate tax at the first spouse's death and to pass the remainder of the estate so that it does not qualify for the marital deduction. This normally results in no tax at the first spouse's death.

This kind of clause might provide, for example, that the smallest fractional share of the estate, when added to other items in the gross estate that have passed to the surviving spouse outside the probate estate or under other parts of the will or trust and that qualify for the marital deduction, will reduce the federal estate tax payable at the first spouse's death to zero or the lowest possible amount, after taking into account deductions from the gross estate (other than this marital deduction) and credits allowed in calculating the federal estate tax, will pass to the surviving spouse in a way that will qualify for the marital deduction (e.g., outright or in a marital trust).[7] Then, the residue of the estate, which normally will equal the applicable exclusion amount, passes in a way that does not qualify for the marital deduction. It may go, for example, to a *nonmarital trust,* in which the surviving spouse may (or may not) be given some or all of the almost-owner powers during his or her lifetime (overlife) and then with the corpus going to their children or others upon the surviving spouse's death. It also may go outright to other family members. The property in this trust or gift will not be in the surviving spouse's gross estate upon his or her death. Any state death taxes (and other nondeductible amounts) may be paid from this nonmarital trust or gift under a tax clause. This method of using marital and nonmarital trusts (sometimes called A and B trusts or marital and family trusts) or marital and nonmarital gifts to qualify the right amount or share for the marital deduction is commonly used.

To illustrate the reduce-to-zero formula clause, let us return to the facts in Example 2, except that Harry Carter follows a reduce-to-zero marital strategy

[6] Note that this formula provision or other marital deduction provision may be in a person's will or revocable living trust (described in Chapter 30), whichever document is the main vehicle for disposing of the person's estate at death. Neither vehicle has an advantage over the other in this respect.

[7] In terms of how the marital deduction is funded, this is a fractional share marital gift with the residue to a bypass gift. See further discussion under "Types of Marital Gifts" later in this chapter.

in his will or revocable trust. In this situation (Example 4), if Harry dies in 2009, his estate situation will be as follows:

Example 4

Adjusted gross estate	$4,500,000
Marital deduction (which goes under the formula to the marital trust or gift or qualifies outside of the will or trust)[8]	–$1,000,000
Taxable estate (which goes to the bypass or credit-shelter trust or gift)	$3,500,000
Tentative estate tax	$1,455,800
Applicable credit amount	–$1,455,800
Federal estate tax payable	$0

If Martha dies later, her estate situation will be:

Adjusted gross estate	$2,500,000 (in her own name)
	$1,000,000 (from Harry's will or trust as the marital gift or qualifying outside the will or trust)
	$3,500,000
Marital deduction	$0
Taxable estate	$3,500,000
Tentative estate tax	$1,455,800
Applicable credit amount	–$1,455,800
Federal estate tax payable	$0

There is no estate tax at either death in Example 4 if the order of deaths is as shown. This can be contrasted with the situations in Examples 2 and 3, where the Carters' estates were overqualified for the marital deduction and an estate tax of $1,575,000 was due at the second death. As can be seen from Example 4, if the combined adjusted gross estates of both spouses are equal to or less than their combined applicable exclusion amounts, there may be no

[8] This is the total amount of marital deduction (probate property and nonprobate property) that will result in zero tax in this situation. If the entire $4,500,000 of AGE were in Harry's probate estate (e.g., owned in his name), the $100,000 would be in the marital trust or gift under his will. Normally, however, there will be several items of nonprobate property in an estate. If we assume, therefore, that Harry's AGE consists of $600,000 in a 401(k) account, with Martha named as beneficiary (a nonprobate asset qualifying for the marital deduction), and the remainder in stocks, bonds, and real estate in his own name, the $600,000 in 401(k) account balance would go directly to Martha and $400,000 would be in the marital trust or gift under the will. The marital deduction still would be $100,000, but it would consist of $600,000 of nonprobate property and $400,000 of probate property. The wording of the formula clause automatically adjusts the marital bequest for nonprobate property that qualifies for the marital deduction.

federal estate tax payable at either death, provided there is proper planning. Of course, if the estates were larger, say Harry's AGE was $10,000,000, there would be some tax payable by the estate of the second spouse to die. Again, it may be observed that this marital trust (gift)-nonmarital trust (gift) strategy (the optimal marital) would no longer be necessary for purely estate tax savings reasons if unused unified credits were transferable between spouses, as has been proposed (see Chapter 26). In that case, each spouse could leave as much as he or she wished to the other spouse (up to the full marital deduction) and then any unused unified credit in the estate of the first spouse to die would be transferred to the estate of the second to die. Even in this situation, there may be non tax reasons to establish marital and nonmarital trusts.

However, if the order of deaths in Example 4 were reversed (i.e., Martha predeceased Harry), as matters now stand, there would be federal estate tax at Harry's subsequent death, even if Martha left her estate so as to bypass Harry's estate (for example, in trust for their children with almost-owner powers for Harry so that the corpus would not be in his gross estate at his death). The solution for this could be for Harry to make lifetime gifts to Martha so that the available applicable credit amount would shield both of their estates from taxation no matter who died first. Here again, the possible change in the law of allowing "portability" of unified credit between spouses, if enacted, would solve this problem without lifetime gifts between spouses.

Status of Surviving Spouse Under the "Optimal Marital" Particularly after EGTRRA with its increased unified credit, an issue with respect to reduce-to-zero formula clauses is that they may cause too much wealth to flow into credit-shelter trusts (bypass or family trusts) that perhaps are mainly for children or others, as compared to wealth passing to the surviving spouse (in trust or outright). This may or may not be a problem, depending on the circumstances.

An example may help illustrate this issue. Suppose now that Harry and Martha were both married before, and each has one child from his or her prior marriage. There also is one child from their present marriage. Also suppose that Harry owns the bulk of their wealth ($4,000,000) and Martha only has about $200,000. Now assume Harry has a standard reduce-to-zero formula provision in his will under which two trusts are created: a martial trust (a Q-TIP trust) for Martha and a credit-shelter trust (the "family trust") which mainly benefits Harry's children. At Harry's death, under this formula, the least amount necessary to reduce the federal estate tax to zero is to go into the marital Q-TIP trust and the remainder is to go into the nonmarital family trust to take full advantage of the existing applicable exclusion amount.

In this situation, if Harry dies in 2009, the formula provision would act as follows:

Adjusted gross estate	$4,000,000
Marital deduction (by way of the Q-TIP trust)	–$500,000
Taxable estate (which goes to the family trust)	$3,500,000
Tentative tax	$1,455,800
Unified credit	–$1,455,800
Federal estate tax payable	$0

Thus, only $500,000 would go to Martha (in trust) and $3,500,000 would be in the family trust.

Also note that, aside from EGTRRA, this same issue can arise if estate values were to decline substantially, such as during a recession or depression.

Various suggestions have been made for dealing with this issue. Some of these include:

- Give the surviving spouse various rights in or powers over the credit-shelter trust. For example, the spouse could be an income beneficiary (mandatory or discretionary), could be given limited powers of appointment over trust corpus, could be trustee if distributions are limited to an ascertainable standard, or could have other rights or powers that will not cause the corpus to be in his or her gross estate at the surviving spouse's subsequent death.
- Use a dollar or fractional cap on the credit-shelter trust.
- Provide for a minimum marital bequest (outright or in trust).
- Use three trusts: a marital trust (Q-TIP trust) for the spouse, a credit-shelter trust for the spouse but with no Q-TIP election, and a traditional credit-shelter trust for children or other beneficiaries.
- Make a bequest to the surviving spouse (outright or in trust) and provide for a possible disclaimer by the spouse (discussed later in this chapter) to a nonmarital family trust.
- Provide alternative trusts (marital and nonmarital) with authority in the executor or trustee to select amounts to fund each.
- Separate marital and nonmarital trusts would not be needed (for tax reasons) if "portability" of unified credits were enacted.

Each of these approaches has its advantages and limitations. They vary in the power they give to the spouse or others to make final decisions at an estate owner's death. Of course, depending on family circumstances, nothing may need to be done.

Equalization of Estates or Equalization of Rates Formula Provisions An alternative formula provision in a will or trust was designed to equalize the spouses' estates or to equalize the tax rates in both estates at the first death. This results in some tax at the first death and some tax at the second death, but perhaps less aggregate tax on both estates. However, at present, this approach is no longer attractive because effectively there is a flat 45 percent federal estate tax rate over the exclusion amount.

Planning For Each Spouse

In planning the appropriate use of the marital deduction, a common procedure is to assume one spouse dies followed by the other and to determine the taxes payable (if any) and the estate shrinkage at each death. Estate liquidity and income needs for the survivor can be evaluated after each death. Then the order of deaths is reversed and the analysis repeated. This is sometimes called the *hypothetical probate.* Recommendations then can be made for improvements in the situation.

How Should Property Be Qualified for the Marital Deduction?

Property can pass to a surviving U.S. citizen spouse in a variety of ways to qualify for the marital deduction.[9] It can make considerable difference in planning how property qualifies.

Outright Gifts or Bequests This is the most direct way and gives the surviving spouse sole ownership and complete control over the property.

Joint Ownership with Spouse (WROS) Property held jointly by the spouses (with right of survivorship) will qualify to the extent that the property is included in the deceased spouse's gross estate (normally one-half). Here again, the surviving spouse has sole ownership and complete control over the property after the first spouse's death.

Life Insurance Proceeds Payable to Surviving Spouse or to a Qualifying Trust for His or Her Benefit Life insurance proceeds that are in the deceased spouse's gross estate and that are payable to the surviving spouse as beneficiary in a lump sum or under a settlement arrangement giving the spouse full withdrawal rights or only a life income will qualify. Also, life insurance proceeds payable to a trust which itself meets the requirements for qualifying its corpus will qualify.[10]

[9] QDOTs can be used for transfers to noncitizen spouses (see Chapter 26).

[10] It may be noted, however, that if a person's estate is going to be subject to federal estate taxation, it normally is better tax-wise to have life insurance on his or her life owned by and payable to an ILIT, as explained in Chapter 29. This allows the proceeds to be removed from the gross estates of both spouses and to go in trust for the benefit of their children, grandchildren, or others as beneficiaries of the ILIT.

Other Beneficiary Designations Payable to Surviving Spouse This can include a variety of situations. Probably most important are qualified retirement plans and IRAs.

The next items involve leaving or giving property in trust for a surviving spouse so that the trust corpus qualifies for the marital deduction.

General Power of Appointment Trusts Prior to the Economic Recovery Tax Act of 1981, this was the traditional way to qualify property in trust for the marital deduction. To meet the requirements for a general power-of-appointment trust, all trust income must be payable at least annually to the surviving spouse for his or her lifetime, and the surviving spouse must have a general power of appointment over the trust corpus exercisable in all events during the spouse's lifetime, at the spouse's death (i.e., exercisable by his or her will), or both.

Q-TIP Trusts These probably are by far the most common choice of marital trusts today. To qualify the corpus for the marital deduction as a Q-TIP trust, all trust income must be payable, at least annually, to the surviving spouse for life, with no person having power to appoint any part of the property to anyone other than the surviving spouse during the spouse's lifetime. However, the original estate owner (or another person) can create powers over, or control the ultimate disposition of, the trust property, which will take effect after the surviving spouse's death. For a trust that meets the requirements just stated to become a Q-TIP trust, the deceased spouse's executor must make an irrevocable election on a timely filed (with extensions)[11] estate tax return to treat the whole trust or only a specific portion (fraction or percentage) of it as a Q-TIP trust. A trust also may be divided by an executor after a decedent's death into two or more separate trusts, with one being a Q-TIP while the other is not.

At the surviving spouse's death, the corpus of a Q-TIP trust is included in the surviving spouse's gross estate. However, the surviving spouse's estate is entitled to reimbursement from the Q-TIP trust for any additional estate tax due because of the inclusion of the Q-TIP property in the estate, unless the surviving spouse affirmatively waives this right to reimbursement.

Estate Trusts In this case, trust income may be payable to the surviving spouse or accumulated in the trust at the trustee's discretion. At the surviving spouse's death, trust corpus and any accumulated income are payable to the

[11] As noted in Chapter 26, the federal estate tax return normally must be filed within nine months after a decedent's death, but a 6-month extension often can be secured. Thus, an executor may have up to 15 months after a decedent's death to decide whether to qualify some or all of an otherwise-qualifying trust for Q-TIP marital deduction treatment, depending on the circumstances. This affords significant postmortem planning opportunities and is an important advantage of the Q-TIP trust.

surviving spouse's estate to be distributed, along with the surviving spouse's own probate property, under the terms of his or her will. Estate trusts are used under some circumstances.

CRT with Spouse as Sole Unitrust or Annuity Trust Beneficiary When established during a donor's lifetime, charitable remainder trusts (CRTs) can qualify a surviving spouse's remaining lifetime annuity trust or unitrust interest (provided there is no other noncharitable beneficiary) for the marital deduction at the donor's death, as well as provide the lifetime advantages noted in Chapter 19. When CRTs are established at death (under a will), the same can be true, except then they should be compared with a Q-TIP trust, with the charity named as remainderperson, as to which is the most efficient approach.

Factors in Choice of Method In terms of planning for the spouse and family, this can be an important decision.

Control Issues: Depending on the circumstances, a married estate owner may wish to retain control over the ultimate disposition of marital property after his or her death and after the death of his or her surviving spouse. This may be true because it is a second marriage with children from a prior marriage; out of concern about his or her spouse's money management interests or abilities, or about demands that may be placed on the surviving spouse by others; out of concern about the "dreaded" new spouse, possibly with children of his or her own; or for other reasons.

The only method for qualifying property for the marital deduction that will give the original estate owner such control is the Q-TIP trust.[12] With a Q-TIP, the first spouse to die can designate the recipients of the corpus after the surviving spouse's death, or the property can remain in trust for such recipients. The surviving spouse can be limited to a life income interest only in the Q-TIP, although a trustee can be given (but is not required to be given) discretionary power to distribute corpus to the surviving spouse.

On the other hand, from the surviving spouse's viewpoint, he or she would have greatest control over marital property with an outright marital bequest, jointly owned property (although this may present overqualification problems), and outright beneficiary designations.

Management of Property: If management of property is desired, a trust is the logical choice.

[12] The CRT with the surviving spouse as sole remaining noncharitable unitrust or annuity trust beneficiary also gives a measure of such control, but in that case the property must go to charity after the surviving spouse's death.

Creditor and Marital Protection: Similarly, a trust with a spendthrift clause normally can protect trust corpus from the surviving spouse's creditors. A marital trust also generally would be protected from any marital property claims of a new spouse against the surviving spouse.

Possible Incapacity of Surviving Spouse: Again, depending on the circumstances, if the surviving spouse is, or may become, physically or mentally incapacitated, a trust (and probably a Q-TIP trust) seems appropriate.

Availability of Postmortem Estate Planning: The Q-TIP trust has an advantage here because, as indicated in Footnote 11 of this chapter, the executor of the estate of the first spouse to die can decide within the time period for filing a timely estate tax return with extensions (which could be as long as 15 months after the first spouse's death) how much, if any, of an otherwise eligible trust contained in a will to elect to qualify for Q-TIP treatment. This allows the executor to make this decision well after the first spouse's death, when circumstances often are much clearer than when the estate planning documents were drafted. This delayed election is only possible under a Q-TIP trust because only it requires an affirmative irrevocable election by the executor to be activated.[13]

Flexibility After EGTRRA: The need for estate planning flexibility after EGTRRA has made the Q-TIP trust even more attractive. The executor can make full, partial, or no Q-TIP election, depending on the circumstances at the time of the estate owner's death.

One technique in this regard is the so-called "single-fund Q-TIP trust." In this case, the will or revocable trust provides that at the death of the estate owner, the entire residuary estate is placed in a single Q-TIPable trust. Then, the executor can make whatever Q-TIP election for a portion, all, or none of this trust, as is appropriate given the circumstances at that time.

How Should the Marital Gift Be Funded?

This is the final component of a marital deduction strategy. It essentially deals with the type of marital gift to be used. This is a complex area, and a full discussion of it is beyond the scope of this book. Only a brief outline of the issues is presented here.

[13] However, as will be explained in the section entitled "Postmortem Estate Planning," the same kind of adjustment can be made by a surviving spouse through a qualified disclaimer of part or all of a marital interest he or she would have received under a deceased spouse's will or revocable living trust.

Types of Marital Gifts There are two basic types of formula marital deduction gifts. One is a *pecuniary amount marital,* where the marital gift is defined as an amount of money (or value of assets to be distributed in kind). The other is a *fractional share marital,* where the marital gift is expressed as a fraction of the estate. The numerator of this fraction is the amount of the marital deduction desired, and the denominator is the value of the assets available for funding the deduction.

Order of Funding For pecuniary amount maritals, one approach is for the will or revocable trust to make the *pecuniary bequest or gift to the marital* (i.e., outright to the surviving spouse or to a marital trust), with the residue going to the credit-shelter (bypass) trust or gift. This may be referred to as a *preresiduary marital.* Assuming estate assets are valued at date-of-distribution values, this freezes the amount of the marital gift and protects the surviving spouse from depreciation of asset values from the date of death to the date of distribution. On the other hand, if there is appreciation in asset values between these dates, it results in the appreciation going into the credit-shelter (bypass) trust or gift, which will not be included in the surviving spouse's gross estate at his or her subsequent death. Any such growth goes to the bypass trust or gift.

The other approach is for the will or revocable trust to make the pecuniary bequest or gift to the nonmarital trust or gift (e.g., to the trustee of a trust), with the residue going to the marital gift or trust. This has the reverse effects from those just described. In effect, appreciation or depreciation of asset values from the date of death to the date of distribution goes to the marital. This approach may be called a *reverse pecuniary,* a *residuary marital,* or a *front-end credit-shelter,* among other names.

Values or Shares in Funding A pecuniary amount formula can use the following valuation methods for estate assets used to fund the marital gift or bequest. One is a *true-worth pecuniary gift,* in which assets distributed in kind are valued at their date-of-distribution values.[14] Thus, for example, one could have a reduce-to-zero, true-worth, pecuniary to the marital formula clause. Another is a *fairly representative approach,* under which assets generally are valued at their federal estate tax values (i.e., their values as of the date of death),

[14] The amount of the marital deduction as reported on the estate tax return is determined as of the date of death based on estate asset values at that time. These are also referred to as the estate tax values of the assets in the estate. But estate assets can appreciate or depreciate in value between the date of death and the date of distribution (i.e., when they are used to fund a marital bequest or trust or a nonmarital bequest or trust), which may be some time from the date of death. This is essentially the issue here.

and the assets used to fund the marital and nonmarital gifts are fairly representative in each case of appreciation and depreciation in their values from the date of death until the date of distribution.[15] Finally, there can be a *minimum-worth* pecuniary gift or bequest. In this case, each asset is valued for funding purposes at the smaller of its estate tax value or its date-of-distribution value.

On the other hand, a fractional share formula can use two different approaches to funding the marital and nonmarital shares. One is a *pro rata allocation* of assets in which the marital share is allocated a pro rata portion of each asset in the estate. The other is a so-called *pick-and-choose* approach in which a fractional share formula is used but assets can be distributed in whole or in part to the marital and nonmarital shares.

Postmortem Estate Planning

This means, in effect, that an estate plan need not be "cast in concrete" at the time of a decedent's death, but rather, with proper planning, it can be modified in certain respects after death to better fit the circumstances then. Following are some common postmortem planning techniques.

Making the Q-TIP Election

The need for a decedent's executor to make an affirmative Q-TIP election with respect to an otherwise eligible Q-TIP trust on a timely filed estate tax return in order to effectuate a Q-TIP marital deduction has introduced considerable postdeath flexibility in marital deduction planning, as noted previously.

Use of Qualified Disclaimers

General Considerations The tax law permits persons to give up their rights to property or property interests that they otherwise would be entitled to receive at someone's death by executing a *qualified disclaimer* under the

[15] This approach arises from the rather well-known IRS Revenue Procedure 64-19. In this Rev. Proc., the IRS addressed the concern that if date-of-death values were used in funding the marital gift, an executor might allocate to the marital gift or trust in a disproportionate manner assets that had declined in value from the date of death to the date of distribution. Thus, the marital gift might effectively be diminished when the surviving spouse died. In a fairly representative approach, however, assets would have to be allocated to the marital gift in a way that represented both appreciation and depreciation in their values since date of death and so the concern would be resolved. When assets are valued at their date-of-distribution values (a true-worth approach), the problem does not exist.

rules of the IRC. Disclaimers can also be used for lifetime gifts and GST tax purposes. When a person makes a valid disclaimer of a property interest, it is treated as though the property was never transferred to him or her (i.e., as if he or she had predeceased the transferor of the property). Thus, the disclaimed property interest goes to whomever or wherever the will or applicable state law indicates should take it if the disclaimant (the person making the disclaimer) had predeceased the decedent.

There are several requirements for a qualified disclaimer for federal transfer tax purposes, as follows:

- A qualified disclaimer must be a written, irrevocable, and unqualified refusal to accept an interest in property.
- A qualified disclaimer must be timely. It must be received by the original transferor (or his or her legal representative) no later then nine months after the later of the date the transfer creating the interest in the disclaimant was made or the day on which the disclaimant turns age 21.[16]
- There can be no acceptance of the interest or any of its benefits by the disclaimant.
- The disclaimed property must pass to the surviving spouse or someone other than the disclaimant. The fact that disclaimed property can pass to a surviving spouse (even if he or she is the disclaimant) can be important because it means a spouse can disclaim part or all of the marital bequest, have it pass to a credit-shelter (bypass) trust under the will, and still benefit from the credit-shelter trust (other than having a special power of appointment over the corpus that is not subject to an ascertainable standard).
- Thus, wills or revocable trusts should have an express provision as to what will happen if a property interest is disclaimed. A disclaimer may be of an entire interest, a partial interest, or a pecuniary amount (a specific dollar amount).

CASE EXAMPLE

Ahmed and his wife, Aysha, are in private equity and consulting, and work for different corporations. They have three children. They both would like their estates to pass to the surviving spouse and then to their children in the event of their deaths. However, they want the survivor to be able to make tax-efficient decisions and they are aware of the uncertainties of estate tax legislation.

[16] There are some special rules for disclaimers of jointly owned property, which can be important because jointly owned property can be a source of overqualifying property for the marital deduction.

Therefore, Ahmed and Aysha have executed reciprocal wills in which each leaves everything outright to the other, if living and if the survivor does not disclaim; otherwise, everything goes to a trust for their children in equal shares.

Assume Ahmed dies in 2009 when Aysha is age 56, in good health, and successfully employed. At his death, Ahmed's AGE is $5,000,000 and Aysha's is $4,000,000. Since Ahmed's estate is overqualified for the marital deduction and Aysha feels she has adequate resources, she decides to execute a qualified disclaimer within nine months of Ahmed's death to refuse to accept that part of his AGE equal to $3,500,000. This amount (the applicable exclusion amount in 2009) will go to the trust for their two children under the terms of Ahmed's will (a nonmarital bequest). The remainder, $1,500,000, will go outright to Aysha as a marital bequest and qualify for the marital deduction. Thus, with the use of a qualified disclaimer, an overqualified estate has been adjusted through postmortem planning into a reduce-to-zero marital.

Allocation of GST Lifetime Exemption

A decedent's executor may allocate the decedent's unused exemption to lifetime or other transfers. Also, in cases where the GST exemption has not been used or fully used, first-generation heirs (e.g., children with sizeable estates) can disclaim their interests so that they will pass to skip persons (e.g., grandchildren of the decedent) to the extent necessary to make full use of the decedent's exemption. Furthermore, if there is going to be a GST tax, skip persons may disclaim their interests to the extent they exceed the GST exemption.

Choice of Where to Deduct Estate Administration Expenses

A decedent's executor normally can choose whether to deduct certain estate administration expenses (e.g., executor's commissions, legal fees, and other fees) on the federal estate tax return (for estate tax purposes) or to deduct the expenses on the estate's income tax return (for income tax purposes). Income tax rates are lower than estate tax rates, so this favors an estate tax deduction. However, if a reduce-to-zero formula is used, there will be no estate tax due at the first death, so the effect of an estate tax deduction will be delayed until the second spouse's death, if ever. On the other hand, if a current estate tax is payable, the situation is different. The decision will be based on the facts of each case and the desires of the parties.

Alternate Valuation Date

An executor can choose date-of-death values or the alternate valuation date (six months from date of death) for valuing estate property for federal estate tax purposes. This should be considered if estate values are falling. Refer to Chapter 26 for a discussion on this topic.

Other Techniques

Other techniques, such as special-use valuation of certain real property (see Chapter 26) and selecting a fiscal year for the estate's income tax return, also may be used.

Estate Liquidity

This is the need for cash or assets that can readily be converted into cash to meet the obligations of an estate.

Estimating an Estate's Liquidity Needs

These needs should be estimated for an estate so that planning can include providing the resources to meet them. They may include:

- Estimated funeral expenses
- Estimated last illness expenses not covered by health insurance or Medicare
- Estimated costs of estate administration
- Current debts
- Unpaid mortgages
- Other debts (bank loans, margin or other securities loans, etc.)
- Federal estate tax
- State death tax
- Any specific dollar bequests in the will

The importance of these items will depend on the facts of each case.

Providing Estate Liquidity

Liquidity can be a serious problem for some estates, but of minor importance for others. Much depends on the composition of the estate and what previous planning has been done. Estate liquidity may be a problem when a large part of an estate consists of relatively unmarketable assets, such as closely held business interests and undeveloped real estate.

Meeting the claims and taxes against an estate generally is the responsibility of the executor, who does this using probate assets. These are the only assets directly available to the executor. However, other assets, such as life insurance proceeds payable to a third-party beneficiary or owned by and payable to an ILIT, that pass outside the probate estate may be made available to the executor by the person or trustee receiving them as a loan to the estate or by purchasing assets from the estate. This is discussed further in Chapter 29.

29
Life Insurance in Estate Planning

Competence Objectives for This Chapter After reading this chapter, planners should understand:

- The federal income taxation of life insurance
- Federal estate tax status of life insurance
- Federal gift tax status of life insurance
- Federal GST tax status of life insurance
- Valuation of life insurance policies for tax purposes
- How to arrange life insurance ownership and beneficiary designations
- The structure and uses of irrevocable life insurance trusts (ILITs)
- Life insurance owned by business entities
- Life insurance owned by qualified retirement plans
- Gifts of life insurance
- The advantages and limitations of gifts of life insurance
- Gifts of group term life insurance
- Deciding which policies to give
- Gifts of life insurance subject to loans

Life insurance occupies an important place in many estates and has unique advantages in estate planning. The characteristics of life insurance itself were covered in Chapter 21.

Taxation of Life Insurance

The tax advantages of life insurance were first mentioned in Chapter 21. In this chapter, we shall consider these advantages in more detail.

Federal Income Taxation

Death Benefits The face amount of a life or accident insurance policy paid by reason of the insured's death normally is not gross income to the beneficiary. When life insurance death proceeds are held by the insurance company under a settlement option, the proceeds themselves remain income tax–free, but any interest earnings on the proceeds will be taxable income. Correspondingly, when life insurance death proceeds are paid to a trust, the proceeds themselves are income tax–free, but the trust investment income from them will be taxed under the normal rules for trust taxation.

Benefits Paid for Terminally Ill Insureds As explained in Chapter 23, life insurance contracts often provide for accelerated death benefits to terminally ill insureds. Also, viatical companies have purchased insurance policies from such insureds, as well as from others. The tax law provides that accelerated death benefits and amounts received from viatical settlement providers for a "terminally ill individual"[1] may be excluded from gross income. The nature and limits of this exclusion are explained in Chapter 23.

Transfer-for-Value Rule An important exception to the general principle that life insurance death proceeds are income tax–free is the transfer-for-value rule. This tax rule provides that if a life insurance policy is transferred for a valuable consideration (sold), at the insured's death the beneficiary must include in gross income the difference between the death proceeds and the consideration paid for the policy plus any subsequent premiums paid by the transferee (buyer).

Suppose, for example, that a viatical company buys a $500,000 (face amount) life insurance policy from a terminally ill owner-insured for $400,000 and pays an additional $10,000 in premiums. Eighteen months later, the insured dies. The $400,000 received from the viatical settlement provider is not gross income to the owner–insured. However, the viatical company (the purchaser and beneficiary of the policy) has gross income of $90,000 ($500,000 death proceeds – $410,000 [$400,000 consideration paid plus $10,000 in subsequent premiums]).

There are, however, some important exceptions to the transfer-for-value rule. First, when the transferee (buyer) is the insured, a partner of the insured, a partnership in which the insured is a member, or a corporation in which the insured is a shareholder or officer, the transfer-for-value rule does not apply. This removes from the rule many common transactions. The

[1] The law also may allow death benefits and other benefits paid to a "chronically ill individual" to be excluded from gross income, but only for amounts paid under a part of the policy that is treated as a qualified long-term care contract.

other exception is when the basis in the policy in the hands of the transferee is determined in whole or in part by reference to the basis in the policy in the hands of the transferor (seller).

Premiums Paid Premiums for personally owned life or accident insurance or an employee's contribution to group life or accident insurance (other than under cafeteria plans) are not deductible for income tax purposes.

Inside Buildup of Cash Values Annual increases in the cash value of a life insurance policy (fixed-dollar or variable) are not currently taxable to the policyowner. This is the tax-deferred (or, hopefully, tax-free) buildup of life insurance cash values.

Policy Dividends Life insurance policy dividends do not constitute taxable income to a policyowner until they exceed the policyowner's income tax basis in the policy. Furthermore, when policy dividends are used to buy paid-up additional amounts of life insurance (paid-up additions), there is also a tax-free buildup of the cash value of these additions.

Surrender or Maturity of Policies If a life insurance contract is surrendered, is sold (other than for terminally ill insureds), or matures during the insured's lifetime, the policyowner will have ordinary income to the extent the amount received exceeds the policyowner's investment in the contract (income tax basis in the policy). This investment in the contract normally is the sum of the net premiums paid (gross premiums minus dividends received in cash). Life insurance policies normally allow the policyowner to leave the surrender value with the insurance company under one or more settlement options. In this case, the entire gain still will be taxed as ordinary income, but it will be spread out over a period of time, depending on the nature of the settlement option (see Chapter 21).

Partial Withdrawals For some policies (e.g., UL and VUL), policyowners can make *partial cash withdrawals.* In the case of policies that are not MECs, the general rule is that such cash distributions are not taxed until they exceed the policyowner's basis in the contract (a FIFO-type rule). However, if such cash distributions are received as a result of certain changes in the contract that reduce benefits and occur during the first 15 years of the contract, different rules apply, and such distributions may be taxable in whole or in part.[2]

For example, suppose that Henry Libowitz has a $750,000 face-amount (type A death benefit) VUL policy on his life that he purchased 20 years ago. The policy permits partial withdrawals. Henry has paid $100,000 in

[2] This is sometimes referred to as the *forced-out gain,* or FOG, provision.

premiums during this period (his investment in the contract or basis), and the policy cash value (invested in a common stock subaccount) is $225,000. Henry can withdraw up to his $100,000 basis without receiving any taxable income, but his basis (and possibly the face of the policy) will be reduced by any such withdrawals. If Henry withdraws more than his $100,000 basis, amounts over basis are taxed as ordinary income to him.

Policy Loans For policies that are not MECs, policy loans are not viewed as distributions from the policy for income tax purposes and, hence, are not gross income even if they exceed the policyowner's basis in the contract. For example, in the situation of Henry Libowitz just described, if Henry took a $200,000 policy loan from his VUL policy, it would not result in any gross income to him.

Changes in Asset Allocations within Variable Policies Changes in cash values among subaccounts in variable life insurance are not currently taxable sales or exchanges for capital gains (or loss) purposes.

Planning for Taking Cash (Benefits) from Life Insurance Policies Policyowners normally do not want to surrender policies for cash before the insured's death, because if the cash value exceeds basis, the owner will realize ordinary income on the difference. Also, he or she will no longer have the insurance protection. There often are other options. First, a policyowner can just continue the policy in force until the insured dies, at which time the death proceeds will be received income tax–free. The policyowner can continue paying premiums or just enough premiums (with the existing cash value) to keep the policy in force for its full amount. A vanishing-premium approach also may do this.

Second, a policyowner can decide to stop paying premiums and take a reduced paid-up amount of life insurance without any current income taxation. If the policy is participating, the policyowner may allow policy dividends to continue to accumulate and, for example, be used to purchase paid-up additions (without current tax liability), or the policyowner could take the policy dividends in cash and pay income tax on the dividends only when they cumulatively exceed the policyowner's basis in the policy. Correspondingly, a policyowner of a flexible premium contract normally can elect to reduce the amount of insurance (if necessary) to where the existing cash value can be expected to carry the policy without further premium payments. In either case, the death benefit will be income tax–free at the insured's death.

Third, if a policyowner under a flexible-premium contract wants to take cash from the policy (which will reduce the cash value and may reduce death proceeds), he or she can take tax-free partial withdrawals up to the investment in the contract. Then, the remaining cash value may carry the policy (with perhaps some additional premiums as needed) until the insured's death, when the proceeds will be received income tax–free.

Finally, cash can be taken tax free from a life insurance policy by way of policy loans. If the policy is to be continued in force, additional premiums normally will have to be paid. Also, a policy loan will require nondeductible interest and may be subject to direct recognition for policy dividend purposes. At the insured's death, the proceeds, minus any outstanding policy loans, will be paid income tax–free to the beneficiary.

Reasons for Taking Cash from Life Insurance Policies A policyowner may need cash for children's educations, business opportunities, or other purposes, but still want to maintain the life insurance, or most of it, in force for family protection or estate conservation purposes. Or a policyowner may need cash for retirement income purposes. Of course, he or she could surrender the policy and perhaps take the cash surrender value over a period of years in installments or perhaps as a life income. On the other hand, the policyowner may want to take cash from the policy (or stop premium payments) at retirement without losing the life insurance protection and hopefully without income taxation. In this event, one of the other strategies just noted may be appropriate.

Finally, a policyowner may want to take cash from a policy prior to transferring it as a gift to an ILIT or an individual donee. This will lower or even eliminate any gift tax value in the policy. It also will enable the policyowner to benefit from at least some of the cash-value buildup in the policy.

Taxation of Economic Benefit of Life Insurance in Some Situations Under some circumstances, the economic value of life insurance protection is gross income to the insured.

Group Term Life Insurance: The first $50,000 of group term life insurance does not result in gross income to insured employees or to retired former employees whose insurance is continued into their retirement years. For amounts in excess of $50,000, the cost of group term life insurance on an employee's (or retiree's) life, minus any employee (or retiree) contributions, is gross income to the employee (or retiree).[3] The cost (economic benefit) of group term life insurance for this purpose is calculated by using uniform premiums (Table I rates) promulgated under IRS regulations, or the actual cost of the insurance, if lower. As we shall see later in the discussion of gifts of group term life insurance, these Table I rates (or actual cost, if lower) also are used to value gifted group term life insurance.

[3] The income tax treatment of employees and retirees under group term life insurance plans is governed by Section 79 of the IRC. Thus, group term life plans sometimes are called *Section 79 plans.*

Split-Dollar Life Insurance Plans: These arrangements are described later in this chapter. At this point, however, it may be noted that a split-dollar arrangement between an employer and employee may produce annual gross income to the insured employee.

Life Insurance Included in Qualified Retirement Plans: Sometimes, life insurance is purchased by qualified retirement plans on the lives of plan participants. Here again, the life insurance will produce annual gross income to the insured employee, as described later in this chapter.

Federal Estate Taxation

Inclusion in Gross Estate Life insurance death proceeds will be included in the insured's gross estate if the insured's estate is named as beneficiary, or if another named beneficiary (such as a trust) is required to or actually does provide the proceeds to meet the estate's obligations, or if the insured at the time of death owned any incidents of ownership (i.e., ownership rights) in the policy. Incidents of ownership include such rights as the power to change the beneficiary, the right to surrender or cancel the contract, the right to assign the contract, and the power to borrow against the policy. Other powers may also be incidents of ownership. However, paying premiums and receiving dividends under participating policies are not considered incidents of ownership.

Gifts of Life Insurance within Three Years of Death If life insurance policies are given away within three years of the insured's death, the proceeds generally will automatically be included in the insured's gross estate. But if the policy is given away more than three years before the insured's death, the proceeds cannot be included in the gross estate.

In situations where the insured makes cash gifts to third parties or an ILIT, which they then use to purchase and own a newly issued life insurance policy on the insured's life, the courts have held that the proceeds are not in the insured's gross estate, even if the insured should die within three years of the gifts. Thus, for newly issued policies that are to be owned by, say, an ILIT, the proper strategy would seem to be to create the ILIT; make a cash gift to the trustee; and then let the trustee purchase, own, and be the beneficiary of life insurance on the grantor's life. Then the three-year automatic inclusion rule would not apply. Of course, an existing policy owned by the insured would have to be transferred to a third party or an ILIT to remove the proceeds from the gross estate, and so the three-year rule cannot be escaped.

Corporate-Owned Life Insurance (COLI) In general, when life insurance is owned by a corporation of which the insured is a stockholder, the proceeds are not included in the insured's gross estate at death because the insured has no direct incidents of ownership in the policy. However, under IRS regulations, if the insured was the sole or a controlling stockholder (owning stock with more than 50 percent of the combined voting power over the corporation), the incidents of ownership in the insurance held by the corporation will be attributed to the sole or controlling stockholder and the proceeds included in his or her gross estate, but only to the extent that the proceeds are not payable to the corporation or for a valid business purpose of the corporation.

Thus, for example, if a trust for the benefit of a sole or controlling stockholder's family is named as beneficiary of the COLI, the death proceeds (to that extent) will be included in the stockholder's gross estate. But if the corporation is named as beneficiary, they will not. However, when the corporation is named as beneficiary (such as for key person life insurance, for example), the death proceeds will be considered in valuing its stock in the deceased stockholder–insured's gross estate. On the other hand, the estate may be entitled to a discount in valuing the stock because of the loss to the corporation of the stockholder–insured's services. This might be called a *key person discount.*

Life Insurance on the Lives of Others Suppose one person owns life insurance on the life of another and the policyowner (not the insured) dies. In this case, the value of the policy (not the death proceeds) will be included in the deceased policyowner's gross estate.

Valuation of Life Insurance Policies for Tax Purposes

The general rules for valuing property for gift and estate tax purposes also apply to life insurance contracts. However, some special principles are relevant because of the nature of life insurance. A newly issued policy (with periodic premiums or a single premium) normally is valued at the actual premium paid. A paid-up policy that has been in force for some time is valued at its replacement cost (the single premium as of the valuation date for the same policy). For cash-value policies that have been in force for some time and on which additional premiums are payable, the value normally is the policy's interpolated terminal reserve plus the pro rata unearned premium (plus any dividend accumulations and minus any policy loans). This value is essentially the policy's cash value, but is not exactly the same. For previously issued individual term policies, the value will be the unearned premium for the year as of the valuation date. As noted previously, the continuing value of group term life insurance is the Table I rate times the full amount of insurance gifted.

Federal Gift Taxation

Taxable Transfers in General If a policyowner absolutely assigns a life insurance policy to someone else, he or she has made a current gift of the then value of the policy. If the donor (normally the insured) continues to pay premiums on the policy, each premium constitutes an additional gift to the new owner. Correspondingly, for gifts of group term life insurance, the annual value of the economic benefit would be a continuing gift each year to the donee. When policies are owned by an ILIT (either purchased directly by the trustee or absolutely assigned to the trustee by the insured), the grantor may make periodic gifts to the trust so that the trustee can pay the premiums.

Possible Indirect Gifts by Third-Party Individual Owners An unusual gift situation can arise when a life insurance policy on the life of one person is owned by a third person and the beneficiary is yet another person. In this situation, upon the insured's death, the owner of the policy is considered to have made a taxable gift of the full policy proceeds to the beneficiary. This can be referred to as an *inadvertent gift* because the policyowner usually has no idea that he or she is making such a taxable gift. Therefore, when the owner of a life insurance policy is other than the insured, the owner should name himself or herself as beneficiary.

Federal GST Tax

Life insurance may be subject to the GST tax. In most cases, this will result from having life insurance in an ILIT that itself is a generation-skipping or dynasty trust. Hence, GST tax planning may be necessary.

How to Arrange Life Insurance

When life insurance is purchased for family protection purposes, the insured may name his or her spouse as primary beneficiary and their children or a trust as contingent beneficiaries. This may be fine in many cases, but various other possibilities may be considered. A basic issue is whether the insured will be owner of the insurance and thus have the proceeds included in his or her gross estate at death, or whether another person or an ILIT will own the insurance and thus have the proceeds escape federal estate taxation at the insured's death. When the insured's estate is large enough to attract federal estate taxation, it is increasingly common to have another person other than the insured's spouse, or more commonly an ILIT, own the life insurance.

Policy Owned by the Insured

Policies owned by the insured can be made payable in the following ways.

To the Insured's Estate This usually is not done unless the insured wants to make sure the proceeds will be available to his or her executor for estate settlement purposes.

To a Third-Party Beneficiary or Beneficiaries in a Lump Sum This is a common arrangement, frequently with the insured's spouse as primary beneficiary and children (or a trust) as contingent or secondary beneficiaries. Upon the insured's death, however, this arrangement may leave the beneficiary with a sizeable sum of money to manage, perhaps at the very time he or she is least able to manage it.

To a Third-Party Beneficiary or Beneficiaries Under Policy Settlement Options The settlement options generally included in life insurance policies were described in Chapter 21. Most insurance companies give the insured wide latitude in the settlement arrangements he or she can make for beneficiaries, or for himself or herself for policy surrender values. Beneficiaries also usually can elect settlement arrangements for themselves after the insured's death if the insured has not already done so.

To a Revocable Unfunded Life Insurance Trust The basic decision a policyowner–insured often must make is, "Should life insurance proceeds be left with the insurance company under a settlement arrangement or with a bank or other trustee to be administered under a trust agreement?" There are arguments on both sides, but the trend decidedly has been toward the use of revocable insurance trusts.

To a Testamentary Trust Sometimes life insurance proceeds are payable to the trustee of a trust set up under the insured's will.

Policy Owned by a Person Other Than the Insured

Ownership can be placed in a third party at the inception of the policy or after it has been issued. Placing ownership in another can be effected by an ownership clause in the policy at inception or by an absolute assignment of the policy. When an ownership clause is used, successive owner(s) can be designated in the event the first owner dies prior to the insured.

Policies may be owned outright by various members of the insured's family, such as adult children. However, there may be drawbacks in this. For example, assuming the insured dies before the policyowner, the proceeds will be paid to the policyowner as beneficiary and will be included in the policyowner's gross estate upon his or her subsequent death, unless he or she makes lifetime gifts or consumes them. In other words, generation skipping (except possibly for one skip person donee) is not possible. On the other hand, the insured may only be interested in keeping the proceeds out of his or her gross estate and the gross estate of his or her spouse, if married.

Another issue is what happens if the individual policyowner (donee) predeceases the insured. Generally, the policyowner's will should leave the policy to someone else who would be a logical owner or to an ILIT, or policy ownership might pass to a successive owner under an ownership clause in the policy.

Still another possible drawback is that policy proceeds paid to an individual in a lump sum may be subject to claims of the individual's creditors or possibly to marital claims against the individual. Furthermore, when ownership is placed in an individual, the policy is subject to that person's control.

Finally, there generally is no tax advantage in giving life insurance to the insured's spouse. Because of the unlimited marital deduction, the same tax result can be achieved simply by naming the spouse as beneficiary. For example, suppose Harry Branson is married, has a sizeable estate, and owns a $700,000 life insurance contract on his own life. If he absolutely assigns this policy to his wife, Mary, and survives three years, it will be out of his gross estate at death, but the $700,000 proceeds will be paid to Mary as beneficiary and will be in her gross estate at her subsequent death. On the other hand, if Harry keeps ownership of the policy and just names Mary as revocable beneficiary, the $700,000 proceeds will be in his gross estate at death, but since they are payable to his surviving spouse, they qualify for the marital deduction and so are deductible in full from his gross estate to arrive at his taxable estate. However, since they are paid to Mary as beneficiary, they will be in her gross estate at her subsequent death. Thus, either way, the $700,000 proceeds will not be taxable at Harry's death, but will be at Mary's subsequent death, absent remarriage, gifts, or consumption of its proceeds. Thus, the normal approach is to make gifts of life insurance to another person or, more commonly, to an ILIT. That way, the proceeds can escape federal estate taxation in both the insured's estate and his or her spouse's estate.

Policy Owned by an ILIT

General Considerations In this case, the insurance policies are owned by and payable to the trustee of an *inter vivos* irrevocable life insurance trust (an ILIT). Upon the insured's death, the proceeds are paid to the trustee and are administered according to the terms of the trust, usually for the benefit of the insured's family. The trust owns and administers the policy(ies) during the insured's lifetime, but it is otherwise unfunded in that usually only a small amount of other assets are also placed in the trust. Payment of premiums may be handled by the insured's making periodic gifts to the trustee, who then uses the funds to pay the premiums.

Transfer Tax Advantages Both the insured's gross estate and the insured's spouse's gross estate normally are skipped in these arrangements. If desired, other trust beneficiaries' estates also can be skipped, provided the beneficiaries (and the insured's spouse, if he or she is also a trust beneficiary) are given only those powers that will not cause the corpus to be included in their gross estates.

However, when a trust is arranged to skip the gross estates of, say, children and other descendents of the grantor, it will be a generation-skipping trust and so may be subject to the GST tax. In this event, the grantor may want to allocate part of his or her exemption to each gift he or she makes to the trust to keep the trust entirely exempt from GST tax. This provides a substantial leveraging effect for the GST tax exemption, since it is allocated only to each periodic gift to the trust to pay premiums, while the entire policy proceeds (as trust corpus) are exempted from the GST tax.

Gift Tax Annual Exclusion A potential problem for ILITs is that any gift of a policy, and any subsequent gifts by the insured, may not be gifts of a present interest and, hence, not eligible for the annual exclusion.

Crummey Powers–General Considerations: However, if a trust gives the beneficiary(ies) a noncumulative annual right to withdraw for a limited period that year's contribution to the trust (a Crummey power), the annual exclusion can be secured for the contribution up to stated limits. The annual limit on Crummey withdrawal powers for each trust beneficiary normally is the lesser of the beneficiary's pro rata share of that year's contribution to the trust or a stated limit.

Setting Annual Limits: A planning issue is how to state this limit. It could be set at the available annual exclusion or twice that amount if split gifts are planned. However, as explained in Chapter 27, a Crummey power is a general power of appointment, and when not exercised, it would be a lapse of a general power. The IRC provides that a lapse of a general power of appointment is only considered a release of the power to the extent it exceeds the larger of $5,000 or 5 percent of the total property value from which the power could have been exercised.[4] This so-called 5 and 5 power often is

[4] This is the same provision that underlies the "5 and 5 power" discussed previously.

referred to as the *lapse-protected amount.* Thus, lapses of a general power in excess of this amount will be a release of the power. The release of a general power may give rise to a taxable transfer for gift-tax purposes from the donee of a power (e.g., a trust beneficiary with a Crummey power) to the other trust beneficiaries and may result in the inclusion of at least a portion of the trust corpus in the gross estate of the donee (the trust beneficiary), depending on the terms of the trust. Therefore, when the annual stated limit is set at, say, the currently available annual exclusion or twice that amount, it exceeds the $5,000 or 5 percent lapse-protected amount.[5] The excess may be a taxable gift by the Crummey powerholder, and there may be inclusion in his or her gross estate. The taxable gift issue normally can be avoided by giving each powerholder a separate share of the trust and a testamentary power of appointment (normally a special power) over his or her share. This makes gifts by the powerholder incomplete. The estate tax issue remains. However, as a practical matter, this may not be a problem if the corpus of the ILIT will be distributed to the powerholder anyway (and hence be in his or her gross estate at some point). Of course, as explained in Chapter 27, the limit could just be set at the $5,000 or 5 percent lapse-protected amount and then there would be no issue, but this would be less than the available annual exclusion.

Generation-Skipping Transfers: If the ILIT is to be a generation-skipping trust, inclusion of a portion of the corpus in a powerholder's gross estate normally would frustrate the generation-skipping purpose of the trust. In this case (and possibly other cases), planners may limit the Crummey withdrawal power to the smaller of the annual exclusion or the lapse-protected amount. In this event, depending on the amount of gifts made to the ILIT, some of the grantor's gift-tax applicable credit amount may have to be used. Also, some of the grantor's GST tax lifetime exemption would be allocated to the gifts to the trust to make it entirely exempt for GST tax purposes.

Hanging Crummey Powers: Another approach suggested by some planners is the "hanging Crummey power." This is a withdrawal right up to the full applicable annual exclusion that will lapse if not exercised within a specified period, but only to the extent of the lapse-protected amount for that year. Thus, to the extent the withdrawal right exceeds the lapse-protected

[5] Note that this $5,000 or 5 percent (whichever is larger) lapse-protected amount applies *per trust beneficiary* each year and not per gift or per trust. Therefore, if a person is, say, beneficiary of several trusts with Crummey powers, he or she is entitled to only one 5 and 5 lapse-protected amount per year, and gifts to the trusts should be coordinated to reflect this.

amount, it will continue to be exercisable (i.e., it will "hang") into the future until it can lapse in some later year within the lapse-protected amount for that year.

Provisions of Crummey Powers: The power to withdraw generally should be available to beneficiaries for a reasonable period (such as 30 days), and the beneficiaries should have actual notice of their Crummey withdrawal rights and probably of contributions to the trust. Also, the persons having Crummey powers should be trust beneficiaries.

There normally should be enough value in an ILIT to satisfy the Crummey withdrawal power if it should be exercised by the powerholder. This depends on the type(s) of insurance contracts in the trust and their values. Sometimes planners consider it advisable to have separate liquid assets in the trust sufficient to cover one year's gifts to the trust so that a Crummey withdrawal could be satisfied if necessary.

Cautions Concerning Crummey Powers: Since 1981, the IRS has not been willing to issue private letter rulings with respect to certain life insurance trusts containing Crummey powers. Furthermore, in recent years, the IRS has increased its scrutiny of and concern over Crummey powers in general. Therefore, planners should be on their guard with respect to Crummey powers and plan for them carefully.

Providing Liquidity and Estate Balance Through ILITs Since there will be a large amount of life insurance proceeds paid to the trustee upon the insured–grantor's death, the ILIT can be an excellent source for providing liquidity to the grantor's estate, the grantor's spouse's estate, or possibly for other purposes. However, care must be taken in how this liquidity is provided. The trustee should not be required to pay or, if authorized to do so, should not actually pay directly the estate taxes and other death costs that are obligations of the insured's estate. This is because these situations will cause the life insurance proceeds to be in the insured's gross estate and the whole purpose of the ILIT will be lost.

Instead, the trustee should be authorized (but not required) to make loans to the deceased insured's estate (or revocable trust) or to buy assets from the estate (or revocable trust) to provide liquidity. This authority also can be extended to the insured's spouse's estate, which may bear the brunt of estate taxes, and possibly to business interests of the insured, which may need cash at his or her death.

An ILIT can also be used to balance an estate among heirs. For example, suppose John Able, who is divorced, owns 100 percent of the stock of a corporation that he would like to leave under his will to his son, who is active with him in the business. The corporation is worth $2 million, and John has about $2,500,000 of other assets. However, John has two other children who are not interested in the business, and he wants to be fair with them. To provide balance among his children, John could establish an ILIT with about $2 million of insurance on his life and with his two other children as trust beneficiaries. He then could leave his corporation stock to his son in the business. His other assets might be used to pay death taxes and other costs and then divided among his children so as to equalize their inheritances.

Life Insurance in the Estate Plan With the increasing excluded amounts and possible repeal of the federal estate tax, questions have arisen in the past about the role of life insurance for estate liquidity and conservation purposes. Life insurance is important for these purposes. The time of death is uncertain and life insurance is the most logical financial product for providing estate liquidity and estate conservation at that time. Also, life insurance is an income tax–favored product it can be removed from the gross estates of both, the insured and his or her spouse through ILITs, and all of its traditional functions in family and business planning remain. Finally, when the internal rate of return (IRR) on insurance death benefits (assuming death at the end of life expectancy) for many policies is considered. Life insurance is an attractive investment in any event. Earlier death, of course, provided an even greater return.

Other Policy Arrangements

Split-Dollar Plans These are arrangements under which benefits and often premiums for cash-value policies are divided between two parties. When the parties are an employer and an insured employee, it may be referred to as *employer-provided split-dollar.* When the parties are other than employer and employee (e.g., a split-dollar arrangement between a parent and a child or between an ILIT established by the insured and the insured's spouse), it is referred to as *private split-dollar.* The remainder of this discussion will be based on employer-provided split-dollar unless the contrary is indicated.

Basic Characteristics: The employer may pay that part of each annual premium equal to the increase in the policy's cash value for that year, the annual premium minus a contribution from the insured employee, or the whole annual premium, depending on the nature of the plan. The employee, or an ILIT established by the employee to own the employee's interest in the policy, pays the part of the annual premium, if any, not paid by the employer. There may be other variations in the split of premiums under these plans.

If the insured dies while the plan is in effect, the employer receives a portion of the death proceeds equal to the policy's cash value or the premiums it has paid (depending on the terms of the plan), and the employee's personal beneficiary or an ILIT receives the balance of the proceeds. If the arrangement is terminated other than by the insured–employee's death, the employer would be entitled to the policy's cash value or the premiums it has paid (again depending on the terms of the plan).

Policy Ownership: The ownership of split-dollar life insurance can be structured in several ways. Under the *endorsement plan,* the employer owns the policy and the division of proceeds and premiums is provided for in an endorsement to the contract. Under the *collateral assignment plan,* the employee owns the policy and the employer's interest is protected by a collateral assignment of the life insurance. An insured employee's interest in a split-dollar arrangement to be transferred to an ILIT or entered into initially between the employer and the ILIT. This is done to remove the proceeds from the insured's gross estate. In these arrangements, the insured employee is considered to make annual indirect gifts to the ILIT of the plan's value each year to the employee.

Income Tax Status: This depends on when the split-dollar arrangement was created. Unless IRS arrangements (arrangements entered into after September 17, 2003, or entered into previously, but materially modified after September 17, 2003), are taxed under a loan system (generally for collateral assignments-type plans) or under an economic benefit system (generally for endorsement-type plans).

Under the *loan system,* the nonowner (e.g., the employer) is treated as making loans (the premium payments) to the owner (e.g., the employee) which would be taxed under the below-market loan rules (see Chapter 3). Under the *economic benefit system,* the owner (e.g., the employer) is considered to be providing an economic benefit (the value of the life insurance provided) to the nonowner (e.g., the employee). In either case, there is income taxation (or other taxation) arising from the split-dollar plan. For split-dollar arrangements entered into before September 18, 2003, the previous (more taxable) IRS rules and guidance apply.

Life Insurance Owned by Business Entities Individual life insurance policies may be purchased and owned by business entities on the lives of one or more of their owners or employees. The entities normally are the beneficiaries of the insurance. In the case of corporations, this often is referred to as corporate-owned life insurance (COLI).

Insurance purchased and owned in this manner can have a variety of purposes, such as key-person life insurance, life insurance to fund buy–sell agreements, life insurance to informally fund nonqualified deferred-compensation agreements, and life insurance to finance Section 303 stock redemptions. The business entities do not get an income tax deduction for the premiums paid on such insurance, but the death proceeds are received income tax–free. The other tax advantages of life insurance also apply.

Life Insurance in Qualified Retirement Plans While qualified retirement plans are primarily for retirement purposes, life insurance can be part of, or carried in, such plans. When this is the case, employee–participants must include the value of the current life insurance protection in their gross income each year. This currently taxable term cost is determined by applying one-year term rates (the lower of the IRS's P.S. 58 rates or the insurer's initial-issue yearly renewable term rates on standard lives) as of the insured's attained age to the difference between the face value of the policy and the policy's cash value as of the end of the year. Policy cash values are plan assets and are taxable as ordinary income when distributed from the plan. The pure protection element, however, is received by the beneficiary income tax–free as life insurance death proceeds. Whether life insurance should be provided under qualified retirement plans is a somewhat controversial issue that is beyond the scope of this book.

Gifts of Life Insurance

Many persons with estates sufficiently large to attract federal estate taxation have made gifts of their life insurance policies as an integral part of their estate planning.

Advantages of Gifts of Life Insurance

Life insurance generally is attractive gift property since it normally can be removed from the insured's gross estate by giving away all incidents of ownership in the policy. Furthermore, insureds can continue to pay the premiums or make periodic gifts to ILITs to enable the trustee to pay them. Also, the gift tax value of insurance contracts, the premium payments, and any indirect gifts normally are small, and in any event are relatively much less than the amount removed from the taxable estate (the policy face). In fact, with the use of Crummey powers and annual exclusions, there may be no actual gift tax involved. Furthermore, an insured may want to make an ILIT into a generation-skipping trust by allocating part of his or her GST tax lifetime exemption to gifts made to the trust. Finally, people may be more willing to give away life insurance (particularly term or low cash-value policies) than, say, securities, because life insurance usually is not producing income currently and is normally intended for the benefit of the policy beneficiaries anyway.

Pitfalls in Gifts of Life Insurance

Despite these advantages, there are some issues to consider. First, the unlimited marital deduction has eliminated any estate tax advantage that may have existed in giving life insurance to one's spouse. Second, donors should be careful to divest themselves of all their interests and rights in the policy. Finally, a life insurance policy normally is valuable property. Therefore, insureds should consider carefully whether they want to relinquish ownership and control over their policies, particularly if the policy has a sizeable cash value.

Gifts of Group Life Insurance

Changes in state law and group contracts have made it possible in most cases for employees to absolutely assign their group term life insurance to an ILIT or another person and remove the proceeds from their gross estate. This can be attractive because the face amounts of group term life insurance in some cases can be quite substantial. Also, since it is term insurance, employees really are not giving away much in the way of policy values. However, there will be annual indirect gifts, as described previously.

What Policies to Give?

Most kinds of life insurance can be placed in, or purchased by, an ILIT. However, lower premium and lower (or no) cash-value forms may be desirable to minimize gift tax issues. This means group term life insurance, an individual term policies, universal life and variable universal life policies with low (or withdrawn) cash values, and low cash-value whole life insurance often are attractive policies to give away. Another popular kind of policy to place in ILITs is a second-to-die policy covering a husband and wife. Also, it is possible to reduce the cash value of an existing policy by the policyowner taking a policy loan and then gifting the encumbered policy to the ILIT or other donee. However, in this case, it is important that the policy loan not exceed the policyowner's income tax basis in the policy for the reason explained in the next section. Finally, it is possible to withdraw each value up to basis in a UL or VUL policy prior to the gift.

Gifts of Policies Subject to Loans

A policy loan reduces the gift tax value of a policy by the amount of the loan and provides assets for the donor's own use. However, loans will reduce the ultimate death benefit. Also, funds need to be provided to pay interest on loans, or additional loans must be taken to pay the interest (although there is a limit to this or the policy will lapse). In addition, there is a *transfer-for-value issue* when policies are given away subject to loans. This is viewed as a sale of the policy to the donee for the amount of the loan, and it is a transfer for value. However, an exception to the transfer-for-value rule is when the basis of the policy in the hands of the transferee (donee in this case) is determined in whole or in part by reference to the basis in the hands of the transferor (donor). This is referred to as the *carryover basis exception.*

If a policy loan on a gifted policy is less than its basis (net premiums paid) in the hands of the donor, the carryover basis exception applies because it is viewed as part sale and part gift, and thus the donee's basis is determined in part (the gift part) by reference to the donor's basis. As an example, assume the following facts about a gifted policy:

Face amount	$500,000
Policy value before policy loan	$80,000
Policyowner's (donor's) basis in policy	$70,000
Policy loan	$65,000

In this case, the policy value for gift tax purposes is $15,000 ($80,000 – $65,000). The donee's basis is determined in part by the presumed sale (the $65,000 loan) and in part by the carryover gift basis of the donor ($15,000). Hence, the carryover basis exception applies and the transfer is not subject to the transfer-for-value rule. The donor also realizes no gain because the presumed sale proceeds (the $65,000 loan) are less than the donor's basis in the policy ($70,000).

On the other hand, if we change our assumptions so that the loan is more than the policy's basis in the hands of the donor, there is a different and less happy result.

Face amount	$500,000
Policy value before loan	$80,000
Policyowner's (donor's) basis in policy	$70,000
Policy loan	$75,000

In this case, the policy value for gift tax purposes is only $5,000 ($80,000 – $75,000). However, now the donee's basis is determined by the presumed sale (the $75,000 loan) and there is no carryover gift basis from the donor.

Hence, the carryover basis exception does not apply and, unless some other exception applies, the transfer is subject to the transfer-for-value rule. This will subject the proceeds at the insured's death (minus the donee's basis in the policy) to taxation as ordinary income. In addition, the donor realizes a $5,000 gain on the policy transfer (taxed as ordinary income) since the presumed sale proceeds (the $75,000 loan) exceed the donor's basis in the policy ($70,000).

This is a complex issue, and it can be a tax trap for the unwary. The principle involved is that when giving away a life insurance policy subject to indebtedness, be sure the outstanding loan is less than the donor's income tax basis in the policy. In some cases, part of a loan may have to be repaid to achieve this result.

30

Revocable Living Trusts and Property Management Arrangements

Competence Objectives for This Chapter After reading this chapter, planners should understand:

- The use of revocable living trusts as a will substitute
- The purposes of revocable living trusts
- The advantages and limitations of jointly owned property
- The various property management arrangements to deal with possible physical or mental incapacity
- The use of durable general powers of attorney
- Some planning issues regarding property arrangements to deal with possible incapacity
- Health-care decision making and uses of health-care powers and living wills

This chapter deals with several methods (i.e., revocable living trusts and jointly owned property WROS) for transferring property to others at a person's death other than by the traditional will. These may be broadly referred to as *will substitutes.* However, elsewhere in the book we have discussed various kinds of property or property interests that can pass to others at the direction of the owner outside the probate estate. These also can be referred to as will substitutes. They include beneficiaries under qualified retirement plans and IRAs, life insurance beneficiary designations, noncharitable beneficiaries under charitable remainder trusts, other beneficiary designations (e.g., under nonqualified annuities, U.S. savings bonds, and some bank accounts), and transfer-on-death (TOD) arrangements for securities in states that permit them. These interests will not be discussed further here. Also covered in this chapter are various arrangements for managing property in the event of the owner's physical or mental incapacity.

Revocable Living Trusts as a Will Substitute

A possibly advantageous way of managing property during an owner's lifetime and then transmitting it to others at death is the *revocable living trust.* These are trusts that can be terminated or changed by the creator during his or her lifetime.

Basic Characteristics

During their lifetime, estate owners create a revocable trust into which they may place some or the major part of their property. The trustee administers and invests the property and pays the income to the creator (grantor) or as the creator directs. Since creators can alter, amend, or revoke the trust at any point during their lifetime, they can change the trustee, change the beneficiaries, change other terms of the trust, or revoke the trust and get the property back. Upon the creator's death, the trust becomes irrevocable, and the corpus is administered according to its terms for the benefit of the creator's beneficiaries. In this sense, it acts like a will.

If desired, the trust can contain marital and nonmarital trust provisions to make proper use of the federal estate tax marital deduction. Life insurance on the estate owner's life and other death benefits can be made payable to the trust. Also, property normally can be poured over from an estate owner's will into such a trust. This is referred to as a *pour-over will.* Thus, a revocable trust can unify an estate so that it can be administered under one instrument. Property can be placed in a revocable living trust as soon as it is created, and assets can be added to it from time to time. Or, the trust can have minimal assets in it when created, and another party under a power of attorney can have authority to transfer the owner's assets into the trust in the event of the owner's physical or mental incapacity.

Tax Status

Since a revocable trust can be terminated by its creator at will, it is a grantor trust and trust income will be taxable to the creator during his or her lifetime. For transfer tax purposes, the corpus will be included in the grantor's gross estate for federal estate tax purposes since it is revocable by the grantor until his or her death. Furthermore, there is no taxable transfer for gift tax purposes when the trust is created because there is no completed gift. Thus, tax savings by the creator are not the motivation for setting up such trusts.

CASE EXAMPLE

Assume that John Mature, age 55, owns securities and other income-producing property worth approximately $4,000,000.

This property yields about $120,000 per year in investment income. John is a busy, successful business executive who also is active in church and civic affairs. He is married and has two married children and four grandchildren.

John decides to transfer the $4,000,000 of income-producing property to a revocable living trust, with the XYZ Bank and Trust Company and John as cotrustees. The bank handles the investment of trust funds with John's consent. Trust income is paid to John during his lifetime. Following his death, the trust is to be continued for the benefit of John's wife, children, and grandchildren. The trust agreement contains marital and nonmarital trust provisions so that at John's death his estate can make proper use of the federal estate tax marital deduction. John's will pours over the balance of his probate estate into this trust.

John also owns $1,000,000 of life insurance (including group term life insurance) on his life and has named the revocable living trust as beneficiary. (However, since his estate has grown in size, he is planning to absolutely assign his life insurance to an ILIT for the reasons given in the previous chapter.) The account balance under John's Section 401(k) plan is payable outright to his wife, Elena, as beneficiary, and their principal residence and a summer home are held by John and Elena as joint tenants with right of survivorship. It can be seen in this situation that relatively little (other than some assets John still owns in his own name) will be in John's probate estate and pass under the terms of his will.

Goals of Revocable Living Trusts

Property Management The XYZ Bank and Trust Company will manage and invest the trust property for John and pay him the income. Thus, John can be relieved of these duties and has the benefit of the bank's expertise in these areas. However, if for any reason John becomes dissatisfied with the arrangement, he can revoke the trust and recover his property or change trustees. Also, if he wishes, John can participate in investment management and, depending on state law, can even be the sole current trustee.

Protection Against Incapacity If John should become physically or mentally incapacitated or otherwise unable to manage his own affairs, the trust would become irrevocable and the successor trustee would continue to manage and invest trust property for John's benefit without interruption.

Investment Diversification If trust property is invested in, say, mutual funds under the prudent investor rule, the advantages of investment diversification can be secured.

Acting as a Will Substitute Upon John's death, the trust becomes irrevocable and the successor trustee will continue to manage and invest trust property for the surviving beneficiaries (John's family) and pay trust income to them without interruption. Ultimately, the property will be distributed to the trust beneficiaries according to the terms of the trust.

Choice of Law John also may decide in what state the trust is to be created and hence determine what law will govern the creation and operation of the trust.

Avoidance of Ancillary Probate If John owns real estate located in a state or states other than the state of his domicile, it can be placed in the revocable living trust, and ancillary administration in the state where the real estate is located (its situs) after John's death can be avoided.[1]

Confidentiality How, to whom, and what property passes at death under a revocable living trust is private information. It is not available to the public, although the other trust beneficiaries can know. A will, on the other hand, is a matter of public record, and anyone who wishes to can see its terms.

Less Vulnerable to Contestation Some feel it may be more difficult for disgruntled heirs to attack a revocable living trust than to contest a will.

Possibly Lower Cost A revocable trust may be a less costly way for John to transfer his estate. This factor is difficult to evaluate and depends on the circumstances. A professional trustee, like the XYZ Bank and Trust Company, will charge an annual trustee's fee, which in this case might be around $26,000 per year for an individually managed trust (see the illustrative fee schedule in Chapter 25). However, because such trustee's fees may be income tax–deductible, the after-tax cost could be less. Also, the trustee is providing investment management and other services to John while he is alive. Thus, annual trustee's fees can be viewed as analogous to the investment management fees for other investment intermediaries (e.g., the expense ratio for mutual funds or fees for investment advisers). Furthermore, if John is the trustee or the trustee does not charge a fee, there would be no annual trustee's fee.

Executors' commissions and other fees of estate administration are usually based on a percentage of the probate estate. This may also be true for the

[1] When property is left under a will, the estate normally is administered under the law of the state where the decedent was domiciled (intended to make his or her home). However, real estate in the probate estate is administered under the law of the state where the real estate is located (its situs). Thus, if a decedent is domiciled in one state but has real estate in another, there must be two administrations, with the attendant costs and possible delays. The administration in the second (or more) state(s)—the situs state(s)—is called *ancillary administration.*

fees of the attorney for the estate. Thus, John's estate could save at least part of the fees that otherwise would have been levied on the $4,000,000 had it passed as part of John's probate estate under his will. These probate costs (which are deductible for estate tax or income tax purposes) might run, say, 3 to 5 percent of the $4,000,000 principal amount. Thus, revocable trusts can result in annual trustee's fees, but can save on probate costs at the creator's death. On the other hand, certain necessary functions at death must be performed and paid for whether a revocable trust or a will is used.

Grantor Can Be Trustee During his lifetime, if he wishes, John may name himself as trustee or one of the trustees of the revocable trust and then name a successor trustee in the event of his incapacity or death.

Avoid Delays in Probate A revocable trust continues uninterrupted after the grantor's death.

Wills are still the traditional way to transmit wealth at death. However, a revocable living trust can be an alternative. In some cases, part of the estate can go by will and part under a revocable living trust. However, in virtually all cases, a will still is necessary because grantors normally retain at least some assets in their own names. Use of revocable living trusts tends to vary considerably among different parts of the United States; however, their use relative to wills seems to be slowly growing.

Joint Property with Right of Survivorship

The characteristics of jointly owned property with right of survivorship (WROS) were described in Chapter 25.

Advantages of Jointly Owned Property

Joint ownership is a convenient, and perhaps natural, way to hold property among family members, particularly husband and wife. At one joint owner's death, the property passes automatically to the other. Also, jointly owned property passes outside the probate estate of the first owner to die and, hence, avoids any costs and delays of probate. Holding property in joint names can avoid inheritance taxes in some states. Finally, jointly owned property may pass to the survivor free of the claims of creditors of the deceased joint owner, depending on state law.

Problems of Jointly Owned Property

An important problem that may arise is a larger-than-necessary federal estate tax because of overqualification of jointly owned property for the marital deduction. This was explained in Chapter 28. Also, when joint ownership is created and one of the joint owners contributes all or more than a proportionate share of the purchase price, a gift for gift tax purposes is made if the transfer is irrevocable.

There are no cut-and-dried rules on how much property should be held in joint names. In situations where the federal estate tax is not a factor, people generally can hold property jointly if they wish. Even where the estate tax is a factor, some joint ownership normally is acceptable. Married couples often hold the family residence and perhaps some bank accounts in joint names for convenience.

Property Management Arrangements to Deal with Physical or Mental Incapacity

Durable Powers of Attorney

A *power of attorney* is a written instrument in which one person (called the *principal*) names another person or persons as his or her attorney-in-fact or agent to act on the principal's behalf, as provided for in the instrument. In essence, it is an agency relationship. A *durable power of attorney* is one that continues in effect, or becomes effective, after the principal's incapacity. To be a durable power, the instrument must specifically so state, unless state law provides otherwise. Powers of attorney can also be *general* or *limited.* A general power of attorney authorizes the agent to act for the principal generally in all matters, while a limited power applies only to certain specified matters.

One approach to planning for incapacity is to execute an *immediately effective durable general power of attorney* naming one or more highly trusted persons as attorney-in-fact. The understanding among all involved should be that the power will not be used unless the person executing the power becomes incapacitated and unable to manage his or her affairs. Another approach is to execute a *springing durable general power of attorney.* A springing power becomes effective only in the event the principal becomes incapacitated, as defined in the document. However, in this case, a clear and workable definition of incapacity or disability is important.

Durable Powers of Attorney in Conjunction with Revocable Living Trusts

Still another approach is to have an existing (or springing) durable power of attorney under which the attorney-in-fact has the power to transfer some or all of the principal's assets to a previously existing revocable living trust. Thus, in the event of the principal's incapacity, the attorney-in-fact can use the power to fund or add assets to the revocable trust and have those assets administered for the principal. At the person's incapacity, the formerly revocable trust becomes irrevocable.

Funded Revocable Living Trusts

These trusts have been described previously. One of their main advantages is to provide property management in the event of the creator's incapacity and inability to manage his or her own affairs.

"Convenience" Joint Tenancies (Accounts)

Sometimes, people attempt to deal with the issue of property management in case of incapacity by creating joint bank accounts, CDs, or other accounts with another person. Should one of them (presumably the older one) become incapacitated or die, the other joint owner would simply use the money or other assets to take care of the incapacitated joint owner or distribute the assets in the event of his or her death. This seems quite simple, and it may be in some cases. However, the essential problem with this approach is that assuming both owners can withdraw freely from the account, the funds may be used other than as intended. Thus, as a practical and legal matter, convenience joint accounts are a questionable solution to the incapacity problem in many cases.

Planning Issues with Regard to Incapacity

This can be a complex and difficult financial planning problem. Professional help normally is advisable. A durable general power of attorney (either existing or springing) may be a satisfactory solution in many cases where there are relatively modest assets. On the other hand, when there are more extensive assets and perhaps other estate and family issues, a revocable living trust may be desirable. Frequently, both a revocable living trust (either unfunded or funded) and a durable power of attorney will be used.

An overriding issue in all of these arrangements is the selection of a person or persons (or institutional trustee) in which the property owner can have complete confidence to be attorney-in-fact or trustee of a living trust. This may be the truly difficult part. After all, this party may be handling the property owner's affairs when he or she is incapacitated. Of course, everyone hopes this will not happen, but it is a possibility to be aware of.

Health-Care Decision Making

The previous section dealt with the sensitive issue of how one can arrange for the management of his or her property in the event of physical or mental incapacity. Now we are dealing with the even more sensitive and controversial issue of health-care decision making when the individual is no longer able to make those decisions for himself or herself.

It is generally recognized that competent persons have the right to accept or refuse medical care for themselves. Unfortunately, however, persons may reach the point where they are no longer competent to make such decisions. Therefore, they may want to make advance arrangements for this unhappy contingency.

Durable Powers of Attorney for Health-Care Decisions This essentially is an extension of the durable power of attorney idea. It allows an attorney-in-fact to make health-care decisions for the principal, within the limits of any applicable law and any limits set by the principal in the power-of-attorney instrument, if the principal becomes incompetent to do so. This obviously can be an important power. The health-care power can be part of a power also covering property management or a separate power. Some states have enacted statutes that specifically allow persons to execute durable powers of attorney for health-care decisions. However, even in states without authorizing statutes, many authorities believe such powers still can be legally effective.

Living Wills Most states have statutes permitting persons to execute valid documents (*living wills*) that can direct in specified circumstances how medical treatment should be rendered or withheld in terminal situations after the person has become incompetent to make his or her own health-care decisions. While living wills and durable powers of attorney for health-care decisions have some similarities of purpose, they differ in several respects. First, living wills apply only in terminal situations. Second, not all kinds of care can be refused under the living-will statutes of various states. Third, durable powers permit the principal, in drafting the instrument, to set such terms and conditions on the power as the principal deems appropriate. Finally, a durable power allows the principal to name a specific party to make health-care decisions if the principal is not competent to do so.

PART IX

Planning for Business Interests

31

Types of Business Entities and Business Planning

Competence Objectives for This Chapter After reading this chapter, planners should understand:

- Some potential issues in planning for business interests
- The characteristics of closely held business interests
- The nature and characteristics of the various types of business entities, including:
  - Sole proprietorships
  - General partnerships
  - Limited partnerships (LPs)
  - Limited liability partnerships (LLPs)
  - C corporations
  - S corporations
  - Limited liability companies (LLCs)
- Issues involving the legal liability of business owners for the debts and obligations of their businesses
- The check-the-box regulations in the choice of a business entity
- The income tax bases of business entities
- The factors in choosing a business entity
- Issues involving the disposition of business interests
- Sales of business interests
- Liquidation of business interests
- Gifts of business interests
- Exchange of stock in a tax-free reorganization
- Sale of stock to an employee stock ownership plan (ESOP)

- Sale or redemption of business interests at death under a buy–sell agreement
- The significance of IRC Chapter 14 special valuation rules
- Issues involving the retention of business interests
- Estate liquidity through IRC Section 303 redemptions

When an individual or family has an interest in a closely held business, proper planning normally will be needed for various aspects of the business, such as its formation; operation; possible sale or liquidation; possible gifts of business interests; its disposition in the event of death, disability, or retirement of an owner; or its possible retention by the family.

Potential Issues

These may include but are not limited to the following:

- What kind of business entity or entities should be used for the business?
- Who will control the business?
- Will there be a market for the business if it has to be sold?
- How will the business provide adequate income for the owners?
- What will be the income tax status of the business and its owners?
- How will the value of the business affect the taxes and liquidity needs of the owners' estates?
- Will the business be able to continue if one of the owners dies, and what will happen to the business interest of a deceased owner?
- How can the business best be sold to a new owner, if desired?
- What will happen to the business and the owner if an owner becomes disabled?
- How can the retirement of an owner be best planned for?
- Should the owners be making gifts of business interests within the family and, if so, how much and in what form?
- What is the legal status of the owners with respect to their personal liability for the debts, obligations, and tort claims against the business?

Characteristics of Closely Held Businesses

We are all familiar with large publicly traded corporations whose shares are listed on various organized exchanges. When we discussed common stocks as an investment in Chapter 5, we were primarily concerned with the stocks of these publicly traded companies.

On the other hand, closely held businesses have a number of different characteristics, including the following:

- They can be formed as one or more of several types of business entities, including LLCs, partnerships, sole proprietorships, S corporations, and C corporations.
- They often are formed as pass-through entities (as described in Chapter 10) in that their profits and losses are not taxed at the business-entity level, but flow through to the owners individually and are taxed to (or deductible by) them personally. Thus, there normally is only one level of income taxation—at the individual owner's level.
- They usually have only a small number of owners, and in many cases these are family members.
- There normally is no ready market for these businesses.
- Due to these and other factors, there usually is limited marketability of closely held business interests. Depending on the circumstances, there also may be lack of control over the business by some owners. These factors may provide a rationale for substantial valuation discounts, when such interests are given to family members or at their death.
- Many owners of closely held businesses are also involved in the day-to-day management of those businesses. They are owner-managers. They may be stockholder–employees of closely held corporations, principals of partnerships, member-managers of LLCs, or sole proprietors. Regardless of the form, the point is that they often manage and control the businesses they own. This is in contrast to the situation of most stockholders of publicly traded companies, who effectively have no control over the corporation's affairs.
- Again, due to the just-stated factors, the owner-managers of closely held businesses often can coordinate their business planning with their own personal and estate planning.

Types of Business Entities

One important decision for a person or persons planning to start a business or who are already in business is what kind of business entity or entities to use in organizing their business.

Sole Proprietorships

In this case, the business's assets, liabilities, and operations are simply part of the owner's personal financial affairs. There is no separate business entity. There can be only one owner. No formal documents or registrations are required. The business's profits and losses are automatically passed through to the sole proprietor for tax and other purposes. The sole proprietor has unlimited personal liability for the debts, tort liability, and other obligations of the business. Adequate commercial liability insurance is the owner's best protection against tort claims arising out of the business.

General Partnerships

A partnership can be viewed as an association of two or more persons to carry on, as co-owners, a business for profit. There must be at least two partners to form a partnership, and it must have a business purpose. The term *person* in this definition is broad and can include virtually any individual or entity, such as U.S. citizens, resident aliens, nonresident aliens, corporations, LLCs, trusts, or other partnerships. Thus, there is essentially no limitation on who or what can be a partner in a partnership.

The partners of a general partnership (aside from an LLP, described in the next section) are jointly and severally liable for the debts, tort claims, and other obligations of the partnership. This means they have unlimited personal liability for any claims against the business, including those arising from the actions of other partners or other persons when acting for the business (so-called vicarious liability).

The state laws governing general partnerships generally are the Uniform Partnership Act (UPA), the Revised Uniform Partnership Act (RUPA), or variations of them. However, the partners in a written partnership agreement can modify the terms of these state laws with respect to their partnership if they wish. In the absence of such an agreement, the state partnership law applies. A general partnership is easy to form, and no state registration is required. There also does not need to be a written partnership agreement, although such an agreement is desirable.

General partnerships are pass-through entities for federal income tax purposes. Thus, the partnership itself pays no tax, and all items of partnership income, gains, losses, deductions, and credits flow through to the partners and are taxable to them individually. Each partner's share of these items normally is determined by the partnership agreement. However, the partnership must compute these items for tax purposes. Thus, a partnership can be viewed as a tax-reporting but not a taxpaying entity. The rules for partnership taxation are contained in Subchapter K of the IRC. These rules also apply to LPs, LLPs, and LLCs (assuming they are treated as partnerships).

Limited Partnerships (LPs)

Limited partnerships are defined by state law and must be registered with the state. They have already been described in Chapter 27 with respect to the creation of FLPs. An LP must contain at least one general partner and one limited partner.

The general partner(s) of an LP has unlimited personal liability for the debts, tort claims, and other obligations of the partnership. However, other entities whose owners have limited liability, like LLCs and S corporations, can be the general partner. The liability of the limited partners for partnership obligations, on the other hand, normally is limited to their investment in the partnership. However, in return for this limited liability, limited partners cannot take part in the active management or conduct of the partnership to the extent specified in the applicable state law. If they do, they may be treated as general partners and lose their limited liability. As in the case of a general partnership, virtually any individual or entity can be a partner in an LP. The state laws governing LPs generally are the Uniform Limited Partnership Act (ULPA), the Revised Uniform Limited Partnership Act (RULPA), or variations of them. There must be a written partnership agreement, and the formalities of these laws must be observed.

Limited Liability Partnerships (LLPs)

These may be formed under state laws that permit general partners to limit their personal liability for some partnership obligations. In many states, general partners in an LLP are not liable for the acts or omissions of other partners or of employees or agents of the partnership (other than those the general partner is directly supervising). In other words, general partners in LLPs essentially are relieved of their vicarious liability. In some states, they are also relieved of other partnership liabilities, like contractual claims. An LLP must register as such under the applicable state law.

Limited Liability Limited Partnerships (LLLPs)

These are formed under some state laws that expressly permit limited partnerships to register as LLLPs. In this case, the general partner(s) can limit their personal liability generally for the act of others.

C Corporations

These are corporations established under state corporation laws. They can have one or more stockholders, and virtually any person or entity can be a stockholder. There are no limits on the number or nature of C corporation stockholders. They can have one or more classes of stock in their capital structure. Thus, for example, a C corporation could have several classes of common stock or one or more classes of common stock and one or more classes of preferred stock. The liability of stockholders for corporate obligations normally is limited to their investment in the corporation. Also, stockholders can actively participate in the management and conduct of the corporation without losing this limited liability. In fact, stockholders of closely held C corporations often are stockholder–employees of the corporation.

C corporations are taxable entities under Subchapter C of the IRC. They are subject to the corporate income tax, the corporate alternative minimum tax,[1] the tax on unreasonable accumulation of earnings, and other levies. Thus, among all the forms of business organization discussed here, the C corporation is the only form that is not a pass-through entity. It and its shareholders are exposed to the corporate double-tax. However, its shareholders are only taxed on dividends that are declared and paid by the corporation, and so as a practical matter, closely held C corporations often elect not to pay dividends to their common stockholders to the extent possible. The strategy of their stockholders often is to take profits out of the corporation in other ways so they will be deductible by the corporation and taxable only once at the stockholder level. Strategies for doing this are discussed later in this chapter. C corporations also are subject to double taxation of capital gains on a corporate liquidation (the so-called repeal of the General Utilities doctrine). However, again as noted in Chapter 11, there is a 50 percent (75 percent from 2009 until 2011) exclusion of gain from the sale or exchange of qualified small business stock in a C corporation, subject to certain conditions.

S Corporations

An S corporation is a regular corporation under state corporation law that meets certain qualification requirements under the tax law and elects (under Subchapter S of the IRC) not to be taxed as a corporation. In most other respects, an S corporation is like a C corporation. For example, S corporation stockholders normally have limited liability for corporate obligations and they often actively participate in the management and conduct of the corporation as stockholder–employees.

Tax Status An S corporation is taxed in most respects like a partnership, rather than a corporation. The S corporation itself generally pays no tax,[2]

[1] However, as noted in Chapter 10, the corporate AMT does not apply to C corporations that are small business corporations for this purpose (i.e., generally those with annual gross receipts not exceeding $5 million).

[2] In certain situations, an S corporation may incur tax at the corporate level if it had formerly been a C corporation (i.e., had a C history). One situation is when the built-in gains in assets as of the date of conversion from C to S are sold or exchanged during the 10-year period after conversion. Another is when the former C was on LIFO inventory accounting. In this

and all items of corporate income, gains, losses, deductions, and credits flow through to the stockholders in proportion to their stockholdings and are taxable to them individually. However, the corporation must compute these items for tax purposes.

Thus, stockholders of S corporations are taxed on the net profits and gains of the corporation even if they do not receive any dividends from the corporation.[3] In fact, since profits have already been taxed to the stockholders, dividends paid by S corporations normally are not taxable to the stockholders.[4] This may put a financial strain on S corporation stockholders, particularly stockholders with minority interests, who may be receiving taxable income from the corporation but who perhaps have little or no control over whether the corporation pays any dividends with which the taxes might be paid. To provide these funds, and perhaps to avoid a situation in which minority stockholders in effect could be forced to sell their stock, S corporations in their bylaws or charters often require the payment of minimum dividends expressed as a percentage of their profits.

Eligibility Requirements Only a small business corporation can elect S corporation status. To be a small business corporation for this purpose, a corporation must meet the following requirements (among others):

- It must be a domestic corporation.
- It must have no more than 100 shareholders (with a husband and wife and all "members of a family" counted as one shareholder).
- S corporations can have only certain classes of eligible shareholders. These can include:
  - Individuals (i.e., U.S. citizens or residents—nonresident aliens cannot be shareholders).
  - Grantor trusts. (Thus, for example, a revocable living trust created by an individual grantor who is a U.S. citizen or resident can be an S corporation shareholder. After the grantor's death, the trust can continue to be an S shareholder for two years.)
  - A trust created under a will (testamentary trust), but only for two years.
  - An estate of a deceased shareholder.

case, there will be LIFO recapture on conversion from C to S. Third, there may be tax on excess net passive income, and the S election may be terminated due to such income for three consecutive years.

[3] This is also true of other pass-through entities, like partnerships and LLCs, with respect to profits and distributions.

[4] When an S corporation has earnings and profits (e.g., resulting from a C history), some dividends may be taxable when they exceed the accumulated adjustments account.

- A qualified subchapter S trust (QSST). These are trusts that meet special requirements, which include the following:
  - The QSST has only one current income beneficiary, who is a U.S. citizen or resident.
  - All trust income must be distributed currently to the one individual.
  - The income interest of the current income beneficiary must terminate at the earlier of the beneficiary's death or the termination of the trust.
  - Any corpus distributed during the current income beneficiary's lifetime can be distributed only to that beneficiary.
  - Upon termination of the trust during the current income beneficiary's lifetime, the trust must distribute all its assets to the beneficiary.
- An electing small business trust (ESBT). These also are trusts that must meet special requirements, which include the following: The trust does not have beneficiaries other than individuals, an estate, or charitable organizations; no interest in the trust was acquired by purchase; and the trustee elected ESBT status. ESBTs are taxed on S corporation income at the highest individual income tax rate.
- Voting trusts.
- Certain exempt organizations (i.e., trusts for qualified retirement plans, such as ESOPs, and charitable organizations).

■ S corporations can have only one class of stock. However, if the only difference among the shares of common stock is in their voting rights, they are still considered as comprising one class of stock. Thus, an S corporation can have voting and nonvoting common stock. It can also have stock option plans for its employees and buy–sell agreements without violating the one-class-of-stock rule. Finally, an S corporation can have straight debt (i.e., a promise to pay a certain sum on demand or at a specified date, at an interest rate not contingent on profits and that is not convertible into stock, among other requirements) without that being considered a second class of stock.

If any of these conditions cease to be met, the S election normally is broken (terminated) and the corporation is taxed as a C corporation from that point on.

Other Issues All stockholders initially must consent to an S election. However, once made, an S election can be revoked (as opposed to being terminated when the requirements for being a small business corporation are no longer met) only by shareholders with more than 50 percent of the stock. Also, in general, once revoked or terminated, an election cannot be made again for five taxable years.

S corporations can have certain subsidiaries. They can own some or all the stock of C corporations, be members (or a single member) of LLCs, and be partners in a partnership. An S corporation also can own 100 percent of a qualified subchapter S subsidiary, which will be combined with its parent for tax purposes. However, C corporations, partnerships, LLCs, and trusts (other than those described previously) still are not eligible shareholders of S corporations.

The just-noted rules apply to the federal income taxation of S corporations. However, states also may have S corporation statutes. Some of these mirror federal law; others have different provisions. Also, some states tax S corporations in varying degrees.

Limited Liability Companies (LLCs)

The limited liability company is a newer form of business organization that probably is the fastest-growing type today. It combines the advantages of limited liability and freedom to have management control of corporations with the pass-through and other tax advantages of partnerships. It also is free from the eligibility requirements of S corporations.

LLCs are created under state law and must be registered with the state. All 50 states and the District of Columbia have LLC statutes.[5] A number of these laws either permit or do not forbid single-member LLCs. However, with respect to many matters, the members of an LLC in their written operating agreement can alter the terms of these state laws with respect to their LLC if they wish. Usually, in the absence of a contrary provision in the operating agreement, the state LLC law applies.

Persons or entities that have ownership interests in an LLC and can influence its management and operations are referred to as *members*. However, there also can be equity owners (nonmembers) who do not have a say in management. Also, LLCs can have managers who manage the affairs of the business. Thus, LLCs may be member-managed (where the members are engaged in running the operation) or manager-managed (where the members select a manager to run the business).

LLC statutes normally relieve the members from personal liability for the debts, obligations, and liabilities of the LLC. However, they can still actively participate in management without losing this limited liability.

[5] A Uniform Limited Liability Company Act has been adopted in some states.

Tax Status Under the check-the-box regulations (described next), an LLC normally will elect to be taxed like a partnership. Thus, it is a pass-through entity and pays no tax itself. All items of income, gains, losses, deductions, and credits flow through to the members and are reported on their individual tax returns. Each member's share of these items normally is determined by the operating agreement.

Other Factors LLCs can be flexible in their formation, structure, and operation. They are relatively easy to form, usually by filing their articles of organization with the state. LLCs can have any number of members (including only one member in many states), and the members essentially can be any person or entity. LLCs can have more than one class of equity interest. They normally do not have to observe many of the formalities often required of corporations under state corporation laws. These might include annual shareholder meetings, certain financial statements, boards of directors, appointment of officers, bylaws, minutes of proceedings, and so forth.[6] State tax laws also apply to LLCs. Some states follow the federal tax approach; others may levy some taxes on LLCs.

Business Trusts

Some states allow businesses to organize as business trusts. These are not common, however.

Use of Multiple Entities

Businesses often employ several of these forms of organization. For example, an S corporation or an LLC can be the general partner of a limited partnership. This would provide flow-through tax treatment and limited liability for all interests. Also, an S corporation can have subsidiary LLCs (or subsidiary S corporations). This would provide flow-through tax treatment, limited liability, and separation of businesses or operations. Furthermore, C corporations could have subsidiary LLCs or be partners in a partnership.

[6] On the other hand, it should be noted that many states have adopted so-called close corporation statutes in various forms. These laws are intended to relieve smaller, closely held corporations from many of the formalities required of larger, publicly traded corporations. They may also relieve shareholders from personal liability for the debts and obligations of their corporation on the ground that the corporation did not observe the usual formalities in the exercise of its corporate powers and management. The failure to observe such formalities has been a basis for creditors to "pierce the corporate veil" in some cases.

Further Thoughts on the Legal Liability Issue

Business owners usually are anxious to have freedom from personal liability for the debts, obligations, and tort claims against their business interests. Of the business forms just described, all provide at least some degree of limited liability, except for general partners not in LLPs or LLLPs.

However, even with the protection afforded by these forms of business organization, some cautions are in order. First, business owners (and everyone else for that matter) are personally liable for tort and other liability arising from their own conduct or misconduct. No form of business organization protects against this, and since closely held business owners often are involved in the management and conduct of their businesses, they may find themselves personally liable for their own actions in this regard. Second, some forms may not provide complete protection from personal liability, such as LLPs and LLLPs possibly for contractual claims and LPs for limited partners who take part in management. Third, many times, owners of closely held businesses will be asked to personally endorse bank or other loans for the business. This will make them personally liable for their payment. Finally, some courts may find stockholders personally liable for certain claims against or obligations of their corporations because they are stockholders. This is referred to as the *corporate veil doctrine.* It is not the general rule, but such liability is possible.

Therefore, commercial liability insurance with adequate limits (or umbrella coverage) still is important for closely held businesses and their owners. Such insurance not only will indemnify insureds for covered liability claims against them, but will also defend them (and pay the defense costs) for such claims. Also, owners should be included as insureds under such coverage.

Check-the-Box Regulations

Check-the-box regulations have already been discussed in Chapter 10. In essence, they provide that an entity organized under a state or federal law as a corporation will be taxed as a C corporation or an S corporation. Other organizations, called *eligible entities,* can elect how they wish to be taxed. Eligible entities essentially would be partnerships and LLCs. Eligible entities with two or more owners can elect to be taxed as a corporation or as a partnership. Eligible entities with a single owner (e.g., single-member LLCs) can elect to be disregarded as a separate entity for tax purposes—they will simply be taxed as part of their owners. Eligible entities generally will elect to be taxed as partnerships or disregarded for tax purposes.

Income Tax Basis in Business Interests

Like other assets, owners of closely held business interests have an income tax basis in their interests. This is referred to as their *outside basis* in their interests. It is analogous to the basis that stockholders of publicly traded corporations have in the stock they own, although it may be acquired and operate differently in the context of closely held business interests.

On the other hand, the basis a business has in its own assets is called its *inside basis.* This difference from outside basis exists because a business is a separate entity from its owners. In the case of pass-through entities, gains or losses from the sale of assets by the business and depreciation on assets flow through to the individual owners for tax purposes. Thus, a pass-through entity's inside basis in its assets will directly affect its owners.

At the formation of a business, the new owners will acquire basis in their interests. In a nontaxable transaction, this basis normally will equal the cash contributed plus the adjusted basis of assets contributed to form the business.[7] When a business interest is purchased, its basis normally is the purchase price (cost). When interests are received as gifts, there is a carryover basis, and when inherited, the basis is the fair market value at death. From this point on, however, there are significant differences between C corporations and pass-through entities.

For C corporations, the stockholders' bases in their stock generally do not change because of the operations of the business.[8] On the other hand, for pass-through entities, the owners' bases do change because of the operations of the business. For example, a partner's outside basis in his or her partnership interest will be increased by his or her share of taxable income of the partnership, capital gains of the partnership, income of the partnership which is tax exempt—e.g., life insurance proceeds, the amount of cash and the adjusted basis of assets contributed by him or her to the partnership plus

[7] For corporations, when appreciated property is transferred to them as part of their formation, it normally will be a nontaxable event if the transferors receive only stock in return and immediately after the exchange, the transferors own 80 percent or more of the stock of the corporation. For partnerships, generally, contributions of appreciated property to a partnership in return for a partnership interest is a nontaxable event at any time. These are tax-free exchanges, as described in Chapter 10. However, there may be gain if the property contributed is subject to liabilities, and there normally will be income if stock or a partnership interest is received in return for services.

[8] There are some exceptions to this. For example, if stockholders receive dividends in excess of the earnings and profits of the corporation, the excess is a return of basis and reduces basis.

any gain recognized on such contributions, and generally, liabilities incurred by the partnership (called entity-level debt). Correspondingly, a partner's outside basis will be decreased by his or her share of partnership losses, nondeductible partnership expenditures not chargeable to a capital account, generally any reduction of partnership liabilities, and distributions he or she receives from the partnership. The same treatment applies to members of LLCs that are taxed as partnerships. For shareholders of S corporations, the same generally is true, except that their bases are not increased by entity-level debt, but a shareholder's basis for purposes of deducting losses is increased by *his or her loans* to the corporation. Basis is necessary to determine gain or loss on the sale or liquidation of a business interest. Also, the owner of an interest in a pass-through entity cannot deduct losses in excess of his or her basis.

Factors in Choice of Entity

Choice of entity often involves consideration of a number of issues—many of which are outlined here. These issues can be complex, and a detailed discussion of them is beyond the scope of this book.

Liability of Owners

The owner liability issue has been discussed previously.

Tax Status of Entity and Owners

This also has been discussed previously. The trend seems to be toward pass-through entities, as opposed to C corporations, which are potentially exposed to double taxation. However, there may be various business reasons for the use of C corporations (e.g., intention to go public or desire for more than one class of stock). Also, closely held C corporations in practice may be able to avoid or mitigate potential double taxation through several strategies, as described next. However, each of these strategies has practical limits.

- *Payment of salaries, bonuses, and so forth, to stockholder–employees.* These are deductible at the corporate level and taxable as compensation to stockholder–employees. However, the limit on such payments is that the compensation must be reasonable and customary for tax purposes. This is a facts-and-circumstances test and depends on the situation. But in the case of unreasonable compensation, the IRS will recharacterize the compensation as nondeductible dividends.

- *Compensation to family members on the payroll.* Here again, the limit is that the compensation must be reasonable for the services performed.
- *Employee benefits for stockholder–employees.* These are currently deductible at the corporate level and are either not taxable or not currently taxable to the shareholder-employees, depending on the employee benefit. However, the limits on such benefits are that total compensation (including the employee benefits) must be reasonable and customary, and most employee benefits cannot discriminate in favor of highly compensated employees who, as a practical matter, often would be the stockholder–employees.[9]
- *Deferred compensation for stockholder–employees.* Here again, these payments will be deductible by the corporation and taxable as ordinary income to the shareholder-former employees when actually made. These arrangements can be discriminatory. The limits on such arrangements are that they must be entered into in advance, must be reasonable, and probably should be justified by compensation studies.
- *Leasing assets from stockholders.* In this case, the rental payments are deductible by the C corporation and are taxable as rent (ordinary income) to the stockholder-owners. Stockholders often will retain real estate used in the business in their own names and rent it to their business. This not only takes money from the corporation with only one level of taxation (to the property owner), but also gives the stockholder-owners the tax advantages of owning real estate directly. The limit to this strategy is that the rent must not exceed a fair market rental value.
- *Lending money to the corporation.* Here, the stockholders make loans to their corporation at fair market interest. The interest is deductible by the corporation and taxable to the stockholder-creditors as ordinary income. The limits on this strategy are that the interest should be reasonable, the interest must be on true debt and not a disguised dividend, debt should not be an excessive proportion of the corporation's capitalization, and the fact that debt may be a financial burden on the corporation.
- *Gifts of closely held stock to charity and then redemption of the stock by the corporation.* This is the *charity bailout* described in Chapter 19. The limits on this technique are that the stockholder should want to make a charitable contribution in any event (since he or she receives only a deduction, not income) and the general limits on charitable contributions.

[9] Disability income benefits and insured health (medical expense) benefits do not have to be nondiscriminatory.

- *While not a strategy to produce only one level of taxation, there has been the approach of paying income tax at the corporate level (perhaps at the 15 or 25 percent bracket), accumulating earnings and profits inside the C corporation, and then liquidating or selling the corporation and paying capital gains tax at the shareholder level.*[10] To be successful, the combined taxes on corporate income and on capital gains at liquidation or sale should be less than the individual tax rates of the shareholders because that is the amount that will be paid on profits in a flow-through entity. While this strategy will be helped by the reduction in capital gains rate on eligible qualified small business stock and by reductions in tax rate on capital gains (and dividends) in general, it is less likely to be attractive when individual income tax rates are reduced relative to corporate income tax rates.

Ease of Formation and Operation

Partnerships and LLCs generally are easier to form and operate than corporations.

Number and Nature of Owners

If the business is to have only one owner, a sole proprietorship, single-member LLC, S corporation, or C corporation must be used. On the other hand, if a business is to have more than 100 owners (e.g., shareholders), an S corporation cannot be used. There also are other eligibility requirements on who can own S corporation stock.

Nature of Management and Control Desired

The forms can differ in this respect, as noted previously.

Transferability of Interests

Traditionally, stock of corporations has been viewed as being freely transferable, while full transfers of partnership interests have required the consent of the other partners or at least some of them. In practice, however, the bylaws of closely held corporations often limit the transferability of their stock.

[10] There may also be capital gains tax on appreciated assets at the corporate level under the repeal of the General Utilities doctrine concept.

This may be particularly true in the case of S corporations where the S election can be broken by a transfer to an ineligible person or entity.

Continuity of Life

Here again, corporations traditionally have had continuity of life, regardless of the death, retirement, bankruptcy, or other condition of the stockholders. For general partnerships and generally under LLC statutes, however, the death, retirement, bankruptcy, and certain other conditions of a partner or member will cause dissolution of the entity. Even so, the business can continue with the agreement of all or a majority of the owners.

For limited partnerships, only the death, retirement, bankruptcy, and so forth of the last remaining general partner will dissolve the partnership. Here again, the partnership can continue with the consent of all or a majority of the limited partners.

Ease of Termination

A partnership (or a partner's interest) generally can be liquidated (terminated) without taxable gain to the partners, except to the extent that the cash (generally including marketable securities) distributed exceeds a partner's basis in his or her partnership interest, with certain exceptions. Thus, in effect, partnership assets generally can be distributed in kind to a liquidating partner or partners without current taxation. The same treatment is true for LLCs that are taxed as partnerships.

For corporations, however, there may be taxable gain on liquidation (termination). In the case of S corporations with appreciated assets, there will be taxable gain at the corporate level, which will be passed through to the shareholders. However, the bases of the shareholders' stock will increase by the amount of the gain and so there often will not be double taxation for liquidating S corporation shareholders—only a single level of capital gains taxation at the shareholder level. For C corporations with appreciated assets, under the so-called repeal of the General Utilities doctrine, there will be taxable gain at the corporate level and then capital gain at the shareholder level on the difference between the cash and the value of the property distributed in liquidation and the stockholders' income tax bases in their stock. Thus, there will be double taxation on liquidation of C corporations.

Also, the conversion of a partnership or LLC to a corporation generally will not be a taxable event. However, there generally will be tax on the conversion of a corporation to a partnership or LLC.

These tax flexibilities tend to favor the partnership and LLC forms. They are easier to form and operate and to terminate.

Future Plans for the Business

If the plans are that the business will soon go public (perhaps in an IPO) or be sold to another firm, a C corporation may be preferred. This may also be true if the business is to be kept in a family for a long time. On the other hand, if it is planned for the business to terminate or for capital distributions to be taken from it fairly soon, this may favor a partnership or LLC.

Availability of Special Allocations

Partnership agreements and operating agreements of LLCs can allocate items of income, gain, loss, deductions, or credits among the partners or members other than according to their interests in the entity, provided the allocation has substantial economic effect.[11] These are referred to as *special allocations.* Corporations generally cannot have such allocations (i.e., profits and losses are allocated according to shares of stock owned), although C corporations can have more than one class of stock with different distribution rights.

Availability of Tax-Favored Employee Benefits for Owners

This is a complex and changing issue. It centers on the fact that stockholders who work for their own corporations are employees of the corporation, while partners and members of LLCs who similarly work in their businesses are principals or owners but not technically employees. Tax-favored employee benefit plans are for employees, unless there are specific statutory provisions stating otherwise.

Qualified Retirement Plans Stockholder–employees of corporations can be covered as employees under these plans and secure their full benefits. Also, self-employed persons (i.e., sole proprietors, partners, and LLC members) who have self-employment earnings as a result of rendering personal services can be covered on essentially the same basis under HR-10 plans. Thus, there is substantial parity or equality under qualified retirement plans between stockholder–employees and self-employed persons.

[11] In general, this means they are likely to affect the economic positions of the partners or members.

Health (Medical Expense) Insurance Stockholder–employees of C corporations can be covered as employees for full benefits on a tax-favored basis under their corporation's health insurance plan. This means employer contributions for employee and dependent coverage are deductible by the C corporation and not gross income to the stockholder–employees.

Self-employed persons are allowed a deduction on their personal tax returns for the amount paid for health insurance for the self-employed person, his or her spouse, and his or her dependents. A more-than-2-percent shareholder of an S corporation is treated as a partner (self-employed person) for this purpose.

Other Welfare (Fringe) Benefits Stockholder–employees of C corporations can be covered as employees for full benefits on a tax-favored basis under a variety of other welfare benefits. These include the cost of the first $50,000 of group term life insurance, the cost of disability income insurance, benefits under a cafeteria plan, and the value of certain miscellaneous fringe benefits. Thus, employer contributions for such benefits are deductible by the C corporation and are not gross income to the stockholder–employees.

For self-employed persons and more-than-2-percent S corporation shareholders, however, there is no tax deduction for contributions for these benefits. In effect, they are purchased with after-tax dollars. Thus, C corporation stockholder–employees have an advantage here over self-employed persons and more-than-2-percent S corporation shareholders.

Other Factors

A variety of other factors might be considered when selecting the business entity form, including state tax issues.

Disposition of Business Interests

At a certain point, closely held business interests may be disposed of by the owner or owners for value in a variety of ways. Alternatively, interests may be given away to or retained for the owner's family.

Sales of Business Interests

Owners may decide to sell their businesses or business interests during their lifetime. The sales may be to co-owners, key employees, family members, or unrelated parties. Also, the business itself may redeem the stock of a stockholder (a stock redemption) or liquidate the interest of a partner.

The economic and tax consequences can differ, depending on the type of business organization and the form of the sale.

When sole proprietors sell their businesses, they are essentially selling the assets. They may have gains or losses on individual assets. When a partner sells or exchanges his or her partnership interest, the selling partner will realize and recognize capital gain or loss on the difference between the amount realized from the sale and his or her adjusted basis in the partnership interest. A partnership interest generally is a capital asset for tax purposes. However, under the collapsible partnership rules, gain will be ordinary income to the extent there is substantially appreciated inventory or unrealized receivables as partnership assets.[12]

There is a special rule for partnerships that allows the partnership to elect to adjust the bases of the partnership assets (i.e., the inside bases) with respect to a purchaser's interest to reflect the difference between the purchaser's outside basis in the partnership interest being purchased (the purchase price plus the purchaser's share of partnership liabilities) and the purchaser's share of the original (before adjustment) inside bases of the partnership assets. In effect, this permits a partnership to elect to allow a purchaser to force his or her outside basis into his or her share of the inside bases of partnership assets.[13] While this may involve some complicated accounting, it can be an attractive election on behalf of a purchasing (or inheriting) partner because his or her share of inside basis will affect his or her share of partnership gains, profits, or losses. There is no comparable IRC provision applying to corporations.

These partnership tax rules also apply to LLCs that have elected to be taxed as partnerships under the check-the-box rules.

For sales of corporations, there is a fundamental choice between sale of stock and sale of assets. In the case of sales of stock, the owners sell their stock to the purchaser, who then acquires the stock (ownership) of the existing corporation. The selling stockholders will realize and recognize capital gain or loss on the difference between the amount realized on the sale and their adjusted bases in their stock. There will be one level of tax for them. The purchaser will acquire the stock of the corporation for the purchase price, the bases of the assets inside the corporation will remain the same, and the

[12] These are sometimes called Section 751 assets or *hot assets*.

[13] This election is permitted under Section 754 of the IRC. It also can apply when a partnership interest is inherited. This could be under a deceased partner's will or under a successor-in-interest provision in a partnership agreement. In either case, the inheriting partner's outside basis would be the partnership interest's fair market value at the date of death (i.e., its stepped-up basis at death).

purchaser generally cannot amortize the cost of any assets.[14] The purchaser also will be responsible for the liabilities of the corporation, such as contractual claims, possibly underfunded pension plans, and environmental liability. On the other hand, the purchaser may get the benefit of favorable contracts, permits, and licenses held by the purchased corporation.

In the case of an asset sale, the buyer purchases the assets from the corporation. The selling corporation may then be liquidated and pay off its liabilities and distribute its remaining assets to the shareholders. If it is a C corporation, there will be two levels of tax for the sellers. First, the corporation will recognize gain on the sale of its assets at the corporate tax rate. Then, when it is liquidated, the shareholders will realize and recognize capital gain at the individual level on the difference between the amount they receive in liquidation and their bases in their stock. If it is an S corporation, there normally will be only one level of tax because it is a flow-through entity. The corporation will recognize gain on the sale of its assets, but this gain will be passed on to the shareholders and be taxable to them. The gain will increase their bases in the corporation, which may eliminate any gain to them on liquidation of the corporation. However, for S corporations that had been C corporations, there will be a corporate-level tax on the gain from any appreciated assets held by the corporation at the date of conversion from C to S and sold within 10 years after conversion. This corporate-level gain is measured by the values of the assets at the date of conversion. This is called the *built-in-gain* provision.

The buyer in an asset sale secures an increased basis in the assets acquired (the purchase price allocated to them) and can amortize the cost of intangible assets (e.g., customer lists) and goodwill over 15 years. This allows the buyer an income tax deduction over this 15-year period. Also, the buyer is not liable for corporate obligations since he or she has not acquired the corporation itself. However, some potential liabilities, such as environmental exposures from assets, still may be passed on to the buyer.

Due to these factors, sellers often prefer to sell stock, while buyers want to purchase assets. Sometimes, the price or terms of a sale can be adjusted to satisfy the goals of both parties. Structuring sales can be complex and often requires professional advice.

Closely held business interests may be the subject of an installment sale, since they are not publicly traded. In this case, care should be taken that the

[14] The purchaser can, however, amortize the cost (over 15 years) of items acquired coincident with the purchase of stock, such as a reasonable noncompetition agreement with the former owner or owners. Also, the corporation can deduct payments when made under a previously made and reasonable nonqualified deferred-compensation agreement with the former owner that, in effect, is part of the sale transaction.

buyer will be able to carry out his or her obligations. Sometimes, the price paid for a business or business interest will not be fixed, but will depend in part on the future profits of the business. This is called an *earnout.* Earnouts may seem attractive to both buyer and seller, but again, care should be taken because it can be difficult to determine just what the profits of a closely held business are.

Liquidation of Business Interests

As just noted, businesses can be liquidated during the owners' lifetimes. For partnerships and LLCs taxed as partnerships, there generally will not be any taxable gain to the partners on liquidation, unless cash (including marketable securities) distributed exceeds the partners' bases in their partnership interests. In the case of S corporations, there generally will be one level of taxation at the shareholder level on liquidation (aside from the built-in-gain issue). For C corporations, there generally will be double taxation on liquidation: once at the corporate level and again as capital gain at the shareholder level.

Gifts of Business Interests

Owners of closely held businesses may want to make gifts of part of their interests during their lifetimes, normally to family members. Older business owners may want to bring their children or other family members into the business and reward them with gifts of stock, partnership interests, or interests in LLCs. Family members with controlling interests may begin to turn the business over to younger family members through gifts in tax-effective ways. Closely held business interests also may be placed in FLPs or LLCs.

However, an issue with respect to such gifts is control of the business. Older family members may or may not wish to maintain control. If they want to retain control, they can organize the business into different interests (e.g., voting and nonvoting stock of C or S corporations) and give away noncontrolling interests (e.g., nonvoting stock) in trust or outright. Or, they can put the business or part of it in an FLP and be the general partner or control an entity that is the general partner. Or, they may not give away enough of an interest to shift control from themselves.

When the owner of a controlled corporation[15] transfers the corporation's stock to an irrevocable trust (or otherwise) but retains the right to vote the stock for his or her lifetime or for a period that does not end before his or her death, it is viewed for transfer tax purposes as the owner's retaining the enjoyment of the transferred stock for his or her lifetime. This will cause

[15] For this purpose, control means retention of the right to vote 20 percent or more of the combined voting stock.

the full value of the transferred stock to be included in the transferor's gross estate at his or her death (like the retention of a life income). The same control generally can be secured by reorganizing the corporation in a tax-free organization to have voting and nonvoting stock and then giving away the nonvoting stock in trust or otherwise.

In giving partnership interests or membership interests in LLCs taxed as partnerships to family members, the family partnership rules need to be considered. These require that before such gifts will be recognized for income tax purposes, the donor partner's personal contributions to the partnership must be recognized in the sharing of profits, and capital must be a material income-producing factor in the partnership. For gifts of S corporation stock within the family, the IRS has statutory authority to reallocate the profits of the S corporation among the shareholders if a donor shareholder's personal services to the corporation are not adequately recognized by a reasonable salary. These provisions are intended to prevent using gifts of interests in pass-through entities to, in effect, shift personal earnings from a donor–owner to lower-bracket family members.

Closely held business interests also may be contributed to a CRT and then sold by the CRT, as explained in Chapter 19.

Exchange of Stock in a Tax-Free Reorganization

In this situation, owners of a closely held corporation exchange their stock tax free for stock of a publicly traded corporation. They can retain this stock until death, at which time it gets a stepped-up income tax basis, or sell it, provided they do not immediately have it redeemed by the issuing corporation. The former owner(s) may even remain on as employees of the publicly traded company. The approach was described and illustrated in Chapter 11.

Sale of Stock to an Employee Stock Ownership Plan (ESOP)

In this case, the stockholder normally sells some or all of his or her stock to the corporation's own leveraged ESOP. This technique also was explained and illustrated in Chapter 11.

Sale or Redemption at Death Under a Buy–Sell Agreement

Assuming an immediate sale, liquidation, or tax-free exchange of a business interest is not contemplated, the owner(s) must consider what will happen to their business upon the death or disability of one of them. One commonly used approach to this issue is a previously existing buy–sell agreement to operate at death and perhaps at disability as well.

Partnerships

Business Continuation Issues: The death of a general partner legally dissolves the partnership, and the deceased partner's interest in the business must be settled. Normally, in the absence of an agreement to the contrary, the surviving partner or partners succeed to the ownership of the firm's assets as *liquidating trustees*. Thus, in the absence of an agreement entered into during the partners' lifetimes providing for the continuation of the business, there may be two alternatives at a partner's death: the business may be reorganized or it may be terminated (i.e., liquidated or wound up).

A Partnership Buy–Sell Agreement: This is a written agreement entered into during the partners' lifetimes between the individual partners (cross-purchase type of agreement) or between the partnership and the partners (entity type of agreement), providing for the sale and purchase of a deceased partner's interest. It establishes a mutually agreeable price for each partner's interest and should contain a provision for adjusting the purchase price if the value of the business changes. Life insurance can be used to fund the agreement by providing the immediate cash to purchase a deceased's interest. There are two main kinds of partnership buy–sell agreements—the *cross-purchase plan* and the *entity plan*. Table 31.1 illustrates both for a partnership of three equal partners valued at $1,200,000.

Tax Aspects: The income tax aspects of partnership buy–sell agreements can be complicated and are only summarized here. Life insurance premiums, whether paid by the individual partners or the partnership, are not deductible for income tax purposes since the premium payor(s) are either directly or indirectly beneficiaries under the life insurance policies. Such payments are considered personal rather than business expenses. Life insurance death proceeds are received by the beneficiary(ies) income tax–free.

The proceeds received by the partnership or the partners are used as payments to purchase the deceased partner's interest from his or her estate. The estate normally will not realize gain or loss on the sale because the deceased's interest usually gets a stepped-up income tax basis at death (except for unrealized receivables and substantially appreciated inventory). Correspondingly, in a cross-purchase-type agreement, the buying partners can increase their bases in their partnership interests by the amount they paid for the decedent's interest. In an entity-type agreement, the surviving partners receive substantially the same effect on their outside bases because of the pass-through nature of a partnership, although this may depend on the timing of the sale and receipt of the insurance proceeds.

For estate tax purposes, upon a partner's death, the value of his or her partnership interest will be included in the deceased's gross estate, just like

Table 31.1. Partnership Value $1,200,000

Partner A Owns a One-Third Interest: $400,000	Partner B Owns a One-Third Interest: $400,000	Partner C Owns a One-Third Interest: $400,000
Cross-purchase agreement		
The three partners agree in writing on the value of their interests and that in the event of the death of a partner, the estate of the deceased will sell the interest of the deceased and the surviving partners will buy it.		
Life insurance to fund agreement		
A insures:	B insures:	C insures:
B for $200,000	A for $200,000	A for $200,000
C for $200,000	C for $200,000	B for $200,000
Each partner is the applicant, owner, premium payor, and beneficiary of the policies on the other two partners.		
At death		
Each surviving partner utilizes the insurance proceeds on the deceased partner's life that he or she receives as beneficiary to purchase one-half of the deceased partner's interest from his or her estate, according to the terms of the buy–sell agreement. (There may be a disability provision in the agreement to meet this risk as well.)		
Entity agreement		
The three partners agree in writing on the value of their interests and that in the event of the death of a partner, the estate of the deceased will sell the interest of the deceased and the partnership will buy it.		
Life insurance to fund agreement		
Partnership insures A for $400,000, B for $400,000, and C for $400,000. The partnership is the applicant, owner, premium payor, and beneficiary of all policies.		
At death		
The partnership utilizes the insurance proceeds on the deceased partner's life that it receives as beneficiary to purchase the deceased partner's interest from his or her estate, according to the terms of the buy–sell agreement. (There may be a disability provision in the agreement to meet this risk as well.)		

any other asset he or she owns. However, a difficulty with closely held business interests is that they often are difficult to value. But when a properly drawn buy–sell agreement exists, normally only the purchase price set in the agreement will be included in a deceased partner's gross estate, provided the requirements of Chapter 14 of the IRC (described later) and the common-law rules regarding valuation are met.

Close Corporations In a close corporation (either a C or an S corporation), stock ownership normally is limited to a small group of individuals, the stockholders often are employees of the corporation, and the stock is, of course, not publicly traded. Unlike a general partnership, which by law technically is dissolved upon a partner's death, a corporation continues in existence after a stockholder's death. However, in practice, the death of a close-corporation stockholder usually has far-reaching and often negative consequences for the other stockholders and the corporation itself. These consequences frequently make a buy–sell agreement taking effect at the death or disability of a stockholder desirable.

A Corporate Buy–Sell Agreement: This is a written agreement between the individual stockholders (a cross-purchase agreement) or between the corporation and its stockholders (a stock retirement or stock redemption agreement) providing for the sale and purchase of the stock of a deceased stockholder. The agreement would establish the purchase price for the stock and should provide for periodic adjustments of the price as the value of the business changes over time. Life insurance on the stockholders' lives is normally used to fund the agreement. Table 31.2 illustrates how a cross-purchase and a stock retirement buy–sell arrangement would operate for a close corporation with three equal stockholders and is valued at $1,200,000.

Tax Aspects: As in the case of partnerships, the tax aspects of buy–sell agreements can be complex. Only the basic rules are summarized here.

- *Income Taxation.* Whether paid by the stockholders or by the corporation, life insurance premiums are not deductible, since the premium payor(s) are either directly or indirectly beneficiaries under the policies.

Life insurance death proceeds generally are received by beneficiaries free of federal income tax. This normally is true whether the beneficiary is the corporation or the individual stockholders.[16]

[16] When the individual stockholders are the beneficiaries (in a cross-purchase plan), a special rule—the *transfer-for-value* rule (described in Chapter 29)—possibly could apply under certain circumstances and cause a portion of the proceeds to be taxed as income. This would happen if a surviving stockholder should purchase a policy on another stockholder's life from a deceased stockholder's estate. In this case, there would be no exception under the transfer-for-value rule for the sale of the policy. Therefore, such a purchase should not be made in a corporate cross-purchase-type agreement.

Table 31.2. Corporation Value $1,200,000

Stockholder A Owns One-Third of the Stock: $400,000	Stockholder B Owns One-Third of the Stock: $400,000	Stockholder C Owns One-Third of the Stock: $400,000
Cross-purchase agreement		
The three stockholders agree in writing on the value of the stock and that in the event of the death of a stockholder, the estate of the deceased will sell the stock of the deceased and the surviving stockholders will buy it.		
Life insurance to fund agreement		
A insures: B for $200,000 C for $200,000	B insures: A for $200,000 C for $200,000	C insures: A for $200,000 B for $200,000
Each stockholder is the applicant, owner, premium payor, and beneficiary of the policies on the other two stockholders.		
At death		
Each surviving stockholder uses the insurance proceeds to purchase one-half of the deceased stockholder's stock from his or her estate, according to the terms of the buy–sell agreement. (There may also be a disability provision in the agreement to meet this risk.)		
Stock retirement agreement		
The three stockholders and the corporation agree in writing on the value of the stock and that in the event of the death of a stockholder, the estate of the deceased will sell the stock of the deceased and the corporation will buy it.		
Life insurance to fund agreement		
Corporation insures: A for $400,000 B for $400,000 C for $400,000		
The corporation is the applicant, premium payor, owner, and beneficiary of all policies.		
At death		
The corporation uses the insurance proceeds to purchase the deceased stockholder's stock from his or her estate, according to the terms of the buy–sell agreement. (There may also be a disability provision in the agreement to meet this risk.)		

In addition, for C corporations, a complication is introduced by the corporate AMT. For C corporations, an amount that increases alternative minimum taxable income (AMTI) is 75 percent of the amount by which a corporation's adjusted current earnings (ACE) exceeds its AMTI (without regard to its ACE) for the year. The tax-deferred (tax-free) investment growth of life insurance cash values would be included in ACE for this purpose, as would the difference between life insurance death proceeds and the policy's basis for AMT purposes. As a practical matter, this means that 75 percent of these otherwise nontaxable items for regular tax purposes may be subject to the corporate AMT rate. This will be true only for COLI by C corporations. However, this AMT issue has been eliminated for many closely held corporations by the repeal of the AMT on small business corporations, as described in Chapter 10.

A stock interest in a corporation is considered a capital asset. Thus, the purchase price normally will not result in a capital gain or loss for the estate because the estate would have a stepped-up income tax basis following the stockholder's death.

In the case of a cross-purchase buy–sell agreement, the purchasing stockholders will be able to increase their bases in their stock by the purchase price. This will not be true, however, in the case of a stock retirement agreement for a C corporation.

- *Estate Taxation.* If the appropriate items are included in the buy–sell agreement, normally only the purchase price actually paid for the stock will be included in a deceased stockholder's estate for federal estate tax purposes. This again depends on meeting the rules for Chapter 14 of the IRC, as described next.

Sole Proprietors A sole proprietorship is not a separate entity apart from the individual proprietor. The sole proprietor, in an economic sense, is the business, and unless plans are made during his or her lifetime, the business often will die with its owner. However, three alternatives for disposing of the business may be available: orderly liquidation or sale, family retention, and sale to an employee (perhaps through a buy–sell agreement entered into in advance).

Chapter 14 Special Valuation Rules

As explained in Chapters 11 and 26, Chapter 14 of the IRC deals with certain special valuation rules for gift tax and estate tax purposes with regard to certain transfers of interests among family members. These valuation rules are quite complex, and a complete discussion of them is beyond the scope of this book.

One section of Chapter 14 (Section 2703–Certain Rights and Restrictions Disregarded) provides certain requirements for valuation provisions in buy–sell agreements. This section provides that the value of any property (such as a business interest under a buy–sell agreement) shall be determined without regard to any option, agreement, or other right to acquire or use the property at a price less than the fair market value of the property, or any restriction on the right to sell or use the property, unless the option, agreement, right, or restriction meets three requirements. These requirements are that it is a bona fide business arrangement, it is not a device to transfer such property to objects of the decedent's bounty for less than full and adequate consideration, and its terms are comparable to similar arrangements entered into by persons in an arm's-length transaction.

By regulation, the IRS has ruled that these statutory requirements do not apply to agreements among unrelated parties. Furthermore, agreements already in existence on October 8, 1990, are grandfathered, and these statutory requirements do not apply to them unless they are "substantially modified" after October 8, 1990. However, the former common-law rules still apply in all situations. These common-law rules generally involve the first two statutory rules, as well as requiring a written agreement that sets a determinable price, which also applies to sales during life (i.e., a first-offer commitment).

Therefore, if the parties wish the value set for a business interest in a buy–sell agreement to fix the value of the interest for federal estate tax purposes (as they normally do), the statutory requirements of Section 2703 of Chapter 14 must be met, unless the agreement is grandfathered or is among unrelated parties, or is otherwise excepted, in which case, the common-law rules still must be met.

Retention of Business Interests

Should a Business Interest Be Sold or Retained for the Family?

When business owners are planning their estates, they have two initial alternatives regarding the fate of the business. One plan may be to dispose of the business interest entirely during their lifetime or upon their death or retirement. Another may be to arrange for its retention in the family.

Retention may be practical when the family owns a majority interest, when some member of the family is interested in the business and is capable of managing it successfully, when the outlook for the business is promising, and when there are other assets in the owner's estate, including perhaps existing or new life insurance. This way, the owner can arrange adequate liquidity for his or her estate and equalize the distribution of the estate among those heirs who will receive a business interest and those who will not. If these elements are missing, the business owner should carefully consider whether to attempt retention.

Estate Liquidity through Section 303 Redemptions

A number of approaches that may facilitate retention have already been covered elsewhere in this book. However, one other approach is the Section 303 redemption. When certain conditions are met, Section 303 of the IRC allows a corporation to redeem sufficient stock from a deceased stockholder's estate or heirs to pay death taxes, funeral costs, and estate administration expenses without creating a taxable dividend to the estate or heirs. The proceeds received under a Section 303 redemption need not actually be used for meeting these death expenses. Section 303 merely sets a limit on the amount that can be received from a partial redemption of stock before it may be considered a taxable dividend. Thus, under the proper circumstances, Section 303 can be an attractive way to get cash out of a closely held corporation upon the death of a stockholder without danger of an income tax liability.

To qualify for a Section 303 redemption, the value of a deceased stockholder's stock in the corporation must comprise more than 35 percent of his or her adjusted gross estate. Assume, for example, the following estate situation for a divorced business owner:

Gross estate	$4,400,000
Minus: Assumed debts, funeral, and estate administration expenses	–400,000
Adjusted gross estate	$4,000,000

In this case, if the deceased stockholder owned stock in the corporation valued at $2,000,000, the estate would be eligible for a Section 303 redemption because 35 percent of the adjusted gross estate in this case is $1,400,000 and so the $2,000,000 stock interest qualifies. So assuming $40,000 for funeral and estate administration expenses and combined federal and state death taxes of $300,000, this estate could offer for redemption a total of $500,000 ($200,000 + $300,000) of stock to the corporation without its being considered a taxable dividend.

However, stock qualifying for a Section 303 redemption and, hence, protecting the proceeds of a redemption from tax treatment as ordinary dividend income is limited to stock redeemed from a stockholder whose interest is reduced directly by the payment of death taxes, funeral expenses, or administration expenses. Hence, some stockholders may not be able to take advantage of Section 303. Life insurance owned by the corporation may be used to finance a Section 303 redemption.

Index

F

J

K

L

Q

R

S

T

U

About the Authors

G. Victor Hallman is an attorney and a lecturer in estate and financial planning at The Wharton School of the University of Pennsylvania. He is a consultant and frequent speaker on wealth management topics and is the author on numerous books and articles, including *Financial Planning for Retirement* and *Employee Benefit Planning*. He holds a Ph.D. from the University of Pennsylvania and a J.D. from Rutgers School of Law.

Jerry S. Rosenbloom is the Frederick H. Ecker Emeritus Professor of Insurance and Risk Management and the academic director of the Certified Employee Benefit Specialist Program at The Wharton School, at the University of Pennsylvania. A popular and well-respected financial consultant, he has written many articles and books, including *The Handbook of Employee Benefits* and *Retirement Planning*. He holds a Ph.D. from the University of Pennsylvania.